P9-CKP-302
Landmark Middle School
15261 Legendary Drive
Moreno Valley, CA 92555

MVFOL
MV

Bowling, Beatniks, and Bell-Bottoms

Pop Culture of 20th-Century America

Bowling, Beatniks, and Bell-Bottoms

Pop Culture of 20th-Century America

Volume 1
1900s-1910s

Sara Pendergast and
Tom Pendergast, Editors

U·X·L®

THOMSON GALE™

Detroit • New York • San Diego • San Francisco • Cleveland • New Haven, Conn. • Waterville, Maine • London • Munich

THOMSON GALE

Bowling, Beatniks, and Bell-Bottoms: Pop Culture of 20th-Century America

Sara Pendergast and Tom Pendergast, Editors

Project Editors
Lawrence W. Baker, Allison McNeill

Editorial
Sarah Hermsen

Permissions
Kim Davis

Imaging and Multimedia
Leitha Etheridge-Sims, Luke Rademacher, Robyn Young

Product Design
Jennifer Wahi

Manufacturing
Rita Wimberley

Composition
Evi Seoud

©2002 by U•X•L. U•X•L is an imprint of The Gale Group, Inc., a division of Thomson Learning, Inc.

U•X•L™ is a registered trademark used herein under license. Thomson Learning™ is a trademark used herein under license.

For more information, contact
The Gale Group, Inc.
27500 Drake Rd.
Farmington Hills, MI 48331-3535
Or you can visit our Internet site at http://www.gale.com

ALL RIGHTS RESERVED
No part of this work covered by the copyright hereon may be reproduced or used in any form or by any means—graphic, electronic, or mechanical, including photocopying, recording, taping, Web distribution, or information storage retrieval systems—without the written permission of the publisher.

For permission to use material from this product, submit your request via Web at http://www.gale-edit.com/permissions, or you may download our Permissions Request form and submit your request by fax or mail to:

Permissions Department
The Gale Group, Inc.
27500 Drake Rd.
Farmington Hills, MI 48331-3535
Permissions Hotline:
248-699-8006 or 800-877-4253, ext. 8006
Fax: 248-699-8074 or 800-762-4058

Cover photographs reproduced by permission of AP/Wide World Photos ("His Master's Voice" painting [dog/phonograph] and Oreo cookies), the Corbis Corporation (Levi's jeans), the Kobal Collection (Austin Powers, the Beatles, and *The Cosby Show* cast), and UPI Corbis/Bettmann (flappers).

While every effort has been made to ensure the reliability of the information presented in this publication, The Gale Group, Inc. does not guarantee the accuracy of the data contained herein. The Gale Group, Inc. accepts no payment for listing; and inclusion in the publication of any organization, agency, institution, publication, service, or individual does not imply endorsement of the editors or publisher. Errors brought to the attention of the publisher and verified to the satisfaction of the publisher will be corrected in future editions.

LIBRARY OF CONGRESS CATALOGING-IN-PUBLICATION DATA

Bowling, beatniks, and bell-bottoms : pop culture of 20th-century America / Sara Pendergast and Tom Pendergast, editors.
p. cm.
Summary: Recounts the enduring products, innovative trends, and fun fads of the past ten decades. In 5 volumes. Includes bibliographical references and indexes.
ISBN 0-7876-5675-5 (set : alk. paper)
1. United States—Civilization—20th century—Miscellanea—Juvenile literature. 2. Popular culture—United States—History—20th century—Miscellanea—Juvenile literature. [1. United States—Civilization—20th century. 2. Popular culture—History—20th century.] I. Pendergast, Sara. II. Pendergast, Tom.
E169.1 .B7825 2002
306'.0973'0904—dc21

2002001829

ISBN 0-7876-5675-5 (set); 0-7876-5676-3 (v. 1); 0-7876-5677-1 (v. 2); 0-7876-5678-X (v. 3); 0-7876-5679-8 (v. 4); 0-7876-5680-1 (v. 5)

Printed in the United States of America
10 9 8 7 6 5 4 3 2 1

CONTENTS

Entries by Alphabetical Order xxix
Entries by Topic Category xlvii
Advisory Board lxv
Contributors lxvii
Reader's Guide lxxi
Timeline lxxv

Volume 1

1900s
The Birth of the American Century 1
1900s: At a Glance (box) 2

Commerce
Overview 7
Aunt Jemima 8
Brownie Cameras 10
Dime Stores 11
Dixie Cups 14
Fuller Brush Company 14
Harley-Davidson 16
J. Walter Thompson Company 18
Kellogg's Cereals 19
Louisville Slugger 21
Model T 22
Plastic 24

Contents

Sears, Roebuck Catalog 26
Stereoscopes 28
Teddy Bears 30

Film and Theater
Overview 33
Broadway 34
Buffalo Bill's Wild West Show 36
The Great Train Robbery 38
Harry Houdini (1874–1926) 39
Minstrel Shows 40
Nickelodeons 42
Silent Movies 44
Vaudeville 47
Ziegfeld Follies 50

Food and Drink
Overview 53
Chewing Gum/Bubble Gum 54
Coca-Cola 56
Cracker Jack 58
Diners 60
Hot Dogs 62
Ice-Cream Cone 64
Jell-O 65
Soda Fountains 67

Music
Overview 71
Jazz 72
Scott Joplin (1868–1917) 75
Phonograph 76

Print Culture
Overview 79
Argosy 80
Buster Brown 81
Dime Novels 82
Gibson Girl 84
Good Housekeeping 85
The Katzenjammer Kids 86
Kewpie Dolls 87
Jack London (1876–1916) 88
Mutt & Jeff 89
National Geographic 90
New York Times 92

Saturday Evening Post 93

Sports and Games
Overview 95
Baseball 96
Ty Cobb (1886–1961) 99
James J. Corbett (1866–1933) 100
Jack Johnson (1878–1946) 101
Kentucky Derby 102
Lionel Trains 104
Milton Bradley Company 106
Negro Leagues 107
Olympics 109
Ouija Boards 111
Rose Bowl 113

The Way We Lived
Overview 115
Avon 116
Catalog Houses 117
Chautauqua Movement 118
Coney Island 120
Dancing 122
Electric Appliances 125
Evangelism 127
Ferris Wheel 128
General Motors 130
Hairstyles 132
Postcards 134
Roller Coasters 136
Billy Sunday (1862–1935) 138
Telephone 139
World's Fairs 142

1910s
A Tumultuous Decade 145
1910s: At a Glance (box) 146

Commerce
Overview 153
AT&T 154
L. L. Bean 155

Fashion
Overview 157
Arrow Collar Man 158

Bra. 159
Tennis Shoes 161
T-Shirt. 163
Zipper 164

Film and Theater

Overview 167
The Birth of a Nation. 168
Charlie Chaplin (1887–1977) 170
Felix the Cat 171
Gertie the Dinosaur 172
Lillian Gish (1896–1993) 174
Keystone Kops. 175
Movie Palaces 177
Will Rogers (1879–1935) 178

Food and Drink

Overview 181
Campbell's Soup 181
Oreo Cookies 184

Print Culture

Overview 187
Fu Manchu 188
Krazy Kat 189
Norman Rockwell (1894–1978) 191
Tarzan 192
Tom Swift Series 194
True Story 195
Vogue. 196
World Book Encyclopedia 197
Zorro 199

Sports and Games

Overview 201
Erector Sets 202
Indianapolis 500 204
National Hockey League 207
Raggedy Ann and Raggedy Andy 208
Babe Ruth (1895–1948) 210
Tinkertoys 211

The Way We Lived

Overview 213
Bridge 214
Father's Day. 215

Greyhound Buses 216
Ku Klux Klan 217
Mother's Day 220
Refrigerators 222
Ringling Bros. and Barnum & Bailey Circus 223
Scouting (Boy and Girl) 226
Titanic 228
War Bonds 231

Where to Learn More cxxxi
Index cxxxv

Volume 2

1920s
The Roaring Twenties 235
1920s: At a Glance (box) 236

Commerce
Overview 243
Advertising 244
Band-Aid 247
Betty Crocker 248
Burma-Shave 250
Cigarettes 251
Department Stores 254
Eddie Bauer 256
Kleenex 256
La-Z-Boy Loungers 257
Macy's Thanksgiving Day Parade 258
Marlboro Man 259

Fashion
Overview 261
Flappers 261
Lipstick 263
Raccoon Coats 264

Film and Theater
Overview 267
Josephine Baker (1906–1975) 267
Clara Bow (1905–1965) 268
Charlie Chan 269
Disney 270
The Jazz Singer 275

MGM 276
Steamboat Willie 278
Rudolph Valentino (1895–1926) 280

Food and Drink
Overview 283
Fast Food 283
Gerber Baby Food 286
7-Up 287
Velveeta Cheese 289
Wheaties 289
Wonder Bread 290

Music
Overview 293
Blues 293
Grand Ole Opry 297
Jimmie Rodgers (1897–1933) 298

Print Culture
Overview 301
Better Homes and Gardens 302
Book-of-the-Month Club 303
Buck Rogers 304
Gossip Columns 306
Hardy Boys Series 308
Little Blue Books 309
Little Orphan Annie 310
New Yorker 312
Popeye 314
Reader's Digest 316
Ripley's Believe It or Not! 318
Time 319
Weird Tales 320
Winnie-the-Pooh 321

Sports and Games
Overview 325
Charles Atlas 326
Crossword Puzzles 327
Jack Dempsey (1895–1983) 328
Harlem Globetrotters 329
Lincoln Logs 331
Miniature Golf 332
National Football League 334
Yo-Yo 336

TV and Radio
Overview 339
Radio 339

The Way We Lived
Overview 345
Air Travel 345
Baseball Cards 347
Bungalows 349
Al Capone (1899–1947) 350
The Charleston 351
Chrysler Building 352
Cocktail Hour 353
Charles Lindbergh (1902–1974) 354
Miss America Pageant 355
Penicillin 356
Prohibition 357
Prom 358
Red Scare 360
Route 66 361
Scopes Monkey Trial 363
Standardized Testing 365

1930s
The Great Depression Disrupts America 367
1930s: At a Glance (box) 368

Commerce
Overview 373
Alka-Seltzer 374
Ballpoint Pens 375
Clairol Hair Coloring 377
Fisher-Price Toys 377

Fashion
Overview 379
Nylon 379
Nylon Stockings 380

Film and Theater
Overview 383
Andy Hardy Movies 384
"B" Movies 386
Betty Boop 388
Humphrey Bogart (1899–1957) 389
James Cagney (1899–1986) 390

Charlie McCarthy 391
Gary Cooper (1901–1961) 391
Dracula 392
Frankenstein 394
Clark Gable (1901–1960) 396
Gone with the Wind 396
Cary Grant (1904–1986) 399
Hollywood 400
King Kong 403
Laurel and Hardy 404
Marx Brothers 406
Mr. Smith Goes to Washington 407
Rockettes 408
Snow White and the Seven Dwarfs 410
Shirley Temple (1928–) 411
Three Stooges 412
John Wayne (1907–1979) 414
The Western 415
The Wizard of Oz 417

Food and Drink
Overview 419
Frozen Dinners 419
The Joy of Cooking 421
Spam 423

Music
Overview 425
Big Bands 426
Billie Holiday (1915–1959) 428
Robert Johnson (1911–1938) 428
Jukeboxes 429

Print Culture
Overview 433
Batman 434
Blondie 436
Dale Carnegie (1888–1955) 438
Comic Books 439
Detective Fiction 441
Dick and Jane Readers 443
Dick Tracy 444
Doc Savage 446
Esquire 448
Flash Gordon 449

The Grapes of Wrath 451
Life 452
Li'l Abner 454
Nancy Drew Series 455
Paperback Books 457
Perry Mason 458
Pulp Magazines 459
The Shadow 461
Superman 462

Sports and Games
Overview 467
Babe Didrikson (1911–1956) 468
Little League 469
Joe Louis (1914–1981) 471
Monopoly 471
Jesse Owens (1913–1980) 473
Stock Car Racing 474

TV and Radio
Overview 477
Amos 'n' Andy 478
Fibber McGee and Molly 482
Guiding Light 483
The Lone Ranger 485
Soap Operas 486
The War of the Worlds 489

The Way We Lived
Overview 493
Apollo Theater 494
Bonnie and Clyde 496
Drive-In Theater 497
Empire State Building 499
Goldfish Swallowing 500
Great Depression 500
Hoover Dam 501
Ranch House 502
Skyscrapers 502
Twelve-Step Programs 504
Wall Drug 505

Where to Learn More cxxxi
Index cxxxv

Volume 3

1940s
The Pivotal Decade 509
1940s: At a Glance (box) 510

Commerce
Overview 517
Best-Sellers 517
Jeep 519
Tupperware 520

Fashion
Overview 523
Bobbysoxers 524
Zoot Suit 525

Film and Theater
Overview 529
Abbott and Costello 530
Casablanca 531
Citizen Kane 533
Fantasia 535
Film Noir 537
It's a Wonderful Life 538
Lassie 540
Elizabeth Taylor (1932–) 542

Food and Drink
Overview 545
Dunkin' Donuts 545
M & M's 546
McDonald's 548
Pizza 550

Music
Overview 553
Bluegrass 554
Country Music 555
Long-Playing Record (LP) 558
Pop Music 560
Rhythm and Blues 564
Frank Sinatra (1915–1998) 565

Print Culture
Overview 567

Archie Comics 568
The Bobbsey Twins Series 570
Brenda Starr, Reporter 571
Captain America 572
Curious George 574
Ebony 576
Golden Books 577
Green Lantern 578
Highlights 579
Rudolph the Red-Nosed Reindeer 581
Seventeen 582
Wonder Woman 583

Sports and Games
Overview 587
Bowling 588
National Basketball Association 590
Jackie Robinson (1919-1972) 592
Scrabble 592
Slinky 594
Tonka Trucks 596

TV and Radio
Overview 597
Jack Benny (1894–1974) 597
Bugs Bunny 598
The Howdy Doody Show 601
Kukla, Fran, and Ollie 603
News Anchors 604
Road Runner and Wile E. Coyote 606
Studio One 608
Television 610

The Way We Lived
Overview 615
Baby Boom 616
The Bomb 618
Cold War 621
Federal Bureau of Investigation 624
Hot Rods 626
Las Vegas 627
Levittown 629
Spring Break 631
Teen Idols 632
UFOs 635

1950s
Pop Culture Explodes in a Decade of Conformity 637
1950s: At a Glance (box) 638

Commerce
Overview 643
Barbie 644
Credit Cards 646
Malls 648
Saran Wrap 649
Timex Watches 650
Trading Stamps 651
Volkswagen Beetle 652

Fashion
Overview 657
Jeans 658
Levi's 659

Film and Theater
Overview 661
The Day the Earth Stood Still 661
James Dean (1931–1955) 663
Francis the Talking Mule 664
Godzilla 666
Marilyn Monroe (1926–1962) 667
North by Northwest 668
On the Waterfront 669
Peyton Place 671
Shane 673
3-D Movies 674

Food and Drink
Overview 677
Burger King 677
French Fries 678
Hamburger 680
TV Dinners 680

Music
Overview 683
Disc Jockeys 684
Electric Guitar 686
B. B. King (1925–) 688
Elvis Presley (1935–1977) 689
Rock and Roll 690

Top 40 694

Print Culture

Overview 697
Beatniks and the Beat Movement 698
The Catcher in the Rye 700
Dr. Seuss 701
Frosty the Snowman 702
MAD Magazine 704
National Enquirer 707
On the Road 708
The Organization Man 710
Peanuts 710
Playboy 712
J. R. R. Tolkien (1892–1973) 713
TV Guide 714

Sports and Games

Overview 717
Etch A Sketch 718
Jack LaLanne (1914–) 718
LEGOs 720
Skateboarding 722
Sports Illustrated 724

TV and Radio

Overview 727
The Adventures of Ozzie and Harriet 728
Alvin and the Chipmunks 729
American Bandstand 731
Candid Camera 733
Captain Kangaroo 734
Davy Crockett 736
Dobie Gillis 737
Dragnet 738
The Ed Sullivan Show 739
Game Shows 741
Gunsmoke 743
The Honeymooners 744
I Love Lucy 746
The Lawrence Welk Show 748
Leave It to Beaver 749
The Mickey Mouse Club 751
The Price Is Right 753
Sitcoms 754

The $64,000 Question 757
This Is Your Life 758
Today 760
The Tonight Show 761
Transistor Radios 763
The Twilight Zone 764

The Way We Lived
Overview 767
Amusement Parks 768
Army-McCarthy Hearings 769
Blacklisting 771
Diets 774
Highway System 775
Hula Hoop 777
The Pill 778
Satellites 779
Suburbs 780

Where to Learn More cxxxi
Index cxxxv

Volume 4

1960s
An Era of Pessimism and Activism 785
1960s: At a Glance (box) 786

Commerce
Overview 793
Budweiser 794
Gap 795
G.I. Joe 796
Kmart 797
Nike 799
Valium 801
Wal-Mart 802
Xerox Copiers 804

Fashion
Overview 807
Bell-Bottoms 807
Doc Martens 809
Mary Kay Cosmetics 810

Miniskirts 811
Twiggy (1949–) 813

Film and Theater

Overview 815
Beach Movies 816
Dr. Strangelove 818
Easy Rider 820
The Graduate 822
Hair 824
A Hard Day's Night 826
Horror Movies 827
James Bond Films 830
Mary Poppins 832
The Odd Couple 833
Planet of the Apes 834
Psycho 836
2001: A Space Odyssey 838

Music

Overview 841
Altamont 842
Beach Boys 844
Beatles 846
Bob Dylan (1941–) 848
Eight-Track Tapes 849
Folk Music 851
Grateful Dead 852
Monkees 854
Motown 856
Rolling Stones 857
Simon and Garfunkel 859
Barbra Streisand (1942–) 861
Woodstock 862

Print Culture

Overview 865
Advocate 866
Cosmopolitan 867
Dune 868
Marvel Comics 869
Rolling Stone 871
Spider-Man 873
Whole Earth Catalog 875

Sports and Games

Overview 877
Muhammad Ali (1942–) 878
Dallas Cowboys 880
Frisbee 881
Evel Knievel (1938–) 881
Joe Namath (1943–) 883
Super Bowl 884
Twister 885
Wide World of Sports 887

TV and Radio

Overview 889
The Andy Griffith Show 890
The Beverly Hillbillies 891
Bewitched 893
Bonanza 895
Johnny Carson (1925–) 896
Daytime Talk Shows 897
Dr. Kildare 900
Flipper 901
The Fugitive 902
Gilligan's Island 903
Hawaii Five-O 905
Mister Ed 906
Mister Rogers' Neighborhood 908
Public Broadcasting System 909
Rowan & Martin's Laugh-In 911
Saturday Morning Cartoons 912
60 Minutes 916
Speed Racer 917
Star Trek 918

The Way We Lived

Overview 921
Civil Rights Movement 922
Gay Liberation Movement 926
Ghettos 928
Haight-Ashbury 929
Hippies 931
Lottery 933
Mafia 934
Marijuana 936
Martial Arts 937
National Aeronautics and Space Administration 938

National Organization for Women 940
Sexual Revolution 941
Students for a Democratic Society 945

1970s
The Me Decade 947
1970s: At a Glance (box) 948

Fashion
Overview 955
Hot Pants 955
Ralph Lauren (1939–) 956
Leisure Suit 956
Mood Rings 958
Polyester 959

Film and Theater
Overview 961
A Clockwork Orange 962
Disaster Movies 963
The Exorcist 965
The Godfather 966
Jaws 968
Rocky 970
The Rocky Horror Picture Show 971
Saturday Night Fever 974
Shaft 976
Star Wars 977

Music
Overview 981
Disco 982
Funk 984
The Hustle 985
KISS 987
Led Zeppelin 989
Barry Manilow (1946–) 990
Punk 991
Sex Pistols 992
Walkman 994

Print Culture
Overview 997
Judy Blume (1938–) 998
Cathy 998
Garfield 999

Harlequin Romances 1001
Hustler 1002
Ms. 1004
People 1005

Sports and Games
Overview 1009
Aerobics 1010
Atari 1011
Dungeons and Dragons 1013
Hacky Sack 1015
Jogging 1016
Monday Night Football 1017
Pong 1019
Video Games 1020

TV and Radio
Overview 1023
All in the Family 1024
The Brady Bunch 1025
Cable TV 1027
CB Radio 1030
Charlie's Angels 1032
The Dukes of Hazzard 1034
ESPN 1035
Fantasy Island 1036
The Gong Show 1038
Happy Days 1040
Hee Haw 1042
Little House on the Prairie 1043
The Love Boat 1045
The Mary Tyler Moore Show 1046
*M*A*S*H* 1049
Monty Python's Flying Circus 1051
Muppets 1053
The Partridge Family 1054
Roots 1057
Saturday Night Live 1058
Schoolhouse Rock 1060
Sesame Street 1062
Taxi 1063
The Waltons 1066

The Way We Lived
Overview 1069

Apple Computer 1070
Chia Pets 1072
Communes 1072
Cults 1073
Divorce 1075
Earth Day 1077
Environmentalism 1079
Equal Rights Amendment 1080
The Joy of Sex 1082
Kent State Massacre 1083
Personal Computers 1085
Pet Rocks 1088
Roe v. Wade 1089
Serial Killers 1091
Sexually Transmitted Diseases 1093
Smiley Face 1094
Streaking 1095
Tanning 1096

Where to Learn More cxxxi
Index cxxxv

Volume 5

1980s
Prosperity and Conservatism 1099
1980s: At a Glance (box) 1100

Commerce
Overview 1105
Home Shopping Network 1106
IBM 1107
J.Crew 1109
Starbucks 1110

Fashion
Overview 1113
Goth Culture 1114
Preppy 1115
Supermodels 1117

Film and Theater
Overview 1119
Airplane! 1120
Blade Runner 1122

Do the Right Thing 1123
E.T.: The Extra-Terrestrial 1125
Fatal Attraction 1126
Friday the 13th 1127
Ghostbusters 1128
Indiana Jones Movies 1130
Rambo 1131

Music
Overview 1135
Compact Disc 1136
Farm Aid 1138
Heavy Metal 1139
Michael Jackson (1958–) 1141
Karaoke 1142
Live Aid 1143
LL Cool J (1969–) 1145
Madonna (1958–) 1146
MTV 1147
Rap and Hip-Hop 1149
Run-DMC 1151
2 Live Crew 1152

Print Culture
Overview 1155
The Bonfire of the Vanities 1156
The Far Side 1157
Sassy 1159
USA Today 1160
Zines 1162

Sports and Games
Overview 1165
Wayne Gretzky (1961–) 1166
Pac-Man 1167
Rubik's Cube 1169
Trivial Pursuit 1170
World Wrestling Federation 1171

TV and Radio
Overview 1175
The A-Team 1176
Cheers 1177
CNN 1179
The Cosby Show 1181
Dallas 1183

David Letterman (1947–) 1185
Miami Vice. 1186
Roseanne 1187
Shock Radio. 1188
The Simpsons. 1190
Talk Radio 1193
Teenage Mutant Ninja Turtles 1194

The Way We Lived
Overview 1197
AIDS 1198
Cabbage Patch Kids 1200
Cocaine 1201
Gangs 1204
Generation X. 1206
Minivans 1208
Political Correctness 1209
Prozac 1211
Road Rage 1212
Skinheads 1214
Sport Utility Vehicles (SUVs) 1215
Urban Legends. 1217
Yuppies 1218

1990s
The Decade America Went Digital 1223
1990s: At a Glance (box) 1224

Commerce
Overview 1229
Mall of America. 1230
Microsoft 1231

Fashion
Overview 1235
Abercrombie & Fitch 1235

Film and Theater
Overview 1237
Austin Powers 1238
Forrest Gump. 1239
JFK 1240
The Lion King 1242
Pulp Fiction. 1244
Scream. 1245
Toy Story 1247

Wayne's World 1249

Music

Overview 1251
Alternative Country Music 1252
Alternative Rock 1253
Grunge 1255
Lollapalooza and Lilith Fair 1256
Nirvana 1258
Raves 1259
Britney Spears (1981–) 1261
Tejano Music 1262

Print Culture

Overview 1265
Harry Potter Series 1266
Jurassic Park 1268

Sports and Games

Overview 1271
Extreme Sports 1272
Michael Jordan (1963–) 1274
Tiger Woods (1975–) 1275

TV and Radio

Overview 1277
Ally McBeal 1278
Anime 1280
Barney and Friends 1281
Baywatch 1283
The Beavis and Butt-Head Show 1284
Beverly Hills 90210 1286
ER 1288
Frasier 1289
Friends 1290
The Real World 1292
Reality TV 1294
Seinfeld 1296
South Park 1298
Thomas the Tank Engine 1299
Who Wants to Be a Millionaire? 1300

The Way We Lived

Overview 1303
Aromatherapy 1305
Beanie Babies 1306
Branch Davidians 1307

Cellular Phones 1308
Chat Rooms 1309
Coffee 1311
Ecstasy 1313
E-Mail 1314
Hackers 1317
Internet 1319
Pokémon 1322
O. J. Simpson (1947–) 1324
WWJD? (What Would Jesus Do?) 1328
Y2K Scare 1329

Where to Learn More cxxxi
Index cxxxv

ENTRIES BY ALPHABETICAL ORDER

Bold type indicates volume numbers.

A

The A-Team **5:** 1176
Abbott and Costello **3:** 530
Abercrombie & Fitch **5:** 1235
The Adventures of Ozzie and Harriet **3:** 728
Advertising **2:** 244
Advocate **4:** 866
Aerobics **4:** 1010
AIDS **5:** 1198
Air Travel **2:** 345
Airplane! **5:** 1120
Alka-Seltzer **2:** 374
All in the Family **4:** 1024
Ally McBeal **5:** 1278
Altamont **4:** 842
Alternative Country Music **5:** 1252
Alternative Rock **5:** 1253
Alvin and the Chipmunks **3:** 729
American Bandstand **3:** 731
Amos 'n' Andy **2:** 478
Amusement Parks **3:** 768
The Andy Griffith Show **4:** 890
Andy Hardy Movies **2:** 384
Anime **5:** 1280
Apollo Theater **2:** 494
Apple Computer **4:** 1070

Archie Comics 3: 568
Argosy 1: 80
Army-McCarthy Hearings 3: 769
Aromatherapy 5: 1305
Arrow Collar Man 1: 158
AT&T 1: 154
Atari 4: 1011
Charles Atlas 2: 326
Aunt Jemima 1: 8
Austin Powers 5: 1238
Avon 1: 116

B

"B" Movies 2: 386
Baby Boom 3: 616
Josephine Baker (1906–1975) 2: 267
Ballpoint Pens 2: 375
Band-Aid 2: 247
Barbie 3: 644
Barney and Friends 5: 1281
Baseball 1: 96
Baseball Cards 2: 347
Batman 2: 434
Baywatch 5: 1283
Beach Boys 4: 844
Beach Movies 4: 816
Beanie Babies 5: 1306
Beatles 4: 846
Beatniks and the Beat Movement 3: 698
The Beavis and Butt-Head Show 5: 1284
Bell-Bottoms 4: 807
Jack Benny (1894–1974) 3: 597
Best-Sellers 3: 517
Better Homes and Gardens 2: 302
Betty Boop 2: 388
Betty Crocker 2: 248
The Beverly Hillbillies 4: 891
Beverly Hills 90210 . . . . . 5: 1286
Bewitched 4: 893
Big Bands 2: 426
The Birth of a Nation 1: 168
Blacklisting 3: 771
Blade Runner 5: 1122
Blondie 2: 436

Bluegrass 3: 554
Blues 2: 293
Judy Blume (1938–) 4: 998
The Bobbsey Twins Series 3: 570
Bobbysoxers 3: 524
Humphrey Bogart (1899–1957) 2: 389
The Bomb 3: 618
Bonanza 4: 895
The Bonfire of the Vanities 5: 1156
Bonnie and Clyde 2: 496
Book-of-the-Month Club 2: 303
Clara Bow (1905–1965) 2: 268
Bowling 3: 588
Bra 1: 159
The Brady Bunch 4: 1025
Branch Davidians 5: 1307
Brenda Starr, Reporter 3: 571
Bridge 1: 214
Broadway 1: 34
Brownie Cameras 1: 10
Buck Rogers 2: 304
Budweiser 4: 794
Buffalo Bill's Wild West Show 1: 36
Bugs Bunny 3: 598
Bungalows 2: 349
Burger King 3: 677
Burma-Shave 2: 250
Buster Brown 1: 81

C

Cabbage Patch Kids 5: 1200
Cable TV 4: 1027
James Cagney (1899–1986) 2: 390
Campbell's Soup 1: 181
Candid Camera 3: 733
Al Capone (1899–1947) 2: 350
Captain America 3: 572
Captain Kangaroo 3: 734
Dale Carnegie (1888–1955) 2: 438
Johnny Carson (1925–) 4: 896
Casablanca 3: 531
Catalog Houses 1: 117
The Catcher in the Rye 3: 700
Cathy 4: 998

CB Radio 4: 1030
Cellular Phones 5: 1308
Charlie Chaplin (1887–1977) 1: 170
The Charleston. 2: 351
Charlie Chan 2: 269
Charlie McCarthy. 2: 391
Charlie's Angels. 4: 1032
Chat Rooms 5: 1309
Chautauqua Movement 1: 118
Cheers 5: 1177
Chewing Gum/Bubble Gum 1: 54
Chia Pets 4: 1072
Chrysler Building. 2: 352
Cigarettes. 2: 251
Citizen Kane 3: 533
Civil Rights Movement 4: 922
Clairol Hair Coloring 2: 377
A Clockwork Orange 4: 962
CNN 5: 1179
Ty Cobb (1886–1961). 1: 99
Coca-Cola 1: 56
Cocaine 5: 1201
Cocktail Hour 2: 353
Coffee. 5: 1311
Cold War 3: 621
Comic Books 2: 439
Communes. 4: 1072
Compact Disc. 5: 1136
Coney Island 1: 120
Gary Cooper (1901–1961) 2: 391
James J. Corbett (1866–1933) 1: 100
The Cosby Show 5: 1181
Cosmopolitan. 4: 867
Country Music. 3: 555
Cracker Jack 1: 58
Credit Cards. 3: 646
Davy Crockett 3: 736
Crossword Puzzles. 2: 327
Cults 4: 1073
Curious George 3: 574

D

Dallas 5: 1183
Dallas Cowboys. 4: 880

Dancing 1: 122
The Day the Earth Stood Still 3: 661
Daytime Talk Shows 4: 897
James Dean (1931–1955) 3: 663
Jack Dempsey (1895–1983) 2: 328
Department Stores 2: 254
Detective Fiction 2: 441
Dick and Jane Readers 2: 443
Dick Tracy 2: 444
Babe Didrikson (1911–1956) 2: 468
Diets 3: 774
Dime Novels 1: 82
Dime Stores 1: 11
Diners 1: 60
Disaster Movies 4: 963
Disc Jockeys 3: 684
Disco 4: 982
Disney 2: 270
Divorce 4: 1075
Dixie Cups 1: 14
Do the Right Thing 5: 1123
Dobie Gillis 3: 737
Doc Martens 4: 809
Doc Savage 2: 446
Dr. Kildare 4: 900
Dr. Seuss 3: 701
Dr. Strangelove 4: 818
Dracula 2: 392
Dragnet 3: 738
Drive-In Theater 2: 497
The Dukes of Hazzard 4: 1034
Dune 4: 868
Dungeons and Dragons 4: 1013
Dunkin' Donuts 3: 545
Bob Dylan (1941–) 4: 848

E

Earth Day 4: 1077
Easy Rider 4: 820
Ebony 3: 576
Ecstasy 5: 1313
The Ed Sullivan Show 3: 739
Eddie Bauer 2: 256
Eight-Track Tapes 4: 849

Electric Appliances 1: 125
Electric Guitar 3: 686
E-Mail 5: 1314
Empire State Building 2: 499
Environmentalism 4: 1079
Equal Rights Amendment 4: 1080
ER 5: 1288
Erector Sets 1: 202
ESPN 4: 1035
Esquire 2: 448
E.T.: The Extra-Terrestrial 5: 1125
Etch A Sketch 3: 718
Evangelism 1: 127
The Exorcist 4: 965
Extreme Sports 5: 1272

F

Fantasia 3: 535
Fantasy Island 4: 1036
The Far Side 5: 1157
Farm Aid 5: 1138
Fast Food 2: 283
Fatal Attraction 5: 1126
Father's Day 1: 215
Federal Bureau of Investigation 3: 624
Felix the Cat 1: 171
Ferris Wheel 1: 128
Fibber McGee and Molly 2: 482
Film Noir 3: 537
Fisher-Price Toys 2: 377
Flappers 2: 261
Flash Gordon 2: 449
Flipper 4: 901
Folk Music 4: 851
Forrest Gump 5: 1239
Francis the Talking Mule 3: 664
Frankenstein 2: 394
Frasier 5: 1289
French Fries 3: 678
Friday the 13th 5: 1127
Friends 5: 1290
Frisbee 4: 881
Frosty the Snowman 3: 702
Frozen Dinners 2: 419

Fu Manchu 1: 188
The Fugitive 4: 902
Fuller Brush Company 1: 14
Funk 4: 984

G

Clark Gable (1901–1960) 2: 396
Game Shows 3: 741
Gangs 5: 1204
Gap 4: 795
Garfield 4: 999
Gay Liberation Movement 4: 926
General Motors 1: 130
Generation X 5: 1206
Gerber Baby Food 2: 286
Gertie the Dinosaur 1: 172
Ghettos 4: 928
Ghostbusters 5: 1128
G.I. Joe 4: 796
Gibson Girl 1: 84
Gilligan's Island 4: 903
Lillian Gish (1896–1993) 1: 174
The Godfather 4: 966
Godzilla 3: 666
Golden Books 3: 577
Goldfish Swallowing 2: 500
Gone with the Wind 2: 396
The Gong Show 4: 1038
Good Housekeeping 1: 85
Gossip Columns 2: 306
Goth Culture 5: 1114
The Graduate 4: 822
Grand Ole Opry 2: 297
Cary Grant (1904–1986) 2: 399
The Grapes of Wrath 2: 451
Grateful Dead 4: 852
Great Depression 2: 500
The Great Train Robbery 1: 38
Green Lantern 3: 578
Wayne Gretzky (1961–) 5: 1166
Greyhound Buses 1: 216
Grunge 5: 1255
Guiding Light 2: 483
Gunsmoke 3: 743

H

Hackers 5: 1317
Hacky Sack 4: 1015
Haight-Ashbury. 4: 929
Hair. 4: 824
Hairstyles. 1: 132
Hamburger 3: 680
Happy Days. 4: 1040
A Hard Day's Night. 4: 826
Hardy Boys Series 2: 308
Harlem Globetrotters. 2: 329
Harlequin Romances 4: 1001
Harley-Davidson 1: 16
Harry Potter Series 5: 1266
Hawaii Five-O. 4: 905
Heavy Metal. 5: 1139
Hee Haw 4: 1042
Highlights 3: 579
Highway System 3: 775
Hippies 4: 931
Billie Holiday (1915–1959) 2: 428
Hollywood. 2: 400
Home Shopping Network 5: 1106
The Honeymooners 3: 744
Hoover Dam 2: 501
Horror Movies. 4: 827
Hot Dogs 1: 62
Hot Pants. 4: 955
Hot Rods 3: 626
Harry Houdini (1874–1926). 1: 39
The Howdy Doody Show 3: 601
Hula Hoop. 3: 777
The Hustle. 4: 985
Hustler. 4: 1002

I

I Love Lucy 3: 746
IBM 5: 1107
Ice-Cream Cone 1: 64
Indiana Jones Movies. 5: 1130
Indianapolis 500 . . . . . 1: 204
Internet 5: 1319
It's a Wonderful Life 3: 538

J

J.Crew 5: 1109
J. Walter Thompson Company 1: 18
Michael Jackson (1958–) 5: 1141
James Bond Films 4: 830
Jaws 4: 968
Jazz 1: 72
The Jazz Singer 2: 275
Jeans 3: 658
Jeep 3: 519
Jell-O 1: 65
JFK 5: 1240
Jogging 4: 1016
Jack Johnson (1878–1946) 1: 101
Robert Johnson (1911–1938) 2: 428
Scott Joplin (1868–1917) 1: 75
Michael Jordan (1963–) 5: 1274
The Joy of Cooking 2: 421
The Joy of Sex 4: 1082
Jukeboxes 2: 429
Jurassic Park 5: 1268

K

Karaoke 5: 1142
The Katzenjammer Kids 1: 86
Kellogg's Cereals 1: 19
Kent State Massacre 4: 1083
Kentucky Derby 1: 102
Kewpie Dolls 1: 87
Keystone Kops 1: 175
B. B. King (1925–) 3: 688
King Kong 2: 403
KISS 4: 987
Kleenex 2: 256
Kmart 4: 797
Evel Knievel (1938–) 4: 881
Krazy Kat 1: 189
Ku Klux Klan 1: 217
Kukla, Fran, and Ollie 3: 603

L

L. L. Bean 1: 155
Jack LaLanne (1914–) 3: 718

Las Vegas. 3: 627
Lassie. 3: 540
Laurel and Hardy. 2: 404
Ralph Lauren (1939–) 4: 956
The Lawrence Welk Show 3: 748
La-Z-Boy Loungers 2: 257
Leave It to Beaver 3: 749
Led Zeppelin 4: 989
LEGOs 3: 720
Leisure Suit 4: 956
David Letterman (1947–) 5: 1185
Levi's. 3: 659
Levittown 3: 629
Life 2: 452
Li'l Abner 2: 454
Lincoln Logs 2: 331
Charles Lindbergh (1902–1974). 2: 354
The Lion King 5: 1242
Lionel Trains 1: 104
Lipstick 2: 263
Little Blue Books. 2: 309
Little House on the Prairie. 4: 1043
Little League 2: 469
Little Orphan Annie. 2: 310
Live Aid. 5: 1143
LL Cool J (1969–). 5: 1145
Lollapalooza and Lilith Fair. 5: 1256
Jack London (1876–1916) 1: 88
The Lone Ranger 2: 485
Long-Playing Record (LP) 3: 558
Lottery. 4: 933
Joe Louis (1914–1981) 2: 471
Louisville Slugger 1: 21
The Love Boat 4: 1045

M

M & M's 3: 546
Macy's Thanksgiving Day Parade 2: 258
MAD Magazine 3: 704
Madonna (1958–). 5: 1146
Mafia. 4: 934
Mall of America. 5: 1230
Malls 3: 648
Barry Manilow (1946–) 4: 990

Marijuana 4: 936
Marlboro Man 2: 259
Martial Arts 4: 937
Marvel Comics 4: 869
Marx Brothers 2: 406
Mary Kay Cosmetics 4: 810
Mary Poppins 4: 832
The Mary Tyler Moore Show 4: 1046
*M*A*S*H* 4: 1049
McDonald's 3: 548
MGM 2: 276
Miami Vice 5: 1186
The Mickey Mouse Club 3: 751
Microsoft 5: 1231
Milton Bradley Company 1: 106
Miniature Golf 2: 332
Miniskirts 4: 811
Minivans 5: 1208
Minstrel Shows 1: 40
Miss America Pageant 2: 355
Mister Ed 4: 906
Mister Rogers' Neighborhood 4: 908
Mr. Smith Goes to Washington 2: 407
Model T 1: 22
Monday Night Football 4: 1017
Monkees 4: 854
Monopoly 2: 471
Marilyn Monroe (1926–1962) 3: 667
Monty Python's Flying Circus 4: 1051
Mood Rings 4: 958
Mother's Day 1: 220
Motown 4: 856
Movie Palaces 1: 177
Ms. 4: 1004
MTV 5: 1147
Muhammad Ali (1942–) 4: 878
Muppets 4: 1053
Mutt & Jeff 1: 89

N

Joe Namath (1943–) 4: 883
Nancy Drew Series 2: 455
National Aeronautics and Space Administration 4: 938
National Basketball Association 3: 590

National Enquirer 3: 707
National Football League. 2: 334
National Geographic 1: 90
National Hockey League. 1: 207
National Organization for Women. 4: 940
Negro Leagues 1: 107
New York Times. 1: 92
New Yorker 2: 312
News Anchors 3: 604
Nickelodeons 1: 42
Nike. 4: 799
Nirvana 5: 1258
North by Northwest 3: 668
Nylon 2: 379
Nylon Stockings 2: 380

O

The Odd Couple. 4: 833
Olympics 1: 109
On the Road. 3: 708
On the Waterfront 3: 669
Oreo Cookies 1: 184
The Organization Man 3: 710
Ouija Boards. 1: 111
Jesse Owens (1913–1980) 2: 473

P

Pac-Man 5: 1167
Paperback Books 2: 457
The Partridge Family 4: 1054
Peanuts 3: 710
Penicillin. 2: 356
People 4: 1005
Perry Mason 2: 458
Personal Computers. 4: 1085
Pet Rocks. 4: 1088
Peyton Place 3: 671
Phonograph. 1: 76
The Pill 3: 778
Pizza 3: 550
Planet of the Apes. 4: 834
Plastic 1: 24
Playboy 3: 712
Pokémon 5: 1322

Political Correctness 5: 1209
Polyester 4: 959
Pong 4: 1019
Pop Music 3: 560
Popeye 2: 314
Postcards 1: 134
Preppy 5: 1115
Elvis Presley (1935–1977) 3: 689
The Price Is Right 3: 753
Prohibition 2: 357
Prom 2: 358
Prozac 5: 1211
Psycho 4: 836
Public Broadcasting System 4: 909
Pulp Fiction 5: 1244
Pulp Magazines 2: 459
Punk 4: 991

R

Raccoon Coats 2: 264
Radio 2: 339
Raggedy Ann and Raggedy Andy 1: 208
Rambo 5: 1131
Ranch House 2: 502
Rap and Hip-Hop 5: 1149
Raves 5: 1259
Reader's Digest 2: 316
The Real World 5: 1292
Reality TV 5: 1294
Red Scare 2: 360
Refrigerators 1: 222
Rhythm and Blues 3: 564
Ringling Bros. and Barnum & Bailey Circus 1: 223
Ripley's Believe It or Not! 2: 318
Road Rage 5: 1212
Road Runner and Wile E. Coyote 3: 606
Jackie Robinson (1919-1972) 3: 592
Rock and Roll 3: 690
Rockettes 2: 408
Norman Rockwell (1894–1978) 1: 191
Rocky 4: 970
The Rocky Horror Picture Show 4: 971
Jimmie Rodgers (1897–1933) 2: 298
Roe v. Wade 4: 1089

Will Rogers (1879–1935) 1: 178
Roller Coasters 1: 136
Rolling Stone 4: 871
Rolling Stones 4: 857
Roots 4: 1057
Rose Bowl 1: 113
Roseanne 5: 1187
Route 66 . . . . . 2: 361
Rowan & Martin's Laugh-In 4: 911
Rubik's Cube 5: 1169
Rudolph the Red-Nosed Reindeer 3: 581
Run-DMC 5: 1151
Babe Ruth (1895–1948) 1: 210

S

Saran Wrap 3: 649
Sassy 5: 1159
Satellites 3: 779
Saturday Evening Post 1: 93
Saturday Morning Cartoons 4: 912
Saturday Night Fever 4: 974
Saturday Night Live 4: 1058
Schoolhouse Rock 4: 1060
Scopes Monkey Trial 2: 363
Scouting (Boy and Girl) 1: 226
Scrabble 3: 592
Scream 5: 1245
Sears, Roebuck Catalog 1: 26
Seinfeld 5: 1296
Serial Killers 4: 1091
Sesame Street 4: 1062
Seventeen 3: 582
7-Up 2: 287
Sex Pistols 4: 992
Sexual Revolution 4: 941
Sexually Transmitted Diseases 4: 1093
The Shadow 2: 461
Shaft 4: 976
Shane 3: 673
Shock Radio 5: 1188
Silent Movies 1: 44
Simon and Garfunkel 4: 859
O. J. Simpson (1947–) 5: 1324

The Simpsons 5: 1190
Frank Sinatra (1915–1998) 3: 565
Sitcoms 3: 754
60 Minutes 4: 916
The $64,000 Question 3: 757
Skateboarding 3: 722
Skinheads 5: 1214
Skyscrapers 2: 502
Slinky 3: 594
Smiley Face 4: 1094
Snow White and the Seven Dwarfs 2: 410
Soap Operas 2: 486
Soda Fountains 1: 67
South Park 5: 1298
Spam 2: 423
Britney Spears (1981–) 5: 1261
Speed Racer 4: 917
Spider-Man 4: 873
Sport Utility Vehicles (SUVs) 5: 1215
Sports Illustrated 3: 724
Spring Break 3: 631
Standardized Testing 2: 365
Star Trek 4: 918
Star Wars 4: 977
Starbucks 5: 1110
Steamboat Willie 2: 278
Stereoscopes 1: 28
Stock Car Racing 2: 474
Streaking 4: 1095
Barbra Streisand (1942–) 4: 861
Students for a Democratic Society 4: 945
Studio One 3: 608
Suburbs 3: 780
Billy Sunday (1862–1935) 1: 138
Super Bowl 4: 884
Superman 2: 462
Supermodels 5: 1117

T

Talk Radio 5: 1193
Tanning 4: 1096
Tarzan 1: 192
Elizabeth Taylor (1932–) 3: 542

Taxi 4: 1063
Teddy Bears 1: 30
Teen Idols 3: 632
Teenage Mutant Ninja Turtles 5: 1194
Tejano Music 5: 1262
Telephone 1: 139
Television 3: 610
Shirley Temple (1928–) 2: 411
Tennis Shoes 1: 161
This Is Your Life 3: 758
Thomas the Tank Engine 5: 1299
Three Stooges 2: 412
3-D Movies 3: 674
Time 2: 319
Timex Watches 3: 650
Tinkertoys 1: 211
Titanic 1: 228
Today 3: 760
J. R. R. Tolkien (1892–1973) 3: 713
Tom Swift Series 1: 194
The Tonight Show 3: 761
Tonka Trucks 3: 596
Top 40 . . . . . 3: 694
Toy Story 5: 1247
Trading Stamps 3: 651
Transistor Radios 3: 763
Trivial Pursuit 5: 1170
True Story 1: 195
T-Shirt 1: 163
Tupperware 3: 520
TV Dinners 3: 680
TV Guide 3: 714
Twelve-Step Programs 2: 504
Twiggy (1949–) 4: 813
The Twilight Zone 3: 764
Twister 4: 885
2 Live Crew 5: 1152
2001: A Space Odyssey 4: 838

U

UFOs 3: 635
Urban Legends 5: 1217
USA Today 5: 1160

V

Rudolph Valentino (1895–1926) 2: 280
Valium 4: 801
Vaudeville 1: 47
Velveeta Cheese 2: 289
Video Games 4: 1020
Vogue 1: 196
Volkswagen Beetle 3: 652

W

Walkman 4: 994
Wall Drug 2: 505
Wal-Mart 4: 802
The Waltons 4: 1066
War Bonds 1: 231
The War of the Worlds 2: 489
John Wayne (1907–1979) 2: 414
Wayne's World 5: 1249
Weird Tales 2: 320
The Western 2: 415
Wheaties 2: 289
Who Wants to Be a Millionaire? 5: 1300
Whole Earth Catalog 4: 875
Wide World of Sports 4: 887
Winnie-the-Pooh 2: 321
The Wizard of Oz 2: 417
Wonder Bread 2: 290
Wonder Woman 3: 583
Tiger Woods (1975–) 5: 1275
Woodstock 4: 862
World Book Encyclopedia 1: 197
World Wrestling Federation 5: 1171
World's Fairs 1: 142
WWJD? (What Would Jesus Do?) 5: 1328

X

Xerox Copiers 4: 804

Y

Yo-Yo 2: 336
Y2K Scare 5: 1329
Yuppies 5: 1218

Z

Ziegfeld Follies **1:** 50
Zines **5:** 1162
Zipper **1:** 164
Zoot Suit **3:** 525
Zorro **1:** 199

ENTRIES BY TOPIC CATEGORY

Bold type indicates volume numbers.

Commerce

Advertising **2:** 244
Alka-Seltzer **2:** 374
AT&T **1:** 154
Aunt Jemima **1:** 8
Ballpoint Pens **2:** 375
Band-Aid **2:** 247
Barbie **3:** 644
Best-Sellers **3:** 517
Betty Crocker **2:** 248
Brownie Cameras **1:** 10
Budweiser **4:** 794
Burma-Shave **2:** 250
Cigarettes **2:** 251
Clairol Hair Coloring **2:** 377
Credit Cards **3:** 646
Department Stores **2:** 254
Dime Stores **1:** 11
Dixie Cups **1:** 14
Eddie Bauer **2:** 256
Fisher-Price Toys **2:** 377
Fuller Brush Company **1:** 14
Gap **4:** 795
G.I. Joe **4:** 796
Harley-Davidson **1:** 16
Home Shopping Network **5:** 1106

IBM 5: 1107
J.Crew 5: 1109
J. Walter Thompson Company 1: 18
Jeep 3: 519
Kellogg's Cereals 1: 19
Kleenex 2: 256
Kmart 4: 797
La-Z-Boy Loungers 2: 257
L. L. Bean 1: 155
Louisville Slugger 1: 21
Macy's Thanksgiving Day Parade 2: 258
Mall of America 5: 1230
Malls 3: 648
Marlboro Man 2: 259
Microsoft 5: 1231
Model T 1: 22
Nike 4: 799
Plastic 1: 24
Saran Wrap 3: 649
Sears, Roebuck Catalog 1: 26
Starbucks 5: 1110
Stereoscopes 1: 28
Teddy Bears 1: 30
Timex Watches 3: 650
Trading Stamps 3: 651
Tupperware 3: 520
Valium 4: 801
Volkswagen Beetle 3: 652
Wal-Mart 4: 802
Xerox Copiers 4: 804

Fashion

Abercrombie & Fitch 5: 1235
Arrow Collar Man 1: 158
Bell-Bottoms 4: 807
Bobbysoxers 3: 524
Bra 1: 159
Doc Martens 4: 809
Flappers 2: 261
Goth Culture 5: 1114
Hot Pants 4: 955
Jeans 3: 658
Ralph Lauren (1939–) 4: 956
Leisure Suit 4: 956

Levi's 3: 659
Lipstick 2: 263
Mary Kay Cosmetics 4: 810
Miniskirts 4: 811
Mood Rings 4: 958
Nylon 2: 379
Nylon Stockings 2: 380
Polyester 4: 959
Preppy 5: 1115
Raccoon Coats 2: 264
Supermodels 5: 1117
Tennis Shoes 1: 161
T-Shirt 1: 163
Twiggy (1949–) 4: 813
Zipper 1: 164
Zoot Suit 3: 525

Film and Theater

Abbott and Costello 3: 530
Airplane! 5: 1120
Andy Hardy Movies 2: 384
Austin Powers 5: 1238
"B" Movies 2: 386
Josephine Baker (1906–1975) 2: 267
Humphrey Bogart (1899–1957) 2: 389
Clara Bow (1905–1965) 2: 268
Beach Movies 4: 816
Betty Boop 2: 388
The Birth of a Nation 1: 168
Blade Runner 5: 1122
Broadway 1: 34
Buffalo Bill's Wild West Show 1: 36
James Cagney (1899–1986) 2: 390
Casablanca 3: 531
Charlie Chaplin (1887–1977) 1: 170
Charlie Chan 2: 269
Charlie McCarthy 2: 391
Citizen Kane 3: 533
A Clockwork Orange 4: 962
Gary Cooper (1901–1961) 2: 391
The Day the Earth Stood Still 3: 661
James Dean (1931–1955) 3: 663
Disaster Movies 4: 963
Disney 2: 270

Do the Right Thing 5: 1123
Dr. Strangelove 4: 818
Dracula 2: 392
E.T.: The Extra-Terrestrial 5: 1125
Easy Rider 4: 820
The Exorcist 4: 965
Fantasia 3: 535
Fatal Attraction 5: 1126
Felix the Cat 1: 171
Film Noir 3: 537
Forrest Gump 5: 1239
Francis the Talking Mule 3: 664
Frankenstein 2: 394
Friday the 13th 5: 1127
Clark Gable (1901–1960) 2: 396
Gertie the Dinosaur 1: 172
Ghostbusters 5: 1128
Lillian Gish (1896–1993) 1: 174
The Godfather 4: 966
Godzilla 3: 666
Gone with the Wind 2: 396
The Graduate 4: 822
The Great Train Robbery 1: 38
Hair 4: 824
A Hard Day's Night 4: 826
Hollywood 2: 400
Horror Movies 4: 827
Harry Houdini (1874–1926) 1: 39
Indiana Jones Movies 5: 1130
It's a Wonderful Life 3: 538
James Bond Films 4: 830
Jaws 4: 968
The Jazz Singer 2: 275
JFK 5: 1240
Keystone Kops 1: 175
King Kong 2: 403
Lassie 3: 540
Laurel and Hardy 2: 404
The Lion King 5: 1242
Marx Brothers 2: 406
Mary Poppins 4: 832
MGM 2: 276
Minstrel Shows 1: 40
Mr. Smith Goes to Washington 2: 407

Marilyn Monroe (1926–1962) 3: 667
Movie Palaces 1: 177
Nickelodeons 1: 42
North by Northwest 3: 668
The Odd Couple 4: 833
On the Waterfront 3: 669
Peyton Place 3: 671
Planet of the Apes 4: 834
Psycho 4: 836
Pulp Fiction 5: 1244
Rambo 5: 1131
Rockettes 2: 408
Rocky 4: 970
The Rocky Horror Picture Show 4: 971
Will Rogers (1879–1935) 1: 178
Saturday Night Fever 4: 974
Scream 5: 1245
Shaft 4: 976
Shane 3: 673
Silent Movies 1: 44
Snow White and the Seven Dwarfs 2: 410
Star Wars 4: 977
Steamboat Willie 2: 278
Elizabeth Taylor (1932–) 3: 542
Shirley Temple (1928–) 2: 411
Three Stooges 2: 412
3-D Movies 3: 674
Toy Story 5: 1247
2001: A Space Odyssey 4: 838
Rudolph Valentino (1895–1926) 2: 280
Vaudeville 1: 47
John Wayne (1907–1979) 2: 414
Wayne's World 5: 1249
The Western 2: 415
The Wizard of Oz 2: 417
Ziegfeld Follies 1: 50

Food and Drink

Burger King 3: 677
Campbell's Soup 1: 181
Chewing Gum/Bubble Gum 1: 54
Coca-Cola 1: 56
Cracker Jack 1: 58
Diners 1: 60

Dunkin' Donuts 3: 545
Fast Food. 2: 283
French Fries. 3: 678
Frozen Dinners 2: 419
Gerber Baby Food 2: 286
Hamburger 3: 680
Hot Dogs 1: 62
Ice-Cream Cone 1: 64
Jell-O. 1: 65
The Joy of Cooking 2: 421
M & M's 3: 546
McDonald's 3: 548
Oreo Cookies 1: 184
Pizza 3: 550
7-Up 2: 287
Soda Fountains 1: 67
Spam. 2: 423
TV Dinners 3: 680
Velveeta Cheese. 2: 289
Wheaties 2: 289
Wonder Bread 2: 290

Music

Altamont. 4: 842
Alternative Country Music 5: 1252
Alternative Rock 5: 1253
Beach Boys 4: 844
Beatles. 4: 846
Big Bands 2: 426
Bluegrass. 3: 554
Blues 2: 293
Compact Disc. 5: 1136
Country Music. 3: 555
Disc Jockeys 3: 684
Disco 4: 982
Bob Dylan (1941–). 4: 848
Eight-Track Tapes 4: 849
Electric Guitar 3: 686
Farm Aid 5: 1138
Folk Music. 4: 851
Funk 4: 984
Grand Ole Opry 2: 297
Grateful Dead 4: 852
Grunge 5: 1255

Heavy Metal 5: 1139
Billie Holiday (1915–1959) 2: 428
The Hustle 4: 985
Michael Jackson (1958–) 5: 1141
Jazz 1: 72
Robert Johnson (1911–1938) 2: 428
Scott Joplin (1868–1917) 1: 75
Jukeboxes 2: 429
Karaoke 5: 1142
B. B. King (1925–) 3: 688
KISS 4: 987
Led Zeppelin 4: 989
Live Aid 5: 1143
LL Cool J (1969–) 5: 1145
Lollapalooza and Lilith Fair 5: 1256
Long-Playing Record (LP) 3: 558
Madonna (1958–) 5: 1146
Barry Manilow (1946–) 4: 990
Monkees 4: 854
Motown 4: 856
MTV 5: 1147
Nirvana 5: 1258
Phonograph 1: 76
Pop Music 3: 560
Elvis Presley (1935–1977) 3: 689
Punk 4: 991
Rap and Hip-Hop 5: 1149
Raves 5: 1259
Rhythm and Blues 3: 564
Rock and Roll 3: 690
Jimmie Rodgers (1897–1933) 2: 298
Frank Sinatra (1915–1998) 3: 565
Britney Spears (1981–) 5: 1261
Rolling Stones 4: 857
Barbra Streisand (1942–) 4: 861
Run-DMC 5: 1151
Sex Pistols 4: 992
Simon and Garfunkel 4: 859
Tejano Music 5: 1262
Top 40 . . . . . 3: 694
2 Live Crew 5: 1152
Walkman 4: 994
Woodstock 4: 862

Print Culture

Advocate 4: 866
Archie Comics 3: 568
Argosy 1: 80
Batman 2: 434
Beatniks and the Beat Movement 3: 698
Better Homes and Gardens 2: 302
Blondie 2: 436
Judy Blume (1938–) 4: 998
The Bobbsey Twins Series 3: 570
The Bonfire of the Vanities 5: 1156
Book-of-the-Month Club 2: 303
Brenda Starr, Reporter 3: 571
Buck Rogers 2: 304
Buster Brown 1: 81
Captain America 3: 572
Dale Carnegie (1888–1955) 2: 438
The Catcher in the Rye 3: 700
Cathy 4: 998
Comic Books 2: 439
Cosmopolitan 4: 867
Curious George 3: 574
Detective Fiction 2: 441
Dick and Jane Readers 2: 443
Dick Tracy 2: 444
Dime Novels 1: 82
Doc Savage 2: 446
Dr. Seuss 3: 701
Dune 4: 868
Ebony 3: 576
Esquire 2: 448
The Far Side 5: 1157
Flash Gordon 2: 449
Frosty the Snowman 3: 702
Fu Manchu 1: 188
Garfield 4: 999
Gibson Girl 1: 84
Golden Books 3: 577
Good Housekeeping 1: 85
Gossip Columns 2: 306
The Grapes of Wrath 2: 451
Green Lantern 3: 578
Hardy Boys Series 2: 308
Harlequin Romances 4: 1001

Harry Potter Series 5: 1266
Highlights 3: 579
Hustler. 4: 1002
Jurassic Park 5: 1268
The Katzenjammer Kids 1: 86
Kewpie Dolls 1: 87
Krazy Kat. 1: 189
Life 2: 452
Li'l Abner 2: 454
Little Blue Books 2: 309
Little Orphan Annie. 2: 310
Jack London (1876–1916) 1: 88
MAD Magazine 3: 704
Marvel Comics. 4: 869
Ms. 4: 1004
Mutt & Jeff 1: 89
Nancy Drew Series. 2: 455
National Enquirer 3: 707
National Geographic 1: 90
New York Times. 1: 92
New Yorker 2: 312
On the Road. 3: 708
The Organization Man 3: 710
Paperback Books 2: 457
Peanuts 3: 710
People 4: 1005
Perry Mason 2: 458
Playboy 3: 712
Popeye. 2: 314
Pulp Magazines. 2: 459
Reader's Digest 2: 316
Ripley's Believe It or Not! 2: 318
Norman Rockwell (1894–1978) 1: 191
Rolling Stone 4: 871
Rudolph the Red-Nosed Reindeer. 3: 581
Sassy 5: 1159
Saturday Evening Post. 1: 93
Seventeen 3: 582
The Shadow. 2: 461
Spider-Man 4: 873
Superman 2: 462
Tarzan 1: 192
Time 2: 319
J. R. R. Tolkien (1892–1973) 3: 713

Tom Swift Series 1: 194
True Story 1: 195
TV Guide 3: 714
USA Today 5: 1160
Vogue 1: 196
Weird Tales 2: 320
Whole Earth Catalog 4: 875
Winnie-the-Pooh 2: 321
Wonder Woman 3: 583
World Book Encyclopedia 1: 197
Zines 5: 1162
Zorro 1: 199

Sports and Games

Aerobics 4: 1010
Atari 4: 1011
Charles Atlas 2: 326
Baseball 1: 96
Bowling 3: 588
Ty Cobb (1886–1961) 1: 99
James J. Corbett (1866–1933) 1: 100
Crossword Puzzles 2: 327
Dallas Cowboys 4: 880
Jack Dempsey (1895–1983) 2: 328
Babe Didrikson (1911–1956) 2: 468
Dungeons and Dragons 4: 1013
Erector Sets 1: 202
Etch A Sketch 3: 718
Extreme Sports 5: 1272
Frisbee 4: 881
Wayne Gretzky (1961–) 5: 1166
Hacky Sack 4: 1015
Harlem Globetrotters 2: 329
Indianapolis 500 . . . . . 1: 204
Jogging 4: 1016
Jack Johnson (1878–1946) 1: 101
Michael Jordan (1963–) 5: 1274
Kentucky Derby 1: 102
Evel Knievel (1938–) 4: 881
Jack LaLanne (1914–) 3: 718
LEGOs 3: 720
Lincoln Logs 2: 331
Lionel Trains 1: 104
Little League 2: 469

Joe Louis (1914–1981) 2: 471
Milton Bradley Company 1: 106
Miniature Golf 2: 332
Monday Night Football 4: 1017
Monopoly 2: 471
Muhammad Ali (1942–) 4: 878
Joe Namath (1943–) 4: 883
National Basketball Association 3: 590
National Football League 2: 334
National Hockey League 1: 207
Negro Leagues 1: 107
Olympics 1: 109
Ouija Boards 1: 111
Jesse Owens (1913–1980) 2: 473
Pac-Man 5: 1167
Pong 4: 1019
Raggedy Ann and Raggedy Andy 1: 208
Jackie Robinson (1919-1972) 3: 592
Rose Bowl 1: 113
Rubik's Cube 5: 1169
Babe Ruth (1895–1948) 1: 210
Scrabble 3: 592
Skateboarding 3: 722
Slinky 3: 594
Sports Illustrated 3: 724
Stock Car Racing 2: 474
Super Bowl 4: 884
Tinkertoys 1: 211
Tonka Trucks 3: 596
Trivial Pursuit 5: 1170
Twister 4: 885
Video Games 4: 1020
Wide World of Sports 4: 887
Tiger Woods (1975–) 5: 1275
World Wrestling Federation 5: 1171
Yo-Yo 2: 336

TV and Radio

The A-Team 5: 1176
The Adventures of Ozzie and Harriet 3: 728
All in the Family 4: 1024
Ally McBeal 5: 1278
Alvin and the Chipmunks 3: 729
American Bandstand 3: 731

Amos 'n' Andy 2: 478
The Andy Griffith Show 4: 890
Anime 5: 1280
Barney and Friends 5: 1281
Baywatch 5: 1283
The Beavis and Butt-Head Show 5: 1284
Jack Benny (1894–1974) 3: 597
The Beverly Hillbillies 4: 891
Beverly Hills 90210 . . . . . 5: 1286
Bewitched 4: 893
Bonanza 4: 895
The Brady Bunch 4: 1025
Bugs Bunny 3: 598
Cable TV 4: 1027
Candid Camera 3: 733
Captain Kangaroo 3: 734
Johnny Carson (1925–) 4: 896
CB Radio 4: 1030
Charlie's Angels 4: 1032
Cheers 5: 1177
CNN 5: 1179
The Cosby Show 5: 1181
Davy Crockett 3: 736
Dallas 5: 1183
Daytime Talk Shows 4: 897
Dobie Gillis 3: 737
Dr. Kildare 4: 900
Dragnet 3: 738
The Dukes of Hazzard 4: 1034
The Ed Sullivan Show 3: 739
ER 5: 1288
ESPN 4: 1035
Fantasy Island 4: 1036
Fibber McGee and Molly 2: 482
Flipper 4: 901
Frasier 5: 1289
Friends 5: 1290
The Fugitive 4: 902
Game Shows 3: 741
Gilligan's Island 4: 903
The Gong Show 4: 1038
Guiding Light 2: 483
Gunsmoke 3: 743
Happy Days 4: 1040

Hawaii Five-O 4: 905
Hee Haw 4: 1042
The Honeymooners 3: 744
The Howdy Doody Show 3: 601
I Love Lucy 3: 746
Kukla, Fran, and Ollie 3: 603
The Lawrence Welk Show 3: 748
Leave It to Beaver 3: 749
David Letterman (1947–) 5: 1185
Little House on the Prairie 4: 1043
The Lone Ranger 2: 485
The Love Boat 4: 1045
The Mary Tyler Moore Show 4: 1046
*M*A*S*H* 4: 1049
Miami Vice 5: 1186
The Mickey Mouse Club 3: 751
Mister Ed 4: 906
Mister Rogers' Neighborhood 4: 908
Monty Python's Flying Circus 4: 1051
Muppets 4: 1053
News Anchors 3: 604
The Partridge Family 4: 1054
The Price Is Right 3: 753
Public Broadcasting System 4: 909
Radio 2: 339
The Real World 5: 1292
Reality TV 5: 1294
Road Runner and Wile E. Coyote 3: 606
Roots 4: 1057
Roseanne 5: 1187
Rowan & Martin's Laugh-In 4: 911
Saturday Morning Cartoons 4: 912
Saturday Night Live 4: 1058
Schoolhouse Rock 4: 1060
Seinfeld 5: 1296
Sesame Street 4: 1062
Shock Radio 5: 1188
The Simpsons 5: 1190
Sitcoms 3: 754
60 Minutes 4: 916
The $64,000 Question 3: 757
Soap Operas 2: 486
South Park 5: 1298
Speed Racer 4: 917

Star Trek 4: 918
Studio One 3: 608
Talk Radio 5: 1193
Taxi 4: 1063
Teenage Mutant Ninja Turtles 5: 1194
Television 3: 610
This Is Your Life 3: 758
Thomas the Tank Engine 5: 1299
Today 3: 760
The Tonight Show 3: 761
Transistor Radios 3: 763
The Twilight Zone 3: 764
The Waltons 4: 1066
The War of the Worlds 2: 489
Who Wants to Be a Millionaire? 5: 1300

The Way We Lived

AIDS 5: 1198
Air Travel 2: 345
Amusement Parks 3: 768
Apollo Theater 2: 494
Apple Computer 4: 1070
Army-McCarthy Hearings 3: 769
Aromatherapy 5: 1305
Avon 1: 116
Baby Boom 3: 616
Baseball Cards 2: 347
Beanie Babies 5: 1306
Blacklisting 3: 771
The Bomb 3: 618
Bonnie and Clyde 2: 496
Branch Davidians 5: 1307
Bridge 1: 214
Bungalows 2: 349
Cabbage Patch Kids 5: 1200
Al Capone (1899–1947) 2: 350
Catalog Houses 1: 117
Cellular Phones 5: 1308
The Charleston 2: 351
Chat Rooms 5: 1309
Chautauqua Movement 1: 118
Chia Pets 4: 1072
Chrysler Building 2: 352
Civil Rights Movement 4: 922

Cocaine 5: 1201
Cocktail Hour 2: 353
Coffee. 5: 1311
Cold War 3: 621
Communes. 4: 1072
Coney Island 1: 120
Cults 4: 1073
Dancing. 1: 122
Diets 3: 774
Divorce 4: 1075
Drive-In Theater 2: 497
Earth Day. 4: 1077
Ecstasy. 5: 1313
Electric Appliances 1: 125
E-Mail 5: 1314
Empire State Building 2: 499
Environmentalism 4: 1079
Equal Rights Amendment 4: 1080
Evangelism 1: 127
Father's Day. 1: 215
Federal Bureau of Investigation. 3: 624
Ferris Wheel. 1: 128
Gangs 5: 1204
Gay Liberation Movement. 4: 926
General Motors 1: 130
Generation X. 5: 1206
Ghettos 4: 928
Goldfish Swallowing. 2: 500
Great Depression. 2: 500
Greyhound Buses. 1: 216
Hackers 5: 1317
Haight-Ashbury. 4: 929
Hairstyles. 1: 132
Highway System 3: 775
Hippies 4: 931
Hoover Dam 2: 501
Hot Rods 3: 626
Hula Hoop. 3: 777
Internet 5: 1319
The Joy of Sex 4: 1082
Kent State Massacre. 4: 1083
Ku Klux Klan 1: 217
Las Vegas. 3: 627
Levittown 3: 629

Charles Lindbergh (1902–1974) 2: 354
Lottery 4: 933
Mafia 4: 934
Marijuana 4: 936
Martial Arts 4: 937
Minivans 5: 1208
Miss America Pageant 2: 355
Mother's Day 1: 220
National Aeronautics and Space Administration 4: 938
National Organization for Women 4: 940
Penicillin 2: 356
Personal Computers 4: 1085
Pet Rocks 4: 1088
The Pill 3: 778
Pokémon 5: 1322
Political Correctness 5: 1209
Postcards 1: 134
Prohibition 2: 357
Prom 2: 358
Prozac 5: 1211
Ranch House 2: 502
Red Scare 2: 360
Refrigerators 1: 222
Ringling Bros. and Barnum & Bailey Circus 1: 223
Road Rage 5: 1212
Roe v. Wade 4: 1089
Roller Coasters 1: 136
Route 66 . . . . . 2: 361
Satellites 3: 779
Scopes Monkey Trial 2: 363
Scouting (Boy and Girl) 1: 226
Serial Killers 4: 1091
Sexual Revolution 4: 941
Sexually Transmitted Diseases 4: 1093
O. J. Simpson (1947–) 5: 1324
Skinheads 5: 1214
Skyscrapers 2: 502
Smiley Face 4: 1094
Sport Utility Vehicles (SUVs) 5: 1215
Spring Break 3: 631
Standardized Testing 2: 365
Streaking 4: 1095
Students for a Democratic Society 4: 945
Suburbs 3: 780

Billy Sunday (1862–1935) **1:** 138
Tanning **4:** 1096
Teen Idols **3:** 632
Telephone **1:** 139
Titanic **1:** 228
Twelve-Step Programs. **2:** 504
UFOs **3:** 635
Urban Legends. **5:** 1217
Wall Drug **2:** 505
War Bonds **1:** 231
World's Fairs **1:** 142
WWJD? (What Would Jesus Do?) **5:** 1328
Y2K Scare **5:** 1329
Yuppies **5:** 1218

ADVISORY BOARD

Special thanks are due to U•X•L's Bowling, Beatniks, and Bell-Bottoms *advisors for their invaluable comments and suggestions:*

Catherine Bond, Department Chair, Library and Media Services, Conestoga High School, Berwyn, Pennsylvania

Cathy Chauvette, Assistant Regional Branch Manager, Fairfax County Public Library, Fairfax County, Virginia

Nancy Schlosser Garabed, Library Media Specialist, Council Rock High School, Newtown, Pennsylvania

Ann West LaPrise, Junior High/Elementary Media Specialist, Huron School District, New Boston, Michigan

Nina Levine, Library Media Specialist, Blue Mountain Middle School, Cortlandt Manor, New York

CONTRIBUTORS

Timothy Berg. Visiting assistant professor, Western Michigan University. Ph.D., History, Purdue University, 1999.

Charles Coletta, Ph.D. Instructor, Department of Popular Culture, Bowling Green State University. Contributing writer, *St. James Encyclopedia of Popular Culture* (2000).

Rob Edelman. Instructor, State University of New York at Albany. Author, *Baseball on the Web* (1997) and *The Great Baseball Films* (1994). Co-author, *Matthau: A Life* (2002); *Meet the Mertzes* (1999); and *Angela Lansbury: A Life on Stage and Screen* (1996). Contributing editor, *Leonard Maltin's Movie & Video Guide, Leonard Maltin's Movie Encyclopedia,* and *Leonard Maltin's Family Viewing Guide.* Contributing writer, *International Dictionary of Films and Filmmakers* (2000); *St. James Encyclopedia of Popular Culture* (2000); *Women Filmmakers & Their Films* (1998); *The Political Companion to American Film* (1994); and *Total Baseball* (1989). Film commentator, WAMC (Northeast) Public Radio.

Tina Gianoulis. Freelance writer. Contributing writer, *World War I Reference Library* (2001–2); *Constitutional Amendments: From Freedom of Speech to Flag Burning* (2001); *International Dictionary of Films and Filmmakers* (2000); *St. James Encyclopedia of Popular Culture* (2000); and mystories.com, a daytime drama Web site (1997–98).

Sheldon Goldfarb. Archivist, Alma Mater Society of the University of British Columbia. Ph.D., English, University of British

Columbia. Author, *William Makepeace Thackeray: An Annotated Bibliography, 1976–1987* (1989). Editor, *Catherine,* by William Makepeace Thackeray (1999).

Jill Gregg Clever, A.A., B.A., M.L.I.S. Graduate of Michigan State University, Thomas Edison State College, and Wayne State University. Business-technology specialist, Toledo–Lucas County Public Library.

Justin Gustainis. Professor of communication, State University of New York at Plattsburgh. Author, *American Rhetoric and the Vietnam War* (1993).

Audrey Kupferberg. Film consultant and archivist. Instructor, State University of New York at Albany. Co-author, *Matthau: A Life* (2002); *Meet the Mertzes* (1999); and *Angela Lansbury: A Life on Stage and Screen* (1996). Contributing editor, *Leonard Maltin's Family Viewing Guide.* Contributing writer, *St. James Encyclopedia of Popular Culture* (2000); *Women Filmmakers & Their Films* (1998); and *The American Film Institute Catalog of Feature Films.*

Edward Moran. Writer of American culture, music, and literature. Associate editor, *World Musicians* (1999); *World Authors* (1996); and *Random House Dictionary of the English Language* (1987; 1991). Contributing writer, *St. James Encyclopedia of Popular Culture* (2000). Editor, *Rhythm,* a magazine of world music and global culture (2001).

Sara Pendergast. President, Full Circle Editorial. Vice president, Group 3 Editorial. Co-editor, *St. James Encyclopedia of Popular Culture* (2000). Co-author, *World War I Reference Library* (2001), among other publications.

Tom Pendergast. Editorial director, Full Circle Editorial. Ph.D., American studies, Purdue University. Author, *Creating the Modern Man: American Magazines and Consumer Culture* (2000). Co-editor, *St. James Encyclopedia of Popular Culture* (2000).

Karl Rahder. M.A., University of Chicago Committee on International Relations. Author, several articles on international history and politics.

Chris Routledge. Freelance writer and editor. Ph.D., American literature, University of Newcastle upon Tyne (UK). Author, "The Chevalier and the Priest: Deductive Method in Poe, Chesterton, and Borges," in *Clues: A Journal of Detection*

(2001). Editor, *Mystery in Children's Literature: From the Rational to the Supernatural* (2001).

Robert E. Schnakenberg. Senior writer, History Book Club. Author, *The Encyclopedia Shatnerica* (1998).

Steven Schneider. Ph.D. candidate, philosophy, Harvard University; Ph.D. candidate, cinema studies, New York University. Author, *An Auteur on Elm Street: The Cinema of Wes Craven* (forthcoming). Co-editor, *Horror International* (forthcoming) and *Dark Thoughts: Philosophic Reflections on Cinematic Horror* (forthcoming). Contributing writer, *British Horror Cinema* (2002); *Car Crash Culture* (2001); and numerous film journals.

Robert C. Sickels. Assistant professor of American film and popular culture, Whitman College. Ph.D., English, University of Nevada. Author, "A Politically Correct Ethan Edwards: Clint Eastwood's The Outlaw Josey Wales" in *Journal of Popular Film & Television* (forthcoming); "'70s Disco Daze: Paul Thomas Anderson's Boogie Nights and the Last Golden Age of Irresponsibility" in *Journal of Popular Culture* (forthcoming). Contributor, *St. James Encyclopedia of Popular Culture* (2000).

READER'S GUIDE

Popular culture—as we know it—was born in America, though historians disagree as to exactly when. Was it in 1893, when magazine publishers used new technologies to cut the costs of their magazines to a dime and sell hundreds of thousands of copies? Or was it in 1905, when the invention of the nickelodeon brought low-cost films to people all across the nation? Or was it back in 1886, when Richard Sears and Alvah Roebuck sent out their first catalog, which allowed people from all over to choose from among hundreds and then thousands of the same goods?

No matter the exact date, by the turn of the twentieth century, American magazine publishers, retailers, moviemakers, and other entertainers were bringing their goods before larger numbers of Americans than ever before. These magazines, movies, advertisements, shopping experiences, sports teams, and more were what we know as "popular culture," because they could be enjoyed firsthand by masses of Americans.

The story of America as revealed by its popular culture is complex and fascinating. Readers of *Bowling, Beatniks, and Bell-Bottoms: Pop Culture of 20th-Century America* will discover, for example, that the comedic forms first developed by vaudeville comedians at the turn of the century lived on in film, radio, and finally television. They will learn that black musicians created the musical forms that are most distinctly American: blues and jazz. And they will realize that popular culture reacted to things like war and economic depressions in ways that were surprising and unexpected. The study of popular culture has a great deal to teach the student who is interested in how people use entertainment and consumption to make sense of their lives and shape their experience.

Bowling, Beatniks, and Bell-Bottoms gathers together essays that reflect the variety, diversity, and excitement of American popular culture of the twentieth century. This collection focuses more on events, fads, programs, performances, and products than on biographies of people, which are well documented in other sources. Even so, brief biographies of notables are sprinkled throughout. With approximately 750 essays on individual topics and dozens of overviews of pop culture trends, *Bowling, Beatniks, and Bell-Bottoms* covers a great deal of American popular culture, though not nearly enough. There are hundreds more people, bands, TV programs, films, and products that were worthy of mention but were left out due to space consideration. Our advisory board of media specialists, however, helped assure that the most prominent and studied subjects were included.

Have you ever wondered how the Slinky was invented, what Velveeta cheese is made of, or what people danced to before rock and roll? Those answers are in *Bowling, Beatniks, and Bell-Bottoms,* along with many others. It is our hope that this collection will bring both information and pleasure to all students of American culture.

Organization

Bowling, Beatniks, and Bell-Bottoms is arranged chronologically by decade over five volumes (two decades per volume). The approximately 750 entries are grouped into nine topic sections: Commerce, Fashion, Film and Theater, Food and Drink, Music, Print Culture, Sports and Games, TV and Radio, and The Way We Lived (though not all topics appear in every decade). Many subjects can easily appear in several different decades, so those essays are placed in either the decade in which the product was invented or the fad initiated, or in the decade in which the subject was most prominent or popular. In addition, several of the essays could have appeared under different topics (such as a book that was made into a movie), so those essays appear under the topic where it was best known. Users should make frequent use of the index or the two additional tables of contents (arranged alphabetically by entry name and by topic category) to locate an entry.

Essays range in length from 150 to 1000 words, with the majority averaging less than 500 words. Every essay aims to describe the topic and analyze the topic's contribution to popular culture. Each essay lists additional sources on the topic, including books, magazine or journal articles, and Web sites. Whenever possible, references to books are geared to younger readers. The editors have personally visited every Web site mentioned and believe that these sites contain content that will assist the reader in understanding the subject. Due to the nature of the World Wide Web, it is possible that not all Web links will still function at the time of publication.

Bowling, Beatniks, and Bell-Bottoms also provides these features:

- A timeline that highlights key historic and pop culture events of the twentieth century
- A general overview of each decade
- A multipaged "At a Glance" box that breaks down "What We Said," "What We Read," "What We Watched," "What We Listened To," and "Who We Knew"
- An overview of each topic section in each decade
- More than 300 photos and illustrations
- Extensive use of cross references (pointing to decade, topic, and volume)

Acknowledgments

This collection simply could not have been created without the diligent efforts and true professionalism of some of the best writers we know: Timothy Berg, Charles Coletta, Rob Edelman, Tina Gianoulis, Justin Gustainis, Audrey Kupferberg, Edward Moran, Chris Routledge, and Bob Schnakenberg. Also worthy of mention are the contributions of Jill Gregg Clever, Sheldon Goldfarb, Karl Rahder, Steven Schneider, and Robert Sickels.

At U•X•L, we would like to thank Julia Furtaw for suggesting that we revisit the subject of American popular culture for younger readers, and Larry Baker for his good humor and skilled handling of the various stages of book production. Much appreciation goes to Theresa Murray, who thoroughly copyedited all five volumes and compiled the detailed subject index, as well as to Jim Buchanan and Bookcomp Inc./Nighthawk Design for their typesetting work. We'd like also to thank the staff of the Snohomish, Washington, branch of the Sno-Isle Regional Library for processing our innumerable book requests with such efficiency and good cheer. Rebecca, Mike, Penny, Vina, Eileen, and everyone else: Thank you. We truly appreciate the work you do.

This book is dedicated to our children, Conrad and Louisa, who provided valuable insights into the entries on Pokémon and Beanie Babies, and who will soon be old enough to find this book in their school libraries. Happy reading, kids!

Comments and Suggestions

We welcome your comments on *Bowling, Beatniks, and Bell-Bottoms*. Please send correspondence to: Editors, *Bowling, Beatniks, and Bell-Bottoms,* U•X•L, 27500 Drake Rd., Farmington Hills, MI 48331-3535; call toll-free: 800-877-4253; fax to 248-414-5043; or send e-mail via www.gale.com.

—Sara Pendergast and Tom Pendergast, Editors

TIMELINE

1900 On January 29, Ban Johnson forms the American League to compete against baseball's National League.

1900 In February, Eastman Kodak introduces the Brownie Camera.

1900 In March, the Good Roads Campaign tries to build support for better roads. At the time, there are only ten miles of paved roads in the nation.

1900 On March 31, the first ad for an automobile appears in *The Saturday Evening Post.*

1900 On April 23, Buffalo Bill Cody's *Wild West Show* opens at Madison Square Garden in New York City.

1900 On November 6, Republican William McKinley is reelected U.S. president, with New York governor Theodore Roosevelt as his vice president.

1900 On November 12, *Floradora,* one of the most popular theatrical musicals of the decade, premieres in New York. It runs for more than five hundred performances.

1901 On February 25, U.S. Steel is formed out of ten companies and becomes the world's largest industrial corporation.

1901 On March 13, steel tycoon Andrew Carnegie donates $2.2 million to fund a New York public library system.

1901 On September 6, President William McKinley is shot by an assassin in Buffalo, New York, and dies eight days later from complications from gangrene due to improperly dressed wounds. Theodore Roosevelt becomes president.

1901 On October 16, President Theodore Roosevelt starts a national controversy when he dines with black leader Booker T. Washington in the White House.

1902 The Teddy Bear is introduced, named after President Theodore Roosevelt.

1902 On January 1, in the first Rose Bowl football game, the University of Michigan defeats Stanford 49-0.

1902 On March 18, Italian opera singer Enrico Caruso produces his first phonographic recording.

1902 On April 16, Tally's Electric Theater, the first theater solely devoted to presenting motion pictures, opens in Los Angeles, California.

1902 On December 21, Guglielmo Marconi transmits the first wireless signals across the Atlantic Ocean.

1903 *Redbook* magazine is founded.

1903 The Portage Lakers of Houghton, Michigan—the first professional hockey team from the United States—win the International Hockey League championship.

1903 On January 22, the United States signs a 99-year lease on what will become the Panama Canal Zone, where they will build a canal that connects the Caribbean Sea to the Pacific Ocean.

1903 In February, the *Ladies' Home Journal* becomes the first American magazine to reach one million paid subscriptions.

1903 On May 23, two men make the first transcontinental automobile trip from San Francisco to New York in sixty-four days. Upon returning home, one driver is ticketed for exceeding the speed limit of six miles per hour.

1903 On August 14, Jim Jeffries defeats James J. "Gentleman Jim" Corbett to retain the world heavyweight boxing title.

1903 On September 12, Scott Joplin's ragtime opera *A Guest of Honor* begins a midwest tour.

1903 In October, the Boston Pilgrims defeat the Pittsburgh Pirates in the first World Series to pit an American League team against a National League team.

1903 On December 1, Edwin S. Porter's film *The Great Train Robbery* is considered the first Western and the first American film with a plot.

1903 On December 17, Wilbur and Orville Wright make the first sustained flight at Kitty Hawk, North Carolina.

1904 The Ford Motor Company sells fourteen hundred of its Model A cars.

1904 On April 20, the World's Fair opens in St. Louis, Missouri.

1904 On May 5, Cy Young pitches baseball's first perfect game.

1904 On November 8, Theodore Roosevelt is reelected president.

1905 The German navy launches the first submarine.

1905 African American leader W. E. B. Du Bois helps found the Niagara Movement, an organization to advance African American issues.

1905 On May 5, the *Chicago Defender,* the first major black newspaper, begins publication.

1905 In June, the era of the nickelodeon begins when Harry Davis's Pittsburgh, Pennsylvania, movie theater offers continuous movie showings. By the end of the decade, more than eight thousand nickel-admission movie theaters are in operation.

1905 On June 18, the Twentieth Century Limited begins train service between Chicago, Illinois, and New York City and boasts a travel time of only eighteen hours.

1906 Kellogg's Corn Flakes breakfast cereal is introduced.

1906 In February, Upton Sinclair publishes *The Jungle,* a novel depicting the horrible conditions in the meat-packing industry. The work prompts the passage of the Meat Inspection Act.

1906 On April 14, President Theodore Roosevelt coins the term "muckraking" when he criticizes journalists who expose abuses and corruption and miss the larger social picture.

1906 On April 18, a major earthquake and fire destroy much of San Francisco, California.

1906 On May 3, the First Annual Advertising Show in New York City heralds the beginning of an important American industry.

1906 On November 21, the first voice radio transmission travels eleven miles from Plymouth to Brant Rock, Massachusetts.

1907 Work begins on the Panama Canal.

1907 On January 23, in what newspapers call the "trial of the century," millionaire Harry K. Thaw is tried for the murder of world-famous architect Stanford White over the honor of Thaw's wife, showgirl Evelyn Nesbit.

1907 On June 10, French motion picture pioneers Auguste and Louis Lumière announce they have developed a method for producing color film.

1907 On July 8, Florenz Ziegfeld's musical revue, the *Ziegfeld Follies,* opens in New York.

1907 On December 3, actress Mary Pickford makes her stage debut in *The Warrens of Virginia.*

1908 The world's first skyscraper, the forty-seven-story Singer Building, is completed in New York City.

1908 The General Motors Corporation is formed and soon becomes the biggest competitor of the Ford Motor Company.

1908 In March, the Original Independent Show, organized in New York, includes works by American painters Edward Hopper, George Bellows, and Rockwell Kent.

1908 On September 6, Isreal Zangwill's play *The Melting Pot* opens in New York City; the title becomes an internationally recognized description of the United States.

1908 On October 1, the Ford Motor Company unveils its Model T with a price tag of $825. It soon becomes the best-selling automobile of its time.

1908 On November 3, former U.S. secretary of war William Howard Taft is elected president.

1908 On December 26, Jack Johnson defeats Tommy Burns to become the first black world heavyweight boxing champion. His victory is considered an outrage by white racists.

1909 The fifty-story Metropolitan Life Insurance Tower in New York City becomes the world's tallest building.

1909 The Ford Motor Company manufactures nineteen thousand Model T cars.

1909 On March 16, the Federal Bureau of Investigation is created as a federal law enforcement agency.

1909 On March 23, former president Theodore Roosevelt leaves for a safari in Africa. He is paid $50,000 by *Scribner's* for his account of the trip.

1909 On April 6, U.S. Navy commander Robert Peary reaches the North Pole.

1909 On May 3, the first wireless press message is sent from New York City to Chicago, Illinois.

1909 On July 12, the U.S. Congress asks the states to authorize a national income tax.

1910 Western novelist Zane Grey's book *Heritage of the Desert* becomes a huge commercial success, starting his career of bringing the American West to the reading world.

1910 Levis Strauss and Company begins making casual play clothes for children.

1910 The Boy Scouts of America are founded in Chicago, Illinois.

1910 On February 28, Russian ballerina Anna Pavlova makes her American debut at the Metropolitan Opera House in New York City.

1910 On March 28, the first one-man show by artist Pablo Picasso opens at photographer and editor Alfred Stieglitz's 291 Gallery in New York City.

1910 In November, the National Association for the Advancement of Colored People (NAACP) publishes the first issue of *The Crisis* magazine, edited by W. E. B. Du Bois.

1910 On November 3, the Chicago Grand Opera opens with a production of *Aida,* by Giuseppe Verdi.

1911 Irving Berlin composes "Alexander's Ragtime Band," the song that popularized ragtime music.

1911 Air conditioning is invented.

1911 *Photoplay,* the first movie fan magazine, is published.

1911 On March 25, in New York City, 146 female workers are killed in the Triangle Shirtwaist Factory fire, alerting Americans to the dangers women face in industrial labor.

1911 On May 23, President William Howard Taft dedicates the New York Public Library.

1911 On May 30, the first Indianapolis 500 auto race is won by Ray Harroun with an average speed of 74.59 mph.

1911 On August 8, *Pathe's Weekly,* the first regular newsreel to be produced in the United States, is released to motion picture theaters.

1911 On December 19, the Association of American Painters and Sculptors is founded.

1912 New Mexico and Arizona become the forty-seventh and forty-eighth states.

1912 The Little Theater in Chicago, Illinois, and the Toy Theater in Boston, Massachusetts, the first influential little theaters in the United States, are founded.

1912 Dancers Irene and Vernon Castle start a craze for ballroom dancing.

1912 On April 15, the *Titanic* sinks on its maiden voyage from Ireland to the United States, killing 1,517.

1912 In August, photographer and editor Alfred Stieglitz devotes an entire issue of his periodical *Camera Work* to the modern art movement.

1912 On August 5, former president Theodore Roosevelt is nominated as the presidential candidate of the newly formed Progressive Party.

1912 On October 31, *The Musketeers of Pig Alley,* a film by D. W. Griffith that points out the social evils of poverty and crime on the streets of New York, is released.

1912 On November 5, New Jersey governor Woodrow Wilson is elected president.

1912 On December 10, the Famous Players Film Company registers for copyright of the five-reel feature film *The Count of Monte Cristo,* directed by Edwin S. Porter.

1913 The 792-foot-high Woolworth Building in New York City becomes the world's tallest building, a record it holds until 1930.

1913 The first crossword puzzle is published.

1913 The Jesse Lasky Feature Play Co., which later would become Paramount Pictures, is established in Hollywood, California.

1913 The Panama Canal is completed, and officially opens on August 15, 1914.

1913 On February 17, the International Exhibition of Modern Art, known as the Armory Show, opens in New York City. It is the first opportunity for many Americans to view modern art.

1913 On February 25, the Sixteenth Amendment to the Constitution is approved, authorizing a federal income tax.

1913 On March 24, the million dollar, eighteen-hundred-seat Palace Theatre opens in New York City.

1913 On May 31, the Seventeenth Amendment to the Constitution is approved, providing for the direct election of U.S. senators.

1914 On February 13, the American Society of Composers, Authors, and Publishers (ASCAP), an organization that seeks royalty payments for public performances of music, is founded in New York City.

1914 In March, comedian Charles Chaplin begins to evolve the legendary character of the Little Tramp in the film *Mabel's Strange Predicament.*

1914 On July 3, the first telephone line connects New York City and San Francisco, California.

1914 On August 3, World War I starts in Europe when Germany invades Belgium. Soon all of Europe is drawn into the conflict, though the United States remains neutral.

1914 On September 5, a German submarine scores its first kill, sinking the British cruiser *Pathfinder,* as World War I intensifies.

1914 In September, in the World War I Battle of the Marne, Germany's advance into France is halted.

1914 On November 3, the first American exhibition of African sculpture opens at the 291 Gallery in New York City.

1914 On December 3, the Isadorables, six European dancers trained by American dancer Isadora Duncan, perform at Carnegie Hall in New York City after escaping with Duncan from her war-torn Europe.

1915 The first taxicab appears on the streets of New York City.

1915 The first professional football league is formed in Ohio and is called simply the Ohio League.

1915 Modern dancers Ruth St. Denis and Ted Shawn found the Denishawn School of Dancing in Los Angeles, California.

1915 Five hundred U.S. correspondents cover World War I in Europe.

1915 On March 10, the Russian Symphony Orchestra plays the American debut performance of the symphony *Prometheus* by Aleksandr Scriabin at Carnegie Hall in

New York City. Color images are projected onto a screen as part of the show.

1915 On December 10, the Ford Motor Company completes its one millionth Model T automobile.

1916 The Boeing Aircraft Company produces its first biplane.

1916 Newspaper publisher William Randolph Hearst inaugurates the *City Life* arts section as a supplement to his Sunday newspapers.

1916 In November, inventor and radio pioneer Lee De Forest begins to transmit daily music broadcasts from his home in New York City.

1916 On November 7, Woodrow Wilson is reelected president after campaigning on the pledge to keep the United States out of the war in Europe.

1917 The Russian Revolution brings communism to Russia, setting the stage for nearly a century of intermittent conflict with the United States.

1917 Showman George M. Cohan composes the song that was a musical call-to-arms during World War I: "Over There."

1917 Motion picture pioneer Cecil B. DeMille directs *The Little American,* a patriotic melodrama starring Mary Pickford.

1917 On April 6, the United States declares war on Germany after German submarines continue to attack U.S. merchant ships.

1917 On May 28, Benny Leonard wins the lightweight boxing championship, which he holds until his retirement in 1924 while building a record of 209-5; he makes a comeback in 1931.

1917 On August 19, the managers of the New York Giants and Cincinnati Reds are arrested for playing baseball on Sunday.

1917 On October 27, sixteen-year-old Russian-born violinist Jascha Heifetz makes his debut American performance at Carnegie Hall in New York City.

1918 The annual O. Henry Awards for short fiction are inaugurated in honor of short story writer O. Henry (a pseudonym for William Sydney Porter).

1918 On January 8, President Woodrow Wilson delivers his "Fourteen Points" address before Congress, outlining his plans for the shape of the postwar world.

1918 In March, *The Little Review* begins to serialize the novel *Ulysses,* by James Joyce, which features stream of consciousness techniques and a kind of private language.

1918 On November 11, Germany signs an armistice with the Allies, ending the fighting in World War I.

1918 In December, the Theatre Guild is founded in New York City.

1919 *Maid of Harlem,* an all-black-cast musical starring "Fats" Waller, Mamie Smith, Johnny Dunn, and Perry Bradford, draws enthusiastic crowds at the Lincoln Theatre in New York City.

1919 On January 29, Prohibition begins with the adoption of the Eighteenth Amendment to the Constitution, which bans the manufacture, sale, and transportation of intoxicating liquors.

1919 On February 5, United Artists, an independent film distribution company, is founded by Charles Chaplin, Douglas Fairbanks, D. W. Griffith, and Mary Pickford.

1919 On June 28, the Treaty of Versailles is signed by the Allied powers, officially ending World War I. Germany is forced to pay costly reparations for the damage it caused during the war.

1919 On July 4, Jack Dempsey defeats Jess Willard to win the world heavyweight boxing championship.

1919 On October 31, the Provincetown Players stage *The Dreamy Kid,* by Eugene O'Neill, with an all-black cast.

1919 On December 22, Attorney General A. Mitchell Palmer authorizes government raids on communists, anarchists, and other political radicals. These "Palmer raids" are part of a nationwide "red scare."

1920 Sinclair Lewis publishes the novel *Main Street.*

1920 Douglas Fairbanks stars in the film *The Mark of Zorro.*

1920 On January 5, the Radio Corporation of America (RCA) is founded and becomes a leading radio broadcaster.

1920 On February 12, the National Negro Baseball League is founded.

1920 On August 20, the first radio news bulletins are broadcast by station 8MK in Detroit, Michigan.

1920 On August 26, the Nineteenth Amendment to the Constitution gives women the right to vote.

1920 On September 28, eight Chicago White Sox players are charged with throwing the 1919 World Series in what becomes known as the "Black Sox Scandal." They are eventually banned from the game for life.

1920 On September 29, New York Yankee Babe Ruth breaks his own single-season home run record with 54 home runs.

1920 On November 1, Eugene O'Neill's play *The Emperor Jones* opens in New York City.

1920 On November 6, U.S. senator Warren G. Harding of Ohio is elected president.

1921 The Ford Motor Company announces a plan to produce one million automobiles a year.

1921 The Phillips Gallery in Washington, D.C., becomes the first American museum of modern art.

1921 In this year, 13 percent of Americans own telephones.

1921 On March 10, the first White Castle hamburger chain opens in Wichita, Kansas.

1921 On April 11, radio station KDKA in Pittsburgh, Pennsylvania, broadcasts the first sports event on radio, a boxing match between Johnny Ray and Johnny Dundee. Later that year, the World Series is broadcast.

1921 On May 23, *Shuffle Along* is the first black Broadway musical written and directed by African Americans.

1921 On July 29, Adolf Hitler is elected dictator of the Nazi Party in Munich, Germany.

1921 On September 8, the first Miss America pageant is held in Washington, D.C.

1921 On November 2, Margaret Sanger founds the American Birth Control League in New York City, raising the anger of many religious groups, especially Catholic groups.

1922 Robert Flaherty releases the documentary film *Nanook of the North.*

1922 Irish author James Joyce publishes *Ulysses,* which is banned in some countries for its alleged obscenity.

1922 F. Scott Fitzgerald publishes *Tales of the Jazz Age.*

1922 The American Professional Football Association changes its name to the National Football League (NFL).

1922 *Reader's Digest* magazine is founded.

1922 Al Jolson pens the popular song "Toot Toot Tootsie."

1922 On May 5, Coco Chanel introduces Chanel No. 5, which becomes the world's best-known perfume.

1922 On August 28, the first advertisement is aired on radio station WEAF in New York City.

1922 On December 30, the Union of Soviet Socialist Republics (USSR) is established with Russia at its head.

1923 Cecil B. DeMille directs the epic film *The Ten Commandments.*

1923 Charles Kettering develops a method for bringing colored paint to mass-produced cars.

1923 Bessie Smith's "Down Hearted Blues" is one of the first blues songs to be recorded.

1923 *Time* magazine begins publication.

1923 On April 6, trumpet player Louis Armstrong records his first solo on "Chimes Blues" with King Oliver's Creole Jazz Band.

1923 On August 3, President Warren G. Harding dies and Vice President Calvin Coolidge takes office.

1924 John Ford directs the Western film *The Iron Horse.*

1924 The Metro-Goldwyn-Mayer (MGM) film studio is formed in Hollywood, California.

1924 Evangelist Aimee Semple McPherson begins broadcasting from the first religious radio station, KFSG in Los Angeles, California.

1924 The stock market begins a boom that will last until 1929.

1924 On January 1, there are 2.5 million radios in American homes, up from 2,000 in 1920.

1924 On February 12, the tomb of King Tutankhamen, or King Tut, is opened in Egypt after having been sealed for four thousand years.

1924 On February 24, George Gershwin's *Rhapsody in Blue* is performed by an orchestra in New York City.

1924 On March 10, J. Edgar Hoover is appointed director of the Federal Bureau of Investigation.

1924 In June, the Chrysler Corporation is founded, and competes with General Motors and Ford.

1924 On November 4, incumbent Calvin Coolidge is elected president.

1925 In one of the most famous years in American literature, F. Scott Fitzgerald publishes *The Great Gatsby,* Ernest Hemingway publishes *In Our Time,* and Theodore Dreiser publishes *An American Tragedy.*

1925 Lon Chaney stars in the film *The Phantom of the Opera.*

1925 *EWSM Barn Dance* radio program begins broadcasting from Nashville, Tennessee; the name is later changed to *Grand Ole Opry* and it becomes the leading country music program.

1925 The magazine *The New Yorker* begins publication and features the prices paid for bootleg liquor.

1925 In February, the Boeing aircraft company builds a

plane capable of flying over the Rocky Mountains with a full load of mail.

1925 On May 8, the Brotherhood of Sleeping Car Porters, founded by A. Philip Randolph, is one of the first black labor unions.

1925 In July, in the Scopes "Monkey" trial, a Tennessee teacher is tried and found guilty of teaching evolution in a trial that attracts national attention.

1925 On August 8, forty thousand Ku Klux Klan members march in Washington, D.C., to broaden support for their racist organization.

1926 Latin idol Rudolph Valentino stars in the film *The Son of the Sheik.*

1926 Ernest Hemingway publishes *The Sun Also Rises.*

1926 The Book-of-the-Month Club is launched to offer quality books to subscribers.

1926 On March 7, the first transatlantic radiotelephone conversation links New York City and London, England.

1926 On March 17, *The Girl Friend,* a musical with songs by Richard Rodgers and Lorenz Hart, opens on Broadway.

1926 On April 18, dancer Martha Graham makes her first professional appearance in New York City.

1927 Al Jolson stars in the film *The Jazz Singer,* the first film to have sound. Clara Bow—the "It" girl—stars in *It.*

1927 On January 1, the Rose Bowl football game is broadcast coast-to-coast on the radio.

1927 On April 7, television is first introduced in America, but investors are skeptical.

1927 On May 21, Charles Lindbergh completes his nonstop flight from New York City to Paris, France, and is given a hero's welcome.

1927 On May 25, the Ford Motor Company announces that production of the Model T will be stopped in favor of the modern Model A.

1927 On September 22, the Jack Dempsey–Gene Tunney heavyweight championship fight becomes the first sports gate to top $2 million.

1927 On December 4, Duke Ellington's orchestra beings a long run at the Cotton Club nightclub in Harlem, New York.

1927 On December 27, the Oscar and Hammerstein musical *Show Boat* opens on Broadway in New York City.

1928 On April 15, the New York Rangers become the first American team to win the National Hockey League Stanley Cup.

1928 On May 11, WGY in Schenectady, New York, offers the first scheduled television service, though the high price of televisions keeps most people from owning them.

1928 On July 30, the Eastman Kodak company introduces color motion pictures.

1928 On November 6, former U.S. secretary of commerce Herbert Hoover is elected president.

1928 On December 13, George Gershwin's *An American in Paris* opens at Carnegie Hall in New York City.

1928 On December 26, swimmer Johnny Weissmuller retires from competition after setting sixty-seven world records.

1929 Mickey Mouse makes his first appearance in *Steamboat Willie,* an animated film made by Walt Disney.

1929 Commercial airlines carry 180,000 passengers in the year.

1929 Ernest Hemingway publishes *A Farewell to Arms,* a novel set during World War I.

1929 Nick Lucas's "Tiptoe through the Tulips with Me" and Louis Armstrong's "Ain't Misbehavin'" are two of the year's most popular songs.

1929 On February 14, in the Saint Valentine's Day Massacre, gunmen working for Chicago, Illinois, mobster Al Capone gun down seven members of a rival gang.

1929 On October 29, the stock market collapses on a day known as "Black Tuesday," marking the start of what will become the Great Depression.

1930 Grant Wood paints *American Gothic.*

1930 The Continental Baking company introduces Wonder Bread, the first commercially produced sliced bread.

1930 Unemployment reaches four million as the economy worsens.

1930 On January 14, jazz greats Benny Goodman, Glenn Miller, Jimmy Dorsey, and Jack Teagarden play George and Ira Gershwin's songs, including "I've Got a Crush on You," in the musical *Strike Up the Band* at the Mansfield Theater in New York City.

1930 On March 6, General Foods introduces the nation's first frozen foods.

1930 On May 3, Ogden Nash, a poet who will become famous for his funny, light verse, publishes "Spring Comes to Murray Hill" in the *New Yorker* magazine and soon begins work at the magazine.

1930 On September 8, the comic strip *Blondie* begins.

1930 On October 14, *Girl Crazy,* starring Ethel Merman, opens at New York's Guild Theater. The musical features songs by George Gershwin, Walter Donaldson, and Ira Gershwin, including "I Got Rhythm" and "Embraceable You."

1931 The horror films *Dracula* and *Frankenstein* are both released.

1931 Nevada legalizes gambling in order to bring revenue to the state.

1931 On March 3, "The Star Spangled Banner" becomes the national anthem by congressional vote.

1931 On April 30, the Empire State Building, the tallest building in the world, opens in New York City.

1931 On June 3, Fred and Adele Astaire perform for the last time together on the first revolving stage.

1931 On July 27, *Earl Carroll's Vanities,* featuring naked chorus girls, opens at the three-thousand-seat Earl Carroll Theater in New York City.

1931 On October 12, the comic strip *Dick Tracy* begins.

1932 Edwin Herbert Land, a Harvard College dropout, invents Polaroid film.

1932 On May 2, *The Jack Benny Show* premieres as a variety show on radio and runs for twenty-three years and then another ten years on television.

1932 On July 30, the Summer Olympic Games open in Los Angeles, California, and feature record-breaking performances by Americans Babe Didrikson and Eddie Tolan.

1932 On July 31, in German parliamentary elections, the Nazi Party receives the most seats but is unable to form a government.

1932 On November 7, the radio adventure *Buck Rogers in the Twenty-Fifth Century* premieres on CBS, and runs until 1947.

1932 On November 8, New York governor Franklin D. Roosevelt is elected president, promising to take steps to improve the economy. In his first one hundred days in office, Roosevelt introduces much legislation to use the government to aid those harmed by the Great Depression.

1932 On December 27, Radio City Music Hall opens at the Rockefeller Center in New York City.

1933 President Franklin D. Roosevelt presents the nation with his first radio address, known as a "fireside chat."

1933 Walt Disney releases the feature film *The Three Little Pigs.*

1933 On January 3, *The Lone Ranger* radio drama premieres on WXYZ radio in Detroit, Michigan.

1933 On January 30, Nazi leader Adolf Hitler becomes chancellor of Germany. Hitler soon seizes all power and sets out to attack his party's political enemies.

1933 On May 27, fan dancer Sally Rand attracts thousands with her performance at the Chicago World's Fair that celebrated the Century of Progress.

1933 On September 30, *Ah, Wilderness,* acclaimed American playwright Eugene O'Neill's only comedy, opens at the Guild Theater in New York City.

1933 On December 5, the Twenty-first Amendment to the Constitution puts an end to Prohibition.

1934 The first pipeless organ is patented by Laurens Hammond. The Hammond organ starts a trend toward more electrically amplified instruments.

1934 Dashiell Hammett publishes *The Thin Man,* one of the first hard-boiled detective novels.

1934 The Apollo Theater opens in Harlem, New York, as a showcase for black performers.

1934 German director Fritz Lang flees Nazi Germany to make movies in the United States.

1934 On May 5, bank robbers and murderers Bonnie Parker and Clyde Barrow are killed by lawmen in Louisiana.

1934 On July 1, the Motion Picture Producers and Distributors of America (MPPDA) association creates the Hay's Office to enforce codes that limit the amount and types of sexuality and other immoral behavior in films.

1934 On July 22, "Public Enemy No. 1" John Dillinger is shot and killed outside a Chicago, Illinois, theater by FBI agents and local police.

1934 On August 13, Al Capp's *Li'l Abner* comic strip debuts in eight newspapers.

1934 On August 19, Adolf Hitler is declared president of Germany, though he prefers the title Führer (leader).

1935 One out of four American households receives government relief as the Depression deepens.

1935 Twenty million Monopoly board games are sold in one week.

1935 The first Howard Johnson roadside restaurant opens in Boston, Massachusetts.

1935 The Works Progress Administration Federal Arts Projects, some of President Franklin D. Roosevelt's many New Deal programs, give work to artists painting post offices and other federal buildings.

1935 In April, *Your Hit Parade* is first heard on radio and offers a selection of hit songs.

1935 On April 16, the radio comedy-drama *Fibber McGee and Molly* debuts on NBC and runs until 1952.

1935 On May 24, the first nighttime major league baseball game is played in Cincinnati, Ohio.

1935 On October 10, *Porgy and Bess,* known as the "most American opera of the decade," opens in New York City at the Alvin Theater. The music George Gershwin wrote for the opera combined blues, jazz, and southern folk.

1936 American Airlines introduces transcontinental airline service.

1936 Ten African American athletes including Jesse Owens win gold medals in the Summer Olympics held in Berlin, Germany, embarrassing Nazi leader Adolf Hitler, who had declared the inferiority of black athletes.

1936 Dust storms in the Plains states force thousands to flee the region, many to California.

1936 Popular public-speaking teacher Dale Carnegie publishes his book *How to Win Friends and Influence People.*

1936 To increase feelings of nationalism, the Department of the Interior hires folksinger Woody Guthrie to travel throughout the U.S. Southwest performing his patriotic songs such as "Those Oklahoma Hills."

1936 In the Soviet Union, the Communist Party begins its Great Purge, executing anyone who resists the party's social and economic policies. By 1938, it is estimated that ten million people have been killed.

1936 Throughout Europe, countries scramble to form alliances with other countries for what seems to be a likely war. Germany and Italy join together to support the military government of Francisco Franco in Spain, while Great Britain and France sign nonaggression pacts with the Soviet Union.

1936 On July 18, the Spanish Civil War begins when Spanish military officers rise up against the Republican government of Spain.

1936 In October, the New York Yankees win the first of four World Series in a row.

1936 On November 3, Franklin D. Roosevelt is reelected as president of the United States.

1936 On November 23, the first issue of *Life* magazine is published.

1937 Dr. Seuss becomes a popular children's book author with the publication of *And to Think That I Saw It on Mulberry Street.*

1937 The Hormel company introduces Spam, a canned meat.

1937 A poll shows that the average American listens to the radio for 4.5 hours a day.

1937 *Porky's Hare Hunt,* a short animated cartoon by Warner Bros., introduces audiences to the Bugs Bunny character and the talents of Mel Blanc, the voice of both Bugs Bunny and Porky Pig.

1937 The first soap opera, *Guiding Light,* is broadcast. It continues as a radio program until 1956 and moves to television.

1937 British writer J. R. R. Tolkien publishes *The Hobbit.*

1937 On June 22, black boxer Joe Louis knocks out Jim Braddock to win the world heavyweight boxing championship.

1937 On December 21, *Snow White and the Seven Dwarfs,* the first feature-length animated film, is presented by Walt Disney.

1938 Glenn Miller forms his own big band and begins to tour extensively.

1938 On January 17, the first jazz performance at Carnegie Hall in New York City is performed by Benny Goodman and His Orchestra, with Duke Ellington, Count Basie, and others.

1938 In June, the character Superman is introduced in *Action Comics #1*. By 1939, he appears in his own comic book series.

1938 On August 17, Henry Armstrong becomes the first boxer to hold three boxing titles at one time when he defeats Lou Ambers at New York City's Madison Square Garden.

1938 On October 31, Orson Welles's radio broadcast of H. G. Wells's science fiction novel *The War of the Worlds* is believed to be a serious announcement of Martian invasion by listeners and panic spreads throughout the country.

1938 On November 11, singer Kate Smith's performance of "God Bless America" is broadcast over the radio on Armistice Day.

1939 Singer Frank Sinatra joins the Tommy Dorsey band, where he will soon find great success.

1939 Federal spending on the military begins to revive the economy.

1939 Pocket Books, the nation's first modern paperback book company, is founded.

1939 The National Collegiate Athletic Association (NCAA) holds it first Final Four championship basketball series, which is won by the University of Oregon.

1939 *Gone with the Wind,* David O. Selznick's epic film about the Civil War, stars Vivien Leigh and Clark Gable.

1939 *The Wizard of Oz* whisks movie audiences into a fantasyland of magic and wonder. The film stars Judy Garland and includes such popular songs as "Somewhere Over the Rainbow," "Follow the Yellow Brick Road," and "We're Off to See the Wizard."

1939 On May 2, baseball great Lou "The Iron Man" Gehrig ends his consecutive game streak at 2,130 when he removes himself from the lineup.

1939 On September 1, German troops invade Poland, causing Great Britain and France to declare war on Germany and starting World War II. Days later, the Soviet Union invades Poland as well, and soon Germany and the Soviet Union divide Poland.

1940 The radio program *Superman* debuts, introducing the phrases "Up, up, and away!" and "This looks like a job for Superman!"

1940 On February 22, German troops begin construction of a concentration camp in Auschwitz, Poland.

1940 The first issue of the comic book *Batman* is published.

1940 On May 10, German forces invade Belgium and Holland, and later march into France.

1940 On June 10, Italy declares war on Britain and France.

1940 On June 14, the German army enters Paris, France.

1940 On August 24, Germany begins bombing London, England.

1940 On November 5, President Franklin D. Roosevelt is reelected for his third term.

1940 On November 13, the Disney film *Fantasia* opens in New York City.

1941 "Rosie the Riveter" becomes the symbol for the many women who are employed in various defense industries.

1941 *Citizen Kane,* which many consider the greatest movie of all time, is released, directed by and starring Orson Welles.

1941 On January 15, A. Philip Randolph leads the March on Washington to call for an end to racial discrimination in defense-industry employment. President Franklin D. Roosevelt eventually signs an executive order barring such discrimination.

1941 On March 17, the National Gallery of Art is opened in Washington, D.C.

1941 On July 1, CBS and NBC begin offering about fifteen hours of commercial television programming each week—but few consumers have enough money to purchase television sets.

1941 On October 19, German troops lay siege to the Russian city of Moscow.

1941 On December 7, Japanese planes launch a surprise attack on the U.S. naval and air bases in Pearl Harbor, Hawaii, and declare war against the United States.

1941 On December 11, the United States declares war on Germany and Italy in response to those countries' declarations of war.

1941 On December 15, the annual Rose Bowl football game is moved from Pasadena, California, to Durham, North Carolina, to avoid the chance of a Japanese bombing attack.

1942 Humphrey Bogart and Ingrid Bergman star in *Casablanca,* set it war-torn Europe.

1942 On February 19, President Franklin D. Roosevelt signs an executive order placing all Japanese Americans on the West Coast in internment camps for the rest of the war.

1942 On May 5, sugar rationing starts in the United States, followed by the rationing of other products.

1942 In June, American troops defeat the Japanese at the Battle of Midway.

1942 On December 25, the comedy team of Abbott and Costello is voted the leading box-office attraction of 1942.

1943 Gary Cooper and Ingrid Bergman star in *For Whom the Bell Tolls,* the film version of the novel by Ernest Hemingway.

1943 On January 25, the Pentagon, the world's largest office complex and the home to the U.S. military, is completed in Arlington, Virginia.

1943 On March 14, composer Aaron Copland's *Fanfare for the Common Man* premieres in Cincinnati, Ohio.

1943 On March 30, the musical *Oklahoma!* opens on Broadway in New York City.

1943 During the summer, race riots break out in Detroit, Michigan, and Harlem, New York.

1943 On September 8, Italy surrenders to the Allies.

1943 On November 9, artist Jackson Pollock has his first solo show in New York City.

1943 On December 30, *Esquire* magazine loses its second-class mailing privileges after it is charged with being "lewd" and "lascivious" by the U.S. Post Office.

1944 *Seventeen* magazine debuts.

1944 *Double Indemnity,* directed by Billy Wilder, becomes one of the first of a new genre of movies known as *film noir.*

1944 On March 4, American planes bomb Berlin, Germany.

1944 On June 6, on "D-Day," Allied forces land in Normandy, France, and begin the liberation of western Europe.

1944 On June 22, the Serviceman's Readjustment Act, signed by President Franklin D. Roosevelt, provides funding for a variety of programs for returning soldiers, including education programs under the G.I. Bill.

1944 On August 25, Allied troops liberate Paris, France.

1944 On November 7, Franklin D. Roosevelt is reelected for an unprecedented fourth term as president.

1945 Chicago publisher John H. Johnson launches *Ebony* magazine.

1945 The radio program *The Adventures of Ozzie and Harriet* debuts.

1945 On January 27, the Soviet Red Army liberates Auschwitz, Poland, revealing the seriousness of German efforts to exterminate Jews.

1945 On April 12, President Franklin D. Roosevelt dies of a cerebral hemorrhage and Vice President Harry S. Truman takes over as president.

1945 On April 21, Soviet troops reach the outskirts of Berlin, the capital of Germany.

1945 On April 30, German leader Adolf Hitler commits suicide in Berlin, Germany, as Allied troops approach the city.

1945 On May 5, American poet Ezra Pound is arrested in Italy on charges of treason.

1945 On May 8, Germany surrenders to the Allies, bringing an end to World War II in Europe.

1945 On August 6, the United States drops the first atomic bomb on the Japanese city of Hiroshima, killing more than fifty thousand people.

1945 On August 9, the United States drops a second atomic bomb on Nagasaki, Japan.

1945 On September 2, Japan offers its unconditional surrender onboard the U.S.S. *Missouri* in Tokyo Bay, bringing an end to World War II.

1946 The Baby Boom begins as the birthrate rises 20 percent over the previous year.

1946 *It's a Wonderful Life,* starring Jimmy Stewart and directed by Frank Capra, becomes one of the most popular Christmas movies of all time.

1946 On January 10, the first General Assembly of the United Nations meets in London, England.

1946 On June 19, Joe Louis knocks out Billy Conn in the first heavyweight boxing match ever shown on television, retaining his title.

1946 On December 11, country singer Hank Williams cuts his first single, "Calling You."

1947 On January 29, Arthur Miller's play *All My Sons* opens in New York City.

1947 On March 12, President Harry S. Truman announces his "containment" policy aimed at stopping the spread of communism. It will later become known as the Truman Doctrine.

1947 On March 21, Congress approves the Twenty-second

Amendment which limits the president to two four-year terms in office. The amendment is ratified in 1951.

1947 On April 10, Jackie Robinson breaks the "color barrier" when he signs a contract to play for professional baseball's Brooklyn Dodgers. He is later named "Rookie of the Year" by *The Sporting News*.

1947 Beginning September 30, the World Series is televised for the first time as fans watch the New York Yankees defeat the Brooklyn Dodgers in seven games.

1947 On October 13, the Hollywood Ten, a group of film directors and writers, appears before the House Un-American Activities Committee (HUAC).

1947 On December 3, Tennessee Williams's *A Streetcar Named Desire* opens on Broadway in New York City.

1948 The Baskin-Robbins ice cream chain opens.

1948 On April 3, Congress approves $6 billion in Marshall Plan aid for rebuilding European countries.

1948 On May 14, the state of Israel is established.

1948 On May 29, the play *Oklahoma!* closes after a record 2,246 performances.

1948 On June 25, heavyweight boxing champion Joe Louis knocks out Joe Walcott for his twenty-fifth title defense and announces his retirement from boxing following the fight.

1948 On September 13, Margaret Chase Smith of Maine becomes the first woman elected to the U.S. Senate.

1948 On November 2, incumbent Harry S. Truman is elected president.

1949 Builder Abraham Levitt and his sons begin construction on a Long Island, New York, suburb called Levittown which will become a symbol for the postwar housing boom.

1949 On February 10, Arthur Miller's *Death of a Salesman* opens on Broadway in New York City.

1949 On April 4, the North Atlantic Treaty Organization (NATO) is formed by the United States and twelve other mainly European countries to provide for mutual defense.

1949 On September 23, American, British, and Canadian officials reveal that the Soviet Union has successfully detonated an atomic bomb.

1949 On October 1, the Communist People's Republic of China is proclaimed.

1950 The first Xerox copy machine is produced.

1950 Miss Clairol hair coloring is introduced, making it easy for women to dye their hair at home.

1950 Desegregation continues when Charles Cooper becomes the first black player in the National Basketball Association and Althea Gibson becomes the first black woman to compete in a national tennis tournament.

1950 In March, the Boston Institute of Contemporary Art and New York's Metropolitan Museum and Whitney Museum release a joint statement on modern art opposing "any attempt to make art or opinion about art conform to a single point of view."

1950 On May 8, President Harry S. Truman sends the first U.S. military mission to Vietnam.

1950 On June 30, U.S. combat troops enter the Korean War.

1950 On October 2, *Peanuts,* the comic strip written and drawn by Charles Schulz, debuts in seven U.S. newspapers.

1951 *The Caine Mutiny,* a war novel by Herman Wouk, is published and soon becomes one of the longest lasting best-sellers of all time, holding its place on the *New York Times* list for 48 weeks.

1951 On April 5, Julius and Ethel Rosenberg receive death sentences for allegedly giving secret information to the Soviet Union.

1951 On June 25, CBS offers the first color television broadcast.

1951 On August 5, the soap operas *Search for Tomorrow* and *Love of Life* premiere on CBS.

1951 On October 15, the sitcom *I Love Lucy* premieres on CBS.

1951 On November 18, the news program *See It Now,* hosted by Edward R. Murrow, premieres on CBS.

1952 *Gunsmoke* debuts as a radio drama. In 1955, the Western drama moves to TV where it lasts until 1975. The show, which starred James Arness as Marshal Matt Dillon, becomes the longest running prime-time TV show with continuing characters.

1952 In January, *American Bandstand,* a popular teen-oriented music program, debuts as a local show in Philadelphia, Pennsylvania. Dick Clark, its most famous host, joins the show in 1956.

1952 On January 14, *The Today Show* debuts on NBC.

1952 In September, *The Old Man and the Sea,* a short novel by Ernest Hemingway, is printed in *Life* magazine, and is the Book-of-the-Month Club's co-main selection.

1953 On October 5, the New York Yankees become the first team in history to win five consecutive World Series when they defeat the Brooklyn Dodgers.

1952 In November, *Bwana Devil,* the first 3-D movie, is released.

1952 On November 4, World War II general Dwight D. Eisenhower is elected president.

1953 *Playboy* becomes the first mass-market men's magazine and rockets to popularity when it publishes nude pictures of rising movie star Marilyn Monroe.

1953 IBM introduces its first computer, the 701.

1953 On January 1, Hank Williams, the father of contemporary country music, dies at age 29 from a heart disease resulting from excessive drinking.

1953 On April 3, the first national edition of *TV Guide* is published.

1953 On July 27, the Korean War ends.

1953 On September 13, Nikita Khrushchev is named first secretary of the Soviet Union's Communist Party.

1953 In November, an eleven-day photoengravers strike leaves New York City without a daily newspaper for the first time since 1778.

1954 Senator Joseph McCarthy leads hearings into the presence of communists in the U.S. Army; his actions are later condemned by the Senate.

1954 *Sports Illustrated* becomes the first glossy weekly magazine about sports.

1954 Swanson Foods introduces the first TV dinners.

1954 On April 4, legendary conductor Arturo Toscanini makes his final appearance conducting the NBC Symphony Orchestra. The concert is broadcast on the radio live from New York City's Carnegie Hall.

1954 On April 4, Walt Disney signs a contract with ABC to produce twenty-six television films each year.

1954 On May 14, the Soviet Union joins with seven Eastern European countries to form the Warsaw Pact, a union of nations pledged to mutual defense.

1954 On May 17, with its *Brown v. Board of Education* decision, the U.S. Supreme Court ends segregation in public schools.

1954 In July, the Newport Jazz Festival debuts in Newport, Rhode Island.

1954 On July 19, "That's All Right, Mama" and "Blue Moon of Kentucky," the first professional records made by Elvis Presley, are released on Sun Records.

1954 On September 27, *The Tonight Show* debuts on NBC.

1954 In October and November, Hungary tries to leave the Warsaw Pact but is attacked and reclaimed by the Soviet Union.

1955 Velcro is invented.

1955 *The $64,000 Question* debuts and soon becomes the most popular game show of the 1950s.

1955 In January, Marian Anderson becomes the first black singer to appear at the Metropolitan Opera.

1955 On January 19, President Dwight D. Eisenhower holds the first televised presidential news conference.

1955 In March, *The Blackboard Jungle,* the first feature film to include a rock and roll song on its soundtrack—"Rock Around the Clock," by Bill Haley and The Comets—opens. The song becomes the country's number-one single in July.

1955 On April 12, large-scale vaccinations for polio are administered throughout the United States.

1955 On July 17, the Disneyland amusement park opens in Anaheim, California.

1955 On September 30, actor James Dean dies after his Porsche roadster slams into another car on a California highway.

1955 On October 13, poet Allen Ginsberg gives the first public reading of *Howl,* his controversial poem-in-progress.

1955 On December 5, Rosa Parks refuses to give up her seat to a white man on a bus in Montgomery, Alabama, sparking a bus boycott that will become a key moment in the Civil Rights Movement.

1956 On June 20, Loew's Inc. releases MGM's pre-1949 film library—excluding *Gone with the Wind* (1939)—for television broadcast.

1956 On November 6, President Dwight D. Eisenhower is reelected.

1956 On November 30, videotape is first used commercially on television, during the broadcast of CBS's *Douglas Edwards with the News.*

1957 On September 26, the landmark musical *West Side Story,* a modern-day adaptation of *Romeo and Juliet* by William Shakespeare, opens on Broadway at the Winter Garden Theatre in New York City.

1957 On October 5, the Soviet Union launches the satellite *Sputnik,* the first man-made satellite in space.

1958 On August 26, Alaska becomes the forty-ninth state.

1958 On October 2, Leonard Bernstein begins his first season as director of the New York Philharmonic.

1958 On October 16, sponsors drop the NBC quiz show *Twenty-One* after a grand jury investigation determines that contestants were provided with pre-show answers.

1959 On January 2, revolutionary leader Fidel Castro assumes power in Cuba.

1959 On February 3, rock and roll legends Buddy Holly, Ritchie Valens, and J. P. Richardson (known as "The Big Bopper") die in a plane crash outside Clear Lake, Iowa.

1959 On August 21, Hawaii becomes the fiftieth state.

1959 On October 21, the Solomon R. Guggenheim Museum, designed by architect Frank Lloyd Wright, opens in New York City.

1960 Designer Pierre Cardin introduces his first fashion designs for men.

1960 On January 3, the Moscow State Symphony begins a seven-week tour at New York City's Carnegie Hall, becoming the first Soviet orchestra to perform in the United States.

1960 On February 11, Jack Paar, host of *The Tonight Show,* walks off the show when an NBC censor deletes a joke from his performance.

1960 On February 20, black students in Greensboro, North Carolina, stage sit-ins at local lunch counters to protest discrimination.

1960 In April, the New York state legislature authorizes the City of New York to purchase Carnegie Hall, which was scheduled for demolition.

1960 On April 1, Lucille Ball and Desi Arnaz appear for the last time as Lucy and Ricky Ricardo on *The Lucy-Desi Comedy Hour.*

1960 On May 5, the Soviet Union announces the capture of American pilot Francis Gary Powers, whose U-2 spy plane was shot down over the Soviet Union.

1960 On September 26, U.S. senator John F. Kennedy of Massachusetts and Vice President Richard M. Nixon appear in the first televised presidential debate.

1960 On October 13, jazz trumpeter Louis Armstrong begins a goodwill tour of Africa, partially sponsored by the U.S. State Department.

1960 On November 8, U.S. senator John F. Kennedy of Massachusetts is elected president.

1961 On January 20, Robert Frost reads his poem "The Gift Outright" at the inauguration of President John F. Kennedy.

1961 On January 27, soprano Leontyne Price first performs at New York's Metropolitan Opera.

1961 In April, folk singer Bob Dylan makes his debut at Gerde's Folk City in New York City's Greenwich Village.

1961 On April 12, Soviet cosmonaut Yuri Gagarin becomes the first man to orbit the Earth.

1961 During the summer, Freedom Rides across the South are aimed at desegregating interstate bus travel.

1961 On August 15–17, East Germany constructs the Berlin Wall, separating communist East Berlin from democratic West Berlin.

1961 On October 1, Roger Maris sets the single-season home run record with 61 homers.

1962 On February 10, Jim Beatty become the first person to run a mile in less than four minutes with a time of 3:58.9.

1962 On May 30, jazz clarinetist Benny Goodman begins a six-week, U.S. State Department–arranged tour of Russia.

1962 On July 10, the *Telstar* satellite is launched and soon brings live television pictures to American television viewers.

1962 On August 5, actress Marilyn Monroe dies from an overdose of barbiturates.

1962 On September 25, Philharmonic Hall, the first completed building of New York's Lincoln Center for the Performing Arts, is inaugurated by Leonard Bernstein and the New York Philharmonic.

1962 On September 29, *My Fair Lady* closes on Broadway after 2,717 performances, making it the longest-running show in history.

1962 In October, the United States and the Soviet Union clash over the presence of Soviet missiles in Cuba.

1962 On October 1, James Meredith becomes the first black person to enroll at the University of Mississippi as federal troops battle thousands of protestors.

1963 On January 8, *Mona Lisa,* by Leonardo da Vinci, is shown at Washington's National Gallery, the first time the painting ever has appeared outside the Louvre in Paris, France.

1963 On May 7, the Guthrie Theatre in Minneapolis, Minnesota, the first major regional theater in the Midwest, opens.

1963 On November 22, President John F. Kennedy is assassinated in Dallas, Texas, and Vice President Lyndon B. Johnson assumes the presidency.

1963 On November 24, the murder of alleged presidential assassin Lee Harvey Oswald is broadcast live on television.

1964 Ford introduces its Mustang, a smaller sporty car.

1964 On February 9, the Beatles make their first appearance on American television, on *The Ed Sullivan Show.*

1964 On February 25, Cassius Clay (who later changes his name to Muhammad Ali) beats Sonny Liston to become the heavyweight boxing champion of the world.

1964 In May, the just-remodeled Museum of Modern Art in New York City reopens with a new gallery, the Steichen Photography Center, named for photographer Edward Steichen.

1964 On July 2, President Lyndon B. Johnson signs the

Civil Rights Act of 1964, which bans racial discrimination in public places and in employment.

1964 On August 7, in the Gulf of Tonkin Resolution, Congress gives President Lyndon B. Johnson the power to use military force to protect U.S. interests in Vietnam.

1964 On November 3, incumbent Lyndon B. Johnson is elected president.

1965 In January, Bob Dylan plays an electric guitar on his new single, "Subterranean Homesick Blues."

1965 On February 21, black leader Malcolm X is murdered in Harlem, New York.

1965 On March 8, the first U.S. combat troops are sent to Vietnam.

1965 On April 26, *Symphony No. 4* by Charles Ives is performed in its entirety for the first time by the American Symphony Orchestra, conducted by Leopold Stokowski.

1965 On May 9, piano virtuoso Vladimir Horowitz returns to the Carnegie Hall stage after a twelve-year "retirement."

1965 On June 2, in a letter to President Lyndon B. Johnson, Pulitzer Prize-winning poet Robert Lowell declines an invitation to attend a White House arts festival, citing his "dismay and distrust" of American foreign policy.

1965 In July, Bob Dylan and his electric guitar are booed off the Newport Folk Festival stage.

1965 On September 29, President Lyndon B. Johnson signs into law the Federal Aid to the Arts Bill.

1965 On October 15, demonstrations against the Vietnam War occur in forty U.S. cities.

1965 On December 9, *A Charlie Brown Christmas* becomes the first *Peanuts* special to air on TV.

1966 The National Organization for Women (NOW) is established.

1966 On June 8, the National Football League and the American Football League merge.

1966 On July 12, rioting by blacks breaks out in twenty U.S. cities over racial discrimination.

1966 On August 29, the Beatles play their last live concert.

1966 On December 8, philanthropist, horse breeder, and art collector Paul Mellon donates his collection of British rare books, paintings, drawings, and prints, valued at over $35 million, to Yale University.

1967 On January 15, in the first Super Bowl, the Green Bay Packers defeat the Kansas City Chiefs, 35-10.

1967 On February 18, the National Gallery of Art arranges to purchase Leonardo da Vinci's *Ginevra dei Benci* for between five and six million dollars, the highest price paid to date for a single painting.

1967 In June, the Monterey International Pop Festival, an important early rock music event, is held in California.

1967 On June 20, Muhammad Ali is stripped of his boxing titles after being found guilty of tax evasion.

1967 On July 23, federal troops are called in to put a stop to rioting in Detroit, Michigan. Forty-three people are killed in the rioting, which lasts a week.

1967 On November 9, the first issue of *Rolling Stone* magazine is published. On the cover is a portrait of the Beatles's John Lennon.

1967 In December, Universal News, the last of the movie newsreel companies, closes because it is unable to compete with television news.

1968 On January 30, North Vietnam launches the Tet Offensive, escalating the war in Vietnam.

1968 On April 4, civil rights leader Martin Luther King Jr. is murdered in Memphis, Tennessee.

1968 On April 19, *Hair* opens on Broadway, at New York City's Biltmore Theatre.

1968 On June 5, presidential candidate Robert F. Kennedy is murdered in Los Angeles, California.

1968 On September 16, presidential candidate Richard Nixon appears as a guest on TV's *Rowan and Martin's*

Laugh-In and delivers one of the show's signature lines: "Sock it to me."

1968 On November 1, the Motion Picture Association of America inaugurates its film ratings system.

1968 On November 5, former vice president Richard Nixon is elected president.

1969 Hot pants make their first appearance.

1969 On July 20, U.S. astronaut Neil Armstrong becomes the first man to walk on the moon when the *Apollo XI* mission succeeds.

1969 On August 15–17, the Woodstock Music and Art Fair is held on a six-hundred-acre hog farm in upstate New York.

1969 On November 15, a quarter million Vietnam War protestors march in Washington, D.C.

1969 On December 6, a festivalgoer is murdered during the Altamont Rock Festival in California.

1970 Soviet cosmonauts spend seventeen days in space, setting a new record for space longevity.

1970 Across the nation, protests continue over the ongoing Vietnam War.

1970 Rock stars Jimi Hendrix and Janis Joplin die within three weeks of each other, both as a result of drug overdoses.

1970 In March, three women—Elizabeth Bishop, Lillian Hellman, and Joyce Carol Oates—win National Book Awards.

1970 On May 4, National Guard members shoot antiwar protesters at Kent State University in Ohio.

1970 On April 10, the Beatles disband.

1970 On April 30, U.S. and South Vietnamese troops invade Cambodia, which has been sheltering North Vietnamese troops.

1970 On September 6, four airliners bound for New York

are hijacked by Palestinian terrorists, but no passengers are harmed.

1970 On September 19, *The Mary Tyler Moore Show* debuts on CBS.

1970 On September 21, *Monday Night Football* debuts on ABC.

1970 On October 2, the Environmental Protection Agency (EPA) is created to regulate environmental issues.

1971 Disney World opens in Orlando, Florida.

1971 Hot pants become a fashion sensation.

1971 On January 2, cigarette advertising is banned from television and radio.

1971 On February 6, British troops are sent to patrol Northern Ireland.

1971 On February 9, the European Economic Community, a precursor to the European Union, is established.

1971 On March 8, Joe Frazier defeats Muhammad Ali to retain the world heavyweight boxing title.

1971 On April 20, the U.S. Supreme Court rules that students can be bused to end racial segregation in schools.

1971 In June, the Twenty-sixth Amendment to the Constitution lowers the legal voting age to eighteen.

1971 On June 13, the *New York Times* publishes the "Pentagon Papers" which reveal Defense Department plans for the Vietnam War.

1971 In September, a prison uprising in Attica, New York, ends with forty-three people killed, including ten hostages.

1971 On October 12, the rock musical *Jesus Christ Superstar* opens on Broadway in New York City.

1971 On October 13, baseball teams play in the first night World Series game.

1971 On December 25, "Christmas bombing" occurs in North Vietnam.

1972 In a sign of the cooling of Cold War tensions, East and West Germany and North and South Korea each enter into negotiations to normalize relations.

1972 *Ms.* magazine begins publication.

1972 Pong, the first video game available to play at home, becomes popular, as does the first video game machine, Odyssey, introduced by Magnavox.

1972 On February 14, the musical *Grease* opens on Broadway in New York City.

1972 On February, 21, President Richard Nixon begins a seven-day visit to Communist China.

1972 On May 22, President Richard Nixon begins a nine-day visit to the Soviet Union.

1972 On June 17, the Watergate scandal begins with the arrest of five men caught trying to bug the Democratic National Committee headquarters at the Watergate building in Washington, D.C. The investigation soon reveals deep corruption in the Nixon administration.

1972 On July 24, the United Nations asks the United States to end its bombing of North Vietnam.

1972 On August 12, the last American combat troops leave Vietnam.

1972 On November 8, cable TV channel HBO premieres in Pennsylvania with 365 subscribers.

1973 Three major American cities—Los Angeles, California; Atlanta, Georgia; and Detroit, Michigan—elect a black mayor for the first time.

1973 Investigations into the Watergate affair capture the public attention and shatter the Nixon administration.

1973 The Sears Tower, the world's tallest building, is completed in Chicago, Illinois.

1973 Ralph Lauren designs the costumes for the film *The Great Gatsby,* helping build his reputation.

1973 Fantasy-adventure game Dungeons and Dragons is created by Dave Arneson and Gary Gygax.

1973 The first Internet is set up by the U.S. Department of Defense as a way of connecting all the department's computers.

1973 On January 14, the Miami Dolphins win the Super Bowl and become the first professional football team to finish a season undefeated.

1973 On October 16, the Organization of Petroleum Exporting Countries (OPEC) declares an embargo (ban) on the export of oil to the United States and other Western countries.

1973 On October 23, the House of Representatives begins impeachment proceedings against President Richard Nixon.

1974 The Ramones launch the American punk movement with their performances at the New York City club CBGB.

1974 The streaking fad sweeps the country.

1974 President Richard Nixon tours the Middle East and the Soviet Union.

1974 On January 18, Israel and Egypt sign a peace accord that ends their long armed conflict.

1974 On April 8, Hank Aaron of the Atlanta Braves breaks Babe Ruth's lifetime home run record when he hits his 715th career homer.

1974 In May, screenwriter Dalton Trumbo, who had been blacklisted in the 1950s during Senator Joseph McCarthy's anticommunist crusades, receives an Oscar award for the 1957 film *The Brave One*.

1974 On August 8, Richard Nixon becomes the first U.S. president to resign from office amid evidence of a cover-up of the Watergate affair.

1974 On August 9, Vice President Gerald Ford is sworn in as president. Less than a month later, he officially pardons former president Richard Nixon.

1974 On September 8, motorcycle stunt rider Evel Knievel tries to jump a rocket over the Snake River Canyon in Idaho but falls short.

1974 On October 3, Frank Robinson joins the Cleveland Indians as major league baseball's first black manager.

1974 On October 30, boxer Muhammnad Ali regains his world heavyweight boxing title by defeating George Foreman.

1974 In December, unemployment hits 6.5 percent amid a prolonged economic slump, and rises to 8.9 percent by May 1975.

1975 The video cassette recorder (VCR) is invented by Sony Corporation in Japan.

1975 The first personal computer, the Altair 8800, is sold in a kit form.

1975 The cult film *The Rocky Horror Picture Show* is released.

1975 Skateboarding becomes popular, and mood rings and pet rocks are popular fads.

1975 Rock star Bruce Springsteen appears on the cover of both *Time* and *Newsweek* thanks to his popular album *Born to Run*.

1975 The Soviet Union and the United States cooperate in the manned *Apollo-Soyuz* space mission.

1975 On January 5, the all-black musical *The Wiz* opens on Broadway in New York City. It eventually tallies 1,672 performances.

1975 On April 30, Saigon, the capital of South Vietnam, is invaded by the communist North Vietnamese, ending the Vietnam War.

1975 On October 1, the Organization of Petroleum Exporting Countries (OPEC) raises crude oil prices by 10 percent.

1975 On October 11, *Saturday Night Live* debuts on NBC.

1976 The first personal computer, the Apple, is developed by Steve Jobs and Steve Wozniak. The Apple II, introduced a year later, offers color graphics.

1976 Model and actress Farrah Fawcett-Majors sets a trend with her feathered haircut and appears on millions of posters in her tiny red bathing suit.

1976 On July 4, the United States celebrates its bicentennial.

1976 On November 2, former Georgia governor Jimmy Carter is elected president.

1976 On November 6, *Gone with the Wind* is broadcast on TV for the first time.

1977 The film *Saturday Night Fever* helps make disco music popular.

1977 Studio 54 becomes New York City's hottest nightclub featuring disco music.

1977 Egyptian artifacts from the tomb of King Tutankhamen, or King Tut, draw huge audiences across the nation.

1977 Alex Haley's book *Roots* becomes a best-seller after the airing of the TV miniseries based on the book.

1977 On January 21, President Jimmy Carter signs an unconditional pardon for most Vietnam-era draft evaders.

1977 On February 8, *Hustler* magazine publisher Larry Flynt is convicted of obscenity.

1977 In April, the Christian Broadcasting Network (CBN) makes its debut.

1977 On August 16, Elvis Presley, the king of rock and roll, dies at Graceland, his Memphis, Tennessee, mansion.

1978 The Walkman personal cassette player is introduced by Sony.

1978 On July 25, the first human test-tube baby is born in England.

1978 On September 17, U.S. president Jimmy Carter hosts negotiations between Israeli prime minister Menachem Begin and Egyptian president Anwar Sadat at Camp David, Maryland.

1978 On October 13, punk rock musician Sid Vicious of the Sex Pistols is arrested for the stabbing death of his girlfriend.

1978 On November 18, Jim Jones and over nine hundred followers of his People's Temple cult are found dead after a mass suicide in Jonestown, Guyana.

1978 On December 5, the Soviet Union and Afghanistan sign a treaty of friendship, and within a year U.S. support for the Afghan government disappears.

1979 Eleven people are trampled to death at a Who concert in Cincinnati, Ohio.

1979 Jerry Falwell organizes the Moral Majority to lobby politicians regarding the concerns of Christian fundamentalists.

1979 On January 1, the United States and the People's Republic of China establish formal diplomatic relations.

1979 On March 28, a major accident in the nuclear reactor at the Three Mile Island power plant near Harrisburg, Pennsylvania, raises concerns about nuclear power.

1979 On November 4, Iranian militants seize the U.S. embassy in Tehran, Iran, and take fifty-two hostages, whom they will hold for nearly a year.

1979 On December 27, the Soviet Union invades Afghanistan, beginning more than two decades of war and disruption in that country.

1980 Post-it notes are created by 3M chemist Arthur Fry.

1980 On February 22, the U.S. Olympic ice hockey team wins the gold medal, sparking national celebration.

1980 On April 12, the United States votes to boycott the Summer Olympics in Moscow to protest the Soviet presence in Afghanistan.

1980 On April 21, the Mariel boatlift begins, bringing 125,000 refugees from Cuba to Florida before being halted in September.

1980 In June, the CNN cable TV network debuts.

1980 On August 19, a report issued by the *Los Angeles Times* indicates that 40 to 75 percent of NBA players use cocaine.

1980 On November 4, former California governor Ronald Reagan is elected president.

1980 On November 21, the "Who Shot J.R.?" episode of *Dallas* draws the largest television audience of all time.

1980 On September 4, Iraq begins an eight-year war with Iran.

1980 On October 2, in his last fight, heavyweight boxer Muhammad Ali is defeated by World Boxing Council champion Larry Holmes.

1980 On December 8, former Beatles musician John Lennon is shot and killed in New York City.

1981 Nintendo's "Donkey Kong" is the most popular coin-operated video game.

1981 NASA launches and lands the first reusable spacecraft, the space shuttle.

1981 On January 13, the National Collegiate Athletic Association (NCAA) votes to sponsor women's championships in twelve sports after the 1981–82 season.

1981 On January 20, American hostages held at the U.S. embassy in Tehran, Iran, are released on the day of President Ronald Reagan's inauguration.

1981 On January 23, the United States withdraws support for the Marxist government of Nicaragua and begins to support antigovernment rebels known as Contras.

1981 On March 26, comedian Carol Burnett wins a $1.6 million libel lawsuit against the tabloid *National Enquirer.*

1981 On July 29, Great Britain's Prince Charles marries Lady Diana Spencer in an event televised around the world.

1981 On August 1, the Music Television Network (MTV) starts offering music videos that soon become as important as the actual music.

1981 On September 21, Sandra Day O'Connor is confirmed as the first woman to serve on the U.S. Supreme Court.

1982 The compact disc is introduced.

1982 The popular movie *E.T.: The Extra-Terrestrial* sets box office records.

1982 Michael Jackson's album *Thriller* is the year's most popular recording.

1982 Americans frustrate themselves trying to solve Rubik's Cube, a popular puzzle.

1982 On April 2, Argentina invades the Falkland Islands off its coast, sparking a short war with Great Britain, which claims the islands.

1982 On June 7, Graceland, the late Elvis Presley's Memphis, Tennessee, home, is opened as a tourist attraction.

1982 On July 27, AIDS is officially named.

1982 On September 15, *USA Today* becomes the first national newspaper.

1982 On October 7, *Cats* opens on Broadway in New York City and will become the decade's most popular musical.

1983 First lady Nancy Reagan announces a "War on Drugs."

1983 Sally Ride becomes the first woman astronaut in space when she joins the crew of the space shuttle *Challenger.*

1983 Actor Paul Newman introduces his own line of spaghetti sauces to be sold in grocery stores; he uses the proceeds to benefit charities.

1983 On February 28, the farewell episode of the sitcom *M*A*S*H* is seen by 125 million viewers.

1983 On March 23, President Ronald Reagan proposes a space-based antimissile defense system that is popularly known as "Star Wars."

1983 On April 18, terrorists bomb the U.S. embassy in Beirut, Lebanon, killing sixty-three.

1983 On September 1, the Soviet Union shoots down a

Korean Air Lines flight that has strayed into its airspace, killing 269.

1983 On October 25, three thousand U.S. soldiers invade the Caribbean island nation of Grenada to crush a Marxist uprising.

1983 In November, Cabbage Patch Kids dolls, with their soft faces and adoption certificates, become the most popular new doll of the Christmas season.

1984 Trivial Pursuit becomes the nation's most popular board game.

1984 *The Cosby Show* debuts on NBC.

1984 Rap group Run-DMC is the first rap group to have a gold album.

1984 Apple introduces a new personal computer, the Macintosh, with a dramatic advertising campaign.

1984 On November 6, Ronald Reagan is reelected president.

1984 On December 3, a Union Carbide plant in Bhopal, India, leaks poison gas that kills two thousand and injures two hundred thousand.

1985 Nintendo Entertainment System, a home video game system that has brilliant colors, realistic sound effects, and quick action, is introduced to the United States.

1985 On March 16, U.S. journalist Terry Anderson is kidnapped in Lebanon; he will be held until December 4, 1991.

1985 In April, Coca-Cola changes the formula of its popular soft drink and the public reacts with anger and dismay, prompting the company to reissue the old formula as Classic Coke.

1985 On July 13, British rock star Bob Geldof organizes Live Aid, a charity concert and album to aid the victims of African famine.

1985 On October 2, the death of handsome movie star Rock Hudson from AIDS raises awareness about the disease.

1986 Country singer Dolly Parton opens a theme park in Tennessee called Dollywood.

1986 On January 28, the space shuttle *Challenger* explodes upon liftoff, killing all astronauts and one teacher who were aboard.

1986 On February 26, Robert Penn Warren is named the first poet laureate of the United States.

1986 On April 26, a serious meltdown at the Chernobyl nuclear power plant near Kiev, Ukraine, releases a radioactive cloud into the atmosphere and is considered a major disaster.

1986 On May 1, in South Africa, 1.5 million blacks protest apartheid (the policy of racial segregation). Around the world, foreign governments place sanctions on South Africa.

1986 On June 10, Nancy Lieberman becomes the first woman to play in a men's professional basketball league when she joins the United States Basketball League.

1986 On July 15, the United States sends troops to Bolivia to fight against drug traffickers.

1986 On July 27, Greg LeMond becomes the first American to win France's prestigious Tour de France bicycle race.

1986 In October, it is discovered that members of the Reagan administration have been trading arms for hostages in Iran and illegally channeling funds to Contras in Nicaragua. This Iran-Contra scandal will eventually be investigated by Congress.

1986 On November 22, twenty-one-year-old Mike Tyson becomes the youngest heavyweight boxing champion when he defeats World Boxing Council champ Trevor Berbick.

1987 On March 19, televangelist Jim Bakker resigns after it is revealed that he has been having an adulterous affair with church secretary Jessica Hahn.

1987 On June 25, Soviet leader Mikhail Gorbachev announces *perestroika,* a program of sweeping economic reforms aimed at improving the Soviet economy.

1987 On October 3, Canada and the United States sign a free-trade agreement.

1987 On October 17, the stock market experiences its worst crash in history when it drops 508 points.

1987 On November 11, Vincent van Gogh's painting *Irises* is sold for $53.9 million.

1988 McDonald's opens twenty restaurants in Moscow, Russia.

1988 Singer Sonny Bono is elected mayor of Palm Springs, California.

1988 On February 5, former Panamanian dictator General Manuel Noriega is charged in a U.S. court with accepting bribes from drug traffickers.

1988 On February 14, Ayatollah Khomeini of Iran calls author Salman Rushdie's book *The Satanic Verses* offensive and issues a death sentence on him. The author goes into hiding.

1988 On April 14, Soviet forces withdraw from Afghanistan after ten years of fighting in that country.

1988 On July 3, believing it is under attack, a U.S. warship shoots down an Iran Air passenger liner, killing 290 passengers.

1988 On November 8, Vice President George Herbert Walker Bush is elected president.

1988 On December 21, Pan Am Flight 747 explodes over Lockerbie, Scotland, killing 259 on the flight and 11 on the ground. Middle Eastern terrorists are eventually charged with the crime.

1989 On March 24, the Exxon *Valdez* oil tanker runs aground in Alaska, spilling 240,000 barrels of oil and creating an environmental disaster.

1989 In May, more than one million Chinese demonstrate for democracy in Beijing.

1989 In June, Chinese troops crack down on demonstrators in Tiananmen Square, drawing attention to the repressive government.

1989 On August 9, Colin R. Powell becomes the United States's first black chairman of the Joint Chiefs of Staff.

1989 On August 23, the Soviet states of Lithuania, Latvia, and Estonia demand autonomy from the Soviet Union. Later, across the former Soviet dominated region, Soviet republics and satellite countries throw off communist control and pursue independence.

1989 On August 24, former baseball star Pete Rose is banned from baseball for life because it is believed that he bet on games in which he was involved.

1989 On October 15, Wayne Gretzky of the Los Angeles Kings becomes the National Hockey League's all-time leading scorer with his 1,850th point.

1989 On October 17, a major earthquake hits the San Francisco, California, area.

1989 On December 16, American troops invade Panama and seize dictator General Manuel Noriega. Noriega will later be convicted in U.S. courts.

1989 On December 22, the Brandenburg Gate in Berlin is officially opened, allowing people from East and West Berlin to mix freely and signaling the end of the Cold War and the reunification of Germany.

1990 The animated sitcom *The Simpsons* debuts on the FOX network.

1990 Ken Burns's documentary *The Civil War* airs on PBS.

1990 British scientist Tim Berners-Lee invents the World Wide Web.

1990 On April 25, the Hubble Space Telescope is deployed in space from the space shuttle *Discovery.*

1990 On July 26, President George Herbert Walker Bush signs the Americans with Disabilities Act, which provides broad protections for those with disabilities.

1990 On August 2, Iraq invades Kuwait, prompting the United States to wage war on Iraq from bases in Saudi Arabia. Much of this conflict, called the Persian Gulf War, is aired live on television and makes CNN famous for its coverage.

1990 On October 3, East and West Germany are reunited.

1991 Mass murderer Jeffrey Dahmer is charged with killing fifteen young men and boys near Milwaukee, Wisconsin.

1991 On March 3, U.S. general Norman Schwarzkopf announces the end of the Persian Gulf War.

1991 In October, confirmation hearings for U.S. Supreme Court justice nominee Clarence Thomas are carried live on television, and feature Anita Hill's dramatic accusations of sexual harassment. Despite the charges, Thomas is confirmed.

1991 On November 7, Los Angeles Lakers basketball star Earvin "Magic" Johnson announces that he has contracted the HIV virus.

1991 On December 8, leaders of Russia and several other former Soviet states announce the formation of the Commonwealth of Independent States.

1992 On April 29, riots erupt in Los Angeles, California, following the acquittal of four white police officers in the beating of black motorist Rodney King. The brutal beating had been filmed and shown widely on television.

1992 On May 21, Vice President Dan Quayle criticizes the CBS sitcom *Murphy Brown* for not promoting family values after the main character has a child out of wedlock.

1992 In August, the Mall of America, the nation's largest shopping mall, opens in Bloomington, Minnesota.

1992 On August 24, Hurricane Andrew hits Florida and the Gulf Coast, causing a total of over $15 billion in damage.

1992 On October 24, the Toronto Blue Jays become the first non–U.S. team to win baseball's World Series.

1992 On November 3, Arkansas governor Bill Clinton is elected president, defeating incumbent George Herbert Walker Bush and strong third party candidate H. Ross Perot.

1992 On December 17, the United States, Canada, and Mexico sign the North American Free Trade Agreement (NAFTA).

1993 Jack "Dr. Death" Kevorkian is arrested in Michigan for assisting in the suicide of a terminally ill patient, his nineteenth such action.

1993 On February 26, six people are killed when terrorists plant a bomb in New York City's World Trade Center.

1993 On April 19, more than eighty members of a religious cult called the Branch Davidians are killed in a mass suicide as leaders set fire to their compound following a fifty-one-day siege by federal forces.

1993 In July and August, the Flood of the Century devastates the American Midwest, killing 48.

1994 Tiger Woods becomes the youngest person and the first black to win the U.S. Amateur Golf Championship.

1994 Special prosecutor Ken Starr is appointed to investigate President Bill Clinton's involvement in a financial scandal known as Whitewater. The investigation will ultimately cover several scandals and lead to impeachment proceedings against the president.

1994 In January, ice skater Nancy Kerrigan is attacked by associates of her rival, Tonya Harding, at the U.S. Olympic Trials in Detroit, Michigan.

1994 On May 2, Nelson Mandela is elected president of South Africa. The black activist had been jailed for decades under the old apartheid regime and became the country's first black president.

1994 On August 11, major league baseball players go on strike, forcing the cancellation of the playoffs and World Series.

1994 On November 5, forty-five-year-old boxer George Foreman becomes the oldest heavyweight champion when he defeats Michael Moorer.

1995 On April 19, a car bomb explodes outside the Alfred P. Murrah Federal Office Building in Oklahoma City, Oklahoma, killing 168 people. Following a manhunt, antigovernment zealot Timothy McVeigh is captured, and later is convicted and executed for the crime.

1995 On September 1, the Rock and Roll Hall of Fame opens in Cleveland, Ohio.

1995 On September 6, Cal Ripken Jr. of the Baltimore Orioles breaks the long-standing record for most consecutive baseball games played with 2,131. The total reaches 2,632 games before Ripken removes himself from the lineup in 1998.

1995 On October 3, former football star O. J. Simpson is found not guilty of the murder of his ex-wife and her friend in what many called the "trial of the century."

1996 Three years after the introduction of H. Ty Warners's Beanie Babies, the first eleven toy styles are retired and quickly become collector's items.

1996 On September 26, American astronaut Shannon Lucid returns to Earth after spending 188 days in space—a record for any astronaut.

1996 On November 5, Bill Clinton is reelected to the presidency.

1997 Researchers in Scotland successfully clone an adult sheep, named Dolly.

1997 The Hale-Bopp comet provides a nightly show as it passes by the Earth.

1997 Actress Ellen DeGeneres becomes the first openly gay lead character in her ABC sitcom *Ellen*.

1997 On January 23, Madeleine Albright becomes the first woman sworn in as U.S. secretary of state.

1997 On March 27, thirty-nine members of the Heavens Gate religious cult are found dead in their California compound.

1997 On April 13, Tiger Woods becomes the youngest person and the first black to win a major golf tournament when he wins the Masters with the lowest score ever.

1997 On June 19, the play *Cats* sets a record for the longest-running Broadway play with its 6,138th performance.

1997 On June 20, four major tobacco companies settle a lawsuit with states that will cost companies nearly $400 billion.

1997 On June 28, boxer Mike Tyson is disqualified when he bites the ear of opponent Evander Holyfield during a heavyweight title fight.

1997 On July 5, the *Pathfinder* spacecraft lands on Mars and sends back images and rock analyses.

1997 On August 31, Britain's Princess Diana is killed in an auto accident in Paris, France.

1998 Mark McGwire of the St. Louis Cardinals sets a single-season home run record with 70 home runs.

1998 The final episode of the popular sitcom *Seinfeld* is watched by an estimated audience of seventy-six million.

1998 On January 22, Unabomber Ted Kaczynski is convicted for a series of mail bombings and sentenced to life in prison.

1998 On March 24, the movie *Titanic* wins eleven Academy Awards, tying the record set by *Ben-Hur* in 1959.

1998 On April 10, a new drug for male impotence known as Viagra hits the market and is a popular sensation.

1998 On August 7, terrorists explode bombs outside the U.S. embassies in Nairobi, Kenya, and Dar es Salaam, Tanzania.

1998 In November, Jesse "The Body" Ventura—a former professional wrestler—is elected governor of Minnesota.

1998 On December 19, the House of Representatives initiates impeachment proceedings against President Bill Clinton, but the U.S. Senate acquits Clinton on two charges in early 1999.

1999 The U.S. women's soccer team wins the World Cup by defeating China.

1999 On March 24, NATO launches a bombing campaign against Serbia to stop its actions in Kosovo.

1999 On March 29, the Dow Jones Industrial Average closes above 10,000 for the first time in history thanks to a booming stock market dominated by high-tech companies.

1999 On April 20, in Littleton, Colorado, two students go on a vicious shooting spree, killing themselves and twelve other students.

1999 On September 24, *IKONOS,* the world's first commercial, high-resolution imaging satellite, is launched into space; it can detect an object on Earth as small as a card table.

Bowling, Beatniks, and Bell-Bottoms

Pop Culture of 20th-Century America

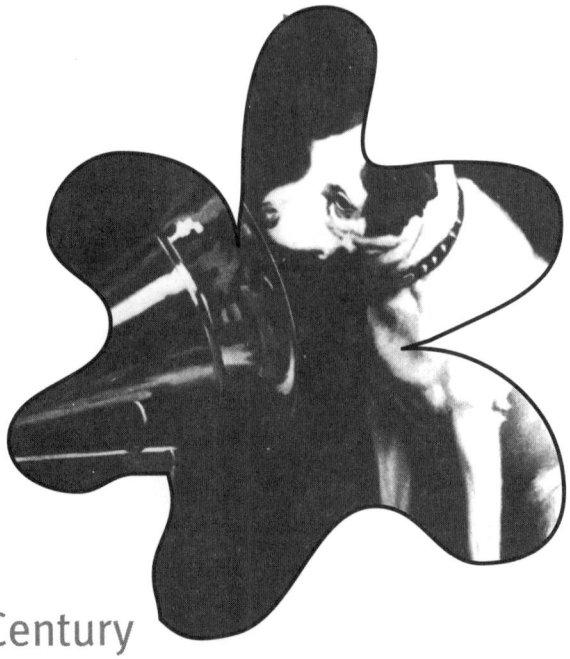

1900s

The Birth of the American Century

The United States entered the twentieth century during a period of sweeping change. In fact, change and transformation were the norm in the first decade of what has since become known as the "American Century." The United States came to be the leading economic and military power in the world. American democracy became the model for political reform in countries around the world. American publishers, musicians, artists, film makers, and performers of all sorts participated in an outpouring of work that made American popular culture the popular culture of much of the Western world.

The social and economic changes that were sweeping the country were striking. Although it had once been a nation of small towns, rapid changes in living styles led to the concentration of more and more Americans into cities; by 1910, fully 54 percent of the population lived in urban areas. The ethnic makeup of America was changing dramatically as well, as some 8,795,386 immigrants arrived in the United States between 1901 and 1910. This surge in immigration made up a large portion of the 21-percent population growth that occurred in the decade, pushing the country's population from 75,994,575 to 91,972,266.

Many of these new immigrants lived in the major urban centers, where they worked in the giant factories that were beginning to dominate American industry. The United States had

1900s At a Glance

What We Said:

As Tom Dalzell, author of *Flappers 2 Rappers: American Youth Slang,* points out, slang did not become an important element of American speech until the 1920s. Slang, it should be remembered, is language that attains special meaning because of its use by a subgroup of the larger society. It was not until the rise of the youth, music, and racial subcultures in the 1920s that slang truly rose to its present importance as an element of popular culture. However, three of the more popular terms of the decade were:

"23 Skidoo!": The most popular expression of the decade, this phrase could be used to mean almost anything, though it was generally used to express approval.

Babe: A pretty girl.

"Good to the last drop" (1907): This enduring advertising slogan for Maxwell House Coffee was rumored to have been invented by President Theodore Roosevelt, who remarked that his cup of coffee he had just drank was "good to the last drop."

What We Read:

Sears, Roebuck catalog: Also known as the "Wish Book," this department store catalog was popular reading in many households. Started in 1891, the catalog was so popular at the turn of the century that people often joked that it was one of the two books rural people ever read!

Comic strips: The "funnies" became a daily part of many newspapers after the *New York Journal* published the first eight-page comics section on October 18, 1896.

Dime novels: These inexpensive books were tremendously popular. George Patten wrote the adventures of Frank Merriwell for *Tip Top Weekly.* Starting in 1896, Patten's new stories reached about 125 million readers each week.

***The Jungle* (1906):** Upton Sinclair wrote this damning account of the dangerous conditions in the meat packing industry. The nation responded to his discovery by pushing for new laws for food and drug handling and the sales of meat dropped by half.

Ladies' Home Journal* and *Collier's Weekly: These two popular magazines wrote to inform and entertain women. *Ladies' Home Journal* often included romantic stories.

What We Watched:

For the most part, people during this decade entertained themselves at public and private gathering places such as saloons, sporting clubs, private clubs, churches, and barbershops.

Traveling entertainment: Acts that visited towns throughout the country included vaudeville and minstrel shows. During the decade, there were more than four hundred touring companies in the country. Almost every town had a vaudeville theater.

once been dominated by small businesses, but a wave of mergers (the combining of businesses) contributed to the growth of what was becoming known as "big business"—the domination of the American economy by huge companies that had branches throughout the nation. The Ford Motor Company (cars), the Standard Oil Company (oil), the United States Steel Corporation (steel), the J. C. Penney Company (retail), and the Philip Morris Corporation (tobacco) were among the largest.

1900s At a Glance (continued)

Circuses: Many circus companies toured the country, with the Ringling Bros. Circus and Barnum & Bailey Circus each trying to be the "greatest". Some were supported by ninety railcars full of animals, entertainers, and props.

Sporting events: Crowds in cities across the country gathered to watch their favorite games. The first game of the first World Series was held on October 4, 1903, and drew a crowd of twenty-five thousand fans in Boston. The American League's Boston Pilgrims beat Pittsburgh's National League Pirates to win the series on October 14.

***The Great Train Robbery* (1903):** This flick was the first movie to provide true suspenseful drama. Five years after its release, there were ten thousand nickelodeons in towns across the nations, ready to offer moviegoers the latest entertainment.

World's Fair: The World's Fair of 1904 in St. Louis, Missouri, drew record crowds.

Olympics: The third Olympics Games were held in 1904 to accompany the World's Fair.

Air meets: Once Wilbur and Orville Wright proved that men could fly in 1908, many people tried to build their own flying machines in their backyards. Air meets, where daredevils would gather to show off their lasted inventions, were especially popular spectacles during the decade.

What We Listened To:

"Meet Me in St. Louis" (1904): This hit song was inspired by the World's Fair of 1904 that was held in St. Louis. The fair attracted more than twenty million visitors.

"In My Merry Oldsmobile" (1905): This song by Vincent Bryan and Gus Edwards boasted pride in the decade's new technology.

"You're a Grand Old Flag" (1906): This song by George M. Cohan highlighted patriotism.

Who We Knew:

Henry Ford (1863–1947): Soon after the establishment of the Ford Motor Company in 1903, Henry Ford and his affordable cars became wildly popular with Americans. By the middle of the next decade, Ford would make half of all the cars in the country.

Immigrants: In 1907 alone, 1.2 million immigrants landed at Ellis Island, near the island of Manhattan, New York. By 1910, one of every seven Americans was an immigrant.

Jack Johnson (1878–1948): In 1908, Jack Johnson became the first black to win the heavyweight boxing champion title.

Theodore Roosevelt (1858–1919): Upon the assassination of President William McKinley in 1900, Vice President Theodore Roosevelt became president. His dynamism and charisma defined the age. He guided the country during the building of the Panama Canal and won the Nobel Peace Prize, among other noted accomplishments.

The Wright Brothers (Wilbur, 1867–1912; Orville, 1871–1948): Aviation pioneers, the Wright brothers are credited with the first motor-powered airplane flight at Kitty Hawk, North Carolina, December 17, 1903.

Leading America during this time of change was its youngest president in history, Theodore "Teddy" Roosevelt (1858–1919). Speaking about America's role in the world, Roosevelt once told an older opponent: "You and your generation have had your chance. . . . Now let us of this generation have ours!" When elected president William McKinley (1843–1901) was assassinated in 1901, Vice President Roosevelt assumed the presidency. He led the country though an era of political and economic reform known as the "Progressive Era." Progressive reformers tried to tame the growth of big business and sprawling cities by passing laws and creating government organizations to regulate areas of American life; many of those laws and organizations remain intact today. In this decade, the United States also created a more powerful military. The United States began to exert its power overseas, extending its influence in the Caribbean and Latin America and protecting its interests in China and the Far East.

In this era of political, economic, and population change, American popular culture was going through a period of transformation as well. In the nineteenth century, limited transportation and communication networks kept forms of popular entertainment from being spread throughout the country. Newspapers, magazines, and theater were mostly local, not national. But that began to change in the 1890s, when magazine publishers used new technologies to print and distribute hundreds of thousands—and then millions—of their magazines to people across the country. These magazines, including the *Saturday Evening Post* and *Argosy,* contained a growing number of advertisements for products that were available everywhere, like Kellogg's cereals and Coca-Cola. Syndication—the placing of a single article or comic strip in many independent newspapers—brought comic strips such as *Mutt & Jeff* and *The Katzenjammer Kids* into homes across the country. The Sears, Roebuck and Company also took advantage of printing advances to send catalogs offering its goods to people all over the land.

Older forms of entertainment still thrived in America. Buffalo Bill Cody (1846–1917) and his Wild West Show, a sensation in the nineteenth century, toured America. Smaller circuses visited towns big and small. But a new media began to take hold in the 1900s: film. The groundbreaking silent film *The Great Train Robbery* (1903) thrilled audiences with its realistic portrayal of a train robbery and helped drive the growth of nickelodeons, storefront theaters that showed the latest short silent films. For as little as a nickel, Americans could see the latest films from the nation's growing movie studios.

Advances in technology and innovation changed American popular culture, but widespread racism kept African Americans from joining in the growth of cultural activity. In fact, one popular form of entertainment—the minstrel show—was based on negative stereotypes of African Americans. The national forms of popular culture—magazines, advertising, films, sports, and book publishing—mostly excluded African Americans. There were, however, some notable exceptions. Black boxer Jack Johnson (1878–1946) gained national fame when he beat a white boxer to gain the heavyweight championship; the ragtime tunes of African American composer Scott Joplin (1868–1917) were some of the most popular sheet music of the decade; and in towns across the South, Negro baseball leagues began to produce players every bit as talented as those in white baseball leagues, from which black players were excluded. It would be years, however, before African Americans were welcome participants in American popular culture.

The advances of the decade—and the century—allowed Americans to share a truly national popular culture in ways they never had before. They could read the same magazines and novels, go to the same movies, and buy the same brands of food, toys, and cars. In the 1900s, Americans drank out of Dixie cups, drove a Ford Model T, ate in local diners, read *National Geographic,* took pictures with their new Brownie cameras, and drank Coke. American kids ate Kellogg's cereals for breakfast, played baseball with a Louisville Slugger bat, chewed gum and ate Cracker Jack popcorn, and went to bed at night with a companion named after their popular president, the teddy bear. This sharing of a common culture was just beginning. In the coming decades of the century, American culture would be further influenced by the movies, radio programs, TV shows, and other forms of entertainment that would provide enjoyment to people living in all regions of the country.

1900s

Commerce

In the last thirty years of the nineteenth century, the American economy had been wracked by a series of economic depressions. By the dawn of the twentieth century, business was booming. In most American industries, business owners were learning the lesson of the day: Bigger is better. When the United States Steel Corporation was incorporated at a value of $1 billion in 1901, it became the world's largest corporation. Other companies followed the lead of U.S. Steel in buying up or merging with competitors to give themselves the advantage of size. Many of the companies in existence at the beginning of the twenty-first century were founded in the 1900s, including the Firestone Tire and Rubber Company (1901), the Quaker Oats Company (1901), the J. C. Penney Company (1902), the Pepsi-Cola Company (1902), Texaco (1903), the Ford Motor Company (1903), the Harley-Davidson Motor Company (1907), the Hershey Chocolate Company (1908), and the General Motors Company (1908). These large companies employed a growing number of professional managers, a new occupation whose practitioners tried to bring logic and order to the huge operations they managed. New management techniques included building elaborate assembly lines, using machines to speed up production times, and encouraging worker efficiency.

Although the rise of big business increased economic activity in the nation, many worried that these large companies were becoming too powerful. Politicians used laws such as the Sherman Antitrust Act of 1890 to limit the power of large corporations to control the marketplace. In fact, President Theodore Roosevelt (1858–1919) gained a reputation as a "trustbuster" for his efforts to break the power of large trusts. (A trust is a combination of companies that work together to reduce competition in an industry.) Congress also passed laws to regulate business practices in the areas of transportation, consumer protection, and banking. Labor unions also stepped up their efforts to protect the rights of workers, whom union leaders said were threatened by the growth of big companies. Unions staged many strikes against American businesses, including the famous Anthracite Coal Strike of 1902, which nearly crippled American business.

Though most Americans learned about the changing economic climate of the day through their newspapers, they also began to experience those changes directly as they purchased and used a variety of new products. The single most notable product to emerge from this decade was the Model T automobile manufactured by the Ford Motor Company beginning in 1908. The self-propelled vehicle known as the car was still in its infancy when Henry Ford (1863–1947) used his assembly line process to make a car that was affordable to more Americans than ever before. The Harley-Davidson Motor Company began to manufacture its motorcycles in this decade as well, and both Ford and Harley-Davidson continue production into the twenty-first century. Though few consumers knew of it, two brothers named Wilbur (1867–1912) and Orville (1871–1948) Wright invented a product in 1903 that would revolutionize travel in the years to come: the airplane.

A range of other products that would have a lasting impact were also introduced in this decade. The Brownie camera, made by Kodak, allowed common people to create their own photographs. The popular stereograph allowed them to view three-dimensional (3-D) images from around the world. Both products changed the way people saw the world.

The way that people bought things also changed. The dime store, and especially dime store giant Woolworth's, brought a version of the department store to lower-income Americans, providing a variety of low-cost goods. Sears, Roebuck used its famous catalog to offer Americans in even the most distant locations access to the growing array of consumer goods. By 1908, the company mailed out 3.6 million copies of a catalog offering ten thousand different items, from guns to pianos to, eventually, houses made from a kit.

Aunt Jemima

Aunt Jemima is best known as a brand of pancake mixes and syrups sold by the Quaker Oats Company since 1889. The image of Aunt Jemima has been controversial for over a hundred years. Based on the pre–Civil War (1861–65) stereotype of the fat, jolly, no-nonsense black "mammy," the character of Aunt Jemima was first introduced in **minstrel shows** (see entry under 1900s—Film and Theater in volume 1) in the late 1800s.

The image of Aunt Jemima as a stereotypical black "mammy," viewed by many as offensive, was used to advertise pancake mixes and syrups for over one hundred years before being made-over in the 1990s. *Corbis Corporation. Reproduced by permission.*

Quaker Oats is thought to have chosen the image of Aunt Jemima to promote the very first packaged pancake mix because the image of the kind and funny black mammy was comforting and safe to many white consumers. From the beginning, many African Americans found the image of the fat, smiling Aunt Jemima with a bandanna on her head to be an insulting glorification of slavery. Some fought to eliminate what they viewed as an offensive trademark. In response, Quaker Oats gave Aunt Jemima a makeover in the 1990s by removing the bandanna and making her fashionably thin. The company also hired famous black spokespeople like singer Gladys Knight (1944–) to advertise its products.

—Tina Gianoulis

For More Information

Kern-Foxworth, Marilyn. *Aunt Jemima, Uncle Ben, & Rastus: Blacks in Advertising, Yesterday, & Tomorrow.* Westport, CT: Greenwood, 1994.

Manring, M. M. *Slave in a Box: The Strange Career of Aunt Jemima.* Charlottesville, VA: University Press of Virginia, 1998.

Patton, Phil. "Mammy: Her Life and Times." *American Heritage* (Vol. 44, no. 5, September 1993): pp. 78–86.

Quaker Oats Company. *Aunt Jemima.* http://www.auntjemima.com (accessed December 12, 2001).

Easy to use and affordable, Kodak's Brownie camera made photography available to everyone. Here, the man on the left holds the new Brownie camera, circa 1900. *Courtesy of the Library of Congress.*

Brownie Cameras

In the 1800s, before the Brownie camera, photography was a difficult and often expensive process. This process made it hard for ordinary people to take pictures. When the Eastman Kodak Company introduced its new Brownie cameras in February of 1900, photography became available to everyone, including children. In fact, the Brownie was designed and marketed especially for kids.

The Brownie camera was very easy to use. It was a simple box with an opening in the front for light to reach the film, a small viewing screen on top, and a switch to expose the film. The film came on easy-to-load rolls. Kodak named the Brownie camera after popular characters created by Palmer Cox (1840–1924), a children's book author and illustrator, in the late 1800s. Using Cox's characters, Kodak marketed the camera in popular magazines where children would see them. Kodak encouraged kids to enter picture contests and join Brownie clubs. Brownie cameras were an instant success. They cost only one dollar, plus fifteen cents for film. Approximately 150,000 cameras shipped the first year, triple the previous sales record. Kodak produced the Brownie for 70 years, eventually offering 125 different Brownie models. Brownies were usually brown or black, but some models were bright colors. Some Brownies had flash bulb attachments for taking pictures in dim light.

The Brownie cameras were such a success because now everyone could take pictures. People could make photo albums of family pictures that captured parents, friends, relatives, and images of daily life. These photos helped preserve cherished memories for generations of people. In a story told on the Kodak Web site, one man remembered, "During a recent family reunion, my aunt shared many of the pictures she had taken with that [Brownie] camera over the years. Those pictures brought back many cherished memories of all the good times that have passed. As she went through the pictures, my aunt told me a story about each one. I heard how my Uncle Tommy won a photo contest at the boys club back in the fifties using that camera." In bringing photography to everyone because of its affordability and ease of use, the Brownie camera became a cherished part of American family life.

—Timothy Berg

For More Information

Auer, Michel. *The Illustrated History of the Camera, from 1839 to the Present.* Boston: New York Graphic Society, 1975.

"The Brownie Camera @ 100: A Celebration." *Kodak.com.* http://www.kodak.com/US/en/corp/features/brownieCam/index.shtml (accessed December 13, 2001).

Collins, Douglas. *The Story of Kodak.* New York: Harry Abrams, 1990.

Dime Stores

The five-and-ten-cent store, also called the five-and-dime, was one of the most popular institutions in the United States from the late 1880s to the middle of the twentieth century. The dime store was more than a place where shoppers met to find a bargain and sip a limeade at the lunch counter. It also sparked a revolutionary change in American shopping habits and was the direct ancestor of the modern discount store. Dime stores

Woolworth's stores were a familiar sight in cities across the United States during most of the twentieth century. *Archive Photos. Reproduced by permission.*

have figured in films, such as *Come Back to the Five and Dime, Jimmy Dean, Jimmy Dean* (1982), and in popular music, as in the 1920s song by Billy Rose (1899–1966) and Fred Fisher (1875–1942), "I Found a Million Dollar Baby (in a Five and Ten Cent Store)." Although they have disappeared from American streets, the five-and-dime still has a firm place in American popular culture.

The father of the dime store was Frank Winfield Woolworth (1852–1919). As a youth, Woolworth did not enjoy working on his family's farm in upstate New York, so he eagerly accepted a job as a sales clerk at the local store, Moore and Smith. At that time, stores kept all their goods behind the counter with no prices marked. Customers had to ask a sales clerk for what they wanted and try to negotiate with the clerk if they could not afford the stated price. Woolworth, who had heard of a new sales technique, placed a variety of items on a counter marked "Everything Five Cents." When that proved successful, he got the idea of opening an entire store selling items for five cents. His employers agreed that his idea was an interesting one and loaned him $315.41 to buy the inventory for his new store.

On February 22, 1879, F. W. Woolworth opened his first five-cent store in Utica, New York. On November 6, 1880, he raised the top price to a dime and opened the first five- and ten-cent store in Pennsylvania. The stores were popular among working people who needed to shop economically. By 1907, Woolworth had twenty-three stores nationwide, serving around a million customers a day. That year, the first Woolworth's lunch counter opened, serving inexpensive meals in an informal setting. By 1930, there were 2,247 Woolworth's around the world along with many successful imitators, including Grant's, Kresge's, Murphy's, and McCrory's. In 1932, the ten-cent top price was dropped and dime stores became simply bargain stores.

Woolworth's gained an immortal place in the **civil rights movement** (see entry under 1960s—The Way We Lived in volume 4) in 1960 when four black college students sat down at a racially segregated Woolworth's lunch counter in Greensboro, North Carolina. Their action led to a statewide boycott of Woolworth's and eventually to civil rights reforms across the South. The Greensboro lunch counter was bought as an historical artifact by the Smithsonian Institute in Washington, D.C.

By the 1980s, many dime stores had become shabby relics of the past. They were replaced on city streets by small "dollar stores" and in **malls** (see entry under 1950s—Commerce in volume 3) and suburban locations by huge modern discount stores like **Wal-Mart** (see entry under 1960s—Commerce in volume 4). In 1998, the last Woolworth's closed its doors, although the Woolworth Corporation still exists. The corporation owns the Footlocker and Kenny shoe-store chains.

—Tina Gianoulis

For More Information

Brough, James. *The Woolworths*. New York: McGraw-Hill, 1982.

Glassner, Lester. *Dime-Store Days*. New York: Penguin Books, 1981.

Gustaitis, Joseph. "The Nickel and Dime Empire." *American History* (Vol. 33, no. 1, March 1998): pp. 40–48.

Hubbell, Sue. "You Can Still Get It at the 'Dime Store,' But Not for a Dime." *Smithsonian* (June 1994): pp. 104–12.

Plunkett-Powell, Karen. *Remembering Woolworth's: A Nostalgic History of the World's Most Famous Five-and-Dime*. New York: St. Martin's Press, 1999.

Wolff, Miles. *Lunch at the 5 & 10*. Chicago: Ivan R. Dee, 1990.

Dixie Cups

The paper cup emerged in the early twentieth century as part of the battle to fight the spread of disease. Before the invention of the paper cup, individuals would often use a common drinking cup placed next to a sink in a school, in a courthouse, or on a train. Legend has it that Kansas doctor Samuel Crumbine (1862–1954) saw a girl with tuberculosis (a contagious disease affecting the lungs) drinking from such a cup and called for the invention of disposable drinking cups. The first such cup was invented in 1904. The disposable drinking cup was perfected in 1908 by Lawrence Luellen, who marketed the "Luellen Cup & Water Vendor," which sold a cup of cold water for a penny.

Luellen's breakthrough invention fused two pieces of paper together with wax, which kept the water from ruining the paper. His water-vending units, soon sold in public places around the United States, were widely hailed for reducing or halting the spread of disease. Luellen's invention was marketed most famously beginning in 1912 by the Health Kup Company, which changed its product name to the Dixie cup in 1919. Like Kleenex and the **Xerox copier** (see entry under 1960s—Commerce in volume 4), the Dixie brand name soon came to stand for the product itself. Dixie advertised and marketed its name widely. Although owned by different corporations through the twentieth century, Dixie was consistently the leading brand of paper cups.

—Tom Pendergast

For More Information

King, Norman. "Dixie Cup." *The Almanac of Fascinating Beginnings*. New York: Citadel Press, 1994.

Lafayette College Libraries. "Dixie Cup Company History." *Hugh Moore Dixie Cup Company Collection, 1905–1986*. [Online] http://ww2.lafayette.edu/~library/special/dixie/company.html (accessed January 2, 2002).

Fuller Brush Company

Founded in 1906 by Alfred C. Fuller (1885–1973), the Fuller Brush Company has for many years been one of the world's most successful direct marketing companies, employing a large sales force that in the twentieth century sold brushes, brooms, and other household products door to door. Just as the Avon Lady sold cosmetics by ringing doorbells, the "Fuller Brush Man" offered an array of more practical merchandise during an era when most women were at home during the daytime. Despite having doors slammed in his face by customers who resented being interrupted, the Fuller Brush Man gained a reputation for persistence and ingenuity in making his sales pitches. Comic strips and skits often satirized an aggressive Fuller Brush Man sticking his foot in a customer's door in a frantic attempt to make his plea. Comedian Red Skelton (1913–1997) starred in *The Fuller Brush Man,* a 1948 film about murder and mayhem in the world of door-to-door sales. A sequel, *The Fuller Brush Girl,* starring Lucille Ball (1911–1989), was released in 1950.

From its earliest days, the Fuller Brush Company adopted three basic principles to achieve its mission: "Make it work, make it last, and guarantee it no matter what." The company promotes the fact that its product line is American made. By 2001, its five-hundred-thousand-square-foot plant near Great Bend, Kansas, was manufacturing more than two thousand items, including household-cleaning aids, industrial cleaners, polishes and wax products, mops, floor brushes, brooms, sponges, wire hangers, lotions and fragrances, hair-care aids, silk-screened graphics, aerosols, and chemicals. The company, now part of CPAC, Inc., consists of nine independent divisions, including Stanley Home Products.

Sensitive to changing lifestyles that have all but eliminated the door-to-door salesman from American life, the Fuller Brush Company sells its products through factory outlets and mail order and has established an online shopping catalog with nearly five hundred items available. Still, the company encourages one-on-one customer contact by offering distributorships to citizens or permanent residents who live in the continental United States.

—Edward Moran

For More Information

"Alfred Fuller." *The Canadians.* http://www.histori.ca/historica/eng_site/resources/the_cdns/alf.html (accessed January 2, 2002).

Fuller, Alfred Carl, as told to Hartzall Spence. *A Foot in the Door: The Life Appraisal of the Original Fuller Brush Man.* New York: McGraw-Hill, 1960.

Fuller Brush Company. http://www.fullerbrush.com (accessed January 2, 2002).
Fuller Brush Man (video). Burbank, CA: Columbia TriStar Home Video, 1991.

Harley-Davidson

In 1903, when William S. Harley (1880–1943) and Arthur Davidson (c. 1880–1950) produced their first motorcycle in their backyard in Milwaukee, Wisconsin, there were 15 motorcycle manufacturers in the United States. By 1911, there were 151 manufacturers. In 2001, only one American motorcycle maker remains: Harley-Davidson. Its bikes have become a major cultural icon around the world, representing not only efficient transportation but freedom, rebellion, and a romantic outlaw image. Harley-Davidson has weathered the arrival of the cheap automobile in the mid-1920s and the appearance of the cheap, high-quality Japanese motorcycle in the mid-1970s, to remain one of the most well-known American corporations in the world.

Harley and Davidson only produced one motorized bicycle the first year they set up shop. The next year they made two; in 1905, eight. In 1910, thirty-two hundred hundred motorcycles rolled away from the Milwaukee factory. By 1920, Harley-Davidson was the largest motorcycle manufacturer in the world, producing twenty-eight thousand bikes. The military used twenty thousand Harleys during World War I (1914–18), and in World War II (1939–45), ninety thousand Harleys joined the army. After the war ended, many returning soldiers bought Harleys for their personal use. Accustomed to bold wartime driving, these soldiers often drove their bikes recklessly and fast. When groups of them gathered to ride together, they formed the first motorcycle "gangs."

Motorcycle gangs have traditionally been associated with Harleys, perhaps because the loud rumbling of their engines and the high vibration of their ride appeals to bikers who wish to project a tough, wild image. Hell's Angels, perhaps the most famous motorcycle gang, founded in 1950, requires members to drive Harleys. However, in recent decades, Harley ownership has spread far beyond the outlaw bikers to those who wish to become "weekend outlaws." By 2001, the average income of a

By the 1920s, Harley-Davidson motorcycles were found everywhere, including the ranks of the New York State Police. *Archive Photos. Reproduced by permission.*

Harley owner reached $70,000 per year. One Harley rider out of ten is a woman. Many who don leather, helmet, and Harley T-shirt are doctors, lawyers, and other professional people. They call their bikes "hogs," and gather with other Harley riders at weekend rallies all around the country, two of the largest being in Daytona Beach, Florida, and Sturgis, South Dakota.

—Tina Gianoulis

For More Information

Bolfert, Thomas C. *The Big Book of Harley-Davidson.* Milwaukee: Harley-Davidson, Inc., 1991.

Harley-Davidson Motorcycles. http://www.harley-davidson.com/hd_main/hd_select_country.jsp (accessed January 2, 2002).

Johnson, David, and Scott Rouseau. "The Bikes That Made Milwaukee Famous." *Cycle World* (Vol. 32, no. 9, September 1993): pp. 48–54.

Krakauer, Jon. "A Hog Is Still a Hog, But the 'Wild Ones' Are Tamer." *Smithsonian* (Vol. 24, no. 8, November 1993): pp. 88–97.

Taylor, Rich. "The Mystique: Harley-Davidson Motorcycles." *Popular Mechanics* (Vol. 175, no. 11, November 1998): pp. 64–73.

J. Walter Thompson Company

Headquartered in New York City, the J. Walter Thompson **advertising** (see entry under 1920s—Commerce in volume 2) agency is one of the world's largest, with more than 250 offices and affiliates in 88 countries. For half a century, from 1922 to 1972, it led the industry in billings (the amount of business done by an ad agency within a certain period of time). Founded in 1864 as Carlton & Smith, the agency was originally a broker of advertising space in religious periodicals. In 1877, William James Carlton (1838–1902), one of the original owners, sold the business to one of its employees, James Walter Thompson (1847–1928), for $500, plus $800 for the furniture. Over the next two decades, the J. Walter Thompson Company became the first full-service advertising agency. As a full-service agency, the company offered creative services like ad design and placement, package design, and logo design to its clients. One of its first logos, created in 1896, was the Rock of Gibraltar symbol for the Prudential Insurance Company, still in use.

During the first decades of the twentieth century, the company helped develop the catchy and concise advertising slogans that have since become a mainstay of consumer marketing. One of J. Walter Thompson's first successes was its 1912 campaign designed to convince women to use deodorant products, using the slogan "You can't vote. But you can smell nice." Under the director of Stanley Resor (1879–1962), who purchased the agency in 1916, J. Walter Thompson commissioned market-research studies and was the first agency to open a research department. These moves helped define the way the advertising industry has functioned ever since. In 1920, the agency hired John B. Watson (1878–1958), the noted behavioral psychologist, to assist in the development of campaigns that would appeal to basic human wants and needs.

After World War I (1914–18), the J. Walter Thompson Company began representing some of America's most familiar brand-name products, such as Libby's, Kraft, **Aunt Jemima** (see entry under 1900s—Commerce in volume 1), and Fleischmann's. Its clients sponsored many popular **radio** (see entry under 1920s—TV and Radio in volume 2) shows during the 1930s, complete with clever jingles that described their products in a few memorable lines. In 1947, one client, Kraft Foods, sponsored the first network television program, "The Kraft Television Theater." Other major clients have been the Ford Motor Company, Pan American Airways, Nestlé, Eastman Kodak, Warner-Lambert, Rolex, Merrill Lynch, and Wendy's (for whom it coined the "Where's the Beef?" slogan). In 1988, the year after it was sold to the WPP Group, J. Walter Thompson did $665 million in new business, a one-year record for the agency.

—Edward Moran

For More Information

Fox, Stephen R. *The Mirror Makers: A History of American Advertising and Its Creators.* New York: Morrow, 1997.

J. Walter Thompson Corporation. http://www.jwt.com (accessed January 18, 2002).

Meyers, William. *The Image Makers: Power and Persuasion on Madison Avenue.* New York: Times Books, 1984.

Sivulka, Juliann. *Soap, Sex, and Cigarettes: A Cultural History of American Advertising.* Belmont, CA: Wadsworth, 1998.

Strasser, Susan. *Satisfaction Guaranteed: The Making of the American Mass Market.* New York: Pantheon Books, 1989.

Kellogg's Cereals

With its headquarters in Battle Creek, Michigan, the Kellogg's Company is the world's largest manufacturer of packaged, ready-to-eat breakfast cereals and related snack products. Many of the company's products, like Corn Flakes, Frosted Flakes, Froot Loops, and Rice Krispies, have become familiar breakfast foods around the globe. In 2001, the company reported more than $6 billion in sales worldwide.

Kellogg's evolved from the religiously based "health industry" of the late nineteenth and early twentieth centuries. The company can trace its roots to the work of two brothers, John Harvey Kellogg (1852–1943) and Will Keith Kellogg (1860–1951). Both men were Seventh Day Adventists, although both men were expelled from the church for worldliness and heresy in 1907. Seventh Day Adventists have traditionally adhered to high nutritional standards, and the Kellogg brothers were active in helping that denomination develop its early programs. John Harvey was medical superintendent of the Adventist Battle Creek Sanitarium, where he promoted a vegetarian diet, hydrotherapy (water therapy), and abstinence from alcohol, coffee, tea, and tobacco. He also served as editor of the church's monthly publication, *Good Health.*

A 1906 advertisement for Kellogg's Toasted Corn Flakes. *Archive Photos. Reproduced by permission.*

In 1894, the Kellogg brothers invented flaked cereals, which they marketed as an easily digestible food product. In 1906, Will founded the Battle Creek Toasted Corn Flake Company to sell sweetened versions of these products as cereals, not just as health foods. By 1909, the brothers had become bitter rivals, and Will won the right to use the Kellogg's name as a trademark in 1920, after which he established the company as it is known today.

By the second half of the twentieth century, Kellogg's was arguably the nation's most recognized cereal brand, with some thirty-five different products, ranging from All-Bran to Strawberry Mini-Wheats. It also manufactures Pop-Tarts and Nutri-Grain snack products. Many of the cartoon characters it developed to promote its various brands have become familiar icons, most notably Tony the Tiger (and his familiar slogan, "They're gr-r-reat!") from Frosted Flakes, and the Snap!, Crackle!, and Pop! gnomes from Rice Krispies. Kellogg's and other cereal manufacturers are often criticized by nutritionists and educators. Nutritionists disapprove of the high sugar content of their products, and educators protest how cereals are aggressively marketed to children, especially on **Saturday-morning television** (see entry under 1960s—TV and Radio in volume 4).

—Edward Moran

For More Information

Hunnicutt, Benjamin Kline. *Kellogg's Six-Hour Day.* Philadelphia: Temple University Press, 1996.

Kellogg's Company. http://www.kelloggs.com (accessed January 2, 2002).

Lindsay, David. *House of Invention: The Secret Life of Everyday Products.* New York: Lyons Press, 2000.

Money, John. *The Destroying Angel: Sex, Fitness & Food in the Legacy of Degeneracy Theory, Graham Crackers, Kellogg's Corn Flakes & American Health History.* Buffalo: Prometheus Books, 1985.

Louisville Slugger

Baseball is called America's National Pastime, and Louisville Slugger is the name of the most famous and popular wooden bat employed by professional ballplayers to smash singles, bash doubles, belt triples, and pound home runs in a ballpark.

The roots of the Louisville Slugger date to 1884 and involve John A. "Bud" Hillerich (1866–1946). Hillerich's father operated a woodworking shop that produced bedposts, bowling pins, handrails, and ornaments. At the time, most ballplayers whittled their own bats and often owned only one. The story goes that Hall-of-Famer-to-be Pete Browning (1861–1905), playing for the Louisville Eclipse of the American Association (the forerunner of the National League), broke his bat during a game. Additionally, he was in the middle of a batting slump. Young Hillerich, who was just eighteen at the time, happened to be at the game and offered to produce a bat for Browning. The ballplayer agreed, and Hillerich spun one out of white ash, to Browning's specifications. The following day Browning busted out of his slump, getting three hits in three times at bat, and requested that Hillerich produce additional bats. Soon other ballplayers began ordering Hillerich's product. At first, they were known as Fall City Sluggers, but in 1894 Hillerich copyrighted the name Louisville Slugger, which was imprinted in an oval on every bat. Each ballplayer's signature also was burned into each bat, allowing him to keep track of his lumber.

In 1905, another future Cooperstown inductee, Pittsburgh Pirate shortstop Honus Wagner (1874–1955), became the first professional athlete to earn endorsement money for allowing his name to be linked to a product when he signed a contract with Hillerich that resulted in bats with his name burned into them to be sold in stores. Ten years later, the Hillerich factory was destroyed in a fire. During the rebuilding process, Frank W. Bradsby (1878–1937), a former buyer of athletic equipment, was hired to market the bats. In 1916, the company name became Hillerich & Bradsby (H&B).

To this day, H&B still produces bats for major leaguers, designed to the specifications of each ballplayer. The history of the company—and the history of its baseball bats—is chronicled in the Louisville Slugger Museum. Located in downtown Louisville, Kentucky, visitors to the museum can observe actual bat production. Despite the present-day use of aluminum bats by schools and Little Leagues, H&B produces hundreds of thousands of wooden bats per year. The company also produces approximately seventy-two bats per season for each major leaguer.

—Rob Edelman

For More Information

Arnow, Jan. *Louisville Slugger: The Making of a Baseball Bat.* New York: Pantheon Books, 1984.

Model T

The Ford Motor Company's mass-produced and affordable Model T made the car an essential part of American life. Before the Model T, cars were luxury items that could be purchased only by the rich. With the Model T, Henry Ford (1863–1947), who founded the Ford Motor Company in 1903, figured out how to make the car a necessary component of everyday life for regular working people.

To construct the Model T, Henry Ford devised labor-saving techniques that would increase production and reduce costs. Unlike his competitors, Ford Motor Company offered only one type of car. The parts for the Model T were interchangeable, and Ford said that people could buy the Model T "in any color they want so long as it's black." As the popularity of the car grew, Ford continued to fine-tune his production line, implementing a system of management that would become known as "Fordism." Fordism was based on the assembly line and increased wages for his workers. Ford's assembly line divided labor into small tasks that required less skill and craftsmanship. But Ford reasoned that workers would only accept the more mundane jobs if they were well paid. The Ford Motor Company paid more than double the average daily wage of other industries. When Ford introduced the eight-hour, five-dollar day in 1914, job seekers flocked to the company. Henry Ford's genius revolutionized the automobile industry and helped increase sales.

Although people had been fascinated with motorized vehicles since the first cars were produced, cars had only been affordable for the very rich. The Model T was introduced for $850, a price far lower than other cars and within reach of many people. For the first time, working men and women could afford a motorized vehicle and Ford aggressively marketed the Model T to them. Ford publicized the Model T by winning a transcontinental race with it. Even though the Model T's victory was later disqualified, the public had already fallen in love with it. It was fast, it was cheap, and it was truly American.

Produced from 1908 to 1927, the Model T changed the way people thought about traveling, distances, and time. The Model T became the best selling car in history, at the time. By 1915, Ford Motor Company had produced one million Model Ts. By the mid-1920s, the Model T had made the car an essential part of American life. The car promoted the development of the **suburbs** (see entry under 1950s—The Way We Lived in volume 3) of the 1920s. Americans began to demand the paving of million of miles of roads. By the time of the stock market crash in 1929 that began the Great Depression (1929–41), the Model T had become so much a part of American life that as people began losing their jobs and savings, they held on to their cars, sometimes pulling them with horses when they could not afford gas. The Model T had made America a nation of drivers.

—Sara Pendergast

For More Information

Gourley, Catherine. *Wheels of Time: A Biography of Henry Ford.* Brookfield, CT: Millbrook Press, 1997.

McCalley, Bruce W. *The Model T Ford: The Car That Changed the World.* Iola, WI: Krause Publications, 1994.

Simonds, Christopher. *The Model T Ford.* Englewood Cliffs, NJ: Silver Burdett Press, 1991.

Plastic

Plastic is a synthetic material made out of petroleum products that can be shaped and molded into an infinite variety of shapes without breaking. Few other products have influenced American culture as much as plastic. In the early twentieth century, plastic proved that it could be used as a substitute for all kinds of natural materials. It soon began to appear in all kinds of products that Americans used. Americans' use of plastic as a cheap imitation of natural substances led some to call American culture a "plastic" or artificial culture, focused on cheap imitations rather than on items of genuine quality. Whether or not that was true, plastics became a part of most Americans' daily lives.

Plastic began as a search for a man-made alternative to natural materials such as marble, ivory, and bone. Those items were used in all kinds of consumer goods in the 1800s and earlier, but depending on the substance they could be somewhat rare and expensive. The first plastic-like substance was celluloid, invented in 1869 by John Wesley Hyatt (1837–1912) as a substitute for ivory. That discovery led to later innovations, including the development of chemically synthetic plastics in the early twentieth century. The invention of other plastic forms such as **nylon** (see entry under 1930s–Fashion in volume 2), rayon, polyvinyl chloride, vinyl, lucite, plexiglas, and teflon followed.

The development of plastic as a scientific story is important, but, like many scientific inventions, its use by ordinary people is what made plastic such an important part of everyday American life. As the twentieth century progressed, plastics crept into American life in more and more unique ways. For instance, celluloid, the first plastic substance, revolutionized photography, enabling film to be used easily in portable cameras by all kinds of people. No longer did one need to be a professional photographer to take pictures. Celluloid was also crucial to the development of motion pictures. All the classic images Americans enjoy on the screens of their local movie theaters are due to plastic celluloid. Cellophane, a close relative of celluloid, was used as plastic wraps to help keep food fresh and in such products as "Scotch" tape. Plastics found their way into clothing in the form of **nylon stockings** (see entry under 1930s–Fashion in volume 2), or nylons, for women's legs; in rayon dresses that simulated natural, and therefore more expensive, silk; and in **polyester** (see entry under 1970s–Fashion in volume 4) suits for men.

Plastics also entered the home in increasing numbers. People spoke into new, one-piece plastic telephone receivers and sat on Naugahyde (artificial leather) recliners. Plastics were especially popular in the kitchen. Vinyl flooring stood up to lots of rough treatment and spills wiped up easily from its surface. Plastic Tupperware, kitchen bowls made out of plastic, proved very popular in the 1940s and after. Plastic could form all kinds of convenient shapes for bowls, glasses, and containers. Plastic kitchenware could be dropped without breaking, and it was inexpensive to buy. Teflon proved it could be used as a nonstick cooking surface. As a result of these innovations, homeowners loved plastic. Plastic was also found elsewhere in the home—in children's toys, such as **LEGO** (see entry under 1950s–Sports and Games in volume 3) blocks and **Fisher-Price toys** (see entry under 1930s–Commerce in volume 2); in teenagers' bedrooms, with vinyl rock-and-roll records; in plastic swimming pools in the backyard; and in plastic doormats that resembled green grass.

By the 1960s, plastics were an inescapable part of American life. The substance was even immortalized in the 1967 film ***The Graduate*** (see entry under 1960s–Film and Theater in volume 4), starring Dustin Hoffman, when an older neighbor tells Hoffman's character that he could describe a bright future for him in one word: "plastics." By that time, however, although millions of people were using plastic in their everyday lives, some people became disturbed by the American tendency to replace natural things with synthetic plastics. Even as early as the 1920s, plastic was used as a negative word for artificial. Living in a "plastic society" meant living in an artificial world cut off from nature. Indeed, plastics had been phenomenally successful in replicating natural materials. But by the 1970s, the costs of this material were slowly becoming known. Plastics, it turned out, caused cancer in many workers who breathed in fumes during its manufacture. It also proved a big environmental problem. Plastic made possible a throw-away culture centered around convenience. Many items, like styrofoam cups, were used once and then thrown away, piling up along roadsides as litter and taking up precious space in landfills. Plastics also do not degrade into their base materials as natural substances do, so the plastic cup someone threw away in 1955 still exists today, sitting in a landfill somewhere. These problems even led some people to boycott styrofoam cups and to urge people to reconsider their use of plastic.

By the end of the twentieth century, plastics were an inescapable part of American life. Plastics helped make life easier in a multitude of ways but also proved that few, if any, innovations come without some cost to society.

—Timothy Berg

For More Information

Fenichell, Stephen. *Plastic: The Making of a Synthetic Century.* New York: HarperBusiness, 1996.

Katz, Sylvia. *Plastics: Common Objects, Classic Designs.* New York: Harry N. Abrams, 1984.

Meikle, Jeffrey L. *American Plastic: A Cultural History.* New Brunswick, NJ: Rutgers University Press, 1995.

Sears, Roebuck Catalog

From the time of its origin in 1888, the Sears, Roebuck catalog was more than just a listing of store merchandise. Called the "Big Book" or the "Wish Book" by the millions of people who eagerly awaited its arrival each year, the catalog brought the wider world into the isolated homes of rural America. From it, working-class Americans who lived far from cities or even shops, could order anything from shoes, clothes, furniture, and appliances to wagons and machinery. More than this, they could keep up to date on advances in equipment, technology, and fashion and even take a peek at a drawing of a member of the opposite sex in underwear. By bringing honesty and dependability to mail-order shopping, Sears, Roebuck and Company was able to reach out to the seventy percent of Americans who lived in the rural United States at the end of the nineteenth

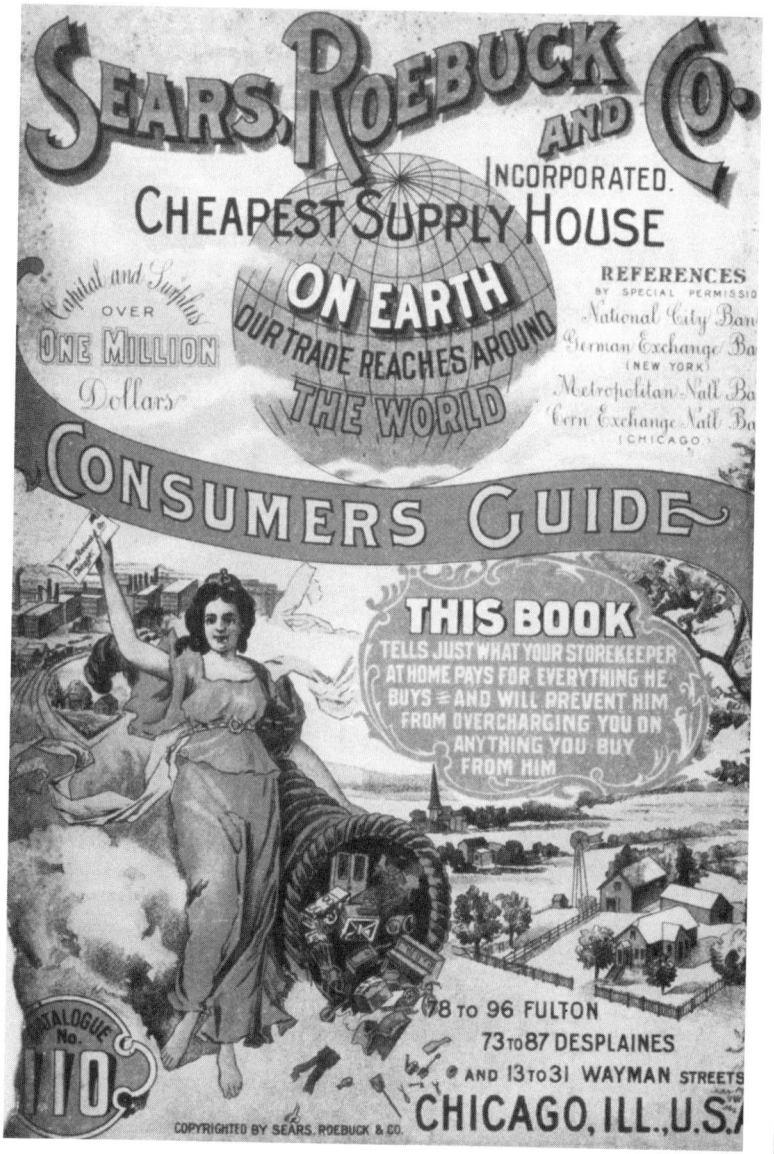

The Sears, Roebuck catalog, pictured here around 1910, helped connect Americans by bringing the latest fashions, appliances, and more to everyone's doorstep. *Archive Photos. Reproduced by permission.*

century. Many of these Americans joked that the Bible and the Sears, Roebuck catalog were the only books that they read.

Richard W. Sears (1863–1914) was working as a station agent for the railroad, passing the time by reading the various catalogs that came through on mail trains, when he began to think that he could develop his own successful mail-order business. He and his partner Alvah C. Roebuck (1864–1948) issued their first catalog in 1888, selling jewelry and watches. Each year the two expanded their catalog and their inventory, offering free trials and money-back guarantees to boost sales. Cleverly, they designed their catalog a little smaller than that of their biggest competitor, Montgomery Ward. That way, they reasoned, the Sears, Roebuck catalog would be placed on top when the catalogs were stacked. By 1895, the company had incorporated, and the catalog had grown to over 500 pages. It now included clothes, guns, farm equipment, and furniture. In 1908, Sears and Roebuck began to sell mail-order houses, with a selection of 450 models. Houses were shipped in thousands of parts, with detailed instructions for building. By the early 1900s, Sears, Roebuck and Company was earning $10 million in sales.

The Sears, Roebuck catalog continued to represent a successful mail-order business for over a century. In 1993, finally overwhelmed by competition and changing shopping habits, the catalog portion of Sears, Roebuck and Company closed. Although a catalog can still be ordered from the company, the Sears Web site now continues the tradition of the famous mail-order catalog.

—Tina Gianoulis

For More Information

Emmett, Boris, and John E. Jeuck. *Catalogues and Counters: A History of Sears, Roebuck and Company.* Chicago: University of Chicago Press, 1950.

Gustaitis, Joseph. "Closing the Book." *American History Illustrated* (Vol. 28, no. 3): pp. 36-42.

Hicks, L. Wayne. "The House Is in the Mail." *American History* (Vol. 35, April 2000): pp. 38-43.

Liggett, Lori. "The Founders of Sears, Roebuck and Company." *Bowling Green State University American Culture Studies Program.* http://www.bgsu.edu/departments/acs/1890s/sears/sears.html (accessed January 2, 2002).

McGinty, Brian. "Mr. Sears and Mr. Roebuck." *American History Illustrated* (Vol. 21, no. 2, June 1986): pp. 34-8.

Sears.com. http://www.sears.com (accessed January 2, 2002).

Worthy, James C. *Shaping An American Institution.* Champaign: University of Illinois Press, 1984.

Stereoscopes

Stereoscopes were the first mass-produced viewers for three-dimensional (3-D) photography. Stereoscopes allowed people to view two photographs of a single scene taken from slightly different perspectives (called stereographs) as one 3-D image. The

3-D images brought a realism and a depth to photography that had never before been seen.

Stereoscopy, popular from 1850 to 1920, was a forerunner of cinema and **television** (see entry under 1940s—TV and Radio in volume 3). From the comfort of their own homes, people could use the stereoscope to see images of important people, places, and historic events. The device also enabled them to entertain themselves with erotica (pictures meant to arouse sexual interest), images of tourist destinations, and fine works of art. Invented by British physicist Charles Wheatstone (1802–1875) in 1832, the stereoscope truly became popular when it was introduced to America. Between 1860 and 1890, more than four hundred million stereographs were produced in assembly-line fashion in large factories in America. Stereographs were the main source of visual information about the American West, the Civil War (1861–65), the Spanish-American War (1898), and the world in general. With the rise in popularity of cinema in the 1920s, however, stereoscopes soon lost their adult audience. Stereoscopic images were relegated to children's toys like the View-Master, which was introduced in 1939.

The stereoscope, pictured here circa 1870, was the first device that allowed people to view 3-D images. *Hulton/Archive. Reproduced by permission.*

Stereoscopic imagery has never ceased to fascinate viewers. The imagery enjoyed a brief revival in the 1950s with **3-D movies** (see entry under 1950s—Film and Theater in volume 3) and **comic books** (see entry under 1930s—Print Culture in volume 2). By the 1990s, computer-generated Magic Eye stereograms, which allowed viewers to see stereoscopic images without a viewer, had become tremendously popular, selling more than twenty-five million books of images by 1995. Computerized holographic and virtual-reality technologies have broadened the usefulness and appeal of stereoscopic imagery to interactive games and even to military training programs for surveillance, weapons targeting, and flight schools.

—Sara Pendergast

For More Information

Earle, W. E., ed. *Points of View: The Stereograph in America–A History.* Rochester, NY: Visual Studies Workshop, 1979.
Jones, John. *Wonders of the Stereoscope.* New York: Knopf, 1976.
Wing, Paul. *Stereoscopes: The First One Hundred Years.* Nashua, NH: Transition, 1996.

Teddy Bears

Most Americans carry fond memories of a childhood teddy bear. Although contemporary stuffed animals are manufactured in the form of every creature from aardvarks to zebras, the bear remains the most popular choice. Today, the making, selling, and collecting of teddy bears represent significant human and economic activities.

The teddy bear has origins both in the United States and in Europe, each dating back to 1902. When U.S. president Theodore Roosevelt (1858–1919) took a hunting trip to Mississippi that year, one of his companions captured a black bear cub and brought it to Roosevelt to shoot. The president saw no sport in such an act and refused to shoot it. A *Washington Post* reporter traveling with the hunting party wrote a story about the incident, which was printed with an illustration showing Roosevelt declining to shoot the helpless cub. A Brooklyn variety store owner, Morris Michtom, saw the cartoon and got an idea about how to sell some stuffed bears that his wife had made. He placed them in his shop window with a sign reading "Teddy's Bears." Demand for the product was so great that Michtom founded the Ideal Novelty and Toy Corporation and went into mass production.

The same year, German Richard Steiff saw trained bears performing at a circus and thought a toy based on the creatures might sell. He took his idea and some drawings to his aunt, Margarete Steiff (1847–1909), who was a well-known toy and doll maker. She designed and made a few sample bears, which she brought to the 1903 Leipzig Toy Fair. European dealers were uninterested, but an American distributor ordered several thousand bears for export to the United States.

Today, teddy bears are big business, with an estimated 2.5 million collectors in the United States alone. The industry distinguishes between two kinds of bears: toys (which have hug-

The Teddy Bear and the Doll at Christmas

How to Dress Them: By Ida Cleve Van Auken

3673

3673—This Teddy-Bear Outfit Consists of a Pajama Suit, Shown on the Left, a Rough-Rider Suit, in the Centre, and a Play Suit, on the Right

3673

An ad from the December 1907 *Ladies Home Journal* depicting the well-dressed teddy bear. *Courtesy of Henry Ford Museum and Greenfield Village.*

gable, soft stuffing) and collectibles (with firm interiors and jointed limbs). Experts acknowledge Gund, Inc. as the premier maker of cuddly toy bears, whereas Germany's Steiff company remains the leader in collectibles. Some of Steiff's classic bears have fetched as much as ten thousand dollars at auction.

—Justin Gustainis

For More Information

Bull, Peter. *The Teddy Bear Book.* New York: Random House, 1970.

Severin, Gustav. *Teddy Bear: A Loving History of the Classic Childhood Companion.* Philadelphia: Courage Books, 1995.

1900s

Film and Theater

The first decade of the twentieth century was one of the last decades in which entertainment was still largely local and non-commercial. Movies were still in their infancy. Broadway had not yet gained a reputation as the center of serious and popular theater. Most Americans sought their entertainment in small local theaters, at vaudeville shows, and—in a growing number of cities—in storefront nickelodeons. Although wealthier Americans in large cities could attend serious professional performances of opera and of classic plays, such as the works of Shakespeare, most Americans enjoyed rougher, less polished fare. In the 1900s, twenty-first-century-style film and theater—polished productions that can be enjoyed by the masses in a variety of locations—simply did not exist.

The most popular form of entertainment in the decade was vaudeville. The core of a vaudeville show was variety: each show contained nine to twelve acts, with comedy, stunts, dramatic skits, and singing. Vaudeville acts toured from city to city, and the best and most famous made stars of some of the performers. The impact of vaudeville on later forms of popular culture—especially radio and TV—was enormous, as many vaudeville performers went on to become the first stars of radio and TV. Another popular form of live entertainment was the minstrel show, a form of variety show in which the performers often presented stereotypical and racist impersonations of African Americans. Many white performers performed "blackface" minstrelsy (MIN-strul-see), which meant that they applied makeup to look black, but minstrel shows also offered a rare opportunity for African Americans to appear on stage. Buffalo Bill Cody (1846–1917) and his Wild West Show provided another form of entertainment, a variety show meant to dramatize the mythical American West.

Film was in its infancy at the beginning of the decade, but it soon made great strides. Technological limitations only allowed films to be about thirty seconds long, limiting the ability of film to tell a story, and they contained no sound. Early films were thus novelties, and they were often shown along with live entertainment, as in a vaudeville show. The creation of the silent film *The Great Train Robbery* in 1903 revolutionized the industry, however. At about twelve minutes long, the film told a dramatic story about a train robbery, and it thrilled audiences across the country. Throughout the decade more and more Americans began to see short films in nickelodeons, essentially storefront theaters that charged a small admission fee. By 1908, it was estimated that eighty million nickelodeon tickets were sold every week. By the 1910s, the rise of more skilled directors and famous "movie stars" would make film one of the most popular forms of entertainment.

Broadway

Even though the roadway named "Broadway" extends the length of the New York City borough of Manhattan, the name has come to indicate the area, in midtown Manhattan, in which a majority of the city's primary theaters are located. The word "Broadway" has come to represent bright, flashing lights and oversized billboards towering over playgoers as they crowd around theater entrances most every evening just before 8 P.M. (and on Wednesday and Saturday for matinees, or afternoon performances). For those who choose to devote their life to the stage, appearing on Broadway is a significant accomplishment and starring on the Broadway stage is a dream come true.

New York City's status as the hub of American theater dates to 1826, when the three-thousand-seat Bowery Theatre opened; it was the first playhouse to feature glass-shaded gas-jet lighting. By the 1880s, "Broadway" had become the general term for American theater, and the New York theater district was nearby the street, only farther downtown, at East 14th Street and Union Square. As the city expanded, clusters of playhouses opened further uptown, in what today is midtown Manhattan. Eventually, most were constructed in the crosstown streets of the West Forties, by and directly above Times Square. The first major playhouse in the area arrived in 1893, when the American Theatre opened on West 42nd Street.

In the early twentieth century, revues featuring music, dance, and comedy were especially popular on Broadway. As the

The original cast of *Oklahoma!* (1943), one of Broadway's most celebrated musicals. *AP/Wide World Photos. Reproduced by permission.*

American musical theater evolved, scores of significant composers and performers earned fame writing music for and appearing in Broadway hits. Before **radio** (see entry under 1920s—TV and Radio in volume 2) and **television** (see entry under 1940s—TV and Radio in volume 3), countless popular songs originated on Broadway. For example, during World War I (1914–18), "Over There," a patriotic national rallying cry composed by George M. Cohan (1878–1942), was introduced at the New Amsterdam Theatre before becoming a hit record. Musical theater flourished on Broadway during a good portion of the twentieth century, but serious dramas and nonmusical comedies were increasingly staged. One notable Broadway dramatist who emphasized realism in his writing was Eugene O'Neill (1883–1953), who during the 1920s authored *The Emperor Jones, Anna Christie,* and *Strange Interlude.*

Many film actors started out on Broadway. Marlon Brando (1924–), for one, became a theater legend in 1947 with his riveting performance as Stanley Kowalski in *A Streetcar Named Desire.* Brando made his screen debut in 1950, replayed Kowalski in the film version of *Streetcar* the following year, and never came back to Broadway. Meanwhile, other actors preferred stage over screen, even though a successful movie actor will have far more international fame than a counterpart on the stage. Such Broadway legends as Laurette Taylor (1884–1946), Eva Le Gallienne (1899–1991), Katherine Cornell (1893–1974), Alfred Drake (1914–1992), and the husband-and-wife team of Alfred Lunt (1892–1977) and Lynn Fontanne (1887–1983) became major stage personalities, while barely, if ever, appearing on screen.

For several decades, theater-lovers have lamented the general decline in quality of the American theater. Yet Broadway—also known as the Great White Way—remains one of New York's top tourist attractions and symbolizes American theater.

—Rob Edelman

For More Information

Atkinson, Brooks. *Broadway.* New York: Macmillan, 1970.

Blum, Daniel. *A Pictorial History of the American Theatre, 1860–1970.* New York: Crown, 1969.

Brown, Gene. *Show Time: A Chronology of Broadway and the Theatre from Its Beginnings to the Present.* New York: Macmillan, 1997.

Dunlap, David W. *On Broadway: A Journey Uptown over Time.* New York: Rizzoli, 1990.

Frommer, Myrna Katz, and Harvey Frommer. *It Happened on Broadway: An Oral History of the Great White Way.* New York: Harcourt, 1998.

League of American Theatres and Producers. *The Internet Broadway Database.* http://www.ibdb.com (accessed April 16, 2002).

Buffalo Bill's Wild West Show

The mythology of the Old West is an essential part not so much of American history as American folklore. While much of this vision derives from countless dime novels (inexpensive, melodramatic books that originally cost ten cents) and Hollywood movies that depict the settling of the American West, the origin of this mythology may be traced to one man: William F. Cody (1846–1917), more commonly known as Buffalo Bill. Cody was a U.S. cavalry scout, buffalo hunter, Indian fighter, Pony Express rider, gold miner, ox team driver—and entertainer. He created Buffalo Bill's Wild West Show, a traveling extravaganza that celebrated and glorified the settling of the American West.

Legend has it that Cody was dubbed "Buffalo Bill" after being hired to help supply buffalo meat to workers building the cross-country railroad; he claimed to have killed 4,280 buffalo. His fame was spread by Ned Buntline (1823–1886), a dime novelist who made him the hero of a series of stories published in *The New York Weekly.* Buntline was not a chronicler of Cody's real-life deeds; he fictionalized and exaggerated them, thus creating the mythology surrounding his subject.

In 1872, Buntline persuaded Cody to act in his play, *The Scouts of the Plains,* which was Buffalo Bill's entry into show business. Supposedly, upon observing a Nebraska Independence Day celebration in 1883, Cody concocted the idea of Buffalo Bill's Wild West Show, which recreated a Pony Express ride, a stagecoach attack, and various rodeo events. The finale included a spectacle involving cowboys, Indians, and stampeding animals. Wherever possible, Cody hired real-life Western notables to appear in his show.

For an 1884 appearance at the Cotton Exposition in New Orleans, Louisiana, Cody acquired the services of his top drawing card: Annie Oakley (1860–1926), the famed sharpshooter. The following year, he hired Sitting Bull (1831–1890), fabled chief of the Teton Sioux Indians, who had led the final major Indian resistance against western settlement. In retrospect, Cody's employment of Indians is controversial. Although he was one of the few who dared hire Native Americans, his depiction of them attacking stagecoaches and settlers perpetuated the image of the Indian as a dangerous savage.

Cody's extravaganza reached its height in popularity in 1887, when he took it to London, England, to celebrate the fiftieth anniversary of the reign of Queen Victoria (1819–1901). Two years later, Cody toured throughout Europe, beginning with a performance in Paris. After returning to the United States in 1893 and savoring one last successful season, Cody's show began to decline. Its luster faded because of competition from similar traveling extravaganzas and internal upheaval. However, Cody did manage to keep the show afloat until his death in 1917.

—Rob Edelman

For More Information

Buffalo Bill and the Indians, Or Sitting Bull's History Lesson (film). United Artists, 1976.

Cody, William F. *An Autobiography of Buffalo Bill (Colonel W. F. Cody).* New York: Cosmopolitan Book Corporation, 1923.

Cody, William F. *The Business of Being Buffalo Bill: Selected Letters of William F. Cody, 1879–1917*. New York: Praeger, 1988.
Leonard, Elizabeth Jane. *Buffalo Bill, King of the Old West*. New York: Library Publishers, 1955.

The Great Train Robbery

The Great Train Robbery (1903) is one of the most popular and important early silent films. It was directed by Edwin S. Porter (1869–1941) for the Edison Company and was enjoyed by audiences for several years after its initial release. What makes this film outstanding is its ambitious length and style of storytelling. Most films of the period lasted only two or three minutes and contained less than a handful of shots. *The Great Train Robbery* told its story in about twelve minutes, linking fourteen individual shots together to complete a cohesive plotline. It is also often called the first recognizably modern **Western** (see entry under 1930s—Film and Theater in volume 2)

The original publicity for this audience pleaser stated that it was meant to present "a faithful duplication of the genuine 'Hold Ups' made famous by various outlaw bands in the far West." The plot is action packed. Bandits enter a telegraph office and tie up the telegraph operator. Then they stop a train and rob the express car and its passengers before escaping on horseback. Next, the telegraph operator's daughter finds her father and unties him. He alerts the people of the town, and they form a posse (PAH-see; a group of people who search for someone) to capture the bandits. The posse chases the bandits and succeeds in killing them.

The film made use of interesting special effects to highlight parts of the story. Two new techniques were especially thrilling to the audience. First, Porter created a sense of realism by stopping the action to insert a dummy for a real-life actor and restarting the camera as the dummy was tossed from a moving train. To tell the story, Porter filmed all the action from a distance, in a series of long shots. Then, after the completion of the story, he zoomed in for a close-up. In a close-up, the camera is placed so close to the subject that the viewer sees him or her only from the chest up; in the movie theater, Porter's close-up shot showed a bandit firing a gun at the camera—and simultaneously at the audience! Early movie audiences had not experienced seeing close-ups and were quite entertained by this powerful final shot.

Compared to today's films, *The Great Train Robbery* is not really an example of clever editing or technological innovation, but it is an illustration of a highly entertaining, longer narrative film that offered early cinema audiences a more detailed story-telling format.

—Audrey Kupferberg

For More Information

Fenin, George N., and William K. Everson. *The Western.* New York: Grossman Publishers, 1973.

Musser, Charles. *The Emergence of Cinema: The American Screen to 1907.* Berkeley: University of California Press, 1990.

Harry Houdini (1874–1926)

During the early twentieth century, Harry Houdini was the world's most celebrated illusionist and escape artist. He won world renown performing death-defying stunts that captured media attention and the imaginations of his audiences.

Houdini was born in Budapest, Hungary, in 1874; his birth name was Erich (or Ehrich) Weiss. His family came to America in 1878. He first became intrigued by trickery and illusion while a teenager and renamed himself after famed French magician Jean Eugene Robert-Houdin (1805–1871). Determined to forge a career as a magician, he labored for several years in obscurity before winning national acclaim in **vaudeville** (see entry under 1900s—Film and Theater in volume 1) and, then, international acclaim upon performing in England.

Houdini started out executing simple magic tricks but eventually developed and perfected the escape acts that won him notoriety. In these acts, he would free himself from straitjackets, prison cells, packing crates, coffins, mail pouches, milk cans, giant paper bags, and Chinese Water Torture chambers (large glass boxes filled with water). Often, he would be tied with rope, handcuffed, or manacled. As his fame grew, Houdini also became known for exposing fake spiritualists.

Master escape artist Harry Houdini. *Courtesy of the Library of Congress.*

In 1918, Houdini began acting in movies. In 1925, he opened on Broadway in *Magic,* a two-and-a-half-hour extravaganza. He died the following year. Legend has it that his death was the direct result of his being punched in the stomach by an overenthusiastic college student who wished to test the strength of Houdini's abdominal muscles. In the Hollywood biography *Houdini* (1953), his demise comes as he fails to complete an underwater escape trick. In fact, Houdini died of peritonitis, caused by a ruptured appendix—which may or may not have been connected to the stomach punch.

—Rob Edelman

For More Information

Hass, E. A. *Houdini's Last Trick: The Amazing True Story of the World's Greatest Magician.* New York: Random House, 1995.

Houdini Tribute. http://www.houdinitribute.com (accessed January 3, 2002).

Library of Congress. *Houdini.* "American Memory Project." http://lcweb2.loc.gov/ammem/vshtml/vshdini.html (accessed January 3, 2002).

Silverman, Kenneth. *Houdini!!! The Career of Erich Weiss.* New York: HarperCollins, 1996.

Woog, Adam. *Harry Houdini.* San Diego: Lucent Books, 1995.

Minstrel Shows

Minstrel shows were an extremely popular form of entertainment in which white performers wearing blackface makeup impersonated African Americans. The shows originated in the nineteenth century as professional stage productions. In the first half of the twentieth century professional productions disappeared, but putting on a minstrel show became a popular activity for amateur groups.

Impersonations of African Americans became popular in the northern United States around 1830. Thomas D. Rice (c. 1808–1860) performed songs and dances as the plantation slave Jim Crow. George Washington Dixon (c. 1801–1861) gained fame by pretending to be a northern black man named Zip Coon.

Dozens of minstrel troupes performed to audiences across the United States during the first half of the 1900s. *Courtesy of the Library of Congress.*

Out of these individual acts came the full-fledged minstrel show, with the first one generally said to be the performance by Dan Emmett (1815–1904) and his Virginia Minstrels on February 6, 1843, in New York City. (Emmett gained greater fame years later, when he wrote the popular Southern anthem "Dixie.")

The Virginia Minstrels were a great success. Soon there were dozens of minstrel troupes, including the Christy Minstrels, led by E. P. Christy (1815–1862). The Christy Minstrels established the standard pattern for the minstrel show: four or more performers in a semi-circle on stage, with a banjo player and a fiddler in the middle and two "endmen," one playing the tambourine and one the bone castanets. The endmen, called Mr. Tambo and Mr. Bones, wore outlandish clothes and makeup and made jokes at the expense of the somewhat pompous master of ceremonies, or Interlocutor, seated in the middle.

In the mid-nineteenth century, the minstrel show was the most popular form of entertainment in America. After 1900, the professional version of it disappeared, losing out in competition with **vaudeville** (see entry under 1900s—Film and Theater in volume 1), **radio** (see entry under 1920s—TV and Radio in volume 2), and the movies. But blackface performers continued to appear in vaudeville shows, in movies like ***The Jazz Singer*** (1927; see entry under 1920s—Film and Theater in volume 2), and in the popular radio show ***Amos 'n' Andy*** (1928–55; see entry under 1930s—TV and Radio in volume 2). There continued to be a craze for amateur minstrel shows until, after the **civil rights movement** (see entry under 1960s—The Way We Lived in volume 4) of the 1960s, they came to be regarded as racist.

Some commentators have defended the minstrel shows, saying that they expressed not just racist derision but also admiration and sympathy for African Americans. Some say the performances were less about race than about the liberating effect of putting on a mask. The general view by the end of the twentieth century, however, was that the minstrel shows were a shameful part of American history.

—Sheldon Goldfarb

For More Information

Comer, Jim. *Every Time I Turn Around: Rite, Reversal, and the End of Blackface Minstrelsy.* http://www.angelfire.com/oh/hydriotaphia/crow.html (accessed January 3, 2002).

Huggins, Nathan Irvin. "Personae: White/Black Faces—Black Masks." In *Harlem Renaissance.* New York: Oxford University Press, 1971, pp. 244–301.

"Minstrel Shows: 'That Shuff-a-lin' Throng.'" *Musicals101.com.* http://www.musicals101.com/minstrel.htm (accessed January 3, 2002).

Toll, Robert C. *Blacking Up: The Minstrel Show in Nineteenth-Century America.* New York: Oxford University Press, 1974.

Wittke, Carl. *Tambo and Bones: A History of the American Minstrel Stage.* Durham, NC: Duke University Press, 1930.

Nickelodeons

During the first decade and a half of the twentieth century, movies were fast becoming a diversion for the masses. However, the popular venues for watching movies, from the thousand-seat **movie palaces** (see entry under 1910s—Film and Theater in volume 1) built during the 1910s and 1920s to the present-day multiplex theaters, had not yet come into being. So motion pictures were projected in nickelodeons—small storefronts that were converted into makeshift theaters. The term "nickelodeon" derived from two words: "nickel," their usual admission price; and "odeon," the Greek word for theater.

Before the development of large movie houses, motion pictures were shown in small storefronts converted into makeshift theaters known as nickelodeons. *Corbis Corporation. Reproduced by permission.*

Nickelodeons played a key role not only in the exhibition of early motion pictures but also because they were one of the first forms of affordable entertainment for the masses. Legend has it that the first nickelodeon came into being in Pittsburgh, Pennsylvania, in 1904, when a local businessman converted a store into a theater. As motion pictures then were **silent** (see entry on silent movies under 1900s—Film and Theater in volume 1), the businessman installed a piano to be used for musical accompaniment. Before the year was out, over one hundred similar establishments sprang up across the city. By 1908, between eight thousand and ten thousand nickelodeons were in use nationwide. Many were located in immigrant and working-class communities, allowing those with modest incomes to indulge themselves in moviegoing. Nickelodeons thus spread the seeds for the development of motion pictures as a form of mass entertainment.

As befitting their status as amusement halls, nickelodeon exteriors were usually brightly painted and lit. They were decorated with posters advertising current and future programs. Live barkers (people who advertise at a show entrance) shouted the latest attractions to passersby. Inside, paying customers sat on wooden benches or folding chairs and watched the movies' images flicker on a canvas screen. The projection booth, located in the rear, was a small box, six feet square, with sufficient room for the projector and projectionist who cranked the film by hand. A nickelodeon's seating capacity ranged from fifty to six hundred seats.

The average nickelodeon program lasted about thirty minutes; it consisted of three separate films, each one reel (or approximately ten minutes) long. Programs often changed daily, to encourage a steady flow of return customers. The content of these one-reelers included adaptations of Shakespeare and the Bible, dramatizations of current events as well as famous novels and plays, depictions of the realities of everyday working-class life, and scenes of faraway places.

Several of Hollywood's business pioneers started out as nickelodeon operators. Among them were Marcus Loew (1870–1927), Adolph Zukor (1873–1976), and William Fox (1879–1952) as well as the Warner brothers: Harry (1881–1958), Albert (1884–1967), Sam (1888–1927), and Jack (1892–1978). Eventually, nickelodeons gave way to more spacious and comfortable movie houses. During the short time of their existence, however, they played an essential role in offering the working and immigrant classes their first exposure to mass entertainment and American popular culture.

—Rob Edelman

For More Information

Nasaw, David. *Going Out: The Rise and Fall of Public Amusements.* New York: BasicBooks, 1993.

Wagenknecht, Edward. *The Movies in the Age of Innocence.* Norman: University of Oklahoma Press, 1962.

Silent Movies

At the beginning of the twenty-first century, the age of digital recording and surround-sound, it is difficult to imagine a time when movie actors did not speak on screen. Yet during the first twenty-five years of the twentieth century, it was difficult to imagine them ever doing so. Silent movies were watched in silence or accompanied by live musicians in the theater. Speech was displayed in print (known as intertitles) on the screen between the action sequences.

Thomas Edison (1847–1931) and his assistant William Dickson (1860–1935) were the first to make moving pictures possible with their Kinematograph in 1891. Dickson later designed the Kinetoscope, a boxlike apparatus that allowed a single viewer to watch moving pictures. Early silent films, known as "actualities," lasted only a few seconds and recorded events as they happened using a fixed camera. In the late 1990s and into

Silent-film star Buster Keaton (on chair) saves the damsel in distress in the 1924 silent comedy *Sherlock, Jr.* *The Kobal Collection. Reproduced by permission.*

the early twenty-first century, **reality TV** (see entry under 1990s—TV and Radio in volume 5) shows used similar filming techniques. For around twenty-five cents—the hourly wage for a skilled worker in 1894—spectators could view a short film on one of the Kinetoscopes set up in "parlors" around the country.

Before long small movie theaters charging a nickel a time were set up in storefronts. By 1910, there were over ten thousand of these **nickelodeons** (see entry under 1900s—Film and Theater in volume 1) in America. Future movie businessmen such as the Warner brothers (Harry, 1881–1958; Albert, 1884–1967; Sam, 1888–1927; and Jack, 1892–1978) and William Fox (1879–1952) began as nickelodeon owners. But some people thought movies were immoral. Edison's film *The Kiss,* which simply shows a couple kissing, caused a scandal in 1908. A small number of films did contain nudity, but as titles such as *The Chinese Laundry* and *Dancing Bears* suggest, most early silent films were tame by the standards of the twenty-first century.

Storytelling in American movies began around 1902 with the short *The Life of an American Fireman* by Edwin S. Porter (1869–1941). In 1905, his fifteen-minute adaptation of the abolitionist tale *Uncle Tom's Cabin* was one of the longest and most expensive movies ever made. But America's racist past is in evidence in many early silent movies such as *The Cheat* (1915) by Cecil B. DeMille (1881–1959) and the *Sambo* series of comedies. Even in 1915, many people found the classic ***The Birth of a Nation*** (see entry under 1910s—Film and Theater in volume 1) directed by D. W. Griffith (1875–1948) shockingly racist. It was banned in several states.

Film shorts used a single reel of film and lasted a maximum of around fifteen minutes. By 1914, "features" used up to twelve reels and lasted over two hours. Classic novels and plays began to be adapted for film on a large scale. Techniques of editing and camera movement improved quickly. But in the 1920s, the studios began to make movies using tested formulas. The formula **Western** (see entry under 1930s—Film and Theater in volume 2) and "swashbuckling" adventure movies such as *The Three Musketeers* and the ***Zorro*** (see entry under 1910s—Print Culture in volume 1) series emerged in the 1920s. **Rudolph Valentino** (1895–1926; see entry under 1920s—Film and Theater in volume 2), Douglas Fairbanks (1883–1939), and young Greta Garbo (1905–1999) were the movie stars of the time. Scandals in Hollywood eventually led to heavy-handed censorship, but in Europe directors continued to experiment. From 1918 onwards, German filmmakers like Carl Meyer (1894–1944) and Fritz Lang (1890–1976) and Russian Sergei Eisenstein (1898–1948) treated film as more than just entertainment. Eisenstein is widely described as the most important filmmaker of the silent era. His *Battleship Potemkin* (1925) is one of the most influential films of all time.

But slapstick comedy and mime are silent film's lasting legacy. Buster Keaton (1895–1966) and Harold Lloyd (1893–1971) enjoyed huge silent success. Charlie Chaplin (1889–1977; see entry under 1910s—Film and Theater in volume 1) crafted brilliant and profitable comedies; *The Immigrant* (1917) and *The Kid* (1921) remain classics.

The first "talkie" film, ***The Jazz Singer*** (see entry under 1920s—Film and Theater in volume 2), marked the end of an era in movie history when it was released in 1927. In it, Al Jolson (1886–1950) heralded the coming of the "talkie" with the famous spoken line: "Wait a minute. Wait a minute. You ain't heard nothing yet!"

Although "talkies" quickly made films more popular than ever, some people clung to the silent film format. Many stars of the silent era had terrible speaking voices and the arrival of sound ended their careers. *Sunset Boulevard* (1950) tells the dark story of Norma Desmond, an ex-silent screen star washed up in the era of sound. When told she used to be a big star, Desmond declares: "I *am* big. It's the pictures that got small." Famously, Chaplin resisted the arrival of sound. His almost-silent film *Modern Times* (1936) is partly an attack on the sound film.

Despite the efforts of the studios to turn out silent films in a production line process, talkies soon became the twentieth century's greatest form of entertainment. Sound simply made movies more powerful. Yet during the transition to sound many argued that silent movies were the purer form of filmmaking. Some of the most highly praised movies of all time come from the silent era.

—Chris Routledge

For More Information

Acker, Ally. *Reel Women: Pioneers of the Cinema 1896 to Present.* New York: Continuum, 1991.

Cook, David A. *A History of Narrative Film.* New York: W. W. Norton, 1996.

Karney, Robyn, ed. *Chronicle of the Cinema: 100 Years of the Movies.* New York: Dorling Kindersley Publishing, 1995.

Silvester, Christopher. *The Penguin Book of Hollywood.* New York: Viking, 1998.

Vaudeville

For decades during the late nineteenth and early twentieth centuries, vaudeville was a primary means of spreading mainstream entertainment in the United States. Vaudeville came before the establishment of a popular dramatic theater movement on **Broadway** (see entry under 1900s—Film and Theater in volume 1), and before movies, **radio** (see entry under 1920s—TV and Radio in volume 2), and then television gained footholds on American popular culture. Vaudeville programs consisted of groups of diverse performers—including singers, dancers, actors, comedians, jugglers, acrobats, animal acts, and magicians—who were hired by talent bookers to tour through regions of the country, performing live, on what was known as the vaudeville "circuit."

The term vaudeville was derived from one of two sources. The first source was the French Val de Vire (or Vau de Vire), the

The Crystal Hall theater, circa 1900, a "big time" vaudeville theater in the heart of New York City.

valley of the Vire River in Normandy. The valley was famed for the comic songs and ballads originating in the region back in the fifteenth century. The second source is the "voix de ville" ("voice of the city"), the French term for urban folk songs. Vaudeville came to the forefront during the 1880s, when forward-thinking entrepreneurs (perhaps the best known was Benjamin Franklin Keith [1846–1914]) began to market entertainment for the masses. These entrepreneurs remodeled their theaters, sometimes to lavish proportions, and booked better-quality performers. Some vaudeville theaters were "small time." These theaters were the less ornate venues (sites of events), many located in smaller towns, where lesser-known performers worked longer hours and earned more modest paychecks. Meanwhile, others were "big time." These theaters, located in the major cities, were large, extravagantly designed entertainment palaces. The most popular, highest-salaried performers worked the major theaters, where schedules were less grueling and working conditions were far superior. Part of a vaudevillian's professional status depended upon whether he or she worked a three-a-day or five-a-day schedule, referring to the number of performances per day.

A typical vaudeville bill consisted of between nine and twelve individual acts. Shows generally were fast paced. As the decades passed, styles and standards were altered to fit the changing American scene. Into the early 1900s, even with an emphasis on bringing in family audiences, sensationalism was a great attraction in vaudeville. Customers were treated to such scandalous theatrics as wiggling exotic dancers removing layers of clothing while performing the "dance of the seven veils." Customers came to the theater for star glimpses of such notorious beauties as Evelyn Nesbit (1884–1967), who had been the "other woman" in a celebrated murder case, and swimming champion Annette Kellerman (1887–1975), who had been arrested in Boston for wearing a one-piece bathing suit that had been deemed indecent.

In addition, the humor occasionally was rowdy. Vaudeville programs featured songs and jokes that featured ethnic slurs against Irish, German, Italian, and Jewish immigrants. These insults provided laughs for both deeply rooted Americans and recent European immigrants. Nor were African Americans spared from being the butt of humor based on stereotype; however, many songs spotlighting black behavior actually were sentimental, particularly those that waxed nostalgic for a peaceful life down South. These numbers were performed mainly by white performers who "corked up" (used the black ash off burned corks as makeup) and appeared in blackface, which then was an acceptable practice.

Among the many great stars of early vaudeville were singing comediennes Nora Bayes (1880–1928), Elsie Janis (1889–1956), and Eva Tanguay (1878–1947); juggler-comedian W. C. Fields (1879–1946); Julian Eltinge (1883–1941), a female impersonator; the comedy teams of Joe Weber (1867–1942) and Lew Fields (1867–1941) and Joe Smith (1884–1981) and Charlie Dale (1881–1971), specialists in ethnic humor; and Bert Williams (1874–1922), a renowned African American comedian.

Around the turn of the twentieth century, motion picture shorts were added to many vaudeville bills. These were considered novelties, and few vaudevillians realized that the growth of the motion picture industry eventually would result in the death of vaudeville. While many vaudevillians made appearances in early motion pictures, W. C. Fields and other stars became movie headliners. Joining Fields were singer-comedian Eddie Cantor (1892–1964); and the comedy teams of Bert Wheeler (1895–1968) and Robert Woolsey (1889–1938), the

Marx Brothers (Harpo [1888–1964], Groucho [1890–1977], Chico [1886–1961], and Zeppo [1901–1979]), and the husband-and-wife duo of George Burns (1896–1996) and Gracie Allen (1902–1964).

Vaudeville began its decline in the late 1920s, with the expanding mass popularity of motion pictures. Back then, a typical screen program included two feature films and, perhaps, a newsreel or travelogue, a comedy short, and a cartoon. When compared with the easy profits that could be made showing films to the public, the coordination and presentation of live vaudeville shows became financially prohibitive—and so "canned entertainment" won the day.

—Audrey Kupferberg

For More Information

Gilbert, Douglas. *American Vaudeville: Its Life and Times.* New York: Dover Publications, 1940, 1968.

Green, Abel, and Joe Laurie Jr. *Show Biz: From Vaude to Video.* New York: Henry Holt, 1951.

Laurie, Joe, Jr. *Vaudeville: From the Honky Tonks to the Palace.* New York: Henry Holt, 1953.

Snyder, Robert. *The Voice of the City: Vaudeville and Popular Culture in New York.* New York: Oxford University Press, 1989.

Staples, Shirley. *Male/Female Comedy Teams in American Vaudeville, 1865–1932.* Ann Arbor, MI: UMI Research Press, 1984.

Ziegfeld Follies

Between 1907 and the early 1930s, the *Ziegfeld Follies* was the most spectacular and famous American revue (a theatrical production consisting of songs, skits, and dance numbers). The *Follies* was conceived by theatrical impresario (the promoter and manager of a theater company) Florenz Ziegfeld (1869–1932) and his first wife, European performer Anna Held (1873–1918). The revues featured singers introducing the day's top musical numbers, dancers performing elaborately choreographed routines, comedians tickling funny bones, and actors performing one-act plays. Most of all, however, the *Ziegfeld Follies* was fabled for featuring scores of young, beautiful, elaborately costumed showgirls, who often would do little more than parade about or pose prettily, amid settings that formed a living picture, or tableau.

The *Follies* began as an American version of sophisticated yet risqué (bordering on indecent) French revues such as the *Folies Bergère*. The American *Follies* quickly created a formula all its own: the production of romantic musical performances as well as the inclusion of more low-brow fare. The romantic musical performances featured ornate art-nouveau settings designed by artist Joseph Urban (1972–1933). (The term *art nouveau* refers to a movement in art, lasting from the 1890s to about 1914, that evolved into a decorative style.) The more unrefined low-brow fare highlighted the pretty showgirls, whose costumes included elaborate accessories such as headdresses but were quite revealing of the wearer's body. Other revues might spotlight a couple dozen showgirls, but a typical *Ziegfeld Follies* would feature more than 120 attractive women. During the course of a show, there might be five or six costume changes. All the clothes, and the materials from which they were made, were handpicked by Ziegfeld. Ziegfeld viewed his showgirls—who came to be known as the Ziegfeld Girls—not as performers but as art objects to be adorned, creatures inhabiting an elaborate fantasy world.

However, the Ziegfeld Girls were far from the entire show. Dozens of legendary singers, dancers, and comic performers appeared in the *Follies,* among them Bob Hope (1903–), **Will Rogers** (1879–1935; see entry under 1910s—Film and Theater in volume 1), Bert Lahr (1895–1967), Eddie Cantor (1892–1964), Fanny Brice (1891–1951), Marilyn Miller (1898–1936), Bert Williams (1874–1922), and Leon Errol (1881–1951). Famed songwriters Irving Berlin (1888–1989), Oscar Hammerstein (1895–1960), and Jerome Kern (1885–1945) composed musical numbers for Ziegfeld. Many of the songs that debuted in the *Follies* went on to become standards of popular American music.

The initial revue was called *The Follies of 1907*. Ziegfeld kept the *Follies* going for the next twenty-three years, until the advent of the Great Depression (1929–41). The Depression made the expensive productions impractical for both Ziegfeld to fund and potential ticket buyers to attend. His life and his Follies were captured on screen in several films: *The Great Ziegfeld* (1936), a biography featuring William Powell (1892–1984) in the title role, which became a Best Picture Academy Award winner; *Ziegfeld Girl* (1941), a tale of three *Follies* showgirls; and *Ziegfeld Follies* (1946), which featured skits, dances, and songs, all introduced by a fantasized Ziegfeld (played again by Powell) who now resided in heaven.

—Audrey Kupferberg

For More Information

Cantor, Eddie. *The Great Glorifier.* New York: A. H. King, 1934.
Carter, Randolph. *The World of Flo Ziegfeld.* New York: Praeger, 1974.
Farnsworth, Marjorie. *The Ziegfeld Follies.* New York: Bonanza Books, 1956.
The Great Ziegfeld (film). Metro-Goldwyn-Mayer, 1936.
Higham, Charles. *Ziegfeld.* Chicago: Regnery, 1972.
Ziegfeld Follies (film). Metro-Goldwyn-Mayer, 1946.
Ziegfeld Girl (film). Metro-Goldwyn-Mayer, 1941.

1900s

Food and Drink

Like much else in America during the first decade of the twentieth century, how Americans prepared and ate their meals was also changing. At the heart of these changes was the movement from preparation of food in the home from scratch, using primitive appliances, to the preparation of prepackaged foods using modern, electric appliances. Although these changes occurred over the first thirty years of the century, they trace their beginnings to the 1900s.

Here is a look at this transition from the vantage point of a typical middle-class kitchen. In 1901, Mrs. Jones, a middle-class housewife (a woman who did not have any servants in the house, which was still a common practice in this day in well-to-do households), spent the majority of her day cooking and cleaning. She tended a small garden that produced food for the family. In the fall, she canned fruit and vegetables to last through the winter. Mrs. Jones kept a fire burning in the wood- or coal-burning stove on which she cooked the meals, although getting the heat level right was never easy. She fetched water in a bucket from the well out behind the house. She bought unbranded foods in bulk from the local grocer.

By 1910, keeping house was beginning to get easier. The Jones family moved to the city, and their new apartment had running water, indoor toilets, and a gas stove. (Electric stoves were available, but too expensive.) Now Mrs. Jones did not have to spend most of her day tending a fire or fetching water—she simply turned on the flame or the faucet. Though she no longer had a garden, Mrs. Jones was lucky that a new A&P grocery store had opened just down the block. The A&P carried all types of dry food, fruits and vegetables (both fresh and canned), and refrigerated goods. Now that canned goods were readily available, Mrs. Jones no longer canned food of her own. She did not have to worry about the quality of the canned foods, because Congress had passed the Pure Food and Drug Act in 1906 to ensure the safety of mass-produced food. Among the Jones family's favorite branded foods were products that were introduced in this decade: Coca-Cola, Cracker Jack popcorn, and Jell-O gelatin. When the

Joneses wanted a change of pace, they could walk three blocks to the local diner, a low-cost restaurant that served good family food, or head out to the amusement park, where they could buy a hot dog and an ice-cream cone—new, popular fast foods.

The growth of mass-produced, branded food products began to make life easier in this decade, and the food industry would expand dramatically through the century. The A&P Grocery Company pioneered the concept of the grocery chain, but it soon faced competition from regional and, later, national grocery chains. In diners and at hot dog stands, Americans got their first taste of fast food.

Chewing Gum/Bubble Gum

Chewing gum dates back thousands of years, but only in the last two centuries has the practice become a widespread phenomenon, enjoyed by children and adults alike. With the mass marketing of chewing gum, and later bubble gum, those in need of fresh breath, sweet taste, and what the commercials call "pure chewing satisfaction" have many options from which to choose.

The Ancient Greeks were probably the first gum chewers. They chewed a resin from the lentisk, or mastic tree. During the same period, the Mayans of Central America chewed chicle (pronounced CHI-kull), the milky sap of the sapodilla tree. More than twenty centuries later, chicle is still one of the primary ingredients of modern chewing gum. Other chewers of olden times include the native North Americans, who chewed the sap from red spruce trees. European colonists later picked up the habit and began trading the resin.

The birth of modern chewing gum can be traced back to the mid-nineteenth century, when chicle, imported to the United States, was combined with waxes and various additives to enhance its chewability. In 1848, John B. Curtis (1827–1897) made and sold the first commercial chewing gum, called the State of Maine Pure Spruce Gum. Shortly thereafter, chewing gum began being produced in a variety of flavors. U.S. troops serving in Europe in World War I (1914–18) introduced chewing gum to the local population. It proved an immediate hit, and a multimillion dollar industry was born. Popular brands of chewing gum have included Chiclets, Wrigley's Spearmint,

An early 1900s ad for Chiclets gum. *Bettmann/Corbis. Reproduced by permission.*

Doublemint, and Big Red. There are a wide variety of sweet, sugarless, and breath-freshening varieties.

Gum technology took a major step forward when bubble gum was invented in 1928. Walter Diemer (c. 1904–1998), an accountant for the Fleer Chewing Gum Company in Philadelphia, Pennsylvania, was experimenting with new gum recipes when he hit upon the bubble gum formula by accident. "I was doing something else," Diemer later explained, "and ended up with something with bubbles." He colored his concoction pink because that was the only color he had on hand. The result, dubbed Dubble Bubble, became a hit with consumers and has remained so ever since.

Throughout the twentieth century and into the twenty-first, bubble gum has been marketed in a variety of novel and interesting ways. It has been included in packets of baseball cards, nested inside lollipops, and packaged with a humorous comic strip chronicling the adventures of the fictional character "Bazooka Joe." However it is made or sold, it continues to win the hearts and exercise the jaws of children of all ages.

–Robert E. Schnakenberg

For More Information

Landau, Elaine. *Chewing Gum: A Sticky Treat.* Vero Beach, FL: Rourke Press, 2001.

Wardlaw, Lee. *Bubblemania: A Chewy History of Bubble Gum.* New York: Aladdin, 1997.

Young, Robert. *The Chewing Gum Book.* Minneapolis: Dillon Press, 1989.

Coca-Cola

In 1886, an Atlanta, Georgia, pharmacist named John "Doc" Pemberton (1831–1888) concocted a thick, sweet brown syrup that he claimed would cure headaches and upset stomachs. Mixed with carbonated water and served for a nickel a glass at the counter of his pharmacy, Doc Pemberton's drink grew in popularity and soon he was selling up to nine glasses a day. He named his creation Coca-Cola, after its most powerful ingredients, cocaine from the coca plant of South America and caffeine from the kola nut of Africa.

From such humble beginnings, Coca-Cola has grown to become one of the most powerful corporations on earth. Sold in 195 countries, Coca-Cola is the largest selling soft drink, and the Coca-Cola bottling system is the most widespread production and distribution network in the world. More than that, "Coke" has come to represent American culture and lifestyle in both positive and negative ways at home and abroad.

Pemberton may have been a creative inventor, but he was not an aggressive businessman. Soon after he introduced Coke in Atlanta, ownership of the product passed to Asa Candler (1851–1929), who was a sharp businessman and increased sales dramatically. He improved the original recipe, removing the cocaine, which was beginning to be considered a dangerous drug. By 1895, Candler was distributing Coca-Cola in every state and territory in the United States. In 1919, Candler sold the business for $25 million dollars to a group of investors headed by Ernest Woodruff. It was Woodruff's son, Robert (1889–1985), who would make Coke an international household word.

When he assumed the presidency of the company in 1923, Robert Woodruff concentrated on creating the Coca-Cola image. His first step was the mystification of the "secret formula" for the drink. Mostly as an advertising trick, he made a very public show of hiding the handwritten copy of Pemberton's original formula in a bank vault. Only two or three Coke executives would have access to the formula, he said, and their identities would be secret. Supposedly, these executives would not be allowed to travel together, so that in case of a car, train, or airplane crash, the formula would not be lost. The American public responded well to Woodruff's little drama. He followed up by producing hundreds of products with the Coca-Cola logo. Trays, glasses, napkins, and calendars bearing the red-and-white script logo appeared in thousands of homes across the United States. However, it was the role of Coke in World War II (1939–45) that established the soft drink globally.

Coke's "Santa Claus" ad campaign has delighted consumers since the 1960s. *Corbis Corporation. Reproduced by permission.*

When the United States joined World War II in 1941, Woodruff continued his campaign to identify his soft drink with basic American values. One of his smartest marketing moves was to supply Cokes to American servicemen at the U.S. price of five cents a bottle, no matter how far away they were stationed. Though this policy cost the company money, it was money well spent. Coca-Cola became a patriotic symbol of home to homesick soldiers, and the journalists who wrote about the war gave the drink priceless advertising in their stories. In 1943, General Dwight D. Eisenhower (1890–1969) set up ten Coca-Cola bottling plants in Northern Africa to supply American troops there. Although other soft drink companies, like Pepsi-Cola, tried to compete, none achieved the popularity of Coke. By the time the war ended, the Coca-Cola company had sixty-three bottling plants set up in Europe, Africa, and Asia, ready to begin peacetime soft drink sales.

Woodruff's aggressiveness in advertising lived on at the company after his death, and the company's advertising slogans have become almost as much a part of American culture as the soda itself. Coke has been called "the real thing," "the pause that refreshes," and "it." A 1971 ad campaign identified Coke with world peace by gathering dozens of singers on an Italian hillside to sing "I'd like to teach the world to sing in perfect harmony. I'd like to buy the world a Coke and keep it company." More than a soda with doubtful health benefits and some peculiar uses—bottles of Coca-Cola syrup are still offered by some pharmacies as a remedy for indigestion, and many household-hints books recommend its acid for cleaning automobile battery terminals—Coca-Cola has become a symbol of the American way of life. As such, many people outside the United States see the soft drink as a symbol of an American invasion of their country, both culturally and economically.

Coca-Cola is now a gigantic corporation that also produces Minute Maid juices and soft drinks Tab and Sprite, along with sport drinks, bottled water, and coffee drinks. However, that fizzy brown soda pop that some call "Georgia champagne" continues to convince generations of Americans that "things go better with Coke."

—Tina Gianoulis

For More Information

Brands, H. W. "Coca Cola Goes to War." *American History* (Vol. 34, no. 3, August 1999): pp. 30-37.

Coca-Cola Web Site. http://www.cocacola.com (accessed December 14, 2001).

Kahn, Ely Jacques. *The Big Drink: The Story of Coca-Cola.* New York: Random House, 1960.

Oliver, Thomas. *The Real Coke, The Real Story.* New York: Random House, 1986.

Pendergrast, Mark. *For God, Country and Coca-Cola: The Unauthorized History of the Great American Soft Drink and the Company That Makes It.* New York: Collier Books, 1994.

Cracker Jack

Children love popcorn, especially if a caramel coating adds sweetness and flavor to each piece. Mix in some peanuts, and

Landmark Middle School
15261 Legendary Drive
Moreno Valley, CA 92555

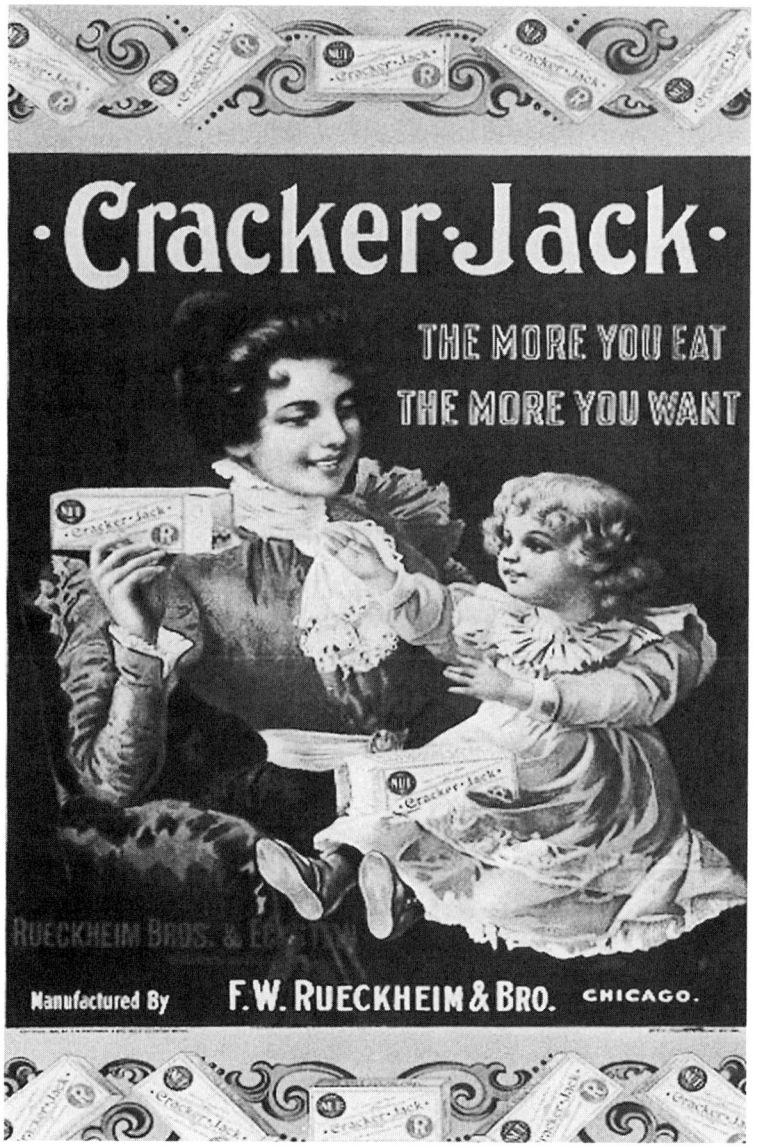

The label used on the 1902 Cracker Jack boxes, nearly ten years before "prizes" were added to each treat. *AP/Wide World Photos. Reproduced by permission.*

the result is a simple yet surefire taste treat. These three ingredients—popcorn, caramel, and peanuts—make up Cracker Jack, a snack that is an essential part of the American childhood experience. Adding to the fun of purchasing Cracker Jack is that included in each box is a small toy, made even more enticing by being labelled a "prize."

The origin of Cracker Jack dates to 1871, when a German immigrant named Frederick William Rueckheim (1846–1934) began selling a popcorn snack on a Chicago street corner. Customers loved his confection (sweet treat), but they were bothered by the stickiness of the caramel. This problem was resolved when Louis Rueckheim (1849–1927), Frederick's brother, invented a secret process that kept the caramel dry and crispy. Around this time, Louis offered the popcorn-peanuts-caramel mixture to a salesman, who declared, "That's a crackerjack" (a popular slang term meaning very good). The brothers liked the salesman's pronouncement and named their product Cracker Jack. The new popcorn snack made its debut in 1893 at Chicago's Columbian Exposition, the city's first **World's Fair** (see entry under 1900s—The Way We Lived in volume 1).

In 1908, Cracker Jack was immortalized in a song that was to become a favorite of baseball fans. In "Take Me Out to the Ball Game," lyricist Jack Norworth (1879–1959) penned the line, "Buy me some peanuts and Cracker Jack." Then in 1912, small toys were added to each box. In ensuing decades, over seventeen billion prizes have been "awarded" to Cracker Jack purchasers. Among the numerous Cracker Jack prizes offered across the years are miniature plates, puzzles, books, bookmarks, pinball games, plastic figurines, and self-adhesive stickers. The product's logo, consisting of an illustration of a boy named Sailor Jack and his dog Bingo, was introduced during World War I (1914–18).

Over the years, Cracker Jack has been marketed in a Butter Toffee flavor and in a fat-free version. The Cracker Jack company also sells other products, including Checkers Popcorn, Campfire Marshmallows, and Angelus Marshmallows. Still, its first product, based on Frederick William Rueckheim's original formula, remains the company favorite.

—Rob Edelman

For More Information

The Cracker Jack Box. http://pw1.netcom.com/~jeepers/CJBhome.html (accessed December 14, 2001).

White, Larry. *Cracker Jack Toys: The Complete, Unofficial Guide for Collectors.* Atglen, PA: Schiffer Publishing, 1997.

Diners

Before the dominance of national **fast food** chains (see entry under 1920s—Food and Drink in volume 2) in the 1950s, the

An example of a diner in 1952. *AP/Wide World Photos. Reproduced by permission.*

diner was the most popular type of inexpensive restaurant for many Americans. Like their fast food cousins, diners emerged as a response to the expanding automobile culture in the United States. Many diners were located along highways, where they offered short-order, home-style meals, complete with apple pie and coffee, to hungry travelers.

The diner itself evolved from horse-drawn lunch wagons of the late nineteenth century. These lunch wagons also served take-out meals in the downtowns of many cities after the restaurants had closed for the night. By the 1890s, stationary diners were being built. The stationary diners resembled lunch wagons, with counters, stools, and grills efficiently laid out in a compact, horizontal format. Simple dishes like hamburgers, hot dogs, eggs, soups, and desserts were served. These early diners were sometimes converted railroad or trolley cars, or were mass produced by such entrepreneurs as Thomas H. Buckley, who had planted them in more than 275 cities across the country. By the 1930s, diners took on a streamlined look, often clad in shiny, chromelike materials and featuring Formica or stainless-steel counters, giving them a sleek Art moderne, or art deco, signature that emphasized cleanliness and efficiency. (Art deco, also called art moderne, was an artistic movement of the 1920s and 1930s influenced by the machine age and characterized by geometric patterns and curving forms.)

After the 1960s, as a response to the standardized look and menu of fast-food outlets such as **McDonald's** (see entry under 1940s—Food and Drink in volume 3) and **Burger King** (see entry under 1950s—Food and Drink in volume 3), many diners were expanded to include table service and also redesigned to express a unique atmosphere, such as Grecian, Mediterranean, colonial, Polynesian, or Googie (a futuristic, space-age decor that emerged in Los Angeles, named for a coffee shop of the same name built there in 1949).

From the 1970s, spurred by architectural historians and others, there has been a revival of interest in the diner as a center of American popular culture, where feisty, overworked employees "slung hash" to impatient customers. The 1982 film *Diner,* directed by Barry Levinson (1942–), helped perpetuate this image. So, too, did one of the most famous television commercials of all time, which featured a harried waitress easily mopping up spills in a New Jersey diner with Bounty paper towels (the "quick picker-upper!"). The Henry Ford Museum in Dearborn, Michigan, includes a fully equipped 1946 diner as part of its collection of cultural artifacts.

—Edward Moran

For More Information

Baeder, John. *Diners.* New York: Harry N. Abrams, 1978.

Googie Architecture Online. http://www.spaceagecity.com/googie (accessed January 4, 2002).

Gutman, Richard J. S. *American Diner Then and Now.* New York: HarperCollins, 1993.

Hess, Alan. *Googie: Fifties Coffee Shop Architecture.* San Francisco: Chronicle Books, 1985.

Hot Dogs

A hot dog is a sandwich that Americans by the millions enjoy at sporting events, picnics, and backyard cookouts. Along with a **hamburger** (see entry under 1950s—Food and Drink in volume 3) and **French fries** (see entry under 1950s—Food and Drink in volume 3), it is a simple, all-American food, as common to the American table as crepes are to the French, tacos are to Mexicans, and fish and chips are to the British. In 2000, Americans consumed some twenty billion hot dogs.

A hot dog consists of a boiled or grilled frankfurter on a soft bun that is long and thin, to follow the shape of the frank. Most often, the sandwich is garnished with mustard or ketchup. Sauerkraut, onions, and pickle relish are often added, singly or in combination. Frankfurters, also known as wieners, are smoked sausages that have been enclosed in several-inch-long cylindrical casings. Their main ingredient is beef or a combination of beef and pork. The origin of the frankfurter is imprecise. Some say that, many centuries ago, the Babylonians devised it by stuffing spiced meat into animal intestines. Others claim that it was invented in Frankfurt, Germany, during the fifteenth century.

Frankfurters and buns supposedly were wedded when Charles Feltman (1841–1910), a German immigrant, concluded that visitors to the Brooklyn, New York, seaside community of **Coney Island** (see entry under 1900s—The Way We Lived in volume 1) might enjoy a hot sandwich they could hold in their hands while strolling about. In 1867, Feltman attached a small charcoal stove to a pushcart and began selling freshly cooked frankfurters on rolls. Feltman parlayed his profits into a restaurant, Feltman's German Beer Garden, which he opened in Coney Island. At Feltman's, seven grills prepared thousands of frankfurters each day, which were sold for ten cents apiece. In 1916, Nathan Handwerker (1892–1974), an ex-Feltman's employee, began selling "hot dogs" from a small building located at Surf and Stillwell Avenues in Coney Island, right by a subway station entrance. Handwerker priced his hot dogs at five cents. They proved so popular that his enterprise became a Coney Island landmark that exists to this day. The business eventually evolved into Nathan's Famous, a fast-food chain. Unlike **McDonald's** (see entry under 1940s—Food and Drink in volume 3), **Burger King** (see entry under 1950s—Food and Drink in volume 3), and Wendy's, where hamburger variations are the signature products, hot dogs still are spotlighted at Nathan's Famous. In the 1930s, the Oscar Meyer Company became the first company to sell frankfurters in supermarkets. Oscar Meyer also began targeting children in its marketing campaigns. Beginning in 1936, its Weinermobile embarked on promotional cross-country trips.

The hot dog made its debut at sporting arenas just after the turn of the twentieth century. Harry Stevens (1855–1934), a concession-stand operator at New York's Polo Grounds, a ballpark located in upper Manhattan, was having difficulty selling ice cream and cold sodas during early-season New York Giants baseball games. On a whim, he replaced them with franks and buns. Legend has it that T. A. "Tad" Dorgan (1877–1929), a newspaper cartoonist, heard Stevens's vendors yelling, "Get your dachshund sausages while they're red hot." He caricatured them as dachshund dogs, and from then on the sandwiches were known as hot dogs.

—Rob Edelman

For More Information

Graulich, David. *The Hot Dog Companion: A Connoisseur's Guide to the Food We Love.* New York: Lebhar-Friedman Books, 1999.

"History of the Hot Dog." *National Hot Dog & Sausage Council.* http://www.hot-dog.org/hd_history.htm (accessed January 4, 2002).

Sebak, Rick, writer and producer. *A Hot Dog Program* (video). Alexandria, VA: PBS Home Video, 1999.

Ice-Cream Cone

One of the most popular American snacks, it is generally believed the ice-cream cone was initially popularized at the 1904 St. Louis Exposition. At that time, Ernest Hamwi, a Syrian waffle vendor, created the "World's Fair Cornucopia" by taking portions of ice cream being dispensed by a fellow vendor who had run out of dishes and serving them up inside waffles that were folded into a cone-like shape. However, other sources, including the Library of Congress, claim that the ice-cream cone was invented on July 23, 1904, by Charles E. Menches of St. Louis and that it did not make its debut as a "walk-away" treat until later that year, at the St. Louis Exposition. A year earlier, a patent for a cone maker had been granted to Italo Marchiony (1868–1954), a New York pushcart vendor, who claimed to have been serving ice-cream cones (paper and later pastry) since 1896. But it was Hamwi who apparently popularized the concept through his Cornucopia Waffle Company and, later, his Missouri Cone Company.

Since the early 1900s, billions of this confectionery treat have been enjoyed all over the world. (They are known as "cornets" in the United Kingdom.) During the 1920s and 1930s, consumers enjoyed cones in a variety of shapes, including **skyscrapers** (see entry under 1930s—The Way We Lived in volume 2) and battleships. Since the 1940s, two kinds of cones have emerged as standards: "sugar" cones, which can be flat-bottomed or pointy, and "waffle" cones made from a large folded wafer. In recent years, hand-baked and hand-rolled waffle cones, often in a variety of flavors like chocolate, oat bran, or honey, have become popular. Environmentalists like the concept because the package and the product are consumed together, leaving no waste or litter behind.

—Edward Moran

For More Information

Damerov, Gail. *Ice Cream! The Whole Scoop.* Lakewood, CO: Glenbridge Publishing, Ltd., 1995.

Dickson, Paul. *The Great American Ice Cream Book.* New York: Atheneum, 1972.

Funderburg, Anne. *Vanilla, Chocolate, and Strawberry: A History of American Ice Cream.* Bowling Green, OH: Bowling Green University Popular Press, 1995.

Gustaitis, John. "Who Invented the Ice Cream Cone?" *American History Illustrated* (Vol. 23, 1988): pp. 42-44.

"Ice Cream Cone." http://www.fspronet.com/archive/iccone.html (accessed January 4, 2002).

Library of Congress. "The Invention of the Ice Cream Cone." *America's Story from America's Library.* http://www.americaslibrary.gov/pages/jb_0723_icecream_1.html (accessed January 4, 2002).

Jell-O

Jell-O is the brand name for a powdered, fruit-flavored gelatin dessert invented in 1897 and widely popularized after the 1920s. The dessert first appealed to busy American housewives seeking low-cost, convenient dishes to serve to their families. Over the years, its makers took full advantage of new advertising and marketing strategies to promote the brand image of Jell-O, making it arguably the nation's most recognizable and popular convenience-food product.

Powdered gelatin was invented in 1845 by Peter Cooper (1791–1883) but the concept did not catch on until 1897, when Pearl B. Wait developed a fruit-flavored version that his wife named Jell-O. He sold the patent to Orator Francis Woodward in 1899 for $450, who began marketing the product in 1902 through the Genesee Pure Food Company of LeRoy, New York. At the time, gelatin desserts required much labor and time to prepare, making them available only to wealthier consumers who had the proper equipment. The advent of powdered Jell-O made these desserts available to the general public for the first time. Jell-O introduced its first pudding products in 1929.

From its earliest days, Jell-O's manufacturers were masters at promoting their product. They created recipe booklets and offered promotional items such as molded dishes to persuade housewives to use the new product. (They even handed out jello molds to immigrants at Ellis Island.) In 1903, Jell-O representatives promoted the product using a fictionalized character called the Jell-O Girl. The character was refashioned in 1908 by Rose O'Neill (1874–1944), creator of the **Kewpie doll** (see entry under 1900s—Print Culture in volume 1). Through the 1920s, O'Neill's Kewpie dolls appeared in many advertisements for Jell-O. Artists like **Norman Rockwell** (1894–1978; see entry under 1910s—Print Culture in volume 1) and Maxfield Parrish (1870–1966) contributed illustrations to promote the brand. L. Frank Baum (1856–1919), author of ***The Wizard of Oz*** (see entry under 1930s—Film and Theater in volume 2), published an edition of his Oz books as a tie-in with Jell-O. In later years, the product was promoted on **radio** (see entry under 1920s—TV and Radio in volume 2) by **Jack Benny** (1894–1974; see entry under 1940s—TV and Radio in volume 3) and Kate Smith (1907–1986) and on television by Roy Rogers (1911–1998), **Andy Griffith** (1926–; see entry on *The Andy Griffith Show* under 1960s—TV and Radio in volume 4), and Ethel Barrymore (1879–1959). From the 1970s through the 1990s, **Bill Cosby** (1937–; see entry under 1980s—TV and Radio in volume 5) was the chief spokesperson for Jell-O and Jell-O Pudding.

Often sneered at by critics who see it as a low-class dessert suitable only for cafeterias and truck-stop diners, Jell-O, despite its wiggly texture, has become a symbol of fast-food convenience for millions of time-starved homemakers.

—Edward Moran

For More Information

Armitage, Shelley. *Kewpies and Beyond: The World of Rose O'Neill.* Jackson: University Press of Mississippi, 1994.

Celebrating One Hundred Years of Jell-O. Lincolnwood, IL: Publications International, Ltd., 1997.
Kraft Foods. *The Cool History of Jell-O.* http://www.kraftfoods.com/jell-o/history (accessed January 4, 2002).

Soda Fountains

From the late 1800s through the 1950s, Americans gathered at drug store soda fountains to gossip, flirt, chat, and drink elaborate new concoctions of sugary syrup, ice cream, and carbonated water. In an era when drinking alcohol was being criticized more and more, the clean, ornate soda fountains provided a socially acceptable alternative to bars and saloons, and the frothy new "soda pop" they dispensed was thought to be the height of health and modernity. The invention of home refrigeration and bottled sodas, along with a population spread out in **suburbs** (see entry under 1950s—The Way We Lived in volume 3) instead of gathered in town centers, helped end the golden age of the soda fountain. However, soda fountains still have a place in American culture, readily visible in films and television, from the 1919 film *True Heart Susie,* starring **Lillian Gish** (1883–1993; see entry under 1910s—Film and Theater in volume 1), to the 1970s television series about the 1950s, ***Happy Days*** (see entry under 1970s—TV and Radio in volume 4).

Philadelphia, Pennsylvania, became the birthplace of the soda fountain in 1825, when apothecary Elias Durand (1794–1873) opened the first modern drugstore there, selling the newly invented "soda water" by the glass. Soda water was supposed to have numerous health benefits, but soon people began to gather at Durand's shop as much to socialize as to drink the carbonated water. Soon, drugstores added cream and syrups flavored with sugars, herbs, and spices to their soda water. They built elaborately decorated counters with seats for patrons and ornate faucets for serving their drinks. The people, mostly men, who worked behind the counters creating the delicious drinks were called "soda jerks," because they jerked the handles on the dispensers to spray foamy carbonation into the syrup. Formulas for chocolate, lemon, strawberry and sarsparilla (root-beer-flavored) sodas as well as for more complex sodas were found in large recipe books behind the counter.

One day in 1874, another Philadelphian, Robert Green, ran out of cream for making sodas. When he added vanilla ice

A soda jerk awaits customers at this Minnesota soda fountain in 1905. *Minnesota Historical Society/Corbis. Reproduced by permission.*

cream instead, he had created another mainstay of the soda fountain, the ice cream soda. Soon ice cream sundaes and milkshakes joined sodas on the fountain menu. By 1910, there were over one hundred thousand soda fountains across the United States, many serving food as well as sodas and ice cream.

World War II (1939–45) brought severe rationing of many of the ingredients used at soda fountains as well as a shortage of men to work at them. After the war, the fountains revived briefly, receiving a boost from the **juke-box** rock music of the 1950s (see entry on juke boxes in 1930s–Music in volume 3), but they did not make enough money for their owners and soon disappeared. They are still a beloved part of American history however, and nostalgia has prompted restaurants in the 1990s and 2000s to adopt the decorative style of old-fashioned soda fountains.

—Tina Gianoulis

For More Information

Funderburg, Anne Cooper. *Sundae Best: A History of Soda Fountains.* Bowling Green, OH: Bowling Green State University Popular Press, 2001.

Pearce, Elizabeth R. "Brown Cows and Walking Sundaes: A Soda Fountain Memoir." *Gourmet* (Vol. 43, July 1983): pp. 20–28.
Rapoport, Roger. "Restored Soda Fountains of Yesteryear." *Americana* (Vol. 19, no. 3, July-August 1991): pp. 60–64.
Schwartz, David M. "Life Was Sweeter, and More Innocent, in Our Soda Days." *Smithsonian* (Vol. 1, July 1986): pp. 114–23.

1900s

Music

Music was an immensely popular form of entertainment in America in the first decade of the century, though not in the same way it is today. Americans did not buy prerecorded records or CDs and play them on stereo equipment. Instead, most American popular music was produced in the home, most likely on a piano, from sheet music purchased from one of many sheet music companies.

Most music was produced by amateurs for small audiences of family and friends, but music was also a developing form in this decade. In fact, this was a decade of vibrant musical production. The sheet music publishing industry was centered in a district of New York City known as Tin Pan Alley, where skilled musicians composed popular music to sell to the masses. Between 1900 and 1909, nearly one hundred of the Tin Pan Alley songs had sold more than one million copies of sheet music. Ragtime music was one of the most popular forms of sheet music, and the king of ragtime was an African American named Scott Joplin (c. 1867–1917). African Americans as a whole fared better in the field of music than they did elsewhere in American popular culture in the decade. Bert Williams (1875–1922), George Walker (1873–1911), Bob Cole (1868–1911), and the Johnson Brothers (J. Rosamond, 1873–1954; James Weldon, 1871–1938) were among the most successful composers of the decade.

Two of the most important American musical forms trace their roots to this decade. Performers W. C. Handy (1873–1958) and Ma Rainey (1886–1939) published and performed the first songs recognized as the blues in this decade. Jazz originated in New Orleans, Louisiana, out of music that combined the rhythms of blues, ragtime, and other musical forms. Both blues and jazz emerged as uniquely American music forms in the 1920s, and some of the earliest and greatest practitioners of these forms were African Americans.

Thomas Edison (1847–1931) invented the phonograph in 1877, a device that could play music that had been recorded on a metal cylinder. Other phonographs, first called gramophones, played music recorded on a vinyl disc. The first recordings to be sold to a wide audience were recorded in 1902 by opera singer Enrico Caruso (1873–1921). Soon, other opera and concert singers began recording their songs. More popular singers began to record songs, but their recordings did not become a mass phenomena until the 1910s, when recording companies improved their manufacturing and marketing systems.

Jazz

Jazz music is one of the most original and innovative of American musical forms. Throughout the twentieth century, jazz evolved to encompass a variety of complex styles and it produced some of the century's greatest composers and musicians.

Jazz originated in the early 1900s, mostly in the South, and especially in New Orleans, Louisiana. Drawing from African American blues and ragtime music, jazz added more complex rhythms and a wider range of tones to create a new style. As it developed in the 1910s and 1920s, a number of important early innovators took jazz in new directions, including Joseph "King" Oliver (1885–1938), Sidney Bechet (1897–1959), Jelly Roll Morton (1890–1941), and especially trumpeter Louis Armstrong (1901–1971). Armstrong was a phenomenal soloist, and he moved the solo instrument to the forefront of jazz. Jazz music often began with a single melody, and then various soloists would add their own touches to it until it became their own. While African American jazz artists such as Armstrong were creating new innovations in jazz, white musicians and band leaders, such as Paul Whiteman (1890–1967), brought a softer version of jazz to white audiences for **dancing** (see entry under 1900s—The Way We Lived in volume 1) in the 1920s.

In the 1930s and early 1940s, jazz moved into what was called the "swing era." Bands got bigger and the music became more popular. Rather than consisting of small groups of five to seven musicians, now the **big bands** (see entry under 1930s—Music in volume 2) might be as large as twenty people, including four to five trumpet players, four to five saxophone players, a drummer, a bassist, and often vocalists. During this time, African American bands continued to be the most innovative. The band led by Fletcher Henderson (1897–1952) was extremely popular, as was the band of Count Basie (1904–1984). Both were known for their driving rhythms and great sound. Even more important was Duke Ellington (1899–1974), who led his own band but was even more important for his songwriting. Ellington wrote popular songs such as "Take the 'A' Train" and "It Don't Mean a Thing If It Ain't Got That Swing." He also extended jazz in a new direction by writing longer pieces of music that resembled classical music in their complexity. His composition "Black, Brown, and Beige," a musical history of African Americans, is a notable example of this development. Following these African American musical leaders, white band leaders such as Benny Goodman (1909–1986), Tommy Dorsey (1905–1956), and Glenn Miller (1904–1944) also made jazz music that excited dancers and listeners, both black and white.

Jazz great Jelly Roll Morton. *Archive Photos. Reproduced by permission.*

Jazz's popularity as "swing" or "big band" music led younger black musicians in the mid-1940s to break out in a new direction. Feeling that popular jazz music was too simple and bland, musicians such as Charlie Parker (1920–1955), Dizzy Gillespie (1917–1993), Thelonious Monk (1917–1982), and Bud Powell (1924–1966) created a new style called "bebop." Bebop was not dance music. It had complex rhythms and lightning-fast solo note runs that favored innovation and personal expression over melody. Parker and Gillespie showcased this new style in such compositions such as "Ornithology," "Ko-Ko," and "Salt Peanuts." Both big bands and swing music faded in the 1950s as **rock and roll** (see entry under 1950s—Music in volume 3) became more popular, but jazz in the bebop style continued. Bebop did not draw the large crowds of dancing fans, but it continued to excite loyal listeners in jazz clubs and concert halls across the United States.

In the 1950s and 1960s, jazz moved in new directions again. Bebop continued, including a more soulful version called "hard bop," but the music also developed in other ways. "Cool jazz" emerged under the influence of trumpeter Miles Davis (1926–1991). This style was more introspective and subdued, evoking a wider range of moods than the fiery-fast bebop style. Davis' album *The Birth of the Cool* remains a landmark work in this style. This period also saw the rise of new and important jazz musicians. Bassist Charles Mingus (1922–1979) brought gospel and blues back into jazz. Mingus also wrote musical works that expressed political views and commented on the problems of racism in America. John Coltrane (1926–1967) emerged on the saxophone as one of the most impressive soloists in the history of jazz on albums such as *Blue Train, Giant Steps,* and *A Love Supreme.* This era also produced important white jazz musicians, including pianist and composer Dave Brubeck (1920–), who had hits with his songs "Take Five" and "Blue Rondo à la Turk," both of which used complex time signatures and rhythms, and saxophonist Stan Getz (1927–1991), who helped fuse Brazilian bossa nova styles with jazz in a way that became very popular in the early 1960s.

In the later 1960s and into the 1970s, jazz continued to move in new directions. "Free" jazz or "avant-garde" jazz took bebop one step further in exciting but difficult compositions that moved away from the standard song and melody composition form. Musicians such as Ornette Coleman (1930–) and Cecil Taylor (1929–) experimented with new and often dissonant sounds (sounding harsh and lacking harmony) in their music. In the 1970s, jazz fusion emerged as a way to combine jazz and rock styles. Musicians such as John McLaughlin (1942–), Chick Corea (1941–), and Herbie Hancock (1940–) used electric guitars and keyboards to extend jazz's sound.

In the 1980s, 1990s, and beyond, jazz music moved on a number of levels. Fusion merged into a lighter, more commercial, form of jazz that many people did not consider jazz at all. Young players continued to emerge, both in the traditional jazz styles and in new innovative ways. Among the most popular of the traditionalists was Wynton Marsalis (1961–). He was also instrumental in forming and leading the Lincoln Center Jazz Orchestra, a group dedicated to keeping alive the classics of jazz. Thus, by the end of the twentieth century, jazz no longer had the popularity it did in the 1930s and 1940s, but it had kept its loyal fans and continued to attract new ones. Because jazz includes so many diverse styles and artists that there is something for everyone to enjoy, jazz keeps its place as one of the most important of American musical styles.

—Timothy Berg

For More Information

Burns, Ken, writer and director. *Jazz* (video). PBS-TV, 2000.
Collier, James Lincoln. *The Making of Jazz: A Comprehensive History.* New York: Houghton Mifflin, 1978.
Giddins, Gary. *Visions of Jazz.* New York: Oxford University Press, 1998.
Gioia, Ted. *The History of Jazz.* New York: Oxford University Press, 1986.
Hentoff, Nat, and Nat Shapiro. *Hear Me Talkin' to Ya: An Oral History of Jazz.* New York: Dover, 1966.
Lee, Jeanne. *Jam!: The Story of Jazz Music.* New York: Rosen, 1999.
Meltzer, David, ed. *Reading Jazz.* San Francisco: Mercury House, 1993.
Public Broadcasting System. *Jazz: A Film by Ken Burns.* http://www.pbs.org/jazz (accessed January 7, 2002).
Seymour, Gene. *Jazz: The Great American Art.* New York: Franklin Watts, 1995.

Scott Joplin (1868–1917)

When one thinks of ragtime, one thinks of Scott Joplin, a pioneering African American musician and composer. Ragtime is a lively, melodic style of music that, at the turn of the twentieth century, was acknowledged as fresh and uniquely American. At the time, it was labeled "the folk music of the American city," and Joplin was famed as the "King of Ragtime Writers."

While growing up in Texas amidst a family of sharecroppers, Joplin heard—and was influenced by—African American work songs and spirituals as well as European waltzes and marches. He began playing the piano and studied music with a German-born teacher, from whom he learned the manner in which European musical compositions were structured. He blended all of these influences into his own rhythmically adventurous brand of music, which he began performing while still an adolescent. In the 1890s, he found himself in Sedalia, Missouri, where he took music courses at the George R. Smith College for Negroes and became a member of the Queen City Band, an all-black group that performed at public and private events. Joplin's compositions soon were published; during his lifetime, his most fabled was "Maple Leaf Rag" (1899). It was followed by "Peacherine Rag" (1901), "Augustan Club Waltz" (1901), "A Breeze from Alabama" (1902), "Elite Syncopation" (1902), "The Entertainer" (1902), "The Strenuous Life" (1902), "Gladiolus Rag" (1907), "Pine Apple Rag" (1908), and "Solace—A Mexican Serenade" (1909).

Joplin earned his living from sheet music sales and by teaching and performing. He viewed himself not as a writer of popular music, however, but as a serious composer. His more important compositions—which, predictably, were not his most popular in the mass market—included *The Ragtime Dance* (1902), a ragtime ballet, and *The Guest of Honor* (1903), a ragtime opera. During the final decade of his life, he worked on *Treemonisha* (1911), a second ragtime opera, whose key theme was the desperate need for education within the African American community. Unfortunately, *Treemonisha* was performed only once during Joplin's lifetime, in 1915.

Scott Joplin was long forgotten by the public at the time of the release of *The Sting* (1973), a film whose score consisted of Joplin rags. The success of the film, which won many Academy Awards, initiated a ragtime renaissance.

—Rob Edelman

For More Information

Benson, Kathleen, and James Haskins. *Scott Joplin.* Garden City, NY: Doubleday, 1978.

Berlin, Edward. "A Biography of Scott Joplin." *The Scott Joplin International Ragtime Foundation.* http://www.scottjoplin.org/biog.htm (accessed January 7, 2002).

Berlin, Edward. *The King of Ragtime: A Biography of Scott Joplin.* New York: Oxford University Press, 1994.

Curtis, Susan. *Dancing to a Black Man's Tune: A Life of Scott Joplin.* Columbia: University of Missouri Press, 1994.

Phonograph

The phonograph gave birth to the modern recording industry. Without it, there would not be records, cassette tapes, compact discs, or digital MP3s. Invented by Thomas Edison (1837–1931) in 1877, the phonograph proved to be one of the most influential technologies in history. The phonograph revolutionized entertainment and the field of music throughout the twentieth century until cassette tapes began crowding out the medium in the 1970s and then **compact disc** (see entry under 1980s—Music in volume 5) technology replaced it in the 1990s.

Edison's invention came from his experiments attempting to record and preserve phone conversations. When he discovered that a human voice could cut a signal into tinfoil, the origins

In the well-known painting (c. 1895) by Francis Barraud, titled "His Master's Voice," Nipper the dog marvels at hearing sounds coming through the phonograph's horn. *AP/Wide World Photos. Reproduced by permission.*

of the modern phonograph were born. Edison improved the device using wax cylinders and later adopted a disc format developed by Emile Berliner (1851–1929). Although the phonograph did not take off as a way to record and preserve phone calls, it did find great popularity in the entertainment world, spawning the modern recording industry in the 1910s. Before this time, people could only hear music played live or make their own music, and most people heard only a limited amount and variety of music. The phonograph changed all that. As phonographs became cheaper to buy, more people could afford them. Record companies responded by producing records of all sorts. There were **blues** (see entry under 1920s—Music in volume 2) and **jazz** (see entry under 1900s—Music in volume 1) records, **country music** (see entry under 1940s—Music in volume 3), **big band** (see entry under 1930s—Music in volume 2) music, ethnic songs, dance music, classical symphonies, speeches, and many more kinds of records. The phonograph was especially popular with people in rural areas and with poor and middle-class people. People in rural areas lived too far away to attend live music concerts, and poor and middle-class people could not afford to hear symphony orchestras very often, if at all.

The phonograph proved to be an instrument of social change as well. In the 1950s, **rock and roll** (see entry under 1950s—Music in volume 3) was successful largely because teenagers could afford to purchase rock-and-roll 45-rpm singles to play on their phonographs. (Singles were called 45s because the recordings were played at a speed of 45 revolutions of the turntable per minute.) Because they could choose the records, rather than having adults on the **radio** (see entry under 1920s–TV and Radio in volume 2) choose their music, teenagers helped spur rock and roll on to great success, spawning a whole era of teen rebellion. In the 1960s, that tradition continued as the phonograph provided a means for **folk musicians** (see Folk Music entry under 1960s–Music in volume 4) to have their protest songs heard. Rock music continued pushing the boundaries of social convention and bringing new insights to young people around the world.

Few mass technologies have had such an important social impact. Eventually, the phonograph was eclipsed by the development of cassette tapes in the 1970s and of compact discs in the 1990s. Both technologies were more durable, portable, and lightweight than phonographs (by now, also called turntables). Despite this, many people still collect vinyl records and restore old phonographs, keeping the technology alive.

–Timothy Berg

For More Information

Eisenberg, Evan. *Recording Angel: Music, Records and Culture.* London: Picador, 1987.

Koenigsbert, Allan. *The Patent History of the Phonograph.* Brooklyn, NY: APM Press, 1990.

Millard, Andre. *America on Record: A History of Recorded Sound.* New York: Cambridge University Press, 1995.

1900s

Print Culture

In an age before radio and television claimed the attention of Americans, reading was one of the most popular leisure-time activities. American writers and publishers churned out a variety of reading material to suit the tastes of every reader, from comic strips to magazines to dime novels to classics.

The comic strip was created just before the turn of the century when Richard Outcault (1863–1928) created a character known as the Yellow Kid in a series known as *Hogan's Alley.* Later strips such as *The Katzenjammer Kids* and *Mutt & Jeff* made such characteristics as word balloons, a distinctive cast of characters, and the use of a series of panels the common conventions of the comic strip. Still, by 1908 there were only five newspapers that ran daily comic strips.

Although magazines—collections of fiction and nonfiction often published on a weekly or a monthly schedule—had been around for many years, the so-called "magazine revolution" of 1893 made it possible to produce massive numbers of magazines and sell them for very little money—sometimes as little as a nickel an issue—thanks to the financial support of advertisers. By 1900, magazines such as *Argosy, Cosmopolitan,* the *Ladies' Home Journal, McClure's, Munsey's,* the *Saturday Evening Post,* and others were read by millions of readers. American advertisers enthusiastically sought space in these magazines, for they provided the best possible way to reach the greatest number of potential consumers.

The same technological advances in printing that allowed for the mass-circulation magazine also spurred the sales of the dime novel, a cheaply produced paperback book that sold for a dime. Dime novels were usually written by unknown writers who worked from outlines provided by the publisher; the stories involved romance, mystery, and adventure. Westerns were one of the most popular forms. Although he did not write dime novels, Jack London (1876–1916) wrote adventure stories set at sea or in the West, and his books sold millions. London was considered by many at the time as a "hack" writer—a writer who writes solely to make money or who writes over and over in the same way, almost as if using a formula. Today, London is considered one of the greater American novelists and is read widely in schools.

Argosy

A popular men's magazine published in the United States from 1888 until 1979, *Argosy* was the first of the **"pulp" magazines** (see entry under 1930s—Print Culture in volume 2), so called because of the cheap, rough paper on which they were printed. It was also the first adult magazine to rely almost exclusively on fiction for its content, usually adventure, detective, science fiction, or western stories that were thought to appeal to a male readership.

Argosy traced its roots to *Golden Argosy: Freighted with Treasures for Boys and Girls,* a magazine created by Frank Munsey (1854–1925) in 1882 to appeal to young people. By 1886, Munsey was publishing adult stories in the magazine, whose name he changed to *Argosy* two years later. In 1896, he shifted to pulp paper and began publishing serial fiction (stories that were "serialized," or broken into sections across several issues) exclusively, with an emphasis on action, adventure, and mystery stories. By the time of Munsey's death in 1925, *Argosy* had helped popularize fictional characters like **Tarzan** (see entry under 1910s—Print Culture in volume 1), **Zorro** (see entry under 1910s—Print Culture in volume 1), **The Shadow** (see entry under 1930s—Print Culture in volume 2), and Sam Spade. It featured stories from some of the most noted authors of the day.

By 1907, *Argosy* had a circulation (the total number of copies sold) of five hundred thousand, but the magazine had a checkered history in the twentieth century. Circulation declined to forty thousand by 1940. The magazine was renamed *New Argosy* in 1942 but was banned from the mails for "obscenity." Sold to Popular Publications, a major publishing company, the magazine was renamed *Argosy: The Complete Men's Magazine* in 1946 and became a "slick" periodical with four-color layouts and better-quality adventure, sports, and humorous stories. By

1953, the circulation had increased to 1.25 million. Popular Publications was dissolved in 1972 and the magazine was sold to Blazing Publications, Inc. It finally folded in 1979, a victim of rising postal rates.

—Edward Moran

For More Information

"The Argosy & Related Magazines." *Magazine Issues.* http://www.pulpgen.com/pulp/biglist/mags/argosy.html (accessed December 14, 2001).
Moonan, Willard. "Argosy." In *American Mass-Market Magazine.* Edited by Alan and Barbara Nourie. Westport, CT: Greenwood Press, 1990.
Server, Lee. *Danger Is My Business: An Illustrated History of the Fabulous Pulp Magazines, 1896–1953.* New York: Chronicle, 1993.

Buster Brown

Though Buster Brown and his bulldog Tige are best known today as trademarks for a brand of clothing and shoes, they got their start as one of America's first comic strips. The beloved pair were created in 1902 by cartoonist Richard Felton Outcault (1863–1928), who also created the very first comic strip in the United States, *The Yellow Kid.* Buster Brown, dressed in his familiar red smock and bloomers, with blond bangs and an angelic face, was a mischievous little boy whose antics always got him into trouble. His loyal companion Tige was the first talking animal in a cartoon strip.

Buster Brown's popularity led manufacturers to pay to use his image on over two hundred products. Besides advertising such items as shoes and clothes, Buster and Tige appeared in books and **silent movies** (see entry under 1900s—Film and Theater in volume 1). Today, though almost no one remembers Outcault's comic strip, which ended during the early 1920s, most Americans are familiar with Buster Brown shoes and clothes, and know what a Buster Brown haircut looks like.

—Tina Gianoulis

For More Information

Markstein, Donald D. "Buster Brown." *Don Markstein's Toonopedia.* http://www.toonopedia.com/buster.htm (accessed January 8, 2002).

An example of a Buster Brown cartoon from 1905. *Illustration by R. F. Outcault. Field Newspaper Syndicate.*

Dime Novels

Dime novels captivated readers with sensational fictitious stories in the late nineteenth and early twentieth centuries. Called dime novels because the first examples cost just ten cents, dime novels appeared at regular intervals and told exciting stories of adventure, mystery, and romance. Readers were encouraged to collect and read whole series of novels featuring a favorite hero or a type of adventure. Costs were kept down by printing the novels on low-quality paper, often with drawn illustrations. By 1900, several publishers had entered the market and in their heyday each title could sell millions of copies. The popularity of **pulp magazines** (see entry under 1930s—Print Culture in volume 2), **radio** (see entry under 1920s—TV and Radio in volume 2), and cinema squeezed dime novels out of the entertainment market by the 1920s. No original titles appeared after that decade.

The first dime novel was *Maleska, the Indian Wife of the White Hunter.* It was published in 1860 by Irwin P. Beadle and was a romance set in the American West. Beadle's mass-market dime novels took advantage of the growing number of readers and cheaper printing technology. By the early 1900s, the range of settings for the stories was huge, although the plots were mostly the same. Dime novel subjects included the American West, the Revolutionary War, Native Americans, the circus, the railroad, sports, science fiction, and detective mysteries. Polar exploration was also common.

Title page from Beadle and Adams' dime novel, *The Deadwood Dick on Deck; or Calamity Jane, the Heroine of Whoop-Up,* by E. L. Wheeler. *The University of Michigan Library. Reproduced by permission.*

Dime novels were written to very strict guidelines, often by groups of writers working under the same name. Writers were instructed to make them exciting, entertaining, and moral. Even so, these tales of violence and passion were thought by some to be a corrupting influence on their young readers. These same arguments continued into the twenty-first century against films, cartoons, and pop stars like Eminem (1972–) and Marilyn Manson (1969–). Writers of dime novels included Edward Stratemeyer (1962–1930), who created the girl detective Nancy Drew, and Louisa May Alcott (1832–1888), the author of *Little Women.* Alcott wrote dime novels under the name A. M. Bernard to protect her reputation as a serious novelist.

Because they were printed on cheap paper and because they were seen as disposable, few dime novels exist outside of libraries in the twenty-first century. As literature, dime novels were considered by scholars to have little value. But as historical artifacts, they reveal a great deal about American life in the late nineteenth and early twentieth centuries.

—Chris Routledge

For More Information

Stanford University Special Collections. "Dime Novels and Penny Dreadfuls." http://www-sul.stanford.edu/depts/dp/pennies/home.html (accessed on December 14, 2001).

Sullivan, Larry E., and Lydia Schurman, eds. *Pioneers and Passionate Ladies: Dime Novels, Series Books, and Paperbacks.* New York: Haworth Press, 1996.

Gibson Girl

In the late 1800s, the socially restrained Victorian era was coming to an end, giving way to the more permissive modern era. In the last days of the Victorian age, a young American artist named Charles Dana Gibson (1867–1944) began to publish sketches of a new kind of American woman who was emerging in the new era. More women were going to work, and the money they earned gave them a new independence and confidence. Gibson was impressed with these dynamic young women, and he drew them over and over, at home, at work, and at play. Once women saw the romantic and elegant images of these "Gibson Girls"—which appeared in popular magazines like ***Life*** (see entry under 1930s—Print Culture in volume 2) *Harpers,* and *Collier's Weekly*—they began to imitate their style, creating a period of fashion that lasted from 1890 to 1910.

Gibson Girls were tall, athletic, and poised, with upswept hair and practical yet feminine clothes. At work, they might wear a tailored dress with long sleeves and a high collar with a necktie; at a party, a low-cut flowing dress with no sleeves was stylish. Their figures were trained into a fashionable "S" shape by a new kind of corset (an undergarment used to support and shape the waist, hips, and bust), called the "health corset" because it allowed the spine to remain straight. The "S" shape, formed by tightly corseted waists between a large bosom and large hips, was exaggerated further by wearing many layers of slips and underclothes. There was a Gibson Man as well. The men's fashion featured trimmed mustaches and jackets with padded shoulders.

The most important distinguishing feature of the Gibson Girl was that she was capable and adventurous as well as beautiful.

By 1900, there were over five million working women in the United States, and across the country, women wanted to imitate the image and style of the Gibson Girl. Many new developments helped them follow the fashion, such as mass-circulation magazines and mail-order catalogs. Newly invented home sewing machines and pattern catalogs also helped women reproduce the clothes they admired in Gibson's magazine drawings.

—Tina Gianoulis

For More Information

CDGibson.com http://www.cdgibson.com/ (accessed January 8, 2002).

Emery, Josiah, writer, director, and producer. *Charles Dana Gibson: Portrait of an Illustrator* (video). Acre Island Productions, 1996.

Gibson, Charles Dana. *The Gibson Girl and Her America: The Best Drawings of Charles Dana Gibson.* New York: Dover Publications, 1969.

Patterson, Martha. "Survival of the Best Fitted: Selling the American New Woman as Gibson Girl, 1895–1910." *ATQ (The American Transcendental Quarterly)* (Vol. 9, no. 2, June 1995): pp. 73-88.

Drawings of "Gibson Girls" helped shaped women's fashions from 1890 to 1910. *Corbis-Bettmann. Reproduced by permission.*

Good Housekeeping

Good Housekeeping magazine was founded in 1885 in the United States by Clark W. Bryan, whose stated goal was the creation of "perfection . . . in the household." When the British version of the journal was launched in 1922, its advertising promised, "infinitely more than a magazine—a New Institution, destined to play an important part in the lives of thousands of women." For over a century, *Good Housekeeping* has been just such an institution. The magazine offers advice and advertises products to help housewives run their homes, although some critics feel that the magazine is outdated because it assumes that only women do housework.

Good Housekeeping was part of a wave of women's magazines that emerged in the early twentieth century to glorify housework and to encourage women to stay in the home. Working-class women were leaving their jobs as household servants for factories, forcing middle-class women to learn to do their own housework. The makers of new "labor-saving" devices such as the electric iron (invented in 1914) and the vacuum cleaner (invented in 1917) needed somewhere to advertise their products. Magazines like *Good Housekeeping* served the dual purpose of instructing women about housework and turning them into consumers who would buy these new products.

From the first, *Good Housekeeping* took its commitment to its readers seriously. In 1900, the Good Housekeeping Institute was founded to evaluate household products. Only products that passed the Institute's tests could be advertised in the pages of the magazine. In 1909, *Good Housekeeping* introduced its famous "Seal of Approval," which guaranteed that if any product bearing the seal proved to be defective within two years of purchase, *Good Housekeeping* itself would refund the money to the consumer. The Good Housekeeping Institute has been responsible for many consumer reforms. An early example of this interest occurred in 1905 when the Institute began inspecting packaged foods and published a "Roll of Honor for Pure Food Products" listing approved foods. The passage by Congress of the 1906 Pure Food and Drug Act was a direct result of the Institute's work.

—Tina Gianoulis

For More Information

"Good Housekeeping." *iVillage.com*. http://magazines.ivillage.com/good-housekeeping (accessed January 9, 2002).

Holzman, Paul, and Micki Siegel. "90 years of the Good Housekeeping Institute." *Good Housekeeping* (February 1990): pp. 69–114.

Horwood, Catherine. "Housewives' Choice: Women as Consumers Between the Wars." *History Today* (Vol. 47, no. 3, March 1997): pp. 23–29.

The Katzenjammer Kids

The Katzenjammer Kids is the longest-running comic strip in American history. The strip, which began appearing in newspapers in 1897, was created by cartoonist Rudolph Dirks

(1877–1968). The comic strip revolves around the shenanigans of Hans and Fritz Katzenjammer, young twins who delight in creating chaos. The boys outwardly appear to be innocent children, but they are, in reality, destructive brats who constantly torment and abuse everyone around them. Their favorite target is The Captain, who can never convince Mama Katzenjammer her sons are incorrigible (beyond reform). The word *katzenjammer* literally translates as "the howling of cats" and is German slang for a hangover.

The strip greatly popularized the emerging comic strip medium. Dirks was one of the first comic artists to employ word balloons containing his characters' speech. Much of the strip's humor resulted from the vaudeville German dialect the characters spoke. In 1912, a legal battle between Dirks and his publisher resulted in competing versions of the strip that ran for decades. *The Katzenjammer Kids* continues to appear in newspapers and holds the distinction of being the only comic strip from the nineteenth century to survive into the new millennium.

—Charles Coletta

For More Information

Dirks, Rudolph. *Komical Katzenjammers—The Katzenjammer Kids Color.* New York: Dover Publications, 1974.

Horn, Maurice, ed. *100 years of American Newspaper Comics.* New York: Gramercy Books, 1996.

Marschall, Richard. *America's Great Comic-Strip Artists.* New York: Abbeville Press, 1989.

Kewpie Dolls

Originally appearing in the form of magazine illustrations between 1905 and 1909, Kewpie dolls made their appearance in 1913 in a design patented by Rose Cecil O'Neill (1874–1944). During O'Neill's lifetime, the dolls were a popular novelty item, often associated with carnivals and country fairs, where they were given as prizes. The Kewpie doll is one of the earliest and most successful examples of a mass-marketed toy. It has since become a sought-after collectable and an enduring symbol of "cuteness."

O'Neill's earliest versions of the Kewpies began appearing in the pages of the *Ladies' Home Journal* between 1905 and 1909 and took the Kewpie name in 1909. In 1910, O'Neill moved her characters to the *Women's Home Companion*. Three years later, she designed a babylike doll with its characteristic rotund shape and plume of wispy hair. The doll became an instant sensation and its sales made O'Neill a millionaire within a year. Just as **Barbie dolls** (see entry under 1950s—Commerce in volume 3) would later be dressed as a variety of characters, Kewpies came dressed as cowboys, farmers, bellboys, and firemen, and in the uniforms of U.S., British, French, and German soldiers. There was also a line of black Kewpies known as Hottentots. Besides the dolls, O'Neill created Kewpie images for a wide variety of products like chinaware, picture frames, clocks, greeting cards, wallpaper, and vases. O'Neill also wrote and illustrated a series of Kewpie books as well as a comic-strip version in the mid-1930s.

The Kewpie dolls were originally made of china or bisque (unglazed china). They were manufactured in Europe until World War I (1914–18), when U.S. firms like the Mutual Doll Company began making the Kewpies from a variety of materials, including fabric. To this day, Kewpie dolls remain sought after among doll collectors.

—Edward Moran

For More Information

Armitage, Shelley. *Kewpies and Beyond: The World of Rose O'Neill.* Jackson: University Press of Mississippi, 1994.

Formanek-Brunell, Miriam. *Made to Play House: Dolls and the Commercialization of American Girlhood, 1830–1930.* New Haven, CT: Yale University Press, 1993.

O'Neill, Rose Cecil. *The Story of Rose O'Neill: An Autobiography.* Columbia: University of Missouri Press, 1997.

Jack London (1876–1916)

One-time vagrant, gold miner, and socialist politician, Jack London is famous for his adventure stories and tales of the Yukon basin region in Alaska and Northwest Canada. Most famous of all are *The Call of the Wild* (1903) and *White Fang* (1906). Although often dismissed as a writer of simple adventures, much of London's work has a tough, adult edge. Novels like *The Sea Wolf* (1904) also explore the savagery of the human soul.

Always ready for new experiences, London was a war correspondent in Japan, suffered scurvy (a disorder resulting from lack of Vitamin C) in the Klondike, and lived in wretched and filthy conditions in an English slum while researching *The People of the Abyss* (1903). Despite having no formal education, his writing entertained and informed millions of readers during his short working life. At one time, he was the best-selling author in the world. Although few of his many books are even in print in 2002, London's life and works anticipated the "hard-boiled" writers of the 1930s and 1940s.

—Chris Routledge

For More Information

Berkeley Digital Library SunSITE. *The Jack London Collection.* http://sunsite.berkeley.edu/London (accessed January 9, 2002).

Dyer, Daniel. *Jack London: A Biography.* New York: Scholastic Press, 1997.

Labor, Earle, and Jeanne Campbells Reesman. *Jack London.* New York: Twayne, 1994.

Lisandrelli, Elaine Slivinski. *Jack London: A Writer's Adventurous Life.* Berkeley Heights, NJ: Enslow, 1999.

Mutt & Jeff

Mutt & Jeff, which appeared in American newspapers from 1907 to 1983, was the first successful daily comic strip. Created by Harry "Bud" Fisher (1885–1954), the strip revolved around the comic misadventures of two mismatched friends—Augustus Mutt, who was tall and smart, and Jeff, who was short and simple minded. Where earlier strips appeared only sporadically, *Mutt & Jeff* was the first feature to run six days a week, use the multiple panel format, and present a regular cast of characters. In 1911, the strip was seen in one of the first **comic books** (see entry under 1930s—Print Culture in volume 2).

Fisher's strip made its debut on the *San Francisco Chronicle* sports page on November 15, 1907. Initially, Mutt was the feature's solo star and its stories revolved around the born-loser's hapless attempts to become wealthy. The focus of the strip changed forever on March 27, 1908, when Mutt encountered Jeff in an insane asylum. The little fellow was convinced he was the celebrated prizefighter Jim Jeffries (1875–1953). The pair became fast friends and behaved much like a stereotypical **vaudeville** (see entry under 1900s—Film and Theater in volume 1) team.

While the strip was crudely drawn and its humor simplistic, it was also innovative. It is credited with bringing topical humor (humor relating to current events) to the comics page. The pair trained with prizefighter Max Schmeling (1905–) and became friends with President Herbert Hoover (1874–1964) in 1929. The strip also poked fun at modern politics. In 1908, Mutt became the first comic strip character to run for president. He later ran for the office again in 1916 and 1932.

Fisher was known as a skilled businessman. In 1915, he won a $1,000-a-week guarantee plus 80 percent of the gross profits from his strip. He was the first cartoonist to copyright his strip and, thus, own all rights to his characters. A flood of *Mutt & Jeff* merchandise further enhanced his income. The pair was featured on toys, books, cartoons, and even served as the inspiration for a ballet.

As early as the 1920s, Fisher delegated much of the work on the strip to several ghostwriters and artists. Although the strip ran until 1983, its last decades saw a steadily declining readership and few creative highlights. Still, Mutt and Jeff are recalled as two of the comics' earliest superstars.

—Charles Coletta

For More Information

Blackbeard, Bill, and Martin Williams. *The Smithsonian Collection of Newspaper Comics.* Washington, D.C.: Smithsonian Institution Press, 1977.

Horn, Maurice, ed. *100 Years of American Newspaper Comics.* New York: Gramercy Books, 1996.

Markstein, Don. "Mutt & Jeff." *Don Markstein's Toonopedia.* http://www.toonopedia.com/muttjeff.htm (accessed January 9, 2002).

Robinson, Jerry. *The Comics: An Illustrated History of Comic Strip Art.* New York: Berkley Publishing Corporation, 1974.

National Geographic

The National Geographic Society was founded at the end of the 1800s, a time of change and discovery all over the world. Its monthly journal, *National Geographic,* reflects the thirst for travel, discovery, and new experiences that marked the turn of the century from the nineteenth to the twentieth. From its first issue in 1888, it was clear that *National Geographic* was not a boring scientific journal. Filled with color pictures of people and lands that were exotic and unusual to its American audience, the journal captured the imagination of readers of all ages.

In 1888, thirty-three members of the Cosmos Club, an elite Washington, D.C., club of professional men, joined together to form a society to learn and spread knowledge about the lands and peoples of the earth. The leaders of this National Geographic Society, whose early presidents included famed inventor Alexander Graham Bell (1847–1922), were determined that it should not be an exclusive organization, limited to scientists and scholars. Instead, they wished to attract a wide range of people who were interested in exploration, discovery, and the world around them.

The magazine became part of the plan to win a broad base of support for the Society. At a time when color photographs were rare, the magazine pioneered new photography techniques in order to give readers a truly vivid look at the wonders of the world. The Society also funded expeditions into unknown regions, such as the 1909 journey to the North Pole by Robert Peary (1856–1920) and Matthew Henson (1866–1955) and the many undersea explorations of Jacques Yves Cousteau (1910–1997). The stories of these adventures appeared in the pages of *National Geographic*.

Although the Society's journal has received high praise for its photography, maps, and wide range of subject matter, it has also received criticism for its strictly nonpolitical stance and its tendency to present a rosy view of the world. For example, a feature about Berlin published just before the start of World War II (1939–45) contained no criticism of the Nazi government and no mention of its anti-Jewish policies. Since the 1970s, the magazine has taken a more critical approach to its subjects. It has published articles about such political topics as apartheid (a-PAR-tayt; racial segregation) in South Africa and the French Canadian separatist movement.

The National Geographic Society has continued to grow and modernize. Its projects include television cable channels, Web sites, and computer software, along with the still-popular magazine and maps.

—Tina Gianoulis

For More Information

Bryan, C. D. B. *The National Geographic Society: 100 Years of Adventure and Discovery.* New York: Harry N. Abrams, 1987.

The Complete National Geographic: 111 Years of National Geographic Magazine on CD-ROM. Washington, D.C.: The Society, 2000. CD-ROM.
National Geographic. http://www.nationalgeographic.com (accessed January 9, 2002).
Patterson, Carolyn Bennett. *Of Lands, Legends, and Laughter: The Search for Adventure with National Geographic.* Golden, CO: Fulcrum Press, 1998.

New York Times

The *New York Times* was founded in 1851 as a four-page paper called the *New-York Daily Times.* It tried to provide objective, serious coverage of the daily news. In 1896, the *Times* was bought by Adolph S. Ochs (1858–1935) and began to establish itself as New York's premier newspaper and the nation's "newspaper of record." Since 1897, it has carried a front-page motto: "All the News That's Fit to Print." In 1905, the paper even gave its name to one of the most famous squares in New York—Times Square.

Apart from being a news source for politicians around the world, the *Times* has also fought for freedom of the press and set the standard for investigative journalism. Always best at reporting on federal government and international news, it won a Pulitzer prize for reporting on World War I (1914–18) in 1918. In the 1960s, critics claimed that the paper had grown too friendly with federal government. In 1971, however, the *Times* once again proved its commitment to free speech when it reported on the "Pentagon Papers." These documents revealed that many prominent public supporters of America's war in Vietnam had grave doubts about it in private. Agents of President Richard M. Nixon (1913–1994) tried to stop publication of the "Pentagon Papers." The *Times* and the *Washington Post* defended their constitutional right to publish without censorship and won their case in the U.S. Supreme Court.

Although famous for its news coverage, the *Times* became a powerful cultural force in other fields as well. Its critics can make or break the careers of writers, actors, and film and theater directors. Its stories on society, culture, and science are highly regarded. Although in many ways an old-fashioned, establishment newspaper, the *Times* has managed to hang onto its reputation for quality journalism. Still owned by Ochs's descendants, the paper entered the twenty-first century with over sixty-five Pulitzer Prizes, more than any other paper. The Pulitzer Prizes are America's most prestigious journalism awards.

–Chris Routledge

For More Information

Diamond, Edwin. *Behind the Times: Inside the New New York Times.* New York: Villard Books, 1994.

Fireside, Harvey. *New York Times v. Sullivan: Affirming Freedom of the Press (Landmark Supreme Court Cases).* New York: Enslow Publishers, 1999.

The New York Times on the Web. http://www.nytimes.com (accessed January 9, 2002).

The New York Times Page One: One Hundred Years of Headlines as Presented in the New York Times. New York: Budget Book Service, 2000.

Saturday Evening Post

The *Saturday Evening Post* was one of the most influential and popular magazines in America from 1900 to 1930. With its mix of business news, nonfiction, romance stories, sports, humor, and illustrations, the *Post*–as it was known–set the standard for the weekly variety magazine. Although the *Post* remained in print for most of the twentieth century, its influence faded after the 1930s.

Publisher Cyrus H. K. Curtis (1850–1933) purchased the struggling *Saturday Evening Post* in 1897. He hired George Horace Lorimer (1867–1937) to edit his magazine. Lorimer believed in honesty, integrity, hard work, and self-reliance. He edited the magazine to promote these values, but he also knew that the purpose of a magazine was to entertain. He hired some of the best writers and illustrators in America.

Lorimer tried to provide the *Post*'s readers with a little bit of everything; he wanted to create a magazine for the entire family. Under Lorimer's guidance the *Post*'s circulation reached one million a week in 1908, two million in 1913, and three million in 1937. The contents of the magazine stayed roughly the same during these years and so did the price: until 1942, an issue cost just five cents.

After Lorimer, the person most associated with the magazine was illustrator **Norman Rockwell** (1894–1978; see entry under

A boy sells the *Saturday Evening Post* in Rochester, New York, in 1910. *Photograph by Lewis W. Hine. Corbis Corporation. Reproduced by permission.*

1910s—Print Culture in volume 1). Rockwell, who began to paint covers for the *Post* in 1916, perfectly captured the tone of the magazine. He painted typical American scenes: a family sitting at a dinner table, a boy scout helping an older lady cross the street, a doctor listening to a doll's heartbeat. Many Americans clipped Rockwell's *Post* covers and framed them. Rockwell provided illustrations for the magazine for forty-seven years.

The *Post* began to fall out of touch with the mainstream in the 1930s. Editor Lorimer did not like the policies of Democratic president Franklin Delano Roosevelt (1882–1945), and he complained loudly about Roosevelt's policies. Soon the *Post* stopped seeming like the voice of American common sense and began to sound conservative and old fashioned. In the 1950s, advertisers moved their accounts to magazines popular with younger readers or to the new medium of television. The Curtis Company stopped publishing the failing magazine in 1969. In the years since that time, the *Post* has returned in one form or another, but never as a major magazine.

—Tom Pendergast

For More Information

Cohn, Jan. *Creating America: George Horace Lorimer and the "Saturday Evening Post."* Pittsburgh: University of Pittsburgh Press, 1989.

Saturday Evening Post. http://www.satevepost.org (accessed January 9, 2002).

Schwartz, Lew, and Doug Horton, eds. *Norman Rockwell and the Saturday Evening Post* (video). Video Arts Inc., 1986.

1900s

Sports and Games

Just like today, Americans were sports crazy in the first decade of the century. The sports of baseball, basketball, football, and boxing all expanded in popularity. The Olympics became an international spectacle of sports. Not content to remain spectators, Americans participated in bowling, golf, and lawn tennis.

Baseball had grown in popularity throughout the nineteenth century and was dominated at the beginning of the decade by the eight-team National League. The American League was formed in 1900 to challenge the National League. By 1903, the two leagues began to cooperate and play games against each other. Attendance at professional baseball games boomed in the decade, growing from 3.6 million in 1901 to 7.2 million in 1910. Fans across America became obsessed with the World Series, which pitted the American League and National League champions against each other. Until 1947, professional baseball was segregated, which meant that black players could not play in the major leagues. Undaunted, African Americans formed their own baseball leagues. Several of the players established reputations that rivaled those of white baseball greats like Ty Cobb (1886–1961).

College football was the second most popular sport in the nation and the dominant sport in colleges throughout the nation. The University of Michigan was the dominant team of the decade, rolling up a 55–1–1 record between 1901 and 1905. Michigan defeated Stanford in the first Rose Bowl game in 1902, setting the stage for major bowl contests between the top football teams. College football was controversial, however; its extreme violence sometimes led to the death of players, and some teams kept players on the roster (list of participants) even when they were not students. College football was reformed in 1906, setting the stage for the modern rules that still govern football today.

The most controversial sport of the decade was boxing. Often conducted without gloves, boxing matches could be bloody affairs. Boxing was outlawed in many states and reformed in most others. But the so-called sport of gentlemen had its fans, and professional boxing matches, especially in the heavyweight class, drew a great deal of attention. No boxer drew more attention than Jack Johnson (1878–1946), who became the first African American to hold the heavyweight title when he defeated Tommy Burns (1881–1955) in 1908. Racist white fight fans were outraged, and they searched for a "Great White Hope" to defeat Johnson. But Johnson did not lose his title until 1915.

Invented in 1891, basketball was in its infancy in the first decade of the century. It was played first in YMCA clubs and Amateur Athletic Union (AAU) leagues and was soon taken up by colleges. By 1908, the University of Chicago played the University of Pennsylvania in the first collegiate national championship game. Professional basketball also existed, but it would be years before pro basketball drew much attention.

Baseball

Despite having to endure labor strikes, scandals, and the rise in popularity of football and basketball, baseball—America's National Pastime—has managed to maintain its allure and produce an array of legendary larger-than-life heroes. Among Americans' most prized cultural traditions are still "baseball, hotdogs, and apple pie."

The origin of baseball has long been a subject of controversy. What is certain is that the game initially was played in the United States before the mid-nineteenth century; in the 1840s, the New York Knickerbockers, the first baseball team in the United States, played in Madison Square in Manhattan, New York, and at Elysian Fields in Hoboken, New Jersey. During the following decade, teams began sprouting up throughout the Northeast, and even in the Midwest and the Far West. After the Civil War (1861–65), teams started charging admission to games. In 1869, the Cincinnati Red Stockings became the first team to field a complete squad of salaried players.

Meanwhile, the rules of the game kept changing and evolving. In 1876, the eight-team National League came into being. The rival American League, also consisting of eight teams, was formed in 1901. At the conclusion of the 1903 season, the top team from each league began meeting each other in the World Series. Thus was born the sport's modern era. Concrete ballparks that seated thousands of fans were constructed in the major league cities. Among the game's early, colorful personalities: outfielders **Ty Cobb** (1886–1961; see entry under 1900s—Sports and Games in volume 1) and Tris Speaker (1888–1958); second baseman Napoleon Lajoie (1874–1959); pitchers Cy Young (1867–1955), Christy Mathewson (1880–1925), and Walter Johnson (1887–1946); and managers Connie Mack (1862–1956) and John McGraw (1873–1934).

Pitcher Cy Young of the Cleveland Naps in 1910. *Archive Photos. Reproduced by permission.*

The game was almost destroyed in the wake of the 1919 World Series, in which eight members of the Chicago White Sox conspired to accept bribes and throw the series to their opponents, the Cincinnati Reds. The sport's savior was **Babe Ruth** (1895–1948; see entry under 1910s—Sports and Games in volume 1), nicknamed The Bambino and The Sultan of Swat, a pitcher-turned-home-run-hitter who during the 1920s became baseball's most illustrious personality. A slew of celebrated ballplayers made the majors during the 1920s and 1930s and established impressive records. Rogers Hornsby (1896–1963) hit over .400 three times, and in 1924 compiled a record .424 batting average. Lou Gehrig (1903–1941) played in 2,130 straight games. Ruth smashed 60 round-trippers (home runs) in 1927 and amassed 714 home runs for his career. The 1934 All-Star game saw pitcher Carl Hubbell (1903–1988) strike out Ruth, Gehrig, Jimmie Foxx (1907–1967), Al Simmons (1902–1956), and Joe Cronin (1906–1984) in succession. All were future Hall of Famers. The Baseball Hall of Fame and Museum in Cooperstown, New York, a shrine to the game's greatest players, opened in 1939. The 1941 season was highlighted by two stellar accomplishments: Joe DiMaggio (1914–1999), a classy and elegant centerfielder, hit in 56 straight games; and Ted Williams (1918–), perhaps the greatest hitter the sport has ever seen, became the last major leaguer to date to hit over .400.

Since the nineteenth century, African Americans had been banned from playing major and minor league baseball. Another milestone for the sport came in 1945, when Brooklyn Dodgers executive Branch Rickey (1881–1965) signed **Jackie Robinson** (1919–1972; see entry under 1940s—Sports and Games in volume 3) to a contract. Robinson debuted with the Dodgers two years later. This event transcended baseball, becoming one of the milestones in the evolution of the fight for equal rights for African Americans.

During the 1950s and 1960s, a new generation of baseball stars emerged, including slugging outfielders Willie Mays (1931–), Mickey Mantle (1931–1995), and Hank Aaron (1934–); outfielder Roberto Clemente (1934–1972), the initial great Latin player; and fireballing pitcher Sandy Koufax (1935–). The 1950s also saw the relocation of the first National and American League franchises since 1903, with the Boston Braves, Philadelphia Athletics, and St. Louis Browns becoming, respectively, the Milwaukee Braves, Kansas City Athletics, and Baltimore Orioles. At that time, St. Louis was the westernmost major league city; the 1958 season saw the Brooklyn Dodgers and New York Giants resettle on the West Coast, in Los Angeles and San Francisco. Then in 1961, the American League added two new franchises, the Los Angeles (later California and Anaheim) Angels and Washington Senators, with the original Senators relocating to Minnesota. The following year, the National League added the New York Mets and Houston Colt .45s (later Astros). In 1972, the "new" Washington Senators moved to Arlington, Texas, to become the Texas Rangers. Four teams were added to the major leagues in 1969; two in 1977; two in 1993; and two in 1998.

The cliche that records are made to be broken is ever the case in baseball. In 1961, slugger Roger Maris (1934–1985) hit 61 homers, breaking Babe Ruth's single season mark. In 1974, steady Hank Aaron topped Ruth's career total of 714 homers; Aaron eventually retired with 755 round-trippers. Pete Rose (1941–), whose nickname is Charlie Hustle, ended his career with 4,256 hits, topping Ty Cobb's 4,189. In 1973, sturdy hurler Nolan Ryan (1947–) struck out 383 batters, the single season mark; during his twenty-seven-year career he amassed a record 5,714 strikeouts, and also pitched seven no-hitters.

Despite these individual accomplishments, baseball is a team sport. Of all major league baseball teams across the decades, the New York Yankees have been the most dominating by far. During the twentieth century, the Bronx Bombers won approximately one out of every four World Series played, including five in a row between 1949 and 1953 and four in a row from 1936 to 1939.

The 1994 season saw the venerable sport suffer through another crisis: a player strike, which not only shut down the season in August but canceled the World Series. Fans by the millions lost interest in the game at the major league level. Two events helped rekindle its popularity. In 1995, Iron Man Cal Ripken (1960–) broke Lou Gehrig's consecutive games played streak; he voluntarily ended his streak three years later, at 2,632 straight games. Also in 1998, sluggers Mark McGwire (1963–) and Sammy Sosa (1968–) battled each other to break Roger Maris' season home-run record. Both of them did, with Sosa ending the year with 66 round-trippers and McGwire topping him with 70. McGwire's record did not last long, however, as Barry Bonds (1964–) of the San Francisco Giants set his own record in 2001 with 73 homers. The 1990s also saw the emergence of a new generation of baseball heroes, including Ken Griffey Jr. (1969–), Alex Rodriguez (1975–), Pedro Martinez (1968–), Nomar Garciaparra (1973–), and Derek Jeter (1974–).

Finally—and, perhaps, most tellingly—baseball is not played just at the professional level. Among the rites of childhood are the tossing, hitting, and catching of baseballs in sandlots and little leagues across America and around the world.

—Rob Edelman

For More Information

Edelman, Rob. *Baseball on the Web.* New York: MIS Press, 1998.

The Editors of Total Baseball. *Baseball: A Biographical Encyclopedia.* New York: Total Sports, 2000.

Hernandez, Keith, and Mike Bryan. *Pure Baseball.* New York: HarperCollins, 1994.

Neyer, Rob, and Eddie Epstein. *Baseball Dynasties: The Greatest Teams of All Time.* New York: Norton, 2000.

Pietrusza, David, Lloyd Johnson, and Bob Carroll. *The Total Baseball Catalog.* New York: Total Sports, 1998.

Rader, Benjamin. *Baseball: A History of America's Game.* Urbana: University of Illinois Press, 1992.

Thorn, John, Pete Palmer, and Michael Gershman, eds. *Total Baseball.* 7th ed. New York: Total Sports, 2001.

Ty Cobb (1886–1961)

Beginning in 1905, Tyrus Raymond Cobb—nicknamed the Georgia Peach—enjoyed a record-breaking twenty-four-year career as a major league **baseball** (see entry under 1900s–Sports and Games in volume 1) player. He compiled a lifetime batting average of .367, which has never been and may never be equaled. He hit over .300 for twenty-three consecutive seasons. Cobb led the American League in hitting an astounding twelve times. For decades, he held the major league record for the most hits—4,189, since eclipsed by Pete Rose (1941–)—and the modern-era stolen base record—892, since eclipsed by Lou Brock (1939–) and Rickey Henderson (1958–). In 1936, he was the first player elected to the Baseball Hall of Fame.

However, Cobb's career and legacy have been tainted by his vicious temper and violent mode of play. He may have been brilliant and unrelentingly aggressive on the playing field, but he was despised by his fellow players—including his teammates—for his humorless demeanor, stiff Southern formality, and inclination to spike infielders for no reason.

Perhaps the key to understanding Cobb is his relationship with his father William, who wished his son to become a doctor, a lawyer, or a military man, rather than a professional ballplayer. That William was killed, accidentally or otherwise, by a shotgun blast fired by his wife Amanda on the eve of Ty's major league debut only added fuel to Cobb's explosive personality.

Ty Cobb was an early advocate of unionizing ballplayers and was a vocal opponent of the Reserve Clause, which bound a player for life to the team that owned his contract. In his retirement, he also supported impoverished former ballplayers. But he continued squabbling with others in the game. When he died in 1961, no one representing major league baseball—and only three ballplayers of his era—bothered to attend his funeral.

—Rob Edelman

For More Information

Jacobs, William Jay. *They Shaped the Game: Ty Cobb, Babe Ruth, Jackie Robinson.* New York: C. Scribner's Sons, 1994.

Macht, Norman L. *Ty Cobb.* New York: Chelsea House, 1993.

The Official Web Site of Ty Cobb. http://www.cmgww.com/baseball/cobb/index.html (accessed December 14, 2001).

James J. Corbett (1866–1933)

James J. "Gentleman Jim" Corbett is more than a boxing legend. He was the first of a new breed of modern-era boxers who approached the sport of boxing methodically. The fast, sleek Corbett believed in training for his fights and in employing speed and strategy rather than uncontrolled power to outmaneuver an opponent.

Through the late nineteenth century, professional boxing was not so much an organized sport as a barbaric fight-to-the-finish free-for-all in which bare-knuckled combatants wrestled and clawed their way to victory. Boxers were more like hooligans who exuded a rough, crude manliness. The sport became more orderly with the institution of the Marquis of Queensberry rules (named after Sir John Sholto Douglas [1844–1900], the eighth Marquis of Queensberry, who helped draft the new boxing rules). Bouts consisted of three-minute rounds featuring minute-long rest periods in between, and to protect their hands, boxers wore five-ounce, padded gloves. On September 7, 1892, the first modern-era heavyweight championship match was held with the Marquis of Queensberry rules in effect. The reigning champion was John L. Sullivan (1858–1918), nicknamed "The Boston Strongboy," an old-style, bare-knuckle boxer. Corbett was the challenger. Their match is the most significant in the sport's history. The smaller, quicker Corbett avoided Sullivan's bullish assaults and wore him down. He knocked out the exhausted champ in the twenty-first round to claim the heavyweight crown—and the modern era of boxing was born.

Unlike other boxers of his time, Corbett hailed from a middle-class family and attended college. While still the champ, he performed on the stage and in vaudeville. He continued doing so after losing his title to Bob Fitzsimmons (1863–1918) in 1897.

—Rob Edelman

For More Information

Fields, Armond. *James J. Corbett: A Biography of the Heavyweight Boxing Champ and Popular Theater Headliner.* Jefferson, NC: McFarland, 2001.

"'Gentleman' Jim Corbett." *The Cyber Boxing Zone.* http://cyberboxingzone.com/boxing/corbett.htm (accessed December 14, 2001).

Myler, Patrick. *Gentleman Jim Corbett: The Truth Behind a Boxing Legend.* London: Robson Book Ltd., 1998.

Jack Johnson (1878–1946)

Jack Johnson, a free-living, highly individualistic heavyweight boxing champion, was a black man who came of age and came to fame at a time when African Americans faced severe discrimination in American culture. When Johnson earned his boxing title in 1908, African Americans faced many forms of racial bias. They were consigned to the back of the bus. They were limited to attending inferior schools and working at menial jobs. They were regularly denied their right to vote. If a black man were considered to be "uppity," he might find himself hanging from a tree, lynched by a white mob. In comparison, here was Jack Johnson, no lowly field worker or janitor but the heavyweight champion of the world. Furthermore, Johnson showed no humility as he savored his fame. He drove expensive cars, tossed extravagant parties, and broke the ultimate social taboo for a black man at that time by dating white women.

Johnson went on to defeat white opponent after white opponent. One of his most famous bouts, in 1910, came against former champ James J. Jeffries (1875–1953). Their fight was advertised as a battle between "The Hope of the White Race vs. The Deliverer of the Negroes." Much to the shock of white America, Johnson pummeled the aging, overweight Jeffries.

No "Great White Hope" boxer could stop Johnson in the ring, and so the federal government stepped in. In 1912, he was convicted of violating the Mann Act, which prohibited the transportation of women across state lines for "immoral purposes." Johnson fled the country, lost his title to a six-foot, six-inch hulk named Jess Willard (1883–1968), and eventually faded into obscurity. But his athletic prowess, and his status as a black champion in a white-dominated world, can never be denied.

—Rob Edelman

For More Information

Fradella, Sal. *Jack Johnson.* Boston: Branden Publishing Co., 1990.
Jakoubek, Robert E. *Jack Johnson.* New York: Chelsea House, 1990.
Schomburg Center for Research in Black Culture. "Jack (John Arthur) Johnson (1876–1946)." *Harlem, 1900–1940.* http://www.si.umich.edu/CHICO/Harlem/text/jajohnson.html (accessed January 9, 2002).

Kentucky Derby

The "Run for the Roses," otherwise known as the Kentucky Derby, is the world's most fabled horserace—as well as the oldest continuous athletic competition held in the United States. It is the first of three annual races, followed by the Preakness and Belmont Stakes, in which three-year-old thoroughbreds compete for the Triple Crown. Each spring, over one hundred thousand racing fans congregate at the Churchill Downs racetrack in Louisville, Kentucky, to witness what has come to be known as the "greatest two minutes in sports."

The race dates back to May 1875, when Colonel Meriwether Lewis Clark (1846–1899) staged the first Derby, which he modeled after the English Derby held at Epsom Downs in Surrey, England. The original Kentucky Derby course was a mile and a half; eventually, it was reduced to a mile and a quarter. Aristides, a chestnut colt, was the first winner. Subsequent contests featured the top American thoroughbreds hailing from Kentucky and the Northeast. However, the Derby did not attain its status as racing's premiere event until the twentieth century. At the turn of the twentieth century, Clark's racetrack was a failing enterprise. Between 1899 and 1914, the top northeastern stables bypassed Churchill Downs for the American Derby at Chicago's Washington Park, and the Kentucky Derby became a regional meet. Then in 1915, financier, socialite, sportsman, and horse breeder Harry Payne Whitney (1872–1930) entered a filly named Regret, which became the lone female thoroughbred to win the Derby until the 1980s. This race signaled the beginning of the Derby's modern era. Matt Winn (1861–1949), a former Louisville tailor and Churchill Downs's longtime vice president and general manager, noted that Regret's victory "made the Kentucky Derby an American institution."

Isaac Murphy (1859–1896), an African American and the son of a former slave, was one of the most honored early jockeys, riding Buchanan, Riley, and Kingman to victory in 1884, 1890, and 1891. His three Derby triumphs were not duplicated until 1930, when Earl Sande (1898–1968) won his third race on Gallant Fox. The record was broken when Eddie Arcaro (1916–1997), who won a total of five Derbys, rode his fourth winner, Citation, in 1948. Bill Hartack (1932–) joined Arcaro as a five-time victor, while Willie Shoemaker (1931–) rode into the winner's circle on four occasions and Angel Cordero (1942–) won three times.

Among the legendary horses who raced at Churchill Downs are Gallant Fox and Omaha, the only father-son combination to win the Triple Crown, in 1930 and 1935; Whirlaway, another Triple Crown victor, who set a record pace while winning the

Derby in 1941; Citation, the 1948 Triple Crown winner and the first horse ever to earn $1 million; and Secretariat, the 1973 Triple Crown champion, the first horse to run the Derby in under two minutes.

—Rob Edelman

For More Information

Bolus, Jim. *Derby Dreams.* Gretna, LA: Pelican, 1996.
Bolus, Jim. *Derby Fever.* Gretna, LA: Pelican, 1995.
Bolus, Jim. *Derby Magic.* Gretna, LA: Pelican, 1995.
Bolus, Jim. *Kentucky Derby Stories.* Gretna, LA: Pelican, 1993.
Bolus, Jim. *Remembering the Derby.* Gretna, LA: Pelican, 1993.
Chew, Peter. *The Kentucky Derby: The First Hundred Years.* Boston: Houghton Mifflin, 1974.
Doolittle, Bill. *The Kentucky Derby: Run for the Roses.* Del Mar, CA: Tehabi Books, 1999.
Longrigg, Roger. *The History of Horse Racing.* New York: Stein and Day, 1972.

Lionel Trains

For generations of Americans, gazing at a spanking new Lionel train set as it chugged along loops of tracks laid out beneath a brightly lit Christmas tree is an extra-special childhood memory. Lionel trains are not the only electricity-powered toys marketed to American children and hobbyists. But of all electric train manufacturers, Lionel is by far the most famous, a status it earned for the quality, craftsmanship, and durability of its product.

Joshua Lionel Cowen (1877–1965), a young man who since childhood had been fascinated by trains and railroads, founded the Lionel Manufacturing Company in lower Manhattan, New York, in 1900. The story goes that, when he was seven, Cowen carved a small locomotive out of wood, which exploded upon his attempting to attach it to a miniature steam engine. Although Cowen did not invent the electric train—one had been displayed at the 1893 Chicago World's Fair—he was the first to produce miniature, electric trains as playthings. For his initial Lionel train, he hooked a small motor onto a red-stained wooden box with attached wheels, and added a gold-painted "Electric Express" to the side. He sold the car, along with thirty inches of track, for the then-hefty sum of $6. The product

Lionel trains captivated baby boomers in the mid-1900s, and remain popular collectibles in the twenty-first century. *Hulton/Archive by Getty Images. Reproduced by permission.*

became a smash-hit. Soon Cowen was manufacturing meticulously designed and painted miniature reproductions of diesel locomotives, steam engines, cabooses, and trolleys as well as coal, cattle, and passenger cars, all operated electrically. He produced his first accessory, a suspension bridge, in 1902, and eventually added tunnels and train stations. In 1915, he introduced smaller, less-expensive O-gauge trains. The term "gauge" refers to the width of the track, and O-gauge models are designed to fit on tracks that are one and one-quarter inches between rails.

By the mid-1920s, Cowen's company completely dominated the toy train business. Across the decades, it sold over fifty million trains. Among the many Lionel classics were the 400E steam locomotive, first marketed in 1931; the 700E New York Central-Hudson steam locomotive, from 1937; and the F3 diesel locomotive, from 1948. In 1953, as parents by the thousands were buying Lionel trains for their **baby boomer** (see entry under 1940s—The Way We Lived in volume 3) offspring, Lionel recorded its highest profits ever. However, beginning in the late 1950s, Lionel trains—and all electric trains—went out of fashion, primarily because airplanes were replacing trains as the primary mode of cross-country travel.

Today, original Lionel trains are collectors items, highly coveted by vintage toy and train enthusiasts. They are especially beloved by baby boomers. In fact, in the 1990s, one celebrated baby boomer, rock musician Neil Young (1945–), even became a part owner in the company.

—Rob Edelman

For More Information

Carp, Roger. *The World's Greatest Toy Train Maker: Insiders Remember Lionel.* Waukesha, WI: Kalmbach, 1997.

Hollander, Ron. *All Aboard! The Story of Joshua Lionel Cowen and His Lionel Train Company.* New York: Workman, 1981.

McComas, Tom, and James Tuohy. *A Collector's Guide and History of Lionel Trains.* Wilmette, IL: TM Productions, 1975.

Milton Bradley Company

The Milton Bradley Company is best known as the manufacturer of classic games, from **Scrabble** (see entry under 1940s—Sports and Games in volume 3) to **Twister** (see entry under 1960s—Sports and Games in volume 3), that have brought fun to players of all ages for over 140 years. The company was founded by Milton Bradley (1836–1911). Bradley was working as a printer in Springfield, Massachusetts, when he produced a new family diversion called The Checkered Game of Life, a board game whose goal was a moral life and peaceful retirement.

Bradley continued to create games and publish educational materials for young children. By 1968, his company was the largest manufacturer of games in the United States. The popularity of such Milton Bradley games as Parcheesi, Yahtzee, Candy Land, Chutes and Ladders, Mousetrap, and Go to the Head of the Class has spanned generations. Books published by Milton Bradley Publishing teach children about everything from numbers and letters to problem solving and computer skills.

The company became part of Hasbro Toys in 1984, but the Milton Bradley name is still used on its classic games. The Game of Life is still one of the most popular, though the goal has been updated. In the modern game, the player who retires with the most money wins.

—Tina Gianoulis

For More Information

Lee, Laura. "Milton Bradley." *The Name's Familiar: Mr. Leotard, Barbie, and Chef Boy-ar-dee.* Gretna, LA: Pelican Publishing, 1999.

"Milton Bradley Company History." *Hasbro.* http://www.hasbro.com (accessed January 9, 2002).

Negro Leagues

In 1947, **Jackie Robinson** (1919–1972; see entry under 1940s—Sports and Games in volume 3) became the first African American to play major league **baseball** (see entry under 1900s—Sports and Games in volume 1) in the twentieth century. Before the late 1940s, African American players could not pitch, hit, and field alongside such greats as **Babe Ruth** (1895–1948; see entry under 1910s—Sports and Games in volume 1), **Ty Cobb** (1886–1961; see entry under 1900s—Sports and Games in volume 1), Lou Gehrig (1903–1941), Walter Johnson (1887–1946), and other white baseball heroes, but that did not deter them from playing the game. The best black ballplayers swatted home runs, stole bases, and hurled shutouts in leagues of their own, all of which are informally known as the Negro Leagues.

All-black baseball clubs existed in the nineteenth century and even took on white opponents. Back in 1869, the Pythian Baseball Club of Philadelphia, Pennsylvania, an all-black team, played—and beat—the all-white City Items. For several decades during this time period, blacks and whites did play side by side. But integrated baseball ended in 1887 when Cap Anson (1852–1922), one of the most influential white ballplayers, declared that he never would play with or against black opponents. Anson's highly publicized declaration eventually evolved into a gentleman's agreement between the major league owners to exclude black players.

African Americans now were restricted to playing on segregated teams. One of the top turn-of-the-twentieth-century teams was the Chicago American Giants, who put together an extraordinary 123-6 record one season while barnstorming cross-country. The Giants' star was pitcher-manager Andrew "Rube" Foster (1879–1930), who after World War I (1914–18) helped establish the eight-team Negro National League. Upon the league's success, a group of white owners formed the rival six-team Eastern Colored League. In 1924, each league's top team met in the first Black World Series.

The next two decades produced its share of legendary Negro League teams, beginning with the Kansas City Monarchs, Pittsburgh Crawfords, Homestead Grays, and Birmingham Black Barons. Among the top stars were gangly pitcher Leroy "Satchel" Paige (1906–1982), a master showman who was the leagues' biggest draw; James "Cool Papa" Bell (1903–1991), a lightning-fast base stealer; and brawny home-run hitter Josh Gibson (1911–1947), who may have belted close to one thousand home runs during his career. On occasion, Negro all-star teams would play similar squads composed of the top major leaguers. On these occasions, the African American ballplayers proved that the best of them could have been major league all-stars. Paige once struck out Hall of Famer Rogers Hornsby (1896–1963) five times in the same contest. New York Yankee legend Joe DiMaggio (1914–1999) called Paige "the best and fastest pitcher I've ever faced." Meanwhile, in these exhibitions, Gibson hit .412 facing formidable major league pitching.

The integration of major league baseball signaled the beginning of the end of the Negro Leagues. Now, the very best African American prospects could be signed by the Brooklyn Dodgers, the Cleveland Indians, or the New York Giants. The could develop their skills in their team's farm systems and make it to the majors. But if the top pre-1947 African American players were not allowed to play alongside their Caucasian counterparts, they at least have joined them in the National Baseball Hall of Fame and Museum in Cooperstown, New York. Beginning in 1971, with the induction of Satchel Paige, Negro Leaguers have been elected to the Hall of Fame.

—Rob Edelman

For More Information

Black Baseball's Negro Baseball Leagues. http://www.blackbaseball.com (accessed January 9, 2002).

Holway, John B. *Black Diamonds: Life in the Negro Leagues.* New York: Stadium Books, 1991.

McKissack, Patricia C., and Fredrick McKissack, Jr. *Black Diamond: The Story of the Negro Baseball Leagues.* New York: Scholastic, 1994.

Negro Leagues Baseball Museum. http://www.nlbm.com (accessed January 9, 2002).

Peterson, Robert. *Only the Ball Was White: A History of Legendary Black Players and All-Black Professional Teams.* New York: Oxford University Press, 1992.

Ward, Geoffrey C., and Ken Burns, with Jim O'Connor. *Shadow Ball: The History of the Negro Leagues.* New York: Knopf, 1994.

Olympics

The earliest Olympic games took place in ancient Greece possibly as far back as the fourteenth century B.C.E. The ancient Olympics mixed sport with pagan religion, and the Romans banned them in 393 C.E. Baron Pierre de Coubertin (1862–1937) staged the first "modern" summer Olympic games for amateur athletes in Athens, Greece, in 1896. The first official winter games were held in 1928 in St. Moritz, Switzerland, though the events of the eleven-day "International Winter Sports Week" in Chamonix, France, are usually called the first winter games. In the 1960s, the first "Paralympics" allowed athletes with disabilities to compete on a world stage. For years and years, both the summer and winter Olympics were held in different cities the same year, every four years; beginning in 1994, however, the winter and summer Olympics began alternating every two years.

The Olympics began in a spirit of fair play and honor among nations, but they have always reflected their times. The Stockholm, Sweden, games of 1912 saw women compete for the first time, though women could not take their place in track and field events until 1928. In 1936, Nazi leader Adolf Hitler (1889–1945) hoped that the Berlin, Germany, Olympics would show the superiority of the "Aryan" race (non-Jewish Caucasians), but African American runner **Jesse Owens** (1913–1980; see entry under 1930s—Sports and Games in volume 2) had other ideas. He went on to win four gold medals. Many Olympics make household names of its stars. Swimmer Johnny Weissmuller (1904–1984) won four medals in 1924 and became famous as "Tarzan" in a series of films; swimmer Mark Spitz (1950–) managed seven swimming golds in 1972. Boxer Cassius Clay, who later changed his name to **Muhammad Ali** (1942–; see entry under 1960s—Sports and Games in volume 4), went on to be one of the best-known sportsmen of all time. Track stars such as Carl Lewis (1961–) and Florence Griffith Joyner (1959–1998) thrilled spectators with breathtaking performances. And, as a team, members of the 1980 U.S. men's hockey team became instant Olympic legends when they defeated the highly favored Soviet hockey team, and then went on to win the gold medal.

In the late twentieth century, the influence of politics grew stronger. The United States and the Soviet Union boycotted one another's games in the 1980s at the height of the **Cold War** (see

One of the most memorable Olympic moments in recent history was when the men's U.S. Olympic hockey team won the gold medal at the 1980 Winter Games in Lake Placid, New York. *AP/Wide World Photos. Reproduced by permission.*

entry under 1940s—The Way We Lived in volume 3). Terrorists disrupted the games in Munich, Germany, in 1972 and in Atlanta, Georgia, in 1996. The Olympic Games have served as an opportunity for host nations to showcase their artistic, cultural, and political values. Since the 1980s, many of the athletes are well-paid professionals. Still, it is the courage, speed, and skill of the athletes that make the Olympics special. Politics, commercialization, drug abuse, and other scandals never quite manage to overshadow the spectacle of the games themselves.

—Chris Routledge

For More Information

Anderson, Dave, and Carl Lewis. *The Story of the Olympics*. New York: HarperCollins, 2000.
Chronicle of the Olympics. London: Dorling Kindersley, 1998.
International Olympic Committee. http://www.olympic.org/ (accessed January 10, 2002).

Ouija Boards

Invented in the late 1800s, the Ouija (WEE-juh) board was part of a fascination with spiritualism and the occult (supernatural phenomena) that swept the United States and Europe during the last half of the nineteenth century. What made the "talking board" special was that the average person could use it to try to contact the spirit world without the help of a psychic or a medium (someone said to be naturally sensitive to the spirit world and able to communicate with its spirits). Since its invention, the Ouija board has been marketed and sold as a toy. Both its fans and its critics, however, have taken it much more seriously at times, viewing it as the key to an unseen world of spirits that some think is better left alone.

In 1848, two sisters, Kate Fox (1839–1892) and Margaret Fox (1833–1893) of Hydesville, New York, became famous when they said they had communicated with the spirit of a long-dead peddler. Soon, people all over the country were holding seances (meetings at which people try to talk to spirits). Some seances included mediums who supposedly went into trances in which dead people could speak directly through them. (A trance is a sleeplike condition in which the medium appears conscious but unable to move or act.) For those without the special skills of a medium, several methods were used to enable the dead to speak. Table turning involved placing hands around a table, which would then rock and thump to indicate the presence of spirits. A planchette (a heart-shaped piece of wood with a pencil attached and wheels or sliders to allow it to glide across paper) would write a spirit message. Fascinated and thrilled by the frightening world of ghosts, most fans of spiritualism cheerfully ignored the likelihood that one of them was pushing the table or the pencil around, consciously or unconsciously.

The Ouija board was a variation of the planchette. It eliminated the paper and substituted a board painted with the alphabet and a few common words like "yes," "no," and "maybe" to

The Ouija board is viewed by some as a harmless game and by others as a link to the spirit world better left alone. *Corbis/Bettmann. Reproduced by permission.*

simplify the spirit writing process. The first Ouija board was invented in 1890 by toy manufacturer Charles Kennard, who named it for a word the board had told him meant "good luck" in Egyptian. In fact, "ouija" does not mean anything in Arabic, the language spoken in Egypt. When Kennard sold the patent to William Fuld in 1892, Fuld explained the name by saying it was a combination of the French and German words for "yes," *oui* and *ja*. The Ouija board was sold in novelty stores and toy shops, competing with other talking boards with names like "The Wireless Messenger" and "Mystic Tray."

In 1966, Fuld's children sold the Ouija board to Parker Brothers, a game company that continued to market the board as a parlor game. Some people still feel it is better left alone. Religious groups complain that playing with the board comes dangerously close to Satanism. Professional psychics worry that the board may unleash evil spirits. Some psychologists express concern that use of the board may further disturb a mentally unbalanced person. Nevertheless, Ouija board use continues to enchant mystics and enliven parties with its promise of access to the forbidden territory of the dead.

—Tina Gianoulis

For More Information

Covina, Gina. *The Ouija Book*. New York: Simon and Schuster, 1979.
Hunt, Stoker. *Ouija: The Most Dangerous Game*. New York: Barnes and Noble, 1992.
Johnson, James P. "Ouija." *American Heritage* (Vol. 34, February–March 1983): pp. 24–27.
Museum of Talking Boards. http://www.museumoftalkingboards.com (accessed January 10, 2002).
"Ouija Board." *Skeptic's Dictionary*. http://www.skepdic.com/ouija.html (accessed January 10, 2002).

Rose Bowl

On and around every New Year's Day, the top college football teams face off in postseason "bowl games," one of which is the National Championship game. Of all the bowl games, the Rose Bowl, held in Pasadena, California, in early January—usually on January 1—is the oldest and the most fabled.

In 1902, business leaders in Pasadena sponsored a football game that would match a top West Coast team against one from back East. With eighty-five hundred fans looking on, the Michigan Wolverines smashed Stanford, 49–0. Disappointed in the loss by the local team, the Tournament of Roses committee did not follow through on a second contest. The next Rose Bowl was held fourteen years later, when Washington State bested Brown, 14–0—and the game has been played every year since. Starting in 1924, contests have been held in the Rose Bowl stadium, with attendance often topping one hundred thousand. Since 1947, when Illinois trounced UCLA, 45–14, the Rose Bowl opponents have been the champions of what today are known as the Big Ten and Pac-10 college football conferences. That tradition ended—temporarily at least—in 2002 when the Rose Bowl joined other bowl games in hosting the Bowl Championship Series' national championship game.

During the twentieth century, nineteen Rose Bowl winners were crowned national champions. The first was the Michigan team that won the original game. The popularity of the Rose Bowl resulted in the founding of other postseason college bowl games. During the 1930s, the Orange (1933), Sugar (1935), Sun (1936), and Cotton (1937) Bowls were established. Other bowls followed in subsequent decades.

Bowl games usually are preceded by elaborate parades through the streets of the host city. Not surprisingly, the most famous is the Rose Bowl's Tournament of Roses parade. (Historically, the Rose Parade preceded the establishment of the Rose Bowl). The procession is famed for its ornately designed floats, each amply covered with floral arrangements. Watching it on television is a New Year's Day ritual for football fans and nonfans alike.

—Rob Edelman

For More Information

Hendrickson, Joe, with Maxwell Stiles. *The Tournament of Roses: A Pictorial History.* Los Angeles: Brooke House, 1971.

Hibner, John Charles. *The Rose Bowl, 1902–1929: A Game-by-Game History of Collegiate Football's Foremost Event, from its Advent through Its Golden Era.* Jefferson, NC: McFarland, 1993.

Michelson, Herb, and Dave Newhouse. *Rose Bowl Football Since 1902.* New York: Stein and Day, 1977.

"Rose Bowl Game History." *Pasadena Tournament of Roses.* http://www.rosebowl.com/history/bowlhistory.htm (accessed January 9, 2002).

1900s

The Way We Lived

In the first decade of the century, Americans began to experience the first of the technological transformations that would make life in the twentieth century so much different than life in the nineteenth century. Two technological innovations alone were responsible for a great deal of this change: electricity and the automobile. Electricity brought great changes to life in the home, from electric lighting that allowed life to go on while darkness descended outside to the development of electric appliances that made housework so much easier. The electric vacuum cleaner was invented in 1907, for example, although it was too expensive for most Americans.

The automobile brought even more sweeping changes. Developed in the nineteenth century, automobiles began to be mass produced in the 1900s by such companies as Ford and General Motors. With a car, Americans could travel farther than they ever had before. A variety of businesses serving travelers resulted, from diners to gas stations. Another nineteenth-century invention, the telephone, also allowed people to close the distances between themselves. By the 1930s, most Americans had access to a telephone.

Americans spent their leisure time in a number of different ways in the decade. Religion was often the center of many people's lives. Evangelical religion enjoyed a boom in popularity, thanks in part to a number of charismatic traveling preachers. The most notable preacher of the decade was Billy Sunday (1862–1935), a former National League baseball player whose sermons drew great crowds. Americans also sought to improve themselves by attending Chautauqua events, which were traveling variety programs that stressed education and self-improvement. Other Americans enjoyed the escapism of amusement parks, where they rode the Ferris wheels and roller coasters that were becoming ever more popular. The most famous American amusement park of the time was Coney Island, outside New York City.

Avon

For more than a century, the Avon Products company has been known for the direct-selling approach it uses to merchandise its cosmetics and personal-care products. In short, Avon employs women—"Avon Ladies"—to demonstrate items to customers in the privacy of their own homes. Avon's vintage television commercials typically opened with the sound of a chiming doorbell followed by the phrase, "Avon calling."

Originally known as the California Perfume Company, the company was founded in 1886 by David McConnell (1858–1937), who later renamed it Avon to honor the birthplace of his favorite author, William Shakespeare (1564–1616). Avon's direct-selling method was pioneered by Mrs. P. F. E. Albee of Winchester, New Hampshire, who became the first "Avon Lady" soon after the company's founding. By 2001, Avon was the world's largest direct-selling company, employing 3.4 million sales representatives in 139 countries around the world (2 percent of whom are male), and with total sales revenues of $5.7 billion.

Avon suffered a decline in its fortunes in the 1970s and 1980s owing to changing lifestyles. Many women began working outside the home, the arena where most of its demonstrations and sales had traditionally taken place. Also during this period, many salespeople left Avon to pursue more lucrative career opportunities. In the 1990s, the company redesigned its focus and advertising, upgraded its product line, and trained its sales force to make presentations in workplace settings, where 50 percent of sales now take place. Avon also considerably expanded its presence outside of the United States, especially in Brazil and other South American countries, China, and eastern Europe. With nearly one third of its top executives being female, the Avon Company is considered one of the most "women-friendly" enterprises.

—Edward Moran

For More Information

Avon.com: The Company for Women. http://www.avon.com (accessed January 10, 2002).

Morris, Betsy. "If Women Ran the World, It Would Look a Lot Like Avon." *Fortune* (July 21, 1997).

Reynolds, Patricia. "Ding Dong! Avon Lady Is Still Calling." *Minneapolis Star Tribune* (September 9, 1996).

Zajac, Jennifer. "Avon Finally Glowing Thanks to Global Sales—and New Lip-Shtick." *Money* (September 1997).

Catalog Houses

Most people are used to buying clothes and other speciality items from catalogs, but in the first half of the twentieth century, Americans could also buy houses from catalogs. As Americans began moving into cities and their **suburbs** (see entry under 1950s—The Way We Lived in volume 3) in increasing numbers after 1890, they needed affordable housing. Catalog houses offered Americans one way to solve their housing problems.

The catalog house industry began in earnest after 1907 with the founding of the Aladdin Company. It was soon joined by other companies, most importantly **Sears, Roebuck and Company** (see entry under 1900s—Commerce in volume 1). Sears sold catalog houses between 1908 and 1940. In all of these catalogs, customers could select from a number of different housing styles, with bungalows and colonial revival homes being among the most popular. When customers ordered a catalog house, they would receive the complete architectural plans, a complete construction manual, and often the building materials as well. These building materials came precut and numbered for easy assembly. All the homeowner had to do was provide the land; the foundation materials, such as concrete or stone; the labor; and other amenities such as windows, doors, plumbing, and other hardware. Sears and other companies provided guarantees of satisfaction and often easy payment credit plans as well to make the houses even more affordable.

As a cultural phenomenon, catalog houses became a common part of the American landscape, popping up in towns all over the United States. They even became the subject of films, most notably in the 1921 short comic film *One Week* by Buster Keaton (1895–1966). In the film, Keaton assembles the house incorrectly and all sorts of funny problems result. *One Week* was one of the most popular comedies of 1921, an indication of the popularity of catalog houses as well.

During the Great Depression of the 1930s, the popularity of catalog houses declined as fewer people could afford to buy any houses. And although many of their designs still stand, the catalog house never rebounded in popularity after 1940.

—Timothy Berg

For More Information

Clark, Clifford E., Jr. *The American Family Home.* Chapel Hill: University of North Carolina Press, 1986.

Jackson, Kenneth T. *Crabgrass Frontier: The Suburbanization of the United States.* New York: Oxford University Press, 1985.

McAlester, Virginia, and Lee McAlester. *A Field Guide to American Houses.* New York: Alfred A. Knopf, 1994.

Stevenson, Katherine C., and H. Ward Jandl. *Houses by Mail: A Guide to Houses from Sears, Roebuck and Company.* Washington, DC: Preservation Press, 1986.

Chautauqua Movement

In the years between the 1870s and the 1920s, the name Chautauqua came to be synonymous with culture, learning, entertainment, and social activism. Originating at a New York religious institute, the Chautauqua movement—which focused on self-improvement through education—spread across small-town America. Even today, that spirit of lifelong education lives on at the Chautauqua Institution.

In 1873, in the little town of Chautauqua, New York, two Methodist ministers, John Heyl Vincent (1832–1920) and Lewis Miller (1829–1899), developed a unique program of study that combined various nonreligious educational subjects with typical Sunday school topics. By 1874, their idea had become reality and the Chautauqua Institution offered a nine-week summer session of adult education courses. As the word spread, more and more people were drawn to the unusual school. They studied politics, culture, literature, and science, and attended lectures and performances from the most famous people of the day, including feminist Susan B. Anthony (1820–1906), inventors Alexander Graham Bell (1847–1922) and Henry Ford (1863–1947), Helen Keller (1880–1968), and nine presidents of the United States.

The leaders of Chautauqua soon became aware that only a few of those Americans who were hungry for learning and cultural dialogue lived within traveling distance of New York. They mailed courses of home study to interested students and sent

Chautauqua Literary and Scientific Circle Procession held on the grounds of the New York institute. *Chautauqua Institution Archives. Reproduced by permission.*

speakers traveling on a circuit to over two hundred Chautauquas around the country. Soon the arrival of the Chautauqua circuit was greeted with as much enthusiasm as a traveling circus. Lecturers, entertainers, politicians, and preachers made the rounds. They brought much needed information, intellectual stimulation, and diversion to communities that had little contact with urban cultures.

Two major developments of the 1920s brought an end to the era of the Chautauqua: the automobile, which ended the isolation of American small towns; and the motion picture, which provided entertainment nationwide. However, New York's Chautauqua Institution still offers its dynamic study sessions, drawing almost two hundred thousand visitors from all over the country in 2000.

—Tina Gianoulis

For More Information

Case, V., and R. O. Case. *We Called It Culture: The Story of Chautauqua.* Manchester, NH: Ayers Company Publishers, 1977.

Chautauqua Institution. http://www.chautauqua-inst.org (accessed December 14, 2001).

Gould, J. E. *The Chautauqua Movement: An Episode in the Continuing American Revolution.* Albany: State University of New York Press, 1961.

Kostyal, K. M. "An Enduring Tradition." *National Geographic Traveler.* (May-June 1993): pp. 28–32.

Schurr, Cathleen. "Chautauqua: Yesterday and Today." *American History Illustrated* (July-August, 1992): pp. 40–47.

Coney Island

For poor and working-class New York City dwellers in decades past, a luxury resort vacation was a fantasy, an indulgence available only to the wealthy. But almost any New Yorker could travel to Coney Island, a five-mile-long sandy strip in the southern part of the borough of Brooklyn. Once there, they could frolic in the Atlantic Ocean and build sand castles to their delight, dine on hot dogs, and ride on roller coasters and carousels.

Actually, Coney Island had initially attracted well-to-do Manhattanites. In the 1840s, steamships began bringing visitors to its beach; two decades later, horse cars made excursions there. In the 1860s and 1870s, large luxurious resort hotels were built. Given its accessibility, however, Coney Island eventually became a desirable destination for all New Yorkers. Bridge construction between Manhattan and Brooklyn and the development of the New York City subway system in the late nineteenth and early twentieth centuries allowed urban dwellers from all walks of life easy access to Coney Island. Soon, it became a haven for the masses, with its beach becoming, on a sweltering summer day, the most densely populated strip in the world.

According to legend, Charles Feltman (1841–1910) invented the **hot dog** (see entry under 1900s—Food and Drink in volume 1) on Coney Island in 1867. Coney Island's delights included the construction of its first carousel in 1875 and of the first American roller coaster, the Switchback Railway, in 1884. By 1886, Coney Island could boast of three racetracks, making it a horse-racing center. Captain Paul Boyton (1848–1924) bought the land for Sea Lion Park in 1895. The park was the world's first outdoor, enclosed (with a fence) amusement park. It had the first Shoot-the-Chutes ride in America. It was remodeled into a state-of-the-art theme park in 1903 and renamed Luna Park. On opening day, Luna Park attracted forty-three thousand paying customers.

In 1897, the rival Steeplechase Park opened. Its centerpiece was the Steeplechase Race Course, on which couples raced one another atop wooden horses-on-wheels. Steeplechase Park burned in 1907 but was rebuilt. It reopened the following year and remained in operation until 1964. Meanwhile, Luna Park fell into decline. It burned down in 1944, and five years later its land became a parking lot. A third Coney Island amusement park, named Dreamland, opened in 1904 but burned to the ground in 1911.

In 1923, the first section of Coney Island's boardwalk opened. Four years later came the eighty-five-foot-high Cyclone, the area's most famous roller coaster. On July 4, 1955, a record 1.5 million bathers and fun seekers visited Coney Island. Yet ten years later, Coney was in decline as an amusement area. In recent decades, while still attracting the newest wave of poor immigrant New Yorkers, the surrounding neighborhood became a crime-riddled slum. However, 2001 marked the opening of KeySpan Park, built on the former site of Steeplechase Park: a seventy-five-hundred-seat

An aerial view of Coney Island amusement park in Brooklyn, New York, July 4, 1952. *AP/Wide World Photos. Reproduced by permission.*

baseball stadium that houses the minor league Brooklyn Cyclones, the first professional baseball team to play in Brooklyn since 1957. With the arrival of KeySpan Park and the Cyclones, Coney Island in the first decade of the twenty-first century is a community ripe for revival.

—Rob Edelman

For More Information

Glueck, Grace, and Paul Gardner. *Brooklyn: People and Places, Past and Present.* New York: Harry Abrams, 1991.

Kasson, John F. *Amusing the Millions: Coney Island at the Turn of the Century.* New York: Hill and Wang, 1978.

McCullough, Edo. *Good Old Coney Island: A Sentimental Journey into the Past.* New York: Fordham University Press, 2000.

Register, Woody. *The Kid of Coney Island: Fred Thompson and the Rise of American Amusements.* New York: Oxford University Press, 2001.

Dancing

Dancing—rhythmically moving the body, especially the feet, to the sound of music—is a long-treasured social activity and a significant aspect of cultures around the world. People of all ages dance for many reasons: as an act of celebration, at weddings and proms; as an act of recreation or as socialization linked to courtship, in dance halls, nightclubs, discos, and high school gyms; and as a religious or tribal rite, with participants occasionally garbed in elaborate costumes. In the United States, dancing primarily is a social activity. As popular music—and popular culture—evolved through the decades, a range of dance styles and crazes also have emerged.

Immigrants who came to the United States, from the nation's beginnings to the present day, brought with them native dances that remained a rich part of their cultures. Early popular dances included folk dances, most often done in groups, and ballroom dances such as the waltz, which was imported from Europe. All these folk dances and ballroom dances were formal dances, which depended upon learning a pattern of movements or steps. Some dances remain linked to their ethnic origins. For example, Polish Americans perform versions of the polka, a fast-paced dance developed in Bohemia during the early nineteenth century. Polka parties and competitions continue to flourish in Polish American communities to this very day. At the same time, as many early immigrant groups began to meet at social events, their dances became intermingled, leading to the creation of the American square dance. The square dance was a folk dance hybrid that became a primary recreational activity for settlers as they headed west during the nineteenth century. Still other dances originated in North America. One was the cakewalk, created in the nineteenth century by plantation slaves. The cakewalk combined a straight, firm body and a quasi-shuffling movement.

Through the end of the nineteenth century, ballroom and square dances were the most popular American dances. However, with the emergence of ragtime music in the 1890s came a new, less-formal style of dance, based more on freely moving one's body to the sound of the music. One dance employing this style was the one-step, so named because one quick walking step accompanied each beat of the music. The one-step generated other dance variations, including the turkey-trot, the grizzly bear, the bunny hug, and the Boston dip. The celebrated husband-and-wife dance team of Vernon (1887–1918) and Irene (1893–1969) Castle fashioned the one-step into the castle walk, which became popular across America. Another one-step offshoot was the two-step, which was danced to ragtime and, eventually, to swing music.

The most popular early twentieth-century dance, however, was the fox-trot, a one-step variation. The fox-trot became fashionable because it combined slow and quick steps, allowing for an increased diversity of dance-floor movement. With the Roaring Twenties, and America's distancing itself from the prudery (excessive attention to modesty or what is considered proper behavior) of the Victorian Era, came the popularity of the **Charleston** (see entry under 1920s—The Way We Lived in volume 2), an energetic dance distinguished by a twisting step. The Charleston is as much an artifact of 1920s American culture as **Prohibition** (the banning of alcohol; see entry under 1920s—The Way We Lived in volume 2) and speakeasies (places where alcohol was illegally sold). The Charleston, along with other dances of the period, including the shimmy and the black bottom, were variations of the fox-trot.

Then in the 1930s, swing music, which evolved from **jazz** (see entry under 1900s—Music in volume 1), came to the forefront of popular culture. At the time, America was a segregated society (one divided socially by race). Swing music was performed by dance-band orchestras (known as big bands) that were groundbreaking in that they occasionally brought together white and black musicians. Swing music is lively and danceable and, consequently, various dance crazes evolved during its popularity. The first was the lindy hop, an acrobatic dance that originated in Harlem during the late 1920s and was refined by dancers at Harlem's Savoy Ballroom. The jitterbug, an even more physically animated dance, grew out of the lindy hop, and was a favorite between the late 1930s and the end of World War II (1939–45). By the 1950s, the popularity of swing music had subsided, yet the jitterbug and its various offshoots still were embraced by teenagers, who danced them to the sounds of early **rock and roll** (see entry under 1950s—Music in volume 3), music that combined elements of **country music** and of **rhythm and blues** (see these entries under 1940s—Music in volume 3)

In the early 1960s, dancing in America was revolutionized by the twist. In 1960, singer Chubby Checker (1941–) recorded a song titled "The Twist," and a dance craze was born. In order to "do the twist," dancers stood in place and rotated shoulders and hips in opposite directions, often switching their weight from one foot to another. However, they did not touch. Before the twist, the act of dancing required a partner, whom you held in your arms while swaying across the dance floor or at least touched while twirling to the beat of the music. Such dancing was the basis for the expression, "It takes two to tango." However, the appeal of the twist signaled a major evolution in dancing. Because of the lack of physical contact, dancing became more of an individual pursuit. Countless 1960s and post-'60s dances were performed by standing in place and moving one's upper body and arms, but not necessarily the feet. Although dance partners maintained eye contact, they hardly touched. The limbo rock, the mashed potato, the watusi, the pony, and the Bristol stomp were a few post-twist dances that, like the twist, won popularity with the emergence of a hit record.

Other favored twentieth-century dances have been Afro-Latin-based. The first was the tango, which created a sensation in 1913 and remained popular off and on through the century. Other Afro-Latin dances include the rumba, the samba, the mambo, the cha-cha, and salsa. In the 1970s, the hustle and disco (the latter not only a dance but an attitude, as well as a style of music and dress) emerged from New York City dance clubs and won widespread popularity. ***Saturday Night Fever*** (1977; see entry under 1970s—Film and Theater in volume 4), a smash-hit movie starring John Travolta (1954–), helped to popularize **disco** (see entry under 1970s–Music in volume 4). The film and disco itself are as closely linked to late-1970s American culture as the Charleston is to the 1920s.

In the 1980s and 1990s, the fashionableness of **rap and hip hop** (see entry under 1980s–Music in volume 5) music, which originally came forth in opposition to the increasing commercialization of rock music, resulted in the creation of a new dance style, break dancing. In break dancing, solo dancers performed dazzling gymnastic routines that derived from a combination of martial arts and the character of Robot on *Soul Train* (1971–), an African American music-and-dance-oriented television show. Break dancing quickly became mainstream, however, and was spotlighted in another hit movie, *Flashdance* (1983).

As the twentieth century came to a close, hip-hop culture continued to generate break dancing variations. Then in the late 1990s, partner dancing and step-dancing enjoyed a revival with a renewed interest in **big band** (see entry under 1930s–Music in volume 2) music and swing dancing as well as in square dancing and line dancing.

–Rob Edelman

For More Information

Cohen, Selma Jeanne, ed. *International Encyclopedia of Dance*. New York: Oxford University Press, 1998.

Erenberg, Lewis A. *Swingin' the Dream: Big Band Jazz and the Rebirth of American Culture*. Chicago: University of Chicago Press, 1998.

Hager, Steven. *Hip Hop: The Illustrated History of Break Dancing, Rap Music, and Graffiti*. New York: St. Martin's Press, 1984.

Stearns, Marshall, and Jean Stearns. *Jazz Dance: The Story of American Vernacular Dance*. New York: Macmillan, 1968.

Stowe, David. *Swing Changes*. Cambridge, MA: Harvard University Press, 1994.

Electric Appliances

Perhaps nothing has changed everyday life within the American household so much as the invention of electric household appliances. Within the first few decades of the twentieth century, most homes in the United States gained access to electricity, and inventors created and improved many devices that used this new power. The aim of these new electric devices was to shorten the time and decrease the effort required to maintain the household.

Electric Appliances

Before the introduction of electricity and running water, household jobs such as cooking, cleaning, and laundry provided full-time work for the women and children of the family. Laundry required a full day of hauling water in washtubs, scrubbing clothes on ridged metal boards called washboards, and hanging clean clothes out to dry in the sun. Clothes were then ironed with heavy flatirons, which were heated on wood-burning stoves. Cooking, too, was a highly skilled and time-consuming operation, involving baking breads and cakes in wood-stove ovens, and canning and preserving foods for future use.

In 1879, Thomas A. Edison (1847–1931) invented the electric light bulb, and soon after he helped build the first electricity generating plant in New York City. As electricity began to find its way into American homes, inventors began to create new uses for it, and American consumers were ready to try the new inventions. In 1908, janitor James M. Spangler invented the first electric vacuum cleaner. By 1919, the Eureka Vacuum Company was producing two thousand vacuum machines per day. In 1913, the home **refrigerator** (see entry under 1910s—The Way We Lived in volume 1) was invented. By 1931, over one million refrigerators were manufactured and sold. Everyone wanted to own one of the new washing machines, invented in the 1920s, even though they had to be filled and emptied by hand and the clothes fed, piece by piece, into the wringer on top. The fully automatic washer was not developed until the 1940s. In the 1980s, electronic components such as microprocessors made electric appliances even "smarter," with programmable timers and more variety of features.

Although these new appliances changed the housewife's labor considerably, they did not necessarily decrease the amount of time she spent doing housework. In 1924, the average homemaker spent fifty-two hours a week doing housework, while in 1966, surrounded by laborsaving devices, she spent fifty-five hours per week. One reason for this is that, as appliances made cleaning easier, people began to expect more from those who kept the house. For example, whereas once laundry was done once a week and clothes worn several days before being laundered, modern housekeepers may do laundry every day because family members wear an item only once before washing it.

—Tina Gianoulis

For More Information

"American-Made: Turn of the Century Household Items." *American Heritage* (Vol. 31, June-July 1980): pp. 50–58.

National Academy of Engineering. "Household Appliances." *Greatest Engineering Achievements of the 20th Century.* http://www.greatachievements.org/greatachievements/ga_15_2.html (accessed January 10, 2002)

Shapiro, Laura. "Household Appliances: How Appliances Have Changed Housework." *Newsweek* (Vol. 130, no. 24, Winter 1997/98): pp. 36–40.

Strasser, Susan. *Never Done: A History of American Housework.* New York: Henry Holt, 2000.

Evangelism

Evangelism, or enthusiastic preaching of the Christian gospel, has always played an important role in U.S. Protestantism, as in the Great Awakening of colonial days or the Methodist camp meetings on the frontier in the nineteenth century. In the twentieth century, evangelism often took the form of elaborate crusades organized by such preachers as **Billy Sunday** (1862–1935; see entry under 1900s—The Way We Lived in volume 1), Oral Roberts (1918–), or Billy Graham (1918–), or, later, in the multimedia productions of "televangelists" like Pat Robertson (1930–) with his *700 Club,* Jim Bakker (1940–) and his wife, Tammy Faye Bakker (1942–), with their PTL Network, and Jerry Falwell (1933–) with his Moral Majority.

While all Christians, including mainstream Protestants, Roman Catholics, and Orthodox believers, affirm baptism as a prerequisite for church membership, many evangelicals demand a "born-again" experience in which an already baptized Christian undergoes a personal experience with Jesus Christ. To these believers, evangelism involves more than just bringing information about Christ and his teachings; it demands an ongoing process of keeping believers enthusiastic about their faith. Evangelical crusades in large stadiums or on television are viewed by their organizers as revival meetings, designed to give already baptized Christians a chance to reaffirm their faith and be reassured about their salvation

As U.S. society became more urbanized and educated during the twentieth century, some religious leaders feared that it was becoming secularized as well, a phenomenon in which religious values lose their power to influence individuals and the culture at large. This motivated evangelists such as Sunday and Graham to organize tent meetings or crusades that moved from city to city with elaborate programs that included choirs and music, fellowship, personal counseling, and an "altar call" in which people were asked to come forward to reaffirm their faith publicly. The centerpiece of these crusades was always a rousing sermon preached with grand oratorical flourishes, often warning of hellfire and damnation, but also describing the joys of heavenly bliss.

Over the years, critics often charged that evangelism in its worst aspects bred a corrupt system that exploited sincere believers for money or power, as described by Sinclair Lewis (1885–1951) in his 1927 novel *Elmer Gantry.* In more recent years, revelations of sexual and financial misdeeds by some television evangelists have confirmed these suspicions. Among U.S. evangelists of the twentieth century, Billy Graham, consulted by U.S. presidents for spiritual advice, remains evangelism's most prominent role model of moral and intellectual integrity.

—Edward Moran

For More Information

Ahlstrom, Sidney. *A Religious History of the American People.* New Haven, CT: Yale University Press, 1972.

Bruns, Roger. *Preacher: Billy Sunday and Big Time American Evangelism.* New York: W. W. Norton, 1992.

Hardman, Keith. *Seasons of Refreshing: Evangelism and Revivals in America.* Grand Rapids, MI: Baker Books, 1994.

Ferris Wheel

Long a popular ride at state fairs and **amusement parks** (see entry under 1950s—The Way We Lived in volume 3), the Ferris wheel is a tall, upright wheel with seats suspended around its rim. Mounted on a fixed structure, the wheel rotates while the swingable seats remain basically parallel to the ground, allowing riders to enjoy panoramic views of the surrounding area. During the twentieth century, Ferris wheels dominated the midways at amusement parks and state fairs in small towns and rural areas throughout the United States as riders sought rare bird's-eye views of the surrounding landscape.

The Ferris wheel is named for U.S. engineer George Washington Gale Ferris (1859–1896), who had installed the first ride

at Chicago's Columbian Exposition in 1893. It was 250 feet high and weighed 4,800 tons. Its axis (the shaft around which the wheel spun) was the largest single piece of forged steel that had been made up to that time. Two 1,000-horsepower engines powered the wheel, which had thirty-six wooden cars capable of holding sixty people apiece, each of whom paid fifty cents for one ride. The device, which symbolized American engineering ingenuity, has been described as "Chicago's answer to the Eiffel Tower," a much taller structure that had been the focal point of the Paris Exposition of 1889. The Chicago Ferris wheel

The Ferris wheel is a mainstay at almost every amusement park and state and local fair. *Archive Photos. Reproduced by permission.*

was moved to St. Louis, Missouri, for the 1904 exposition there, and was finally scrapped in 1906.

Since that time, Ferris wheel builders have competed to build the biggest and best Ferris wheel. The record so far goes to the "London Eye," a 1,900-ton structure that took riders on a 30-minute "flight" 450 feet above the River Thames in 32 enclosed "capsules" when it was built in 2000. As long as people enjoy the thrill of looking at the world from high above, there are sure to be Ferris wheels.

—Edward Moran

For More Information

Anderson, Norman D., and Walter R. Brown. *Ferris Wheels: An Illustrated History.* New York: Pantheon Books, 1983.

British Airways London Eye. http://www.british-airways.com/londoneye (accessed January 10, 2002).

The Ferris Wheel. http://users.vnet.net/schulman/Columbian/ferris.html (accessed January 10, 2002).

General Motors

General Motors (GM) was founded by Billy Durant (1861–1947) in 1908 with his merger of the Oldsmobile and Buick companies. He added Cadillac the next year and the company just kept on growing. GM was the first company to gross more than $1 billion in a year. It dominated the U.S. and world car markets for most of the twentieth century, while its management structure had a major influence on the way large corporations are run. Ford brought no-nonsense motoring to the masses, but GM made the automobile an international symbol of modern America. From finned Cadillacs to the iconic 1957 Chevy, from unwieldy muscle cars to **sport utility vehicles** (SUVs; see entry under 1980s—The Way We Lived in volume 5), GM has built many of the definitive American cars.

Unlike Henry Ford (1863–1947), whose skill was in manufacturing, Durant was brilliant at striking deals. He started out with car manufacturers but added component suppliers so that he could control every aspect of the business. After Alfred Sloan (1875–1966) took over in 1920, GM's cars became statements about a person's social status, tastes, and desires. The Chevy was a cheap first car; then you worked your way up through

A 1903 Cadillac from General Motors. *American Automobile Association. Reproduced by permission.*

Buick and Oldsmobile. A Cadillac was something to dream about. Until 1961, when television ads took over, road shows called "Motoramas" moved around the country selling GM cars and creating a "car culture." GM updated its models every year. They became more "space-age" and more powerful. But GM has sometimes gone too far in trying to sell its products. In 1949, along with several others, GM was convicted of criminal conspiracy to replace electric trams with GM buses in forty-five American cities.

The attack by consumer advocate Ralph Nader (1934–) on the unsafe Corvair in the 1960s began GM's slow decline. Emissions regulations, oil crises, and stiff competition all took their toll on GM's gas-guzzling model range. A sharply comic film *Roger and Me* (1989) by Michael Moore (c. 1954–) highlights the terrible human cost of GM's failure in the 1980s. But like many large corporations, in the 1990s GM began to revive. With interests in companies around the globe, in the twenty-first century GM remains one of the world's largest and most powerful auto manufacturers.

—Chris Routledge

For More Information

General Motors. http://www.gm.com (accessed January 10, 2002).
Madsen, Axel. *The Deal Maker: How William C. Durant Made General Motors*. New York: John Wiley and Sons, 1999.
Nader, Ralph, and Barbarah Ehrenreich. *The Ralph Nader Reader*. New York: Seven Stories Press, 2000.
Sloan, Alfred P. *My Years with General Motors*. New York: Doubleday, 1996.

Hairstyles

The way that human beings wear their hair can have many meanings. Beyond conforming to the fashion of the day, a hairdo can be an expression of personal style as well as an expression of religious, cultural, and political beliefs. Because of this, society often has strict rules about how hair should be worn. Those who rebel against society often begin with what are considered outlandish hairstyles. It is no accident that institutions like armies and prisons often initiate new members by cutting off their hair, thus removing this means of individual self-expression and encouraging conformity. From the Biblical story of Samson, who lost his superhuman strength when his hair was cut, to the radical student movements of the 1970s, when men's long hair was considered a revolutionary statement, hair has often been given a far greater significance than any other bodily feature.

Preoccupation with the latest hairstyle is far from being only a modern concern. From earliest times, people have adorned their hair in a wide variety of ways for a wide variety of reasons. Hairstyle can indicate economic class and social status. For example, in the second century B.C.E., members of Egyptian nobility shaved their heads and wore wigs made from braided animal hair or palm fronds, often dyed in bright colors. Noblewomen in eighteenth-century England wore powdered wigs that were up to four feet tall and elaborately decorated with stuffed birds and bowls of fruit. Hairstyles can also be practical. Like many modern men, Louis XIV (1638–1715) of France wore his large curled wig in the 1700s to hide his baldness.

The significance of hairstyles has changed through the ages. Short hair was considered a sign of power in ancient Rome, but by the middle ages, short hair had become a symbol of dishonor. In 1644, when the Manchus conquered China, they forced Chinese men to shave the tops of their heads and wear their hair in a long braid at the back, as a sign of being a conquered people. By the 1900s, when the Manchus were ousted from power, the pigtail had become a symbol of Chinese cultural identity. Chinese men kept the pigtail even when they emigrated, and Chinese immigrants to the United States were often persecuted for wearing it.

In the United States, until the beginning of the twentieth century, most women wore their hair long and pinned up on their heads. With the suffrage movement of the early 1900s came the **flapper** (see entry under 1920s–Fashion in volume 2) style, and short, "bobbed" hair became the modern hairdo. Because caring for long hair is time consuming and identified with soft femininity, short hair has often become popular when women have been politically active. Although longer hair soon became popular again, and American soldiers during World War II (1939–45) sighed over pinups of actress Rita Hayworth (1918–1987) and her long, flowing curls, the working women of the 1940s wore shorter, practical styles. The 1950s returned women to the home, and hairstyles became more elaborate. Women wore curls held stiffly in place by permanents or hair spray or tall beehives so rigidly perfect that rumors abounded that nests of mice or bees lived inside. There was a rebellious side to the 1950s, however, and while clean-cut American boys wore crewcuts, the rebel in the leather jacket no doubt sported a greased-back duck tail.

Soon, rebellion became revolution. From the **beatniks** (see entry under 1950s–Print Culture in volume 3) of the early 1960s to the **hippies** (see entry under 1960s–The Way We Lived in volume 4) of the late 1960s and 1970s, young people began to question society's values. Both men and women, especially those who identified with political movements for peace and justice, began to wear their hair long. At the same time, black Americans began to fight for **civil rights** (see entry under 1960s–The Way We Lived in volume 4) and an end to discrimination. Black people, who for decades had felt compelled to force their hair into styles meant for white European hair, began to let their hair grow naturally into a fluffy style they called an Afro. The Broadway musical ***Hair*** (see entry under 1960s–Film and Theater in volume 4), which debuted in 1968, made the connection between hairstyle and the challenges of an entire generation. This connection continued into the 1980s with the rise of the **punk** (see entry under 1970s–Music in volume 4) movement. Perhaps because the hippies of the 1960s had failed to revolutionize society, punks were less idealistic and angrier than the hippies had been, and their style was more extreme. Punks shaved parts of their hair off and dyed the rest in bright, unnatural reds, blues, and purples, using gel to shape it into spikes. The extreme style of the punks opened the door to a new freedom. While most people never attempted the punk look, hair fashions have continued to remain less rigid and more open to individual expression.

The importance of hair fashion has been dramatized in various films and plays, from the serious to the campy. The 1975 film *Shampoo,* directed by Hal Ashby (1936–1988), spoofs pretentious celebrity hair stylists. *Hairspray* (1988) by John Waters (1946–) humorously explores the often uncomfortable transition between the conservative 1950s and the radical 1960s. In the 1989 tearjerker *Steel Magnolias,* by Herbert Ross (1927–2001), Dolly Parton (1946–) plays the owner of a Southern beauty parlor, a time-honored institution of female bonding. In *Blow Dry* (2000), director Paddy Breathnach (1964–) documents the hilarious troubles of a Scottish hair-stylists competition.

—Tina Gianoulis

For More Information

Coates, Simon. "Scissors or Swords: Social Aspects of Medieval Hairstyles." *History Today* (Vol. 49, no. 5, May 1999): pp. 7-15.

"How Important Are Hairstyles in the Workplace?" *Jet* (Vol. 99, no. 26, June 11, 2001): pp. 36-9.

Lassieur, Allison. "Hair Time Line: Evolution of Hair Designs." *National Geographic World* (No. 278, October 1998): pp. 12-16.

Punke, Harold H. *Social Implications of Lawsuits over Student Hairstyles.* Danville, IL: Interstate Publishers, 1973.

Wilkinson, Brian. "Growing Dissent: The Politics of Hair." *Seventeen* (Vol. 49, no. 5, May 1990): pp. 98-100.

Postcards

The picture postcard, with a graphic image on one side and a blank space for a message and an address on the other, made its debut in the late nineteenth century. Before **telephones** (see entry under 1900s—The Way We Lived in volume 1) were in widespread use, the postcard provided a quick and inexpensive way of sending short messages, either for business or social purposes. For more than one hundred years, vacationers have typically mailed postcards of scenes from faraway destinations to impress the "folks back home," often accompanied with clichéd messages like "Having a wonderful time. Wish you were here." Another familiar phrase, "pretty as a postcard," has been used to describe a setting that is pretty enough to be featured on a postcard. Businesses have long used postcards for advertising purposes, and musicians or record labels commonly use them to promote new recordings or club appearances. Over the years, some artists and graphic designers have produced higher-quality images that are especially in demand by deltiologists, more commonly known as postcard collectors.

The government-issue "postcards" sold in post offices, with a stamp already printed on the address side and a blank side for a message, are technically known as "postal cards." Austria-Hungary issued the first one in 1869. It was not until 1898 that the United States permitted "private mailing cards" that could have an image on one side, with the other side reserved for the stamp and the address. Messages on such cards had to be written atop the picture until 1907, when the U.S. Post Office permitted the blank side to be divided into two sections: the left side for a message and the right side for the address and the stamp. This format is still the most commonly used.

Picture postcards were enormously popular during the first two decades of the twentieth century. It has been estimated that nearly a billion of them were produced in the United States during this period. Picture postcards offer a visual overview of U.S. popular culture and a graphic archive of the institutions and tourist locations considered important in their day.

–Edward Moran

For More Information

Carline, Richard. *Pictures in the Post: The Story of the Picture Postcard and its Place in the History of Popular Art.* Philadelphia: Deltiologists of America, 1972.

Klamkin, Marian. *Picture Postcards.* New York: Dodd, Mead and Co., 1974.

Morgan, Hal, and Andreas Brown. *Prairie Fires and Paper Moons: The American Photographic Postcard, 1900–1920.* Boston: David R. Godine, 1981.

Ryan, Dorothy. *Picture Postcards in the United States, 1893–1918.* New York: Clarkson N. Potter, 1982.

Roller Coasters

Travelling at speeds of up to one hundred miles per hour, hundreds of feet up in the air, roller coasters are the most thrilling of all amusement rides. Whether strapped into a miniature "train," dangling chairlift style, or even standing up, roller coaster fans enjoy the sensation of not being in control. Besides being built for the enjoyment of enthusiasts, roller coasters are also objects of local pride. The famous wooden Coney Island Cyclone was a New York City landmark in the early twentieth century. In the 1920s, boardwalk roller coasters helped publicize beach resorts. In the twenty-first century, roller coasters are the centerpieces of all big amusement parks.

However intricate the twists, turns, and loops of the track might be, roller coasters are really very simple. The cars carry enough energy from the first big downhill to take them through the rest of the course. In the twenty-first century, the cars are often launched from the start, rather than climbing a slope, but the principle is the same. With names like Cyclone, Fireball, Superman, and The Big One, roller-coaster design in the twenty-first century is a fusion of high-tech construction, computer control, and big talk. But no modern roller coaster can match the scale or speed of the first American roller coaster. Built to carry coal from the mines in the Pennsylvania mountains, the Mauch Chunk Switchback Railway became a tourist attraction in 1870 and operated safely until 1933. Passengers paid one dollar for the scenic twenty-mile ride up the mountain, where they could eat lunch at a hotel near the summit. On the terrifying return trip, the cars are reputed to have reached speeds of over one hundred miles an hour.

Although rickety wooden roller coasters are still in operation, steel roller coasters, pioneered by **Disney** (see entry under 1920s—Film and Theater in volume 2) in the 1950s, are the most common coasters today. They make possible "corkscrews," loops, and unsettling "inversions." Roller coasters will always be dangerous, because people misbehave or because they react badly to "negative Gs" (the feeling of weightlessness). Designers have pushed at the limits of safety, and mechanical failures occasionally happen. But part of the enjoyment of riding a "coaster" is being afraid while feeling just safe enough.

—Chris Routledge

Roller coasters thrill and terrify thousands of riders each year. *Archive Photos. Reproduced by permission.*

For More Information

Cartmell, Robert. *The Incredible Scream Machine.* Bowling Green, OH: Bowling Green State University Popular Press, 1987.

RCDB: Roller Coaster Database. http://www.rcdb.com/ (accessed January 10, 2002).

Rutherford, Scott. *The American Roller Coaster.* Osceola, WI: Motorbooks International, 2000.

Billy Sunday (1862–1935)

Billy Sunday was an early forerunner of the contemporary religious right. The most famous traveling **evangelist** (see entry on Evangelism under 1900s–The Way We Lived in volume 1) of his day, Sunday crusaded across the nation with performances that united fundamentalist religious teaching and conservative politics with good old-fashioned showmanship.

In his early career, Sunday was a womanizing professional baseball player who liked to drink and fight. But after hearing the services of an evangelistic group from the Pacific Garden Mission in Chicago, Illinois, in 1886, Sunday was soon converted. He gave up drinking, swearing, and womanizing and began offering inspirational talks to his young fans.

Sunday left baseball in 1891 and began a touring ministry four years later. Advance men promoted his appearances as if they were **vaudeville** (see entry under 1900s–Film and Theater in volume 1) shows. Musical entertainment was furnished by choirs and bands. Sunday—the star of the show—combined dramatic gestures and colorful language to preach against sin and for the need to right oneself with God. His preaching produced hundreds of thousands of converts. A staunch right-winger, he also brought politics into religion, advocating the outlawing of alcoholic beverages and the banning of teaching evolution in schools.

—Rob Edelman

For More Information

Bruns, Roger. *Preacher: Billy Sunday and Big Time American Evangelism.* New York: W. W. Norton, 1992.

Dorsett, Lyle W. *Billy Sunday and the Redemption of Urban America.* Grand Rapids: Eerdmans, 1991.

Alexander Graham Bell (seated) tests the newly invented telephone. *Courtesy of the U.S. National Aeronautics and Space Administration.*

Telephone

Although there are others who claim to have done so first, the telephone was invented in 1875 by a Scot, Alexander Graham Bell (1847–1922). His invention enabled people to talk to one another across vast distances. Within twenty years, telephones were widespread in the homes of the wealthy in the United States and in Europe. The laying of the first transatlantic telephone cable in 1956 began to create what is known as the "global village." In the twenty-first century, the principles of telephony invented by Bell are behind innovations such as fax machines and the **Internet** (see entry under 1990s—The Way We Lived in volume 5). Although telephone messages are now transmitted using satellites and digital signals, the telephone of the twenty-first century remains much as Bell anticipated.

Like many other things, the telephone was invented partly by accident. In the 1870s, the telegraph was the quickest way of sending messages over a long distance. But Bell hoped to speed up the system by making it possible to send more than one message at a time. He created a device that could convert sounds into electrical pulses and transmit them down a wire. From there, it was a short step to developing a machine that could carry the human voice. He was issued patent number 174465 on March 7, 1876. Soon after, he made the first telephone call, commanding his assistant Thomas Augustus Watson (1854–1934), who was in the next room: "Mr. Watson, come here! I want you!"

Bell's invention transformed the way people thought about distance, travel, and their communities. The telephone opened the way for long-distance gossip in a way that was impossible by telegraph, the older method of sending messages, yet in many ways the changes brought by the telephone were subtle and gradual. For a start, it did not change much in the way of the physical environment. The device itself was always quite small, stuck out of the way in hallways and booths. Where the telephone had its greatest impact was on the structure of society itself. As home telephones became more affordable in the 1920s and 1930s, people began using them as part of their social lives. For some commentators, this marked the beginning of a trend towards people becoming more private and self-centered. For others, however, the telephone simply freed people from having to travel to deliver simple messages. Either way, the telephone changed the way people lived their lives.

The telephone led to the growth of a whole range of services never before available. Police and firefighters could be called by the public from special telephone boxes on the street. (As more and more people acquired telephones, this practice was replaced beginning in the 1960s by the 911 system of alerting emergency services.) Telephone companies began to offer "wake-up" calls and messaging services. "Cold calling," whereby a salesperson uses the phone book to find new customers, became a useful but hated way to find new business. The arts and the media also felt the effect. The TV or radio phone-in became a cheap way for broadcasters to fill airtime. The plots of **detective fiction** (see entry under 1930s–Print Culture in volume 2) of the 1930s and 1940s often turn on a well-timed telephone call. Comedy routines from the early days of film include telephone jokes. Even in the twenty-first century, the telephone is a source of humor in shows from ***Frasier*** (see entry under 1990s–TV and Radio in volume 5) to ***The Simpsons*** (see entry under 1980s–TV and Radio in volume 5).

By the 1930s, most households in America at least had access to a telephone. People could be contacted more easily, and they in turn could make contact with the outside world. The trend continued throughout the twentieth century and into the twenty-first. By the 1980s, documents could be transmitted by fax while **personal computers** (see entry under 1970s—The Way We Lived in volume 4) "talked" to one another using modems that connected to telephone lines. Car telephones were available in the 1960s, but it was in the 1990s that hand-held mobile telephones became cheap enough for most people to own. They even became a fashion item. By the beginning of the twenty-first century, the video telephone had moved out of science fiction and into offices and some homes. **Cellular phones** (see entry under 1990s—The Way We Lived in volume 5), **satellite** (see entry under 1950s—The Way We Lived in volume 3) links, and the Internet meant that in 2002 there were few places on earth where one could not be reached by telephone.

Voicemail, answering machines, automated information services, and a host of other systems have made the telephone the most powerful communication tool of the early twenty-first century. But perhaps the best measure of the telephone's importance is that it is taken for granted. Telephones work behind the scenes so that in 2002, more than half of all telephone calls take place between machines, with no human intervention. In the twenty-first century, not having access to a telephone is a serious form of deprivation, and the multibillion-dollar telecommunications industry is fundamental to the world economy. Whether for medical emergencies, high-powered business deals, or ordering **pizza** (see entry under 1940s—Food and Drink in volume 3), the telephone remains an essential part of twenty-first century life.

—Chris Routledge

For More Information

Fischer, Claude S. *America Calling: A Social History of the Telephone to 1940.* Berkeley: University of California Press, 1992.

Gearhart, Sarah. *The Telephone.* New York: Atheneum Books for Young Readers, 1999.

Holland, Gini. *Telephones.* New York: Benchmark Books, 1996.

Oxlade, Chris. *Telecommunications.* Austin, TX: Raintree Steck-Vaughn, 1997.

Stern, Ellen, and Emily Gwathmey. *Once Upon a Telephone: An Illustrated Social History.* New York: Harcourt Brace, 1994.

World's Fairs

During the nineteenth and twentieth centuries, a series of international exhibitions in major cities around the globe attracted millions of visitors to national and corporate pavilions that demonstrated their industrial and cultural achievements. Many products now in common use were first seen by the general public at world's fairs, such as the **telephone** (see entry under 1900s—The Way We Lived in volume 1), in Philadelphia, Pennsylvania (1876); the **phonograph** (see entry under 1900s—Music in volume 1), in Paris, France (1889); incandescent lights and the **Ferris wheel** (see entry under 1900s—The Way We Lived in volume 1), in Chicago, Illinois (1893); the **ice-cream cone** (see entry under 1900s—Food and Drink in volume 1), in St. Louis, Missouri (1904); **television** (see entry under 1940s—TV and Radio in volume 3), in New York (1939); and the **IBM** (see entry under 1980s—Commerce in volume 5) computer, in New York (1964).

The first modern world's fair was London's Crystal Palace Exhibition of 1851, organized under the leadership of Prince Albert (1819–1861). The first in the United States was Philadelphia's Centennial Exposition of 1876, which commemorated the one hundredth anniversary of national independence. Chicago's Columbian Exposition of 1893 marked the rebirth of the city after the fire of 1871; it was famous for its "White City" that inspired the City Beautiful movement in architecture and city planning. In 1933, Chicago's Century of Progress fair celebrated the city's centennial. The 1958 Brussels World's Fair celebrated Europe's revival after World War II (1939–45).

With its "World of Tomorrow" theme, the New York's World's Fair that opened in 1939 offered an optimistic view of the future to Depression-weary visitors. The Futurama exhibit of **General Motors** (see entry under 1900s—The Way We Lived in volume 1) imagined the United States as it might appear in 1960, complete with television, an elaborate **highway system** (see entry under 1950s—The Way We Lived in volume 3), high-rise urban centers, **suburbs** (see entry under 1950s—The Way We Lived in volume 3), and modern farms. The fair's symbols were the Trylon and Perisphere, an obelisk next to a sphere that included a prototypical utopian city called "Democracity." Unlike earlier fairs, the New York World's Fair of 1964 had few national pavilions, with most of the exhibits instead constructed by U.S. corporations to promote their products and images.

World's fairs in the later twentieth century had far less of an impact on the general public, for whom television, the **Internet** (see entry under 1990s—The Way We Lived in volume 5), and theme parks provided much of the information and entertainment once offered by international expositions.

—Edward Moran

For More Information

Allwood, John. *The Great Exhibitions.* New York: Studio Vista, 1978.

Badger, Reid. *The Great American Fair: The World's Columbia Exposition and American Culture.* Chicago: Nelson-Hall, 1979.

Findling, John E. *Chicago's Great World's Fairs.* Manchester, England: Manchester University Press, 1994.

Harrison, Helen. *Dawn of a New Day: The New York World's Fair, 1939/40.* New York: New York University Press, 1980.

1910s

A Tumultuous Decade

The 1910s were a decade of great tumult and change in the United States. The decade began at a time of peace and prosperity. America found itself the richest nation in the world, thanks largely to the growth of huge companies that sold goods all over the world. The president, William Howard Taft (1857–1930), had succeeded Theodore Roosevelt (1858–1919) as the leader of the Republican Party, which offered its support to American businesses. Many Americans enjoyed improved living standards, as more people owned cars and used electricity in their homes with every passing year.

Great disruptions soon came in politics, international affairs, and the economy, however. In the presidential elections of 1912, Roosevelt left the Republican Party to become the nominee of the Progressive Party, the first serious challenger to the two-party system in many years. He and Socialist Party candidate Eugene V. Debs (1855–1926) helped steal votes from Taft, which in turn led to the election of Democratic candidate Woodrow Wilson (1856–1924), a champion of progressive political reforms. Wilson led government efforts to reform the federal banking system, regulate large businesses, provide aid to farmers, and enact a progressive income tax (which meant higher tax rates for those who earned more). During the decade, four constitutional amendments were also adopted, calling for direct election of U.S. senators, the progressive income tax, the right

1910s At a Glance

What We Said:

Slang was still a decade away from being a prominent part of popular culture. One slogan did, however, enter the American lexicon:

"When It Rains It Pours" (1911): This advertising slogan let consumers know that Morton salt would not clump up and stick together, but it was made popular in a different way. The expression came to mean that once something happens, it may set in motion a string of unstoppable events.

What We Read:

***The Rosary* (1909):** The best-selling novel of 1910, this sentimental romance was written by an English woman named Florence Barclay. The novel was translated into eight languages and had sold over a million copies by 1921.

Books by Theodore Dreiser: Dreiser became the dominant American realist writer with several books published during the decade: *Jennie Gerhardt* (1911), *Sister Carrie* (1911 [first published in 1900 but suppressed by the publisher]), *The Financier* (1912), *The Titan* (1914), and *The "Genius"* (1915).

***O Pioneers!* (1913) and *My Antonia* (1918):** Author Willa Cather gained fame for her portrayals of people trying to survive in the harsh settings of the American prairie.

***Over the Top* (1917):** Written by Arthur Guy Empey, who served with the British army in the trenches on the Western Front, this war book introduced Americans to the horrors of World War I in Europe.

***The Rise of David Levinsky* (1917):** Abraham Cahan's story told of a Jewish immigrant's experience breaking into the world of business in New York City.

***The U.P. Trail* (1918):** Written by one of the most popular writers of the decade, Zane Grey, this Western tells the story of the creation of the transcontinental railroad. Grey also published such favorites as *Riders of the Purple Sage* (1912), *The Lone Star Ranger: A Romance of the Border* (1915), and *The Desert of Wheat* (1919).

Magazines: *Saturday Evening Post, Collier's Weekly, Cosmopolitan,* and *American Magazine* were among the most popular magazines of the decade.

What We Watched:

Vaudeville shows and **musical revues:** These forms of entertainment, which began in the 1900s, continued their popularity into the 1910s, despite the rise of movies. The annual *Ziegfeld Follies*—with its stage full of chorus girls—was one of the biggest draws in New York, while traveling vaudeville shows brought variety to American cities large and small.

***Queen Elizabeth* (1913):** The first four-reel (60 minute) film, starring Sarah Bernhardt, allowed moviemakers to tell a full-length dramatic story.

to vote for women, and Prohibition (a ban on the sale of alcoholic beverages).

American foreign policy, which had long been concerned with having the United States avoid "entanglement" in foreign conflicts, also changed dramatically during the decade. In 1914, most of Europe became involved in World War I (1914–18), a terrible conflict that would claim nearly nine million lives. The United States tried to stay neutral, for it had economic ties to

1910s At a Glance (continued)

***The Adventures of Kathlyn* (1913):** The first in a thirteen-part serial—a series of movies about one character or set of characters—starred Kathlyn Williams, who was billed as "The Girl without Fear." The most popular serial of the decade was *The Perils of Pauline,* which was released in biweekly installments in 1914.

***Quo Vadis* (1913):** The first eight-reel (two-hour) film, made in Italy, was shown in the United States.

***Gertie the Dinosaur* (1914):** This animated silent film featuring a female dinosaur, created by comic strip artist Winsor McCay, is considered the forerunner to modern animated films, including Walt Disney's *Steamboat Willie* (1929).

***Tillie's Punctured Romance* (1914):** Directed by Mack Sennett, known as the father of film comedy, this six-reel comedy was one of the most popular films starring the Keystone Kops, a group of inept policeman. It starred stage actress Marie Dressler and had Charlie Chaplin and Mabel Normand in supporting roles.

***The Birth of a Nation* (1915):** The decade's most controversial film, directed by D. W. Griffith, tells the story of the American Civil War and Reconstruction, and presents favorable depictions of the racist group the Ku Klux Klan. The film caused great controversy and was banned from many theaters.

***Intolerance* (1916):** Directed by D. W. Griffith, this film is considered the first great American epic. Over three-and-one-half hours long and with a huge cast, the story tells of the impact of historical events on ordinary people.

Western films directed by Thomas Ince: His action-packed movies about cowboys and villains on the frontier included *War on the Plains* (1912), *Custer's Last Raid* (1912), *The Bargain* (1914), *Hell's Hinges* (1916), and *The Gun Fighter* (1917).

Movies about World War I: Moviegoers enjoyed such films as *War Is Hell* (1914), *The War Bride's Secret* (1916), *The Fall of a Nation* (1916), *The Little American* (1917)—directed by Cecil B. DeMille and starring Mary Pickford—and *The Kaiser, Beast of Berlin* (1918).

What We Listened To:

John Philip Sousa: The famed bandmaster toured the world with his one-hundred-piece marching band in 1910.

Tin Pan Alley music: Professional sheet music companies located in New York City's Tin Pan Alley produced some of the decade's most popular music, including Irving Berlin's "Alexander's Ragtime Band" (1911), George M. Cohan's war-themed "Over There" (1917), Richard Whiting's "Till We Meet Again" (1917), and George Gershwin's "Swanee" (1919).

The Victrola: The Victor Talking Machine Company modified Thomas Edison's phonograph into the Victrola in 1915, which soon became the most popular American record player. The first Victrola, with its large, trumpet-like megaphone, is quite expensive,

countries on both sides of the fight. But German attacks on U.S. shipping and the United States' historic friendship with England and France drew the Americans into the war against Germany in 1917. Two million American soldiers served overseas and one hundred thousand died, half of them from disease. Although President Wilson hoped that American involvement in the war would "make the world safe for democracy" and lead to more American engagement overseas, senators in Congress refused to ratify Wilson's peace treaty.

1910s
At a Glance (continued)

however, and does not gain wide popularity until the 1920s.

The Dixieland Jazz Band: This ensemble toured the United States in 1916 and became the first musicians to make a jazz recording in 1917.

War-influenced music: In 1918, World War I influenced popular music, producing such songs as "Would You Rather Be a Colonel with an Eagle on Your Shoulder or a Private with a Chicken on Your Knee?," "I'd Like to See the Kaiser with a Lily in His Hand," and "General Pershing Will Cross the Rhine."

"Oh, How I Hate to Get Up in the Morning": Irving Berlin's song was one of the most popular songs of 1919.

African American musical groups: Several toured the country, introducing Americans to new musical styles that would become jazz and the blues. These groups included the Superior Orchestra, the Onward Brass Band, Ma Rainey's Georgia Jazz Band, and a band led by Jelly Roll Morton.

Who We Knew:

John Dewey (1859–1952): This American philosopher, educator, and psychologist is widely credited for shaping the school system that continues to educate American children today. Dewey believed that American democracy would work best if all students were given an education that balanced academic learning and vocational training. His book *Democracy and Education* (1916) is still hailed as a guide to educating students to contribute to a democratic society.

William C. "Billy" Durant (1861–1947): Billy Durant emerged as one of the best-known businessmen of the decade thanks to his ambitious leadership of the car manufacturer General Motors, for a time the world's largest industrial company. Durant formed General Motors in 1908, and by 1910 the growing company had swallowed up thirty smaller companies, including eleven automakers. After losing control of the company in 1911, Durant regained control in 1915 and rebuilt the company to become an industry leader by 1919, when it was valued at $1 billion. Durant was known as a great innovator in the automobile industry.

Marcus Garvey (1877–1940): An important black leader during the 1910s and 1920s, Marcus Garvey was born in Jamaica and traveled widely before arriving in America in 1916. With the influence of black leaders Booker T. Washington and W. E. B. DuBois fading, Garvey encouraged African Americans to join together to build businesses or, if whites would not accept them, leave the country in a "Back to Africa" movement. Garvey formed the Universal Negro Improvement Association and published a leading African American weekly paper, the *Negro World*. Though Garvey's plans

The war highlighted some of the economic and racial issues facing the country. American businesses were growing increasingly dependent on foreign trade (selling goods to foreign countries). War had threatened foreign trade, and some said that war was fought to keep foreign markets open to American business. American workers, especially those in labor unions, continued to fight for improved wages and working conditions, though strikes ended once America entered World War I. With many workers leaving to join the armed forces, black workers gained access to many jobs they had been barred from before.

910s
At a Glance (continued)

aw little success, he was later hailed by black eader Malcolm X as a visionary.

. C. Handy (1873–1958): Known as the "Father of e Blues," this African American musician toured ith a minstrel show before deciding to specialize a new form of music known as the blues. In 1912, andy published his first song, "Memphis Blues," nd he followed that in 1914 with "St. Louis Blues," e most recorded song in musical history. Handy ecame the first black performer to play in New ork's Carnegie Hall in 1928.

hoeless Joe Jackson (1887–1951): One of the ost tragic figures in the history of baseball, Jackon rose from humble beginnings in the rural outh to become one of baseball's greatest hitters hile playing for the Cleveland Indians and the hicago White Sox. Only Babe Ruth was thought to e a better hitter. But Jackson's reputation was forver ruined when he was implicated in the "Black ox Scandal" in which eight Chicago White Sox layers were paid to lose the 1919 World Series.

ary Pickford (1892–1979): This popular actress, nown as "America's Sweetheart," starred in such ms as *The Poor Little Rich Girl* (1917) and *ebecca of Sunnybrook Farm* (1917). The first merican actress to achieve international stardom, e was mobbed by fans at public appearances and signed a $1 million contract in 1916. Along with husband Douglas Fairbanks, D. W. Griffith, and Charlie Chaplin, Pickford established the United Artists movie company.

Margaret Sanger (1879–1966): An outspoken proponent of the rights of women, Margaret Higgins Sanger was kept from becoming a doctor because of her gender, but she went on to become a pioneer in birth control practices for women. As a nurse, Sanger was alarmed at how many women saw their health and welfare endangered by their failure to avoid unwanted pregnancies. In the 1910s, she lectured widely about sexual practices, published a magazine called *The Woman Rebel,* and opened the nation's first birth-control clinic in 1916. She founded the National Birth Control League in 1914 and later was involved in creating the Planned Parenthood Foundation of America. By the 1950s, Sanger was involved in the development of the first birth control pill.

Jim Thorpe (1888–1953): Frequently named as one of the greatest athletes of all time, Native American Jim Thorpe played a variety of sports in his long career. He first came to fame as a college football player at Carlisle University. In 1912, he set a world record in the decathlon at the Summer Olympic Games in Stockholm, Sweden. Thorpe then played professional baseball for the New York Giants, the Cincinnati Reds, and the Boston Braves, and professional football for the Canton Bulldogs and the New York Giants.

The existence of jobs in wartime industries in the North called forth a "great migration" of blacks from the South.

Once the war ended, labor unrest grew. In 1919, hundreds of thousands of American workers walked off their jobs in steel, coal mining, and other industries. Police went on strike in Boston, Massachusetts, and there was a general strike of all workers in Seattle, Washington. Black workers were outraged at being thrown out of jobs they had recently gained. This wave of strikes and protests scared businessmen and politicians. Police cracked down on strikers, causing riots in several cities.

In what was known as the Red Scare of 1919, thousands of people were arrested and hundreds deported in a crackdown on people thought to be Communists, Socialists, or other radicals. The decade closed in a flurry of riots, arrests, and hysteria.

The 1910s saw a real flowering of popular culture in a number of areas. The most notable development in arts and entertainment was the development of the movie industry. Many Americans still saw short films in nickelodeons (cheap storefront theaters), but the movie industry was changing dramatically. Movies were longer and more polished, and they starred actors who soon became household names, such as Lillian Gish (1893–1993) and Rudolph Valentino (1895–1926). These movies were shown in ornate movie palaces. By 1916, nearly twenty-five million Americans saw a movie on any given day. Movies thus joined magazines in their ability to entertain millions of Americans across the nation. Magazines continued to flourish, with old standards such as *Collier's,* the *American Magazine,* and the *Saturday Evening Post* achieving circulations in the millions, while magazines such as *True Story, Vanity Fair,* and *Vogue* all emerged to provide different forms of reading material.

While movies and magazines provided entertainment to the great masses, other forms of culture also flourished. American artists and writers were thrilled by the Armory Show of European artists in 1913, which sparked a rebirth in American artistic and literary activity. Novelists Theodore Dreiser (1871–1945) and Willa Cather (1873–1947) published important works in the decade. Poet Carl Sandburg (1878–1967) published poems celebrating his home town of Chicago, Illinois. Perhaps the most popular artist of the day was actually a magazine illustrator, Norman Rockwell (1894–1978).

In their daily lives, Americans enjoyed an ever growing variety of amusements. The Ringling Bros. and Barnum & Bailey Circus was formed in this decade and boasted that it was the "Greatest Show on Earth." Sports fans thrilled or booed to the exploits of the New York Yankees. Hockey joined the ranks of professional sports in 1917 with the establishment of the National Hockey League. Two "crazes" swept the nation in this decade—the bridge craze, which saw millions of Americans playing the popular card game, and the crossword puzzle craze, with new word challenges offered each week in newspapers and magazines.

Americans fell in love with two new foods in the 1910s: Campbell's soup, which came in a convenient can, and Oreo cookies. Both products continue to this day as the most popular brand in their class. Homemakers also enjoyed the newest electrical appliance, the refrigerator, which allowed them to keep foods fresh longer and to not make so many trips to the grocery store.

1910s

Commerce

In American business, the 1910s was the decade of organization. Across the country, large corporations sought ways to make their production more efficient. They hired managers in great numbers, and it was the manager's job to get employees to increase production. Many of these managers followed the thinking of an engineer named Frederick W. Taylor (1865–1915), who preached the principles of "scientific management." These new management techniques emphasized efficiency and order and getting the most out of workers. Managers also looked to automation, as more and more American businesses used assembly-line processes to produce their goods. The Ford Motor Company was the shining example of what organization could do for a company; Henry Ford (1863–1947) and his car company boosted automobile production to 730,041 units by 1917.

When President Woodrow Wilson (1856–1924) brought his progressive political ideas to the White House in 1913, critics feared that his pro-reform administration would be antibusiness. In fact, progressive legislation helped business operate more efficiently. Both the Clayton Antitrust Act of 1914 and the creation of the Federal Trade Commission (FTC) helped restore healthy competition to American business by eliminating monopolistic (single company dominance) and anticompetitive business practices. Other acts increased exports by promoting free trade with other nations, helped provide farmers with low-interest loans, and protected workers' rights.

The American economy was boosted dramatically by World War I (1914–18). Before it entered the war in 1917, the United States provided food and other goods to all of the warring countries. Once America entered the war, it was free also to provide military weapons and heavy industrial goods to its allies, France and the United Kingdom. President Wilson's government helped American companies organize their activities to ship war goods; labor unions felt it was unpatriotic to strike; and the economy boomed. During the course of the decade, the value of goods and services produced in the United States rose from $35.3 billion in 1910 to $91.5 billion in 1920. Even more importantly, the United States was now exporting more goods than ever before. Exports exceeded imports by $273 million in 1910. By 1920, they exceeded imports by $2.88 billion.

By the end of the decade, the American economy was the undoubted leader of the world. American companies shared in the boom. The Ford Motor Company, General Motors, General Electric, Eastman Kodak, DuPont, and other companies grew to have values greater than many small nations. The American Telephone and Telegraph Company (AT&T) laid telephone lines from New York to San Francisco, paving the way for transcontinental telephone service—and for AT&T to become the world's largest company eventually.

Individual Americans also enjoyed the country's economic growth. The income of the average American rose from $580 in 1914 to more than $1,300 by the end of the decade. Advertisers and a growing retail industry persuaded Americans to spend some of their disposable income. Department stores such as Wanamaker in Philadelphia and grocery stores like Piggly Wiggly in Tennessee adopted scientific management techniques to sell people more goods. L. L. Bean (1872–1967) founded his outdoor goods company in 1912 and soon shipped goods across the country to people who had received his catalog.

AT&T

An outgrowth of the original Bell Telephone Company founded by Alexander Graham Bell (1847–1922) in 1877, the American Telephone & Telegraph Company is one of the best known companies in the United States. The company is commonly known by its corporate initials, AT&T, or by its familiar nickname, "Ma Bell." Incorporated in 1885, AT&T became the parent company of the Bell System in 1915. In 1915, AT&T also extended its New York-based network to San Francisco, California, permitting the first transcontinental **telephone** (see entry under 1900s—The Way We Lived in volume 1) calls. The company had a controlling interest in Western Electric, its manufacturing unit, and in Bell Labs (now the independent Lucent Technologies), its research and development division. AT&T introduced the first commercial transatlantic telephone service between the United States and London, England, in 1927 and the first transpacific service to Hawaii in 1931 and to Tokyo, Japan, in 1934. AT&T's development of the Telstar I **satellite** (see entry under 1950s—The Way We Lived in volume 3), launched in 1962, opened a new era of global telecommunications from space.

For its first century, AT&T was a government-regulated monopoly (single company dominance) that provided telecommunications services throughout the United States in exchange for its commitment to offer universal service at a low price to consumers. Thanks to AT&T, 50 percent of all households had telephone service by 1945; 70 percent, by 1955; and 90 percent, by 1969. In 1974, however, the U.S. government filed an antitrust suit against AT&T that led to its breakup into eight smaller companies in 1984: a shrunken AT&T, plus seven "baby Bells" that provided local telephone service. The breakup reduced AT&T's assets from $149.5 billion to $34 billion and its employees from 1,009,000 to 373,000. Its familiar logo of a bell within a circle was replaced by a stylized globe and the monogram AT&T. For the next twelve years, AT&T described itself as an "integrated telecommunications services and equipment company" that, along with MCI, Sprint, and other newcomers, was one of many long-distance carriers. Since 1996, AT&T has been reinventing itself as a company that provides businesses and consumers with voice, data, and video services via wireless, data, and cable networks. It reported annual revenues of $66 billion in 2000.

—Edward Moran

For More Information

"About AT&T." *AT&T.* http://www.att.com (accessed January 15, 2002).

Brooks, John. *Telephone: The First Hundred Years.* New York: Harper & Row, 1976.

Coll, Steve. *The Deal of the Century: The Breakup of AT&T.* New York: Atheneum, 1986.

Kleinfield, Sonny. *The Biggest Company on Earth: A Profile of AT&T.* New York: Holt, Rinehart, and Winston, 1981.

Stone, Alan. *Wrong Number: The Breakup of AT&T.* New York: Basic Books, 1989.

L. L. Bean

L. L. Bean—based in Freeport, Maine—is a supplier of outdoor apparel, furnishings, and equipment. Since its inception in 1912, it has become renowned for its products and services and for the rustic, genteel lifestyle that it represents. With a largely unchanging mix of products such as khaki pants, the famous "Bean boot," and camping equipment, L. L. Bean has virtually defined the outdoors-oriented retailing industry. In the 1980s, when the **"preppy"** (see entry under 1980s—Fashion in volume 5) look was in vogue, L. L. Bean was practically revered. In Lisa Birnbach's best-selling book *The Official Preppy Handbook,* she wrote of the preppy rite of passage of going to the Bean store in Freeport at midnight. The L. L. Bean catalog has been a legend for decades. Until the 1990s, there was only one store in Freeport, and all orders were through the catalog. For most people, the catalog *was* L. L. Bean.

Leon Leonwood Bean (1873–1967) got started in the business because he was tired of coming home from outings in the Maine woods with cold, wet feet. He created a lightweight leather boot with rubber bottoms and sold them via mail order. Unfortunately, the stitching came out on most of them. This fault turned out to be a blessing, since he returned his customers' money and thereby established the famous Bean unconditional guarantee. He went back to the drawing board. The improved "Maine hunting shoe" is still sold today as the "Bean boot" and is probably L. L. Bean's best-known product. They have also offered a "field coat" since 1924, widely copied in the 1990s. Other Bean innovations have included keeping the store open for twenty-four hours a day year round, running a fly-fishing school, and offering a variety of environmental programs.

By the late 1990s, L. L. Bean was considered by some to be overly traditional. In an effort to keep up with competition from companies like Lands' End and Recreational Equipment Incorporated (REI), the company expanded the number of stores and tried to be more market savvy. It is hard to tell if the new strategy will work, but as recently as late 2000, upscale fashion houses such as Gucci and Oscar de la Renta were drawing inspiration from L. L. Bean standbys, but charging a lot more for them.

—Karl Rahder

For More Information

"Bean There, Done That." *Harper's* (December 2000): p. 260.

Birnbach, Lisa. *The Official Preppy Handbook.* New York: Workman Publishing, 1980.

"Get to Know More About L. L. Bean." *L. L. Bean.* http://www.llbean. com/customerService/aboutLLBean/index.html?feat=gn (accessed January 15, 2002).

Montgomery, M. R. *In Search of L. L. Bean.* Boston: Little, Brown, 1984.

Symonds, William C. "Paddling Harder at L. L. Bean." *Business Week* (December 7, 1998): pp. 72–73.

1910s

Fashion

Fashion in the 1910s bore little resemblance to fashion in the twenty-first century. There were few if any famous designers or popular brands of clothes and few fashion magazines to publicize the latest clothing styles. The very idea of style would have seemed laughable to most people, whose highest hopes for their clothes were that they were durable. Many Americans still wore clothes that were made at home; those who did not make their own clothes bought them at general stores or department stores based on price and durability, and not on whether the clothes were in style.

Only the wealthiest Americans had the luxury of thinking about the cut and style of the clothes they wore. Wealthy men might have their suits handmade in London, England, while rich women traveled to Paris, France, to view the latest in female fashions. Beginning in 1914, Americans could consult the magazine *Vanity Fair* for advice on stylish attire. This magazine was one of the first to promote stylish clothes for men in its articles and advertisements. The Arrow Collar Man, a stylishly handsome illustrated figure used to sell shirt collars, became the most famous fashion symbol of the decade thanks to his appearance in countless magazine advertisements.

In general, the trends in clothing during the decade were to greater simplicity and ease of use. Both men and women were beginning to enjoy more active lives—bicycling, golfing, and dancing were all becoming very popular—and their clothing changed to suit those lifestyles. Women gave up wearing the cumbersome corset (a heavy, tight undergarment) and began wearing the more comfortable brassiere, or bra, that was invented in 1913. Similarly, men gave up their thick woolen union suits in favor of the light cotton T-shirt that became popular among soldiers fighting in World War I (1914–18). Active people of both sexes also looked for lightweight footwear. Beginning in 1917, they could purchase Converse All Star tennis shoes, with their light uppers and no-skid rubber bottom.

Arrow Collar Man

A 1912 print advertisement featuring the Arrow Collar Man. *Bettmann/Corbis. Reproduced by permission.*

Appearing in hundreds of print advertisements between 1905 and 1930, the Arrow Collar Man presented an iconic image—the ideal representation of a handsome, athletic, self-confident male. Even President Theodore Roosevelt (1858–1919) described him as a superb portrait of the "common man." The Arrow Collar Man was used to sell more than four hundred varieties of detachable collars. In the early decades of the twentieth century, most men's shirts still had detachable collars, often made of celluloid. (Celluloid was the first synthetic **plastic** [see entry under 1900s—Commerce in volume 1]. Made from cellulose and camphor, other plastics replaced celluloid because it was highly flammable.) The Arrow Collar achieved widespread brand recognition to become an advertising icon; if a man wore an Arrow Collar, he must be like that handsome, athletic, self-confident Arrow Collar Man. The Arrow Collar Man was created by J. C. Leyendecker (1874–1951) for its manufacturer, Cluett, Peabody & Company. During the 1920s, he served as an advertising model for Arrow Shirts with their newfangled attached collars.

Leyendecker, who preferred to work from live models, drew the Arrow Collar Man as a polished, Anglo-Saxon figure. The portraits were designed to suggest an ideal image of the can-do American male. He used several prominent actors for models, but his favorite was Charles Beach, Leyendecker's business manager and companion for half a century. It has been reported that the fictional image received more fan mail than movie stars of the period, including **Rudolph Valentino** (1895–1926; see entry under 1920s—Film and Theater in volume 2). At the height of the Arrow Collar Man's popularity in 1920, he was receiving seventeen thousand love letters a week. He was also the subject of a **Broadway** (see entry under 1900s—Film and Theater in volume 1) show and several popular songs and poems.

After the campaigns featuring the Arrow Collar Man ended in 1930, Leyendecker continued his career as a magazine illustrator for the ***Saturday Evening Post*** (see entry under 1900s–Print Culture in volume 1) and other national publications. He was a great influence on another of America's greatest illustrators, **Norman Rockwell** (see entry under 1910s–Print Culture in volume 1).

–Edward Moran

For More Information

"J. C. Leyendecker: A Retrospective." *The Norman Rockwell Museum.* http://www.tfaoi.com/newsmu/nmus21b.htm (accessed January 14, 2002).

"Joseph Christian Leyendecker." *National Museum of American Illustration.* http://www.americanillustration.org/html/jcl/bio.html (accessed January 14, 2002).

Schau, Michael. *J. C. Leyendecker.* New York: Watson-Guptill Publications, 1974.

Bra

Few items of clothing have attracted as much attention–positive and negative–as the brassiere, or bra. Worn by women to support and protect their breasts, the bra has become a symbol of femininity, female sexuality, and womanhood. So closely is the bra equated with the role of women in society that acceptance or rejection of the bra can be a political decision as well as a fashion decision.

The bra was invented in 1913 by New York City socialite Caresse Crosby (1892–1970). Rebelling against the confinement and unattractive lines of the corsets (restrictive undergarments) that the fashion of the day dictated, Crosby directed a servant to sew together two handkerchiefs with ribbons to make a garment to wear over her breasts. Crosby was not the first to think of such a device, but she patented her invention and therefore was able to claim the rights to it. She sold the patent to Warners, a corset manufacturer, for $1500.

Bras have been used throughout the years to help women make their bodies look fashionable. In the 1920s, the bra was a tight band that allowed women to achieve a slim, boyish figure; by the 1930s, bras pushed women's breasts up and in to show off their cleavage (the visual line between the breasts). In 1935, Warners introduced the cup design with different sized cups for a better individual fit. The 1940s and 1950s featured

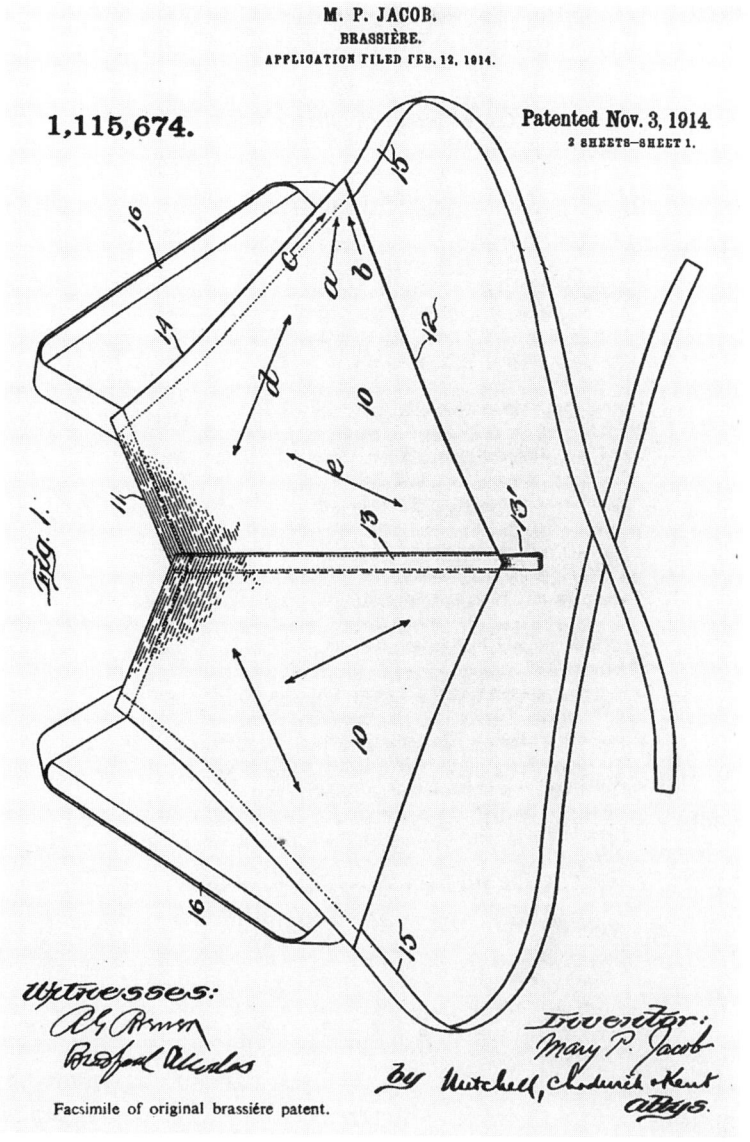

Facsimile of original brassiére patent.

A copy of the original brassiere patent, filed on February 12, 1914. *Hulton/Archive by Getty Images. Reproduced by permission.*

sturdy bras made of cotton and elastic. Big breasts became fashionable, and the 1950s saw the introduction of the padded bra and "falsies," small foam pads placed in the bra to enlarge the bustline.

In the 1960s, as women began to question their role in male-dominated society, men's obsession with women's breasts became a source of anger and dissent. The women's liberation movement accused men of viewing women mainly as objects of sexual desire, and made the bra a symbol of women's confinement to men's expectations. At the 1968 **Miss America**

Pageant (see entry under 1920s—The Way We Lived in volume 2), feminists protested male beauty standards by throwing curlers, makeup, and bras into a garbage can. Although no bras were burned, the media exaggerated the event and "bra-burner" became a synonym for feminist.

Since then, women have continued to wear bras, whether as a social convention or a need for a supportive garment for their breasts. With forty-three separate component parts, the modern bra is an engineering marvel, and manufacturers are constantly working to improve the design. Sports bras have been designed that can be worn under a shirt or alone by female athletes. During the 1990s technological boom, bras were even designed to contain heart monitors, global positioning system locators, cellular phones, and cancer warning sensors. The lingerie company Victoria's Secret scored a marketing triumph with its sophisticated Wonderbra in the 1990s. The bra continues to reflect the tastes and conventions of American society in every era.

—Tina Gianoulis

For More Information

Baldwin, Deborah. "Caresse Crosby and the Brassiere." *Discovery.com.* http://www.discovery.com/stories/deadinventors/dead980910/deadinventors.html (accessed January 15, 2002).

Dowling, Claudia Glenn. "Ooh-la-la! The Bra." *Life.* (June 1989): pp. 88–96.

Hawthorne, Rosemary, and Mary Want. *From Busk to Bra: A Survey of Women's Corsetry.* Cincinnati: Seven Hills Book Distributors, 1987.

Lindsay, David. *House of Invention: The Secret Life of Everyday Products.* New York: Lyons Press, 2000.

Tennis Shoes

The tennis shoe has been called the only new style of shoe to be invented in the past three hundred years. The athletic shoe was first introduced in the 1860s as the plimsoll, a lightweight canvas shoe with a rubber sole for playing lawn croquet. The athletic shoe has since evolved into not only a high-tech piece of sports equipment but also a sign of status and an expression of individual personality. Often called "tennies" or "sneakers," tennis shoes are no longer just for sports. They are a major part of the modern American wardrobe.

In 1916, a shoe company called Keds produced a lightweight canvas and rubber shoe that remained the basic pattern of the tennis shoe for the next fifty years. In the late 1960s, the customized athletic shoe first appeared, when University of Oregon track coach Bill Bowerman (1911–1999) began experimenting with new designs for a lightweight shoe with improved traction. He created a new type of sole by pouring latex rubber into a waffle iron. The odd-looking but efficient shoe he created by attaching his new sole to a nylon upper was dubbed the "moonshoe."

Bowerman became one of the founders of the **Nike** (see entry under 1960s—Commerce in volume 4) shoe company. Nike, along with athletic equipment company Spalding and German company Adidas, continued to improve the design of the running shoe during the 1970s. The **aerobics** (see entry under 1970s—Sports and Games in volume 4) craze of the 1970s and 1980s sparked more experimentation in specific shoe design for different sports. In the 1990s, shoes with technical accessories, such as built-in air pumps to customize fit, became popular.

Modern athletic shoes can cost from $25 to $175 a pair. Manufacturing athletic shoes has become a $12 billion-a-year industry. The most popular sports shoes are often endorsed by well-known athletes, who receive millions of dollars for their endorsements. The teenage boys who identify with those athletes are often drawn to the expensive brand-name shoes that their heroes endorse. Poor youth, who often see success in sports as a way out of poverty, want to own the "best" sneakers, even though the price tag may be out of reach. As a result, a new area of crime has arisen, and many young people have been hurt or killed when their new expensive sneakers have been stolen right off their feet.

—Tina Gianoulis

For More Information

Berendt, John. "The Sneaker." *Esquire* (Vol. 107, May 1987): pp. 26–28.

Kiefer, Michael. "Ode to the Sneaker: A Discourse on Laces, Lore and Sole with Soul." *Chicago* (Vol. 35, May 1986): pp. 164–68.

"The Sneaker Story." *Co-Ed* (Vol. 30, March 1985): pp. 32–37.

Telander, Rick, and Mirko Ilic. "Senseless: In America's Cities, Kids Are Killing Kids over Sneakers and Other Sports Apparel Favored by Drug Dealers; Who's to Blame?" *Sports Illustrated* (Vol. 72, no. 20, May 14, 1990): pp. 36–43.

Wolkomir, Richard. "The Race to Make a 'Perfect' Shoe Starts in the Laboratory." *Smithsonian* (Vol. 20, no. 6, September 1989): pp. 94–103.

T-Shirt

The T-shirt is one of the beacons of American casual fashion. Popularized by U.S. Navy sailors during the first two world wars, the T-shirt has become an essential element of the American wardrobe.

In 1913, the U.S. Navy issued short-sleeved, white cotton crewneck undershirts to sailors. Sailors returning from World War I (1914–18) had grown to prefer the T-shirt to the woolen undershirt that had been the most typical undergarment since 1880. The popularity of the garment grew. By World War II (1939–45), twelve million men were wearing the shirts. News photographs and newsreels showed sailors and soldiers working in only pants and T-shirts. Underwear was exposed to the public for the first time. America had become quite used to the display of American muscle under a thin layer of white T-shirt by war's end.

Although the military persuaded America to embrace the T-shirt as an essential element of a man's wardrobe, films turned the T-shirt into an American cultural phenomenon. In 1951, the sculpted muscles of Marlon Brando (1924–) bulged under his T-shirt in *A Streetcar Named Desire*; his character Stanley Kowalski's powerful masculinity was reflected in Brando's physique and perfectly displayed under his T-shirt. In 1955, **James Dean** (see entry under 1950s—Film and Theater in volume 3) brought a youthful, anti-establishment attitude to the T-shirt in *Rebel Without a Cause*. This anti-establishment theme continued into the 1960s with Peter Fonda (1939–) in *Easy Rider* (1966). The sexual and rebellious characters that actors portrayed in films translated into the behavior of American youths. T-shirts became associated with youthful, American attitudes.

Women made T-shirts their own symbol of youth and rebellion during the **sexual revolution** (see entry under 1960s—The Way We Lived in volume 4) of the 1960s and 1970s. The teasingly revealing anatomy of a T-shirt-clad Jacqueline Bisset (1944–) in *The Deep* (1977) is perhaps the best illustration of women's adoption of the T-shirt. Since the 1970s, young braless women have lined up in wet T-shirts in bars across the country to display their own sexuality.

Soon T-shirts displayed attitudes in type. Although some T-shirts carried printed messages before the 1960s, in the 1970s

T-shirts became personal billboards for individual expression. Anything from "Have a Nice Day" to swear words could be found on T-shirts. By the beginning of the twenty-first century, T-shirts were a staple garment of Americans and many others around the world. Offered in a variety of colors, styles, and with unlimited messages, the T-shirt can still be seen adorning young and old alike.

—Sara Pendergast

For More Information

Grey, Ian. "Tee-Construction a Brief History of the T-Shirt." *Vintagesskivvies.com.* http://www.vintageskivvies.com/pages/archives/articles/readersubmissions/historyofthet-shirt.html (accessed January 15, 2002).

"The History of a T-Shirt." *Teehive.com.* http://shop.store.yahoo.com/teehive/hisoftshir.html (accessed January 15, 2002).

Stern, Jane, and Michael Stern. *The Encyclopedia of Bad Taste.* New York: HarperCollins Publishers, 1990.

Zipper

Zippers provide easy opening and secure fastening to luggage, clothing, and even plastic bags. Although zippers are found in many everyday items today, the zipper did not immediately interest people when it was first invented.

Elias Howe (1819–1867), inventor of the sewing machine, patented the first zipper in 1851. He called it an "automatic, continuous clothing closure." Howe never marketed his invention, though. Whitcomb Judson patented his "clasp locker" in 1893. After its introduction at the **World's Fair** (see entry under 1900s—The Way We Lived in volume 1) in Chicago, Illinois, and the successful marking of his product through his Universal Fastener Company, he became known as the "Inventor of the Zipper."

Judson's invention laid the groundwork for modern zippers. Gideon Sundback, an employee of Universal Fastener Company, designed a zipper in 1913 that is much like the zippers found today. Sundback's "separable fastener" received a patent in 1917. The Universal Fastener Company started producing hundreds of feet of it a day.

The B. F. Goodrich Company put Sundback's fastener on its rubber boots and called the device a "zipper." The name stuck, but it took several years for the zipper to become popular. For the first twenty years of its existence, the zipper only closed boots and tobacco pouches. Other uses seemed impractical; the zipper was expensive, it rusted, and it sometimes broke open. But when designers started using zippers in children's clothing in the 1930s, it did not take long for zippers to replace buttons in the flies of men's trousers. Soon, zippers were the preferred fastener for trousers, jackets, and all sorts of other items. By the beginning of the new millennium, zippers came in thousands of different styles and hundreds of different colors.

—Sara Pendergast

For More Information

Friedel, Robert. *Zipper: An Exploration in Novelty.* New York: W. W. Norton, 1994.

"The History of the Zipper." *About.com.* http://inventors.about.com/library/weekly/aa082497.htm (accessed January 15, 2002).

"The History of the Zipper." *Apparel Search.* http://www.apparelsearch.com/zipper_history.htm (accessed January 15, 2002).

1910s

Film and Theater

One of many amusements in the 1900s, movies began to compete seriously with books and magazines for people's leisure time in the 1910s. By 1916, twenty-five million Americans attended a movie every single day. Advances in technology and in the art of filmmaking helped make movies such an important part of American popular culture. Technologically, films could now be longer and could be shown on a bigger screen. Artistically, directors had developed the art of telling a story on film. They used rising "stars"—actors and actresses loved by their audience—to craft dramatic stories.

Nickelodeons, which showed short, one-reel films (films that fit on a single reel and were generally ten to twelve minutes long) in cramped spaces, faded in popularity during this decade. Soon the little nickelodeons were replaced by large, ornate theaters in many big cities. These "movie palaces," which seated hundreds of viewers who enjoyed the splendor of the setting, made going to the movies a special treat. Filmmakers soon made two-, three-, eight-, and even twelve-reel movies. These movies, called features, were long enough to tell a detailed story. Movies were still silent, of course, for sound would not come to films until the late 1920s.

Film production, which had once been centered in New York, relocated westward, settling in an area near Los Angeles, California, known as Hollywood. Open space and good weather allowed movie studios to make more and better movies. The most notable directors soon became famous. The best-known director of the day was D. W. Griffith (c. 1875–1948), director of the famous *Birth of a Nation* (1915) and *Intolerance* (1916). Cecil B. DeMille (1881–1959) soon built a solid reputation. Griffith and DeMille and other directors also turned to stars to help draw viewers to their movies. Among the best known stars of this early era of filmmaking were "America's Sweetheart" Mary Pickford (1893–1979), "Latin Lover" Rudolph Valentino (1895–1926), Charlie Chaplin (1889–1977), Lillian Gish (1893–1993), Douglas Fairbanks (1883–1939), Tom Mix (1880–1940), and many others.

On the stage, vaudeville was still the most popular form of live entertainment. A form of variety theater that included a range of acts, vaudeville shows were performed all across the nation, in towns large and small. In many cities outside the South, African Americans participated in mixed-race vaudeville performances or toured with vaudeville shows of their own. Many of the most famous vaudeville performers of the day—including Chaplin, the Marx Brothers (Harpo, 1888–1964; Groucho, 1890–1977; Chico, 1886–1961; and Zeppo, 1901–1979), George Burns (1896–1996), and Jack Benny (1894–1974)—went on to star in movies and, several decades later, television. Large cities often had ornate theaters to house their vaudeville shows, and these theaters also showed movies.

Musicals and musical revues also gained in popularity during the decade. The most famous musical revue was the annual Ziegfeld Follies, which ran from 1907 to 1931 but was most popular during this decade. Though Broadway was still struggling to develop a successful theater tradition, a trend called the Little Theater Movement saw the birth of local theater companies across the country. Eugene O'Neill (1888–1953), who would become one of America's most famous playwrights, had his first play performed by the Provincetown Players in New York City in 1916.

The Birth of a Nation

The Birth of a Nation was a groundbreaking 1915 silent film. Directed by D. W. Griffith (1875–1948), the film is set during the American Civil War (1861–65) and Reconstruction period (1865–1877). *The Birth of a Nation* depicts the era through the fictional stories of two white families caught up in the conflict, the Stonemans from the North and the slaveowning Camerons from the South. The film popularized the acting careers of **Lillian Gish** (1893–1993; see entry in 1910s—Film and Theater in volume 1) and her younger sister, Dorothy (1898–1968). The sisters became two of the most familiar stars of the **silent movie** (see entry under 1900s—Film and Theater in volume 1) era. *The Birth of a Nation* introduced many technical and artistic advances in the new medium of film. The film remains controversial to this day because of its interpretation of the historical events it portrayed.

A scene from the controversial 1915 silent film *The Birth of a Nation*. *Bettmann/Corbis. Reproduced by permission.*

Based on *The Clansman,* a 1905 play by Thomas Dixon Jr. (1864–1946), *The Birth of a Nation* sympathized with defeated Southern slaveholders. It portrayed the Confederacy and the **Ku Klux Klan** (see entry under 1910s—The Way We Lived in volume 1) in a generally favorable light, while painting a negative picture of Southern blacks during the period. The film depicted the Cameron plantation before the war as a happy place where slaves and masters lived together in harmony until Northern abolitionists disturbed the balance. After the war, Austin Stoneman sends a friend of mixed race, Silas Lynch, to encourage the emancipated slaves to vote and run for public office, provoking a horrified Ben Cameron to organize the Ku Klux Klan as an organ of white resistance. The narrative is personalized when romantic attachments develop between members of the two families, but these scenes are overshadowed by unflattering depictions of black characters, who are portrayed as uncouth and violence prone. Not surprisingly, protests greeted *The Birth of a Nation* when the film opened in many cities in the spring of 1915. Among those criticizing the film were the National Association for the Advancement of Colored People

(NAACP), and prominent African American educators Booker T. Washington (1856–1915) and W. E. B. DuBois (1868–1963).

Despite these controversies, *The Birth of a Nation* remains a milestone in the history of the early film industry. It was heavily promoted and advertised nationally, making it the prototype of the modern "blockbuster." In the **nickelodeon** (see entry under 1900s—Film and Theater in volume 1) era, *The Birth of a Nation* was the first film for which a two-dollar admission was charged, proving that mass audiences would support serious movies. It also pioneered a number of production techniques still used by filmmakers. These techniques include the use of creative camera angles, such as closeups and panoramic shots, and of artificial lighting for filming at night. Writer and film critic James Agee (1909–1955) declared that *The Birth of a Nation* was full of "tremendous magical images" that could be compared to Abraham Lincoln's speeches, Walt Whitman's poems, and Mathew Brady's photographs in evoking the Civil War era.

—Edward Moran

For More Information

Barry, Iris. *D. W. Griffith: American Film Master.* New York: Museum of Modern Art, 1965.

Gish, Lillian, with Ann Pinchot. *The Movies, Mr. Griffith, and Me.* Englewood Cliffs, NJ: Prentice Hall, 1969.

Silva, Fred, ed. *Focus on "The Birth of a Nation."* Englewood Cliffs, NJ: Prentice Hall, 1971.

Sarris, Andrew. "Birth of a Nation or White Power Back When." Village Voice (July 17 and July 24, 1969).

Charlie Chaplin (1887–1977)

Charlie Chaplin was a brilliant mime artist and a key comic actor and director of Hollywood's **silent movie** (see entry under 1900s—Film and Theater in volume 1) era. Hired by the Keystone Film Company in 1913 for $150 a week, Chaplin quickly became a major star. Just four years later, First National paid him $1 million to make eight films. He once said that all he needed to make a comedy was a park, a policeman, and a pretty girl. But Chaplin's films combine wild visual jokes with serious issues such as immigration and unemployment. He appears as the "Little Tramp" in all his best work. The image of the man in the bowler hat with his turned-out feet is still famous the world over.

English-Chaplin never became an American citizen and left the United States in 1952. In 1972, a special Oscar honored him as one of the most distinguished figures in Hollywood's history. He was made Sir Charles Chaplin in 1975.

—Chris Routledge

For More Information

Cook, David A. *A History of Narrative Film*. New York: W. W. Norton, 1996.

Epstein, Jerry. *Remembering Charlie: A Pictorial Biography*. London: Bloomsbury, 1988.

Mitchell, Glenn. *The Charlie Chaplin Encyclopedia*. New York: Batsford, 1997.

Felix the Cat

A comic-book and animated-cartoon character created around 1920 by Otto Messmer (1892–1983) and Pat Sullivan (1885–1933), Felix the Cat first appeared (under another name) in a 1919 animated cartoon called *Feline Follies*. Felix the Cat was a lively, clever character who overcame difficulties placed in his path by inventive solutions such as changing his body parts into tools. During the next decade, the black-and-white, wide-eyed cat starred in more than 150 short animated cartoons. In 1923, he began appearing in a comic strip distributed by King Features. Felix was the first important animal character to star in his own cartoon series. Felix the Cat was also the first major cartoon character whose image was licensed for use by toy companies and other businesses that used his image on retail products. In 1927, Felix was the first character to appear on balloons in the **Macy's Thanksgiving Day Parade** (see entry under 1920s—Commerce in volume 2).

Through a series of favorable deals Messmer and Sullivan arranged with film distributors, Felix became a familiar presence in movie theaters around the country. Despite his popularity in silent films, his creators were unable to adapt their character when films gained sound in the late 1920s. Competitor **Walt Disney** (see Disney entry under 1920s—Film and Theater in volume 2) soon emerged as the major film animator with another animal: Mickey Mouse.

After an unsuccessful film revival in 1936, Felix the Cat continued to appear in newspaper comic strips and in Dell comic books. In 1959 and again in 1982, Joe Oriolo (1913–1985) created

Cartoonist Otto Messmer poses with his famous creation, Felix the Cat. *AP/Wide World Photos. Reproduced by permission.*

a Felix the Cat cartoon series for television, adding such supporting characters as the Professor and Poindexter. His son, Don Oriolo, continued the tradition by producing *Felix the Cat: The Movie* in the 1980s and developing the "Baby Felix" character. Through such revivals, Felix the Cat remained a durable fixture of twentieth-century popular culture.

—Edward Moran

For More Information

Canemaker, John. *Felix: The Twisted Tale of the World's Most Famous Cat.* New York: Pantheon, 1991.

FelixtheCat.com. http://www.felixthecat.com/ (accessed January 15, 2002).

Gerstein, David. *Classic Felix the Cat Page.* http://wso.williams.edu/~dgerstei/felix/ (accessed January 15, 2002).

Messmer, Otto. *Nine Lives to Live: A Classic Felix Celebration.* Seattle: Fantagraphic Books, 1996.

Gertie the Dinosaur

Gertie the Dinosaur (1914) may not be the first animated cartoon ever created, but it easily is the most famous—and most

Gertie the Dinosaur was the first-ever animated movie star. *The Kobal Collection. Reproduced by permission.*

influential—of its day. The title character is a real charmer: a cuddly, sweetly mischievous prehistoric creature who not only was an audience favorite but became the first-ever animated movie star.

Gertie was the creation of Winsor McCay (1871–1934), a newspaper cartoonist and comic strip artist-turned-pioneering animator. McCay's first animated cartoon was *Little Nemo* (1911), based on his comic-strip creation. *Little Nemo* consisted of four thousand drawings. *Gertie the Dinosaur* was his most celebrated follow-up animation. To create it, McCay used ten thousand drawings, each one representing an individual frame of film. All the drawings were inked on rice paper and mounted on cardboard.

McCay first presented his films as part of an act he performed in **vaudeville** (see entry under 1900s—Film and Theater in volume 1), in which he announced to the audience that he could make his drawings come to life. When presenting *Gertie the Dinosaur,* McCay portrayed the creature's trainer. As his film was projected, he synchronized his movements with those onscreen. McCay thus "talked" to Gertie, interacting with her and giving her commands to which she responded. At the finale,

McCay "walked" into the movie, becoming an animated figure that Gertie carries off on her back. He promoted the routine as "The Greatest Animal Act in the World!!!"

What is most astonishing about Gertie, however, is her fluid, detailed movement. She sways back and forth and, as she breathes, her body expands and contracts. McCay also includes a groundbreaking sense of realism in his animation. For example, as Gertie uproots a tree trunk and chomps away on it, bits of dirt fall to earth.

The film *Gertie the Dinosaur* (which also has been called *Gertie, Gertie the Dinosaurus,* and *Gertie the Trained Dinosaur*) was released to movie theaters in an expanded, one-reel version. McCay surrounded the animation with a live-action story, involving the animator agreeing to a bet with another cartoonist, George McManus (1884–1954), that he can make Gertie come alive. After the animated portion of the film, McCay and McManus are pictured at a dinner party. McManus has lost the bet and pays for the meal.

—Rob Edelman

For More Information

Maltin, Leonard. *Of Mice and Magic: A History of American Animated Cartoons.* New York: Penguin Books, 1980.

Lillian Gish (1896–1993)

Nicknamed "the First Lady of the Silver Screen," Lillian Gish is still considered the best serious film actress of her time. She brought a realism to film acting that had not been seen before. Lillian appeared in many classic films, including ***The Birth of a Nation*** (see entry under 1910s—Film and Theater in volume 1) (1915) and *Way Down East* (1920).

Born Lillan de Guiche, Gish made her screen debut in 1912 along with her sister Dorothy (1898–1968) in *An Uneasy Enemy.* Both sisters would have successful film careers. Dorothy was a comedienne, whereas Lillian appeared in melodramas and in literary classics. Lillian had a far longer career and is more highly regarded today, but Dorothy actually appeared in more films. Lillian's career ended after seventy-five years when she appeared in her last film, *The Whales of August,* in 1987.

—Jill Gregg Clever

For More Information

Estate of Lillian Gish. *Lillian Gish Official Home Page.* http://www.cmgww.com/stars/gish/index.html (accessed January 15, 2002).

Gish, Lillian, and Ann Pinchot. *The Movies, Mr. Griffith and Me.* Denver, Prentice-Hall, 1969.

"Lillian Gish." *American Masters.* http://www.pbs.org/wnet/americanmasters/database/gish_l.html (accessed January 15, 2002).

Keystone Kops

During the first two decades of the twentieth century, comedy was the favorite genre of moviegoers, and no moviemaker was more adept at tickling the funnybones of audiences than Mack Sennett (1880–1960). One of the most famous and everlasting of all his contributions to screen comedy was the Keystone Kops, a fictional gang of well-meaning but hilariously inept policemen. The Keystone Kops have long been synonymous with onscreen slapstick and bungling, chases filled with horseplay, and overall comic chaos.

Sennett was mentor to some of the era's most famous screen comedians, including **Charlie Chaplin** (1889–1977; see entry under 1910s—Film and Theater in volume 1) and Mabel Normand (1894–1930). He also worked with dozens of other comic actors, including Ford Sterling (1883–1939), Chester Conklin (1888–1971), Hank Mann (1887–1971), Fred Mace (1878–1917), Edgar Kennedy (1890–1948), and Roscoe "Fatty" Arbuckle (1887–1933), all of whom at one time or another were members of the Keystone Kops. The head of this band of comic lunatics was a character named police chief Teeheezel. He first was played by Mann, and then by Sterling.

The Kops were named for the Keystone studio, the film production company founded in 1912 by Sennett. They first appeared on screen in the Sennett-directed slapstick *Hoffmeyer's Legacy* (1912), but their popularity soared with the release of *The Bangville Police* (1913). Approximately five hundred short Keystone Kops comedies followed. The Kops also had a prominent role in *Tillie's Punctured Romance* (1914), which starred Chaplin, Normand, and comedienne Marie Dressler (1869–1934). *Tillie's Punctured Romance* was the first-ever feature-length film comedy.

The Kops wore handlebar moustaches and ill-fitting suits. During the course of their films, they would be tossed out of

The Keystone Kops, a fictional group of bumbling policemen, were featured in approximately five hundred short comedy films. *Bettmann/Corbis. Reproduced by permission.*

moving cars, or fall under moving cars, or be thrown over cliffs. Visual humor prevailed, for after all, the films in which they appeared were silent.

The Keystone Kops' stardom began to fade as other screen comics—most notably Chaplin in 1914—began receiving the bulk of the attention at the Keystone studio. But they did keep appearing in Sennett slapsticks and were paid homage decades later in a sound-film farce featuring **Abbott and Costello** (see entry under 1940s—Film and Theater in volume 3). (Bud Abbott [1895–1974] and Lou Costello [1906–1959] were a popular comedy duo in the 1940s and 1950s.) The film was titled *Abbott and Costello Meet the Keystone Kops* (1954). Furthermore, all sound-film comedy masters who rely on physical humor, from Abbott and Costello and the **Three Stooges** (see entry under 1930s—Film and Theater in volume 2) through Jerry Lewis (1926–) and Jim Carrey (1962–), owe a debt to Mack Sennett and his Keystone Kops.

—Audrey Kupferberg

For More Information

Lahue, Kalton C., and Terry Brewer. *Kops and Custards: The Legend of Keystone Films.* Norman: University of Oklahoma Press, 1968.
Sennett, Mack. *King of Comedy.* San Francisco: Mercury House, 1990.

Movie Palaces

From the early days of film until the 1950s, movie theaters really were palaces. As going to the movies became a popular American activity, movie theaters grew from the original storefront **nickelodeons** (see entry under 1900s—Film and Theater in volume 1) into huge, ornate theaters such as The Regent (New York City, built 1913), The Million Dollar (Los Angeles, built 1918), and Radio City Music Hall (New York City, built in 1932). Unfortunately, after the emergence of **television** (see entry under 1940s—TV & Radio in volume 3) and growth of **suburbia** (see entry under 1950s—The Way We Lived in volume 3) in the 1950s, movie palaces began to disappear. Today there are still motion picture theaters, but they no longer play the major role they did during the first half of the twentieth century. During the **Great Depression** (see entry under 1930s—The Way We Lived in volume 2), movie palaces helped audiences forget their troubles for awhile. The theaters even helped modern architecture find wider acceptance than it had previously.

The Strand in New York, although not the first movie palace, began the movie palace era, opening in 1914. The theaters had promotions such as free china, lotteries, and other prizes. Each theater had a different design theme and boasted velvet ropes and crystal chandeliers. Moviegoers received a royal welcome with doormen and ushers. Many theaters provided childcare, and one even boasted a miniature golf course.

By the late 1920s, audiences were becoming jaded, and after the Great Depression began in 1929 attendance took a dive. But people were lured back with low prices. The movie palaces experienced their peak during the late 1940s. Until then, motion picture studios owned the theaters also. A Supreme Court decision in 1948 made studios sell off the theaters.

During the 1950s, the decline of the movie palace began with the advent of television. Between 1947 and 1957, 90 percent of American households acquired a television. The theaters and studios tried to fight this development with movie spectaculars filmed with new techniques such as Widescreen, **3-D** (see entry under 1950s—Film and Theater in volume 3), and Cinerama. Unfortunately for the theaters, their audiences also began to move out to the suburbs. Smaller neighborhood theaters began to appear. The movie palaces all but disappeared after that.

A few palaces have been renovated and reopened, but most either stand empty and falling apart or were torn down years ago. The lavish theater experience that movie palaces once offered audiences can now only be remembered.

—Jill Gregg Clever

For More Information

Hall, Ben. *The Best Remaining Seats: The Story of the Golden Age of the Movie Palace.* New York: Clarson N. Potter, 1961.

Margolies, John, and Emily Gwathmey. *Ticket to Paradise: American Movie Theaters and How We Had Fun.* Boston: Bullfinch Press, 1991.

Valentine, Maggie. *The Show Starts on the Sidewalk: An Architectural History of the Movie Theatre.* New Haven, CT: Yale University Press, 1994.

Will Rogers (1879–1935)

Humorist Will Rogers was one of the most famous and beloved Americans of his time. His persona was that of a simple Everyman who employed common sense and clever good humor to view and comment on politics, lifestyles, and the American scene.

Rogers, part-Irish and part-Cherokee, was born in the Colagah Indian Territory, which is now Oklahoma. He quit school in 1891, became a cowboy in the Texas Panhandle, and performed with a traveling Wild West Circus. He first appeared on the New York stage in 1905 and became a full-fledged star on **Broadway** (see entry under 1900s—Film and Theater in volume 1) in the ***Ziegfeld Follies*** of 1916 (see entry under 1900s—Film and Theater in volume 1). Rogers soon appeared in motion pictures, debuting in *Laughing Bill Hyde* (1918). His popularity grew with the introduction of sound films in the late 1920s. Now, he could entertain moviegoers with his unique brand of verbal humor. He quickly became a top box office star.

Rogers was a lifelong Democrat, and his support helped elect Franklin D. Roosevelt (1882–1945) to the U.S. presidency in

1932. Rogers was not above poking fun at his party's sometimes erratic behavior, however. On one occasion, he noted, "No, I'm not a member of an organized political party—I'm a Democrat." Upon his introduction to Republican president Calvin Coolidge (1871–1933), he quipped, "Didn't catch the name," the first of many times the humorist made the often dour (stern or gloomy) chief executive smile. Rogers was killed in a plane crash in 1935. All America mourned his loss.

—Audrey Kupferberg

For More Information

Carter, Joseph H. *I Never Met a Man I Didn't Like: The Life and Writings of Will Rogers.* New York: Avon Books, 1991.

Malone, Mary. *Will Rogers: Cowboy Philosopher.* Springfield, NJ: Enslow, 1996.

Rogers, Will. *Autobiography.* Boston: Houghton Mifflin, 1949. Reprint, New Brunswick, NJ: Transaction Publishers, 1998.

Sonneborn, Liz. *Will Rogers, Cherokee Entertainer.* New York: Chelsea House, 1993.

Will Rogers Home Page. http://www.willrogers.org (accessed January 24, 2002).

1910s

Food and Drink

Housework continued to become easier in the 1910s, thanks to the continuing spread of electricity and running water, to the invention of new appliances, and to the availability of pre-prepared food and drink. Vacuum cleaners, invented in 1908, made cleaning easier. Refrigerators, first made for home use in 1913, helped cut down on trips to the grocery store. The electric toaster, invented in 1919, made warming bread a snap. But real modern efficiency had not yet come to the home in the 1910s. Homemakers still had to wash clothes by hand and hang them on a line to dry. The high cost of many appliances made them difficult to afford for most people. For example, a refrigerator in 1920 cost about $600, nearly half of the average person's annual income.

Buying and preparing food certainly became easier in the 1910s, continuing a trend started in the previous decade. Grocery stores grew in size, carrying thousands of items to help make home life easier. Food producers kept inventing new ways to package food, hoping to make money by making cooking quick and easy. Two famous products are good examples of the trend toward efficiency in American food preparation. Campbell's Soups—condensed soups that could be mixed with water to make a meal—became a national brand in 1911. Condensed soups allowed cooks to avoid the long preparation time involved in making homemade soup. By 1920, Americans bought more than one million cans of the twenty-one varieties of soup. Oreo cookies, invented in 1912, soon became America's favorite packaged cookie. Both items were helped along by carefully constructed advertising campaigns. Both remain the leading brands in their category.

Campbell's Soup

For more than a century, the Campbell Soup Company has helped revolutionize eating habits around the world by offering

"Some appetite" is surely right!
Here's Campbell's Soup to greet it.
And with this spoon we'll show you soon
The proper way to eat it!

Some appetite!

You'll know you have it when a fragrant, tempting plate of Campbell's Tomato Soup is placed before you! Your appetite may have been indifferent before, but it will sparkle at the very sight and the taste of this delicious blend of all that is tonic and tasty in luscious Jersey tomatoes.

Campbell's Tomato Soup

is made from the finest fruit that grows—sun-ripened aristocrats of the vines, laden with juiciness. We use only the pure tomato juices and the fruity parts strained to a rich, smooth puree, made richer still by butter such as you serve on your own table. A soup so appetizing and refreshing that you never tire of it!

21 kinds **12 cents a can**

Wonderful tomato sauce all ready to serve!

Campbell's Tomato Soup is used by thousands of dainty housewives as an appetizing and delightful sauce for meats, fish and salads and to give extra tastiness to spaghetti, rice, eggs or vegetables.

Campbell's SOUP

LOOK FOR THE RED AND WHITE LABEL

A 1922 print ad for Campbell's tomato soup featuring the Campbell Kids. *Gaslight Advertising Archives. Reproduced by permission.*

a line of convenient, inexpensive canned "condensed soups." All consumers need do is add a can of water to the soup before heating it. Based in Camden, New Jersey, the firm was an outgrowth of the Joseph A. Campbell Preserve Company. The company had been started in 1869 by Joseph A. Campbell (1817–1900), a fruit merchant, and Abraham Anderson, a manufacturer of iceboxes. In 1897, the fortunes of the company changed. General manager Arthur Dorrance reluctantly hired his nephew, Dr. John T. Dorrance (1873–1930), a twenty-four-year-old chemist. John Dorrance invented a process for making the condensed soup by eliminating water from the cans, thus reducing the costs for packing, shipping, and storage. Dorrance's breakthrough allowed the company to reduce the price of a can of soup from thirty cents to a dime. The company introduced its soups on the national market in 1912 and officially changed its name to the Campbell Soup Company in 1922.

Twenty-one flavors, including the perennial favorites, tomato and vegetable, were promoted in the company's first magazine ads in the early 1900s. Chicken noodle and cream-of-mushroom varieties made their debut in 1934. Others were added over the years. The Campbell Kids, a pair of rosy-cheeked cartoon characters, began appearing in ads in 1904. In the 1990s, the Campbell Kids were still promoting the soups by dancing to rap songs in television commercials. Campbell's familiar jingle—"M'm! M'm! Good! M'm! M'm! Good! That's what Campbell's soups are! M'm! M'm! Good!"—was first heard in **radio** (see entry under 1920s—TV and Radio in volume 2) commercials in the 1930s. Generations of Americans were introduced to Campbell's products via celebrity endorsements and through its sponsorship of the *Campbell Playhouse* on radio and ***Lassie*** (see entry under 1940s—Film and Theater in volume 3) and *Peter Pan* on **television** (see entry under 1940s—TV and Radio in volume 3).

The familiar Campbell's soup can was inspired by the red-and-white uniforms of the Cornell University football team that had impressed a company executive with their brilliance and visibility. In the 1960s, pop artist Andy Warhol (1928?–1987) transformed the image into an icon by creating paintings and screenprint editions featuring the cans.

In the latter decades of the twentieth century, Campbell's added several new lines of soup products. The new products included the Chunky line, a heartier soup that needed no water added, and a line of Healthy Request soups with less sodium, cholesterol, fat, and calories. Campbell's is also the parent company of other familiar brand names such as Pepperidge Farm, V8, Franco-American, Prego, Swanson, and Godiva chocolates. In 2001, the company reported net worldwide sales of $6.664 billion and controlled nearly 80 percent of the U.S. soup market.

—Edward Moran

For More Information

"Campbell History." *Campbell's Community.* http://www.campbellsoup.com (accessed January 16, 2002).

Parkin, Katherine. "Campbell's Soup and the Long Shelf Life of Traditional Gender Roles." In *Kitchen Culture in America: Popular Representations of Food, Gender, and Race.* Edited by Sherrie A. Inness. Phladelphia: University of Pennsylvania Press, 2001.

World's Greatest Brands: An International Review. New York: John Wiley & Sons, 1992.

Since their introduction in 1912, Nabisco estimates that more than 362 billion Oreo cookies have been consumed. *AP/Wide World Photos. Reproduced by permission.*

Oreo Cookies

Since their introduction on March 6, 1912, Nabisco's Oreo cookies have become the most popular commercial cookie product in the United States. More than 362 billion of them have been consumed over the years. According to their manufacturer, that number is equivalent to a pile that would stretch between the Earth and the moon five times over. Known officially as Oreo Chocolate Sandwich Cookies, a single Oreo consists of two intricately patterned chocolate-colored wafers, with a cream filling in between.

Nabisco does not offer a definitive conclusion about the origins of the name "Oreo," but cites several theories: it might have been suggested by *or,* the French word for gold, the most prominent color on the original packaging; it might have come from a Greek word for mountain, since early prototypes were mound-shaped; or it might have been invented by surrounding "RE" (two letters in the word "cream") with two "O"s from the word "chocolate." Although Nabisco does make Oreos with chocolate filling, the traditional cream filling (Nabisco spells it "creme") is white in color. This white-between-black combination led to the negative use of the term "Oreo" to describe an African American who betrays his race (i.e., one who is "black on the outside and white on the inside").

Over the years, consumers of Oreos have entered into a great debate over how to eat the cookies. Citing research it has done on the eating habits of Oreo consumers, Nabisco claims that 35 percent of respondents to one survey twist their cookies apart before eating them, 30 percent dunk them in milk, and 10 percent nibble them.

Over the years, some variations have been introduced to the standard Oreo. These variations include Double Stuf, an Oreo with a double portion of cream filling; Fudge Covered Oreo Sandwich Cookies; Oreo Big Stuf large snack cookies; and seasonal Oreos, such as those with orange cream sold at Halloween.

–Edward Moran

For More Information

Only Oreo. http://www.oreo.com/Oreo/Default.htm? (accessed January 16, 2002).

World's Greatest Brands: An International Review. New York: John Wiley & Sons, 1992.

1910s

Print Culture

Although going to the movies became an increasingly popular way to spend leisure time in this decade, books and magazines were still the core entertainment of most Americans. In this decade, the gulf widened between American high literature (fine writing concerned with philosophic ideas) and American popular literature (writing designed to inform and entertain). Some of the finest literary artists of the century published important works in this decade, including novelists Willa Cather (1873–1947), Theodore Dreiser (1871–1945), and Sherwood Anderson (1876–1941); and poets Gertrude Stein (1874–1946), Vachel Lindsay (1879–1931), T. S. Eliot (1888–1965), William Carlos Williams (1883–1963), and Ezra Pound (1885–1972). These writers and many others were discussed in small-circulation "little magazines" that were dedicated to the arts. They were also talked about in more general magazines such as *The Atlantic Monthly, The Smart Set, Vanity Fair,* and *The Seven Arts.* These artists, however, had few readers compared with the great readership enjoyed by popular novelists and contributors to the popular magazines.

American magazines continued to prosper in this decade, thanks largely to the eagerness of advertisers to promote their products to the millions of Americans who read popular magazines. The most popular magazines, including the *Saturday Evening Post,* the *American Magazine, Collier's, Ladies' Home Journal,* and *Good Housekeeping,* often used half of their pages each issue for advertisements. The advertising industry grew dramatically to help encourage Americans to buy, buy, buy. Several new magazines attracted attention in his decade, including *True Story,* a racy confession magazine for working-class readers, and *Vogue,* one of the first magazines devoted to fashion.

Beginning in 1912, the magazine *Publishers Weekly* began to use the term "best-seller" to describe the most popular fiction and nonfiction in America. This magazine and several others tracked those books that sold best, and their publicity helped drive sales even higher. Gene Stratton Porter (1868–1924), Zane Grey (1875–1939), Harold Bell Wright (1872–1944), Mary

Roberts Rinehart (1876–1958), and Winston Churchill (1874–1965) all had several titles on the best-seller list in the decade. During the World War I (1914–18) years, there was a separate list of best-sellers just about war. The *Tom Swift* series of adventure books for boys was one of the publishing sensations of the decade. The *Tom Swift* books set the stage for the *Hardy Boys* and the *Nancy Drew* series that would become so popular during the 1920s. Another surprise hit of the decade was the *World Book Encyclopedia,* whose goal was to provide the accumulated wisdom of the Western world in an easy-to-read format.

Fu Manchu

"Imagine a person, tall, lean and feline, high-shouldered, with a brow like Shakespeare and a face like Satan, a close-shaven skull, and long, magnetic eyes of the true cat green. Invest him with all the cruel cunning of an entire Eastern race . . . and you will have a mental picture of Dr. Fu Manchu, the yellow peril incarnate in one man." This is how mystery writer Sax Rohmer introduced the villain to readers in his first novel featuring the character. The shadowy, sinister Fu Manchu is one of the best known villains of Western literature. More than just an evil outlaw, the Fu Manchu character embodied the racism and fear of foreigners that was all too common in Western culture a century ago.

Fu Manchu was the creation of Sax Rohmer, the pen name of British writer Arthur Henry Sarsfield Ward (1886–1959). His first accounts of Fu Manchu appeared as a series of stories published in a British magazine between 1912 and 1913. These accounts were published in 1913 as a novel, *The Mystery of Dr. Fu Manchu.* This novel was followed by *The Devil Doctor* (1916) and *The Si-Fan Mysteries* (1917). In each of these stories, Fu Manchu is the head of a secret society, the Si-Fan, which carries out sinister plots for the Chinese government. He is opposed in each book by Denis Nayland Smith, a bold and fearless British secret agent.

After the third book, Rohmer left the evil doctor, but he returned to the character in 1931 with *The Daughter of Fu Manchu.* He then produced *The Mask of Fu Manchu* (1932), *Fu Manchu's Bride* (1933), and *The Trail of Fu Manchu* (1934). After a shorter break, Rohmer brought Fu Manchu and his nemesis, Nayland Smith, back in *President Fu Manchu* (1936). The characters reappeared in 1939 in *The Drums of Fu Manchu* and in 1941 in *The Island of Fu Manchu.* Rohmer again abandoned his character for a time but then featured him in three more books: *The Shadow of Fu Manchu* (1948), *Re-Enter Fu Manchu* (1957), and *Emperor Fu Manchu* (1959), Rohmer's last novel.

Five of the novels were adapted into films between 1920 and 1966. Three different versions of *Fu Manchu* dramas were produced for **radio** (see entry under 1920s—TV and Radio in volume 2) during the 1930s, with another appearing during World War II (1939–45). An American **television** (see entry under 1940s—TV and Radio in volume 3) series based on the character was broadcast during from 1956 to 1957.

—Justin Gustainis

Warner Oland portrays Dr. Fu Manchu in the 1929 film *The Mystery of Dr. Fu Manchu.* *UPI/Corbis-Bettmann. Reproduced by permission.*

For More Information

Nevins, Francis M. *The Mystery Writer's Art.* Bowling Green, OH: Bowling Green State University Popular Press, 1970.

Van Ash, Cay, and Elizabeth Sax Rohmer. *Master of Villainy: A Biography of Sax Rohmer.* Bowling Green, OH: Bowling Green State University Popular Press, 1972.

Krazy Kat

Krazy Kat, which appeared in newspapers from 1910 until 1944, is widely regarded as the most significant comic strip in American history. Created by George Herriman (1880–1944), the strip revolved around the misadventures of the androgynous (not clearly male or female) Krazy Kat and his (or her) love for Ignatz Mouse. Ignatz despised this unwanted affection and responded by continually hitting Krazy with an endless supply of bricks. Offisa Bull Pupp, a third character, served as the strip's symbol of law and order. Pupp also completed the strip's central love triangle since he adored Krazy and felt obligated to jail

***Krazy Kat*, which appeared in newspapers from 1910 until 1944, was noted for its unique blend of poetry, wordplay, bold colors, and surrealism.** *King Features Syndicate, Inc. Reproduced by permission.*

the violent Ignatz. Herriman's strip was noted for its unique blend of poetry, wordplay, bold colors, and surrealism. (Surrealism was a twentieth-century movement that involved representing the subconscious mind in pictures and words, often in disconnected or dreamlike ways. The melting watches of artist Salvador Dali (1904–1989) are an example of surrealism.)

Krazy Kat evolved from an earlier Herriman strip titled *The Dingbat Family* (1910–16), part of which highlighted the family's pets. In 1913, the animals were given their own feature that grew increasingly inventive and bizarre. M. Thomas Inge writes in *Comics as Culture* that "the world of *Krazy Kat* is a world of fantasy set against the surreal and abstract landscapes of Herriman's imagination approximating the real Coconino County in the state of Arizona." Krazy's world was a place where anything could happen. Landscapes mutated constantly. The characters spoke in a pun-filled dialect that contained elements of Latin, Greek, Old English, Yiddish, Navajo, and African American. The strip blended broad slapstick with sophisticated, philosophical thoughts on the absurdities of life. Intellectuals were especially devoted to the strip and proclaimed Herriman a cartooning genius. President Woodrow Wilson (1856–1924) was an avid admirer and read *Krazy Kat* at cabinet meetings. The strip has also been the focus of intense academic examination as to its "true meaning." In *America's Great Comic-Strip Artists,* Richard Marschall states, "It has been portrayed as a variation on the eternal triangle of tragic romances; as a grand statement on freedom versus authority; as an allegory on innocence meeting reality; and, of course, as a comic cacophony of obsessions."

Although the strip was critically acclaimed, it was never a financial success. Only the admiration of publisher William

Randolph Hearst (1863–1951) kept *Krazy Kat* in newspapers for decades. When Herriman died in 1944, the strip ended, and the comics page lost some of its luster.

—Charles Coletta

For More Information

Herriman, George. *The Komplete Kolor Krazy Kat.* 2 vols. Princeton, NJ: Remco/Kitchen Sink, 1990-91.

Inge, M. Thomas. *Comics as Culture.* Jackson: University Press of Mississippi, 1990.

"Kartoonist's Kramp." *Sputnik's Krazy Kat Page.* http://retrograde.net/kat/index.html (accessed January 16, 2002).

Marschall, Richard. *America's Great Comic-Strip Artists.* New York: Abbeville Press, 1989.

McDonnell, Patrick, Karen O'Connell, and Georgia Riley de Havenon. *Krazy Kat: The Complete Art of George Herriman.* New York: Abrams, 1986.

Norman Rockwell (1894–1978)

Norman Rockwell is famed for his illustrative paintings that capture everyday American life in the twentieth century. Rockwell began studying art during his freshman year of high school. He quit school when he was fifteen to attend the National Academy of Design. Eventually, he enrolled in the Art Students League. Rockwell was interested in accurately capturing the minutest detail of his subjects and their settings. This technique allowed him to tell their stories and reveal their personalities via their facial expressions and body language.

In 1913, Rockwell was hired as contributing art director of *Boy's Life* magazine. However, it was not until 1916, when he began his association with the ***Saturday Evening Post*** (see entry under 1900s—Print Culture in volume 1), that he arrived as an artist. The *Saturday Evening Post* was then a popular mass-market magazine. For the next forty-seven years, Rockwell was the *Post's* most famous and prolific cover illustrator. Additionally, he illustrated everything from Boy Scout calendars to reprints of *The Adventures of Tom Sawyer* and *Huckleberry Finn* to advertisements for the Massachusetts Mutual Life Insurance Company.

After leaving the *Post* in 1963, Rockwell's art became more issue oriented. Among his most famous works of the period is

Artist Norman Rockwell. *Archive Photos. Reproduced by permission.*

his 1964 *Look* magazine cover depicting the integration of an all-white elementary school. During and after his lifetime, Rockwell was the subject of controversy in relation to the very nature and meaning of art. To some, Rockwell is one of America's greatest artists. Others view him as an overly sentimental illustrator whose concerns were strictly commercial and who depicted a narrow and stereotypical segment of society.

—Rob Edelman

For More Information

Durrett, Deanne. *Norman Rockwell.* San Diego: Lucent Books, 1997.

Gherman, Beverly. *Norman Rockwell: Storyteller with a Brush.* New York: Atheneum Books for Young Readers, 2000.

Norman Rockwell: Pictures for the American People. http://www.rockwelltour.org/frameset.html (accessed January 16, 2002).

Rockwell, Norman. *My Adventures as an Illustrator, by Norman Rockwell, as told to Thomas Rockwell.* Garden City, NY: Doubleday, 1960.

Tarzan

Tarzan, the Lord of the Jungle, has been one of the most enduring heroic figures in American popular culture. Created by writer Edgar Rice Burroughs (1875–1950) in 1912, the Tarzan character first appeared in the pulp fiction *All-Story Magazine.* (**Pulp magazines** [see entry under 1930s—Print Culture in volume 2] of the era consisted of sensational stories printed on low-quality—that is, pulp—paper.) Tarzan has appeared in more than twenty novels, forty films, several **television** (see entry under 1940s—TV and Radio in volume 3) programs, **radio** (see entry under 1920s—TV and Radio in volume 2) serials, comic strips, cartoons, **comic books** (see entry under 1930s—Print Culture in volume 2), toys, and thousands of items of merchandise. The character's stories have been translated into more than fifty languages. He is one of the most famous men who never actually lived.

Burroughs had failed at nearly every endeavor he attempted before he devised Tarzan. In the initial tale of the "Lord of the Apes," Burroughs reveals his animalistic jungle man to be, in actuality, John Clayton, the future Lord Greystoke. As a child, Clayton's parents die while on tour of Africa. A female ape named Kala, who calls him Tarzan ("white-skin" in ape language), adopts him. Raised among the apes, he learns to communicate with all the wild beasts. As an adult, Tarzan encounters African natives as well as white people visiting the continent. His most significant relationship is with Jane Porter, an English woman on expedition with her father. A romance blossoms between the jungle man and the civilized lady. The two face many obstacles in both Africa and England, where Tarzan eventually claims his family's inheritance.

Johnny Weissmuller portrayed Tarzan in a dozen movies filmed between 1932 and 1948.

Tarzan was an immediate hit with the public, who thrilled to his jungle adventures filled with lost cities, fierce animals, evil poachers, and tribal warfare. Tarzan achieved even greater popularity through his many film appearances. In 1918, Elmo Lincoln (1889–1952) was the first movie Tarzan in *Tarzan of the Apes*. Numerous muscular actors would also don the hero's signature loincloth over the years. The performer most associated with the role was Johnny Weissmuller (1904–1984), a former five-time gold medal winner in swimming from the 1924 and 1928 **Olympics** (see entry under 1900s—Sports and Games in volume 1). His powerful physique and great athletic abilities served him well in a dozen Tarzan movies filmed between 1932 and 1948. In film, Tarzan is usually played as a much less well-spoken figure than Burroughs' original character. The famous line of dialogue "Me Tarzan, You Jane" never appeared in a Burroughs tale. The film most closely capturing Burroughs' conception of the character is 1984's *Greystoke: The Legend of Tarzan, Lord of the Apes,* starring Christopher Lambert (1957–)

as Tarzan. A new generation of fans encountered the jungle hero in a 1999 animated **Disney** (see entry under 1920s—Film and Theater in volume 2) feature film.

When Burne Hogarth (1911–1996), writer of the *Tarzan* comic strip, was asked in *Comics: Between the Panels* to account for the jungle man's lasting popularity, he stated: "He is energy, grace, and virtue. He symbolizes the inevitable life source, the earth, the seed, the rain, the harvest, achievement, the triumph of adversity and death."

—Charles Coletta

For More Information

Duin, Steve, and Mike Richardson. *Comics: Between the Panels.* Milwaukie, OR: Dark Horse Comics, 1998.

Edward Rice Burroughs, Inc. *Edgar Rice Burroughs: Creator of Tarzan.* http://www.tarzan.org (accessed January 16, 2002).

Foster, Hal. *Tarzan Vol. 1.* New York: Flying Buttress, 1992.

Horn, Maurice, ed. *100 Years of American Newspaper Comics.* New York: Random House, 1996.

Taliaferro, John. *Tarzan Forever: The Life of Edgar Rice Burroughs, Creator of Tarzan.* New York: Scribner, 1999.

Tom Swift Series

The *Tom Swift* series included more than forty novels for boys published by the Grosset & Dunlap Company between 1910 and 1941. Although most of the books in the series were published under the pen name "Victor Appleton," they were really written by writers working for the Stratemeyer Syndicate. The Stratemeyer Syndicate was a book packager that created juvenile literature under the supervision of its founder, Edward Stratemeyer (1862–1930). The writer responsible for most of the *Tom Swift* series was Howard Roger Garis (1873–1962). Over the years, the *Tom Swift* series sold some six million copies.

Tom Swift, the hero of the series, was an ingenious, plucky lad who used modern technology like electricity or steam power to outwit his rivals by creating new devices. In so doing, Tom Swift became a symbol of American creativity in an era that admired scientists and inventors like Thomas Edison (1847–1931) or the Wright Brothers (Wilbur, 1867–1912; Orville, 1871–1948). In an advertisement for the first set of *Tom Swift* books, Stratemeyer wrote: "It is the purpose of these spirited tales to convey in a realistic way the wonderful advances in land and sea locomotion and to interest the boy of the present in the hope that he may be a factor in aiding the marvelous development that is coming in the future."

In the earliest books in the series, all published in 1910, Tom Swift helps his father, Barton Swift ("the aged inventor"), build or improve airships and submarines. Tom goes on to invent a sky racer (1911), a telephone with photographic capability (1914), a transcontinental air-express service (1926), and "talking pictures" (1928). A regular cast of characters populates the *Tom Swift* series, including Tom's buddy Ned Newton, an eccentric older friend, Wakefield Damon, and their rival, Andy Foger.

In the 1950s, the Stratemeyer Syndicate introduced a series of books about Tom Swift Jr., written under the pseudonym of Victor Appleton II, but the books never achieved the popularity of the originals. In the 1980s, Simon & Schuster published several *Tom Swift* books in a science-fiction format. In 1991, Simon & Schuster returned to the "inventions" format with several volumes published under its Archway imprint.

–Edward Moran

For More Information

Dizer, John T., Jr. *Tom Swift and Company: "Boy's Books" by Stratemeyer and Others.* Jefferson, NC: McFarland, 1982.

Ippolito, Thomas R. *The Tom Swift Book Series (1910–1993).* http://www.web-span.com/raven43/hist.htm (accessed January 16, 2002).

Johnson, Deidre. *Edward Stratemeyer and the Stratemeyer Syndicate.* New York: Twayne, 1993.

"Tom Swift." *Stratemeyer Syndicate.* http://www.larilana.com/stratemeyer/swift/swift.htm (accessed January 16, 2002).

True Story

A popular "confessional" magazine, first published by Bernarr Macfadden (1868–1955) in 1919, *True Story* was enormously popular during the 1920s and 1930s. Its largely working-class readership devoured its sensational and often tawdry tales of sin, sex, and redemption. By challenging mainstream publishing norms and elevating scoundrels into heroes and heroines, *True Story* outraged conventional society with its depictions of vice and undesirable behavior.

Macfadden, the eccentric publisher of *Physical Culture* magazine, got the idea for *True Story* from the personal letters of "confession" he received from his readers about their own involvement with illegitimacy, premarital sex, adultery, and criminal activities. During the magazine's heyday, it was dismissed by serious critics, one of whom complained that it allowed millions of readers to "wallow in the filth of . . . politely dressed confessions." *True Story* was the forerunner of many of the supermarket tabloids that emerged in later years, with their tales of sordid gossip and bizarre occurrences.

By the 1930s, Macfadden succeeded in transforming the publication into a somewhat tamer women's romance magazine. It never lost its appeal to more downscale, poorly educated readers. Although altered in design and style over the years, the periodical has survived into the twenty-first century billed as "a modern woman's guide to love and life." Its first-person stories reflect more contemporary concerns, such as "I'm Going to Blow Up My School," "I'll Be Wife #5," and "War and Hunger."

—Edward Moran

For More Information

Ernst, Robert. *Weakness Is a Crime: The Life of Bernarr Macfadden.* New York: Syracuse University Press, 1991.

True Story Online Magazine. http://www.truestorymail.com (accessed January 16, 2002).

Vogue

Vogue is one of the world's most influential lifestyle magazines covering women's fashion and beauty. Founded as a weekly society paper in 1892 and purchased by Condé Nast in 1909, *Vogue* was the first magazine of its kind to use lavish photographic spreads and colorful graphics to highlight the latest fashion trends. So influential did the magazine become that the phrase "Vogue model" became a synonym for the highest standards in beauty, composure, and sophistication.

Under editor-in-chief Edna Woolman Chase (1877–1957) and art director Mehemed Gehmy Agha (1896–1978), *Vogue* published the work of leading photographers like Edward Steichen (1879–1973), Sir Cecil Beaton (1904–1980), and Baron de Meyer (1868–1949). These photographers presented their models in glamorous settings that reflected the elaborate **Hollywood** (see entry under 1930s–Film and Theater in volume 2) movies of the period. During World War II (1939–45), *Vogue* concentrated more on affordable, ready-to-wear lines of clothing but continued to emphasize quality and style.

In the postwar era, editor-in-chief Jessica Davies collaborated with art director Alexander Liberman (1912–1999) to reform the magazine using simpler, more contemporary graphics. Together with photographers Irving Penn (1917–) and Richard Avedon (1923–), they reinvented the fashion magazine with images that used starker lighting and that put a stronger focus on the model. *Vogue* also upgraded its coverage of contemporary events by including more serious commentaries on art, film, and theater and articles on the lives of celebrities and entertainers.

Editor-in-chief Diana Vreeland (1906–1989), credited with coining the term "youthquake," brought an edgier tone to the magazine by highlighting the colorful and revealing fashions and accessories that were representative of the "swinging sixties." Models such as Twiggy (1949–), Penelope Tree (1950–), and Verushka (1939–) became celebrities in their own right via photo shoots that showed them in action-filled, "real life" poses outside the studio. Vreeland's successor, Grace Mirabella (1929–), guided the magazine through the so-called feminist era of the 1970s, when women wanted to be taken seriously in the workplace without sacrificing elegance and good taste. During this period, *Vogue* itself shrank in size from a large-format magazine and became a monthly. Mirabella was succeeded as editor-in-chief by Anna Wintour (1949–), who promoted fashion trends by new designers.

—Edward Moran

For More Information

Devlin, Polly. Liberman. *Vogue Book of Fashion Photography.* London: Thames and Hudson, 1979.

Kazajian, Dodie, and Calvin Tomkins. *Alex: The Life of Alexander Liberman.* New York: Alfred A. Knopf, 1993.

Lloyd, Valerie. *The Art of Vogue Photographic Covers: Fifty Years of Fashion and Design.* New York: Harmony Books, 1986.

World Book Encyclopedia

Published since 1917, the *World Book Encyclopedia* is a general reference work. The encyclopedia deliberately uses nontechnical language and abundant graphics to make it especially accessible to students and general readers without sacrificing depth and accuracy. The editors of the first edition emphasized the use of "everyday, simple language" in the eight-volume set.

In 1919, *World Book* began the practice of printing annual revisions of its encyclopedia, which has been followed every year since except for 1920, 1924, and 1932. *World Book*'s first major revision took place in 1929, when the set was expanded to thirteen volumes. In 1931, *World Book* adopted the unit-letter system of arrangement, in which each volume was a different-sized book that contained all the entries for one or more letters of the alphabet. The set was expanded to nineteen volumes in 1933, to twenty volumes in 1960, and to twenty-two volumes in 1972. The final volume in the set is a research guide and an index.

World Book has traditionally worked with educators in an attempt to keep its product in line with current teaching practices. In 1936, it created an editorial advisory board of distinguished educators and established a curriculum-analysis program to ensure that the encyclopedia would be especially useful to its student readers. In 1955, *World Book* launched a classroom research program designed to monitor exactly which subjects typical students were looking up in the reference work.

World Book entered the digital age in 1990 with the publication of *Information Finder,* its first CD-ROM encyclopedia, which included the full text of both the encyclopedia and a dictionary. In 1996, *World Book* partnered with IBM to produce a line of electronic reference works and learning products, and with Tiger Electronics to create the *World Book* Learning Center, an electronic learning aid. *World Book Online* was launched in 1998, with an interactive Web site that delivers articles, maps, pictures, sounds, and video to registered subscribers.

World Book has also created other reference products, including *Childcraft,* a resource library for preschool and elementary-school children, first published in 1934, the *World Book Dictionary* (1963), the *World Book Atlas* (1964), *Early World of Learning* (1987), plus annual volumes about science, health, and medicine. The *World Book Student Discovery Encyclopedia,* an introductory general reference set, appeared in 1999.

—Edward Moran

For More Information

Hancock, Susan, ed. *A Guide to Children's Reference Books and Multimedia Material.* Brookfield, VT: Ashgate, 1998.
World Book. http://www2.worldbook.com (accessed January 17, 2002).
World Book Online. http://www.worldbookonline.com (accessed January 17, 2002).

Zorro

Zorro, the masked avenger of the Old Southwest, has been one of the most popular heroic figures of the twentieth century. The character, created by Johnston McCulley (1883–1958) in 1919, first appeared in a story titled "The Curse of Capistrano" in the pulp magazine *All-Story Weekly.* El Zorro ("The Fox") dressed completely in black and wore a mask and a wide-brimmed hat to conceal his identity as he fought evildoers in nineteenth-century California. He rode a jet-black horse named Tornado and was a master with both sword and whip. His trademark was to carve a "Z" with his blade upon his enemies. Without his costume, Zorro was the wealthy Spanish count Don Diego, who assumed a foppish manner to conceal his secret identity. (A fop is a man who is overly concerned about his looks and his clothes.) Zorro's adventures have thrilled Americans for generations as he has appeared in novels, film, **television** (see entry under 1940s—TV and Radio in volume 3), and cartoons, as well as in a multitude of merchandise and collectibles.

Zorro emerged from **pulp magazines** (see entry under 1930s—Print Culture in volume 2) to become a national phenomenon. Readers loved the swashbuckler as he displayed a devil-may-care attitude, great swordsmanship, and compassion for the oppressed (mistreated). McCulley penned sixty-five of the hero's adventures over nearly forty years. Zorro was successful in print, but he was even more popular on film. Douglas Fairbanks Sr. (1883–1939) first portrayed him in *The Mark of Zorro* (1920) to great acclaim. Numerous Zorro films and serials appeared into the 1970s. Perhaps the most popular depiction of Zorro was in the 1940 version of *The Mark of Zorro.* Actor Tyrone Power (1914–1958) perfectly characterized both the weak Don Diego and bold hero Zorro.

Zorro was also often featured on television. Disney produced a Zorro series in the 1950s starring Guy Williams (1924–1989)

Douglas Fairbanks Sr. as Zorro in a scene from *Don Q., Son of Zorro* (1925). *The Kobal Collection/ United Artists. Reproduced by permission.*

that sparked a bonanza of merchandise. In 1980, George Hamilton (1939–) appeared in the campy *Zorro, The Gay Blade*. The film showed Zorro wearing a pink leather costume and was a complete disaster. Between 1989 and 1994, Duncan Regehr (1952–) appeared as the swordsman. The 1980s and 1990s further witnessed several animated Zorro programs. In 1998, Zorro again dominated the national consciousness when Anthony Hopkins (1937–) and Antonio Banderas (1960–) starred in *The Mask of Zorro,* which introduced the character to another generation of fans.

Zorro was one of the twentieth century's first popular heroic icons. He is a dashing, gentleman bandit who performs heroic feats, woos lovely ladies, and fights corruption—all with a charming elegance and flashing blade. Dozens of heroic characters, most notably **Batman** (see entry under 1930s—Print Culture in volume 2), have followed the pattern established by McCulley's masked daredevil.

—Charles Coletta

For More Information

Curtis, Sandra. *Zorro Unmasked: The Official History.* New York: Hyperion, 1998.

Hutchinson, Don. *The Great Pulp Heroes.* Buffalo: Mosaic Press, 1996.

McCulley, Johnston. *The Mark of Zorro.* New York: American Reprint Co., 1924, 1976.

Toth, Alex. *Zorro: The Complete Classic Adventures.* Forestville, CA: Eclipse Books, 1988.

1910s

Sports and Games

Baseball continued to dominate the American sports scene in the 1910s. Attendance at professional baseball games remained high throughout the decade, rising slightly from 6,206,447 in 1910 to 6,532,439 in 1919; the numbers might have been higher without the interruptions of World War I (1914–18). The American League dominated the World Series, winning eight of ten titles in the decade. The games biggest stars were Ty Cobb (1886–1961) of the Detroit Tigers, Walter Johnson (1887–1946) of the Washington Senators, and an emerging star—George Herman "Babe" Ruth (1895–1948) of the Boston Red Sox (and later the New York Yankees). Baseball received a black eye in 1919 when several players on the Chicago White Sox were involved in "throwing" (intentionally losing) the World Series for money; the event became known as the Black Sox Scandal.

Aside from baseball, American professional sports were just getting started in the 1910s. Professional hockey got its start in 1911 with the founding of the Pacific Coast Hockey League, which overshadowed the fledgling National Hockey League, founded in 1917. Auto racing also got a boost in the decade with the founding of the Indianapolis 500. Ray Harroun (1879–1968) won the initial race—and the $10,000 prize—by averaging an amazing 74.6 miles an hour. Horse racing also gained respectability in the decade thanks to the introduction of the Triple Crown, a series of horse races that included the most famous race of all, the Kentucky Derby.

College football continued to be the most popular fall spectator sport, with Notre Dame becoming a dominant team in the decade behind the play of Knute Rockne (1888–1931), who became the team's coach late in the decade. Professional football was still limited to a small league in the Midwest. Unlike professional baseball, the early pro football leagues allowed black players to participate, and several black players starred on early teams. Native American Jim Thorpe (1888–1953) was the star of the decade in professional football, and he remained so into the 1920s.

Black boxer Jack Johnson (1878–1946) continued his reign as heavyweight champion in this decade, enraging racist white fight fans who could not stand the idea of a black man being in a position of dominance. Johnson finally lost his title to white boxer Jess Willard (1883–1968) in 1915. In 1919, a new champion, Jack Dempsey (1895–1983), took the crown. Dempsey would become the most celebrated boxer of the 1920s. Other sports also gained participants in the decade. Golf and tennis—once games of the upper classes—became popular among the American middle class. Golf champion Walter Hagen (1892–1969) became a minor celebrity.

Young Americans also enjoyed some fascinating new toys and games in this decade. Both Tinkertoys and Erector Sets allowed children to create toys modeled after the innovations of their day—cars and skyscrapers. Other children played with the newly popular Raggedy Ann and Andy dolls. Each of these toys remained in production in the early twenty-first century.

Erector Sets

Before **LEGOS** (see entry under 1950s—Sports and Games in volume 3), there were Erector Sets. The Erector Set is a popular construction toy that taught as well as amused youngsters for most of the twentieth century. The primary components of Erector Sets are nuts, bolts, and hole-filled metal girders of varying sizes. Other materials include wheels, pulleys, gears, and electric motors. Following instructions that come in each Erector Set box, children use the nuts and bolts to attach the girders, resulting in the construction of elaborate miniature buildings, airplanes, trucks, cars, bridges, ships, clocks, houses—and even robots.

The toy was first produced in 1913 by the Mysto Magic Company, which sold magic-trick components. It was the creation of A. C. Gilbert (1884–1961), the company founder. Gilbert was a man of varied interests and many talents. In 1908, he won a gold medal for pole-vaulting in the Summer **Olympics** (see entry under 1900s—Sports and Games in volume 1). The following year, he earned a medical degree from Yale University. While a passenger on a train bound from New Haven, Connecticut, to New York City, he observed workmen positioning steal beams. This event inspired him to create a child's construction kit that he called the "Mysto Erector Structural Steel Builder"; the product eventually became commonly known as the Erector Set. Gilbert was aware of simi-

A boy plays with an Erector Set. A. C. Gilbert created the toy so that it would not only provide hours of fun but also promote a greater understanding of science and technology.
Bettmann/Corbis. Reproduced by permission.

lar construction toys already available in the marketplace, such as the English Meccano. However, his sets were an improvement over the competition, because he included square girders and pieces that could bend to a ninety-degree angle. Gilbert's goal was to create a toy that was fun to play with but also allowed the user to gain an increased understanding of science and technology. He believed that "playing is essential to learning."

The instructions that accompanied Erector Sets from decade to decade paralleled twentieth-century technological advances. As architects designed great urban **skyscrapers** (see entry under 1930s—The Way We Lived in volume 2) and expansive suspension bridges, Erector Set owners were encouraged to build their own tall buildings and elevated structures. Instructions for constructing trucks, **Ferris wheels** (see entry under 1900s—The Way We Lived in volume 1), and zeppelins were added to the sets during the 1920s. A parachute jump came in the 1940s, followed by an entire **amusement park** (see entry under 1950s—The Way We Lived in volume 3) in the 1950s.

Gilbert created and marketed additional toys, including Mysto Magic sets, American Flyer trains, a glass-blowing kit, and an Atomic Energy Lab, which included authentic radioactive particles and a real Geiger counter. In his lifetime, Gilbert was credited with over 150 patents and inventions. After his death, the Meccano Company—now Meccano Toys Ltd. and one of Gilbert's chief early competitors—purchased the rights to Erector Sets. The Brio Corporation, known for its wooden trains, began distributing a new line of Erector Sets in the summer of 2001.

—Rob Edelman

For More Information

Bean, William M. and Al M. Sternagle. *Greenberg's Guide to Gilbert Erector Sets, 1913–1932.* Waukesha, WI: Kalmbach Publishing Company, 1993.

Bean, William M. *Greenberg's Guide to Gilbert Erector Sets, Volume Two, 1933–1962.* Waukesha, WI: Kalmbach Publishing Company, 1998.

Dr. Prune's Erector World. http://www.erectorworld.com (accessed October, 2001).

"Kids' Trains: BRIO Brings Back the Erector Set." *Trains.com.* http:// www.trains.com/Content/Dynamic/Articles/000/000/001/109exais.asp (accessed on January 17, 2002).

Indianapolis 500

The Indianapolis 500 is America's most celebrated auto race. It has been held each May on or around Memorial Day, every year since 1911 (except during the world war years), at the Indianapolis Motor Speedway. The race consists of two hundred laps around the track's two-and-a-half-mile oval.

When the race started in 1911, it was called the International Sweepstakes, and it lasted most of the day. Ray Harroun (1879–1968) earned $10,000 for his first-place finish. His car, known as the "Marmon Wax," averaged a then-astounding 74.602 miles per hour. The car reportedly was the first single-seat race car and the first auto ever to employ a rearview mirror. Now contrast Harroun's statistics to those of drivers and cars racing in the 500 during the final quarter of the twentieth century. By then, the race generally was completed in less than three-and-a-half hours. In 1977, Tom Sneva (1948–) became the first driver to top 200 miles per hour during a race; by the 1990s, drivers regularly topped 220 miles on the corners and 240 miles on the straightaways. In 1990, winner Arie Luyendyk

Cars rounding a lap during the 1996 Indianapolis 500 at the Indianapolis Motor Speedway. *Photograph by Amy Sancetta. AP/Wide World Photos. Reproduced by permission.*

(1953–) averaged a course-record 185.981 miles per hour. Harroun's prize money was a tidy sum back in 1911, but it does not compare with the $1,568,150 Luyendyk walked away with for winning the 500 in 1997.

All the great drivers have raced at Indianapolis. In its early days, they included barnstormers like Harroun. Between 1937 and 1940, Wilbur Shaw (1902–1954) came in first place three times. In 1946, Shaw persuaded businessman-philanthropist Anton "Tex" Hulman (1901–1977) to purchase the speedway from its ownership group. Shaw was named its president. Under his and Hulman's stewardship, the Indianapolis 500 earned its status as the world's top auto race. In the 1950s, such innovations as high-octane gasoline, fuel injection, and disc brakes all were tested at Indianapolis.

Of all the drivers to compete in the Indianapolis 500, the most celebrated is A. J. Foyt (1935–). He debuted in the race in 1958. He holds the record for most career starts (thirty-five, all consecutive) and most competitive miles driven (12,273 miles). Foyt emerged victorious a record four times, a feat equaled only by Al Unser (1939–) and Rick Mears (1951–). On the downside, forty drivers have been killed at Indianapolis across the decades, fifteen drivers during the actual race and twenty-five during practice and qualifying runs.

In recent years, because so much money is at stake, race-car owners have become as prominent as their drivers. Perhaps the most famous is Roger Penske (1937–), a former driver who became a car-and-track owner. The decade of the 1990s saw an increase in politics within the racing establishment, and competition between the Indianapolis Racing League (IRL), which sponsors the Indianapolis 500, and its rival Championship Auto Racing Teams (CART). For this reason, many of the sport's top drivers have been forgoing the Indianapolis 500, thus tainting its reputation as "the greatest spectacle in racing."

—Rob Edelman

For More Information

Binford, Tom. *A Checkered Past: My Twenty Years as Indy 500 Chief Steward.* Chicago: Cornerstone, 1998.

Indianapolis 500. http://my.brickyard.com/500/ (accessed January 17, 2002).

Taylor, Rich. *Indy: 75 Years of Auto Racing's Greatest Spectacle.* New York: St. Martin's Press, 1991.

National Hockey League

Ice hockey has been played for more than five hundred years, but the National Hockey League (NHL) has only been around since 1917. Formed by team owners in the aftermath of World War I (1914–18), this new professional league succeeded where previous ones, such as the International Pro Hockey League, the National Hockey Association, and the Pacific Coast League had failed.

The NHL originally consisted of five teams: the Montreal Canadiens, the Montreal Wanderers, the Ottawa Senators, the Quebec Bulldogs, and the Toronto Arenas. The league's first game was held December 19, 1917. By 1926, the league had expanded to ten teams and two divisions and adopted the Stanley Cup as its championship trophy. The financial shocks of the Great Depression (1929–41) claimed three of the franchises, while another folded in 1942, leaving the NHL a six-team league for the next twenty-five years. That period, from 1942 to 1967, saw increasing dominance of the sport by Canadian players. In fact, the two premier Canadian teams, the Toronto Maple Leafs and the Montreal Canadiens, combined to win ten Stanley Cups during the era.

One of the NHL's first American superstars emerged in the late 1960's, as defenseman Bobby Orr (1948–) led the Boston Bruins to two Stanley Cup victories. Orr's success and the development of college hockey programs in the United States spurred renewed American enthusiasm for the sport during the 1970s. The league merged with a rival league, the World Hockey Association, in 1979, adding five teams in one stroke of a pen.

The NHL continued to grow in the 1980s, following the gold medal performance by the U.S. men's team at the 1980 Winter **Olympics** (see entry under 1900s—Sports and Games in volume 1) in Lake Placid, New York. **Wayne Gretzky** (1961–; see entry under 1980s—Sports and Games in volume 5) and his Edmonton Oilers became the dominant team in the sport during the 1980s. The high-scoring Mario Lemieux (1965–) emerged as a star in the 1990s. The collapse of the Soviet Union spurred the emigration of a number of talented Eastern European players, such as Jaromir Jagr (1972–) and Dominik Hasek (1965–). The influx of new players and styles made the game of hockey more dynamic than ever, and this period saw the NHL enjoy its greatest growth. A number of new franchises were added, while others—particularly those

The Detroit Red Wings, who joined the National Hockey League in 1926, emerged as a powerhouse team in the late 1990s and early 2000s. *Photograph by Bill Kostroun. AP/Wide World Photos. Reproduced by permission.*

based in Canada—relocated to growing American cities like Phoenix, Arizona, and Denver, Colorado. A players' strike in 1995 briefly curtailed the NHL's growth, but interest began building again toward the turn of the twenty-first century.

—Robert E. Schnakenberg

For More Information

Goyen, Chrys. *Blades on Ice: A Century of Professional Hockey.* New York: Hushion House, 2000.

NHL.com. www.nhl.com (accessed January 17, 2002).

Strachan, Al, ed. *One Hundred Years of Hockey.* New York: Thunder Bay Press, 1999.

Raggedy Ann and Raggedy Andy

A quarter of a century before the 1995 film ***Toy Story*** (see entry under 1990s—Film and Theater in volume 5) explored the hidden life of toys, a writer named Johnny Gruelle (1880–1938) wrote about the adventures of a pair of dolls and their toy friends and the lives they lived when "real" people were not

Raggedy Ann and Raggedy Andy. *Archive Photos. Reproduced by permission.*

looking. First created in 1918, Raggedy Ann and Andy are still loved by children everywhere.

Dolls made of rags were not uncommon in the eighteenth and nineteenth centuries, when most toys were handmade and not manufactured. In the early 1900s, Gruelle's daughter Marcella had loved the little rag doll she named Raggedy Ann. Marcella died while still a child, and her grieving father began to write down stories about his daughter's favorite doll. Raggedy Ann and, later, her brother Raggedy Andy appeared in a series of popular books with titles like *How Raggedy Ann Got Her Candy Heart* and *Raggedy Ann and Raggedy Andy and the Camel with the Wrinkled Knees.*

Soon, toymakers began making dolls that looked like the ones in Gruelle's books. Modern children cannot only read Raggedy Ann and Andy books and own the dolls but can also watch Raggedy Ann and Andy videos and dress in Raggedy costumes on Halloween.

—Tina Gianoulis

For More Information

Hall, Patricia. *Raggedy Ann and Andy: A Retrospective Celebrating 85 Years of Storybook Friends.* New York: Simon and Schuster, 2001.
Hall, Patricia. *The Real-for-Sure Story of Raggedy Ann.* Gretna, LA: Pelican Publishing, 2001.
"The History of Raggedy Ann." *The Last Great Company.* http://www.raggedyman.com/story.html (accessed January 17, 2002).
Hudson, Patricia L. "Still Smiling at Seventy-Five: What a Doll!" *Americana* (Vol. 18, no. 5, December 1990): pp. 52–56.

Babe Ruth (1895–1948)

With due respect to baseball stars from **Jackie Robinson** (1919–1972; see entry under 1940s—Sports and Games in volume 3) to Mickey Mantle (1931–1995) to Mark McGwire (1963–), Babe Ruth is without doubt the most celebrated **baseball** (see entry under 1900s—Sports and Games in volume 1) hero of the twentieth century.

For over two decades beginning in 1914, George Herman Ruth—whose nicknames included "The Bambino" and "The Sultan of Swat"—ruled the world of baseball. His most prominent records have been broken. His record of sixty home runs in a season in 1927 was eclipsed thirty-four years later by Roger Maris (1934–1985) and broken yet again by McGwire and Sammy Sosa (1968–) in 1998 and Barry Bonds (1964–) in 2001. Ruth's career record of 714 round-trippers was bested in the early 1970s by Hank Aaron (1934–). Yet Ruth remains the most immortal of all baseball immortals for many reasons. His larger-than-life presence, his lovable personality, and his Hall of Fame ability as a pitcher as well as a home-run basher all figure in his reputation. The most significant reason, though, is his single-handed rescue of baseball in the wake of the Black Sox gambling scandal that forever tainted the 1919 World Series, leading to a questioning of the game's integrity by a wary public. In this regard, Ruth was as much a key to the sport's resurgence during the 1920s as the home run derby in 1998 between McGwire and Sosa was to its renewed popularity in the wake of the 1994 baseball strike.

—Rob Edelman

For More Information

Jacobs, William Jay. *They Shaped the Game: Ty Cobb, Babe Ruth, Jackie Robinson.* New York: C. Scribner's Sons, 1994.

Macht, Norman L. *Babe Ruth.* New York: Chelsea House, 1991.
Miller, Ernestine. *The Babe Book: Baseball's Greatest Legend Remembered.* Kansas City: Andrews McMeel Publishing, 2000.
Ruth, George Herman. *Babe Ruth's Own Book of Baseball.* Lincoln: University of Nebraska Press, 1992.

Tinkertoys

Like **LEGOS** (see entry under 1950s—Sports and Games in volume 3), **Lincoln Logs** (see entry under 1920s—Sports and Games in volume 2), and **Erector Sets** (see entry under 1910s—Sports and Games in volume 1), Tinkertoys have a timeless appeal. Introduced in 1914, the simple wooden sticks with connecting wooden hubs remain a favorite among kids into the twenty-first century. In many ways, Tinkertoys are the perfect toy. Simple and durable, they have the capacity to engage a child's imagination as he or she creates an unlimited variety of structures.

A young girl plays with wooden Tinkertoys. *Hulton/Archive by Getty Images. Reproduced by permission.*

Tinkertoys were invented by Charles H. Pajeau, a stone mason. He thought up the toy after watching children play with pencils and wooden spools. Pajeau drilled holes around the sides of a spool and sawed thin wooden dowels into various lengths to create the first set of Tinkertoys. The sticks and spools could be combined to create a huge number of shapes, from cars to boats to the Tinkertoy classic **Ferris wheel** (see entry under 1900s—The Way We Lived in volume 1). Pajeau joined with former stock trader Robert Pettit to form a company called The Toy Tinkers of Evanston, Illinois. In 1914, they set up Tinkertoy Ferris wheels in shop windows in Chicago, Illinois, and their toy became an immediate hit. For the next several decades, demand for their product was high. In 1952, the original owners sold their company. The Tinkertoy brand passed through several owners before being purchased by toy giant Hasbro in 1986.

Tinkertoys have gone through a number of changes over the years. Sets have been sold in different sizes and with motors. Beginning in 1992, wood was replaced with plastic. In 2000, however, Hasbro took Tinkertoys back to its roots and began marketing wooden Tinkertoys in the characteristic cardboard canister. Nearly ninety years after their introduction, classic wooden Tinkertoys remain a favorite among American kids. In recognition of their enduring status, in 2001 Tinkertoys were named "Toy of the Year" in their category by the Toy Manufacturers of America.

—Tom Pendergast

For More Information

"The Classic Tinkertoy Construction Set." *Hasbro . . . Making the World Smile.* http://www.hasbropreschool.com/default.asp?x=tinkertoy (accessed January 17, 2002).

Jailer, Mildred. "Construction Toys." *Antiques and Collecting Hobbies* (May 1988): p. 38.

Strange, Craig. *Collector's Guide to Tinker Toys.* Paducah, KY: Collector Books, 1996.

"Tinker Toys." *Yesterdayland.* http://www.yesterdayland.com/popopedia/shows/toys/ty1079.php (accessed January 17, 2002).

1910s

The Way We Lived

Like the decade before it, the 1910s were characterized by a slow but steady modernizing trend. American society became more urban. People left rural areas for suburbs. Cities expanded thanks to the ease of travel provided by automobiles, buses, and streetcars. As American factories grew larger and more capable of producing a variety of goods, more and more Americans ceased to make clothes, food, and other household goods at home. Instead, they bought those goods from retail stores and from the growing variety of catalog retailers, such as Sears, Roebuck; L. L. Bean; and others.

Several dramatic social movements also helped reshape America in the decade. Racism grew even more intense in the South, as seen in the growing number of Jim Crow laws (which forced blacks into separate and inferior public facilities) and the increase in lynchings (illegal mob killings). By mid-decade blacks began leaving the South in huge numbers, heading north to fill the expanding factories of manufacturers in cities such as Detroit, Michigan; Chicago, Illinois; Cleveland, Ohio; and New York City. This movement of African Americans, quickened by the involvement of the United States in World War I (1914–18) in 1917, is known as the Great Migration (1900–60).

Two other social movements led to constitutional amendments. As more and more women left their roles as homemakers and moved into the workplace, they clamored for the full rights enjoyed by men—including the right to vote. Thanks to leadership from organizers like Carrie Chapman Catt (1859–1947) and Alice Paul (1885–1977), a women's suffrage amendment passed Congress in 1919 and became law in 1920 as the Nineteenth Amendment. Temperance crusaders led a campaign to ban the sale and distribution of alcohol. Their campaign culminated in the Eighteenth Amendment, ratified in 1919 (and repealed in 1933 after the disastrous social experiment known as Prohibition).

World War I brought major changes to the way Americans lived in the decade as well. American leaders kept the United

States out of the war for the first three years, but when America joined the Allies in 1917, Americans threw their support behind the war effort. Two million American soldiers joined the war effort, including several thousand African American soldiers. Millions more Americans supported the war by purchasing war bonds. Though war brought unity to many Americans, it also created divisions. German immigrants were singled out for mistreatment, even though most committed themselves to their new country. Political radicals like Socialists and Communists faced hostility during the Red Scare of 1919.

Despite these major social changes, people still found time for new forms of amusement. There were popular crazes for new games like the card game bridge. Americans by the thousands went to see a new circus that billed itself as the "Greatest Show on Earth"—the Ringling Bros. and Barnum & Bailey Circus. Boys and girls across the nation enjoyed joining the Boy Scouts and the Girl Scouts, two popular organizations that tried to build character in their participants.

Bridge

One of the most popular card games in the world, bridge has been played in one form or another since the sixteenth century. Since modern contract bridge was developed in 1925, bridge has become by far the most organized card game, with bridge clubs and leagues all over the world sponsoring highly competitive tournaments. Though often associated with rich old ladies trading gossip and nibbling delicate snacks between hands, bridge is actually a game of skill and strategy. Its addicts include all sorts of people from college students to business executives.

Although some claim that the game of bridge has its roots in Turkey or Russia, the first real documentation of a bridgelike card game comes from sixteenth-century England. That game, called whist, whisk, triumph, or trump, introduced the "trick," where each player in turn lays a card down, following suit, and the highest ranking card wins the round.

The game went through various developments, but modern contract bridge was invented in 1925 by wealthy American businessman Harold S. Vanderbilt (1884–1970), supposedly to pass the time while cruising through the Panama Canal. Within two years, three major national contract bridge clubs had formed. In 1928, the first national bridge championship tournament was played. The winner of that tournament, Ely Culbertson (1893–1955), went on to popularize bridge nationwide. Culbertson founded *Bridge World* magazine and wrote the *Blue Book* laying out rules and strategies for playing the game. In the 1940s, another champion, Charles Goren (1901–1991), became the national bridge expert, writing a daily newspaper column on bridge tactics.

Though bridge is often thought of as an old-fashioned game, it still has a thriving following. As of 2000, the American Contract Bridge League had 180,000 members nationwide, and the **Internet** (see entry under 1990s—The Way We Lived in volume 5) is also bringing bridge to a wider and younger audience than ever. There are dozens of bridge Web sites where players who are home alone can find partners with whom to play. One of the largest, OKBridge.com, claims it hosts over a thousand players a day.

—Tina Gianoulis

For More Information

ACBL Online. http://www.acbl.com (accessed January 17, 2002).

"Bridge." *Playsite*. http://www.playsite.com/games/list.gsp?root=playsite.card.bridge (accessed January 17, 2002).

D'Amato, Brian. "Bridge: The Game People Play." *Harper's Bazaar* (August 1994): pp. 66–68.

Goodwin, Jude, and Don Ellison. *Teach Me to Play: A First Bridge Book*. Roswell, GA: Pando Publications, 1988.

Koczela, Catherine. "Bridge, Handed Down; Among High Schoolers, Old Game Gaining New Following." *Washington Post* (October 16, 1997): p. M1.

Father's Day

On Father's Day, the third Sunday in June, children young and old show appreciation for their dear-old dads—and uncles, grandfathers, and godfathers. The day serves as a symbol of America's regard not only for fatherhood but for the sanctity of the American family.

The roots of the day are imprecise. In 1910, Sonora Smart Dodd, of Spokane, Washington, wished to honor her father—a man who had raised his six children upon the death of his wife—successfully petitioned the Spokane Ministerial Association to set aside a day of reverence for all fathers. Yet Vancouver, Washington, claimed to be the first American city to officially sanction Father's Day, in 1912. Three years later, Harry Meek, the president of the Uptown Lions Club in Chicago, Illinois, was recognized as the "Originator of Father's Day" when he proposed that the third Sunday in June be set aside to honor fatherhood. He selected that date because it was closest to the birthday of the then-U.S. president, Woodrow Wilson (1856–1924). In 1924, President Calvin Coolidge (1872–1933) advocated the official acknowledgment of Father's Day across the country. Finally, in 1972, President Richard Nixon (1913–1994) signed a law making the day an official national holiday.

Today, Father's Day is exploited commercially, as children are expected not just to honor their fathers but to shower them with cards and gifts. Each year, approximately one hundred million Father's Day cards are purchased, along with endless neckties, power tools, sports shirts, golf balls, and other "male" attire and accessories. Nonetheless, the day remains a reminder of the sacrifice and devotion of fathers across the nation.

—Rob Edelman

For More Information

Klebanow, Barbara. *American Holidays: Exploring Traditions, Customs, and Backgrounds*. Brattleboro, VT: Pro Lingua Associates, 1986.

Myers, Robert. *Celebrations: Complete Book of American Holidays*. New York: Doubleday, 1972.

Santino, Jack. *All Around the Year: Holidays and Celebrations in American Life*. Urbana: University of Illinois Press, 1995.

Schmidt, Leigh Eric. *Consumer Rites: The Buying and Selling of American Holidays*. Princeton, NJ: Princeton University Press, 1995.

Greyhound Buses

With the advice to "Go Greyhound—and leave the driving to us," Greyhound buses have become part of the mythology of the American road. In 1968, songwriter **Paul Simon** (1941–; see Simon and Garfunkel entry under 1960s—Music in volume 4) wrote of exploring America, and finding himself, on a Greyhound bus. Often operating out of bus stations in neglected areas of urban areas, Greyhound still represents the best way to, as Simon sang, "Look for America."

Founded by Carl Eric Wickman (1887–1954) in 1914, Greyhound Buses started life as the Mesaba Transportation Company. Wickman's first bus, a seven-passenger Hupmobile, carried mineworkers between the towns of Hibbing and Alice, Minnesota. The company grew quickly. By 1935, there were seventeen hundred buses with the "racing Greyhound" logo, covering over forty-six thousand route miles. In 2000, the company carried over nineteen million passengers. Over two thousand people every day travel its busiest route, between New York City and Atlantic City, New Jersey.

—Chris Routledge

For More Information

Greyhound Lines, Inc. http://www.greyhound.com/ (accessed on January 17, 2002).

Schisgall, Oscar. *The Greyhound Story: From Hibbing to Everywhere.* Chicago: J. G. Ferguson, 1985.

Ku Klux Klan

The Ku Klux Klan is America's oldest white supremacist organization. It first gained power in the South during Reconstruction (1865–77; the period following the American Civil War when the federal government assisted and policed the former Confederate states), which the Klan resisted with beatings, murder, and terrorism. Although the organization has splintered and its fortunes have declined somewhat, the Klan still maintained a hold on the American consciousness going into the twenty-first century.

The organization's name is derived from the Greek word *kuklos,* meaning "circle," and a corruption of "clan," or family. Its origins lie with a group of six Confederate war veterans who returned to Pulaski, Tennessee, when the Civil War (1861–65) ended in 1865. They relieved boredom by dressing up in white sheets and playing pranks on their neighbors by night. The Klan might have remained a mere gang of bullies were it not for the Congressional Reconstruction Act of 1867. This law mandated Federal military occupation of the South, declared Southern state governments illegitimate, and said that the rights of newly freed black slaves would be guaranteed by the U.S. Army.

The Klan, whose membership grew quickly, responded with violence toward anyone—black or white—who appeared to

The Ku Klux Klan marching down Pennsylvania Avenue in Washington, D.C., in 1925. *Courtesy of National Archives and Records Administration.*

threaten the traditional Southern way of life. There are no reliable statistics for the number of people intimidated, beaten, shot, or lynched (murdered by a mob, usually by hanging) by the Klan, but the violence was bad enough for Congress to pass anti-Klan legislation in 1871 and again in 1872, and to back it up with Federal troops. The Klan did not disappear, but its more public outrages stopped.

The Klan first entered popular culture in 1905, with the publication of a novel by Thomas Dixon Jr. (1864–1946), *The Clansman*. Dixon was a virulent racist. His book both criticized Reconstruction and praised the Klan's response to it. He did the same in the sequel, *The Leopard's Spots,* which appeared the following year. Both books were popular in the South, but their greatest influence involved filmmaker D. W. Griffith (1875–1948), who used material from the two novels in his 1915 epic film ***The Birth of a Nation*** (see entry under 1910s—Film and Theater in volume 1).

The film, regarded as one of the classics of early American cinema, is nonetheless thoroughly racist. Blacks are portrayed as either sex-crazed rapists or as moronic victims of "carpetbaggers," Northerners who came south after the war to take advantage of post-war conditions in the South. The film's protagonists, the Stonemans, are saved from a mob of blacks only by the intervention of the Ku Klux Klan.

The Klan is also portrayed positively in 1918's *The Prussian Cur,* an anti-German propaganda film released in the last year of World War I (1914–18). Director Raoul Walsh (1887–1980) tells the story of a German spy in the United States who is caught and put in jail. A group of disloyal German Americans try to free him, but they are stopped by a patriotic group of robed Klansmen.

The Klan itself began to show renewed signs of life in 1915, courtesy of William Joseph Simmons (1880–1945). He even hired a public relations firm to drum up membership for the organization, now known as the Knights of the Ku Klux Klan. The new Klan reached out to those whites who were troubled by the social changes taking place in America. Consequently, its recruiting material stressed the Klan's opposition to the rising social position of blacks, Jews, Catholics, immigrants, suffragettes, and labor unions. The public relations firm arranged for journalists to interview Simmons, planned elaborate initiation ceremonies for new Klansmen, and even had newspaper ads and billboards spreading the Klan's message.

The Klan played an important role in the best-selling novel ***Gone with the Wind*** (see entry under 1930s—Film and Theater in volume 2) by Margaret Mitchell (1900–1949), published in 1937. Most of the male characters in the book become Klan members. Even Rhett Butler is sympathetic to the group's aims. However, movie producer David O. Selznick (1902–1965) eliminated all mention of the Klan in his 1939 movie version of the book.

The Klan appeared only sporadically in the popular culture of the next several decades, mostly in films. *The Burning Cross* (1948) has its war-veteran hero confront the Klan's power in his hometown. In *Storm Warning* (1951), a crusading district attorney, played by Ronald Reagan (1911–), sets out to convict a group of murderous Klansmen. In *The FBI Story* (1959), Special Agent Chip Hardesty, played by Jimmy Stewart (1908–1997), fights Klan violence in a Southern town.

Portrayals of the Klan surged in the 1980s and beyond. A segment of *Twilight Zone: The Movie* (1983) turns the tables on a bigot, portrayed by Vic Morrow (1929–1982), and includes a scene in which he is the victim of a Klan lynching. Set in 1964, the grimly powerful film *Mississippi Burning* (1988), directed by Alan Parker (1944–), follows the investigation of FBI agents into the Klan murder of three civil rights workers. Klan violence is also portrayed in the films *Fried Green Tomatoes* (1990); *Sommersby* (1992); *A Time to Kill* and *The Chamber* (both 1996 films based on novels by John Grisham, 1955–); and *O Brother Where Art Thou?* (2001).

The actual Klan has not been idle, either. In some areas, Klan groups exploit local public access TV to broadcast their propaganda. Klan leaders have also appeared on talk shows ranging from *Oprah* to *The Jerry Springer Show*. But the biggest boost to the Klan has come from the World Wide Web. Klan organizations have learned that they can reach far more people with a Web site than they ever could with their rallies and leaflets. And so they do—with a message of hate that remains fundamentally unchanged since 1915.

—Justin Gustainis

For More Information

Chalmers, David Mark. *Hooded Americanism: The History of the Ku Klux Klan*. New York: F. Watts, 1981.

Cutlip, Scott M. *The Unseen Power: Public Relations, A History*. Hillsdale, NJ: Lawrence Erlbaum Associates, 1994.

Dessomes, Nancy Bishop. "Hollywood in Hoods: The Portrayal of the Ku Klux Klan in Popular Film." *Journal of Popular Culture* (Spring 1999): pp. 13–22.

Riley, Michael. "New Klan, Old Hatred." *Time* (July 6, 1992): pp. 24–27.

Mother's Day

Since 1914, Mother's Day has been celebrated as a national holiday. On the second Sunday of May, children of all ages honor the parent who by tradition has raised them, and they pay homage to the strength and integrity of the American family, as well. However, because they express their appreciation by giving gifts and sending flowers and greeting cards, Mother's Day has also evolved into a commercial entity.

The roots of the holiday are based on love and respect for motherhood rather than on commercial exploitation. They may be traced to Anna Jarvis (1864–1948), a West Virginian who wished to perpetuate the memory of her own mother while honoring the contributions of all mothers. The intention of Jarvis—who, ironically, was neither wife nor parent herself—was to establish a day of reverence for mothers, to be celebrated across the country. The initial public memorial for her own mother took place in 1907, and the following year similar services were held for all mothers, throughout the nation.

One reason that Mother's Day was embraced as a holiday was that it helped allay fears about the then-emerging "new woman." The new woman was the suffragette who was not satisfied to be compliant in the presence of men. The new woman demanded the right to vote. She might even brazenly smoke **cigarettes** (see entry under 1920s—Commerce in volume 2) or offer her own opinions in public!

Today, Mother's Day primarily is associated with commerce. Children not only pay homage to their mothers but present them with cards, flowers, boxes of candy, and gifts. Each year, approximately 150 million Mother's Day cards are purchased; this compares to 100 million **Father's Day** (see entry under 1910s—The Way We Lived in volume 1) cards, and 900 million Valentine's Day cards. As early as 1910, the Florists' Telegraph Delivery Service (FTD) began encouraging sons and daughters living far away from their mothers to send them flowers. Candy makers, stationers, jewelers, and clothing manufacturers conduct pre-Mother's Day advertising campaigns to boost sales of their products.

Indeed, what Anna Jarvis envisioned as a "holy day" has evolved into a commercial holiday in which the buying, selling, and marketing of products has taken precedence over her initial intention. Similar holidays have followed: Father's Day easily is the most popular; others include Bosses' Day, Secretary's Day, and Grandparents' Day. While Mother's Day does remain a time to honor the sacrifice and devotion of mothers across the nation, it also has evolved into a $9 billion industry.

—Rob Edelman

For More Information

Klebanow, Barbara. *American Holidays: Exploring Traditions, Customs, and Backgrounds.* Brattleboro, VT: Pro Lingua Associates, 1986.

Myers, Robert. *Celebrations: Complete Book of American Holidays.* New York: Doubleday, 1972.

Santino, Jack. *All Around the Year: Holidays and Celebrations in American Life.* Urbana: University of Illinois Press, 1995.

Schmidt, Leigh Eric. *Consumer Rites: The Buying and Selling of American Holidays.* Princeton, NJ: Princeton University Press, 1995.

The first model of the Frigidaire refrigerator, circa 1921.
UPI/Corbis-Bettmann. Reproduced by permission.

Refrigerators

Today, refrigerators are taken for granted as one of the most common appliances in America, but it was not always so. Before refrigerators, people tried to preserve their food in cool places like streams, caves, and snow banks. As more people moved into cities, however, a better solution was needed.

By the early 1800s, people kept blocks of ice in insulated wooden cabinets called "ice cabinets." The widespread use of ice cabinets created the ice-harvesting industry in the northern states. Ice harvesters cut blocks of ice from frozen lakes and shipped them to warmer parts of the country. When the Civil War (1861–65) broke out in 1861, ice was one of the first supplies to be cut off from the southern states, leaving southerners' ice cabinets empty and their food rotting. By the early 1890s, warm winters caused ice supplies throughout the United States to diminish, providing an opportunity for other refrigeration techniques to interest people.

Several inventors experimented with mechanical refrigeration techniques in the 1800s. A method using liquefied ammonia created by French inventor Ferdinand Carré became the basic system used by modern refrigerators. Carré obtained a patent in France in 1859 and in the United States in 1860. It was not until 1914, however, that the first home-use refrigerator—the Dolmere—was introduced in Chicago, Illinois.

Refrigerators soon became tremendously popular; finally, homemakers had a convenient way to store perishable products. By 1916, more than two dozen brands were sold on the market; a number that increased to two hundred by 1920. The first freezers came on the market in the late 1920s. Modern refrigerators started to be mass-produced after World War II (1939–45), making home refrigerators a common consumer product. Home refrigeration systems have not lost their appeal over the years; they have only become more efficient and more environmentally friendly. By the end of the century, refrigerators had become the most common product in American homes; 99.5 percent of American homes had one.

—Sara Pendergast

For More Information

"The History of Household Wonders: History of the Refrigerator." *History Channel.com.* www.historychannel.com/exhibits/hometech (accessed January 17, 2002).

Jones, Joseph C., Jr. *American Ice Boxes: A Book on the History, Collecting, and Restoration of Ice Boxes.* Humble, TX: Jobeco Books, 1981.

Preville, Cherie, and Chris King. "Cooling Takes Off in the Roaring Twenties." *The Achrnews.com.* http://www.achrnews.com/CDA/ArticleInformation/features/BNP__Features__Item/0,1338,24844,00.html (accessed January 17, 2002).

Yenne, Bill. *100 Inventions That Shaped World History.* San Mateo, CA: Bluewood Books, 1993.

Ringling Bros. and Barnum & Bailey Circus

Going to a circus and delighting in the antics of clowns, lion tamers, acrobats, and trapeze artists is one of the rites of childhood. The most famous American circus company is the Ringling Bros. and Barnum & Bailey Circus. ("Bros." is the abbreviation for Brothers.)

The first circuses in the United States appeared in the late eighteenth century. The traditional ones are presented in tents, a practice that dates from 1825. The initial tent circuses were

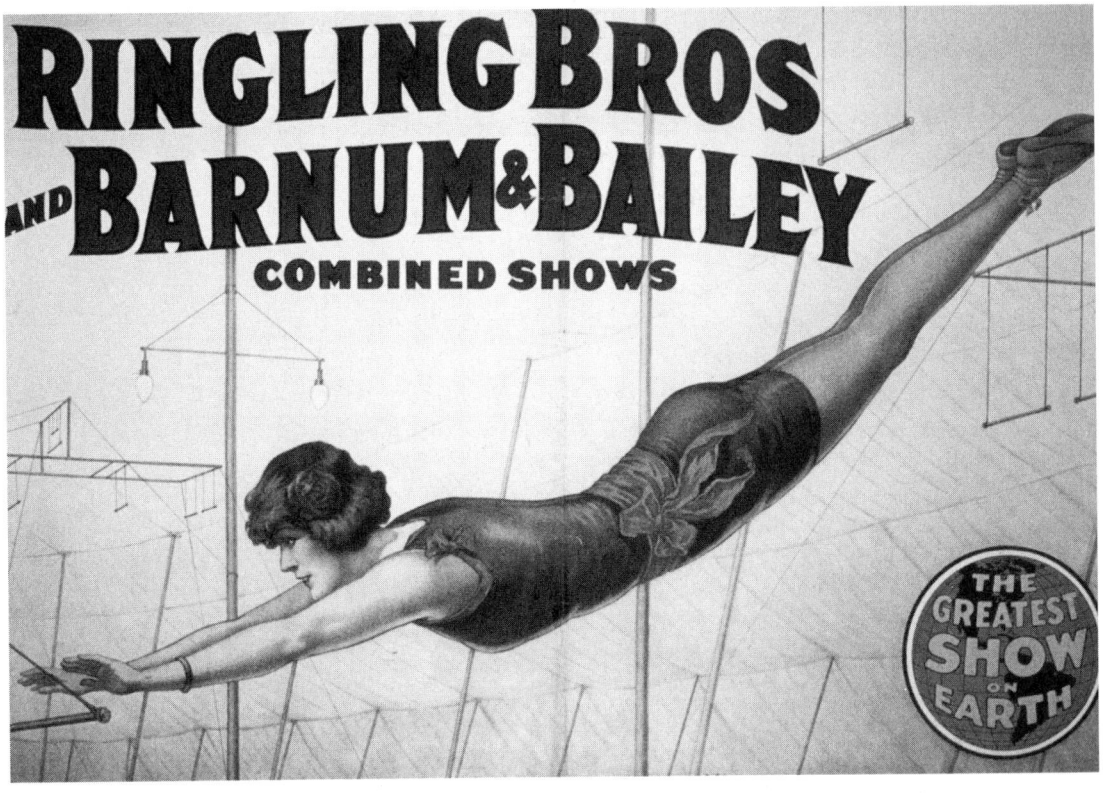

The Ringling Brothers Circus and the Barnum & Bailey Circus combined into one show in 1919. *Bettmann/Corbis. Reproduced by permission.*

small and featured a single ring in which the entertainers performed. As the years passed, the tent size expanded, and the number of rings increased to two and three. Of all the nineteenth-century American circuses, easily the best known was the Barnum & Bailey. It was the brainchild of two men: Phineas T. Barnum (1810–1891) and James A. Bailey (1847–1906), who initially operated their own separate circuses. Barnum was a flamboyant master showman. In 1842, he purchased a five-story building in New York City and converted it into the American Museum, in which he presented freak shows, beauty contests, and theatrical shows. Among his early stars: the Feejee Mermaid, a woman dressed in a fish costume; co-joined twins Chang and Eng (1811–1874); and Charles S. Stratton (1838–1883), a twenty-five-inch-tall man nicknamed General Tom Thumb. In 1871, Barnum began what he labeled "The Greatest Show on Earth," in which he combined traditional circus acts with sideshow performers and caged wild animals. Another of his many successes was his purchase and exploitation of Jumbo, a six-ton elephant.

Bailey, meanwhile, began traveling with circuses while still a boy, and worked his way up to managerial positions with various concerns. In 1872, he became a partner in James E. Cooper's Circus, which first was renamed the Great International Circus and then the Cooper, Bailey & Company Circus. In 1881, Barnum and Bailey merged their operations. For decades, their circus traversed the United States by train, bringing thrills and excitement to towns large and small. After Barnum's death in 1891, Bailey took the show to Europe. Then he expanded it to five rings plus additional stages, and it crossed the country in eighty-five railroad cars. In 1897, the circus spotlighted an act using a record seventy horses, performing together in the same ring. After Bailey died in 1906, the Ringling Brothers Circus, which began as a tent show in 1884, purchased the Barnum & Bailey for $400,000. The two operated as separate entities until 1919, when they combined into one immense enterprise.

Among the most fabled twentieth-century Ringling Bros. and Barnum & Bailey attractions were the Flying Wallendas, a family of high-wire artists founded by Karl Wallenda (1905–1978); Con Colleano (1900–1973), an acrobat known as the Toreador of the Tight Wire; aerialist Lillian Leitzel (1882 or 1892–1931); lion-tamer Clyde Beatty (1903–1965), who later had his own circus; and Emmett Kelly (1898–1979), a sad-faced clown whose best-known character was called Weary Willie.

Despite the popularity of other entertainment media, including motion pictures, **radio** (see entry under 1920s—TV and Radio in volume 2), and **television** (see entry under 1940s—TV and Radio in volume 3), the American circus—and the Ringling Bros. and Barnum & Bailey—endures as a special treat for people of all ages. Across the decades, it remains unchanged in the type of merriment and spectacle it offers as well as in the manner in which it transports itself by rail across the country.

—Rob Edelman

For More Information

Fenner, Mildred Sandison, and Wolcott Fenner. *The Circus, Lore and Legend.* Englewood Cliffs, NJ: Prentice-Hall, 1970.

Hammerstrom, David Lewis. *Behind the Big Top.* New York: Barnes & Noble, 1980.

Kirk, Rhina. *Circus Heroes and Heroines.* New York: Hammond, 1974.

Ringling Bros. and Barnum & Bailey Online. http://www.ringling.com/home.asp (accessed January 17, 2002).

Taylor, Robert Lewis. *Center Ring: The People of the Circus.* Garden City, NY: Doubleday, 1956.

Wallace, Irving. *The Fabulous Showman: The Life and Times of P. T. Barnum.* Norwalk, CT: Easton Press, 1990.

Scouting (Boy and Girl)

Around the world, scouting was the most popular youth movement in the twentieth century. By 2001, scouting organizations for boys and girls were in all but five countries on earth. Founded in Britain by Robert Baden-Powell (1857–1941), the Boy Scouts reached the United States in 1909, when Ernest Thompson Seton (1860–1946) was appointed Chief Scout of America. In Britain, the Girl Scouts (then called Girl Guides) started their own movement in 1910, led by Baden-Powell's sister Agnes (1858–1945). Scouting offered young people the chance to explore the countryside and learn skills such as woodcraft, tracking, and first aid. In 2001, the Boy Scouts of America (BSA) stated that it aimed to help boys build character and physical fitness and become good citizens. Above all, both boy and girl scouts are expected to "Be Prepared."

Scouting began when General Baden-Powell returned from the British campaign at Mafikeng in the South African Boer War (1899–1902). His handbook, *Scouting for Boys,* was published in 1908 and immediately became a **best-seller** (see entry under 1940s—Commerce in volume 3). Chapters entitled "Scoutcraft," "Woodcraft," "Chivalry," and "Our Duties as Citizens" gave advice on subjects such as tying knots, blazing a trail, running a successful camp, and caring for others. Perhaps reflecting Baden-Powell's military background, the handbook even explains what to do if you find a dead body. Through the Boy Scouts and the Girl Guides, Baden-Powell instructed British boys and girls to become loyal subjects of the British Empire.

In the United States, scouting began for different reasons. After the declared "closure" of the frontier in 1893, many Americans worried that the country would lose the pioneering spirit. In 1902, Seton set up the "Woodcraft Indians," a troop of boys who learned how to follow a trail; to recognize different animals, birds, and plants; and to work together as a team in the wilderness. Seton visited Baden-Powell in London in 1906 to exchange ideas. Two years later, scouting came to the attention of American William D. Boyce (1858–1929). Finding himself lost in London, Boyce asked a small boy the way back to his hotel. Boyce was surprised when the boy led him all the way there. He was even more surprised when the boy refused to take money for his trouble, telling Boyce that this was his good turn as a Boy Scout. Impressed, Boyce sought out Baden-Powell to

Boy Scouts gather around their scoutmaster while on a camping trip. *Archive Photos. Reproduced by permission.*

find out about scouting. On his return to the United States, Boyce contacted Seton and together they founded the BSA. The organization was granted its Congressional charter in 1916.

Baden-Powell's aim for the Boy Scouts was to turn boys into "handy, capable men." Organized in army-style "patrols," boy scouts learned teamwork, loyalty, and respect for authority. Early scouting laid down very clear rules about what boys and girls could and should do with their lives. Unlike the boys, who would learn to be leaders and adventurers, Girl Guides would learn to become good companions to their husbands, brothers, and sons. Juliette Gordon "Daisy" Low (1860–1927) began the first American Girl Guide troop in Savannah, Georgia, in 1912. They became known as Girl Scouts in 1915. Already moving away from Baden-Powell's ideas for Girl Guides, Low envisioned an organization that would help girls enjoy an active life outside of the home. Although the first Girl Scout handbook, *Scouting for Girls* (1920) emphasizes domestic skills such as cooking, sewing, and household hygiene, the Girl Scouts also gave girls the chance to live more active and independent lives than before.

Low's Girl Scouts were encouraged to help in their communities, fundraising through annual bake sales and cookie drives. In 1912, ankle-length blue uniforms reflected the accepted view that respectable girls did not play sports, but Low had the girls playing basketball and tennis. Girl Scouts went on hiking and camping trips as well. By 1926, the Girl Scouts had 137,000 members and a national training center in upstate New York. The Girl Scouts organization was always less militaristic than the Boy Scouts. Its religious views sit more easily with modern attitudes and beliefs, and the organization has made a great effort to be tolerant and inclusive. In 2001, it boasted 2.7 million members worldwide, ranging from the kindergarten "Daisies" to seventeen-year-old "Seniors." Remarkably, cookie drives remain an important source of income for the Girl Scouts.

For almost fifty years, parents welcomed scouting as a wholesome influence on youth. But as society became more liberal in the 1960s, the movement lost momentum. Many of the attitudes in *Scouting for Boys* and *Scouting for Girls* seemed very outdated. In the 1990s, the Boy Scouts' opposition to homosexuals and religious nonbelievers drove away many natural supporters. Many people dislike the military style and conservative approach of scouting in general. Even critics of scouting, however, accept that its core values of loyalty, honesty, and respect for others are also the essential qualities of any good citizen.

—Chris Routledge

For More Information

Boy Scouts of America. http://www.scouting.org/ (accessed on January 17, 2002).

Girl Scouts of the U.S.A. http://www.girlscouts.org/ (accessed on January 17, 2002).

Peterson, Robert W. *Boy Scouts: An American Adventure.* New York: American Heritage, 1985.

75 Years of Girl Scouting. New York: Girl Scouts of the U.S.A., 1986.

Titanic

The largest and most luxurious liner of the time, the *R.M.S. Titanic* was a wonder of its age. The ship was a vast symbol of the industrial age and an emblem of the power of the British Empire. But the fame of the *Titanic* before it sailed was nothing compared with what followed. Retold in numerous books, documentaries, and films, the story of the *Titanic* has become a modern folk

tragedy. A warning against pride and overconfidence, it is also a fable of lost dreams, dignified bravery, and greedy self-interest.

The story of the *Titanic* begins in 1907. J. Bruce Ismay (1862–1937), head of the White Star shipping line, commissioned the shipbuilders Harland and Wolff of Belfast, Ireland, to create three new liners for the North Atlantic crossing. The *Olympic,* the *Titanic,* and the *Britannic* would carry passengers and mail between Britain and the United States. Built alongside the larger second vessel, the *Olympic* was the first to be finished. But the *Titanic* was the masterpiece. White Star's ships

The luxury liner *R.M.S. Titanic* struck an iceberg on its maiden voyage. Damaged beyond repair, the ship sank, killing 1,513 passengers. *Painting by Willie Stoewer. UPI/Corbis-Bettmann. Reproduced by permission.*

offered greater stability, luxury, and sheer size than rival Cunard's fleet. The *Titanic,* then the largest moving object ever made, was launched into the river Langan on May 31, 1911.

The ill-fated maiden voyage of the *R.M.S. Titanic* (the R.M.S. stands for Royal Mail Steamer) began from Southampton on April 10, 1912. The ship stopped at Cherbourg, France, and Queenstown (now Cobh), Ireland. Then the *Titanic* left for New York carrying over 2,200 passengers and hundreds of mail bags on April 12. The *Titanic* struck an iceberg on April 14 and sank off Newfoundland with the loss of 1,513 lives. Considered unsinkable, the ship carried lifeboats for only half its passengers. The inquiries that followed pointed blame in many directions, including at Captain Edward John Smith (1850–1912) for hurrying through dangerous waters, and at White Star for ignoring the need for lifeboats. The sinking led to tougher safety rules for shipping, including instructions for dealing with disasters, and the establishment of the International Ice Patrol.

But while the *Titanic* disaster had an effect on rules for shipping, its influence on popular culture was profound. Some religious leaders claimed the wreck was a warning from God against the excesses of the "Gilded Age" (the period of rapid industrialization in the late 1900s). Some women survivors were criticized for not staying behind with their husbands. Groups campaigning for women's rights actually complained about the unfair treatment of men left behind on the sinking ship. At a time when the social classes were strictly divided, the *Titanic* revealed the different experiences of people from different backgrounds. Passengers in the cheaper "steerage" cabins were much less likely to have survived than first-class passengers. It was suspected that lower-class passengers were never meant to be rescued.

Just one month after the disaster, *Saved from the Titanic* was filmed on the *Olympic,* starring survivor Dorothy Gibson (1884–1946). Lawrence Beesley (1877–1967) published the first survivor's account of the tragedy, *The Loss of the S.S. Titanic,* six weeks after the event. Numerous books, magazine articles, and popular songs appeared in the aftermath of the disaster, but by 1913, *Titanic* mania had eased. Among the most interesting of the many early movies are *Atlantic* (1929) and *Titanic* (1943), a German propaganda film. The *Titanic* enjoyed renewed notoriety in the 1950s. The best of the films from that decade is *A Night to Remember* (1958). In 1960, there was even a popular Broadway musical telling the story of survivor Margaret Tobin

Brown (1867–1932), entitled *The Unsinkable Molly Brown. Titanic: A New Musical* revived the story for the stage in 1997.

A second revival in the 1970s included the best-selling novel by Clive Cussler (1931–), *Raise the Titanic* (1976). Many real-life attempts have been made over the years to find and raise the *Titanic*. One of the more unlikely plans was to freeze the water inside the ship. It would then rise to the surface like, of all things, an iceberg. But it was not until September 1985 that American Robert Ballard (1942–) and Frenchman Jean-Louis Michel finally located the wreck. After much debate about whether the ship should be left untouched as a grave site, artifacts were finally recovered from the wreck. An exhibition of objects from the *Titanic* went on tour around the world.

In the twenty-first century, a *Titanic* industry produces everything from models of the ship to reproductions of china and silverware. There is a Titanic Historical Society dedicated to all things *Titanic*, and there are many small *Titanic* museums in Britain, Ireland, and America. Perhaps the most lavish tribute to the ship, its passengers, and its crew is the 1997 film by James Cameron (1954–), *Titanic*, co-starring teen heartthrob Leonardo DiCaprio (1974–). Using near-life-sized models and enhancing them with computer-generated images, Cameron's film was the most expensive ever made. Despite historical inaccuracies, *Titanic* the movie is as much a wonder of its own age as the ship was in 1912.

—Chris Routledge

For More Information

Encyclopedia Titantica. http://www.encyclopedia-titanica.org/ (accessed on January 17, 2002).

Hill, Christine M. *Robert Ballard: Oceanographer Who Discovered the Titanic*. Berkely Heights, NJ: Enslow, 1999.

Lynch, Don. *Titanic: An Illustrated History*. New York: Hyperion, 1992.

Spignesi, Stephen J. *The Complete Titanic: From the Ship's Blueprints to the Epic Film*. New Jersey: Carol Publishing Group, 1998.

Titanic: The Official Archive. http://www.titanic-online.com/titanic/ (accessed on January 17, 2002).

War Bonds

Wars are expensive, and nations at war need to raise a great deal of money. Higher taxes raise some money, but usually not

An American propaganda poster, circa 1917, designed to entice citizens into buying war bonds to support U.S. efforts during World War I. *Courtesy of Hoover Institution Archives.*

enough. The solution in the United States during the twentieth century has been war bonds.

In buying a war bond, a citizen is loaning money to the government, at a given rate of interest, to be repaid years later, when the war is over. In World War I (1914–18), these notes were called Liberty Bonds. They were touted at bond rallies, endorsed by movie stars, and the subject of speeches by civilian volunteers called the Four Minute Men. Similar strategies were used during World War II (1939–45) to sell bonds. Some of the most successful bond rallies, attended by thousands of people and often broadcast live over the **radio** (see entry under 1920s—TV and Radio in volume 2), featured popular entertainer Kate Smith (1907?–1986) singing "God Bless America."

—Justin Gustainis

For More Information

Blum, John Morton. *V Was for Victory: Politics and American Culture during World War II.* New York: Harcourt Brace Jovanovich, 1976.

O'Neill, William L. *A Democracy at War: America's Fight at Home and Abroad in World War II.* New York: The Free Press, 1993.

WHERE TO LEARN MORE

The following list of resources focuses on material appropriate for middle school or high school students. Please note that the Web site addresses were verified prior to publication, but are subject to change.

Books

America A to Z: People, Places, Customs and Culture. Pleasantville, NY: Reader's Digest Association, 1997.

Beetz, Kirk H., ed. *Beacham's Encyclopedia of Popular Fiction.* Osprey, FL: Beacham, 1996.

Berke, Sally. *When TV Began: The First TV Shows.* New York: CPI, 1978.

Blum, Daniel; enlarged by John Willis. *A Pictorial History of the American Theatre.* 6th edition. New York: Crown Publishers, 1986.

Brooks, Tim, and Earle Marsh. *The Complete Directory to Prime Time Network and Cable TV Shows.* 7th rev. ed. New York: Ballantine, 1999.

Cashmore, Ellis. *Sports Culture.* New York: Routledge, 2000.

Craddock, Jim. *VideoHound's Golden Movie Retriever.* 2002 ed. Detroit: Gale, 2002.

Gilbert, Adrian. *The Nineties (Look at Life In).* Austin, TX: Raintree Steck-Vaughn, 2000.

Daniel, Clifton, ed. *Chronicle of the Twentieth Century.* Liberty, MO: JL International Pub., 1994.

Dunning, John. *On the Air: The Encyclopedia of Old-Time Radio.* New York: Oxford University Press, 1998.

Dunning, John. *Tune In Yesterday: The Ultimate Encyclopedia of Old-Time Radio 1925–1976.* New York: Oxford University Press, 1998.

Epstein, Dan. *20th C Pop Culture.* Philadelphia: Chelsea House, 2000.

Finkelstein, Norman H. *Sounds of the Air: The Golden Age of Radio.* New York: Charles Scribner's, 1993.

Flowers, Sarah. *Sports in America.* San Diego: Lucent, 1996.

Gilbert, Adrian. *The Eighties (Look at Life In).* Austin, TX: Raintree Steck-Vaughn, 2000.

Godin, Seth, compiler. *The Encyclopedia of Fictional People: The Most Important Characters of the 20th Century.* New York: Boulevard Books, 1996.

Grant, R. G. *The Seventies (Look at Life In).* Austin, TX: Raintree Steck-Vaughn, 2000.

Grant, R. G. *The Sixties (Look at Life In).* Austin, TX: Raintree Steck-Vaughn, 2000.

Green, Joey. *Joey Green's Encyclopedia of Offbeat Uses for Brand-Name Products.* New York: Hyperion, 1998.

Green, Stanley. *Encyclopedia of the Musical Theatre.* New York: Da Capo Press, 1980.

Hischak, Thomas S. *Film It with Music: An Encyclopedic Guide to the American Movie Musical.* Westport, CT: Greenwood Press, 2001.

Katz, Ephraim. *The Film Encyclopedia.* 4th ed. New York: HarperResource, 2001.

Lackmann, Ron. *The Encyclopedia of American Radio: An A–Z Guide to Radio from Jack Benny to Howard Stern.* New York: Facts on File, 2000.

Lebrecht, Norman. *The Companion to 20th-Century Music.* New York: Simon & Schuster, 1992.

Lissauer, Robert. *Lissauer's Encyclopedia of Popular Music in America: 1888 to the Present.* New York: Facts on File, 1996.

Lowe, Denise. *Women and American Television: An Encyclopedia.* ABC-CLIO: Santa Barbara, CA, 1999.

Maltin, Leonard, ed. *Leonard Maltin's Movie Encyclopedia.* New York: Dutton, 1994.

McNeil, Alex. *Total Television: The Comprehensive Guide to Programming from 1948 to the Present.* New York: Penguin, 1996.

Newcomb, Horace, ed. *Encyclopedia of Television.* Chicago: Fitzroy Dearborn Publishers, 1997.

Pendergast, Tom, and Sara Pendergast, eds. *St. James Encyclopedia of Popular Culture.* Detroit: St. James Press, 1999.

Rosen, Roger, and Patra McSharry Sevastiades, eds. *Coca-Cola Culture: Icons of Pop.* New York: Rosen, 1993.

Schwartz, Richard A. *Cold War Culture: Media and the Arts, 1945–1990.* New York: Facts on File, 1997.

Sies, Luther F. *Encyclopedia of American Radio, 1920–1960.* Jefferson, NC: McFarland, 2000.

Slide, Anthony. *Early American Cinema.* Metuchen, NJ: Scarecrow Press, 1994.

Tibbetts, John C., and James M. Welsh. *The Encyclopedia of Novels into Film.* New York: Facts on File, 1998.

Tibbetts, John C., and James M. Welsh. *The Encyclopedia of Stage Plays into Film.* New York: Facts on File, 2001.

Wilson, Charles Reagan, and William Ferris, eds. *Encyclopedia of Southern Culture.* Chapel Hill: University of North Carolina Press, 1989.

Web Sites

Markowitz, Robin. *Cultural Studies Central.* http://www.culturalstudies.net/ (accessed May 13, 2002).

Pop Culture Club. http://www.popcultureclub.org/ (accessed May 13, 2002).

Washington State University, American Studies. *Popular Culture: Resources for Critical Analysis.* http://www.wsu.edu/%7Eamerstu/pop/tvrguide.html (accessed May 13, 2002).

Yesterdayland. http://www.yesterdayland.com/ (accessed May 13, 2002).

Zupko, Sarah. *Popcultures.com: Sarah Zupko's Cultural Studies Center.* http://www.popcultures.com/ (accessed May 13, 2002).

INDEX

Italic type indicates volume number; **boldface** type indicates main entries and then page numbers; "(ill.)" indicates photos and illustrations.

A

A&P Grocery Company, *1:* 54
The A-Team, *5:* **1176–77,** 1177 (ill.)
AA. *See* Alcohol
Aaron, Hank, *1:* 210; *3:* 717; *4:* 1010
Abbott and Costello, *1:* 176; *3:* 529, **530–31,** 531 (ill.)
Abbott, Bud, *3:* 531 (ill.); 530
ABC (American Broadcasting Company), *3:* 611, 684, 727; *4:* 887, 888; *5:* 1175, 1277
Abdul-Jabbar, Kareem (Lew Alcindor), *4:* 878
Abercrombie & Fitch, *5:* 1235, **1235–36**
Abortion, *4:* 941, 1069, 1089–91, 1090 (ill.)
Acheson, Lila, *2:* 317
Acid rock, *4:* 842
Acquired Immunodeficiency Syndrome (AIDS). *See* AIDS
Action figures, *4:* 796–97, 1130, 1133, 1195, 1195 (ill.)
Action sports, *5:* 1272–74, 1273 (ill.)
Action TV series
  The A-Team, 5: 1176–77, 1177 (ill.)
  The Dukes of Hazzard, 4: 1034
  Flipper, 4: 901–2
Actors and actresses
  African American, *4:* 922–23
  Baker, Josephine, *2:* 267–68, 268 (ill.)
  Bogart, Humphrey, *2:* 389–90
  Bow, Clara, *2:* 268–69
  Broadway, *1:* 35 (ill.), 35–36
  Cagney, James, *2:* 390
  Chaplin, Charlie, *1:* 46, 47, 167, 170–71; *2:* 238, 369
  Cooper, Gary, *2:* 391–92
  Dean, James, *3:* 663–64
  Gable, Clark, *2:* 396
  Gish, Lillian, *1:* 174
  Grant, Cary, *2:* 399–400
  Pickford, Mary, *1:* 149
  Rogers, Will, *1:* 178–79
  silent film, *1:* 46–47
  Taylor, Elizabeth, *3:* 542 (ill.), 542–43
  Temple, Shirley, *2:* 411–12
  Valentino, Rudolph, *2:* 280–81
  Wayne, John, *2:* 414–15
  Welles, Orson, *2:* 489, 490 (ill.); *3:* 533–34, 534 (ill.)
"Actualities," *1:* 44–45
Acuff, Roy, *2:* 425; *3:* 553, 556
Adam's Apple (New York disco), *4:* 896
Adams, Don, *3:* 623
Adams, James Truslow, *2:* 368
Adams, Neal, *3:* 579
Adams, Richard, *4:* 949
Adams, Scott, *5:* 1224
Addams, Charles, *2:* 313

Addiction treatment, *2:* 504
Adolescents. *See* Teenagers
Adult comics, *2:* 440; *5:* 1281
Adult education, Chautauqua movement, *1:* 115, 118–20, 119 (ill.)
Advanced Projects Research Agency Network (ARPANET), *5:* 1319
Advanced Research Projects Agency (ARPA), *5:* 1314
Adventure
  Buck Rogers, 2: 304–6, 305 (ill.)
  Disney live action, *2:* 273
  extreme sports, *5:* 1272–74, 1273 (ill.)
  Indiana Jones movies, *5:* 1130–31
  James Bond films, *4:* 830–31, 831 (ill.)
  King Kong, 2: 403–4
  London, Jack, *1:* 88–89
  Popeye, *2:* 314–16, 315 (ill.)
  Tarzan, *1:* 192–94, 193 (ill.)
  3-D, *3:* 675
  Zorro, *1:* 199–200, 200 (ill.)
The Adventures of Kathlyn, 1: 147
The Adventures of Ozzie and Harriet, *3:* 513, **728–29**
Advertising, *2:* **244–47,** 245 (ill.); *3:* 643; *4:* 890. *See also* Marketing; Slang and slogans
  Alka-Seltzer, *2:* 374–75
  AT&T, *3:* 780
  auto racing, *2:* 475
  Betty Crocker, *2:* 248–50, 249 (ill.); *3:* 638
  The Birth of a Nation, 1: 170
  Budweiser, *4:* 794
  Burma-Shave, *2:* 250–51
  Buster Brown, 1: 81, 82 (ill.)
  Campbell Kids, *1:* 183
  cartoon characters, *1:* 21, 183; *2:* 254; *3:* 712
  celebrity endorsements, *1:* 183
  cigarettes, *2:* 254
  Coca-Cola, *1:* 56–58, 57 (ill.)
  Cracker Jack, *1:* 59 (ill.), 59–60
  extreme sports, *5:* 1273
  Good Housekeeping, 1: 86
  The Hidden Persuaders, 3: 639
  J. Walter Thompson Company, *1:* 18–19
  Jell-O, *1:* 65–66
  Levi's jeans, *3:* 660
  MAD parodies, *3:* 705
  Marlboro Man, *2:* 259 (ill.), 259–60
  Nike, *4:* 799–801, 800 (ill.)
  Peanuts, 3: 712
  Reader's Digest, 2: 317
  sponsorship on radio and TV, *1:* 183
  Super Bowl, *4:* 884–85
  supermodels, *5:* 1117–18, 1118 (ill.)
  television, *3:* 612
  Timex watches, *3:* 650–51
  toy, *4:* 915
  Volkswagen Beetle, *3:* 653–54
  Wheaties, *2:* 289–90
  Wonder Bread, *2:* 291
Advice and Consent, 3: 622
Advocate, *4:* **866–67,** 926
Aerobics, *1:* 162; *4:* **1010–11**
Aerosmith, *5:* 1151
An Affair to Remember, 2: 400
The African, 4: 1058
African American life and culture, *1:* 4–5
  Ali, Muhammad (Cassius Clay), *1:* 109; *4:* 789, 791, 878–80, 879 (ill.)
  Amos 'n' Andy, 2: 479–80
  Apollo Theater, *2:* 494–95, 495 (ill.)
  Aunt Jemima, *1:* 8–9, 9 (ill.)
  Baker, Josephine, *2:* 267–68, 268 (ill.)
  black athletes, *4:* 1009–10. *See also* specific athlete, e.g., Aaron, Hank
  blues, *1:* 149; *2:* 293–96, 294 (ill.)
  the Charleston, *2:* 351
  civil rights movement, *4:* 788–90, 921, 922–25, 924 (ill.)
  The Cosby Show, 5: 1181–83, 1182 (ill.)
  Do the Right Thing, 5: 1123–25, 1124 (ill.)
  Drew, Charles Richard, *3:* 513
  early-century musical groups, *1:* 148
  Ebony, 3: 576–77
  funk, *4:* 981, 984–85
  Garvey, Marcus, *1:* 148–49
  hairstyles, *1:* 133
  Harlem Globetrotters, *2:* 329–31, 330 (ill.)
  impersonation, *1:* 40–42, 41 (ill.)
  Johnson, Robert, *2:* 428–29
  Joplin, Scott, *1:* 5, 75–76
  King, B. B., *3:* 688
  Louis, Joe, *2:* 471

Negro leagues, *1:* 5, 107–8
Owens, Jesse, *2:* 473
politically correct terms, *5:* 1210
racism, *1:* 213; *4:* 788–89. *See also* Racism and racial segregation
rhythm and blues (R&B), *3:* 564–65
Robinson, Jackie, *1:* 98; *3:* 514, 592
Roots, 4: 1057 (ill.), 1057–58
Shaft, 4: 961, 976–77, 977 (ill.)
Simpson, O. J., *5:* 1324 (ill.), 1324–26
suburbs, *3:* 782
TV treatment, *4:* 896
Williams, Venus and Serena, *5:* 1271
zoot suit, *3:* 525–27, 526 (ill.)
Afro, *1:* 133
The Age of Innocence, 2: 236
Agent 007 (James Bond), *4:* 830. *See also* James Bond films
Agha, Mehemed Gehmy, *1:* 196
"The Agrarian ideal," *3:* 782
Agricultural Credit Act, *5:* 1139
Agriculture, *2:* 243–44, 374, *5:* 1138 (ill.), 1138–39
Ahrens, Lynn, *4:* 1061
AIDS (Acquired Immunodeficiency Syndrome), *3:* 778; *4:* 926, 944, 1083, 1093; *5:* 542–43, **1198–99,** 1199 (ill.)
AIDS Memorial Quilt, *5:* 1199, 1199 (ill.)
Aiello, Danny, *5:* 1123
Air meets, *1:* 3
Air travel, *1:* 3, 8, 194; *2:* **345–46,** 354
Airplane!, *5:* **1120–21,** 1121 (ill.)
Airport, 4: 787, 964; *5:* 1120
Aladdin Company, *1:* 117
The Alamo, 3: 736
Alamogordo, New Mexico, *3:* 619
Al-Anon, *2:* 504
Alas, Babylon, 3: 620, 622
Alaska, *1:* 88
Albatross (publishers), *2:* 457
Albee, Edward, *4:* 816
Albee, Mrs. P. F. E., *1:* 116
Albums. *See* Compact Disc; Long-Playing Record (LP)
Alcindor, Lew (Kareem Abdul-Jabbar), *4:* 878
Alcohol
Alcoholics Anonymous (AA), *2:* 504–5
cocktail hour, *2:* 353
hangover relief, *2:* 374
Prohibition, *1:* 123, 213; *2:* 235, 345, 357–58, 370, 419; *4:* 935
slang, *2:* 236
Alcott, Louisa May, *1:* 83
Alda, Alan, *4:* 1050
Aldrin, Buzz, *4:* 789, 939
Alen, William van, *2:* 352
Alexander, Jason, *5:* 1296, 1297 (ill.)
Alexanderson, Ernst F. W., *3:* 610
Alfred E. Neuman, *3:* 705–6, 706 (ill.)
Algar, Garth, *5:* 1250 (ill.)
Ali, Muhammad (Cassius Clay), *1:* 109; *4:* 789, 791, **878–80,** 879 (ill.)
Alienation, *4:* 822
Aliens, *3:* 635–36
The Day the Earth Stood Still, 3: 661–63, 662 (ill.)
E.T.: The Extra-Terrestrial, 5: 1125–26
Alka-Seltzer, *2:* **374–75;** *4:* 948
All I Really Need to Know I Learned in Kindergarten, 5: 1101
All in the Family, *4:* 949, 1023, **1024–25,** 1034
All My Children, 2: 487
All My Sons, 3: 530
"All or Nothing at All," *3:* 512–13
All Quiet on the Western Front, 2: 237, 369
All the President's Men, 4: 949
"All the way," *2:* 368
"All Things Considered," *4:* 950
All-American Girls Baseball League, *3:* 587
Allegretti, Gus, *3:* 735
Allen, Gracie, *1:* 50; *2:* 342, 423, 477
Allen, Paul, *5:* 1231
Allen, Steve, *3:* 761
Allen, Woody, *4:* 951
Alley, Kirstie, *5:* 1179
Allison, Fran, *3:* 603
Allison, Jone, *2:* 484
All-Story Magazine, 1: 192, 199
Ally McBeal, *5:* **1278–79,** 1279 (ill.)
Altair, MITS, *5:* 1232
Altamont, *4:* 842, **842–43,** 843 (ill.), 863, 872
Alternative country music, *3:* 558; *5:* **1252–53,** 1253 (ill.)

Alternative rock, *3:* 687–88; *4:* 981; *5:* 1251, **1253–54,** 1256–58, 1257 (ill.)
Altman, Robert, *2:* 316; *4:* 1050
Alvin and the Chipmunks, *3:* **729–31**
AM radio stations, *5:* 1175–76
Amazon.com, *5:* 1227
America Online, *5:* 1227
American Bandstand, *3:* **731–32,** 732 (ill.)
American Bowling Congress, *3:* 588
American Broadcasting Company (ABC). *See* ABC (American Broadcasting Company)
American Civil Liberties Union (ACLU), *2:* 364
American Communist Party, *3:* 772
American Contract Bridge League, *1:* 215
American Express, *4:* 948
An American Family, *5:* 1294
American Family Association, *5:* 1160
American Football League (AFL), *2:* 335; *4:* 877
American Graffiti, *3:* 677
American League, *1:* 96–97, 201
American literature, *1:* 187. *See also* Books; Fiction; Literature; Novels
American Museum (New York City), *1:* 224
American musical theater. *See* Musical theater
American Professional Football Association (APFA), *2:* 334
American slang. *See* Slang and slogans
American Telephone and Telegraph (AT&T), *1:* **154–55;** *2:* 345
American Tobacco Company, *2:* 347
American Top 40, *3:* 695
Amos 'n' Andy, *1:* 42; *2:* 239, 270, 370, 477, **478–81,** 479 (ill.); *3:* 755; *5:* 1181
Amos, Tori, *2:* 417
Amphetamines, *3:* 774; *5:* 1313
Amusement. *See* Leisure time
Amusement halls. *See* Nickelodeons
Amusement parks, *1:* 115; *3:* **768–69**
  Coney Island, *1:* 115, 120–22, 121 (ill.)
  Disney theme, *2:* 273
  Ferris wheel, *1:* 128–30, 129 (ill.)
  LEGOLAND, *3:* 721
  roller coasters, *1:* 121, 136, 137 (ill.); *3:* 768, 769
Anchors Aweigh, *3:* 565
Anderson, Abraham, *1:* 182
Anderson, Melissa Sue, *4:* 1044, 1044 (ill.)
Anderson, Pamela, *5:* 1284
Anderson, Walt, *2:* 284
Andrews, Julie, *4:* 788, 832
Andrews Sisters, *3:* 512
The Andy Griffith Show, *4:* 788, **890–91**
***Andy Hardy* movies,** *2:* **384–86,** 385 (ill.)
Anheuser-Busch Companies, *4:* 794
Animal characters
  Babe (pig), *3:* 665
  Bingo (dog), *1:* 60
  Eddie (dog), *5:* 1290
  Flipper (dolphin), *4:* 901–2
  Francis the Talking Mule, *3:* 664–65
  King Kong (ape), *2:* 403–4
  Lassie (dog), *3:* 540–41, 541 (ill.)
  Mister Ed (horse), *4:* 906–7
  Tige (dog), *1:* 81
Animal training, *4:* 907
Animals (rock group), *4:* 841
Animals (stuffed), *1:* 30–31, 31 (ill.); *5:* 1306 (ill.), 1306–7
Animation
  Alvin and the Chipmunks, *3:* 729–31
  Anime, *5:* 1280–81
  The Beavis and Butt-Head Show, *5:* 1284–85
  Betty Boop, *2:* 388 (ill.), 388–89
  Bugs Bunny, *3:* 598–601, 599 (ill.)
  color, *2:* 272
  computer generation, *5:* 1237, 1247
  Disney, *2:* 270–74, 271 (ill.); *3:* 511
  Fantasia, *3:* 535–36, 536 (ill.)
  Felix the Cat, *1:* 171–72, 172 (ill.)
  Gertie the Dinosaur, *1:* 172–74, 173 (ill.)
  The Lion King, *5:* 1225, 1237, 1242–43, 1243 (ill.)
  Pokémon, *5:* 1278, 1322–23, 1323 (ill.)
  The Real Ghostbusters, *5:* 1130
  Road Runner and Wile E. Coyote, *3:* 606–8, 607 (ill.)

Rudolph the Red-Nosed Reindeer, *3:* 581–82
Saturday morning cartoons, *4:* 912–16, 913 (ill.)
The Simpsons, 5: 1190–93, 1191 (ill.)
Snow White and the Seven Dwarfs, 2: 384, 410–11, 411 (ill.)
South Park, 5: 1298–99, 1299 (ill.)
Space Jam, 3: 600; *5:* 1275
Speed Racer, 4: 917–18
Steamboat Willie, 2: 278–79, 279 (ill.)
stop-motion, *2:* 404
Toy Story, 5: 1247–49, 1248 (ill.)
Winnie-the-Pooh, *2:* 321–23, 322, 322 (ill.)
Anime, *4:* 917–18; *5:* 1278, **1280–81**
Aniston, Jennifer, *5:* 1225, 1291, 1291 (ill.)
Annie, 2: 311
Anorexia nervosa, *3:* 775
Anson, Cap, *1:* 107
Antacid, *2:* 374
Anthony Adverse, 2: 368–69
Anthracite Coal Strike of 1903, *1:* 7
Antiabortion activism, *4:* 1091
Antibiotics, *2:* 356–56
Anticommunism, *2:* 414–15; *3:* 640, 670–71, 767, 769–71; *5:* 1102
Antiestablishment attitudes, *1:* 163. *See also* Counterculture
Antismoking activism, *2:* 253
Antitrust suit *(U.S. vs. AT&T), 1:* 155
Antiwar movement, *4:* 785, 790–91, 841, 922, 945, 1083–85, 1084 (ill.); *5:* 1209
Apartheid, *1:* 91
Apollo flights, *4:* 789, 939, 940
Apollo Theater, *2:* **494–95,** 495 (ill.); *5:* 1150
Apple Computer, *4:* **1070–71,** 1071 (ill.), 1086
Apple IIGS Computer, *4:* 1071 (ill.), 1086
Appleton, Victor, *1:* 194
Appliances, electric, *1:* **125–26**
Arab oil embargo, *4:* 947
Aragones, Sergio, *3:* 706
Arbuckle, Jon, *4:* 1000
Arby's, *2:* 285
Arcades, *4:* 1021 (ill.)
Archaeology, *5:* 1130–31
Archie comics, *3:* **568–69,** 569 (ill.)
Architecture
bungalows, *2:* 349–50
Chrysler Building, *2:* 352–53
diners, *1:* 60–62, 61 (ill.)
Empire State Building, *2:* 499
Levittown, *3:* 629–31, 630 (ill.)
mail-order houses, *1:* 28
ranch house, *2:* 502
Route 66, *2:* 363
skyscrapers, *2:* 502–4
World's Fairs, *1:* 142–43
Argosy, *1:* **80–81**
Ark of the Covenant, *5:* 1131
Arkoff, Sam, *4:* 816
Arledge, Roone, *4:* 888
Armstrong, Louis, *1:* 72; *2:* 240, 293
Armstrong, Neil, *4:* 789, 939
Armstrong, Robert, *2:* 403
Army-McCarthy hearings, *3:* 767, **769–71,** 770 (ill.)
Arnaz, Desi, *3:* 639, 716, 747, 747 (ill.), 755
Arnaz, Desi, Jr., *3:* 715 (ill.), 715–16
Arness, James, *3:* 640, 743
Arnold, Kenneth, *3:* 636 (ill.)
Arnold, Roseanne, *5:* 1187
Aromatherapy, *5:* **1305**
ARPA (Advanced Research Projects Agency), *5:* 1314
ARPANET (Advanced Projects Research Agency Network, *5:* 1319
Arquette, David, *5:* 1246
Arrow Collar Man, *1:* 157, **158–59,** 159 (ill.)
Art and artists. *See* Illustration
Art deco (art moderne), *1:* 61 (ill.), 61–62; *2:* 353
Art nouveau, *1:* 51
Artificial materials, *2:* 379–80
"As if!," *5:* 1224
Ash, Mary Kay, *4:* 810
Ashe, Arthur, *5:* 1161
Asher, William, *4:* 816
Asian influence
Charlie Chan, *2:* 269
Hawaii Five-O, 4: 906
karaoke, *5:* 1142–43
martial arts, *4:* 937
Asimov, Isaac, *2:* 461
"Ask not what your country can do for you . . .," *4:* 785

Asner, Edward, *4:* 1048
Assassinations, *4:* 791, *5:* 1240–41
Assembly line production (Ford), *1:* 23, 153
Astaire, Fred, *2:* 383
Asteroids, *4:* 1012, 1012 (ill.)
Astronauts, *4:* 789, 939
Atari, *4:* 1011–13, 1012 (ill.), 1086
Athens, Greece, *1:* 109
Atherton, Gertrude, *2:* 237
Athletes
  Thorpe, Jim, *1:* 149
  Wheaties, *2:* 290
  women, *5:* 1271
Athletic shoes. *See* Footwear
Atlanta Braves, *5:* 1271
Atlantic City, New Jersey, *2:* 355, 472
Atlas, Charles, *2:* 239, **326**
Atomic bomb, *3:* 511, **618–21,** 619 (ill.), 641
Atriedes, Paul, *4:* 868
AT&T (American Telephone and Telegraph), *1:* **154–55;** *2:* 345; *3:* 780
Attenborough, David, *5:* 1270
Aunt Jemima, *1:* **8–9,** 9 (ill.)
Austin, Minnesota, *2:* 423
Austin Powers, *5:* 1238 (ill.), **1238–39**
Austin, Steve, *5:* 1171, 1172 (ill.), 1173
Austin, Tracy, *4:* 1009
Auto racing, *1:* 201; *2:* 474–75; *3:* 626–27; *4:* 1009
Automobiles, *1:* 115; *2:* 345
  drive-in theater, *2:* 497–99, 498 (ill.)
  General Motors, *1:* 130–31
  highway system, *3:* 775–76
  hot rods, *3:* 626–27
  Jeep, *3:* 519–20
  minivans, *5:* 1208, 1209 (ill.)
  Model T, *1:* 8, 22–23
  radios, *2:* 239
  road rage, *5:* 1212–13
  Route 66, *2:* 361–63, 362 (ill.)
  sport utility vehicles (SUVs), *5:* 1215–17, 1216 (ill.)
  stock car racing, *2:* 474–75
  Volkswagen Beetle, *3:* 643, 652–55, 653 (ill.)
Automotive industry, *1:* 148; *2:* 345, 373; *4:* 947
Autry, Gene, *2:* 426; *3:* 512, 556, 581
Avalon, Frankie, *3:* 524, 633, 641; *4:* 816
"Avant-garde" jazz, *1:* 74
Avedon, Richard, *1:* 197
Avery, Tex, *3:* 599
Aviation, *1:* 3; *2:* 345–46. *See also* Lindbergh, Charles; Wright brothers
Avildsen, John G., *4:* 971
Avon, *1:* **116**
Aware (guardian organization), *3:* 772
Awdry, Christopher, *5:* 1299
Awdry, Rev. Wilbert, *5:* 1299–1300, 1300 (ill.)
Aykroyd, Dan, *4:* 1059, 1059 (ill.), 1060; *5:* 1129, 1129 (ill.)
Ayres, Lew, *2:* 369

B

B. F. Goodrich Company, *1:* 164
"B" movies, *2:* **386–87,** 497
Babe (pig), *3:* 665
Baby boom, *3:* 514, **616–18,** 637, 767
Baby boomers, *1:* 105; *4:* 820, 950–52, 1025, 1069; *5:* 1104, 1197, 1206, 1215
Baby Bop, *5:* 1281
Baby Pac-Man, *5:* 1168
BabyGap, *4:* 795
Bacall, Lauren, *2:* 253, 390; *5:* 1245
Bach, Catherine, *4:* 1034
Bach, Richard, *4:* 948
"Back in the Saddle Again," *3:* 512
Backstreet Boys, *3:* 563; *5:* 1251
Backus, Jim, *4:* 904
Baden-Powell, Robert and Agnes, *1:* 226
Baer, Max, Jr., *4:* 891, 892 (ill.)
Baer, Ralph, *4:* 1021
Baez, Joan, *4:* 841
Bagdasarian, Ross, *3:* 729–30
Bailey, Jack, *3:* 742 (ill.)
Bailey, James A., *1:* 224
Bailey, Raymond, *4:* 891
Baird, John Logie, *3:* 610
Bajo sexto, *5:* 1262
Baker, Josephine, *2:* **267–68,** 268 (ill.)
Bakker, Jim and Tammy Faye, *1:* 127; *5:* 1103
Baldwin, Alec, *2:* 462
Ball, Harvey R., *4:* 1094–95

Ball, Lucille, *1:* 15; *3:* 639, 641, 716, 740 (ill.), 747 (ill.), 747–48, 755
Ballard, Robert, *1:* 231
Balloons, *2:* 258, 388 (ill.)
Ballpoint pens, *2:* **375–76**
Ballroom dancing, *1:* 123
Balmer, Edwin, *2:* 450
Baltimore Orioles, *4:* 1009
Bamboo Harvester, *4:* 907
Banana Republic, *4:* 795
Bancroft, Anne, *4:* 823
Band-Aid, *2:* **247–48**
Banderas, Antonio, *1:* 200
Bank Americard (Visa), *3:* 647
Banks, Ernie, *3:* 717
Banks, Jane and Michael, *4:* 832 (ill.)
Barbera, Joseph, *4:* 914
Barbie, *3:* 643, **644–46,** 645 (ill.); *4:* 796
Barclay, Florence, *1:* 146
Barker, Bob, *3:* 753
Barlow, Dorothy Hope Smith, *2:* 287
Barnes and Noble, *5:* 1328
Barney and Friends, *5:* 1278, **1281–83,** 1282 (ill.)
Barnum, Phineas T., *1:* 224
Barr, Roseanne, *5:* 1187–88
Barrett, Oliver, *5:* 1115
Barris, Chuck, *4:* 1023, 1038–39, 1039 (ill.)
Barrow, Clyde, *2:* 496, 496, 496 (ill.)
Barry, Rick, *3:* 591
Barrymore, Drew, *4:* 1033; *5:* 1246
Barrymore, Lionel, *2:* 385; *3:* 538
Bars, *5:* 1143, *5:* 1177–79, 1178 (ill.)
BASE (Building, Antennas, Spans, Earth) jumping, *5:* 1272–73
Baseball, *1:* 95, **96–99,** 97 (ill.), 201; *3:* 587; *4:* 1009, 1010; *5:* 1165, 1275
  cards, *2:* 347–49, 348 (ill.)
  Cobb, Ty, *1:* 99–100
  "color barrier," *3:* 592, 717; *4:* 922
  Cracker Jack, *1:* 60
  ESPN, *4:* 1035
  Jackson, Shoeless Joe, *1:* 149
  Little League, *2:* 469–70, 470 (ill.)
  Louisville Slugger, *1:* 21–22
  Negro leagues, *1:* 5, 107–8
  Robinson, Jackie, *3:* 592
  Ruth, Babe, *1:* 210
Baseball cards, *2:* **347–49,** 348 (ill.)
BASIC (programming language), *5:* 1232
Basie, Count, *1:* 72; *2:* 427
Basketball, *1:* 96; *4:* 877–78, 1009; *5:* 1165, 1271
  Harlem Globetrotters, *2:* 329–31, 330 (ill.)
  Jordan, Michael, *5:* 1274–75
  National Basketball Association (NBA), *3:* 590–91, 717; *4:* 877–78; *5:* 1274
"Bat Boy," *3:* 705
Bates, Norman, *4:* 828, 836–37, 1092
Batman, *2:* **434–36,** 435, 435 (ill.), 440
Bats (Louisville Slugger), *1:* 21–22
"Battle of the Sexes," *4:* 1009
The Battleship Potemkin, 1: 46
Bauer, Eddie, *2:* 256
Baum, L. Frank, *1:* 66; *2:* 417
Bavier, Frances, *4:* 890
Baywatch, *5:* **1283–84**
"Bazooka Joe," *1:* 56
Beach Blanket Bingo, 4: 816, 817 (ill.)
Beach Boys, *3:* 693; *4:* 789–90, 842, **844–45,** 845 (ill.)
Beach, Charles, *1:* 158
Beach movies, *4:* **816–18,** 817 (ill.)
Beadle, Irwin P., *1:* 83
Beals, Dick, *2:* 374–75
Bean, Leon Leonwood, *1:* 156
Beanie Babies, *5:* 1304, 1306 (ill.), **1306–7**
Bears
  teddy bears, *1:* 30–31, 31 (ill.)
  Winnie-the-Pooh, *2:* 322, 322 (ill.)
Beastie Boys, *5:* 1135
Beatles, *3:* 560, 562, 685, 687, 693, 740; *4:* 788–89, 791, 841, **846–48,** 847 (ill.), 915, 931
  Beatlemania, *3:* 633–34; *4:* 846
  hairstyle, *3:* 634
  A Hard Day's Night, 4: 826–27, 846, 847 (ill.)
Beatniks and the Beat movement, *3:* 638, **698–99,** 699 (ill.); *4:* 931
  Dobie Gillis, *3:* 737 (ill.), 737–38
  On the Road, 3: 641, 708–9
Beaton, Sir Cecil, *1:* 196
Beatty, Clyde, *1:* 225

Beaumont, Hugh, *3:* 750, 750 (ill.)
The Beavis and Butt-Head Show, *5:* 1148, 1277, **1284–85**
"Bebop," *3:* 553
Bechet, Sidney, *1:* 72
Becker, Casey, *5:* 1246
Becker, Ethan, *2:* 422
Becker, Marion Rombauer, *2:* 422
Bedford, Annie North, *3:* 703
Bee Gees, *4:* 983
Beer, Budweiser, *4:* 794
Bee's knees, *2:* 236
Beesley, Lawrence, *1:* 230
Beetle (Volkswagen), *3:* 643, **652–55,** 653 (ill.)
Beiderbecke, Bix, *2:* 293
Bell, Alexander Graham, *1:* 91, 139 (ill.), 139–40
Bell, James "Cool Papa," *1:* 108
Bell, Rex, *2:* 269
Bell-bottoms, *4:* 807, **807–9,** 808 (ill.)
Bellow, Saul, *4:* 787
Bellows, Gil, *5:* 1279 (ill.)
Belushi, John, *4:* 1059, 1059 (ill.), 1060
Ben & Jerry's, *4:* 930
Benchley, Peter, *4:* 968
Benedict, Dirk, *5:* 1176, 1177 (ill.)
Benefit concerts, *5:* 1138 (ill.), 1138–39, 1143–45, 1144 (ill.)
Ben-Hur, *2:* 238; *3:* 640, 661
Benny, Jack, *1:* 168; *2:* 342, 370, 477; *3:* **597–98**
Benson, Mildred A. Wirt, *2:* 455
Bergen, Edgar, *2:* 342, 391; *4:* 1066
Bergman, Ingrid, *3:* 511, 532
Berkowitz, David "Son of Sam," *4:* 1092, 1092 (ill.)
Berle, Milton, *2:* 483; *3:* 597, 639, 641
Berlin Airlift, *3:* 622
Berlin Wall, *5:* 1103, 1180
Berliner, Emile, *1:* 77
Bernard, A. M. (Louisa May Alcott), *1:* 83
Bernays, Edward, *2:* 252
Berners-Lee, Tim, *5:* 1320
Bernice the Whiffle Hen, *2:* 315
Bernstein, Carl, *4:* 949
Berry, Chuck, *3:* 641, 686
Berry, Ken, *4:* 891
Bert the Turtle, *3:* 622
Besser, Joe, *2:* 414
Best, James, *4:* 1034
Best, Pete, *4:* 846
The Best Years of Our Lives, *3:* 512
Best-sellers, *1:* 187; *3:* **517–18,** 672; *5:* 1288, 1328
"Beth," *4:* 987
Better Homes and Gardens, *2:* **302**
Betty Boop, *2:* 388 (ill.), **388–89**
Betty Crocker, *2:* **248–50,** 249 (ill.); *3:* 638
Beverages
  Coca-Cola, *1:* 56–58, 57 (ill.)
  Coffee, *5:* 1311–13
  7-Up, *2:* 287–88
  Soda fountains, *1:* 67–68, 68 (ill.)
  Starbucks, *5:* 1110–11, 1111 (ill.)
The Beverly Hillbillies, *4:* 788, **891–93,** 892 (ill.), 1042
Beverly Hills 90210, *5:* 1225, **1286–87,** 1287 (ill.)
Bewitched, *4:* **893–95**
Bianculli, David, *5:* 1283, 1284
Bias, Len, *5:* 1202
Bich, Baron, *2:* 376
Bicycle motocross (BMX), *5:* 1273
Big bands, *1:* 72–73; *2:* **426–27;** *3:* 553–54, 561
Big Bird, *4:* 1062–63, 1063 (ill.)
"Big Blue," *5:* 1107
The "Big Book," *1:* 26
"Big business," *1:* 2
Big eyes, *3:* 510
The Big Sleep, *3:* 529, 537
Biggers, Earl Derr, *2:* 269
Bigotry, *4:* 1025
Bikers (motorcycle), *1:* 16
Bikini Atoll, Marshall Islands, *3:* 619 (ill.)
Billboards, *2:* 245
Billingsley, Barbara, *3:* 750, 750 (ill.)
Binet, Alfred, *2:* 365
Bingo (dog), *1:* 60
Biofeedback, *4:* 958
Bionicles, *3:* 722
Biotechnology, *5:* 1227
Biplanes, *2:* 346
Bird, Larry, *3:* 591; *5:* 1165–66
Birds Eye Foods, *2:* 420
Birdseye, Clarence, *2:* 420
Birnbach, Lisa, *1:* 156; *5:* 1116, 1116 (ill.)
Biro, Ladislo, *2:* 375
Birth control, *1:* 149; *3:* 778; *3:* 778–79
The Birth of a Nation, *1:* 46, 147, 167, **168–70,** 169 (ill.), 218–19
Bisset, Jacqueline, *1:* 163

Black, Brown, and Beige, 1: 73
Black Oxen, 2: 237
Black Sabbath, *5:* 1140
Black, Shirley Temple, *2:* 412
"Black sitcoms," *3:* 756
Black Sox Scandal, *1:* 97, 149, 201, 210
Black Tuesday, *2:* 241
Blackface, *1:* 40, 42, 49
Blacklisting, *3:* 669–71, 745, 767, **771–73**
Blackman, Honor, *4:* 831 (ill.)
Blackwood, Nina, *5:* 1148 (ill.)
Blade Runner, *3:* 537; *5:* **1122–23**
Blair, Linda, *4:* 965
The Blair Witch Project, 2: 386; *5:* 1237
Blake, Amanda, *3:* 743
Blanc, Mel, *3:* 599, 599 (ill.)
Blatty, William Peter, *4:* 948–49, 961, 965
Bledsoe, Tempestt, *5:* 1182 (ill.)
Bleeth, Yasmine, *5:* 1284
Blind date, *2:* 236
Bloch, Robert, *2:* 461; *4:* 836
Block, Martin, *3:* 684
Blockbusters, *1:* 170; *4:* 961; *5:* 1155
Blocker, Dan, *4:* 896
Blondie, *2:* 433, **436–38,** 437 (ill.)
Blood bank, *3:* 513
Bloods, *5:* 1205
Bloom County, 3: 711
"Blowin' in the Wind," *4:* 788
Blue jeans, *3:* 658–59, 659 (ill.), 659–60
Blue-collar TV sitcoms. *See also* Comedies, TV
  All in the Family, 4: 1024–25
  The Honeymooners, 3: 744–46, 745 (ill.)
  Roseanne, 5: 1187–88
  Taxi, 4: 1063–65, 1064 (ill.)
Bluegrass, *3:* **554–55;** *4:* 891
Blues, *1:* 71; *2:* **293–96,** 294 (ill.), 425
  Handy, W. C., *1:* 149
  Johnson, Robert, *2:* 428–29
  King, B. B., *3:* 688
Blume, Judy, *4:* 998, **998**
Bluth, Don, *2:* 273
Bluto, *2:* 315 (ill.)
BMX (Bicycle motocross), *5:* 1273
Board games. *See* Games
"Boarders," *3:* 723
Boardwalks, Coney Island, *1:* 120–22, 121 (ill.)
Bobbed hair, *1:* 133; *2:* 262
***Bobbsey Twins* series,** *3:* **570–71**
Bobbysoxers, *3:* **524–25,** 525 (ill.), 566, 633
Bodybuilding, *2:* 326
Bogart, Humphrey, *2:* **389–90;** *3:* 511, 532
Bogue, *4:* 948
"Bohemians," *4:* 808
Bok, Edward, *2:* 349–50
Bolger, Ray, *2:* 417
The Bomb, *3:* **618–21,** 619 (ill.)
Bomb shelters, *3:* 620, 623
Bonaduce, Danny, *4:* 1055, 1055 (ill.)
Bonanza, *4:* 787–88, 792, **895–96**
Bonaparte, Charles, *3:* 624
Bond, James, *3:* 623; *4:* 815, 830–31, 831 (ill.), 865, 937–38; *5:* 1238
Bond, Ward, *3:* 539
Bondi, Beulah, *3:* 539
Bonds, Barry, *1:* 99, 210; *5:* 1228
Bonet, Lisa, *5:* 1182 (ill.)
The Bonfire of the Vanities, *5:* 1155, **1156–57,** 1219
Bonham, John, *4:* 989
Bonnie and Clyde, *2:* **496,** 496 (ill.)
Booke, Sorrell, *4:* 1034
Book-of-the-Month Club, *2:* **303–4**
Books, *1:* 79–80, 187; *2:* 241, 301; *5:* 1265. *See also* Fiction; Literature; Novels; Reading
  best-sellers, *3:* 517–18
  Bobbsey Twins series, *3:* 570–71
  Book-of-the-Month Club, *2:* 303–4
  The Catcher in the Rye, 3: 700–701
  Charlie Chan, *2:* 269, 269 (ill.)
  comic books. *See* Comic books
  condensed, *2:* 316
  Curious George, 3: 574–75, 575 (ill.)
  detective fiction, *2:* 441–43
  dime novels, *1:* 82–84, 83 (ill.)
  Dr. Seuss, *3:* 701–2, 702 (ill.)
  Dracula, *2:* 392–93
  Frankenstein, *2:* 394–95, 395 (ill.)
  Fu Manchu, *1:* 188–89, 189 (ill.)
  Golden Books, *3:* 577–78
  The Grapes of Wrath, 2: 451–52
  Hardy Boys series, *2:* 308–9
  The Joy of Cooking, 2: 421–22

Little Blue Books, *2:* 309–10
mail-order, *2:* 303–4
Nancy Drew series, *2:* 455–56
paperback books, *2:* 457–58; *3:* 510
Perry Mason, *2:* 458–59
Peyton Place, 3: 671–72
Raggedy Ann and Raggedy Andy, *1:* 208–9, 209 (ill.)
On the Road, 3: 708–9
on tape, *5:* 1265
Tarzan, *1:* 192–94, 193 (ill.)
Tom Swift series, *1:* 194–95
Winnie-the-Pooh, *2:* 321–22, 322 (ill.)
World Book Encyclopedia, 1: 197–98
Zorro, *1:* 199–200, 200 (ill.)
Bookspan, *2:* 304
Boomtown Rats, *5:* 1144
Boots, *4:* 809–10
Borglum, Gutzon, *3:* 513
Born on the Fourth of July, 5: 1119
"Born-again" Christian, *1:* 127
Bosley, Tom, *4:* 1040
Boston Bruins, *1:* 207
Boston Celtics, *4:* 878; *5:* 1166
Bostwick, Barry, *4:* 972
Boulder (Hoover) Dam, *2:* 372; *3:* 628
Boulle, Pierre, *4:* 834
Bourke-White, Margaret, *2:* 454
Bow, Clara, *2:* 262, 264, **268–69**
Bowerman, Bill, *1:* 162; *4:* 799
"Bowl games," *1:* 113
Bowling, *3:* **588–89,** 589 (ill.)
Bowman, Dave, *4:* 838
Bowman Gum Company, *2:* 347
Boxing, *1:* 95–96
Ali, Muhammad (Cassius Clay), *1:* 109; *4:* 789, 791, 878–80, 879 (ill.)
Corbett, James J., *1:* 100–101
Dempsey, Jack, *2:* 328–29
Johnson, Jack, *1:* 3, 5, 96, 101–2, 202
Louis, Joe, *2:* 471
Rocky, 4: 970–71
Boy Scouts, *1:* **226–28,** 227 (ill.)
Boyce, William D., *1:* 226
Boy's Life, 1: 191
Boyton, Paul, *1:* 121; *3:* 768
Bra, *1:* 157, **159–61,** 160 (ill.); *5:* 1271
Bradbury, Ray, *2:* 321, 461
Braddock, Benjamin, *4:* 823
Bradley, Milton, *1:* 106
Bradsby, Frank W., *1:* 22
Bradshaw, Terry, *4:* 1009
The Brady Bunch, *4:* 1024, 1025, **1025–27,** 1026 (ill.)
Braless look, *1:* 163
Branagh, Kenneth, *2:* 395
Branch Davidians, *4:* 1074; *5:* 1304, **1307**
Brand, Max, *2:* 460; *4:* 900
Brand names, *1:* 18–19, 54; *2:* 246, 256–57; *5:* 1113. *See also* specific brand, e.g., **Betty Crocker**
Brand, Neville, *2:* 351
Brand, Stewart, *4:* 787, 875
Brando, Marlon, *1:* 35–36, 163; *3:* 657, 658, **669–71,** 670 (ill.); *4:* 961, 966, 967 (ill.); *5:* 1204
Brannum, Hugh "Lumpy," *3:* 734, 735 (ill.)
Brassiere. *See* Bra
Brawl, *2:* 368
Bread, *2:* 290–91
Break dancing, *1:* 125; *5:* 1149
Breakfast foods, *1:* 8–9, 9 (ill.), 19–21, 20 (ill.); *2:* 289–90
Brenda Starr, Reporter, *3:* **571–72**
BR5-49, *5:* 1252
Brice, Fanny, *2:* 370, 477
Bridge (card game), *1:* 150, **214–15**
Bridges, Lloyd, *5:* 1121
The Bridges of Madison County, 5: 1224
Briggs, Donald, *2:* 458
Bright Lights, Big City, 5: 1155, 1203, 1219
Brinkley, David, *3:* 605
British invasion, *3:* 693; *4:* 858
Broadcasts, first, *2:* 238
Broadway, *1:* **34–36,** 35 (ill.); *2:* 267; *3:* 530; *5:* 1120, 1237, 1243
Angels in America, 5: 1199
Annie, 2: 311
Hair, 4: 824–26, 825 (ill.), 932
The Lion King, 5: 1237, 1243
The Odd Couple, 4: 833
Broccoli, Albert, *4:* 830
Brock, Lou, *1:* 100
Broderick, Matthew, *3:* 667
Brodie, *4:* 786
Brokaw, Tom, *3:* 606
Bronco (Ford), *5:* 1216
Bronson, Charles, *4:* 935
Brooklyn Cyclones, *1:* 122
Brooklyn Dodgers, *3:* 587, 592
Brooklyn, New York, *1:* 115, 120–22, 121 (ill.)

Brooks, Garth, *4:* 1043; *5:* 1226, 1251
Brooks, Gwendolyn, *4:* 928
Brooks, Mel, *2:* 395; *3:* 650
Brooks, Walter, *4:* 907
Broslovski, Kyle, *5:* 1298
Brosnan, Pierce, *4:* 831
Brothers Grimm, *2:* 410
Brown, Andrew H., *2:* 478–81
Brown, Betty and Kent, *3:* 580
Brown, Charlie, *3:* 698, 711
Brown, Cheryl, *2:* 356
Brown, David, *4:* 868
Brown, Dee, *4:* 948
Brown, Georg Stanford, 1058
Brown, Helen Gurley, *4:* 867–68, 942
Brown, James, *4:* 981, 984–85
Brown, Louise Joy, *4:* 951
Brown, Margaret Tobin, *1:* 231
Brown v. Board of Education, 4: 924
Browne, Joy, *5:* 1193
Brownie cameras, *1:* 8, 10 (ill.), **10–11**
Browning, Pete, *1:* 21
Browning, Ricou, *4:* 902
Browning, Tod, *2:* 393
Brubeck, Dave, *1:* 74
Brunot, James, *3:* 593
Brussels World's Fair (1958), *1:* 142
Bryan, Clark W., *1:* 85
Bryan, Vincent, *1:* 3
Bryan, William Jennings, *2:* 364
Brzezinski, Anton, *2:* 305 (ill.)
Bubble gum (candy), *1:* **54–56**
Bubble Mower, *2:* 378
Bubblegum (music), *4:* 1056
Bucannon, Mitch, *5:* 1283
Buck, Pearl S., *2:* 368
Buck Rogers, *2:* **304–6,** 305 (ill.)
Buckeroos, *3:* 557
Buckley, Thomas H., *1:* 61
Budinger, Victoria May, *4:* 897
Budweiser, *4:* 793, **794**
Buffalo Bills, *5:* 1324
Buffalo Bill's Wild West Show, *1:* 4, 33, **36–37**
Buffalo Bob, *3:* 602, 602 (ill.)
Buggin' Out, *5:* 1123
Bugs Bunny, *3:* **598–601,** 599 (ill.)
A Bug's Life, 5: 1237
Building, Antennas, Spans, Earth (BASE) jumping, *5:* 1272–73
Building projects, New Deal, *2:* 371–72
Building toys. *See* Construction toys
Bulimia, *3:* 775
Bumstead, Dagwood, *2:* 436
Bundy, Ted, *4:* 1092
Bungalows, *1:* 117; *2:* **349–50**
Buntline, Ned, *1:* 37
Burdick, Eugene, *4:* 819
Bureau of Alcohol, Tobacco, and Firearms, *5:* 1307
Burger King, *2:* 285; *3:* **677–78**
Burgess, Anthony, *4:* 962
Burghoff, Gary, *4:* 1050–51
Burma-Shave, *2:* **250–51**
Burma-Vita Company, *2:* 250
Burnett, Carol, *3:* 708
Burnett, Mark, *5:* 1295
Burns, George, and Gracie Allen, *1:* 50, 168; *2:* 342, 423, 477
Burns, Tommy, *1:* 96
Burr, Raymond, *2:* 459; *3:* 666
Burroughs, Edgar Rice, *1:* 192
Burroughs, William F., *3:* 698, 709
Burrows, James, *5:* 1177
Burstyn, Ellen, *4:* 965
Burton, LeVar, *4:* 1057, 1057 (ill.)
Burton, Richard, *3:* 542; *4:* 815, 965
Burton, Tim, *4:* 836
Bury My Heart at Wounded Knee, 4: 948
Buses, Greyhound, *1:* 216–17
Bush, George, *5:* 1102, 1198, 1223
Bush, George W., *4:* 925, 978
Bushnell, Nolan, *4:* 1012, 1019, 1021
Business and industry, *1:* 1–2, 153.
  See also Economy; Inventions
    General Motors, *1:* 7, 130–31, 148
    IBM, *5:* 1107–9, 1108 (ill.)
    movie industry, *2:* 240–41
    The Organization Man, 3: 710
Buster Brown, *1:* **81,** 82 (ill.)
Butler, Rhett, *2:* 368, 397 (ill.)
Butterfield 8, 3: 542
Butts, Alfred Mosher, *3:* 593
Buzz Lightyear, *5:* 1248, 1248 (ill.)
Buzzi, Ruth, *4:* 911
Bwana Devil, 3: 639, 675
Byrds, *4:* 851
Byrne, John, *2:* 465

C

C. A. Swanson and Sons, *3:* 681
Caan, James, *4:* 966, 967 (ill.)
Cabbage Patch Kids, *5:* **1200–1201,** 1201 (ill.)

The Cabinet of Dr. Caligari, *4:* 827
Cable News Network (CNN), *5:* **1179–80**
Cable TV, *3:* 611–12; *4:* **1027–29;** *5:* 1175
Cable News Network (CNN), *5:* 1175, 1179–80
ESPN, *4:* 1035–36
Home Shopping Network (HSN), *5:* 1106–7
MTV (Music Television), *5:* 1101, 1135, 1147–49, 1148 (ill.)
Cabot, Bruce, *2:* 403
Cadillac (1903), *1:* 131 (ill.)
Cafés, *5:* 1312
Caffeine, *5:* 1311
Cagney, James, *2:* 371, 383, **390;** *3:* 511, 625
Cagney, Jeanne, *3:* 742 (ill.)
Cahan, Abraham, *1:* 146
Cain, James M., *3:* 530
The Caine Mutiny, *3:* 638
Cakewalk, *1:* 123
California Gold Rush, *3:* 658
California lifestyle, *3:* 722–24, 723 (ill.); *4:* 844–45; *5:* 1283–84
The Call of the Wild, *1:* 88
Calloway, Cab, *2:* 389
Calvin and Hobbes, *3:* 711
Cambodia, *4:* 1083
Cameras, Brownie, *1:* 10 (ill.), **10–11**
Cameron, James, *1:* 231; *4:* 963
Campanella, Roy, *3:* 717
Campbell, E. Simms, *2:* 449
Campbell, Joseph A., *1:* 182
Campbell Kids, *1:* 183
Campbell, Luther, *5:* 1152
Campbell, Nell, *4:* 972 (ill.), 973
Campbell, Neve, *5:* 1246
Campbell's soup, *1:* 151, **181–83,** 182 (ill.)
Cancer, cigarettes, *2:* 252
Candid Camera, *3:* **733–34**
Candler, Asa, *1:* 56–57
Candy, *1:* 54–56; *3:* 546–48, 547 (ill.)
Canned goods, *1:* 53; *2:* 423–24
Cantor, Eddie, *1:* 49; *3:* 759
Cape Canaveral, Florida, *4:* 940
Capitalism, *3:* 771
Capone, Al, *2:* 239, **350–51,** 383
Capote, Truman, *4:* 787
Capp, Al, *2:* 455
Capra, Frank, *2:* 407; *3:* 539, 540
Captain America, *3:* **572–73;** *4:* 870
Captain Kangaroo, *3:* **734–35,** 735 (ill.)
Captain Marvel, *2:* 440
Car racing. *See* Auto racing
Caravan (Chrysler), *5:* 1209 (ill.)
Carbine, Patricia, *4:* 949, 1004
Carbonated water, *1:* 67
Cards, *1:* 214–15; *2:* 347–49, 348 (ill.)
Career women, *4:* 867–68, 998–99, 1046–49, 1047 (ill.)
"Carhops," *3:* 548
Carlson, Chester F., *4:* 805
Carlson, Emmons, *2:* 483
Carlton, William James, *1:* 18
Carnegie, Dale, *2:* **438–39**
Carney, Art, *3:* 609, 745, 745 (ill.); *4:* 833
Carothers, Wallace, *2:* 379
Carpenters (musical group), *4:* 951
Carpentier, Georges, *2:* 328
Carradine, David, *4:* 938
Carré, Ferdinand, *1:* 223
Carré, John Le, *4:* 787
Carrey, Jim, *1:* 176; *3:* 701; *4:* 1065
"Carry On" comedy movies, *5:* 1238
Cars. *See* Automobiles
Carson, Johnny, *3:* 762 (ill.), 762–63; *4:* 789, 885, **896–97;** *5:* 1143, 1185
Carson, Lisa Nicole, *5:* 1279 (ill.)
Carter Family (A. P., Sara, and Maybelle), *2:* 425; *3:* 556
Carter, Garnet, *2:* 332
Carter, Jimmy, *4:* 949; *5:* 1099
Carter, Lynda, *3:* 585
Carteris, Gabrielle, *5:* 1286, 1287 (ill.)
Cartland, Barbara, *4:* 997
Cartoon balloons, *2:* 258, 388 (ill.)
Cartoon characters. *See* Animation; Cartoons; Comic strips
Cartoons. *See also* Animation; Comic strips
The Beavis and Butt-Head Show, *5:* 1284–85
Bugs Bunny, *3:* 600
The Far Side, *5:* 1157–58, 1158 (ill.)
Felix the Cat, *1:* 171–72, 172 (ill.); *2:* 258
Gertie the Dinosaur, *1:* 172–74, 173 (ill.)
MAD Magazine, *3:* 704–6, 705 (ill.)

The New Yorker, 2: 312, 313, 313 (ill.)
Ripley's Believe It or Not!, 2: 318–19
Road Runner and Wile E. Coyote, *3:* 606–8, 607 (ill.)
Saturday morning cartoons, *4:* 912–16, 913 (ill.)
Schoolhouse Rock, 4: 1060–62
The Simpsons, 5: 1190–93, 1191 (ill.)
Teenage Mutant Ninja Turtles, *5:* 1194–95, 1195 (ill.)
Caruso, Enrico, *1:* 72
Carvey, Dana, *4:* 1060; *5:* 1249, 1250 (ill.)
Casablanca, *2:* 387, 389; *3:* 511, **531–32**
Caselotti, Adrianna, *2:* 410
Cash and Carry, 3: 741
Casino Royale, 4: 830
Cassady, Neal, *3:* 698, 709
Cassidy, David, *3:* 633 (ill.), 634; *4:* 1055, 1055 (ill.), 1056
Castle, Vernon and Irene, *1:* 123
Castle walk, *1:* 123
Casual dress
Abercrombie & Fitch, *5:* 1235–36
casual Fridays, *5:* 1113, 1235
Eddie Bauer, *2:* 256
J.Crew, *5:* 1109
jeans, *3:* 658–59
L. L. Bean, *1:* 155–56
Levi's, *3:* 659 (ill.), 659–60
T-shirts, *1:* 163–64
"Cat," *2:* 368; *3:* 638
Catalog houses, *1:* **117–18**
Catalogs
Abercrombie & Fitch, *5:* 1235–36
"Dynamic Tension Bodybuilding Course," *2:* 326
Fuller Brush, *1:* 15
J.Crew, *5:* 1109
L. L. Bean, *1:* 155–56
Sears, Roebuck, *1:* 2, 8, 26–28, 27 (ill.)
Whole Earth Catalog, 4: 875
The Catcher in the Rye, *3:* 617, 697, **700–701;** *4:* 865
Catch-22, 4: 786–87
Cather, Willa, *1:* 146, 150; *2:* 241
Catholic Legion of Decency, *4:* 815
Cathy, *4:* **998–99**
Cat's meow, *2:* 236
Catt, Carrie Chapman, *1:* 213
CATV (Community Antennae Television), *4:* 1028
Caulfield, Holden, *3:* 700
"Cautionary tale" urban legend, *5:* 1217
Cavalcade of Stars, 3: 746
Cavilleri, Jenny, *5:* 1115
Cayleff, Susan E., *2:* 468
Cazale, John, *4:* 967 (ill.)
CB Radio, *4:* **1030–31,** 1031 (ill.)
CBS (Columbia Broadcasting System), *2:* 341, 489; *3:* 611, 684, 727; *5:* 1175, 1277
CD (Compact Disc), *5:* **1136–37,** 1137 (ill.). *See also* Long-playing record (LP)
Cellophane, *1:* 25
Cellucotton, *2:* 257
Cellular phones, *5:* **1308–9,** 1309 (ill.), 1315
Celluloid, *1:* 24, 158
Censorship, *3:* 512; *4:* 998
Centennial Exposition (Philadelphia, Pennsylvania), *1:* 142
Centers for Disease Control (CDC), *4:* 1093; *5:* 1198
Central Intelligence Agency (CIA), *4:* 945
Century of Progress (Chicago, Illinois), *1:* 142
Cereal, *1:* 19–21, 20 (ill.); *2:* 289–90
CERN (European Laboratory for Particle Physics), *5:* 1320
Chabon, Michael, *5:* 1203
Chai, *5:* 1110
"Chain" e-mail, *5:* 1316
Chain store, *4:* 797
Chairs, reclining, *2:* 257
Challenger disaster, *4:* 939; *5:* 1180
Chamber of commerce, *2:* 368
Chamberlain, Richard, *3:* 634; *4:* 900
Chamberlain, Wilt, *3:* 590; *4:* 878
Champagne Music Makers, *3:* 748
Championship Auto Racing Teams (CART), *1:* 206
Chan, Charlie, *2:* **269,** 269 (ill.)
Chan, Jackie, *4:* 938
Chandler, Raymond, *2:* 241, 402, 442; *3:* 530; *5:* 1244
Chanel, Coco, *2:* 239; *4:* 1097
Chaney, Lon, *2:* 238
Chang and Eng, *1:* 224
Chapel, Lee, *3:* 626
Chaplin, Charlie, *1:* 46, 47, 167, **170–71;** *2:* 238, 369

Chapman, Graham, *4:* 1052
Chapman, Mark, *3:* 700
Charge cards, *3:* 646–47
Charles, Glen and Les, *5:* 1177
Charles, Prince of Wales, *4:* 1076; *5:* 1103
Charles, Ray, *3:* 565, 683
Charles, Suzette, *2:* 355 (ill.)
The Charleston, *1:* 123; *2:* 293, **351–52,** 352 (ill.)
Charley Horse, *3:* 578
"Charlie," *4:* 786
Charlie Brown, *3:* 698, 711
Charlie Chan, *2:* **269,** 269 (ill.)
Charlie McCarthy, *2:* **391,** 477; *3:* 641
Charlie's Angels, *4:* 1023, **1032–33,** 1033 (ill.), 1036
Chase, Chevy, *4:* 1059, 1060
Chase, Edna Woolman, *1:* 196
Chastain, Brandi, *5:* 1271
Chat rooms, *5:* 1303, **1309–11,** 1316
Chautauqua movement, *1:* 115, **118–20,** 119 (ill.)
Checker, Chubby, *1:* 124
Cheers, *5:* **1177–79,** 1178 (ill.), 1289–90
Cheese, Velveeta, *2:* **289**
Cheever, John, *2:* 313
Cherry, *3:* 638
Chevrolet Corvette, *3:* 643
Chewing gum, *1:* **54–56;** *2:* 347–48
Chia Pets, *4:* **1072**
Chicago American Giants, *1:* 107
Chicago Bears, *2:* 334–35
Chicago blues sound, *2:* 296
Chicago Bulls, *3:* 591; *5:* 1274
Chicago Century of Progress (1933), *2:* 318
Chicago gangsters, *2:* 350
"Chicago Seven," *4:* 945
Chicago Tribune, *3:* 571
Chicago White Sox, *1:* 97, 149, 201
Chicano culture, zoot suit, *3:* 525–27, 526 (ill.)
Chick, *3:* 638
Chicle, *1:* 54
Chiclets gum, *1:* 55 (ill.)
Child stars, *2:* 411–12; *3:* 542 (ill.), 542–43
Children
  and divorce, *4:* 1076
  Gerber baby food, *2:* 286–87
  Little League, *2:* 469–70, 470 (ill.)
Children's entertainment, *2:* 270–742: 271 (ill.)
Children's literature, *3:* 567
  Bobbsey Twins series, *3:* 570–71
  Brownies, *1:* 10
  Curious George, *3:* 574–75, 575 (ill.)
  Dr. Seuss, *3:* 697, 701–2, 702 (ill.)
  Frosty the Snowman, *3:* 703
  Golden Books, *3:* 577–78
  Harry Potter series, *5:* 1266–68, 1267 (ill.)
  Highlights, *3:* 579–80
  Raggedy Ann and Raggedy Andy, *1:* 208–9, 209 (ill.)
  Tom Swift series, *1:* 194–95
Children's television, *4:* 890
  Barney and Friends, *5:* 1281–83, 1282 (ill.)
  Captain Kangaroo, *3:* 734–35, 735 (ill.)
  Crockett, Davy, *3:* 736–37
  Disneyland, *2:* 273
  The Howdy Doody Show, *3:* 601–2, 602 (ill.)
  Kukla, Fran, and Ollie, *3:* 603–4, 604 (ill.)
  The Mickey Mouse Club, *2:* 273; *3:* 751–52
  Mister Rogers' Neighborhood, *4:* 908–9, 909 (ill.)
  Schoolhouse Rock, *4:* 1060–62
  Sesame Street, *4:* 1062–63
  Thomas the Tank Engine, *5:* 1299–1300, 1300 (ill.)
Children's Television Workshop (CTW), *4:* 1062
Childress, Alvin, *2:* 479 (ill.)
Chill, *5:* 1224
China, *1:* 132–33, 188
Chlamydia, *4:* 1093
Chong, Tommy, *4:* 933
Christianity, *4:* 1074
Christiansen, Ole Kirk, *3:* 720
Christie, Agatha, *2:* 457
Christmas, *2:* 255, 258
  Frosty the Snowman, *3:* 702–4
  It's a Wonderful Life, *3:* 538, 540
  Rockettes show, *2:* 409
  Rudolph the Red-Nosed Reindeer, *3:* 581–82
A Christmas Carol, *3:* 540
Christopher, William, *4:* 1051
Christy, E. P., *1:* 41
Christy Minstrels, *1:* 41–42

Chrysler Building, *2:* **352–53**
Chrysler Corporation, *3:* 627; *5:* 1208
Chrysler, Walter, *2:* 352
Church of Scientology, *4:* 1074
Churchill, Winston, *1:* 188
Chutes Park (Chicago, Illinois), *3:* 768
Cigarettes, *2:* **251–54,** 259 (ill.), 259–60, 347, 348 (ill.)
Cimarron, *2:* 368
Cincinnati Red Stockings, *1:* 96, 97
Cincinnati Reds, *4:* 1009; *5:* 1165
Cinema. *See* Film; Movies
Circuses, *1:* 3, 223–25, 224 (ill.)
Citation (horse), *1:* 103, 104
Citizen Kane, *3:* 511, 529, **533–35,** 534 (ill.)
Citizens Band (CB) Radio, *4:* 1030–31, 1031 (ill.)
City Lights, *2:* 369
Civil rights movement, *1:* 13; *2:* 471; *3:* 577, 617; *4:* 789–90, 921, **922–25,** 924 (ill.), 1025; *5:* 1209
Civil War, *1:* 168–70; *2:* 396–99
Clairol hair coloring, *2:* **377**
Clancy, Tom, *5:* 1101
The Clansman, *1:* 169, 218
Clapper, *4:* 1072
Clapton, Eric, *3:* 687, 687 (ill.), 688
Clarabell the clown, *3:* 602, 734
Clark, Dick, *3:* 731–32, 732 (ill.)
Clark, Meriwether Lewis, *1:* 103
Clark, Mike, *5:* 1189
Clark, Roy, *4:* 1042
Clarke, Arthur C., *4:* 838
Clarke, Mae, *2:* 390, 395 (ill.)
Clash, Kevin, *4:* 1063
Clash (musical group), *4:* 991
Clay, Cassius (Muhammad Ali), *1:* 109; *4:* 789, 791, **878–80,** 879 (ill.)
Clayton Antitrust Act of 1914, *1:* 153
Clayton, Don, *2:* 333
Clayton, John, *1:* 193
Clean Air Act, *4:* 1078
Clean Water Act, *4:* 1078
Clear and Present Danger, *5:* 1101
Cleese, John, *4:* 1052
Cleopatra, *3:* 542; *4:* 815
Cleveland Indians, *4:* 1009
Clinton, Bill, *2:* 307; *3:* 708; *4:* 937; *5:* 1223–27, 1239
Clinton, George, *4:* 985
Clinton, Hillary Rodham, *5:* 1225
A Clockwork Orange, *4:* 962, **962–63**
Clooney, George, *5:* 1289
Close, Glenn, *5:* 1126
Close-ups, *1:* 38–39
Clothing
  Abercrombie & Fitch, *5:* 1235–36
  Arrow Collar Man, *1:* 158–59, 159 (ill.)
  bell-bottoms, *4:* 807–9, 808 (ill.)
  blue jeans, *3:* 658–59
  bobbysoxers, *3:* 524–25, 525 (ill.)
  bra, *1:* 157, 159–61, 160 (ill.)
  Eddie Bauer, *2:* 256
  flappers, *2:* 261–63, 262 (ill.)
  Gibson Girl, *1:* 84–85, 85 (ill.)
  Great Depression era, *2:* 379
  grunge, *5:* 1254
  hip-hop, *5:* 1149
  hot pants, *4:* 955–56
  J.Crew, *5:* 1109
  L. L. Bean, *1:* 155–56
  leisure suit, *4:* 956–57, 957 (ill.)
  Levi's, *3:* 659 (ill.), 659–60
  miniskirts, *4:* 811–13, 812 (ill.)
  nylon, *2:* 379–80
  nylon stockings, *2:* 380–82, 381 (ill.)
  polyester, *4:* 959–60
  raccoon coats, *2:* 264–65
  skateboarding, *3:* 723 (ill.), 724
  T-shirts, *1:* 163–64
  zipper, *1:* 164–65
  zoot suit, *3:* 525–27, 526 (ill.)
Clowns, *1:* 225; *3:* 602; *5:* 1192
Cluett, Peabody & Company, *1:* 158
CNN (Cable News Network), *4:* 1029; *5:* 1175, **1179–80**
Coal miners, *2:* 373–74
Coats, raccoon, *2:* **264–65**
Cobain, Kurt, *5:* 1251, 1254, 1256, 1258
Cobb, Lee J., *3:* 670
Cobb, Ty, *1:* 97, **99–100,** 201
COBOL 80 (programming language), *5:* 1232
Coca-Cola, *1:* **56–58,** 57 (ill.)
Cocaine, *4:* 820, 935; *5:* **1201–4,** 1220
Cocktail hour, *2:* **353**
"Code of Wartime Practices for American Broadcasters," *3:* 512
Cody, Buffalo Bill, and His Wild West Show, *1:* 4, 33, **36–37**

Cody, Samuel F., *2:* 346
Coffee, *5:* 1110–11, 1111 (ill.), **1311–13**
Coffin nail, *2:* 368
Cohan, George M., *1:* 3, 35; *2:* 390; *3:* 511
Cohn, Roy, *3:* 770, 771
Cojunto, *5:* 1262
Colasanto, Nicholas, *5:* 1178, 1178 (ill.)
Colbert, Claudette, *2:* 383–84
"Cold calling," *1:* 140
Cold War, *1:* 109–10; *3:* 515, 517, 615–16, 617, 620–21, **621–24,** 638–41, 767, 772; *4:* 939; *5:* 1314
Cole, Nat King, *2:* 363
Coleco, *5:* 1200
Coleman, Ornette, *1:* 74
Colgate University, *3:* 632
Colleano, Con, *1:* 225
Collectibles
  baseball cards, *2:* 348
  G.I. Joe, *4:* 797
  Lionel trains, *1:* 104–6, 105 (ill.)
  MAD Magazine, *3:* 705
  postcards, *1:* 135
  teddy bears, *1:* 30–31, 31 (ill.)
College football. *See under* Football
College students
  antiwar movement, *4:* 791, 922
  goldfish swallowing, *2:* 500
  raccoon coats, *2:* 264–65
  spring break, *3:* 631–32
Collier's Weekly, 1: 2
Collyer, Bud, *2:* 465
"Color barrier," *3:* 592, 717
Color, in animation, *2:* 272
Colors, 5: 1197, 1206
Coltrane, John, *1:* 74
Columbia Broadcasting System (CBS). *See* CBS (Columbia Broadcasting System)
Columbian Exposition, *1:* 60, 129–30, 142
Columbine High School (Littleton, Colorado) shootings, *5:* 1115
Columbus, Christopher, *2:* 251
Columnists, *2:* 306–7, 241
Combustible Edison, *2:* 353
Comedies, Movie
  Baker, Josephine, *2:* 267–68, 268 (ill.)
  Chaplin, Charlie, *1:* 46, 47, 167, 170–71; *2:* 238, 369
  Disney live action, *2:* 273
  "dumb" films, *5:* 1120, 1250
  Francis the Talking Mule, *3:* 664–65
  A Hard Day's Night, 4: 824–26, 825 (ill.)
  Keystone Kops, *1:* 175–76, 176 (ill.)
  Laurel and Hardy, *2:* 404–5, 405 (ill.)
  Marx Brothers, *2:* 406–7
  Rogers, Will, *1:* 178–79
  screwball, *2:* 399–400
  Three Stooges, *2:* 412–14, 413 (ill.)
  Wayne's World, 5: 1249–50, 1250 (ill.)
Comedies, TV
  Abbott and Costello, *3:* 530–31, 531 (ill.)
  The Adventures of Ozzie and Harriet, 3: 728–29
  All in the Family, 4: 1024–25
  Ally McBeal, 5: 1278–79, 1279 (ill.)
  Amos 'n' Andy, 2: 478–81, 479 (ill.)
  Benny, Jack, *3:* 597–98
  Bewitched, 4: 893–95
  The Brady Bunch, 4: 1025–27, 1026 (ill.)
  Cheers, 5: 1177–79, 1178 (ill.)
  The Cosby Show, 5: 1181–83, 1182 (ill.)
  Fibber McGee and Molly, 2: 482–83
  Frasier, 5: 1289–90
  Friends, 5: 1290–92, 1291 (ill.)
  Gilligan's Island, 4: 903–5, 904 (ill.)
  Happy Days, 4: 1040–41, 1041 (ill.)
  The Honeymooners, 3: 744–46, 745 (ill.)
  I Love Lucy, 3: 746–48, 747 (ill.)
  Leave It to Beaver, 3: 749–51, 750 (ill.)
  The Many Loves of Dobie Gillis, 3: 737 (ill.), 737–38
  The Mary Tyler Moore Show, 4: 1046–49, 1047 (ill.)
  *M*A*S*H, 4:* 1049–51
  Mister Ed, 4: 906–7
  The Monkees, 4: 854–55, 855 (ill.)
  Monty Python's Flying Circus, 4: 1051–52
  The Partridge Family, 4: 1054–56, 1055 (ill.)

Roseanne, 5: 1187–88
Rowan & Martin's Laugh-In, 4: 911–12, 912 (ill.)
Saturday Night Live, 4: 1058–60, 1059 (ill.)
Seinfeld, 5: 1296–98, 1297 (ill.)
South Park, 5: 1298–99, 1299 (ill.)
Taxi, 4: 1063–65, 1064 (ill.)
Comedy Central, *4:* 1029
Comfort, Alex, *4:* 949, 1082
Comic books, *2:* 433, **439–40;** *3:* 510, 567; *4:* 866
Archie, 3: 568–69, 569 (ill.)
Batman, 2: 434–36, 435 (ill.)
Captain America, 3: 572–73
Felix the Cat, 1: 171–72, 172 (ill.)
Green Lantern, 3: 578–79
manga, 5: 1281
Marvel Comics, *4:* 869–71
Spider-Man, 4: 873–74, 874 (ill.)
Superman, 2: 462–66, 463 (ill.)
Wonder Woman, 3: 583–85
Comic Code Authority, *2:* 440
Comic strips, *1:* 2, 79; *2:* 433. *See also* Cartoons
Blondie, 2: 436–38, 437 (ill.)
Brenda Starr, Reporter, 3: 571–72
Buck Rogers, 2: 304–6, 305 (ill.)
Buster Brown, 1: 81, 82 (ill.)
Cathy, 4: 998–99
Dick Tracy, 2: 444–46, 445 (ill.)
The Far Side, 5: 1157–58, 1158 (ill.)
Flash Gordon, 2: 449–51, 450 (ill.)
Garfield, 4: 999–1001, 1000 (ill.)
The Katzenjammer Kids, 1: 86–87
Krazy Kat, 1: 189–91, 190 (ill.)
Li'l Abner, 2: 454–55
Little Orphan Annie, 2: 310–11
Mutt & Jeff, 1: 89–90
Peanuts, 3: 698, 710–12, 711 (ill.)
Popeye, 2: 314–16, 315 (ill.)
Secret Agent X-9, 3: 624
Coming of the Saucers, 3: 636 (ill.)
Commerce, *1:* 1–5, 153–54; *2:* 243–44, 373–74; *3:* 517, 643–44; *4:* 793; *5:* 1105, 1229. *See also* Business and industry; specific company, e.g., Ford Motor Company
Commercialization, Holiday, *1:* 215–16, 220–21
Commercials, television. *See under* Television
Commodores, *4:* 985
The Common Sense Book of Baby and Child Care, 3: 511
Communes, *4:* **1072–73**
Communication, *2:* 301
AT&T, *1:* 154–55
cellular phones, *5:* 1308–9, 1309 (ill.)
E-mail, *5:* 1314–17, 1315 (ill.)
postcards, *1:* 134–35
satellites, *3:* 779–80
telephone, *1:* 139 (ill.), 139–41
T-shirts, *1:* 163–64
Communion, 3: 636
Communism, *1:* 150; *2:* 360–61; *3:* 670–71, 767. *See also* Blacklisting; Cold War
Community Antennae Television (CATV), *4:* 1028
Compact discs (CDs), *5:* **1136–37,** 1137 (ill.). *See also* Long-playing record (LP)
The Complete Book of Running, 4: 949, 1016
Computer-generated animation, *5:* 1247–49, 1270
Computers
Apple, *4:* 1070–71, 1071 (ill.)
chat rooms, *5:* 1310–11
E-mail, *5:* 1314–17, 1315 (ill.)
hackers, *5:* 1317–18
HAL, *4:* 838
IBM, *5:* 1107–9, 1108 (ill.)
Internet, *5:* 1319–21, 1320 (ill.)
Microsoft, *5:* 1231–33, 1232 (ill.)
personal, *4:* 1085–87
viruses, *5:* 1304
Conaway, Jeff, *4:* 1064 (ill.), 1065
Concerts
Altamont, *4:* 842–43, 843 (ill.)
Farm Aid, *5:* 1138 (ill.), 1138–39
Grateful Dead, *4:* 853
Live Aid, *5:* 1143–45, 1144 (ill.)
Lollapalooza and Lilith Fair, *5:* 1256–58, 1257 (ill.)
Condé Nast, *1:* 196
Condit, Gary, *3:* 708
Condon, Richard, *3:* 622
Coney Island, *1:* 115, **120–22,** 121 (ill.), 136; *3:* 768
"Confessional" magazines, *1:* 195–96

Conger, Darva, *5:* 1296
Congressional Reconstruction Act of 1867, *1:* 217
Conjunto, *5:* 1262
A Connecticut Yankee, 2: 267
Connery, Sean, *4:* 830, 831 (ill.); *5:* 1131
Conrad, William, *3:* 743
Conservatism, *4:* 910, 944, 1076; *5:* 1104
  Limbaugh, Rush, *5:* 1225–26
  Little Orphan Annie, 2: 311
  Reader's Digest, 2: 316–17
"Conspicuous Consumption," *5:* 1105, 1220
Construction, *2:* 371–72, 493–494, 501–2; *3:* 629–31, 630 (ill.)
Construction toys, *1:* 202
  Erector sets, *1:* 202–4, 203 (ill.)
  LEGOs, *3:* 720–22, 721 (ill.)
  Lincoln Logs, *2:* 331–32
  Tinkertoys, *1:* 211 (ill.), 211–12
"Consumer culture," *3:* 617, 643; *4:* 793
Consumerism
  baby boomers, *5:* 1206
  game shows, *3:* 742, 753–54
  Mall of America, *5:* 1230 (ill.), 1230–31
  MTV, *5:* 1148
  postwar, *3:* 517, 643
  yuppies, *5:* 1218–20
Continental Baking Company, *2:* 291
Convenience foods, *1:* 65–66; *2:* 286–87; *3:* 680–82, 681 (ill.)
Conversation, Chat rooms, *5:* 1310–11
Convoy, 4: 1031
Cook, Ann Turner, *2:* 287
Cook, Paul, *4:* 992
Cookbooks, *2:* 250; *3:* 638
Cookie Monster, *4:* 1063 (ill.)
Cookies, Oreo, *1:* 184 (ill.), **184–85**
Cooking, *1:* 126
  Aunt Jemima, *1:* 8–9, 9 (ill.)
  Betty Crocker, *2:* 248–50, 249 (ill.); *3:* 638
  The Joy of Cooking, 2: 421–22
Cool, *3:* 638
"Cool jazz," *1:* 73–74
Coolidge, Calvin, *1:* 179, 216; *2:* 236, 354, 480
Cooling, *3:* 510
Coon, Zip, *1:* 40
Coonskin caps, *2:* 265; *3:* 736
Cooper, Alice, *4:* 981; *5:* 1140, 1249
Cooper, Gary, *2:* **391–92**
Cooper, James A., *1:* 225
Cooper, Kenneth, *4:* 1010–11
Cooper, Merian C., *2:* 404
Cooper, Peter, *1:* 65
Cooper, Ralph, *2:* 495
Cooperstown, New York, *1:* 108
Cooties, *3:* 638
Copper, Kenneth H., *4:* 1010
Coppola, Francis Ford, *4:* 935, 966
COPS, 5: 1225
Copy machines, *4:* 804–5
Corbett, James J., *1:* **100–101**
Corby, Ellen, *4:* 1066
Corea, Chick, *1:* 74
"Corkscrews" (roller coasters), *1:* 136, 137 (ill.)
Corman, Roger, *2:* 387
Corn Popper (toy), *2:* 378
Cornell, Chris, *5:* 1255 (ill.)
Cornell University, *1:* 183; *5:* 1318
Corolla, Adam, *5:* 1193
Corporate sponsors, *1:* 183; *2:* 246, 291, 339, 475
Corporate world, *1:* 7, 130–31, 148; *3:* 657, 710
Corporation for Public Broadcasting, *4:* 890
Correll, Charles, *2:* 478
Cortez, Ricardo, *2:* 458
Corvairs, *1:* 131
Corwin, Norman, *2:* 342
Cosa Nostra, 4: 934
Cosby, Bill, *1:* 66; *3:* 623; *4:* 913 (ill.); *5:* 1101, 1102, 1104, 1181, 1182 (ill.), 1183
The Cosby Show, *5:* 1102, **1181–83,** 1182 (ill.)
Cosell, Howard, *4:* 1017, 1018 (ill.)
Cosmetics, *1:* 116; *2:* 263–64, 377; *4:* 810–11
Cosmopolitan, *4:* **867–68**
Cosmos, 5: 1100
Cosmos Club, *1:* 91
Costello, Lou, *1:* 176; *3:* 529, 530–31, 531 (ill.)
Costner, Kevin, *5:* 1241
Coubertin, Pierre de, *1:* 109
Coughlin, Fr. Charles E., *2:* 342, 371
Counterculture, *4:* 786, 922
  bell-bottoms, *4:* 809
  communes, *4:* 1072–73
  Easy Rider, 4: 820–21, 821 (ill.)
  Grateful Dead, *4:* 853
  Haight-Ashbury, *4:* 929–30, 930 (ill.)
  Hair, 4: 824–26, 825 (ill.)

heavy metal, *5:* 1139–41, 1140 (ill.)
Rolling Stone, 4: 871–72, 872 (ill.)
T-shirts, *1:* 163
Whole Earth Catalog, 4: 875
Counterintelligence, *3:* 625
Country Club Plaza (Kansas City, Missouri), *3:* 648
Country music, *3:* 553, **555–58,** 691; *5:* 1136, 1262
alternative country music, *5:* 1252–53, 1253 (ill.)
bluegrass, *3:* 554–55
Grand Ole Opry, 2: 297–98, 298 (ill.)
Hee Haw, 4: 1042–43
Rodgers, Jimmie, *2:* 298–99
Coupland, Douglas, *5:* 1206
Courlander, Harold, *4:* 1058
Courrege, Beverly, *5:* 1328
Courrèges, André, *4:* 812
Court TV, *2:* 458; *4:* 1029
Cousteau, Jacques Yves, *1:* 91
Cousy, Bob, *3:* 590
Cowboys, *2:* 426, 259 (ill.), 259–60; *3:* 658, 659
Cowen, Joshua Lionel, *1:* 104
Cowsills, *4:* 1056
Cox, Courteney, *5:* 1247, 1291, 1291 (ill.)
Crabbe, Buster, *2:* 306, 450 (ill.), 451
"Crack" cocaine, *5:* 1202–3
Cracker Jack, *1:* **58–60,** 59 (ill.)
"Cramp your style," *2:* 368
Crane, David, *5:* 1291
"Crap!," *2:* 368
Craven, Wes, *4:* 829; *5:* 1245, 1247
Crawford, Cindy, *5:* 1118 (ill.)
Crawford, Joan, *2:* 371
Credit cards, *3:* **646–47**
"Crib," *5:* 1224
Crichton, Michael, *5:* 1224, 1237, 1268, 1270, 1288
Crime, *4:* 1092
hackers, *5:* 1317–18
Mafia, *4:* 934–35
Perry Mason, *2:* 458–59
Pulp Fiction, 5: 1244–45
serial killers, *4:* 1091–93, 1092 (ill.)
Crips, *5:* 1205
Criss, Peter, *4:* 950 (ill.), 987
Crocker, Betty. *See* Betty Crocker
Crocker, William, *2:* 249
Crockett, Davy, *2:* 265; *3:* **736–37**
Cronkite, Walter, *3:* 605
Crooners, *3:* 561
Crosby, Bing, *3:* 512, 513, 553
Crosby, Caresse, *1:* 159
Crosby, Stills, Nash and Young, *4:* 1085
Crosland, Alan, *2:* 275
Crossover utility vehicles (CUVs), *5:* 1208
Crossword puzzles, *1:* 150; *2:* 326, **327**
Crough, Suzanne, *4:* 1055, 1055 (ill.)
Crow, Jim, *1:* 40
Crumb, Robert, *2:* 440
Crumbine, Samuel, *1:* 14
Crusader Rabbit, 4: 914
Crusades (evangelical), *1:* 115, 127–28, 138; *2:* 240
Crystal Hall Theater (New York City), *1:* 48 (ill.)
Crystal Palace Exhibition (London, England), *1:* 142
Cuban Missile Crisis, *3:* 620, 622
Culbertson, Ely, *1:* 215
Cullen, Bill, *3:* 753, 754 (ill.)
Culp, Robert, *3:* 623
Cult followings, *4:* 853, 919, 973
Cults, *4:* 1069–70, 1073–74, **1073–74;** *5:* 1307
Cultural movements, *1:* 118–20, 119 (ill.)
Cummings, Bill, *2:* 474
Cunningham, Sean S., *5:* 1127
Cups, *1:* 14, 26
Cure (musical group), *5:* 1253
Curious George, *3:* **574–75,** 575 (ill.)
Curry, Tim, *4:* 972, 972 (ill.)
"The Curse of Capistrano," *1:* 199
Curtin, Jane, *4:* 1059, 1059 (ill.)
Curtis, Cyrus H. K., *1:* 93
Curtis, Jamie Lee, *4:* 837
Curtis, John B., *1:* 54
Curtis, Ken, *3:* 743
Curtis, Tony, *3:* 640
Curtiz, Michael, *3:* 532
Cussler, Clive, *1:* 231
CUVs (Crossover utility vehicles), *5:* 1208
Cyberspace, *5:* 1310–11
Cyclone (roller coaster), *1:* 121, 136

D

Dahl, Gary, *4:* 1088–89
Daigneau, Kenneth, *2:* 423

Dallas, *2:* 488; *4:* 1034; *5:* 1101, **1183–85,** 1184 (ill.)
Dallas Cowboys, *4:* 880
Dalton, Timothy, *4:* 831
Daly, Carroll John, *2:* 442
Daly, Tim, *4:* 903
Dams, *2:* 494
Dancing, *1:* **122–25;** *2:* 345; *5:* 1281
aerobic, *4:* 1011
American Bandstand, 3: 731–32, 732 (ill.)
Baker, Josephine, *2:* 267–68, 268 (ill.)
the Charleston, *2:* 351–52, 352 (ill.)
disco, *4:* 982–83, 983 (ill.)
Hustle, *4:* 985–87, 986 (ill.)
marathons, *2:* 326
pop dance music, *3:* 563
prom, *2:* 358–60, 359 (ill.)
raves, *5:* 1259–60, 1260 (ill.)
Saturday Night Fever, 4: 974–75, 975 (ill.)
tango, *1:* 124; *2:* 280
Daniels, Les, *3:* 584
The Danny Thomas Show, 3: 642
Danson, Ted, *5:* 1178, 1178 (ill.)
Danza, Tony, *4:* 1064 (ill.), 1065
Daredevils, *1:* 3; *4:* 881–83, 882 (ill.); *5:* 1272–74, 1273 (ill.)
"Dark cinema." *See* Film noir
The Dark Knight Returns, 2: 435, 440
Darlington International Raceway, *2:* 474
Darrow, Charles B., *2:* 472
Darrow, Clarence, *2:* 239, 309, 364
Darwin, Charles, *2:* 364, 365
Dassin, Jules, *3:* 773
David, Larry, *5:* 1296
Davidson, Arthur, *1:* 16
Davidson, Carol, *4:* 800
Davies, Jessica, *1:* 197
Davies, Michael P., *5:* 1301–2
Davis, Ann B., *4:* 1026
Davis, Jacob, *3:* 658
Davis, Jim, *4:* 999, 1000 (ill.), 1001
Davis, Miles, *1:* 73; *3:* 553
Dawes, Tom, *2:* 375
Dawson's Creek, 5: 1225
The Day the Earth Stood Still, *3:* **661–63,** 662 (ill.)
Day traders, *5:* 1228
The Days of Wine and Roses, 2: 505
Daytime talk shows, *4:* **897–900,** 898 (ill.)
Daytona Beach, Florida, *2:* 474
DC Comics, *2:* 440, 462
De Forest, Lee, *2:* 341
de Graff, Robert, *2:* 457
de Meyer, Baron, *1:* 196
Dead hoofer, *2:* 368
Dead Men Don't Wear Plaid, 3: 537
Deadheads, *4:* 853
The Deadwood Dick on Deck; or Calamity Jane, the Heroine of Whoop-Up, 1: 83 (ill.)
Dean, James, *3:* 609, 634, 657, 658, 661, **663–64;** *5:* 1204
Debs, Eugene V., *1:* 145
Deckard, Rick, *5:* 1122
Deejaying, *5:* 1149
Deejays. *See* Disc jockeys
Defense Department, *5:* 1318
DeGeneres, Ellen, *5:* 1277
Deltiologists, *1:* 135
DeMille, Cecil B., *1:* 46, 167; *2:* 237–38; *4:* 942
Demming, Elling, *2:* 484
Democracy and Education, 1: 148
Democracy vs. communism, *3:* 621–22
Democratic National Convention (Chicago, Illinois), *4:* 945
Dempsey, Jack, *1:* 202; *2:* 239, **328–29,** 467
DeNiro, Robert, *2:* 351
Dent, Lester, *2:* 447
Denver, Bob, *3:* 699, 737; *4:* 904, 904 (ill.)
Denver Broncos, *5:* 1165
DePalma, Brian, *5:* 1203
Department stores, *2:* **254–55,** 258; *3:* 647, 648–49; *4:* 798
DeRita, "Curly Joe," *2:* 414
Dern, Laura, *5:* 1270
deRossi, Portia, *5:* 1279 (ill.)
DeSalvo, Albert "Boston Strangler," *4:* 1092
"Designer" drugs, Prozac, *5:* 1211–12
Designers, fashion, *5:* 1113
Desmond, Norma, *1:* 47
Detective Comics, 2: 434
Detective stories
Blade Runner, 5: 1122–23
Charlie Chan, *2:* 269, 269 (ill.)
Charlie's Angels, 4: 1032–33, 1033 (ill.)
detective fiction, *2:* 441–43
Dick Tracy, *2:* 444–46, 445 (ill.)
Hardy Boys series, *2:* 308–9
Hawaii Five-O, 4: 905–6

Miami Vice, 5: 1186–87
Nancy Drew series, *2:* 455–56
Perry Mason, *2:* 458–59
The Shadow, 2: 461–62
Shaft, 4: 976–77, 977 (ill.)
Detroit, Michigan, *2:* 474; *3:* 565; *4:* 842, 928
Detroit Pistons, *5:* 1166
Detroit Red Wings, 208 (ill.)
DeVito, Danny, *4:* 1064 (ill.), 1065
Dewey, John, *1:* 148
Dey, Susan, *4:* 1055, 1055 (ill.)
Dharma and Greg, 4: 933
Dhiegh, Khigh, *4:* 906
Dial M for Murder, 3: 676
Diana, Princess of Wales, *4:* 1076; *5:* 1103
Diaz, Cameron, *4:* 1033
Diazepam (Valium), *4:* 801–2
DiCaprio, Leonardo, *1:* 231; *2:* 253; *3:* 634; *5:* 1225
Dick and Jane readers, *2:* **443–44**
Dick Tracy, *2:* 433, **444–46,** 445 (ill.); *5:* 1308
Dickens, Charles, *2:* 486; *3:* 540
Dickson, Earle and Josephine, *2:* 247–48
Dickson, J. T., *4:* 959
Dickson, William, *1:* 44
Dictionary of Teleliteracy, 5: 1283
Didrickson, Babe, *2:* 290, 467, **468–69,** 469 (ill.)
Diego, Don, *1:* 199
Diemer, Walter, *1:* 55
Diets, *3:* **774–75**
"Digital age" encyclopedia, *1:* 198
Dilbert, 5: 1224
Dille, John, *2:* 304
Diller, Barry, *5:* 1106
Dillinger, John, *2:* 371
Dillon, Matt, *3:* 640, 743
DiMaggio, Joe, *1:* 97, 108; *3:* 668
Dime novels, *1:* 2, 79, **82–84,** 83 (ill.)
Dime stores, *1:* 8, **11–13,** 12 (ill.)
Diners, *1:* **60–62,** 61 (ill.)
The Dingbat Family, 1: 189
Dinks, *5:* 1219
Dinosaurs, *5:* 1268, 1281
Dion, Celine, *5:* 1226
Dior, Christian, *3:* 523, 657
Direct marketing, *1:* 14–15, 116; *3:* 520–22, 521 (ill.)
Directors
Chaplin, Charlie, *1:* 46, 47, 167, 170–71; *2:* 238, 369
Friedkin, William, *4:* 965
Griffith, D. W., *1:* 46, 147, 167; *2:* 237
Hitchcock, Alfred, *3:* 640, 661, 668–69, 676; *4:* 788, 836, 837, 1092
Kazan, Elia, *3:* 669–71, 773
Kubrick, Stanley, *4:* 838
Lee, Spike, *5:* 1123
Scott, Ridley, *5:* 1122, 1123
Stevens, George, *3:* 673
Welles, Orson, *3:* 533–35, 534 (ill.)
Dirks, Rudolph, *1:* 86
The Dirty Dozen, 5: 1176
Disaster movies, *1:* 230–31; *4:* **963–64,** 964 (ill.); *5:* 1120–21, 1121 (ill.)
Disc jockeys, *2:* 343; *3:* 641, 683, **684–85,** 695; *5:* 1260
Disco, *1:* 124; *4:* 974–75, 975 (ill.), **982–83,** 983 (ill.)
Discount stores, *1:* 11, 13; *4:* 797–99, 802–4
Discovery Channel, *4:* 1029
Disk operating system (MS-DOS), *5:* 1232–33
Disney, *2:* 267, **270–74,** 271 (ill.); *3:* 511; *5:* 1248, 1281
Fantasia, 3: 535–36, 536 (ill.)
Mary Poppins, 4: 832, 832 (ill.)
Snow White and the Seven Dwarfs, 2: 410–11, 411 (ill.)
Steamboat Willie, 2: 238, 267, 270, 278–79, 279 (ill.)
Winnie-the-Pooh, *2:* 321–23, 322 (ill.)
Disney amusement parks, *2:* 271 (ill.); *3:* 769
Disney, Roy, *2:* 278
Disney, Walt, *2:* 278, 322, 369; *3:* 535; *4:* 817, 832
Disneyland (TV show), *3:* 736
"Disposable income," *5:* 1105
Diss, *5:* 1100
Distributorships. *See* Door-to-door sales
Ditko, Steve, *4:* 873
Divorce, *4:* 1026, 1069, **1075–77**
Dixie cups, *1:* **14**
Dixieland Jazz Band, *1:* 148
Dixon, Franklin W., *3:* 570
Dixon, George Washington, *1:* 40
Dixon, Thomas, Jr., *1:* 169, 218
Djerassi, Carl, *3:* 778
DMs (Doc Martens), *4:* 810
Do the Right Thing, *5:* **1123–25,** 1124 (ill.)

"Do They Know It's Christmas?," *5:* 1144
Dobie Gillis, *3:* 737 (ill.), 737–38
Doc Martens, *4:* **809–10**
Doc Savage, *2:* **446–48**
"Dr. Death," *5:* 1227
Dr. Dolittle movies, *3:* 665
Dr. Doodle, *2:* 378
Dr. Evil, *5:* 1238
Dr. Kildare, *4:* **900–901**
Dr. Maertens (Klaus Maertens), *4:* 809
Dr. Octopus, *4:* 874
Dr. Seuss, *3:* 697, **701–2;** *4:* 865
Dr. Strangelove, *3:* 620, 623; *4:* **818–19**
Doctor Zhivago, 4: 788
Documentaries, Disney, *2:* 273
Dodd, Jimmy, *3:* 752
Dodd, Sonora Smart, *1:* 215
Dodge Caravan, *5:* 1209 (ill.)
Dogg, Snoop, *5:* 1150
Dogs, *3:* **540–41,** 541 (ill.)
Doherty, Shannen, *5:* 1286, 1287 (ill.)
Dolenz, Micky, *4:* 854, 855, 855 (ill.)
"Dollar" (discount) stores, *1:* 11, 13
Dolls
  Barbie, *3:* 644–46, 645 (ill.)
  Cabbage Patch Kids, *5:* 1200–1201, 1201 (ill.)
  G.I. Joe, *4:* 796–97
  Kewpie dolls, *1:* 66, 86–87
  Raggedy Ann and Raggedy Andy, *1:* 202, 208–9, 209 (ill.)
Don Juan, 2: 276
Donahue, Phil, *4:* 899
Donkey Kong, *4:* 1021
"Don't leave home without it," *4:* 948
Donuts, *3:* 545–46
"Doomsday Machine," *4:* 819
Door-to-door sales, *1:* 14–15, 116; *4:* 810–11
Dopamine, *2:* 252
Doraemon, 5: 1280
Doren, Charles Van, *3:* 742
Doren, Philip Van, *3:* 538
Dorough, Bob, *4:* 1061
Dorrance, Arthur, *1:* 182
Dorrance, John T., *1:* 182–83
Dorsey, Jimmy, *2:* 427
Dorsey, Tommy, *1:* 73; *2:* 427; *3:* 565
Dot-coms, *5:* 1227, 1229, 1321
Dotrice, Karen, *4:* 832 (ill.)
Douglas, Donna, *4:* 891, 892 (ill.)
Douglas, John Sholto, *1:* 101
Douglas, Kirk, *5:* 1245
Douglas, Lloyd C., *3:* 511
Douglas, Michael, *5:* 1102, 1126
Dow Chemical Company, *3:* 649; *4:* 945
Dow, Tony, *3:* 750, 750 (ill.)
Down parka, *2:* 256
"Downshifting," *5:* 1220
"Downsizing," *5:* 1220
Doyle, Arthur Conan, *2:* 441
Doyle Dane Bernbach (DDB), *3:* 653
Doyle, David, *4:* 1032
Dozier, Lamont, *4:* 856
Dracula, *2:* 369, 383, **392–93**
"Drag races," *3:* 626
Dragnet, *3:* 640, **738–39**
Dragon Ball Z, 5: 1278
Dramas, TV
  Baywatch, 5: 1283–84
  Bonanza, 4: 895–96
  COPS, 5: 1225
  Dr. Kildare, 4: 900–901
  Dragnet, 3: 738–39
  ER, 5: 1225, 1288–89
  Fantasy Island, 4: 1036–37, 1037 (ill.)
  The Fugitive, 4: 902–3
  Hawaii Five-O, 4: 905–6
  Little House on the Prairie, 4: 1043–45, 1044 (ill.)
  The Love Boat, 4: 1045–46
  Miami Vice, 5: 1186–87
  Roots, 4: 1057 (ill.), 1057–58
  Studio One, 3: 608–9
  The Twilight Zone, 3: 764–66
  The Waltons, 4: 1066–67
Dreamland, *1:* 121
Dreiser, Theodore, *1:* 146, 150
Drew, Charles Richard, *3:* 513
Drexler, Millard, *4:* 795
Dreyfuss, Richard, *4:* 968–69, 969 (ill.)
Drinks. *See* Alcohol; Beverages; Soft drinks
Drive-by shooting, *4:* 925
Drive-in theater, *2:* **497–99,** 498 (ill.)
Drivers, road rage, *5:* 1212–13
Dropping out, *4:* 786
Drudge, Matt, *2:* 307
Drug use, *4:* 922, 936–37; *5:* 1165, 1259
Drug-induced music, *4:* 789
Drugs, *4:* 801

Alka-Seltzer, *2:* 374–75
caffeine, *5:* 1311
Cocaine, *5:* 1201–4
diets, *3:* 774
Ecstasy, *5:* 1313–14
hallucinatory, *4:* 852
marijuana, *4:* 936–37
Penicillin, *2:* 356–57
Prozac, *5:* 1211–12
Valium, *4:* 801–2
Drury, Allen, *3:* 622
Dubble Bubble, *1:* 55
DuBois, W. E. B., *1:* 170
"Duck and cover" drills, *3:* 620, 623
Dude, *5:* 1100
The Dukes of Hazzard, *4:* **1034**
Dullea, Keir, *4:* 838
"Dumb" movies, *5:* 1120, 1250
Dumont, Margaret, *2:* 406
Duncan, Donald F., *2:* 336
Dune, *4:* 787, **868–69**
Dungeons and Dragons, *4:* **1013–15,** 1014 (ill.)
Dunkin' Donuts, *3:* **545–46;** *5:* 1110
Dunne, Irene, *2:* 383–84
DuPont Company, *2:* 379
Duran Duran, *5:* 1135
Durand, Elias, *1:* 67
Durant, William C. "Billy," *1:* 130, 148
Dweeb, *4:* 948
Dyer, Wayne, *4:* 949
Dylan, Bob, *3:* 693; *4:* 788, 841, **848–49,** 946; *5:* 1138
Dynasty, 2: 488; *5:* 1101

E

Earhart, Amelia, *2:* 468
Earl, Craig, *3:* 741
Earle, Steve, *5:* 1252
Early film, *1:* 33–34
Earnhardt, Dale, *2:* 474
Earth Day, *4:* 1069, **1077–78**
Earth Wind & Fire, *4:* 985
East of Eden, 3: 664
Eastman, Kevin, *5:* 1195
Eastman Kodak Company, *1:* 10–11; *2:* 240
Eastwood, Clint, *3:* 665; *5:* 1100
Easy Rider, *1:* 163; *4:* **820–21,** 821 (ill.)
Eating disorders, *3:* 775; *4:* 813; *5:* 1279
E-Bay, *5:* 1227
Eberhard-Faber, *2:* 375
Ebony, *3:* **576–77**
E-books, *5:* 1265
Ebsen, Buddy, *3:* 736; *4:* 891, 892 (ill.)
Echo Park, 5: 1150
E-commerce, *5:* 1229
Economy. *See also* Business and industry; Great Depression
downturns, *4:* 928, 947; *5:* 1220, 1223
Great Depression, *2:* 367–68. *See also* Great Depression
growth periods, *2:* 235–36, 243, 283; *3:* 517, 643, 767; *4:* 793; *5:* 1099, 1219–20
post-World War II, *3:* 545
"trickle down," *5:* 1197
World War I, *1:* 153–54; *2:* 235–36, 243
World War II, *3:* 512–14
Ecstasy, *5:* 1259, **1313–14**
The Ed Sullivan Show, *3:* 639, **739–40,** 740 (ill.); *4:* 841, 1053
Eddie Bauer, *2:* **256**
Edelstein, Andrew, *4:* 816
Edgerton, David, *3:* 678
Edison, Thomas, *1:* 44, 45, 71, 76–77, 126, 194; *2:* 394; *3:* 558; *5:* 1202
Edmonton Oilers, *5:* 1166
Education
Chautauqua movement, *1:* 115, 118–20, 119 (ill.)
Cold War era, *3:* 638
Dewey, John, *1:* 148
Dick and Jane readers, *2:* 443–44
Schoolhouse Rock, 4: 1060–62
standardized testing, *2:* 365–66
World Book Encyclopedia, 1: 188, 197–98
Edward VIII, king of England, *4:* 1076
Edwards, Anthony, *5:* 1288
Edwards, Gus, *1:* 3
Edwards, Ralph, *3:* 759
Edwards, Vincent, *4:* 901
Eighteenth Amendment, *1:* 213; *2:* 357–58, 419
Eight-track tapes, *4:* **849–50,** 850 (ill.); *5:* 1163
Einstein, Albert, *3:* 618
Eisenhower, Dwight D., *1:* 57–58; *3:* 637, 641, 776
Eisenstein, Sergei, *1:* 46
Electra, Carmen, *5:* 1284

Electric appliances, *1:* **125–26,** 222 (ill.), 222–23
Electric guitar, *2:* 296; *3:* **686–88,** 687 (ill.); *5:* 1139, 1255
Electricity, *1:* 115
Eli Lilly and Co., *5:* 1211
Ellen, 5: 1277
Ellington, Duke, *1:* 73; *2:* 240, 293, 427, 495
Elliot, Joe, *5:* 1140 (ill.)
Ellis, Bret Easton, *5:* 1155, 1203
Ellis Island, *1:* 3
Elmer Gantry, 1: 128
Elmo, *4:* 1063
Elway, John, *4:* 885
E-mail, *5:* 1218, 1303, **1314–17,** 1315 (ill.), 1319
Emergency services, *1:* 140
Emmett, Dan, *1:* 41
Emmy Awards, *4:* 1065; *5:* 1289
Emoticons, *5:* 1224, 1315
Empey, Arthur Guy, *1:* 146
Empire State Building, *2:* 372, 493, **499**
The Empire Strikes Back, 5: 1101
Encyclopedias, *1:* 197–98
Eng and Chang, *1:* 224
Engel, Georgia, *4:* 1049
Enter the Dragon, 4: 938
Enterprise, 4: 918
"Entertaining Comics (EC)," *3:* 704
Entertainment
  Broadway, *1:* 34–36, 35 (ill.)
  Buffalo Bill's Wild West Show, *1:* 4, 33, 36–37
  children's, Disney, *2:* 270–74*2:* 271 (ill.)
  Houdini, Harry, *1:* 39–40, 40 (ill.)
  minstrel shows, *1:* 2, 8–9, 33, 40–42, 41 (ill.)
  movie palaces, *1:* 177–78
  nickelodeons, *1:* 34, 42–44, 43 (ill.), 45
  vaudeville, *1:* 2, 3, 47–50, 48 (ill.), 146
  Ziegfeld Follies, 1: 50–52, 146
Entertainment and Sports Programming Network (ESPN), *4:* **1035–36;** *5:* 1273–74
"Environmental fragrancing," *5:* 1305
Environmental Protection Agency (EPA), *4:* 1078, 1080
Environmentalism, *1:* 26; *4:* 951–52, 1069, 1079–80, 1077–78, **1079–80**
The Epic of America, 2: 368
Epstein, Julius J. and Philip G., *3:* 532
Equal Rights Amendment, *4:* 921, 1069, **1080–82,** 1081 (ill.)
ER, *5:* 1225, 1277, **1288–89**
Erector sets, *1:* **202–4,** 203 (ill.)
Erving, Julius, *3:* 591; *4:* 1009
Escape artists, *1:* **39–40,** 40 (ill.); *2:* 239
ESPN (Entertainment and Sports Programming Network), *4:* **1035–36;** *5:* 1273–74
Esposito, Giancarlo, *5:* 1123
Espresso, *5:* 1312
Esquire, *2:* **448–49**
Establishment, *4:* 786
E.T.: The Extra-Terrestrial, *5:* 1101, 1119, **1125–26**
Etch A Sketch, *3:* 717, **718,** 719 (ill.)
Etiquette, 2: 237
Eureka Vacuum Company, *1:* 126
European Laboratory for Particle Physics (CERN), *5:* 1320
Evangelism, *1:* 115, 127, 138, **127–28**; *2:* 240; *3:* 513
Evans, Maurice, *4:* 894
Everly Brothers, *3:* 641
Evers, Medgar, *4:* 925
Eversharp, *2:* 375
Evert, Chris, *4:* 1009
Everything You Always Wanted to Know About Sex (But Were Afraid to Ask), 4: 948
Evolution, Scopes Monkey trial, *2:* 239, 363–64
Exercise, *3:* 718–20; *4:* 1010–11, 1016–17; *5:* 1113
Exhibitionism, *4:* 1095
Exhibitions, international, *1:* 142–43
The Exorcist, *4:* 948–49, 950, 961, **965**
Expositions, international, *1:* 142–43
Extreme sports, *5:* **1272–74,** 1273 (ill.)

F

F. W. Woolworth's stores, *1:* 12 (ill.), 12–13
"Fab Four," *3:* 693
Fabian, *3:* 633
Fads, *4:* 953, 1069
  CB Radio, *4:* 1030–31, 1031 (ill.)

Chia Pets, *4:* 1072
Crockett, Davy, *3:* 736–37
diets, *3:* 774–75
goldfish swallowing, *2:* 500
karaoke, *5:* 1142–43
mood rings, *4:* 958 (ill.), 958–59
pet rocks, *4:* 1088 (ill.), 1088–89
raccoon coats, *2:* 264–65
smiley face, *4:* 1094–95
streaking, *4:* 1095–96, 1096 (ill.)
tanning, *4:* 1096–98, 1097 (ill.)
3-D movies, *3:* 675
Fail-Safe, 3: 620, 622
Fairbanks, Douglas, Sr., *1:* 167, 199; *2:* 237
Fairness Doctrine, *5:* 1194
Falwell, Jerry, *1:* 127; *4:* 1003; *5:* 1103, 1198
Family Circle, 2: 433
Family Ties, 5: 1178
Family, "typical" American, *3:* 749–51
Fan clubs, Star Trek, *4:* 919
Fantasia, *2:* 272; *3:* 529, **535–36,** 536 (ill.)
Fantasy
Bewitched, 4: 893–95
Dungeons and Dragons, *4:* 1013–15, 1014 (ill.)
Fantasy Island, 4: 1036–37, 1037 (ill.)
Tolkien, J. R. R., *3:* 713–14
The Twilight Zone, 3: 764–66
Weird Tales, 2: 320–21
The Wizard of Oz, 2: 417–18
Fantasy Island, *4:* 1023, **1036–37,** 1037 (ill.)
"Far Out!," *4:* 786
The Far Side, *5:* 1100, **1157–58,** 1158 (ill.)
Farm Aid, *5:* 1138 (ill.), **1138–39**
Farmer, John, *2:* 337 (ill.)
Farmers, *2:* 243–44, 374
Farr, Jamie, *4:* 1050
Farrakhan, Louis, *5:* 1203
Farrell, Mike, *4:* 1051
Farrell, Perry, *5:* 1256–57
Farrow, Mia, *3:* 672; *4:* 1006 (ill.)
Fascanato, Jack, *3:* 603
Fashion, *1:* 157; *2:* 261, 379; *3:* 523–24, 657–60; *4:* 807, 955; *5:* 1113–14, 1235
advertising, *5:* 1117
Barbie, *3:* 644–46, 645 (ill.)
beatnik, *3:* 699
hairstyles, *1:* 132–34
hip-hop, *5:* 1149
social status, *2:* 261
supermodels, *5:* 1117–18, 1118 (ill.)
Vogue, 1: 196–97
Fashion designers, *5:* 1113
Fast food, *2:* **283–86,** 284 (ill.); *3:* 545. *See also* specific food, e.g., French fries
Burger King, *3:* 677–78
Dunkin' Donuts, *3:* 545–46
frozen dinners, *2:* 419–21
McDonald's, *3:* 548–50, 549 (ill.)
Starbucks, *5:* 1110–11, 1111 (ill.)
White Castle, *2:* 284 (ill.), 284–85
Fat Albert and the Cosby Kids, 4: 913 (ill.); *5:* 1183
Fatal Attraction, *5:* **1126–27**
Father Knows Best, 3: 642
Fatherhood, 5: 1101
Father's Day, *1:* **215–16**
Faulkner, William, *2:* 303, 402; *3:* 697
Faust, Frederick, *2:* 460; *4:* 900
Fawcett-Majors, Farrah, *4:* 1032, 1033 (ill.)
FBI (Federal Bureau of Investigation). *See* Federal Bureau of Investigation (FBI)
FCC (Federal Communications Commission). *See* Federal Communications Commission (FCC)
Federal Bureau of Investigation (FBI), *1:* 219; *3:* 615, **624–26,** 625 (ill.); *4:* 1092
Federal Communications Commission (FCC), *2:* 343, 478; *4:* 1028; *5:* 1189, 1308
Federal Theatre Project (FTP), *2:* 384
Federal Trade Commission (FTC), *1:* 153
Feejee Mermaid, *1:* 224
Feeney, Joe, *3:* 749
Feinberg, Louis, *2:* 412, 413 (ill.)
Feldon, Barbara, *3:* 757
Feldstein, Al, *3:* 705
Felix the Cat, *1:* **171–72,** 172 (ill.); *2:* 258
Felker, Clay, *2:* 449
Feltman, Charles, *1:* 63, 120
The Feminine Mystique, 4: 921, 943
Feminist movement, *1:* 160, 161; *3:* 583; *4:* 790, 940–41, 943, 951,

1004, 1069; *5:* 1126. *See also* Equal Rights Amendment; Women's liberation movement
Fender, Leo, *3:* 686
Ferber, Edna, *2:* 368
Ferlinghetti, Lawrence, *3:* 698
Fernandez, Peter, *4:* 918
Ferris, George Washington Gale, *1:* 128
Ferris wheel, *1:* **128–30,** 129 (ill.); *5:* 1230
Fibber McGee and Molly, *2:* 342, 477, **482–83**
Fiction, *1:* 79–80; *2:* 301; *4:* 997. *See also* Books; Literature; Novels; Reading
Argosy, 1: 80–81
Bonfire of the Vanities, 5: 1155
Brand, Max, *4:* 900
Charlie Chan, *2:* 269, 269 (ill.)
dime novels, *1:* 2, 82–84, 83 (ill.)
Little Blue Books, *2:* 309–10
"trash," *4:* 997
"Field coat," *1:* 156
Fields, W. C., *1:* 49
Filene's department store (Boston, Massachusetts), *2:* 255
Film, *1:* 33–34, 167; *2:* 267, 383; *3:* 529–30, 661; *4:* 815–16, 961; *5:* 1119–20, 1237. *See also* Movies; specific type of movie, e.g. Comedies, Movie; specific movie, e.g., *Gone with the Wind*
Film noir, *3:* 529–30, **537–38,** 539
Film production, *1:* 33–34, 167
Film technology, *1:* 38–39, 168, 170
Filo, John, *4:* 1085
Finance, personal, *3:* 647
Fine, Larry, *2:* 412, 413 (ill.)
"Fireside chats," *2:* 370
Firestone Tire and Rubber Company, *1:* 7
First base, *3:* 638
First Blood, 5: 1131
First broadcasts, *2:* 238
Fish, George Winthrop, *4:* 900
Fisher, Carrie, *4:* 978, 978 (ill.)
Fisher, Dan and Doris, *4:* 795
Fisher, Fred, *1:* 12
Fisher, Harry "Bud," *1:* 89, 90
Fisher, Herman, *2:* 378
Fisher, Terence, *2:* 393
Fisher-Price toys, *2:* **377–78**
Fitness. *See* Physical fitness
Fitzgerald, Ella, *2:* 425
Fitzgerald, F. Scott, *2:* 241, 245, 262, 301, 402, 433, 448; *4:* 942; *5:* 1219
Fitzsimmons, Bob, *1:* 101
Five-and-dime stores, *1:* 11–13, 12 (ill.)
Fixx, Jim, *4:* 949, 1016–17
"Flaming" (E-mail), *5:* 1316
"Flaming youth," *2:* 265
Flamingo (Las Vegas, Nevada), *3:* 514, 629
Flappers, *1:* 133; *2:* **261–63,** 262 (ill.), 268
Flares (pants), *4:* 809
"Flash!," *2:* 370
Flash Gordon, *2:* 305, **449–51,** 450 (ill.)
Flatt, Lester, *4:* 891
Fleer Chewing Gum Company, *1:* 55
Fleischer Studio, *2:* 389
Fleming, Alexander, *2:* 357
Fleming, Ian, *3:* 623; *4:* 830, 865
Fleming, Victor, *2:* 417
Flight attendants, *2:* 346
Flint, Charles Ranlett, *5:* 1107
The Flip Wilson Show, 4: 949
Flipper, *4:* **901–2**
Flockhart, Calista, *5:* 1278, 1279 (ill.)
Floren, Myron, *3:* 749
Flores, Pedro, *2:* 336
Florists' Telegraph Delivery Service (FTD), *1:* 221
Flying saucers. *See* Unidentified Flying Object (UFO)
Flying Wallendas, *1:* 225
Flynt, Larry, *4:* 1003, 1003 (ill.), 1003–4
FM radio stations, *2:* 343; *3:* 685; *4:* 1024; *5:* 1175
Folies Bergère, *2:* 267
Folk music, *2:* 425–26; *3:* 553, 554; *4:* 841, 848–49, **851–52**
Folklore, *1:* 36
Fonda, Henry, *2:* 452; *4:* 821, 1066
Fonda, Jane, *4:* 821, 951; *5:* 1100–1101
Fonda, Peter, *1:* 163; *4:* 820, 821 (ill.)
Fong, Kam, *4:* 906
"The Fonz," *4:* 1040, 1041, 1041 (ill.)
Food, *1:* 53–54, 181; *2:* 283; *3:* 545, *3:* 677. *See also* specific

food, e.g., Jell-O, or a category of food, e.g., Snack food, or by brand name, e.g., Campbell's soup
baby (Gerber), *2:* 286–87
convenience. *see* Convenience foods
fast. *See* Fast food
organic, *2:* 287
processed. *See* Processed foods
"Food courts," *3:* 648
Food industry, *1:* 53–54; *2:* 284–86, 287
Food preparation, *1:* 53–54, 181
Footbags (Hacky Sack), *4:* 1015–16
Football
American Football League (AFL), *2:* 335; *4:* 877
college, *1:* 95, 113–14, 183, 201; *2:* 334
Dallas Cowboys, *4:* 880
ESPN, *4:* 1035
Monday Night Football, 4: 1017–19, 1018 (ill.)
Namath, Joe, *4:* 883–84
National Football League (NFL), *2:* 334–36; *4:* 877; *5:* 1165
pro, *1:* 201; *4:* 877, 1009
Rose Bowl, *1:* 113–14
Simpson, O. J., *5:* 1324 (ill.), 1324–26
Super Bowl, *4:* 884–85
Footwear, *1:* 157
Bean boot, *1:* 156
Doc Martens, *4:* 809–10
Nike, *1:* 162; *4:* 799–801, 800 (ill.)
tennis shoes, *1:* 157, 161–62
"For crying out loud!," *2:* 236
For Whom the Bell Tolls, 3: 510
Ford Bronco, *5:* 1216
Ford, Harrison, *4:* 903, 978, 978 (ill.); *5:* 1122, 1130
Ford, Henry, *1:* 3, 8, 22–23, 153; *2:* 345; *3:* 626, 630
Ford, John, *2:* 414, 416, 452
Ford Motor Company, *1:* 2, 3, 7, 22–23, 153
Ford Thunderbird, *3:* 643
"Fordism," *1:* 23
Fore-Front Records, *5:* 1328
Foreign policy, *1:* 146–47
Foreman, George, *4:* 879
Forever Amber, 3: 511
Forman, Milos, *4:* 1004
Forrest Gump, *5:* **1239–40,** 1240 (ill.)
Forster, Brian, *4:* 1055
Forsythe, John, *4:* 1032
Forsythe, William, *2:* 351
Fort Lauderdale, Florida, *3:* 632
Fort Peck Dam (Montana), *2:* 494
FORTRAN-80 (programming language), *5:* 1232
42nd Street, 2: 369
Foss, Christopher, *4:* 1083
Foster, Andrew "Rube," *1:* 107
Foster, Jodie, *3:* 625
Four Minute Men, *1:* 232
Four Tops, *4:* 842
"Fox," *4:* 786
"The Fox" (El Zorro), *1:* 199
Fox, Harold C. "Zoot Suit," *3:* 526
Fox, Kate, *1:* 111
Fox, Margaret, *1:* 111
FOX network, *5:* 1175, 1180, 1277, 1278, 1285
Fox, William, *1:* 44, 45
Foxx, Jimmie, *2:* 290
Foxx, Redd, *4:* 949–50, 1023
Foyt, A. J., *1:* 206; *4:* 951
Frampton, Peter, *4:* 951
France, Bill, *2:* 474
Franchising, *2:* 284–85; *3:* 546, 549, 677; *5:* 1110–11
Francis the Talking Mule, *3:* **664–65;** *4:* 907
Frank, Anne, *3:* 513
Frank, Pat, *3:* 620
Frankenheimer, John, *4:* 965
Frankenstein, *2:* 383, **394–95,** 395 (ill.); *5:* 1270
Frankfurters, *1:* 63
Franklin, Benjamin, *5:* 1162
Franklin, Bonnie, *4:* 1077
Franklin, Melvin, *4:* 857 (ill.)
"Frankly, my dear, I don't give a damn," *2:* 368
Frappucino, *5:* 1110
Frasier, *5:* 1277, **1289–90**
Frawley Pen Company, *2:* 376
Frawley, William, *3:* 639, 747, 759
Frazier, Joe, *4:* 879
"Free" jazz, *1:* 74
Freed, Alan, *3:* 641, 683, 684
Freedman, Gerald, *4:* 825
Freedom of the press, *1:* 92
Freeman, Leonard, *4:* 905
Free-speech rights, *2:* 364
Frehley, Ace, *4:* 950 (ill.), 987
Frémont, John C., *3:* 628
French fries, *3:* 677–78, **678–79,** 548–50, 679

Fresh, *5:* 1100
Fricke, Aaron, *2:* 360
Friday the 13th, *4:* 828 (ill.), 829; *5:* 1119, **1127–28**
Friedan, Betty, *4:* 921, 940, 943
Friedkin, William, *4:* 965
Friends, *5:* 1225, 1277, **1290–92,** 1291 (ill.)
Frisbee, *4:* **881**
From Hell, 4: 1092
From Here to Eternity, 3: 565, 638
Frosted Flakes, *1:* 21
Frosty the Snowman, *3:* 698, **702–4**
Frozen dinners, *2:* **419–21**
Fry, Stephen, *5:* 1268
Fu Manchu, *1:* **188–89,** 189 (ill.)
The Fugitive, *4:* **902–3**
Fuhrman, Mark, *5:* 1326
Fuld, William, *1:* 112
Fulghum, Robert, *5:* 1101
Full Metal Jacket, 5: 1119
Fuller, Alfred C., *1:* 14
Fuller Brush Company, *1:* **14–15**
Fuller, John G., *3:* 636
Fundamentalism, *1:* 115, 127–28, 138; *2:* 240; *3:* 513; *4:* 944; *5:* 1103, 1198
Funicello, Annette, *3:* 752; *4:* 816
Funk, *4:* 981, **984–85**
Funny Girl, 4: 861
Funt, Allen, *3:* 733
Funt, Peter, *3:* 734
Furniture, *2:* **257**
Fusion (jazz), *1:* 74
Futurama, *1:* 142
Fuzz, *3:* 638

G

Gable, Clark, *2:* 368, 370, **396,** 397 (ill.), 398
Gacy, John Wayne, *4:* 1092
Gaines, William, *3:* 704, 705 (ill.)
Gallant Fox (horse), *1:* 103
Gambling, *3:* 514, 627–29, 628 (ill.); *4:* 933–34
Game shows, *3:* **741–42,** 742 (ill.)
The Price Is Right, 3: 753–54, 754 (ill.)
The $64,000 Question, 3: 640, 757–58, 758 (ill.)
Who Wants to Be a Millionaire, 5: 1300–1302, 1301 (ill.)
Games, *1:* 202; *2:* 326, *2:* 468; *3:* 587. *See also* Sports
Atari, *4:* 1011–13, 1012 (ill.)
board, *1:* 106; *3:* 592–94, 593 (ill.)
card, *1:* 214–15
crossword puzzles, *2:* 327
Dungeons and Dragons, *4:* 1013–15, 1014 (ill.)
frisbee, *4:* 881
Game of Life, *1:* 106
lottery, *4:* 933–34
Milton Bradley Company, *1:* 106
miniature golf, *2:* 332–34, 333 (ill.)
Monopoly, *2:* 471–73
Ouija boards, *1:* 111–12, 112 (ill.)
Pac-Man, *5:* 1167–68, 1168 (ill.)
Pong, *4:* 1019–20, 1021
Rubik's Cube, *5:* 1169 (ill.), 1169–70
Scrabble, *3:* 592–94, 593 (ill.)
Trivial Pursuit, *5:* 1170–71
Twister, *4:* 885–87, 886 (ill.)
video, *4:* 1020–22, 1021 (ill.)
Yo-Yo, *2:* 336–37, 337 (ill.)
Gangs, *1:* 16; *4:* 842–43, 843 (ill.), 962–63; *5:* 1149, 1197, **1204–6**
"Gangsta rap," *5:* 1150, 1206
Gangsters, *2:* 350–51
Gannett Company, *5:* 1160
Ganz, Joan, *4:* 1062, 1063 (ill.)
Gap, *4:* **795–96,** 930; *5:* 1235
Garber, Matthew, *4:* 832 (ill.)
Garbo, Greta, *1:* 46; *2:* 371
Garcia, Jerry, *4:* 853, 933
Gardner, Erle Stanley, *2:* 442, 458, 460
Garfield, *4:* **999–1001,** 1000 (ill.)
Garfield, John, *5:* 1245
Garfunkel, Art, *4:* 859–60
Garis, Howard Roger, *1:* 194
Garland, Judy, *2:* 370, 385 (ill.), 417; *4:* 861
Garrison, Jim, *5:* 1241
Garroway, Dave, *3:* 760
Garth, Jennie, *5:* 1286, 1287 (ill.)
Garvey, Marcus, *1:* 148–49
Gates, Bill, *5:* 1226, 1231–33, 1232 (ill.)
Gay liberation movement, *4:* 866–67, 921, **926–27,** 927 (ill.), 944; *5:* 1209–10
Gaye, Marvin, *4:* 842, 951
Gecko, Gordon, *5:* 1105
Geer, Will, *4:* 1066
Geets, *3:* 510
Gehrig, Lou, *1:* 97; *2:* 290, 392, 468; *5:* 1271

Gein, Ed, *4:* 836, 1092
Geisel, Theodor (Dr. Seuss), *3:* 697, 701–2, 702 (ill.); *4:* 865
Gelatin dessert, *1:* 65–66
Gelb, Lawrence M., *2:* 377
Gelbwaks, Jeremy, *4:* 1055, 1055 (ill.)
Geldof, Bob, *5:* 1144
Gemayel, Bashir, *5:* 1161
General Foods, *2:* 420
General Mills, *2:* 290
General Motors, *1:* 7, **130–31,** 148
General reference books, *1:* 188, 197–98
Generation X, *5:* **1206–7,** 1224, 1235, 1255
  Extreme sports, *5:* 1272–74, 1273 (ill.)
  Friends, 5: 1225, 1290–92, 1291 (ill.)
Genital herpes and warts, *4:* 1093–94
Gentlemen Prefer Blondes, 2: 237; *3:* 667
George Olsen and His Music, *2:* 264
George, Peter, *4:* 818
Gerber baby food, *2:* **286–87**
Gerber, Daniel Frank and Dorothy, *2:* 286
Geritol, *3:* 748
Germann, Greg, *5:* 1279 (ill.)
Gershwin, George, *2:* 240, 293
Gertie the Dinosaur, *1:* 147, **172–74,** 173 (ill.)
"Get a clue!," *4:* 948
Get Smart, 3: 623
Getz, Stan, *1:* 74
Ghettos, *4:* **928–29**
Ghostbusters, *5:* **1128–30,** 1129 (ill.)
G.I. Joe, *3:* 511; *4:* 796, **796–97**
Giant, 3: 664
Gibson, Althea, *3:* 717
Gibson, Charles Dana, *1:* 84; *2:* 453
Gibson, Dorothy, *1:* 230
Gibson Girl, *1:* **84–85,** 85 (ill.); *2:* 453, 453 (ill.)
Gibson Guitar Company, *3:* 686
Gibson, Henry, *4:* 911
Gibson, Josh, *1:* 108
Gibson, Walter Brown, *2:* 461
Gifford, Frank, *4:* 1017, 1018 (ill.)
Gifford, Kathie Lee, *4:* 899, 1043
Giggle water, *2:* 236
Gilbert, A. C., *1:* 202
Gilbert, Melissa, *4:* 1044, 1044 (ill.)
Gillespie, Dizzy, *1:* 73; *3:* 553
Gillespie, Leonard, *4:* 900
Gilliam, Terry, *4:* 1052
Gilligan's Island, *4:* **903–5,** 904 (ill.), 1026
Gillis, Dobie, *3:* 737 (ill.), **737–38**
Gilpin, Peri, *5:* 1290
Gilroy, Zelda, *3:* 737
Gimble's department store, *2:* 255, 376; *3:* 594
Gingrich, Arnold, *2:* 448
Ginsberg, Allen, *3:* 697, 698, 709
Ginzburg, Ralph, *2:* 449
Girl Guides (Britain), *1:* 226, 227
Girl Scouts, *1:* **226–28**
Gish, Dorothy, *1:* 168, 174; *2:* 237
Gish, Lillian, *1:* 150, 167, 168, **174;** *2:* 237
Glass ceiling, *5:* 1100
The Glass Menagerie, 3: 530
Glaucoma, *4:* 936
Gleason, Jackie, *3:* 609, 745, 745 (ill.)
Glenn, John, *4:* 939
Global communication. *See* Communication
Global positioning devices, *3:* 780
"Global village," *1:* 139; *5:* 1148
G-Men, 3: 625
Gnarly, *4:* 948
Go, 3: 698
"Go ahead—make my day!," *5:* 1100
"Go fly a kite!," *2:* 236
The Godfather, *4:* 935, 950, 961, **966–67,** 967 (ill.)
Godzilla, *3:* 661, 666 (ill.), **666–67**
Gojira, 3: 661
Gold Diggers of 1933, 2: 369
Gold Rush, *3:* 658
Goldblum, Jeff, *5:* 1270
Golden Books, *3:* **577–78,** 703
Golden Gate Bridge, *2:* 372
Goldfinger, 4: 937
Goldfish swallowing, *2:* **500**
Goldman, Ronald, *5:* 1325
Goldmark, Peter, *3:* 559
Goldwater, John, *3:* 568
Goldwyn, Samuel, *2:* 277
Golf, *1:* 202; *2:* 325; *5:* 1271
  Didrikson, Babe, *2:* 468–69, 469 (ill.)
  miniature golf, *2:* 332–34, 333 (ill.)
  Woods, Tiger, *5:* 1275–76
Golfer, 5: 1275

Gone with the Wind, *1:* 219; *2:* 369, 370, 383, **396–99,** 397 (ill.)
The Gong Show, *4:* 1023, **1038–39,** 1039 (ill.)
Gonorrhea, *4:* 1094
"Gonzo" journalism, *4:* 872
The Good Earth, 2: 368
Good Housekeeping Institute, *1:* 86
Good Times, 4: 1023; *5:* 1181
"Good to the Last Drop," *1:* 2
Goodbye, Mr. Chips, 2: 369
Goodman, Benny, *1:* 73; *2:* 427
Goodman, John, *5:* 1187
Goodman, Mark, *5:* 1148 (ill.)
"Goodnight Irene," *3:* 640
Goodson, Mark, *3:* 753
Goodstein, David B., *4:* 866
Gorbachev, Mikhail, *5:* 1102
Gordon, Gale, *2:* 482; *3:* 748
Gordon, Jeff, *2:* 474
Gordy, Berry, Jr., *4:* 842, 856
Gore, Tipper, *5:* 1140–41
Goren, Charles, *1:* 215
Göring, Hermann, *3:* 600
Gosden, Freeman, *2:* 478
Gossip columns, *2:* 240, **306–7**; *3:* 707–8, 708 (ill.)
Goths, *5:* **1114–15,** 1235
Gould, Chester, *2:* 444
Gould, Elliott, *4:* 1050
Gould, Sandra, *4:* 894
Government, *2:* 367–68, 407
Grable, Betty, *3:* 510
Grace, Princess of Monaco. *See* Kelly, Grace
Grace Under Fire, 4: 1077
Graceland (Nashville, Tennessee), *3:* 690
The Graduate, *1:* 25; *4:* 788, **822–24,** 823 (ill.), 860
Graff, Robert de, *2:* 457
Graham, Billy, *1:* 127; *3:* 513
Graham, Martha, *2:* 371
Grahame, Gloria, *3:* 539
Grammar, Kelsey, *5:* 1178, 1289
Gramophones, *1:* 71–72
Grand Ole Opry, *2:* **297–98,** 298 (ill.), 426; *3:* 553, 556–57
Grandy, Fred, *4:* 1046
Grange, Harold "Red," *2:* 334–35
Granger, David, *2:* 449
Granny Doodle, *2:* 378
Grant, Cary, *2:* 353, 383–84, **399–400;** *3:* 529, 640, 661, 668
Grant, Maxwell, *2:* 462
The Grapes of Wrath, *2:* 362, 369, 374, 433, **451–52;** *3:* 529
Graphical User Interface (GUI), *4:* 1070, 1086; *5:* 1233
Grassle, Karen, *4:* 1044, 1044 (ill.)
Grateful Dead, *4:* 842, **852–53,** 933
Graves, Peter, *5:* 1121
Gray, Harold, *2:* 310–11
Gray, John, *5:* 1224
Gray, William S., *2:* 444
"Great American Smokeout," *2:* 253
Great Depression, *1:* 23, 51, 117–18; *2:* 241, 284, 367, 373, 419, 476, 493; *3:* **500–501,** 509, 768; *4:* 820
  big bands, *2:* 426–27
  The Grapes of Wrath, 2: 433, 451–52
  movie palaces, *1:* 177
  radio, *2:* 341
  Rodgers, Jimmie, *2:* 298–99
  Route 66, *2:* 361–63, 362 (ill.)
  The Waltons, 4: 1066–67
The Great Gatsby, 2: 245; *5:* 1219
Great Migration, *1:* 213
The Great Train Robbery, *1:* 3, 4, 34, **38–39**
"Great White Hope," *1:* 102
Great White Way, *1:* 36
"The Greatest Gift," *3:* 538–39
"The Greatest Show on Earth," *1:* 150
Green Acres, 4: 890, 893, 1042
Green Bay Packers, *4:* 877, 884
Green, Brian Austin, *5:* 1286, 1287 (ill.)
Green Goblin, *4:* 873
The Green Hornet, 4: 938
Green Lantern, *3:* **578–79**
Green, Robert, *1:* 67–68
Green Stamps (S&H), *3:* 651–52
Greenbush, Lindsay and Sidney, *4:* 1044, 1044 (ill.)
Greene, Charles Sumner and Henry Mather, *2:* 349
Greene, Lorne, *4:* 896
Greene, "Mean" Joe, *4:* 1009
Greenpeace, *4:* 1080
Greensboro, North Carolina, *1:* 13
Greenstreet, Sydney, *3:* 532
Grenada, *5:* 1101
Gretzky, Wayne, *1:* 207; *5:* **1166–67**
Grey, Zane, *1:* 146; *2:* 236, 241
Greyhound buses, *1:* **216–17**
Greystoke: The Legend of Tarzan, Lord of the Apes, 1: 193
Griffin, Merv, *3:* 742

Griffith, Andy, *4:* 788, 890. *See also* ***The Andy Griffith Show***
Griffith, D. W., *1:* 46, 147, 167; *2:* 237
Griffiths, Martha, *4:* 1081
Grimm brothers (Jacob Ludwig Carl and Wilhelm Carl), *2:* 410
"The Grinch," *3:* 701
Grisham, John, *1:* 220
Grocery shopping, *1:* 53, 54
Groening, Matt, *5:* 1190
Grohl, Dave, *5:* 1258
Groovy, *4:* 786
Gross national product (GNP), *3:* 643
Grosset & Dunlap Company, *1:* **194–95**
Groudey Gum Company, *2:* 347
Groupies, *4:* 948
Grover's Mills, New Jersey, *2:* 489
Gruelle, Johnny, *1:* 208
Grunge, *5:* 1251, 1254, **1255–56,** 1258
GUI (Graphical User Interface), *4:* 1070, 1086; *5:* 1233
Guiding Light, *2:* 370, **483–84**
Guilbert, Paul, *2:* 360
Guisewite, Cathy, *4:* 999
Guitar, electric, *2:* 296; *3:* **686–88,** 687 (ill.); *5:* 1255
Gulf War, *5:* 1180, 1223
Gum, chewing/bubble *1:* **54–56**
Gund, Inc., *1:* 31
Gunsmoke, *3:* 640, 642, **743–44**
Guthrie, Janet, *4:* 1009
Guthrie, Woody, *4:* 851
Guyana Tragedy: The Story of Jim Jones, *4:* 1074
Gwynne, Fred, *2:* 395
Gygax, Gary, *4:* 1013–14

H

Hack, Shelley, *4:* 1032
Hackers, *5:* 1304, **1317–18**
Hacky Sack, *4:* **1015–16**
Hadden, Briton, *2:* 319
Hagen, Walter, *1:* 202; *2:* 325
Hagerty, Julie, *5:* 1121
Haggard, Merle, *3:* 557; *5:* 1252
Hagman, Larry, *5:* 1184, 1184 (ill.)
Haight-Ashbury, *4:* **929–30,** 930 (ill.)
Hailey, Arthur, *4:* 787; *5:* 1120
Hair (musical), *4:* 816, 932
Hairstyles, *1:* **132–34;** *4:* 807; *5:* 1235
Beatles, *3:* 634
Clairol hair coloring, *2:* 377
Janssen, David, *4:* 903
mohawk, *4:* 992; *5:* 1177
"Rachel," *5:* 1292
Halas, George, *2:* 334
Haldeman-Julius, Emanuel and Marcet, *2:* 309
Hale, Alan, *4:* 904, 904 (ill.)
Haley, Alex, *4:* 949, 997, 1057
Haley, Bill, and the Comets, *3:* 640
Haley, Jack, *2:* 417
Halloween, *4:* 829; *5:* 1119
Hallucinatory drugs, *4:* 852
Hamburgers, *3:* **680**
Burger King, *3:* 677–78
McDonald's, *3:* 548–50, 549 (ill.)
White Castle, *2:* 284 (ill.), 284–85
Hamill, Mark, *4:* 978, 978 (ill.)
Hamilton, George, *1:* 200
Hamilton, Margaret, *2:* 417
Hamm, Mia, *2:* 468; *5:* 1228
Hammer, Mike, *3:* 511, 638
Hammerstein, Oscar, *4:* 788
Hammett, Dashiell, *2:* 241, 442, 460; *3:* 530, 624; *5:* 1244
Hamner, Earl, Jr., *4:* 1066
Hamwi, Ernest, *1:* 64
Hancock, Herbie, *1:* 74
Handheld computers, *4:* 1070, 1087
Handler, Ruth, *3:* 644
Handles, CB, *4:* 1030–31
Handwerker, Nathan, *1:* 63
Handy, W. C., *1:* 149; *2:* 295
Haney, Chris, *5:* 1170
Hangovers, *2:* 374
Hanks, Tom, *5:* 1157, 1199, 1239, 1240 (ill.)
Hanna, William, *4:* 914
Happy Days, *3:* 677; *4:* 950, 1023, **1040–41,** 1041 (ill.)
A Hard Day's Night, *4:* **826–27,** 846, 847 (ill.)
Hard rock, *3:* 687; *4:* 981
Hardaway, Ben "Bugs," *3:* 599
Hard-boiled detective fiction, *2:* 442
Hardesty, Chip, *3:* 625
Harding, Warren G., *2:* 236
Hardy Boys **series,** *2:* **308–9**
Hardy, Oliver, *2:* **404–5,** 405 (ill.)
Harlan County, Kentucky, *2:* 373
Harlem, *2:* 494
Harlem Globetrotters, *2:* **329–31,** 330 (ill.)
Harlequin romances, *4:* **1001–2**

Harley, William S., *1:* 16
Harley-Davidson, *1:* 7, 8, **16–17,** 17 (ill.)
Harper, Valerie, *4:* 1049
Harrelson, Woody, *5:* 1178
Harris, Thomas, *4:* 787, 1092
Harrison, George, *4:* 826, 846, 847 (ill.), 849
Harrison, John, *4:* 869
Harroun, Ray, *1:* 204
Harry Potter and the Sorcerer's Stone, 5: 1225, 1265
***Harry Potter* series,** *5:* **1266–68,** 1267 (ill.)
Hart, Gary, *3:* 707, 708 (ill.)
The Harvester, 3: 518
Harvey, Paul, *3:* 513; *5:* 1328
Hasbro toys, *1:* 211, 212; *4:* 796
Hasek, Dominik, *1:* 207
Hasselhoff, David, *5:* 1283
Hatch, Richard, *5:* 1295, 1295 (ill.)
Hate crimes, *5:* 1214–15
Hate sites, *1:* 220
Hauer, Rutger, *5:* 1122
The Haunting, 5: 1129
Hauptmann, Bruno, *2:* 371–72
Have Gun Will Travel, 3: 642
Hawaii Five-O, *4:* **905–6,** 1023
Hawkins, Connie, *2:* 331
Hawks, Howard, *2:* 414
Hay, George D., *2:* 297
Hayden, Tom, *4:* 945
Hayes, Isaac, *4:* 976
Hays Commission, *2:* 401
Hays, Robert, *5:* 1121
Hayworth, Rita, *3:* 510
Head, 4: 855
Health
  AIDS (Acquired Immunodeficiency Syndrome), *5:* 1198–99, 1199 (ill.)
  Alka-Seltzer, *2:* 374–75
  aromatherapy, *5:* 1305
  Band-Aid, *2:* 247–48
  cigarettes, *2:* 252, 253, 259 (ill.), 259–60
  Coca-Cola, *1:* 56–58, 57 (ill.)
  diets, *3:* 774–75
  Dixie cups, *1:* 14
  fast food, *2:* 285–86
  jogging, *4:* 1016–17
  Kellogg's cereals, *1:* 19–21, 20 (ill.)
  penicillin, *2:* 356–57
  Wonder Bread, *2:* 291
Health Kup Company, *1:* 14
Healy, Ted, *2:* 413
Hearst Corporation, *2:* 449
Hearst, William Randolph, *1:* 191; *2:* 314; *3:* 533–34
"Heartbreak Hotel," *3:* 640
Heavy metal, *3:* 687; *5:* **1139–41,** 1140 (ill.); *5:* 1255, 1257
Hee Haw, *4:* **1042–43**
Hefner, Christie, *3:* 713
Hefner, Hugh, *3:* 639, 712–13; *4:* 942
Heinlein, Robert, *2:* 461; *4:* 865
Held, Anna, *1:* 50
Heller, Joseph, *4:* 786–87
Hell's Angels Motorcycle Club, *1:* 16; *4:* 821, 842–43, 843 (ill.)
Hellzapoppin', 2: 370
Hemingway, Ernest, *2:* 303, 433; *3:* 510, 697; *4:* 787
Hemp plant *(Cannabis sativa), 4:* 936–37
Hemsley, Sherman, *5:* 1181
Henderson, Fletcher, *1:* 72
Henderson, Florence, *4:* 1026
Henderson, Rickey, *1:* 100
Hendrix, Jimi, *3:* 687, 693; *4:* 842
Henie, Sonja, *2:* 467
Henneberger, J. C., *2:* 320
Henner, Marilu, *4:* 1064 (ill.), 1065
Henning, Paul, *4:* 893
Henreid, Paul, *3:* 532
Henson, Jim, *2:* 391; *3:* 578; *4:* 1053, 1062
Henson, Matthew, *1:* 91
Hepatitis B, *4:* 1094
Hepburn, Audrey, *2:* 353
Hepburn, Katharine, *3:* 529
Herbert, Brian, *4:* 869
Herbert, Frank, *4:* 787, 865, 868, 869
"Here's looking at you, kid," *3:* 510
Here's Lucy, 3: 747
Heroes and superheroes
  Batman, *2:* 434–36, 435 (ill.)
  Buck Rogers, *2:* 304–6, 305 (ill.)
  Captain America, *3:* 572–73
  Doc Savage, *2:* 446–48
  Green Lantern, *3:* 578–79
  Rambo movies, *5:* 1131–33, 1132 (ill.)
  Superman, *2:* 462–66, 463 (ill.)
  Tarzan, *1:* 192–94, 193 (ill.)
  Wonder Woman, *3:* 583–85
  Zorro, *1:* 199–200, 200 (ill.)
Heroin, *4:* 935
Herriman, George, *1:* 189
Herrmann, Bernard, *3:* 533

Hershey Chocolate Company, *1:* 7
Herzog, 4: 787
Heston, Charlton, *3:* 640; *4:* 834, 835, 835 (ill.), 968
Hewitt, Don, *4:* 916
Hick, *2:* 236
Hickman, Dwayne, *3:* 737, 737 (ill.)
The Hidden Persuaders, 3: 639
High Noon, 2: 392
High school prom, *2:* 358–60, 359 (ill.)
Highlights, *3:* **579–80**
Highway system, *2:* 361–63, 362 (ill.); *3:* **775–76**; *5:* 1212–13
Hilfiger, Tommy, *4:* 960
Hill, Anita, *5:* 1226
Hill, Faith, *5:* 1251
Hill, George Roy, *3:* 609
Hill, Lauryn, *5:* 1226
Hillbillies, *2:* 425–26, 454–55; *4:* 788, 891–93, 892 (ill.), 1042
Hillerich, John A. "Bud," *1:* 21
Hilliard, Harriet, *3:* 729
The Hills Have Eyes, 5: 1245
Hilton, James, *2:* 369
Hilton, Lester, *4:* 907
Hip-hop. *See* **Rap and hip-hop**
Hippies, *1:* 133; *3:* 536, 617; *4:* 786, 791, 808–9, 922, **931–33,** 932 (ill.)
  communes, *4:* 1072–73
  Haight-Ashbury, *4:* 929–30, 930 (ill.)
  Volkswagen Microbus, *3:* 654
  Woodstock, *4:* 862–63, 863 (ill.)
Hiroshima, 2: 312
Hiroshima, Japan, *3:* 620
Hirsch, Judd, *4:* 1064 (ill.), 1065
Hispanic American culture, Tejano music, *5:* 1262–63
Hitchcock, Alfred, *3:* 640, 661, 668–69, 676; *4:* 788, 828, 836, 837, 1092
Hitler, Adolf, *1:* 109; *2:* 473; *3:* 509, 573, 600; *5:* 1214
HIV (human immunodeficiency virus), *4:* 1093
The Hobbit, 3: 713
Hockey, *1:* 201; *4:* 1009; *5:* 1166
  Gretzky, Wayne, *5:* 1166–67
  National Hockey League (NHL), *1:* 207–8, 208 (ill.)
  Olympic, *1:* 110 (ill.)
Hoffa, Jimmy, *4:* 951–52
Hoffman, Dustin, *4:* 788, 822, 823 (ill.), 860
Hoffmann-La Roche, *4:* 801
Hogan, Hulk, *5:* 1171, 1173
Hogan's Alley, 1: 79
Hogarth, Burne, *1:* 194
"Hogs," *1:* 17
Holiday, Billie, *2:* 425, **428;** *3:* 513, 553
Holiday Inn, 3: 512
Holidays
  Christmas, *2:* 255, 258
  Father's Day, *1:* 215–16
  Mother's Day, *1:* 220–21
  spring break, *3:* 631–32
  Thanksgiving Day parade, *1:* 171; *2:* 258, 388 (ill.)
Holland, Brian and Eddie, *4:* 856
Holly, Buddy, *3:* 686
Hollywood, *1:* 167; *2:* 307, **400–403,** 401 (ill.); *4:* 820
  blacklisting, *3:* 669–71, 771–73
Hollywood eyes, *3:* 510
Hollywood Production Code, *4:* 943
"Hollywood Ten," *3:* 772
Holmes, John Clellon, *3:* 698
Holmes, Sherlock, *2:* 441
Home Box Office (HBO), *4:* 1028
Home life, *1:* 53–54
Home Shopping Network (HSN), *5:* 1105, **1106–7**
Home study, *1:* 118
Homelessness, *5:* 1100
Homemaking and decorating, *1:* 125–26, *2:* 248–50, 249 (ill.), 302; *3:* 638
Homosexuality, *4:* 866–67, 926–27; *5:* 1198, 1277
Honda, Ishiro, *3:* 666
The Honeymooners, *3:* **744–46,** 745 (ill.)
Hoover Dam, *2:* 372, 494, **501–2**
Hoover, Herbert, *2:* 371, 480
Hoover, J. Edgar, *3:* 624, 625 (ill.)
Hope, Bob, *1:* 51
Hope, Laura Lee, *3:* 570
Hopkins, Anthony, *1:* 200
Hopkins, Claud, *2:* 245
Hopper, Dennis, *4:* 820
Hopper, Hedda, *2:* 307
Hormel, Jay C., *2:* 423
Horn, Bob, *3:* 731
Horn, Maurice, *3:* 572
Hornsby, Lesley. *See* Twiggy
Hornsby, Rogers, *1:* 97, 108
Horror movies, *2:* 497; *4:* **827–29,** 828 (ill.); *5:* 1119, 1237
  Dracula, *2:* 392–93

The Exorcist, 4: 965
Frankenstein, *2:* 394–95, 395 (ill.)
Friday the 13th, 5: 1127–28
King Kong, 2: 403–4
Psycho, 4: 836–37
The Rocky Horror Picture Show, 4: 971–73, 972 (ill.)
Scream, 5: 1245–47, 1246 (ill.)
spoof, *3:* 531
3-D, *3:* 675
Weird Tales, 2: 320–21
Horseracing, *1:* 102–4, 201
Horwitz brothers (Three Stooges), *2:* 412–13, 413 (ill.)
Hosiery, nylon, *2:* **380–82,** 381 (ill.)
"Hot diggity dog!," *2:* 236
Hot dogs, *1:* **62–64**
Hot pants, *4:* **955–56**
Hot Rod (magazine), *3:* 627
Hot rods, *3:* **626–27**
Houdini, Harry, *1:* **39–40,** 40 (ill.); *2:* 239
House of Wax, 3: 675
House Un-American Activities Committee (HUAC), *3:* 670, 772
Housekeeping, *1:* 53, 85–86, **125–26,** 181. *See also* Homemaking and decorating
Houses
Better Homes and Gardens building-plan service, *2:* 302
bungalows, *2:* 349–50
catalog houses, *1:* 117–18
Levittown, *3:* 629–31, 630 (ill.)
mail-order, *1:* 28
ranch house, *2:* 502
suburbs, *3:* 780–83
Housewares, Tupperware, *3:* 520–22, 521 (ill.)
Houston, Whitney, *5:* 1135
"How Much Is That Doggie in the Window?," *3:* 640
Howard, Curly, Moe, and Shemp, *2:* 412–13, 413 (ill.)
Howard, Ron, *4:* 890, 1040, 1041, 1041 (ill.)
Howdy Corporation, *2:* 288
The Howdy Doody Show, *3:* 597, **601–2,** 602 (ill.)
Howe, Elias, *1:* 164
Howell, Vernon (David Koresh), *5:* 1307
"Howl," *3:* 697, 698
HSN (Home Shopping Network), *5:* **1106–7**
HUAC (House Un-American Activities Committee), *3:* 670
Hubbell, Carl, *1:* 97
Hudson, Ernie, *5:* 1129, 1129 (ill.)
Hudson, Rock, *5:* 1103
Hudson's department store (Detroit, Michigan), *3:* 648
Huggins, Roy, *4:* 902
Hughes, Howard, *2:* 371; *3:* 629
Hugo, Victor, *4:* 902
Hula hoop, *3:* 777 (ill.), **777–78**
Hull, Edith M., *2:* 236
Hulman, Anton "Tex," *1:* 206
Human sexuality, *4:* 941–44
Hunter, Alan, *5:* 1148 (ill.)
Hunter, Kim, *4:* 836
Hunter, Meredith, *4:* 843
Hunter, Tab, *3:* 634
Huntley, Chet, *3:* 605
Hurt, Malin, *2:* 483
Hüsker Dü, *5:* 1253
Hussein, Saddam, *5:* 1223
Hustle, *1:* 124; *4:* **985–87,** 986 (ill.)
Hustler, *4:* **1002–4,** 1003 (ill.)
Hyatt, John Wesley, *1:* 24
Hyde Pierce, David, *5:* 1290
Hydrogen bomb, *3:* 620
"Hypertext," *5:* 1320

I

"I Can't Live Without My Radio," *5:* 1102
I Love Lucy, *2:* 341–42; *3:* 639, 641, **746–48,** 747 (ill.); *4:* 1028
I Married a Communist, 3: 623
I Spy, 3: 623; *5:* 1183
I, the Jury, 3: 511
Iacocca, Lee, *5:* 1101, 1208
IBM (International Business Machines), *4:* 1086; *5:* **1107–9,** 1108 (ill.)
ICBMs (Intercontinental ballistic missiles), *3:* 620
Ice cabinets, *1:* 222, 222 (ill.)
Ice T, *5:* 1150
Ice-cream cone, *1:* **64–65**
Ice-cream soda, *1:* 68
Icky drip, *3:* 510
Ideal Novelty and Toy Corporation, *1:* 30
Idle, Eric, *4:* 1052
Illegal drugs, *5:* 1201–4, 1313–14
Illusionists, *1:* 39–40, 40 (ill.); *2:* 239
Illustration

advertising, *2:* 246
Arrow Collar Man, *1:* 157, 158–59, 159 (ill.)
Dr. Seuss, *3:* 701–2, 702 (ill.)
Gerber baby, *2:* 287
Gibson Girl, *1:* 84–85, 85 (ill.); *2:* 453, 453 (ill.)
Kewpie dolls, *1:* 86–87
Rockwell, Norman, *1:* 66, 93–94, 150, 159, 191–92, 192 (ill.)
Saturday Evening Post, 1: 93–94, 94 (ill.), 158
"I'm Looking Over a Four-Leaf Clover," *3:* 513
I'm OK, You're OK, 4: 787
"I'm So Lonesome I Could Cry," *3:* 513
iMac, *4:* 1071
IMAX, *3:* 536
Immigrants and immigration, *1:* 1, 3, 122–23
Imus, Don, *5:* 1189
In Cold Blood, 4: 787
In His Steps, 5: 1328
"In My Merry Oldsmobile," *1:* 3
Ince, Thomas, *1:* 147
Income, discretionary, *4:* 793
The Incredible Hulk, 4: 1034
Independence Day, 4: 963, 980; *5:* 1237
***Indiana Jones* movies, *5:* 1130–31**
Indianapolis 500, *1:* 204–6, 205 (ill.)
Indianapolis, Indiana, *2:* 290
Indians. *See* Native Americans
"Indie rock," *5:* 1253–54
Indoor tanning booths, *4:* 1097
Industrialists, *1:* 1–2, 3, 7–8. *See also* Business and industry
Infared communication, *4:* 1070
Ingalls, Laura, *4:* 1043–44
Inge, M. Thomas, *1:* 190
Ingram, Billy, *2:* 284
Ink Spots, *3:* 512
Integration, *3:* 587, 592, 683, 717
Intelligence Quotient (IQ) test, *2:* 365
Intercontinental ballistic missiles (ICBMs), *3:* 620
Interlocutor, *1:* 42
International Business Machines (IBM), *5:* 1107–9, 1108 (ill.)
International expositions, *1:* 142–43
International No-Diet Day, *3:* 775
International Sweepstakes, *1:* 204
Internet, *4:* 1029; *5:* 1218, 1229, 1268, 1280, 1303, 1305, 1314, **1319–21,** 1320 (ill.)
Internet Worm (computer virus), *5:* 1318
The Interrupted Journey, 3: 636
Interstate highway system, *3:* 775–76
Interview with the Vampire, 2: 393
Intolerance, 1: 147, 167
Invasion of the Body Snatchers, 3: 661
Invasion U.S.A., 3: 623; *5:* 1119
Inventions
ballpoint pens, *2:* 375–76
bra, *1:* 157, 159–61, 160 (ill.)
cellular phones, *5:* 1308–9, 1309 (ill.)
compact discs (CDs), *5:* 1136–37, 1137 (ill.)
Dixie cups, *1:* 14
eight-track tapes, *4:* 849–50, 850 (ill.)
electric appliances, *1:* 125–26
electric guitar, *3:* 686–88, 687 (ill.)
E-mail, *5:* 1314–17, 1315 (ill.)
Etch A Sketch, *3:* 718, 719 (ill.)
flaked cereals, *1:* 20
ice cream cone, *1:* 64–65
Internet, *5:* 1319–21, 1320 (ill.)
nylons, *2:* 379–80
personal computers, *4:* 1085–87
phonograph, *1:* 71, 76–78, 77 (ill.)
plastic, *1:* 24–26
refrigerators, *1:* 126, 181, 222 (ill.), 222–23
Rubik's Cube, *5:* 1169 (ill.), 1169–70
Saran Wrap, *3:* 649–50
satellites, *3:* 779–80
Slinky, *3:* 594–96, 595 (ill.)
telephone, *1:* 139 (ill.), 139–41
Tom Swift series, *1:* 194–95
transistor radios, *3:* 763–64
video games, *4:* 1019–20
Walkman, *4:* 994–95
Xerox copiers, *4:* 804–5
zipper, *1:* 164–65
Investigative journalism, *1:* 92; *4:* 916–17
Iraq, *5:* 1223
Ireland, Kathy, *4:* 799
Irwin, Hale, *2:* 334
Ismay, J. Bruce, *1:* 229
Isolationism, *3:* 509
"It," *2:* 236, 268

It Happened One Night, 2: 369, 383–84, 396
Italy, *4:* 934
It's a Wonderful Life, *3:* 512, **538–40,** 539 (ill.)
Ives, Burl, *3:* 581
Iwatani, Toru, *5:* 1167
Iwerks, Ub, *2:* 278
Izod polo shirts, *5:* 1113

J

J. C. Penney Company, *1:* 2, 7
J.Crew, *5:* **1109**
J. Fred Muggs, *3:* 760
J. Walter Thompson Company, *1:* **18–19**
Jack Frost, 3: 704
Jack the Ripper, *4:* 1092
The Jackie Gleason Show, 3: 746
Jackson, Bee, *2:* 352 (ill.)
Jackson Five, *4:* 951
Jackson, Jesse, *3:* 708
Jackson, Kate, *4:* 1032, 1033 (ill.)
Jackson, Keith, *4:* 1017
Jackson, L. L., *5:* 1148 (ill.)
Jackson, Michael, *3:* 563; *5:* 1102, 1104, 1135, **1141–42,** 1144, 1147
Jackson, Shoeless Joe, *1:* 149
Jacobson, Mark, *4:* 1064
Jaffee, Al, *3:* 706
Jagged Little Pill, 5: 1226
Jagger, Mick, *4:* 858, 858 (ill.)
Jagr, Jaromir, *1:* 207
Jamerson, James, *4:* 856
James Bond films, *4:* 815, **830–31,** 831 (ill.), 937–38; *5:* 1238
James, Dennis, *3:* 741, 753
James, Harry, *2:* 427
James, Richard and Betty, *3:* 594
James, Sheila, *3:* 737
James, Will, *2:* 368
"Jane Roe," *4:* 1090
Janssen, David, *4:* 903, 903 (ill.)
Japanese animation (anime), *5:* 1280–81
Jar Jar Binks, *5:* 1237
Jardine, Al, *4:* 844, 845 (ill.)
Jarvis, Anna, *1:* 220
Jason and the Scorchers, *5:* 1252
Jason (Vorhees), *5:* 1128
Jaws, *4:* 950, 961, **968–69,** 969 (ill.)
Jayhawks, *5:* 1252
Jazz, *1:* 71, **72–74,** 73 (ill.); *2:* 425, 428; *3:* 553, 683–84
"The Jazz Age," *2:* 235, 262; *4:* 942
Jazz fusion, *1:* 74
"Jazz King," *2:* 293
The Jazz Singer, *1:* 42, 46; *2:* 238, **275–76**
Jeans, *3:* **658–59,** 659 (ill.), 659–60
Jeep, *2:* 243; *3:* **519–20;** *5:* 1216
Jefferson Airplane, *3:* 693; *4:* 842, 929, 931
Jefferson, Blind Lemon, *2:* 425
Jefferson, Thomas, *3:* 679
The Jeffersons, 4: 1023, 1025; *5:* 1181
Jeffries, James J., *1:* 89, 102
Jell-O, *1:* **65–66;** *5:* 1183
Jenney, LeBaron, *2:* 503
Jennings, Peter, *3:* 606
The Jenny Jones Show, 4: 899
Jeopardy, 3: 742
Jewelry, *4:* 958 (ill.), 958–59
JFK, *5:* **1240–41**
JFK Stadium (Philadelphia, Pennsylvania), *5:* 1143
"Jiggle TV," *5:* 1283
Jim Crow, *1:* 40
Jimi Hendrix Experience, *4:* 789–90
The Jimmy Dean Show, 4: 1053
Jingles, Burma-Shave, *2:* 250–51
Jitterbug, *1:* 124; *3:* 524
Jobs, Steve, *4:* 1070, 1071
Jockeys, *1:* 103
Joe Camel, *2:* 254
Jogging, *4:* **1016–17**
John, Elton, *4:* 950; *5:* 1243
Johnson & Johnson Company, *2:* 247–48
Johnson, Arte, *4:* 911
Johnson brothers (Robert Wood, James, and Edward), *2:* 247
Johnson, Don, *5:* 1186
Johnson, Dwayne "The Rock," *5:* 1171, 1173
Johnson, Earvin "Magic," *3:* 591; *5:* 1166
Johnson, Harry B., *2:* 444
Johnson, Jack, *1:* 3, 5, 96, **101–2,** 202; *4:* 878
Johnson, John Harold, *3:* 576
Johnson, Lyndon B., *4:* 786, 910, 947
Johnson Publishing Company, *3:* 576, 577
Johnson, Robert, *2:* 295, 425, **428–29**
Johnson, Russell, *4:* 904
Johnson, Virginia E., *4:* 943

Johnson, Walter, *1:* 201
Jolson, Al, *2:* 238, 275
Jonathan Livingston Seagull, 4: 948
Jonathan Winters Show, 4: 1042
Jones, Amos, *2:* 478–81
Jones, Bobby, *2:* 325, 467
Jones, Brian, *4:* 858, 858 (ill.), 859
Jones, Chuck, *3:* 599, 606
Jones, Davy, *4:* 854, 855, 855 (ill.)
Jones, George, *3:* 557; *5:* 1252
Jones, Indiana, 1130–31
Jones, James, *3:* 638
Jones, Jenny, *4:* 899
Jones, Jim, *4:* 1074
Jones, John Paul, *4:* 989
Jones, Louis "Grandpa," *4:* 1042
Jones, Orlando, *2:* 288
Jones, Paula, *5:* 1226
Jones, Sam J., *2:* 451
Jones, Shirley, *4:* 1054, 1055, 1055 (ill.)
Jones, Steve, *4:* 992
Jones, Terry, *4:* 1052
Jonestown, Guyana, *4:* 1070, 1074
Joplin, Janis, *4:* 842, 929, 931
Joplin, Scott, *1:* 5, **75–76**
Jordan, Hal, *3:* 579
Jordan, Jim and Marian, *2:* 477, 482
Jordan, Louis, *3:* 565
Jordan, Michael, *2:* 290, 334; *3:* 591, 601; *4:* 925; *5:* 1226–27, 1228, 1271, **1274–75**
Joseph Enterprises, Inc., *4:* 1072
Josie and the Pussycats, *3:* 569
Journalism, *1:* 92–93; *2:* 306–7; *4:* 872, 916
Journalists, radio, *2:* 342–43
The Joy of Cooking, *2:* **421–22**
The Joy of Sex, *4:* 949, **1082–83**
Joyner, David, *5:* 1282
Joyner, Florence Griffith, *1:* 109
Joyner-Kersee, Jackie, *2:* 468
Judge, Mike, *5:* 1285
"The Judgement," *4:* 902
Judson, Whitcomb, *1:* 164
"Juke joints," *2:* 370–71, 425, 430
Jukeboxes, *2:* 425, **429–30,** 430 (ill.)
Jung, George, *5:* 1204
The Jungle, 1: 2
Jungle Book, 4: 788
Junior Jamboree, 3: 603
Jurassic Park, *2:* 404; *5:* 1224, 1228, 1237, 1265, **1268–70,** 1271 (ill.)
"Just Do It," *5:* 1224
"Just Say No," *5:* 1100
"Just the facts, ma'am," *3:* 638
JVC Jazz Festival, *3:* 683

K

Kaczynski, Ted, *5:* 1227
Kael, Pauline, *2:* 313
Kal-El, *2:* 464
Kaltenborn, Hans von, *2:* 239
Kane, Bob, *2:* 434
Kane, Carol, *4:* 1064 (ill.)
Kane, Charles Foster, *3:* 533
Kansas City Chiefs, *4:* 877
Kansas City, Missouri, *3:* 648
Karan, Donna, *5:* 1113
Karaoke, *5:* **1142–43**
Karloff, Boris, *2:* 394, 395, 395 (ill.); *4:* 828
Kasem, Casey, *3:* 695
The Katzenjammer Kids, *1:* 79, **86–87**
Kauffman, Marta, *5:* 1291
Kaufman, Andy, *4:* 1064 (ill.), 1065
Kaufman, Murray, *3:* 685
Kazan, Elia, *3:* 669–71, 773
KDKA (East Pittsburgh, Pennsylvania), *2:* 341
Kean, Jane, *3:* 746
Keaton, Buster, *1:* 45, 46, 117; *2:* 278
Keats, John, *4:* 849
Keds, *1:* 162
Keene, Carolyn, *3:* 570
Keeshan, Bob, *3:* 602, 734, 735 (ill.)
Keith, Benjamin Franklin, *1:* 48
Kellerman, Annette, *1:* 49
Kelley, Christina, *5:* 1159
Kelley, David E., *5:* 1278
Kelley, DeForest, *4:* 919 (ill.)
Kellogg, John Harvey and Will Keith, *1:* 19
Kellogg's cereals, *1:* **19–21,** 20 (ill.)
Kelly, Chin Ho, *4:* 906
Kelly, Emmett, *1:* 225
Kelly, Grace (Grace, princess of Monaco), *3:* 661; *5:* 1160
Kelly's Heroes, 5: 1176
Kelton, Pert, *3:* 745
Kendricks, Eddie, *4:* 857 (ill.)
Kennard, Charles, *1:* 112
Kennedy, Jamie, *5:* 1246
Kennedy, John F., *3:* 605, 612, 668; *4:* 785, 789, 807, 889, 939, 947; *5:* 1240–41

Kennedy, John F., Jr., *4:* 785
Kennedy (Onassis), Jacqueline, *4:* 807, 1003; *5:* 1113
Kennedy, Robert F., *3:* 612, 668; *4:* 791
Kent, Clark, *2:* 464
Kent State massacre, *4:* **1083–85,** 1084 (ill.)
Kentucky Derby, *1:* **102–4**
Kentucky Fried Chicken (KFC), *2:* 285
Kepner, Jim, *4:* 866
Kerkorian, Kirk, *2:* 277
Kerouac, Jack, *3:* 641, 697, 698, 708–9
Kevorkian, Jack, *5:* 1227
Kewpie dolls, *1:* 66, **86–87**
KeySpan Park, *1:* 121–22
Keystone Film Company, *1:* 170
Keystone Kops, *1:* **175–76,** 176 (ill.)
KFC (Kentucky Fried Chicken), *2:* 285
Khaury, Herbert, *4:* 897
Khrushchev, Nikita, *2:* 423
Kidman, Nicole, *4:* 1098
Kilborn, Craig, *4:* 1036
The Killers, *3:* 537
Killers, serial, *4:* **1091–93,** 1092 (ill.)
Killing Fields, *5:* 1119
Kimberly-Clark, *2:* 256–57
Kimble, Richard, *4:* 902
Kinematograph, *1:* 44
Kinetoscope, *1:* 44–45
King, B. B., *2:* 296; *3:* **688**
King, Billie Jean, *4:* 952, 1009
King Features, *1:* 171; *2:* 389
King Kong, *2:* **403–4;** *4:* 964
King, Martin Luther, Jr., *3:* 577, 612; *4:* 789, 790, 921, 923 (ill.), 924, 925; *5:* 1124
King Records, *3:* 691
King, Rodney, *5:* 1227
King, Stephen, *4:* 997; *5:* 1101, 1128, 1155, 1225
Kingston Trio, *4:* 851
Kinsey, Alfred, *3:* 639; *4:* 942
Kipling, Rudyard, *4:* 788
Kirby, Jack, *3:* 573
Kirk, Captain James T., *4:* 918–19, 919 (ill.)
KISS, *4:* 950, **987–88,** 988 (ill.); *5:* 1140
The Kiss, *1:* 45
Kiss Me Kate, *3:* 675
Kitchen, *1:* 8–9, 9 (ill.); *2:* 248–50, 249 (ill.), 421–22; *3:* 638
Kitty Hawk, North Carolina, *1:* 3
Kleenex, *2:* **256–57**
Klein, Calvin, *4:* 955; *5:* 1113, 1118
Klugman, Jack, *4:* 833
Kmart, *4:* 793, **797–99;** *5:* 1328
Knabusch, Edward M., *2:* 257
Knebel, Fletcher, *4:* 787
Knievel, Evel, *4:* **881–83,** 882 (ill.); *5:* 1272
Knight, Christopher, *4:* 1026
Knight, Eric, *3:* 540
Knight, Gladys, *1:* 9
Knight, Philip, *4:* 799
Knight, Ted, *4:* 1047 (ill.), 1048
Knotts, Don, *4:* 788, 890
Knuckle sandwich, *3:* 638
Knuckling down, *2:* 368
Kodak Company, *1:* 10, 11; *2:* 240
Kool & the Gang, *4:* 951, 985
Kopell, Bernie, *4:* 1046
Korean War, *3:* 622; *4:* 1049–51
Koresh, David (Vernon Howell), *4:* 1074; *5:* 1304, 1307
KOWH (Omaha, Nebraska), *3:* 695
Kraft Foods, *1:* 18–19; *2:* 289
Kraft Television Theatre, *3:* 765
Krakowski, Jane, *5:* 1279 (ill.)
Kramden, Ralph and Alice, *3:* 744–45, 745 (ill.)
Krantz, Judith, *4:* 997
Krazy Kat, *1:* **189–91,** 190 (ill.)
Krebs, Maynard G., *3:* 699, 737
Kreutzmann, Bill, *4:* 853
Kroc, Ray, *2:* 285; *3:* 549
Ku Klux Klan, *1:* **217–20,** 218 (ill.); *2:* 240
Kubelsky, Benjamin, *3:* 598
Kubrick, Stanley, *3:* 620, 623; *4:* 838, 939, 962
Kudrow, Lisa, *5:* 1291
Kukla, Fran, and Ollie, *3:* 597, **603–4,** 604 (ill.)
Kulp, Nancy, *4:* 892
Kung Fu, *4:* 938
Kunta Kinte, *4:* 1057, 1057 (ill.)
Kurobe, Akihiko, *5:* 1143
Kurtzman, Harvey, *3:* 704, 705
Kushner, Tony, *5:* 1199
Kuwait, *5:* 1223

L

L. L. Bean, *1:* **155–56**
"La Revue Negre," *2:* 267
La Salle, Eriq, *5:* 1288
Labor, sweatshop, *4:* 795–96, 804
Labor unions, *1:* 7, 149; *2:* 373–74

Laborsaving devices, *1:* 126
Ladd, Alan, *3:* 579, 673
Ladd, Cheryl, *4:* 1032
Ladies' Home Journal, 1: 2, 31, 87; *2:* 349
Lahr, Bert, *2:* 417
Laird, Peter, *5:* 1195
Lake, Arthur, *2:* 438
LaLanne, Jack, *3:* 718, **718–20**
Lamb Chop, *3:* 578
Lambert, Christopher, *1:* 193
L'Amour, Louis, *2:* 460
Landlord's Game, *2:* 472
Landon, Michael, *4:* 896, 1044, 1044 (ill.)
Landry, Tom, *4:* 880
Lane, Allan "Rocky," *4:* 907
Lane, Drew, *5:* 1189
Lane, Lois, *2:* 464
Lang, Fritz, *1:* 46; *3:* 537
lang, k. d., *2:* 253
Lange, Ted, *4:* 1046
Laptop computers, *4:* 1087
"Lara's Theme," *4:* 788
Larkin, John, *2:* 458
LaRocque, Rod, *2:* 462
Larson, Gary, *5:* 1100, 1157–58, 1158 (ill.)
Las Vegas, *3:* 514, **627–29,** 628 (ill.)
Lasseter, John, *5:* 1248–49
Lassie, *3:* **540–41,** 541 (ill.)
Lassinger, J. M., *2:* 320
"Latch-key kids, *5:* 1206
Latin American culture, Tejano music, *5:* 1251, 1262–63
Latin Hustle. *See* Hustle
Latte, *5:* 1110
Laundry, *1:* 126
Lauper, Cyndi, *5:* 1102
Laurel and Hardy, *2:* **404–5,** 405 (ill.)
Laurel, Stan, *2:* 404–5, 405 (ill.)
Lauren, Ralph, *4:* 955, **956;** *5:* 1113
Laverne & Shirley, 4: 950, 1023
Lawrence, D. H., *4:* 942
The Lawrence Welk Show, *3:* **748–49**
Lawyers, *2:* 458–59; *5:* 1278–79, 1279 (ill.), 1324 (ill.), 1324–26
Lazarus, Fred, *2:* 255
La-Z-Boy Loungers, *2:* **257**
Lazenby, George, *4:* 830
Leach, Archibald, *2:* 399
Leach, Sheryl, *5:* 1282
Leachman, Cloris, *4:* 893, 1049
Leaf Company, *2:* 347
League of Women Voters, *2:* 239
Lean, David, *4:* 788
Lear, Norman, *3:* 756; *4:* 1024
Lear, William Powell, *4:* 849
Learned, Michael, *4:* 1066
Leary, Timothy, *4:* 789–90
Leather jackets, *4:* 992, 1040
Leave It to Beaver, *3:* **749–51,** 750 (ill.), 782
Lebanon, *5:* 1101
LeBeauf, Sabrina, *5:* 1182 (ill.)
LeBlanc, Matt, *5:* 1291, 1291 (ill.)
Lecter, Hannibal, *4:* 829, 1092
Led Zeppelin, *4:* **989–90;** *5:* 1144
Lee, Bruce, *4:* 938
Lee, Christopher, *2:* 393
Lee, Harper, *4:* 786, 865
Lee, Spike, *5:* 1104, 1123, 1124 (ill.)
Lee, Stan, *3:* 573; *4:* 870, 873, 874
Lee, Will, *4:* 1063
Leeves, Jane, *5:* 1290
Legalized gambling, *4:* 933–34
The Legend of Hell House, 5: 1129
LEGOs, *3:* 717, **720–22,** 721 (ill.)
Legosi, Bela, *2:* 393
Leigh, Janet, *4:* 837
Leigh, Vivien, *2:* 370, 397 (ill.), 398
Leisure suit, *4:* **956–57,** 957 (ill.)
Leisure time, *1:* 115, 214; *2:* 345, 494. *See also* Games; Movies; Reading; Sports; Television
  baby boomers, *4:* 943
  bowling, *3:* 588–89, 589 (ill.)
  karaoke, *5:* 1142–43
  La-Z-Boy loungers, *2:* 257
  post-World War II, *3:* 615
  radio, *2:* 339–43, 340 (ill.)
  3-D movies, *3:* 674–76, 675 (ill.)
Leitzel, Lillian, *1:* 225
Lembeck, Harvey, *4:* 818
Lemieux, Mario, *1:* 207
Lemmon, Jack, *3:* 640; *4:* 833
Lemon, Meadowlark, *2:* 330
Lennon, John, *3:* 700; *4:* 826, 846, 847 (ill.), 871
Lennon Sisters, *3:* 749
Leno, Jay, *3:* 763; *4:* 897; *5:* 1185
Leo Burnett Company, *2:* 260
The Leopard's Spots, 1: 218
Leroux, Gaston, *2:* 238
Les Miserables, 4: 902
Lesbians, *4:* 926–27
Lesco Corporation, *5:* 1328
Lesh, Phil, *4:* 853

Less Than Zero, *5:* 1155, 1203
Lester, Richard, *4:* 826
Letterman, David, *3:* 761, 763; *4:* 897; *5:* **1185–86,** 1186 (ill.)
Levi Strauss & Company, *3:* 659
Levinson, Sara, *5:* 1148
Levi's, *3:* 659 (ill.), **659–60**
Levitt, William and Alfred, *3:* 630, 781
Levittown, *3:* **629–31,** 630 (ill.), 781
Lewinsky, Monica, *5:* 1226
Lewis, Al, *2:* 393
Lewis, Carl, *1:* 109
Lewis, Jerry, *1:* 176
Lewis, Jerry Lee, *3:* 641
Lewis, Shari, *3:* 578
Lewis, Sinclair, *1:* 128; *2:* 237, 241, 433
Leyendecker, J. C., *1:* 158
Liberals, *4:* 910, 1024–25; *5:* 1104, 1210
Liberman, Alexander, *1:* 197
Liberty Bonds, *1:* 232
Life, alien, *3:* 635–36
Life in America. *See* The Way We Lived
Life insurance, *2:* 287
Life (magazine), *2:* 433, **452–54,** 453 (ill.)
Life of Brian, *4:* 1052
Lifestyle
  Arrow Collar Man, *1:* 157, 158–59, 159 (ill.)
  baby boomers, *5:* 1206
  cigarettes, *2:* 251–54
  flappers, *1:* 133; *2:* 261–63, 262 (ill.)
  Gibson Girl, *1:* 84–85, 85 (ill.); *2:* 453, 453 (ill.)
  goth culture, *5:* 1114–15
  L. L. Bean, *1:* 155–56
  Marlboro Man, *2:* 259 (ill.), 259–60
  raccoon coats, *2:* 264–65
  television, *3:* 514–15, 610–13, 611 (ill.)
  Vogue, *1:* 196–97
  Volkswagen Beetle, *3:* 652–55, 653 (ill.)
A Light in the Attic, *5:* 1100
"Like," *4:* 948
Li'l Abner, *2:* **454–55**
Li'l Folks, *3:* 710
Lilith Fair, *5:* **1257–58**
Limbaugh, Rush, *2:* 343; *5:* 1176, 1193, 1225–26
Lincoln, Abraham, *2:* 331–32
Lincoln, Elmo, *1:* 193
Lincoln Highway, *3:* 776
Lincoln Jazz Center Orchestra, *1:* 74
Lincoln Logs, *2:* **331–32**
Lindbergh, Charles A., *2:* 239, 241, 320, **354,** 371–72
Lindbergh, Charles A., Jr., *2:* 371–72
Lindsay, George "Goober," *4:* 1042
Lindy hop, *1:* 124
Lingerie, *1:* 160–61
Linus Van Pelt, *3:* 711
Linville, Larry, *4:* 1050
The Lion King, *5:* 1225, 1237, **1242–43,** 1243 (ill.)
Lionel trains, *1:* **104–6,** 105 (ill.)
Lipschitz, Ralph, *4:* 956
Lipstick, *2:* **263–64**
Lish, Gordon, *2:* 448
Liston, Sonny, *4:* 878, 879 (ill.)
Literacy, *2:* 443–44
Literary magazine, *2:* 312–14, 313 (ill.)
Literature, *1:* 187; *2:* 241; *4:* 997. *See also* Books; Fiction; Novels; Reading
  Beatniks and the Beat movement, *3:* 698–99, 699 (ill.)
  Book-of-the-Month Club, *2:* 303–4
  Little Blue Books, *2:* 309–10
Little Blue Books, *2:* **309–10**
Little House on the Prairie, *4:* 1023, **1043–45,** 1044 (ill.)
Little League, *2:* **469–70,** 470 (ill.)
Little, Malcolm (Malcolm X), *4:* 789, 921, 924
Little Orphan Annie, *2:* **310–11**
Little People, *2:* 378
Little Richard, *3:* 641
Little Theater Movement, *1:* 168
Littleton, Colorado, *5:* 1115
Liu, Lucy, *4:* 1033; *5:* 1279 (ill.)
Live Aid, *5:* **1143–45,** 1144 (ill.)
Live entertainment. *See* Entertainment; Vaudeville; *Ziegfeld Follies*
Live with Regis and Kathie Lee, *4:* 899
Live with Regis and Kelly, *4:* 900
Livelong learning, *1:* 115, 118–20, 119 (ill.)
"Living Newspaper" dramas, *2:* 384
LL Cool J, *5:* 1102, 1135, **1145–46,** 1150

Lloyd, Christopher, *4:* 1064 (ill.), 1065
Lloyd, Harold, *1:* 46
Loc, Tone, *5:* 1135
Lockhart, June, *3:* 541 (ill.)
Lockwood, Gary, *4:* 838
Loew, Marcus, *1:* 44
Loew's, Inc., *2:* 277
Logos, *1:* 18, 155; *2:* 247, 248, 302, 457
Lois & Clark: The New Adventures of Superman, 2: 465
Lolita, 3: 639
Lollapalooza and Lilith Fair, *5:* 1251, **1256–58,** 1257 (ill.)
Lombardi, Gennaro, *3:* 550
Lomeli, Lori Lynn, *3:* 778
Lon, Alice, *3:* 749
London, England, *1:* 142
"London Eye" (Ferris wheel), *1:* 130
London, Jack, *1:* 79–80, **88–89;** *2:* 309
Lone Cowboy, 2: 368
Lone Ranger, *2:* 370, **485–86**
Long hair, *1:* 132, 133; *3:* 634; 8807
Long, Shelley, *5:* 1178, 1178 (ill.)
Long-playing record (LP), *3:* **558–60,** 559 (ill.), 685; *4:* 788. *See also* Compact disc
Lookinland, Mike, *4:* 1027
Loos, Anita, *2:* 237
Lord & Thomas, *2:* 245
Lord, Jack, *4:* 905
The Lord of the Rings, 3: 714
Lorimer, George Horace, *1:* 93
Lorne, Marion, *4:* 894
Lorre, Peter, *3:* 532
Los Angeles Advocate, 4: 866
Los Angeles, California, *1:* 167, 177; *4:* 928; *5:* 1122–23, 1205
Los Angeles Kings, *5:* 1166
Los Angeles Lakers, *3:* 591; *5:* 1166
Los Del Rio, *5:* 1226
Losey, Joseph, *3:* 773
Lost in Space, 4: 939
The Lost World, 5: 1270
Lottery, *4:* **933–34**
Loud, John, *2:* 375
Louis XIV, king of France, *1:* 132
Louis, Joe, *2:* 372, 467, **471**
Louis-Dreyfuss, Julia, *5:* 1296, 1297 (ill.)
Louise, Tina, *4:* 904
Louisiana Pete (Narciso Martinez), *5:* 1262
Louisville Slugger, *1:* **21–22**
Lounge lizard, *2:* 236
Loungers, La-Z-Boy, *2:* 257
The Love Boat, *4:* 1023, 1036, **1045–46**
Love, Courtney, *5:* 1258
Love Me Tender, 3: 689
Love, Mike, *4:* 844, 845 (ill.)
Love Story, 4: 948; *5:* 1115, 1117
Lovecraft, H. P., *2:* 461
Lovett, Lyle, *5:* 1252
Low, Juliette Gordon "Daisy," *1:* 227–28
Lowe, Rob, *5:* 1249
LSD (drug), *4:* 943
Lucas, George, *4:* 950, 978; *5:* 1130
Lucas, Henry Lee, *4:* 1092
Luce, Henry R., *2:* 319, 453
The Lucy Show, 3: 747
Lucy Van Pelt, *3:* 711
Ludlum, Robert, *4:* 997; *5:* 1155
Luellen, Lawrence, *1:* 14
Lugosi, Bela, *2:* 369; *4:* 828
Luna Park (Coney Island, New York), *1:* 121; *3:* 768
Lunch counters, *1:* 13
Lung cancer, Cigarettes, *2:* 252
Luyendyk, Arie, *1:* 204
Lydon, John (Johnny Rotten), *4:* 992, 993, 993 (ill.)
Lynch, David, *4:* 869
Lynde, Paul, *4:* 894
Lyne, Adrian, *5:* 1126
Lynne, Jeff, *4:* 849

M

M & M's, *3:* **546–48,** 547 (ill.)
"Ma Bell," *1:* 154
Maas, Peter, *4:* 935
"Macarena," *5:* 1226
MacArthur, James, *4:* 906
MacDermot, Galt, *4:* 825
MacDonald, John D., *2:* 460
Macfadden, Bernarr, *1:* 195
MacGraw, Ali, *4:* 948
Macintosh, *4:* 1070, 1086
MacKenzie, Allison, *3:* 671
MacLachlan, Kyle, *4:* 869
MacLeod, Gavin, *4:* 1046, 1049
MacNicol, Peter, *5:* 1279 (ill.)
MacRae, Sheila, *3:* 745
Macy's department store (New York City), *2:* 255, 258; *3:* 594, 648
Macy's Thanksgiving Day parade, *1:* 171; *2:* **258,** 388 (ill.)

MAD Magazine, *3:* **704–6,** 705 (ill.)
Madden, Dave, *4:* 1055
Madden, John, *4:* 1019
Madison, Oscar, *4:* 833
Madison Square Garden (New York City), *2:* 325
Madonna, *3:* 563; *4:* 812, 1029; *5:* 1102, 1135, **1146**
Maertens, Klaus, *4:* 809
Mafia, *4:* **934–35,** 950, 966; *5:* 1241
"Magalog," *5:* 1236
Magazine illustration
  Arrow Collar Man, *1:* 157, 158–59, 159 (ill.)
  Gibson Girl, *1:* 84–85, 85 (ill.); *2:* 453, 453 (ill.)
  Kewpie dolls, *1:* 86–87
  Saturday Evening Post, 1: 93–94, 94 (ill.), 159
Magazines, *1:* 4, 79, 187; *2:* 241; *3:* 697; *4:* 866, 997; *5:* 1156
  Argosy, 1: 80–81
  Better Homes and Gardens, 2: 302
  Cosmopolitan, 4: 867–68
  Ebony, 3: 576–77
  Esquire, 2: 448–49
  fashion, *5:* 1156
  Highlights, 3: 579–80
  Hustler, 4: 1002–44: 1003 (ill.)
  Life, 2: 452–54, 453 (ill.)
  MAD Magazine, *3:* 704–6, 705 (ill.)
  mass-circulation, *1:* 79
  Ms., 4: 1004–5
  National Geographic, 1: 90–91
  New Yorker, 2: 312–14, 313 (ill.)
  People, 4: 1005–7, 1006 (ill.)
  Playboy, 3: 639, 712–13
  pulp, *2:* 459–61, 460 (ill.). *See also* Pulp magazines
  Reader's Digest, 2: 316–17
  Sassy, 5: 1159–60
  Saturday Evening Post, 1: 93–94, 94 (ill.)
  Seventeen, 3: 582–83
  Sports Illustrated, 3: 639, 724–25
  Time, 2: 319–20
  True Story, 1: 195–96
  Vogue, 1: 196–97
  Yank, 3: 511
  zines, *5:* 1162–64
Magic Eye stereograms, *1:* 29
Magic Kingdom (Disneyland), *2:* 271 (ill.); *3:* 769
Magic Sam, *2:* 296
Magic tricks, *1:* 39–40, 40 (ill.); *2:* 239
The Magnificent Seven, 2: 259
Maguire, Tobey, *4:* 873
Maharis, George, *2:* 363
Mah-Jongg, *2:* 326
Mahoney, John, *5:* 1290
Mail order. *See* Catalogs and under specific retailer, e.g., Sears, Roebuck catalog
Mailer, Norman, *3:* 697
Main Street, 2: 237
"Maine hunting shoe," *1:* 156
Make Room for Daddy, 3: 642
The Make-Believe Ballroom, 3: 684
Make-up. *See* Cosmetics; Lipstick
Malcolm X (Malcolm Little), *4:* 789, 921, 924
Male chauvinist pig, *4:* 948
Maleska, the Indian Wife of the White Hunter, 1: 83
Mall of America, *5:* 1229, 1230 (ill.), **1230–31**
Malloy, Terry, *3:* 670, 670 (ill.)
Malls, *3:* 644, **648–49;** *5:* 1229, 1230 (ill.), 1230–31
The Maltese Falcon, 3: 529, 537
Maltese, Michael, *3:* 606
Malvern, Corinne, *3:* 703
"Mammy" character, *1:* 8–9, 9 (ill.)
The Man from U.N.C.L.E., 3: 623
The Man in the Gray Flannel Suit, 3: 657
Man of Steel, *2:* 465
The Man of the Forest, 2: 236
Management systems, "Fordism," *1:* 23
Management techniques, *1:* 153
Manchu, Fu. *See* Fu Manchu
The Manchurian Candidate, 3: 565, 622
Manchus, *1:* 132–33
Manhattan (New York City), Broadway, *1:* 34–36, 35 (ill.)
Manhattan Project, *3:* 619
Manilow, Barry, *4:* 981, **990**
Mankiewicz, Herman J., *3:* 533
Man-made materials, *2:* 379–80
Mann, Michael, *5:* 1186
Manson, Charles, *4:* 790, 872
Mantle, Mickey, *1:* 210; *2:* 349; *3:* 650
The Many Loves of Dobie Gillis, 3: 699
"March Madness," *5:* 1166
March on Washington (1963), *4:* 921

Marchiony, Italo, *1:* 64
Marconi, Guglielmo, *2:* 340
Marcus Welby, M.D., 4: 949; *5:* 1288
Marguiles, Julianna, *5:* 1288
Marijuana *(Cannabis sativa), 4:* 931, **936–37,** 943; *5:* 1259
Marin, Cheech, *4:* 933
Maris, Roger, *1:* 98, 210; *5:* 1228
The Mark of Zorro, 1: 199; *2:* 237
Marketing. *See also* Advertising
  Anheuser-Busch Companies, *4:* 794
  Buster Brown, 1: 81, 82 (ill.)
  eight-track tape player, *4:* 850
  General Motors, *1:* 130–31
  KISS, *4:* 987–88, 988 (ill.)
  research, *2:* 245–46
Markham, Monte, *2:* 459
Marks, Johnny, *3:* 581
Marland, Douglas, *2:* 484
Marlboro Man, *2:* 254, 259 (ill.), **259–60**
Marlowe, Philip, *2:* 442
Marquez, Gabriel Garciá, *4:* 997
Marquis of Queensberry rules (boxing), *1:* 101
Marriage and divorce, *4:* 943, 1075–77; *5:* 1126–27
Mars, Forrest, *3:* 547
Mars, Inc., *3:* 546
Mars space flights, *4:* 939
Marsalis, Wynton, *1:* 74
Marschall, Richard, *1:* 190; *2:* 450
Marsh, Stan, *5:* 1298
Marshall, Gary, *4:* 1040
Marshall Islands, *3:* 619 (ill.)
Marshall, Mike, *4:* 1015
Marshall, Thurgood, *4:* 790
Marston, William Moulton, *3:* 583
Martial arts, *4:* **937–38**
Martin, Dick, *4:* 911
Martin, Ricky, *5:* 1226, 1251
Martin, Steve, *3:* 537
Martinez, Narciso (Louisiana Pete), *5:* 1262
Martini, *2:* 419
Marvel Comics, *2:* 440; *4:* 866, **869–71**
Marx Brothers (Harpo, Groucho, Chico, Zeppo), *1:* 50, 168; *2:* **406–7**
Mary Hartman, Mary Hartman, 2: 488
Mary Kay Cosmetics, *4:* **810–11**
Mary Poppins, *4:* **832,** 832 (ill.)
The Mary Tyler Moore Show, *4:* 1023, **1046–49,** 1047 (ill.), 1076–77
M*A*S*H, *4:* 950, **1049–51**
"Mash me a fin," *3:* 510
Mason, Bobbie Ann, *3:* 570
Mason, Perry. *See* Perry Mason
Mass market, *1:* 88; *2:* 241; 560–63, 632–33
Mass murders, *4:* 1092
Mass suicides, Jonestown, Guyana, *4:* 1070, 1074
Master Charge (MasterCard), *3:* 647
Masters of Deceit, 3: 625
Masters, William H., *4:* 943
Mathers, Jerry, *3:* 750, 750 (ill.)
Mathis, June, *2:* 280
Mattel, *2:* 378; *3:* 644
Matthau, Walter, *4:* 833
Mauch Chunk Switchback Railway, *1:* 136
Maugham, Somerset, *3:* 608
Maxwell House Coffee, *1:* 2
May, Robert L., *2:* 255; *3:* 581
Mayberry R.F.D., 4: 891
Mayer, Louis B., *2:* 277
Mayfield, Curtis, *4:* 982
Mays, Willie, *3:* 717
McAuliffe, Christa, *4:* 939
McBeal, Ally, *5:* 1278
McCain, John, *4:* 1098
McCall, C. W., *4:* 1031
McCall, David, *4:* 1060
McCarthy, Charlie, *2:* **391;** *3:* 641
McCarthy, Joseph, *3:* 640, 767, 769–71
McCarthy-Army hearings, *3:* **769–71,** 770 (ill.)
"McCarthyism," *3:* 771
McCartney, Paul, *4:* 826, 846, 847 (ill.)
McCay, Winsor, *1:* 147, 173
McConnell, David, *1:* 116
McCormick, Kenny, *5:* 1298
McCormick, Maureen, *4:* 1027
McCorvey, Norma, *4:* 1090
McCoy, Sherman, *5:* 1156
McCoy, Van, *4:* 982, 986
McCulley, Johnston, *1:* 199
McDaniel, Hattie, *2:* 398
McDaniels, Daryl "DMC," *5:* 1151, 1151 (ill.)
McDonald, Dick and Mac, *3:* 548
McDonald's, *2:* 285; *3:* **548–50,** 549 (ill.), 677, 679, 680
McDonough, John, *3:* 735
McDowall, Roddy, *3:* 541; *4:* 836

McDowell, Malcolm, *4:* 962, 1037
McFarlane, Leslie, *2:* 308
McGarrett, Steve, *4:* 905
McGovern, George, *4:* 860
McGowan, Rose, *5:* 1246
McGwire, Mark, *1:* 99, 210; *5:* 1228, 1271
McInerney, Jay, *5:* 1155, 1203, 1219
McKay, Jim, *4:* 887
McKernan, Ron, *4:* 853
McKinley, William, *1:* 3
McLachlan, Sarah, *5:* 1257–58
McLamore, James, *3:* 678
McLaren, Malcolm, *4:* 992
McLaughlin, John, *1:* 74
McMahon, Ed, *3:* 762; *4:* 897
McMahon, Vince, Jr., *5:* 1172–73
McMahon, Vince, Sr., *5:* 1171–72
McManus, George, *1:* 174
McNamara, Frank, *3:* 647
McVeigh, Timothy, *5:* 1227, 1304, 1307
MDMA, *5:* 1313
"The Me Decade," *4:* 947, 958–59, 1069; *5:* 1156
"Me Generation," *4:* 948
Meadows, Audrey, *3:* 745 (ill.), 746
Meal preparation, *1:* 53–54; *2:* 289
The Meaning of Life, 4: 1052
Mears, Rick, *1:* 206
Meat, canned, *2:* 423–24
Meccano, *1:* 202, 203
Media. *See* specific medium, e.g., Television
Medical Center, 5: 1288
Medical dramas. *See also* Dramas, TV
  Dr. Kildare, 4: 900–901
  ER, 5: 1225, 1288–89
Meek, Harry, *1:* 216
"Meet Me in St. Louis," *1:* 3
Mekons, *5:* 1252
Melanoma, *4:* 1098
Mellencamp, John, *5:* 1138
Memorial Quilt (AIDS), *5:* 1199, 1199 (ill.)
Memphis, Tennessee, *3:* 688, 691
Men
  Argosy, 1: 80–81
  Arrow Collar Man, *1:* 158–59, 159 (ill.)
  divorce, *4:* 1069, 1075, 1075–77
  Esquire, 2: 448–49
  gray flannel suit, *3:* 657
  long hair, *4:* 807
  Marlboro Man, *2:* 259 (ill.), 259–60
  "power" suit, *5:* 1113
  raccoon coats, *2:* 264–65
  Sports Illustrated, 3: 725
Men Are from Mars, Women Are from Venus, 5: 1224–25
Menches, Charles E., *1:* 64
Merchandising
  Abercrombie & Fitch, *5:* 1235–36
  Barney and Friends, 5: 1283
  Crockett, Davy, *3:* 736
  Disney, *2:* 274, 322
  Felix the Cat, *1:* 171
  Harry Potter series, *5:* 1267 (ill.), 1267–68
  holidays, *1:* 216
  Kewpie dolls, *1:* 86–87
  KISS, *4:* 987–88, 988 (ill.)
  Mother's Day, *1:* 220–21
  Mutt & Jeff, 1: 90
  Peanuts, 3: 712
  Pokémon, *5:* 1322–23, 1323 (ill.)
  Sesame Street, 4: 1063
  Teenage Mutant Ninja Turtles, *5:* 1194–95, 1195 (ill.)
  toy, *4:* 915
  Winnie-the-Pooh, *2:* 322
"Mercury Radio Theatre of the Air," *2:* 489
Meredith, Don, *4:* 1017, 1018 (ill.)
Meredith, Edwin T., *2:* 302
Merman, Ethel, *2:* 389
Merton, Niles, *4:* 867
Mertz, Fred and Ethel, *3:* 747
Messick, Dalia (Dale), *3:* 571
Metalious, Grace, *3:* 639, 671
Metallica, *5:* 1140, 1257
Metro-Goldwyn-Mayer (MGM), *2:* 276–77
Mexican American culture, Zoot suit, *3:* 525–27, 526 (ill.)
Meyer, Baron de, *1:* 196
Meyer, Carl, *1:* 46
***Miami Vice, 5:* 1186–87**
Michaels, Al, *4:* 1019
Michaels, Lorne, *4:* 1059
Michel, Jean-Louis, *1:* 231
Michener, James, *5:* 1155
Michtom, Morris, *1:* 30
Mickey Mouse, *2:* 238, 267, 270, 272, 278–79, 279 (ill.); *3:* 535, 536 (ill.)
***The Mickey Mouse Club, 2:* 308; *3:* 751–52**

Microbus (Volkswagen), *3:* 654
Microprocessors, *5:* 1232
Microsoft, *4:* 1086; *5:* 1229, **1231–33,** 1232 (ill.)
Microwaves, *5:* 1310
Midnight Cowboy, 4: 815
Mighty Morphin Power Rangers, 4: 938
Mighty Mouse Playhouse, 4: 914
Migrant workers, *2:* 452
Mikan, George, *3:* 590
Milius, John, *4:* 969
Milk, Harvey, *4:* 927 (ill.)
Millennium, 4: 1093
Millennium bug, *5:* 1330
Miller, Arthur, *3:* 530, 668
Miller, Dennis, *4:* 1019
Miller, Frank, *2:* 435
Miller, Glenn, *1:* 73; *2:* 427; *3:* 512
Miller, Henry, *4:* 942
Miller, Jason, *4:* 965
Miller, Jeffrey, *4:* 1085
Miller, Lewis, *1:* 118
Milli Vanilli, *5:* 1103
The Million Dollar (Los Angeles, California), *1:* 177
Milne, A. A., *2:* 237, 322
Milner, Martin, *2:* 363
Milton Bradley Company, *1:* **106;** *4:* 885
Milwaukee, Wisconsin, *1:* 16
Mime artists, *1:* 46, 47, 167, 170–71; *2:* 238, 369
Miner, Worthington, *3:* 609
Miners, jeans, *3:* 658, 659
Mingo, Norman, *3:* 706
Mingus, Charles, *1:* 74
Mini Me, *5:* 1238
Miniature golf, *2:* **332–34,** 333 (ill.)
Miniseries, *Roots, 4:* 1057 (ill.), 1057–58
Miniskirts, *4:* **811–13,** 812 (ill.)
Minivans, *5:* **1208,** 1209 (ill.)
Minneapolis, Minnesota, *3:* 648
Minnie Mouse, *2:* 278
Minow, Newton, *4:* 889
Minstrel shows, *1:* 2, 8–9, 33, **40–42,** 41 (ill.); *2:* 479
Mirabella, Grace, *1:* 197
Miracle on 34th Street, 2: 255
Miracles (musical group), *4:* 842
The Miseducation of Lauryn Hill, 5: 1226
Miss America Pageant, *2:* 355 (ill.), **355–56**
Miss Vicky and Tiny Tim, *4:* 897, 898 (ill.)
Missing in Action, 5: 1119
Mississippi Burning, 1: 220; *3:* 625
Mr. Bones, *1:* 42
Mister Ed, *3:* 665; *4:* **906–7**
Mr. Green Jeans, *3:* 734
Mr. Holland's Opus, 4: 975
Mister Rogers' Neighborhood, *4:* 890, **908–9,** 909 (ill.)
Mr. Smith Goes to Washington, *2:* **407**
Mr. T (Lawrence Tureaud), *5:* 1176–77, 1177 (ill.)
Mr. Tambo, *1:* 42
Mitch, Richard, *4:* 866
Mitchell, Margaret, *1:* 219; *2:* 369, 398
Mitchell, Thomas, *3:* 539
Mitchell, Vinett Beatrice "Jackie," *2:* 468
Mix, Tom, *1:* 167; *2:* 370
Mizell, Jason "Jam Master Jay," *5:* 1151, 1151 (ill.)
"Mod look," *4:* 807, 812
Model T, *1:* 8, **22–23;** *2:* 345
Models, *5:* 1113–14
  supermodels, *5:* 1114, 1117–18, 1118 (ill.)
  swimsuit, *3:* 725
  Vogue, 1: 196
Modern Times, 1: 47
Mohawk hairstyle, *4:* 992; *5:* 1177
"Mom-and-pop" stores, *4:* 798
Monday Night Football, *4:* **1017–19,** 1018 (ill.)
Money, *4:* 933
Monk, Thelonius, *1:* 73; *3:* 553
Monkees, *3:* 562–63; *4:* 789–90, 841, **854–55,** 855 (ill.)
Monkey Trial. *See* Scopes Monkey trial
Monoplanes, *2:* 346
Monopoly (board game), *2:* 468, **471–73**
Monopoly cases, *1:* 155; *5:* 1233
Monroe, Bill, *3:* 554
Monroe, Marilyn, *2:* 396; *3:* 639, 640, 661, **667–68,** 713
Montalban, Ricardo, *4:* 1036–37, 1037 (ill.)
Montana, Bob, *3:* 568
Montana, Joe, *4:* 885
Montand, Yves, *3:* 780
Montgomery, Elizabeth, *4:* 893
Montgomery, Robert, *4:* 894

Monty Python and the Holy Grail, *4:* 1052
Monty Python's Flying Circus, *4:* **1051–52**
Mood, *4:* 958 (ill.), 958–59; *5:* 1305
Moon landing, astronauts, *4:* 789, 939
"Moondog Rock and Roll Party," *3:* 684
Moonshiners, *2:* 474
Moonwalk, *5:* 1141
Moore, Clayton, *2:* 485
Moore, Don, *2:* 450
Moore, Mary Tyler, *4:* 1047 (ill.), 1047–48
Moore, Michael, *1:* 131
Moore, Roger, *4:* 830
Moore, Tim, *2:* 479 (ill.)
Moorehead, Agnes, *4:* 894
Moral Majority, *1:* 127; *5:* 1103, 1160, 1197, 1198
Moran, Erin, *4:* 1040
Morgan, Harry, *4:* 1051
Morgan, Robin, *4:* 1004, 1005
Morganfield, McKinley (Muddy Waters), *2:* 295
Mormonism, *4:* 1074
Morning news and entertainment programs, *3:* **760–61**
Morrell, David, *5:* 1131
Morris, Garrett, *4:* 1059, 1059 (ill.)
Morrisette, Alanis, *5:* 1226
Morrison, Toni, *4:* 997
Morrissey, *5:* 1254
Morrow, Vic, *1:* 219
Mortal Kombat, *4:* 1022
Mortenson, Norma Jeane, *3:* 667
Morton, Jelly Roll, *1:* 72, 73 (ill.); *2:* 240, 293
Morton Salt, *1:* 146
Mosley, Walter, *2:* 442
Moss, Kate, *3:* 774
Most, Donny, *4:* 1040, 1041 (ill.)
Mother's Day, *1:* **220–21**
"Mother's Little Helper," *4:* 802
Mothership Connection, *4:* 985
Motion Picture Association of America, *4:* 815
Motion pictures. *See* Movies
Motocross, *5:* 1273
Motor City 500, *2:* 474
Motor vehicles, *5:* 1208, 1209 (ill.), 1212–13, 1215–17, 1216 (ill.), 1308–9. *See also* Automobiles; Motorcycles; Trucks
"Motoramas," *1:* 130
Motorcycles, *1:* 8, 16–17, 17 (ill.), 163; *4:* 820–21, 821 (ill.), 842–43, 843 (ill.)
Motown, *3:* 565; *4:* 789, 842, **856–57,** 857 (ill.)
Mount Carmel Ranch (Waco, Texas), *5:* 1307
Mount Rainier, Washington, *3:* 635, 636 (ill.)
Mount Rushmore, *3:* 513, 669
Mountain Dew, *5:* 1273
Mouseketeers, *3:* 752
A Moveable Feast, *4:* 787
Movements
  gay liberation movement, *4:* 926–27, 927 (ill.)
  The Joy of Sex, *4:* 1082–83
  Kent State massacre, *4:* 1083–85, 1084 (ill.)
  PC (political correctness), *5:* 1209–11
  Roe v. Wade, *4:* 1089–91, 1090 (ill.)
  sexual revolution, *4:* 941–44
Movie industry, *2:* 240–41, 267; *3:* 661; *4:* 815
  African Americans, *4:* 922–23
  blacklisting, *3:* 772–73
  early development, *1:* 167
Movie palaces, *1:* 167, **177–78**
Movie parodies, *3:* 705; *5:* 1120–21, 1121 (ill.)
Movie stars, *1:* 35–36; *2:* 306–7, 401
Movie studios, *2:* 267, 276–77; *3:* 386–87, 529–30, 661. *See also* specific studio, e.g., RKO Radio Pictures
Movie theaters, *1:* 34, 42–44, 43 (ill.), 177–78
Moviemaking. *See* Movie industry
Movies, *1:* 25, 167. *See also under* Film
  actors' Broadway starts, *1:* 35–36
  beach movies, *4:* 816–18, 817 (ill.)
  counterculture, *4:* 820–21, 821 (ill.)
  disaster movies, *4:* 963–64, 964 (ill.)
  drive-in theater, *2:* 497–99, 498 (ill.)
  early development, *1:* 167. *See also* Nickelodeons
  Harlem Globetrotters, *2:* 330

Hollywood, *2:* 400–403, 401 (ill.)
horror movies, *4:* 827–29, 828 (ill.)
James Bond films, *4:* 830–31, 831 (ill.)
MGM, *2:* 277
science fiction. *See under* Science fiction
silent movies, *1:* 44–47, 45 (ill.)
talking pictures, *2:* 275–76
3-D, *3:* 674–76, 675 (ill.)
Movietone newsreels, *2:* 276
MP3, *3:* 559
Ms., *3:* 585; *4:* 949, **1004–5**
Ms. Pac-Man, *5:* 1168, 1168 (ill.)
MS-DOS (disk operating system), *5:* 1232–33
MSNBC, *5:* 1180
MTV (Music Television), *4:* 1029; *5:* 1101, 1135, **1147–49,** 1148 (ill.), 1277, 1292
The Real World, 5: 1292–94, 1293 (ill.)
Mufasa, *5:* 1242
Muhammad Ali. *See* Ali, Muhammad
Munchkins, *2:* 417
Munsey, Frank, *1:* 80
The Munsters, 2: 395, 393
Muppets, *4:* **1053–54,** 1062, 1063 (ill.)
"Murder!," *3:* 510
The Murder of Roger Ackroyd, 2: 457
Murders, *4:* 1091–93, 1092 (ill.); *5:* 1324 (ill.), 1324–26
Murdock, Buzz, *2:* 363
Murnau, F. W., *2:* 393; *4:* 828
Murphy, Dale, *2:* 470
Murphy, Eddie, *3:* 665; *4:* 908, 1060
Murphy, Isaac, *1:* 103
Murray, Bill, *4:* 1059 (ill.), 1060; *5:* 1129, 1129 (ill.)
"Murray the K," *3:* 685
Murrie, William, *3:* 547
Murrow, Edward R., *2:* 343; *3:* 597, 641
Museum of Modern Shopping, *5:* 1107
Music, *1:* 71–72; *2:* 293, 425–26; *3:* 553–54, 683–84; *4:* 841–42, 981–82; *5:* 1135–36, 1251. *See also* specific musician or musical group, e.g., Beatles
alternative rock, *5:* 1251, 1253–54
American Bandstand, 3: 731–32, 732 (ill.)
beach music, *4:* 844
big bands, *2:* 426–27
bluegrass, *3:* 554–55
blues, *2:* 293–96, 294 (ill.)
compact disc (CD), *5:* 1136–37, 1137 (ill.)
country, *2:* 297–99, 298 (ill.); *3:* 555–58; *5:* 1251
disc jockeys, *3:* 684–85
disco, *4:* 952, 982–83, 983 (ill.)
drug-induced, *4:* 789
easy-listening, *3:* 748–49
electronic, *5:* 1260
folk, *3:* 553; *4:* 848, 851–52
funk, *4:* 984–85
grunge, *5:* 1255–56
jazz, *1:* 72–74, 73 (ill.); *3:* 553
jukeboxes, *2:* 429–30, 430 (ill.)
long-playing record (LP), *3:* 558–60, 559 (ill.), 685; *4:* 788
Motown, *4:* 856–57, 857 (ill.)
MTV (Music Television), *5:* 1135, 1147–49, 1148 (ill.)
new wave, *3:* 693; *4:* 981
phonograph, *1:* 71, 76–78, 77 (ill.)
pop, *3:* 560–63
punk, *4:* 982, 991–92, 992 (ill.)
ragtime, *1:* 5, 71, 75–76
rap and hip-hop, *5:* 1135, 1149–50, 1251
rhythm and blues (R&B), *3:* 564–65
rock and roll, *3:* 641–42, 690–94, 691 (ill.); *4:* 981
soundtrack albums, *4:* 788
teen idols, *2:* 324–525; *3:* 563, 632–34, 633 (ill.), 732 (ill.)
tejano music, *5:* 1251, 1262–63
Tin Pan Alley, *1:* 147
top 40, *3:* 694–95
World War I, *1:* 148
"Music Goes Round and Round," *2:* 370
Music movies
Hair, 4: 824–26, 825 (ill.)
A Hard Day's Night, 4: 826–27, 847 (ill.)
Music sitcoms. *See also* Comedies, TV
The Monkees, 4: 854–55, 855 (ill.)

The Partridge Family, 4: 1054–56, 1055 (ill.)
Music Television (MTV). *See* MTV (Music Television)
Music videos, *4:* 1029; *5:* 1135, 1141, 1147
Musical instruments, *3:* 686–88, 687 (ill.)
Musical revues. *See Ziegfeld Follies*
Musical theater, *1:* 168; *5:* 1237
Annie, 2: 311
Broadway, *1:* 34–36, 35 (ill.), 168; *2:* 267; *3:* 530
Hair, 4: 824–26, 825 (ill.)
minstrel shows, *1:* 2, 8–9, 33, 40–42, 41 (ill.)
vaudeville, *1:* 2, 33, 47–50, 48 (ill.), 146
Ziegfeld Follies, 1: 50–52, 146, 168
"Must See TV," *5:* 1178, 1277, 1291, 1297
Mutt & Jeff, *1:* 79, **89–90**
Mutual Radio Network, *2:* 485
My Antonia, 1: 146
My Fair Lady, 3: 640
My Favorite Husband, 2: 342
My Name Is Barbra, 4: 861
"My Prayer," *3:* 640
My Three Sons, 4: 1076
Myers, Garry Cleveland and Carolyn Clark, *3:* 580
Myers, Mike, *4:* 1060; *5:* 1238, 1238 (ill.), 1249, 1250 (ill.)
Mysteries
Fu Manchu, *1:* 188–89, 189 (ill.)
Hardy Boys series, *2:* 308–9
The Shadow, 2: 461–62
The Mysteries of Pittsburgh, 5: 1203

N

NAACP (National Association for the Advancement of Colored People), *1:* 169–70; *2:* 479
Nab, *3:* 510
Nabisco, *1:* 184
Nabokov, Vladimir, *3:* 639
Nader, Ralph, *1:* 131; *4:* 790
Nagasaki, Japan, *3:* 620
Naismith, James, *3:* 590
The Naked and the Dead, 3: 697
Naked Gun, 5: 1121
Naked Lunch, 3: 698
Namath, Joe, *2:* 335; *4:* 792, **883–84,** 885
Namco, *5:* 1167
***Nancy Drew* series,** *2:* **455–56;** *5:* 1268
"Nannygate," *5:* 1224
Narcotics, *5:* 1201–4
NASA (National Aeronautics and Space Administration), *4:* **938–40**
NASCAR (National Association for Stock Car Racing), *2:* 474, 475
Nashville sound, *3:* 557
Nashville, Tennessee, *3:* 690
Nathan, Syd, *3:* 691
Nathan's Famous, *1:* 63
National Aeronautics and Space Administration (NASA), *4:* **938–40**
National Association for Stock Car Racing (NASCAR), *2:* 474, 475
National Association for the Advancement of Colored People (NAACP), *1:* 169–70; *2:* 479
National Barn Dance, 2: 426
National Baseball Hall of Fame, *1:* 108
National Basketball Association (NBA), *3:* **590–91,** 717; *4:* 877–78; *5:* 1274
National Broadcasting Company. *See* NBC (National Broadcasting Company)
National Collegiate Athletic Association (NCAA), *5:* 1324
National Education Television, *4:* 910
National Enquirer, *3:* **707–8,** 708 (ill.)
National Football League (NFL), *2:* **334–36;** *4:* 1035
National Forest Service, *4:* 1079
National Geographic, *1:* **90–91**
National Guard, *4:* 1084–85
National Hockey League (NHL), *1:* 201, **207–8,** 208 (ill.)
National Hot Rod Association, *3:* 627
National League, *1:* 96–97
National Organization for the Reform of Marijuana Laws (NORML), *4:* 936
National Organization for Women (NOW), *4:* 921, **940–41,** 941 (ill.)
National parks, *4:* 1079
National Public Radio (NPR), *4:* 950; *5:* 1176
National Velvet, 3: 542
National Women's Party, *4:* 1081

National Wrestling Alliance, *5:* 1171
Native Americans, *1:* 37; *2:* 485; *4:* 896; *5:* 1210
Natural Born Killers, 5: 1244
Natural Resources Defense Council, *4:* 1080
Natwick, Grim, *2:* 388
Navaira, Emilio, *5:* 1263
Nazis, modern, *5:* 1214
NBA. *See* National Basketball Association (NBA)
NBC (National Broadcasting Company), *3:* 611, 684, 727; *4:* 898–99; *5:* 1175, 1178, 1277, 1288, 1296
NBC radio network, *2:* 341
NCAA (National Collegiate Athletic Association), *5:* 1324
Neal, Patricia, *4:* 1066
Negro Digest, 3: 576
Negro leagues, *1:* 5, **107–8;** *3:* 592
Negro Theatre Project, *2:* 384
Neill, Sam, *5:* 1270
Nelson, Gaylord, *4:* 1077–78
Nelson, Ozzie, Harriet, David, and Ricky, *3:* 729
Nelson, Ricky, *3:* 633
Nelson, Steve, *3:* 702
Nelson, Willie, *2:* 417; *5:* 1103, 1138, 1138 (ill.), 1252
Neo-Nazis, *5:* 1214
Nesbit, Evelyn, *1:* 49
Nesmith, Mike, *4:* 854, 855, 855 (ill.)
Nestor Film Company, *2:* 400
Netherlands, *5:* 1311
Neuman, Alfred E., *3:* 705–6, 706 (ill.)
Neuwirth, Bebe, *5:* 1179
Nevada, southwestern, *3:* 627–28
Nevermind, 5: 1254
New age health practices, *5:* 1306
New Deal, *2:* 367–68, 384, 493; *3:* 553
"New Economy," *5:* 1227
New Fun Comics, 2: 440
New Jack City, 5: 1206
"New journalism," *5:* 1156
New Kids on the Block, *5:* 1251
New Orleans, Louisiana, *1:* 71, 72; *2:* 293
New Wave music, *3:* 693; *4:* 981
New York City, New York
  Broadway, *1:* 34–36, 35 (ill.)
  Coney Island, *1:* 115, 120–22, 121 (ill.), 136
  Empire State Building, *2:* 493, 499
  King Kong, *2:* 403–4
  movie palaces, *1:* 177–78
  Rockefeller Center, *2:* 493
  World's Fairs, *1:* 142; *2:* 381, 478
New York Jets, *2:* 335; *4:* 877, 883, 884
New York Journal, 1: 2
New York Knickerbockers, *1:* 96
New York Mets, *4:* 877
New York Times, *1:* **92–93;** *3:* 518
New York World, 2: 327
New York Yankees, *3:* 642; *5:* 1271
New Yorker, *2:* **312–14,** 313 (ill.)
Newark, New Jersey, *4:* 928
Newcombe, Don, *3:* 717
Newman, Laraine, *4:* 1059, 1059 (ill.)
Newport Jazz Festival (JVC Jazz Festival), *3:* 683
News. *See also* Newspapers
  Cable News Network (CNN), *5:* 1179–80
  censored, *3:* 512
  news anchors, *3:* 604–6
  radio, *2:* 342–43
  60 Minutes, 4: 916–17
  Time, 2: 319–20
  TV, *3:* 597, 612
News anchors, *3:* **604–6**
Newsmongers, *2:* 307
Newspapers. *See also* News
  Advocate, 2: 301; *4:* 866–67
  comics. *See* Comic strips
  gossip columns, *2:* 306–7
  National Enquirer, 3: 707–8, 708 (ill.)
  New York Times, 1: 92–93
  Stars and Stripes, 3: 511
  syndicated columnists, *2:* 241
  USA Today, 5: 1156, 1160–62
Newsreels, Movietone, *2:* 276
Newsweek, 4: 1089
NFL (National Football League), *2:* **334–36;** *4:* 1035
NHL (National Hockey League, *1:* 201, **207–8,** 208 (ill.)
Nichols, J. C., *3:* 648, 781
Nichols, Mike, *4:* 822, 860
Nicholson, Jack, *4:* 821, 855
Nicholson, James, *4:* 816
Nickelodeons, *1:* 34, **42–44,** 43 (ill.), 45, 167
Nicklaus, Jack, *2:* 334; *5:* 1271
Nicotine, *2:* 252

Nielsen, Leslie, *4:* 965; *5:* 1121
A Night at the Opera, 2: 406
Nightmare on Elm Street, 4: 829; *5:* 1119
Nike, *1:* 162; *4:* 793, **799–801,** 800 (ill.)
Nimoy, Leonard, *4:* 919, 919 (ill.)
911 system, *1:* 140
1999, 5: 1102
Nineteenth Amendment, *1:* 213
Nintendo, *4:* 1021–22
Nirvana, *5:* 1226, 1253, 1254, 1256, **1258**
Nitty Gritty Dirt Band, *5:* 1252
Niven, David, *4:* 1096
Nixon, Agnes, *2:* 484
Nixon, Richard M., *1:* 92, 216; *2:* 336; *3:* 612; *4:* 912, 948, 950, 952, 1083; *5:* 1225, 1315–16
No Depression, 5: 1252
No, No Nanette, 2: 267
Nonsmoking, *2:* 253
North by Northwest, *2:* 400; *3:* 640, 661, **668–69**
Nose twitch, *4:* 894
Nosferatu, A Symphony of Horrors, 2: 393; *4:* 828
"Not!," *5:* 1224
Notorious, 2: 400
The Notorious B.I.G., *5:* 1150
Notre Dame football, *1:* 201
Novels, *1:* 79–80, 187; *2:* 241, 301; *5:* 1265. *See also* Books; Fiction; Literature; Reading
  Bobbsey Twins series, *3:* 570–71
  The Bonfire of the Vanities, 5: 1156–57
  The Catcher in the Rye, 3: 700–701
  Charlie Chan, *2:* 269, 269 (ill.)
  detective fiction, *2:* 441–43
  dime novels, *1:* 82–84, 83 (ill.)
  Dracula, *2:* 392–93
  Frankenstein, *2:* 394–95, 395 (ill.)
  Fu Manchu, *1:* 188–89, 189 (ill.)
  The Grapes of Wrath, 2: 451–52
  Hardy Boys series, *2:* 308–9
  Harlequin romances, *4:* 1001–2
  Little Blue Books, *2:* 309–10
  London, Jack, *1:* 88–89
  Nancy Drew series, *2:* 455–56
  Perry Mason, *2:* 458
  Peyton Place, 3: 671–72
  On the Road, 3: 708–9
  Tarzan, *1:* 192–94, 193 (ill.)
  Tolkien, J. R. R., *3:* 713–14
  Tom Swift series, *1:* 194–95
  Zorro, *1:* 199–200, 200 (ill.)
Novoselic, Chris, *5:* 1258
NOW (National Organization for Women), *4:* **940–41,** 941 (ill.)
NPR (National Public Radio), *4:* 950
*NSYNC, *5:* 1251
Nuclear arms race, *3:* 662. *See also* Cold War
Nuclear attack drills, *3:* 620, 623
Nuclear bombs, *3:* 618–21, 619 (ill.)
Nuclear radiation, Godzilla, *3:* 666 (ill.), 666–67
Nylon, *2:* **379–80**
Nylon stockings, *1:* 25; *2:* **380–82,** 381 (ill.)
NYPD Blue, 5: 1277

O

O Pioneers! (Cather), *1:* 146
Oakland A's, *4:* 1009
Oakland, California, *2:* 372
Oakley, Annie, *1:* 37
Oboler, Arch, *2:* 342
O'Brien, Richard, *4:* 971, 972 (ill.), 973
O'Brien, Willis, *2:* 404
Occult, *1:* 111–12, 112 (ill.)
Ochs, Adolph S., *1:* 92
O'Connor, Carroll, *4:* 1024
O'Connor, Donald, *3:* 664
The Odd Couple, *4:* 816, **833–34**
Odditoriums, *2:* 318
O'Donnell, Rosie, *4:* 1063
The Official Preppy Handbook, 1: 156; *5:* 1115–17, 1116 (ill.)
O'Hara, Scarlett, *2:* 397 (ill.)
O'Horgan, Tom, *4:* 825
Oil embargo, *4:* 947, 1030
"Okey dokey," *2:* 368
"Okies," *2:* 374
Oklahoma!, 1: 35 (ill.); *3:* 511
Oklahoma City, Oklahoma, *5:* 1304
Oland, Warner, *1:* 189 (ill.); *2:* 269
Olbermann, Keith, *4:* 1035
"Old Blood and Guts," *3:* 513–14
The Old Man and the Sea, 3: 697
Old Navy, *4:* 795; *5:* 1235
Old Southwest, *1:* 199
Old West, *1:* 36
Olive Oyl, *2:* 314
Oliver, Joseph "King," *1:* 72
Olsen, George, *2:* 264

Olsen, Johnny, *3:* 753
Olsen, Susan, *4:* 1027
Olympics, *1:* 3, **109–10,** 110 (ill.); *2:* 325, 473; *4:* 888; *5:* 1271, 1273 (ill.), 1274
Omaha (horse), *1:* 103
Omaha, Nebraska, *3:* 695
The Omen, 4: 829
Omerta code of silence, *4:* 935
On the Beach, 3: 620
On the Road, *3:* 641, 697, 698, **708–9**
On the Waterfront, *3:* **669–71,** 670 (ill.)
Onassis, Jackie Kennedy, *4:* 807, 1003; *5:* 1113
Once And Again, 4: 1077
One Day at a Time, 4: 1077
One Life to Live, 2: 487
O'Neal, Ryan, *3:* 672; *4:* 948
Oneidas, *4:* 1073
O'Neil, Denny, *3:* 579
O'Neill, Eugene, *1:* 35, 168; *2:* 241
O'Neill, Rose, *1:* 66
One-step (dance), *1:* 123
Online shopping, *1:* 15, 28; *4:* 795
Oomph girl, *3:* 510
Orbison, Roy, *4:* 849
Oreo cookies, *1:* 151, 181, 184 (ill.), **184–85**
Organic foods, *2:* 287
The Organization Man, *3:* **710**
Organization of the Petroleum Exporting Countries (OPEC), *4:* 1030
Oriolo, Don and Joe, *1:* 171–72
Orphans of the Storm, 2: 237
Orr, Bobby, *1:* 207
Ortega, Santos, *2:* 458
Osbourne, Ozzy, *5:* 1140
Oscar Meyer Company, *1:* 63
Osmond, Ken, *3:* 751
Oswald, Lee Harvey, *5:* 1241
Oswald the Rabbit, *2:* 270
Otis, Elisha Graves, *2:* 503
Ouija boards, *1:* **111–12,** 112 (ill.)
Our Man Flint, 5: 1238
Out, 4: 926
Outcault, Richard, *1:* 79, 81
Outdoor clothing and supplies, *1:* 155–56; *2:* 256
"Outlaw" country music, *3:* 558; *5:* 1252
The Outline of History, 2: 237
Over the Top, 1: 146
Owens, Buck, and His Buckeroos, *3:* 557; *4:* 1042
Owens, Jesse, *1:* 109; *2:* 467, **473**
Oyl, Olive, *2:* 314

P

Paar, Jack, *3:* 761–62
Pace, Harry H., *3:* 576
The Pace That Kills, 5: 1203
Pacino, Al, *4:* 966, 967 (ill.); *5:* 1203
Packard, Vance, *3:* 639
Pac-Man, *5:* **1167–68,** 1168 (ill.)
Page, Jimmy, *4:* 989
Page, Patti, *3:* 640
Paige, Leroy "Satchel," *1:* 108
Pain reliever, *2:* 374
Pajeau, Charles H., *1:* 211
Palin, Michael, *4:* 1052
Palmer, A. Mitchell, *2:* 360
Palmer, Betsy, *5:* 1127
Palmer, Jim, *2:* 470
Paltrow, Gwyneth, *4:* 1098
Pancakes and syrups, *1:* 8–9, 9 (ill.)
Pants, *3:* 658–59, 659 (ill.), 659–60; *4:* 807–9, 808 (ill.)
Pantyhose, *2:* 381
Paper cups, *1:* 14
Paperback books, *2:* **457–58;** *3:* 510
Papermate pens, *2:* 376
Papp, Joseph, *4:* 825
Parachutes, *2:* 380
Parades, *1:* 114; 252, 258, 388 (ill.)
Paralympics, *1:* 109
Paranormal, *5:* 1128–30, 1129 (ill.)
Parapsychology, *5:* 1129
The Parent Trap, 4: 1077
Parental units, *5:* 1224
Parents Music Resource Center, *5:* 1140
Paretsky, Sara, *2:* 442
Paris, France, *2:* 267
Park, *2:* 236
Park, Maud Wood, *2:* 239
Parka, quilted down, *2:* 256
Parker, Alan, *1:* 220
Parker, Bonnie, *2:* 496, 496 (ill.)
Parker, Charlie, *1:* 73; *3:* 512
Parker, Dorothy, *2:* 263, 402
Parker, Fess, *3:* 736
Parker, Peter, *4:* 873, 874
Parker, Ray, Jr., *5:* 1129
Parker, Trey, *5:* 1298
Parks, Gordon, *4:* 976
Parks, Wally, *3:* 627
Parliament/Funkadelic, *4:* 985

Parrish, Maxfield, *1:* 66
Parsons, Gram, *5:* 1252
Parsons, Louella, *2:* 307
The Partridge Family, *3:* 562–63, 634; *4:* 1027, **1054–56,** 1055 (ill.)
"Party" direct sales system, *3:* 521
Pasadena, California, *1:* 113
Passion pit, *3:* 638
Patch, Sam, *5:* 1272
Patman, Wright, *3:* 647
Patrick, Dan, *4:* 1035
Patriotism, *3:* 573; *5:* 1119
Patten, Fred, *2:* 305
Patten, George, *1:* 2
Patton, Charley, *2:* 425
Patton, Gene, *4:* 1038
Patton, George S., *3:* 513–14
Paul, Alice, *1:* 213; *4:* 1081
The Paul Harvey News, 3: 513
Paul, Les, *3:* 686
Paxson, Lowell "Bud," *5:* 1106
"Pay per view," *4:* 1029
"Payola" scandal, *3:* 685
Payton, Walter, *2:* 290
PBS. *See* Public Broadcasting System (PBS)
PC (political correctness), *5:* 1100, 1189, **1209–11,** 1210
PCs (personal computers). *See* Personal computers (PCs)
Peale, Norman Vincent, *3:* 639
Peanut Gallery, *3:* 602
Peanuts, *3:* 698, **710–12,** 711 (ill.)
Pearce, Alice, *4:* 894
Pearl Harbor, *2:* 343; *3:* 509
Pearl Jam, *5:* 1254
Pearl, Minnie, *4:* 1042
Peary, Robert, *1:* 91
Peck, Harry Thurston, *3:* 518
Pegleg Pete, *2:* 278
Pekar, Harvey, *2:* 440
Pemberton, John "Doc," *1:* 56
Pen, ballpoint, *2:* **375–76**
Penguin Books, *2:* 457
Penicillin, *2:* **356–57**
Penn, Arthur, *2:* 496
Penn, Irving, *1:* 197
Penn, Sean, *5:* 1146
Penney's. *See* J. C. Penney Company
Pennsylvania Turnpike, *3:* 776
Penske, Roger, *1:* 206
Pentagon, *3:* 621
"Pentagon Papers," *1:* 92
People, *4:* 949, **1005–7,** 1006 (ill.)
People for the Ethical Treatment of Animals (PETA), *2:* 265
The People vs. Larry Flynt, 4: 1004
People's Temple, *4:* 1074
Peppard, George, *5:* 1176, 1177 (ill.)
Peppermint Patty, *3:* 711
Pepsi-Cola Company, *1:* 7
Percolator, *3:* 510
Perez, George, *3:* 585
The Perils of Pauline, 1: 147
Perkins, Anthony, *4:* 837
Perlman, Rhea, *5:* 1178
Perot, H. Ross, *5:* 1223
Perry, Luke, *5:* 1286, 1287 (ill.)
Perry Mason, *2:* **458–59**
Perry, Matthew, *5:* 1291, 1291 (ill.)
Persian Gulf War, *5:* 1180
Personal care products
  aromatherapy, *5:* 1305
  Avon, *1:* 116
  baby, *2:* 287
  Band-Aid, *2:* 247–48
  Burma-Shave, *2:* 250–51
  Kleenex, *2:* 256–57
Personal computers (PCs), *4:* **1085–87;** *5:* 1231, 1303, 1321
  Apple Computer, *4:* 1070–71, 1071 (ill.)
  chat rooms, *5:* 1310–11
  E-mail, *5:* 1314–17, 1315 (ill.)
  hackers, *5:* 1317–18
  Internet, *5:* 1319–21, 1320 (ill.)
  Microsoft, *5:* 1231–33, 1232 (ill.)
Personal digital assistants (PDAs), *4:* 1087
Personal finance, credit cards, *3:* 647
Personal style. *See* Style
Pet rocks, *4:* 1072, 1088 (ill.), **1088–89**
Pet Sounds, 4: 842, 844–45
Peter, Harry, *3:* 584
Peter, Paul, and Mary, *4:* 841
Peterson, Arthur, *2:* 483
Petronas Towers (Kuala Lumpur, Malaysia), *2:* 503
Pets.com, *5:* 1227
Petticoat Junction, 4: 890, 893
Pettit, Robert, *1:* 211
Petty, Richard, *2:* 474
Petty, Tom, *4:* 849
Peyton Place, *3:* 639, **671–72**
The Phantom of the Opera, 2: 238
Pharmaceuticals. *See* Drugs
Phat, *5:* 1224
Philadelphia, 5: 1199
Philbin, Regis, *4:* 899; *5:* 1301, 1301 (ill.), 1301–2

Philip Morris Corporation, *1:* 2
Phillips, Irna, *2:* 483, 487
Phillips, Sam, *3:* 691
Phonograph, *1:* 71, **76–78,** 77 (ill.)
Photography, *1:* 24–25
advertising, *2:* 244–45
Brownie cameras, *1:* 10 (ill.), 10–11
stereoscopes, *1:* 8, 28–29, 29 (ill.); *3:* 675
Physical fitness, *3:* 717, 718–20; 1010–11, 1016–17
Pickens, Slim, *3:* 623; *4:* 819
Pickford, Mary, *1:* 149, 167; *2:* 237
Pierce, Jack, *2:* 394
Piercings, *5:* 1235
Pig, *4:* 786
Pigtail (Chinese), *1:* 132–33
The Pilgrim, 2: 238
The Pill, *3:* **778–79;** *4:* 943
Pinsky, Drew, *5:* 1193
Pin-up girl, *3:* 510
Pitt, Brad, *5:* 1292
Pittsburgh Pirates, *4:* 1009
Pittsburgh Steelers, *4:* 1009
Pixar, *5:* 1247, 1248
Pizza, *3:* 545, **550–51**
Planchette, *1:* 111
Planes, *2:* 346
Planet of the Apes, *4:* 815, **834–36,** 835 (ill.)
Plant, Robert, *4:* 989
Plastic, *1:* **24–26**; *3:* 520–22, 521 (ill.), 649–50
"Plastic society," *1:* 25
Platters (musical group), *3:* 640
Playboy, *3:* 639, **712–13;** *4:* 942
Playhouse 90, 3: 765
Plessy v. Ferguson, 4: 924
Plimsoll, *1:* 161
"Plop, plop, fizz, fizz," *4:* 948
"Plug and play," *4:* 1070
Plumb, Eve, *4:* 1027
The Plutocrat, 2: 237
Poe, Edgar Allan, *2:* 310, 441
Poitier, Sidney, *4:* 924
Pokémon, *5:* 1278, 1280, 1304, **1322–23,** 1323 (ill.)
Police dramas. *See also* Dramas, TV
COPS, 5: 1225
Dragnet, 3: 738–39
Miami Vice, 5: 1186–87
Police (musical group), *5:* 1102
Polio, *3:* 641
Polish Americans, *1:* 122
Political correctness (PC), *5:* 1100, 1189, **1209–11**
Political humor, *4:* 1060
Political movements, *1:* 133
Politically Incorrect, 5: 1210
Pollution, *4:* 1080
Polo shirts, Izod, *5:* 1113
Polonsky, Abraham, *3:* 773
Polyanna, 2: 237
Polyester, *1:* 25; *4:* **959–60**
Polygamy, *4:* 1074
Pong, *4:* 1010, **1019–20,** 1021
Poodle skirts, *3:* 657; *4:* 1040
Poole, Frank, *4:* 838
Poor Richard's Almanac, 5: 1162
Pop music, *3:* **560–63;** *4:* 1029
dance music, *3:* 563
Jackson, Michael, *5:* 1141–42
karaoke, *5:* 1142–43
Madonna, *5:* 1146
Manilow, Barry, *4:* 990
Monkees, *4:* 854–55, 855 (ill.)
Sinatra, Frank, *3:* 565–66
Spears, Britney, *5:* 1261, 1261 (ill.)
Streisand, Barbra, *4:* 861–62
Pop, soda, *1:* 56–58, 57 (ill.); *2:* 287–88
Popcorn snacks, *1:* 58–60, 59 (ill.)
Pope, Generoso, Jr., *3:* 707
Popeye, *2:* **314–16,** 315 (ill.); *3:* 680
Poppins, Mary, *4:* 832
Popular culture, *1:* 5; *3:* 550
Popular Mechanics, 3: 763
Popular music. *See* Pop music
Porsche, Ferdinand, *3:* 652
"The Port Huron Statement," *4:* 945
Porter, Edwin S., *1:* 38, 45–46; *2:* 415
Porter, Eleanor H., *2:* 237
Porter, Jane, *1:* 193
The Poseidon Adventure, 4: 963, 964 (ill.)
Post, Emily, *2:* 237
Post, Wilbur, *4:* 906
Postal system, *2:* 255
Postcards, *1:* **134–35**
Postmodernism, *5:* 1297
"Post-punk," alternative rock, *5:* 1253–54
Postwar period, *3:* 513–15, 610, 615–16, 625, 637
the Bomb, *3:* 618–21, 619 (ill.)
Cold War, *3:* 621–24
frozen dinners, *2:* 419–21
unidentified flying objects (UFO), *3:* 635–36, 636 (ill.)

Potts, Annie, *5:* 1129
Poverty, *4:* 928
Powell, Bud, *1:* 73
Powell, Colin, *4:* 925; *5:* 1227
Powell, William, *1:* 51
The Power of Positive Thinking, 3: 639
Power, Tyrone, *1:* 199
Powers, Austin, *5:* 1238
The Practice, 5: 1278
Pratt, Jane, *5:* 1159
Prepared foods, *2:* 419–21; *3:* 677, 680–82, 681 (ill.)
Preppy, *1:* 156; *5:* 1113, **1115–17,** 1116 (ill.)
Presley, Elvis, *3:* 561, 633, 640, 641, 683, **689–90,** 690 (ill.), 691, 740; *4:* 788; *5:* 1230, 1239
Press, freedom of, *1:* 92
Preston, John, *4:* 867
Preventative medicine, *4:* 1016
Price, Irving, *2:* 378
The Price Is Right, *3:* **753–54,** 754 (ill.)
Price, Vincent, *3:* 675
PRIDE (Personal Rights in Defense and Education), *4:* 866
Priestley, Jason, *5:* 1286, 1287 (ill.)
Prince, *5:* 1102, 1135
Prince Charles of England, *5:* 1103
Princess Diana, *4:* 1076; *5:* 1103
Princess Mononoke, 5: 1280
Print, *1:* 79–80, 187–88; *2:* 301, 433–34; *3:* 567, 697–98; *4:* 865–66, 997; *5:* 1155–56, 1265–66. *See also* Books; Fiction; Literature; Magazines; Newspapers; Novels
Private investigators. *See under* Detective stories
Prizefighters. *See* Boxing
Pro-abortion (pro-choice), *4:* 1089–91
Processed foods, *2:* 289, 419–21, 423–24
Product advertising. *See* Advertising
Product evaluation, *Good Housekeeping, 1:* 86
Product names. *See* Brand names
Product promotion, *1:* 56–60, 57 (ill.), 59 (ill.), 66. *See also under* Advertising
Production Code Association (PCA), *3:* 529
Production line (Ford), *1:* 23
Professional baseball. *See under* Baseball
Professional basketball. *See under* Basketball
Professional football. *See under* Football
Professional hockey. *See under* Hockey
Professor Quiz, 3: 741
Profiler, 4: 1093
"Progressive era," *1:* 4
Progressive Party, *1:* 145
Prohibition, *1:* 123, 213; *2:* 235, 345, **357–58,** 370, 419; *4:* 935
Pro-life, *4:* 1089–91
Prom, *2:* 345, **358–60,** 359 (ill.)
The Promised Land, 3: 518
Promotional items, *1:* 56–60, 57 (ill.), 59 (ill.), 66. *See also under* Advertising
Protestantism *1:* 115, 127–28, 138; *2:* 240
Protests, *4:* 851, 1083–85, 1084 (ill.)
Provincetown Players, *1:* 168
Provost, Jon, *3:* 541
Prozac, *5:* **1211–12,** 1304
Pryor, Richard, *4:* 952
Pseudodocumentaries, *5:* 1293
Psychedelic art and music, *4:* 842, 852, 931–32
Psycho, *4:* 788, 815, 828, **836–37**
PT Cruiser, *3:* 627
Public Broadcasting Act of 1967, *4:* 910
Public Broadcasting System (PBS), *3:* 611; *4:* 890, 908, **909–10;** *5:* 1281, 1294, 1300
Public Enemy, 2: 369, 390
Public Enemy (rap group), *4:* 929; *5:* 1124, 1135
Public speaking, *2:* 438
Publishers Weekly, 1: 187; *3:* 518
Publishing industry
  best-sellers, *3:* 517–18; *5:* 1155, 1265
  books, *2:* 241, 303–4, 309–10; *4:* 997; *5:* 1155, 1265–66
  encyclopedias, *1:* 188, 197–98
  magazines, *1:* 4; *2:* 241; *3:* 576–77, 697; *5:* 1156
  newspapers, *2:* 241; *5:* 1156
  paperback books, *2:* 457–58
  sheet music, *1:* 71
  zines, *5:* 1162–64
Pulitzer Prizes, *1:* 93; *2:* 451
Pulliam, Keshia Knight, *5:* 1182 (ill.)
Pulp Fiction, *3:* 550; *5:* **1244–45**
Pulp magazines, *2:* 301, 440, 442, **459–61,** 460 (ill.); *3:* 567

Argosy, 1: 80–81
detective fiction, *2:* 441–43
The Shadow, 2: 461–62
Tarzan, *1:* 192
Weird Tales, 2: 320–21
Zorro, *1:* 199–200, 200 (ill.)
Punk, *1:* 133–34; *3:* 687, 693; *4:* 810, 981, **991–92,** 992 (ill.); *5:* 1114, 1253, 1255
Puppets, *3:* 601–2, 603–4, 604 (ill.); *4:* 1053–54, *4:* 1062–63
Pure Food and Drug Act (1906), *1:* 53
Purple Rain, 5: 1135
Putin, Vladimir, *5:* 1316
Putnam, Robert, *3:* 588
Putt-Putt Golf, *2:* 333–34
Puzo, Mario, *4:* 935, 966
Puzzles, *2:* 327; *5:* 1169 (ill.), 1169–70
Pyle, Denver, *4:* 1034
Pyle, Ernie, *3:* 514

Q

Quaker Oats Company, *1:* 7, 8–9, 9 (ill.)
Quant, Mary, *2:* 381; *4:* 807, 812
Quarrymen, *4:* 846
Queen Elizabeth, 1: 146
Queen, Ellery, *2:* 441
Queen Latifah, *5:* 1135
Queen of Sheba, 2: 264
Questel, Mae, *2:* 388
Quilt, AIDS Memorial, *5:* 1199, 1199 (ill.)
Quilted down parka, *2:* 256
Quinn, Don, *2:* 482
Quinn, Martha, *5:* 1148 (ill.)
Quinn, Patricia, *4:* 972 (ill.), 973
Quint, James A., *2:* 248
Quo Vadis, 1: 147
QVC, *5:* 1106

R

Rabinowitz, Jakie, *2:* 275
Raccoon coats, *2:* **264–65**
Raccoon-skin caps, *2:* 265; *3:* 736
Race relations, *5:* 1123–25, 1124 (ill.)
Racer X, *4:* 918
Racial profiling, *4:* 925
Racism and racial segregation, *1:* 4–5, 13, 42, 46, 91, 102, 188, 213; *2:* 268; *3:* 592, 599–600, 617; *4:* 922–25, 928
"Radical chic," *5:* 1156
Radio, *2:* 261, 301, **339–43,** 340 (ill.), 369–70, 425, 467, 477–78; *3:* 514, 597, 683, 691, 728; *4:* 890, 1024; *5:* 1175–76
advertising, *1:* 18–19, 66
AM radio, *3:* 685; *5:* 1175–76
CB radio, *4:* 1030–31, 1031 (ill.)
disc jockeys, *2:* 343; *3:* 684–85
"firsts," *2:* 238–39, 328
FM radio, *2:* 343; *4:* 1024; *5:* 1175
Fu Manchu, *1:* 189
Grand Ole Opry, 2: 297–98; *3:* 553
and phonographs, *1:* 78
rock and roll, *3:* 691
shock radio, *5:* 1188–90, 1189 (ill.)
soap operas, *2:* 487
sound effects, *2:* 477
talk radio, *2:* 343; *5:* 1175–76, 1193–94
Top 40, *3:* 694–95
transistor radios, *3:* 763–64
TV show sources, *2:* 341–42
Radio City Music Hall, *1:* 177; *2:* 408–9, 409 (ill.)
Radio drama, *2:* 342
Radio shows
Abbott and Costello, *3:* 530–31, 531 (ill.)
Amos 'n' Andy, 2: 478–81, 479 (ill.)
Fibber McGee and Molly, 2: 482–83
Guiding Light, 2: 483–84
The Lone Ranger, 2: 485–86
Perry Mason, 2: 458–59
The Shadow, 2: 461–62
soap operas, *2:* 486–88
Radios, *2:* 239; *3:* **763–64**
Radner, Gilda, *4:* 1059, 1059 (ill.), 1060
Rado, James, *4:* 824
Rafelson, Bob, *4:* 854
Raggedy Ann and Raggedy Andy, *1:* 202, **208–9,** 209 (ill.)
Ragni, Gerome, *4:* 824
Ragtime, *1:* 5, 71, 75–76
Raiders of the Lost Ark, 5: 1101
Railroad, national, *2:* 255
Rainbows, *4:* 1076
Rainey, Ma, *1:* 71; *2:* 294 (ill.), 295
Rainey, Puck, *5:* 1293
Rains, Claude, *3:* 532
Raise the Titanic, 1: 231
Ralston, Henry W., *2:* 447

Rambo movies, *3:* 623; *5:* 1119, **1131–33,** 1132 (ill.)
Rambova, Natasha, *2:* 280
Ramis, Harold, *5:* 1129, 1129 (ill.)
Ramones, *4:* 991
Ranch house, *2:* **502**
Rand, Bill, *4:* 866
Randall, Tony, *4:* 833
Randolph, Joyce, *3:* 745 (ill.), 746
Ranma ½, 5: 1280
Rap and hip-hop, *5:* 1135, **1149–50,** 1262
LL Cool J (James Todd Smith), *5:* 1145–46
Run-DMC, *5:* 1151 (ill.), 1151–52
2 Live Crew, *5:* 1152
Rashad, Phylicia, *5:* 1181, 1182 (ill.)
Rather, Dan, *3:* 606
Ratings system (movies), *4:* 815
Ratzenberger, John, *5:* 1178, 1178 (ill.)
Raves, *4:* 809; *5:* **1259–60,** 1260 (ill.), 1313–14
Rawlings, Marjorie Kinnan, *2:* 369
Raymond, Alex, *2:* 450
Raymond, Charles, *4:* 1083
Rayon, *1:* 25
"Reach out and touch someone," *5:* 1100
Reader's Digest, *2:* 301, **316–17**
Reading, *2:* 433. *See also* Books; Fiction; Literature; Magazines; Newspapers; Novels
Dick and Jane readers, *2:* 443–44
Little Blue Books, *2:* 309–10
Reader's Digest, 2: 316–17
Reagan Doctrine, *5:* 1101
Reagan, Nancy, *5:* 1100, 1113
Reagan, Ronald, *1:* 219; *4:* 978, 1076, 1091; *5:* 1099, 1103, 1105, 1113, 1119, 1197, 1198, 1223
The Real World, *5:* 1148, 1278, **1292–94,** 1293 (ill.)
Reality TV, *1:* 45; *3:* 612; *5:* 1292, 1293, **1294–96,** 1295 (ill.)
Candid Camera, 3: 733–34
The Real World, 5: 1278, 1292–94, 1293 (ill.)
Reasoner, Harry, *3:* 606
Rebagliati, Ross, *5:* 1273 (ill.)
Rebel Without a Cause, 1: 163; *3:* 617, 664
Rebellion/revolution (social), *1:* 133–34
Reclining chairs, *2:* 257
Reconstruction, after Civil War, *1:* 168–70, 169 (ill.)
Recorded books, *5:* 1265
Recording technology. *See* Sound-recording technologies
Recreational drugs, *5:* 1313–14
Red Dawn, 3: 623; *5:* 1119
"Red Menace," *3:* 622–23
Red scare, *1:* 150; *2:* **360–61**
Redford, Robert, *4:* 956
Reed, Donna, *3:* 539, 539 (ill.)
Reed, Robert, *4:* 1026
Reefer Madness, 4: 936
Reeve, Christopher, *2:* 465
Reeves, George, *2:* 465
Reference books, *1:* 188, 197–98
Refrigerators, *1:* 126, 181, 222 (ill.), **222–23;** *2:* 420
Regehr, Duncan, *1:* 200
Regency TR-1 (Regency Electronics), *3:* 763
The Regent (New York City), *1:* 177
Regret (horse), *1:* 103
Reid, John, *2:* 485
Reiner, Rob, *4:* 1024
Reitman, Ivan, *5:* 1129
Relationships, Divorce, *4:* 1075–77
Religion, *1:* 115
Branch Davidians, *5:* 1307
cults, *4:* 1069–70, 1073–74
evangelism, *1:* 127–28
Ouija boards, *1:* 111–12, 112 (ill.)
religious right, *5:* 1103
Scopes Monkey trial, *2:* 363–64
Sunday, Billy, *1:* 115, 127, 138; *2:* 240
R.E.M., *5:* 1253
Remarque, Erich Maria, *2:* 237
Rembrandts, *5:* 1292
Rent, 5: 1237
Replacements, *5:* 1253
"Replicants," *5:* 1122
Repossessed, 4: 965
Reproductive rights, *4:* 941
Republican Party, *1:* 145
Reserve Clause, *1:* 100
Reserve Officers' Training Corps (ROTC), *4:* 945, 1084
Reservoir Dogs, 5: 1244
Resor, Stanley, *1:* 18
"Respect," *4:* 789
Retail shopping, *1:* 213; *3:* 643–44. *See also* Stores, e.g., Macy's
Abercrombie & Fitch, *5:* 1235–36
department stores, *2:* 254–55

dime stores, *1:* 8, 11–13, 12 (ill.)
Eddie Bauer, *2:* 256
Fuller Brush Company, *1:* 14–15
Gap, *4:* 795–96
HSN (Home Shopping Network), *5:* 1106–7
J.Crew, *5:* 1109
Kmart, *4:* 797–99
L. L. Bean, *1:* 155–56
Mall of America, *5:* 1230 (ill.), 1230–31
Sears, Roebuck catalog, *1:* 2, 8, 26–28, 27 (ill.)
Wall Drug, *2:* 505–7, 506 (ill.)
Wal-Mart, *4:* 802–4, 803 (ill.)
Woolworth's stores, *1:* 8, 12 (ill.), 12–13
Rettig, Tommy, *3:* 541
Retton, Mary Lou, *2:* 290
Return of the Jedi, 4: 979; *5:* 1101, 1119
Reuben, David, *4:* 948
Reuben, Gloria, *5:* 1288–89
Revere, Ann, *3:* 773
Revival meetings, *1:* 127
Revues, musical, *1:* 50–52, 146
Rey, Hans Augusto (H. A.), and Margaret, *3:* 574
Reynolds, Burt, *4:* 868
Reynolds, Joshua, *4:* 958
Reynolds, Milton, *2:* 376
Rhodes, James, *4:* 1084
Rhyming signs, Burma-Shave, *2:* 250–51
Rhythm and blues (R&B), *3:* **564–65,** 684, 691; *4:* 846; *5:* 1141–42, 1262
Ricardo, Lucy and Ricky, *3:* 747
Rice, Anne, *2:* 393
Rice, Grantland, *2:* 328
Rice Krispies, *1:* 21
Rice, Linda Johnson, *3:* 577
Rice, Thomas D., *1:* 40
Rice, Tim, *5:* 1243
Rich, Robert, *3:* 773
Richards, Keith, *4:* 858, 858 (ill.)
Richards, Michael, *5:* 1296, 1297 (ill.)
Richie, John Simon (Sid Vicious), *4:* 991, 992, 993
Rich's department store (Atlanta, Georgia), *2:* 255
Rickey, Branch, *1:* 98; *3:* 592
Riggs, Bobby, *4:* 1009
"Right On," *4:* 786
The Right Stuff, 4: 940
Rimes, LeAnn, *5:* 1251
Ringling Bros. and Barnum & Bailey Circus, *1:* 3, 150, **223–25,** 224 (ill.)
Rings, Mood, *4:* 958 (ill.), **958–59**
Ripa, Kelly, *4:* 900
Ripken, Cal, Jr., *1:* 99; *2:* 290, 470; *5:* 1271
Ripley, Robert L., *2:* 318
Ripley's Believe It or Not!, *2:* **318–19**
The Rise and Fall of the Third Reich, 4: 786
The Rise of David Levinsky, 1: 146
Ritchie, Lionel, *5:* 1144
RKO Radio Pictures, *3:* 533, 534
Road culture, *1:* 23; *2:* 250–51, 362–63
Road rage, *5:* **1212–13**
Road Runner and Wile E. Coyote, *3:* **606–8,** 607 (ill.)
Road system, *3:* 775–76
"The Roaring Twenties, *2:* 235, 351
Robards, Jason, *2:* 350; *3:* 609
Robbins, Harold, *4:* 997
The Robe, 3: 511, 518, 661
Roberts, Julia, *2:* 273
Roberts, Oral, *1:* 127
Roberts, Parnell, *4:* 896
Roberts, Tanya, *4:* 1032
Roberts, Xavier, *5:* 1200
Robertson, Pat, *1:* 127
Robin, *2:* 434
Robinson, Bartlett, *2:* 458
Robinson, Edward G., *2:* 383
Robinson, Frank, *4:* 1009
Robinson, Jackie, *1:* 98; *3:* 514, 587, **592,** 717; *4:* 924
Robinson, Max, *3:* 606
Robinson, Smokey, *2:* 495; *4:* 842
Robocop, 5: 1119
Rock and roll, *1:* 77–78; *3:* 561, 565, 641–42, 683, **690–94,** 691 (ill.); *4:* 791, 820, 841; *5:* 1255, 1258, 1262
alternative rock, *5:* 1253–54
American Bandstand, 3: 731–32, 732 (ill.)
Beatles, *4:* 846–48, 847 (ill.)
blues roots, *2:* 294, 296
electric guitar, *3:* 686–88, 687 (ill.)
Freed, Alan, *3:* 684–85
hard rock, *3:* 687; *4:* 981
heavy metal, *5:* 1139–41, 1140 (ill.)
Jackson, Michael, *5:* 1141–42

KISS, *4:* 987–88, 988 (ill.)
Led Zeppelin, *4:* 989–90
Madonna, *5:* 1146
new wave music, *3:* 693; *4:* 981
pop-rock. *See* Pop music
Presley, Elvis, *3:* 689–90, 690 (ill.), 691
punk, *4:* 981, 991–92, 992 (ill.)
Rolling Stones, *4:* 857–59, 858 (ill.)
Sex Pistols, *4:* 991, 992–94, 993 (ill.)
teen idols, *3:* 633–34
"Rock Around the Clock," *3:* 640
Rock festivals
Farm Aid, *5:* 1138 (ill.), 1138–39
Live Aid, *5:* 1143–45, 1144 (ill.)
Lollapalooza and Lilith Fair, *5:* 1256–58, 1257 (ill.)
Woodstock, *4:* 862–63, 863 (ill.)
Rockefeller Center (New York City), *2:* 493
Rockettes, *2:* **408–9,** 409 (ill.)
Rockne, Knute, *1:* 201
Rockwell, Norman, *1:* 66, 93–94, 150, 159, **191–92,** 192 (ill.)
Rockwell, Rick, *5:* 1296
Rocky, *4:* 948, **970–71**
The Rocky Horror Picture Show, *4:* 962, **971–73,** 972 (ill.)
Roddy, Rod, *3:* 754
Roden, Ben, *5:* 1307
Rodgers, Bill, *4:* 1017
Rodgers, Jimmie, *2:* **298–99,** 425; *3:* 556
Rodgers, Richard, *4:* 788
Roe v. Wade, *4:* 1069, **1089–91,** 1090 (ill.)
Roebuck, Alvah C., *1:* 27
Roger and Me, 1: 131
Rogers, Anthony "Buck." *See* Buck Rogers
Rogers, Fred (Mr. Rogers), *4:* 908–9, 909 (ill.)
Rogers, Ginger, *2:* 383
Rogers, Roy, *2:* 426; *3:* 556
Rogers, Wayne, *4:* 1050
Rogers, Will, *1:* 51, **178–79**
Rohmer, Sax, *1:* 188
Roller coasters, *1:* 121, **136,** 137 (ill.); *3:* 768, 769; *5:* 1230, 1250
Rolling Stone, *4:* 787, 866, **871–72,** 872 (ill.)
Rolling Stones, *3:* 687; *4:* 841, **857–59,** 858 (ill.), 951
Rollins, Jack, *3:* 703
The Romance of Helen Trent, 2: 487
Rombauer, Irma, *2:* 421
"Romp," *4:* 854
Rooney, Mickey, *2:* 385 (ill.), 385–86; *3:* 665
Roosevelt, Franklin D., *1:* 94, 178; *2:* 255, 342, 354, 372, 419, 425, 477, 478; *3:* 619
New Deal, *2:* 367–68, 493, 494, 501; *3:* 509
Roosevelt, Theodore, *1:* 2, 3, 7, 30, 145, 158; *3:* 624; *4:* 1079
Roost, *3:* 510
Roots, *4:* 949, 1057 (ill.), **1057–58**
Ropin' the Wind, 5: 1226, 1251
The Rosary, 1: 146
Rose, Billy, *1:* 12
Rose Bowl, *1:* 95, **113–14;** *2:* 239
Rose, Pete, *1:* 98, 100; *4:* 1009; *5:* 1165
Roseanne, *5:* 1175, **1187–88**
Roseland Ballroom Orchestra, *2:* 427
Rosenberg, Ethel and Julius, *3:* 641
Rosenberg, William, *3:* 546
Ross, Diana, *4:* 842
Ross, Harold, *2:* 312
Ross, Katharine, *4:* 823
Ross, Marion, *4:* 1040
Roswell, New Mexico, *3:* 635
Roth, Henry, *4:* 928
Roth, Lillian, *3:* 759–60
Rothafel, Samuel "Roxy," *2:* 408
Rotten, Johnny (John Lydon), *4:* 992, 993, 993 (ill.)
Roundtree, Richard, *4:* 961, 976–77, 977 (ill.)
Route 66, *2:* **361–63,** 362 (ill.)
Rowan & Martin's Laugh-In, *4:* 788, **911–12,** 912 (ill.)
Rowan, Dan, *4:* 911
Rowlf the Dog, *4:* 1053
Rowling, J. K., *5:* 1225, 1265–66, 1267
Royal Oak, Michigan, *2:* 342
Rozelle, Pete, *2:* 335
Rubik, Erno, *5:* 1169, 1169 (ill.), 1169–70
Rubik's Cube, *5:* 1169 (ill.), **1169–70**
Rubin, Rick, *5:* 1145
Rudolph the Red-Nosed Reindeer, *2:* 255; *3:* **581–82,** 704
Rueckheim, Frederick William and Louis, *1:* 59–60
The Ruff and Ready Show, 4: 914
Ruffin, David, *4:* 857 (ill.)

Rumrunner, *2:* 236
Run-DMC, *5:* 1102, 1104, 1135, 1151 (ill.), **1151–52**
Rural life, *2:* 236–40; *4:* 890, 893, 1028, 1043
The Andy Griffith Show, 4: 890–91
The Beverly Hillbillies, 4: 891–93, 892 (ill.)
The Dukes of Hazzard, 4: 1034
Little House on the Prairie, 4: 1023, 1043–45, 1044 (ill.)
The Waltons, 4: 1066–67
Rushmore, Mount, *3:* 513
Russell, Bill, *3:* 590, 717; *4:* 878
Ruth, Babe, *1:* 201, **210;** *2:* 240, 241, 467, 468; *4:* 1010
Rutherford, Ann, *2:* 385 (ill.)
Rutherford, Maude Russell, *2:* 351
Ruthledge, John, *2:* 483
Ryan, Irene, *4:* 891, 892 (ill.)
Ryan, Nolan, *1:* 98; *2:* 470
Ryan, Robert, *5:* 1245
Rydell, Bobby, *3:* 633, 732 (ill.)

S

S&H Green Stamps, *3:* 651–52
Sabrina, the Teenage Witch, *3:* 569
Sad Sack, *3:* 511
Safe sex, *4:* 1083
Sagan, Carl, *5:* 1100
Sailor Jack, *1:* 60
Sailor Moon, 5: 1278
Sailors, bell-bottoms, *4:* 808
St. Elmo's Fire, 5: 1102
St. Louis, Missouri, *2:* 288
St. Moritz, Switzerland, *1:* 109
The Saint Valentine's Day Massacre, 2: 350
Sales. *See also* Advertising; Direct marketing
cable TV, *5:* 1106
catalog, *5:* 1109. *See also* Catalogs
IBM, *5:* 1108
"pyramid," *4:* 811
Salinger, J. D., *3:* 617, 697; *4:* 865
Salk, Jonas, *3:* 641
Salon.com, *5:* 1265
Salt-N-Pepa, *5:* 1135
Saltzman, Harry, *4:* 830
Sam 'n' Henry, 2: 238–39
Samples, Alvin "Junior," *4:* 1042
San Francisco, California, *2:* 372; *4:* 853, 929–30, 930 (ill.)
San Francisco Chronicle, 5: 1158
Sandburg, Carl, *1:* 150
Sandler, Adam, *4:* 1060
Sandwiches, *1:* 62–64; *3:* 548–50, 677–78, 680
Sanford and Son, 4: 949–50, 1023; *5:* 1181
Sanger, Margaret, *1:* 149; *2:* 310; *3:* 778
Santa Claus, *2:* 255
Saran Wrap, *3:* 643, **649–50**
Sarandon, Susan, *4:* 972
Sarazen, Gene, *2:* 325
Sargent, Dick, *4:* 894
Sassy, *3:* 583; *5:* **1159–60**
Satellites, *3:* **779–80;** *4:* 939; *5:* 1175
Satirical humor
Beavis and Butt-Head, 5: 1285
MAD Magazine, *3:* 704–6, 705 (ill.)
Monty Python's Flying Circus, 4: 1051–52
Saturday Evening Post, *1:* **93–94,** 94 (ill.); *2:* 505; *4:* 866
Saturday morning cartoons, *3:* 600, 608; *4:* **912–16,** 913 (ill.), 1061; *5:* 1322
The Alvin Show, 3: 730
Godzilla's *Super Power Hour, 3:* 667
Pokémon, *5:* 1322–23, 1323 (ill.)
Rambo, *5:* 1133
Schoolhouse Rock, 4: 1060–62
Teenage Mutant Ninja Turtles, *5:* 1194–95, 1195 (ill.)
Saturday Night Fever, *1:* 124; *4:* **974–75,** 975 (ill.), 982, 983, 984
Saturday Night Live, *4:* **1058–60,** 1059 (ill.); *5:* 1249
Saunders, Jeraldine, *4:* 1045
Savoy Ballroom (New York City), *2:* 345
Scarface, 5: 1203
Scents, *5:* 1305
Schafer, Natalie, *4:* 904
Schaffner, Franklin, *4:* 835
Scheider, Roy, *4:* 968
Schelle, Helen, *2:* 378
Schenectady, New York, *3:* 610
Scherman, Harry, *2:* 303
Schiffer, Claudia, *5:* 1250 (ill.)
Schilling, Mary Kaye, *5:* 1159
Schine, G. David, *3:* 770
Schlessinger, Laura, *2:* 343; *5:* 1193

Schmeling, Max, *2:* 471
Schmidt, Mike, *2:* 470
Schneider, Bert, *4:* 854
Schneider, John, *4:* 1034
Schoedsack, Ernest B., *2:* 404
Schoolhouse Rock, *4:* 915, **1060–62**
Schreck, Max, *2:* 393; *4:* 828
Schulberg, Budd, *3:* 670
Schultz, Dwight, *5:* 1176, 1177 (ill.)
Schultz, Howard, *5:* 1110
Schulz, Charles, *3:* 698, 710–12, 711 (ill.)
Schuster's Department Store (Milwaukee, Wisconsin), *3:* 651
Schwartz, Sherwood, *4:* 904, 1026
Schwimmer, David, *5:* 1291, 1291 (ill.)
Science fiction, *4:* 961
  Blade Runner, 5: 1122–23
  Buck Rogers, 2: 304–6, 305 (ill.)
  A Clockwork Orange, 4: 962–63
  The Day the Earth Stood Still, 3: 661–63, 662 (ill.)
  Doc Savage, *2:* 446–48
  Dr. Strangelove, 4: 818–19
  Dune, 4: 868–69
  E.T.: The Extra-Terrestrial, 5: 1125–26
  Flash Gordon, 2: 449–51, 450 (ill.)
  Ghostbusters, 5: 1128–30, 1129 (ill.)
  Godzilla, *3:* 666 (ill.), 666–67
  Jurassic Park, 5: 1268–70, 1271 (ill.)
  Planet of the Apes, 4: 834–36, 835 (ill.)
  The Rocky Horror Picture Show, 4: 971–73, 972 (ill.)
  Star Trek, 4: 918–20
  Star Wars, 4: 977–80, 978 (ill.)
  The Twilight Zone, 3: 764–66
  2001: A Space Odyssey, *4:* 838, 839 (ill.)
  unidentified flying objects (UFO), *3:* 635–36, 636 (ill.)
  The War of the Worlds, 2: 370, 489–90, 490 (ill.)
  Weird Tales, 2: 320–21
"Scientific management," *1:* 153
Scopes, John, *2:* 239, 364
Scopes Monkey trial, *2:* 239, **363–64**
Scott Foresman and Company, *2:* 443
Scott, George C., *4:* 819, 965
Scott, Lizabeth, *5:* 1245
Scott, Ridley, *5:* 1122
Scott, Stuart, *4:* 1036
Scott, Willard, *3:* 760
Scouting, *1:* **226–28,** 227 (ill.)
Scrabble, *3:* **592–94,** 593 (ill.)
Scragg, Daisy Mae, *2:* 455
Scream, *4:* 829; *5:* 1237, **1245–47,** 1246 (ill.)
Screen Gems, *4:* 841
Screwball comedies, *2:* 399–400
Scruggs, Earl, *3:* 554; *4:* 891
SDS (Students for a Democratic Society), *4:* **945–46**
Sea Lion Park (Coney Island, New York), *1:* 121; *3:* 768
Sea Wolf, 1: 88
Seances, *1:* 111
The Searchers, 4: 979
Sears, Richard W., *1:* 27
Sears, Roebuck catalog, *1:* 2, 8, **26–28,** 27 (ill.), 117
Sears Tower, *5:* 1230
Seattle, Washington, *5:* 1110, 1255
Seaver, Tom, *2:* 470
"Second-hand smoke," *2:* 253
Secret Agent X-9, 3: 624
Secretariat (horse), *1:* 104
See It Now, 3: 641
Seeger, Pete, *4:* 851
Segal, Erich, *4:* 948; *5:* 1115
Segar, Elzie Crisler, *2:* 314
Segregation, *4:* 922–24. *See also* Racism and racial segregation
Seinfeld, *5:* 1225, 1277, **1296–98,** 1297 (ill.)
Seinfeld, Jerry, *5:* 1277, 1296, 1297 (ill.)
Selchow and Righter Company, *5:* 1170
Selective Serotonin Reuptake Inhibitors (SSRIs), *5:* 1211–12
Selena, *5:* 1251, 1263
Self improvement, *4:* 951, 958
  Carnegie, Dale, *2:* 438–39
  Chautauqua movement, *1:* 115, 118–20, 119 (ill.)
  Men Are from Mars, Women Are from Venus, 5: 1224–25
  twelve-step programs, *2:* 504–5
Self-publishing, *5:* 1162–64
Selig Studios, *2:* 400
Sellers, Peter, *4:* 819
Selznick, David O., *1:* 219; *2:* 396, 398
Selznick, Myron, *2:* 398
Semiao, Ron, *5:* 1273

Senate Permanent Subcommittee on Investigations, *3:* 769
Sendak, Maurice, *4:* 865
Sennett, Mack, *1:* 147, 175
"Sensational" magazines, *1:* 195–96
Sensationalism (vaudeville), *1:* 49
The Sensuous Woman, 4: 942
September 11, 2001, terrorist attacks, *2:* 503–4; *3:* 621
Sergeant York, 2: 392
Serial killers, *4:* **1091–93,** 1092 (ill.)
Serling, Rod, *3:* 764–65
Serotonin, *5:* 1211
Sesame Street, *4:* 890, 910, 1053, 1061, **1062–63**
Seuss. *See* Dr. Seuss
Seven, 3: 537–38
Seven Days in May, 4: 787
The Seven Year Itch, 3: 667
Seventeen: A Tale of Youth and the Baxter Family, Especially William, 3: 582
Seventeen (magazine), *3:* **582–83**
Seventh-Day Adventists, *5:* 1307
78-rpm record, *3:* 559
77 Sunset Strip, 3: 642
7-Up, *2:* **287–88**
Seville, David, *3:* 730
Sex, *4:* 1082–83; *5:* 1259–60, 1260 (ill.), 1281
Sex and the Single Girl, 4: 942
Sex Pistols, *4:* 991, **992–94,** 993 (ill.)
Sex symbols, *2:* 372; *3:* 510, 667–68; *5:* 1284
"Sexploitation" magazines, *4:* 1002–4
Sexual Behavior in the Human Female, 3: 639; *4:* 942
Sexual Behavior in the Human Male, 4: 942
Sexual revolution, *4:* 812, **941–44,** 1094
  bra, *1:* 159–61
  Cosmopolitan, 4: 867–68
  The Joy of Sex, 4: 1082–83
  the Pill, *3:* 778–79
  T-shirts, *1:* 163
  Twister, *4:* 886
Sexually transmitted diseases (STDs), *3:* 779; *4:* 944, **1093–94**
Sgt. Pepper's Lonely Hearts Club Band, 3: 693; *4:* 789, 842, 847, 931
Shadburne, Susan, *2:* 360
The Shadow, *2:* **461–62**
Shaft, *4:* 961, **976–77,** 977 (ill.)
Shakers, *4:* 1073
Shakespeare, William, *2:* 384; *3:* 608, 676
Shakur, Tupac, *5:* 1150
Shallek, Alan J., *3:* 575
Shane, *3:* **673–74**
Shankar, Ravi, *4:* 931
Sharecroppers, *2:* 493
Sharman, Jim, *4:* 973
Sharp, Zerna, *2:* 444
Shatner, William, *4:* 919, 919 (ill.)
Shaw, Bernard, *3:* 606
Shaw, Clay, *5:* 1241
Shaw, George Bernard, *2:* 480
Shaw, Robert, *4:* 969, 969 (ill.)
Shaw, Wilbur, *1:* 206
Shawn, William, *2:* 312
"Shebas," *2:* 237, 264. *See also* Flappers
Sheet music publishing industry, *1:* 71
The Sheik, 2: 236, 280
"Sheiks," *2:* 237, 261, 264
Sheldon, Charles M., *5:* 1328
Shelley, Mary, *2:* 394; *5:* 1114
Shepard, Alan, *4:* 939
Shepard, Ernest H., *2:* 322
Shepard, Vonda, *5:* 1279 (ill.)
Sheppard, Sam, *4:* 902
Sherman Antitrust Act of 1890, *1:* 7
She's So Unusual, 5: 1102
Shining Time Station, 5: 1278
Shirer, William, *3:* 597; *4:* 786
Shirts, *1:* 158–59, 159 (ill.), 163–64
"Shock jocks," *5:* 1189, 1193
Shock radio, *5:* **1188–90,** 1189 (ill.)
Shoemaker, Edwin J., *2:* 257
Shoes and footwear
  Bean boot, *1:* 156
  Doc Martens, *4:* 809–10
  Nike, *1:* 162; *4:* 799–801, 800 (ill.)
  tennis shoes, *1:* 157, 161–62
Shoots-the-Chutes, *1:* 121
Shopping
  Abercrombie & Fitch, *5:* 1235–36
  department stores, *2:* 254–55
  dime stores, *1:* 8, 11–13, 12 (ill.)
  Fuller Brush Company, *1:* 14–15
  Home Shopping Network (HSN), *5:* 1106–7

J.Crew, *5:* 1109
mail-order. *See* Catalogs and under specific retailer, e.g., Sears, Roebuck catalog
Mall of America, *5:* 1230 (ill.), 1230–31
postwar, *3:* 643–44
Sears, Roebuck catalog, *1:* 2, 8, 26–28, 27 (ill.)
Woolworth's stores, *1:* 8, 12 (ill.), 12–13
Shopping incentives, *3:* 651–52
Short hair, *1:* 132–33
Show Boat, 2: 267
Shower scene, *4:* 837
Showgirls, *1:* 50, 51
Shuffle Along, 2: 351
Shulman, Max, *3:* 737
Shuster, Joe, *2:* 464
Shute, Nevil, *3:* 620
Sicily, *4:* 934
Siegel, Benjamin "Bugsy," *3:* 514, 628
Siegel, Jerry, *2:* 464
Si-Fan, *1:* 188
Signs, Road, *2:* 250–51, 505–6
The Silence of the Lambs, 3: 625; *4:* 829, 1092
Silent movies, *1:* **44–47,** 45 (ill.); *2:* 275, 400–401
The Birth of a Nation, 1: 168–70, 169 (ill.)
Chaplin, Charlie, *1:* 170–71
Gish, Lillian, *1:* 174
Silent Spring, 4: 787, 1079–80
Silicon Valley, California, *5:* 1229
Silly Symphonies, 2: 270–71
Silverheels, Jay, *2:* 485
Silverstein, Charles, *4:* 1083
Silverstein, Shel, *5:* 1100
Simmons, Gene, *4:* 950 (ill.), 987
Simmons, Joseph "Run," *5:* 1151, 1151 (ill.)
Simmons, William Joseph, *1:* 219
Simon and Garfunkel, *4:* 841, **859–60**
Simon, Joe, *3:* 573
Simon, Neil, *4:* 816, 833
Simon, Paul, *1:* 216; *4:* 859–60
Simpson, Bart, *3:* 723
Simpson, Nicole Brown, *5:* 1325
Simpson, O. J., *4:* 1009; *5:* 1180, 1227, 1304, 1324 (ill.), **1324–26**
Simpson, Wallis Warfield, *4:* 1076
The Simpsons, *4:* 1061; *5:* **1190–93,** 1191 (ill.), 1225, 1277
Sinatra, Frank, *2:* 427; *3:* 512–13, 524, 553, 561, **565–66,** 633, 762 (ill.); *5:* 1123
Sinclair, Upton, *1:* 2
Singers
Baker, Josephine, *2:* 267–68
Dylan, Bob, *3:* 693; *4:* 788, 841, 848–49, 946; *5:* 1138
Holiday, Billie, *2:* 428
Jackson, Michael, *5:* 1141–42
Johnson, Robert, *2:* 428–29
King, B. B., *2:* 296; *3:* 688
LL Cool J, *5:* 1102, 1135, 1145–46, 1150
Madonna, *5:* 1146
Manilow, Barry, *4:* 981, 990
Presley, Elvis, *3:* 689–90
Rodgers, Jimmie, *2:* 298–99
Simon and Garfunkel, *4:* 859–60
Sinatra, Frank, *3:* 565–66
Spears, Britney, *5:* 1261
Streisand, Barbra, *4:* 861–62
Singles bars, *4:* 944
Singleton, Penny, *2:* 438
Siodmak, Robert, *3:* 537
Sitcoms, *2:* 482; *3:* 612, **754–56;** *5:* 1289, 1296. *See also* Comedies, TV; specific TV sitcom, e.g., *All in the Family*
Sitting Bull, *1:* 37
Situation comedies (TV sitcoms). *See* Sitcoms
60 Minutes, *4:* **916–17;** *5:* 1101
The $64,000 Question, *3:* 640, **757–58,** 758 (ill.)
Skateboarding, *3:* 717–18, **722–24,** 723 (ill.)
Skelton, Red, *1:* 15; *3:* 729
Skin cancer, *4:* 1098
Skin magazines, *3:* 712
Skinheads, *4:* 809; *5:* 1198, **1214–15**
Skull and Roses, 4: 853
Skylab, 4: 939
Skyscrapers, *2:* 352–53, 493–94, 499, **502–4;** *5:* 1272
"Slackers," *5:* 1206
Slang and slogans, *1:* 2, 18, 21; *2:* 236, 289, 368; *3:* 510, 638; *4:* 786, 948, 1030–31; *5:* 1224
A Clockwork Orange, 4: 962–63
Coca-Cola, *1:* 58
Slapstick, *2:* 412–14, 413 (ill.)
Slashers, *5:* 1119, 1127–28
Slate.com, *5:* 1265
Slavery, *4:* 1057 (ill.), 1057–58
Sleet, Moneta, Jr., *3:* 577
Slinky, *3:* **594–96,** 595 (ill.)
Sloan, Alfred, *1:* 130

Slogans. *See* Slang and slogans
Smackdown!, 5: 1173
Smallville, 2: 465
Smart, David, *2:* 448
"Smells Like Teen Spirit," *5:* 1226
Smiley face, *4:* **1094–95**
Smith, Al, *2:* 238
Smith, Bessie, *2:* 295
Smith, Denis Nayland, *1:* 188
Smith, Edward John, *1:* 230
Smith, Jaclyn, *4:* 1032, 1033 (ill.)
Smith, James Todd. *See* LL Cool J
Smith, Kate, *1:* 232
Smith, Mamie, *2:* 295
Smith, Robert E., *3:* 601
Smith, Will, *5:* 1150
Smiths, *5:* 1253
Smoking, Cigarettes, *2:* 252, 253, 259 (ill.), 259–60
The Smothers Brothers Comedy Hour, 4: 889
Snack food. *See also* Fast food
  Cracker Jack, *1:* 58–60, 59 (ill.)
  hot dogs, *1:* 62–64
  ice-cream cone, *1:* 64–65
  Jell-O, *1:* 65–66
  pizza, *3:* 550–51
"Snail mail," *5:* 1314
Snap! Crackle! and Pop! gnomes, *1:* 21
"Sneaker game" (football), *2:* 335
Sneakers, *1:* 157, 161–62; *4:* 799–801, 800 (ill.)
Sneva, Tom, *1:* 204
Snoop Dogg, *5:* 1150
Snoopy, *3:* 711
Snoopy Sniffer, *2:* 378
Snow White and the Seven Dwarfs, *2:* 272, 369, 384, **410–11,** 411 (ill.)
Snowboarding, *5:* 1272, 1273 (ill.)
Soap, 2: 488
Soap operas, *2:* 477, **486–88**
  Brenda Starr, Reporter, 3: 571–72
  Dallas, 5: 1183–85, 1184 (ill.)
  Guiding Light, 2: 483–84
  Peyton Place, 3: 671–72
Soapdish, 2: 488
"Soccer mom," *5:* 1208
Soccer, women's, *5:* 1271
Social activism, *2:* 355 (ill.), 355–56; *4:* 921
Social class
  The Beverly Hillbillies, 4: 891–93, 892 (ill.)
  Beverly Hills 90210, 5: 1286–87, 1287 (ill.)
  General Motors, *1:* 130–31
  The Honeymooners, 3: 744–46, 745 (ill.)
  preppy, *5:* 1115–17, 1116 (ill.)
  Roseanne, 5: 1187–88
Social movements, *1:* 213; *3:* 767–68; *4:* 785
  alternative proms, *2:* 360
  Beatniks and the Beat movement, *3:* 698–99, 699 (ill.)
  Chautauqua movement, *1:* 115, 118–20, 119 (ill.)
  civil rights movement, *4:* 921, 922–25, 924 (ill.)
  communes, *4:* 1072–73
  cults, *4:* 1073–74
  divorce, *4:* 1075–77
  environmentalism, *4:* 1069, 1077–80
  gay liberation movement, *4:* 921, 926–27, 927 (ill.)
  Haight-Ashbury, *4:* 929–30, 930 (ill.)
  hairstyles, *1:* 132–34
  hippies, *4:* 931–33, 932 (ill.)
  The Joy of Sex, 4: 1082–83
  Kent State massacre, *4:* 1083–85, 1084 (ill.)
  PC (Political correctness), *5:* 1209–11
  Roe v. Wade, 4: 1089–91, 1090 (ill.)
  Scopes Monkey trial, *2:* 363–64
  scouting, *1:* 226–28, 227 (ill.)
  sexual revolution, *4:* 941–44
  telephone use, *1:* 139 (ill.), 139–41
  temperance, *2:* 357–58
  women's liberation movement, *1:* 160–61; *4:* 921
  women's suffrage movement (right to vote), *1:* 213, 221; *2:* 252
  youth movement, *4:* 921, 922
Socialism, *2:* 360–61
Socialist Party (U.S.), *1:* 145
"Sock it to me!," *4:* 786
Soda, ice cream, *1:* 68
Soda fountains, *1:* **67–68,** 68 (ill.)
"Soda jerks," *1:* 67, 68 (ill.)
Soda pop, *1:* 56–58, 57 (ill.); *2:* 287–88
"Soda water," *1:* 67
Soft drinks, *1:* 56–58, 57 (ill.), 67–68, 68 (ill.); *2:* 287–88
Soft rock, *4:* 981. *See also* Pop music

Software, Microsoft, *5:* 1231–33, 1232 (ill.)
Some Like It Hot, 3: 640, 661, 667
Something for the Boys, 3: 530
Sominex, *3:* 748
Son Volt, *5:* 1252
Sondergaard, Gale, *3:* 773
Song of the South, 3: 512
Sony TR-63 transistor radio, *3:* 764
The Sopranos, 4: 935
"The Sorcerer's Apprentice," *3:* 535, 536 (ill.)
Sosa, Sammy, *1:* 99, 210; *5:* 1228, 1271
Soul music, *3:* 565. *See also* Motown; Rhythm and blues
Soul Train, 1: 125
Sound effects, radio, *2:* 477
The Sound of Music, 4: 788
Soundabout, *4:* 994
Soundgarden, *5:* 1255, 1255 (ill.)
Sound-recording technologies
  Alvin and the Chipmunks, *3:* 729
  compact disc, *5:* 1136–37, 1137 (ill.)
  eight-track tapes, *4:* 849–50, 850 (ill.)
  The Jazz Singer, 2: 275–76
  jukeboxes, *2:* 429–30, 430 (ill.)
  long-playing record (LP), *3:* 558–60, 559 (ill.)
  phonograph, *1:* 71, 76–78, 77 (ill.)
  Steamboat Willie, 2: 278, 279
  Victrola, *1:* 147
  Walkman, *4:* 994–95
Soundtrack albums, *4:* 788
Soup, *1:* 151, 181–83, 182 (ill.)
Sousa, John Philip, *1:* 147
South Park, *5:* 1277, **1298–99,** 1299 (ill.)
South (region), *1:* 169, 218
  The Andy Griffith Show, 4: 890–91
  civil rights movement, *4:* 921, 922
  The Dukes of Hazzard, 4: 1034
  Great Depression, *2:* 493
  Hee Haw, 4: 1042–43
Southdale Shopping Center (Minneapolis, Minnesota), *3:* 648
Southern 500, *2:* 474
Soviet Union
  Cold War, *1:* 109–10; *3:* 515, 622, 638–40; *4:* 939; *5:* 1100–1102
  Sputnik, 3: 779
Space, *3:* 779–80; *4:* 938–40
Space Jam, 3: 600; *5:* 1275
Spain, Bernard and Murray, *4:* 1095
"Spam" (E-mail), *5:* 1316
Spam (food), *2:* **423–24**
Spangler, James M., *1:* 126
Speakeasies, *2:* 236, 345, 357
Spears, Britney, *4:* 1029; *5:* 1251, **1261,** 1261 (ill.)
Special effects, *1:* 38–39; *2:* 404; *4:* 838, 961; *5:* 1119, 1237
Speech, politically correct, *5:* 1210
"Speed" (amphetamines), *3:* 774
Speed climbing, *5:* 1273
"Speed metal," *5:* 1140
Speed Racer, *4:* **917–18;** *5:* 1280
"Speed shops," *3:* 626
Speer, Roy, *5:* 1106
Spelling, Aaron, *4:* 1036–37, 1045; *5:* 1286
Spelling, Tori, *5:* 1286, 1287 (ill.)
Spencer, Diana, princess of Wales, *5:* 1103
Sperlich, Harold, *5:* 1208
Sperry & Hutchinson (S&H) Company, *3:* 651–52
Spider-Man, *4:* 866, **873–74,** 874 (ill.)
Spiegelman, Art, *2:* 440
Spielberg, Steven, *2:* 404; *4:* 950, 961, 968; *5:* 1125, 1130, 1270, 1289
Spillane, Mickey, *3:* 511, 638
Spilsbury, Klinton, *2:* 486
Spinach, *2:* 315
Spiritualism, Ouija boards, *1:* 111–12, 112 (ill.)
Spitz, Mark, *1:* 109; *4:* 952
Splatter movies, *4:* 829
Spock, Benjamin, *3:* 511
Sponsorship (corporate), *1:* 183; *2:* 246, 291, 339, 475; *3:* 576
Spoofs
  Airplane!, 5: 1120–21, 1121 (ill.)
  "Gumby," *4:* 1060
  horror, *3:* 531; *4:* 971–73; *5:* 1246
  James Bond, *4:* 830
  Mister Rogers, *4:* 908

Scream, *4:* 829; *5:* 1237, 1245–47, 1246 (ill.)
soap opera, *2:* 488
Sport utility vehicles (SUVs), *5:* 1208, **1215–17,** 1216 (ill.). *See also* Jeep
Sports, *1:* 95–96, 201–2; *2:* 325–26, 467–68; *3:* 587, 642, 717; *4:* 877–78, 1009–10; *5:* 1165–66, 1271–72. *See also* Games; individual sport, e.g., Baseball
bowling, *3:* 588–89, 589 (ill.)
extreme sports, *5:* 1272–74, 1273 (ill.)
frisbee, *4:* 881
Hacky Sack, *4:* 1015–16
Monday Night Football, *4:* 1017–19, 1018 (ill.)
Nike, *1:* 162; *4:* 799–801, 800 (ill.)
Sports Illustrated, *3:* 724–25
television, *5:* 1165
tennis shoes, *1:* 157, 161–62
Wide World of Sports, *4:* 887–88
World Wrestling Federation, *5:* 1171–73, 1172 (ill.)
Sports Illustrated, *3:* 639, 642, **724–25;** *4:* 1036; *5:* 1276
SportsCenter, *4:* 1035
"Sprawl," *3:* 782
Spring break, *3:* **631–32**
Springer, Jerry, *4:* 899
Springsteen, Bruce, *5:* 1135, 1152
Sprite, *2:* 288
Sputnik, *3:* 779; *4:* 939
Spy stories, *4:* 830–31, 831 (ill.), 997
The Spy Who Came in from the Cold, *4:* 787
Square, *3:* 638
Square dance, *1:* 123
Squaresville, *3:* 638
SSRIs (Selective Serotonin Reuptake Inhibitors), *5:* 1211–12
Stack, Robert, *5:* 1121
Stadiums (sports), *2:* 325, 467
Stagecoach, *2:* 414, 416
Stalberger, John, *4:* 1015
Stallone, Sylvester, *4:* 948, 970; *5:* 1132, 1132 (ill.)
Standard Oil Company, *1:* 2
Standardized testing, *2:* **365–66**
Stanley, Paul, *4:* 950 (ill.), 987
Stapleton, Jean, *4:* 1024
The Star, *4:* 1070
Star Trek, *2:* 305; *4:* **918–20,** 939
Star Wars, *2:* 305; *4:* 950, 961, **977–80,** 978 (ill.); *5:* 1101, 1119
Starbucks, *5:* 1105, **1110–11,** 1111 (ill.), 1312
Stark, Steven, *5:* 1180
Starr, Brenda, *3:* 571–72
Starr, Kenneth, *5:* 1226
Starr, Ringo, *4:* 826, 846, 847 (ill.)
Stars and Stripes, *3:* 511
Starship *Enterprise,* *4:* 918
Staubach, Roger, *4:* 1009
Steamboat Willie, *2:* 238, 267, 270, **278–79,** 279 (ill.)
Steel, Danielle, *5:* 1101, 1155, 1225
Steen, Marguerite, *3:* 510
Steeplechase Park (Coney Island, New York), *1:* 121; *3:* 768
Stefano, Joseph, *4:* 836
Steichen, Edward, *1:* 196
Steiff, Margarete and Richard, *1:* 30–31
Steiger, Rod, *2:* 350
Steinbeck, John, *2:* 303, 362, 369, 433, **451–52,** 455; *3:* 529
Steinem, Gloria, *3:* 584; *4:* 940, 941 (ill.), 949, 952, 1004
Stephenson, David C., *2:* 240
Steppenwolf, *4:* 820
Stereoscopes, *1:* 8, **28–29,** 29 (ill.); *3:* 675
Stern, Howard, *2:* 343; *5:* 1189 (ill.), 1189–90, 1193
Stevens, Harry, *1:* 64
Stevens, Ray, *4:* 1096
Stevenson, McLean, *4:* 1050
Stewardesses, *2:* 346
Stewart, James, *1:* 219; *2:* 407; *3:* 529, 538, 539 (ill.), 625
Stewart, Martha, *4:* 799; *5:* 1227
Stewart, Rod, *4:* 951
Stiers, David Ogden, *4:* 1051
Stiles, Tod, *2:* 363
Stillman, Stacey, *5:* 1295
Sting, *5:* 1102
The Sting, *1:* 76
Stipe, Michael, *5:* 1254
Stock car racing, *2:* **474–75**
Stock market, *5:* 1228, 1321
Stock market crash (October 29, 1929), *2:* 241, 244, 367, 373. *See also* Great Depression
Stockings (nylons), *2:* 380–82, 381 (ill.)
Stoker, Bram, *2:* 392

Stokowski, Leopold, *2:* 272; *3:* 535
Stone, Lewis, *2:* 385
Stone, Matt, *5:* 1298
Stone, Milburn, *3:* 743
Stone, Oliver, *5:* 1102, 1241, 1244
Stonewall Inn (Greenwich Village, New York), *4:* 926, 944
Stop-motion animation, *2:* 404
Stores. *See also* Retailers, e.g., L. L. Bean
  department, *2:* 254–55
  dime, *1:* 11–13, 12 (ill.)
  Kmart, *4:* 797–99
  Wall Drug, *2:* 505–7, 506 (ill.)
  Wal-Mart, *4:* 802–4, 803 (ill.)
Stork Club, *2:* 268
Storytelling, *1:* 45–46; *3:* 609; *5:* 1217–18
Storz, Todd, *3:* 694–95
Stouffer, Nancy K., *5:* 1267
The Strand (New York City), *1:* 177
Stranger in a Strange Land, 4: 865
Stranger Than Paradise, 3: 680
Strategic Defense Initiative (SDI), *4:* 978
Stratemeyer, Edward, *1:* 83, 194; *3:* 570
Stratemeyer Syndicate, *1:* 194–95; *2:* 308–9; *3:* 570–71
Stratocaster guitar, *3:* 687, 687 (ill.)
Stratton, Charles S., *1:* 224
Strauss, Levi, *3:* 658
Strauss, Richard, *4:* 838
"The Streak," *4:* 1096
Streaking, *4:* **1095–96,** 1096 (ill.)
Street & Smith, *2:* 461
Street luge, *5:* 1273
"Street rods," *3:* 627
Street Talk and Tuxes, 2: 360
A Streetcar Named Desire, 1: 35–36, 163
Streisand, Barbra, *4:* **861–62**
Stress reduction, *5:* 1305
Strieber, Whitley, *3:* 636
Strikes (union), *1:* 7; *2:* 373–74
Struthers, Sally, *4:* 1024
Students
  antiwar movement, *4:* 922, 1083–85, 1084 (ill.)
  "duck and cover" drills, *3:* 620, 623
  Kent State massacre, *4:* 1083–85, 1084 (ill.)
  spring break, *3:* 631–32
  standardized testing, *2:* 365
Students for a Democratic Society (SDS), *4:* 922, **945–46**
Studio One, *3:* **608–9**
"Studio system." *See* Movie studios
Stuffed animals, *1:* 30–31, 31 (ill.); *5:* 1306 (ill.), 1306–7
Stuntmen
  Browing, Ricou, *4:* 902
  Houdini, Harry, *1:* 39–40, 40 (ill.); *2:* 239
  Knievel, Evel, *4:* 881–83, 882 (ill.); *5:* 1272
  LaLanne, Jack, *3:* 720
Style, *2:* 261. *See also* Clothing; Youth culture
  Arrow Collar Man, *1:* 158–59, 159 (ill.)
  development of fashion sense, *1:* 157
  flappers, *1:* 133; *2:* 261–63, 262 (ill.)
  Gibson Girl, *1:* 84–85, 85 (ill.); *2:* 453, 453 (ill.)
  hairstyles, *1:* 132–34
Styrofoam cups, *1:* 26
Suburbs, *2:* 302; *3:* 637, 776, **780–83;** *4:* 928
  Levittown, *3:* 629–31, 630 (ill.)
  Mall of America, *5:* 1230 (ill.), 1230–31
  malls, *3:* 648–49
  sprawl, *2:* 286
Succeeding Against the Odds, 3: 576
Suck up, *2:* 368
Sucks, *5:* 1100
Sues, Alan, *4:* 911
Suffrage movement (women's right to vote), *1:* 213, 221; *2:* 263
Sullivan, Ed, *3:* 639, 739–40, 740 (ill.); *4:* 841
Sullivan, John L., *1:* 101
Sullivan, Pat, *1:* 171
Summer, Donna, *4:* 951
Sun and sun bathing, *4:* 1096–98, 1097 (ill.); *5:* 1283–84
The Sun Is My Undoing, 3: 510
Sun lotions, *4:* 1098
Sun Records, *3:* 691
Sunday, Billy, *1:* 115, 127, **138;** *2:* 240; *3:* 513
Sundback, Gideon, *1:* 164
Sunset Boulevard, 1: 47; *3:* 537
Super Bowl, *4:* 877, 883, **884–85**
Superheroes, *2:* 440
  Batman, *2:* 434–36, 435 (ill.)

Captain America, *3:* 572–73
Doc Savage, *2:* 446–48
Green Lantern, *3:* 578–79
Spider-Man, *4:* 866, 873–74, 874 (ill.)
Superman, *2:* 462–66, 463 (ill.); *3:* 512
Wonder Woman, *3:* 583–85
Superman, *2:* **462–66,** 463 (ill.); *3:* 512
Supermodels, *2:* 440; *3:* 725, 774; *4:* 813; *5:* **1117–18,** 1118 (ill.)
Supernatural, *4:* 893–95; 1036–37, 1037 (ill.); *5:* 1128–30, 1129 (ill.)
Superpowers, *3:* 622
Supremes, *4:* 842
Surf music, *4:* 844
"Surfin' U.S.A.," *4:* 789
"Surfing" (Internet), *5:* 1320
Survivor, 5: 1278, 1295, 1295 (ill.)
Susann, Jacqueline, *4:* 787, 802, 943
Suspense, *3:* 668–69; *4:* 836–37, 902–3
Sutherland, Donald, *4:* 1050
SUVs. *See* Sport utility vehicles (SUVs)
Swank, Hilary, *5:* 1287
Swanky, *2:* 236
Swanson, Clark, *3:* 681
Swanson frozen foods, *2:* 420
Swarthout, Glendon, *3:* 632
Swashbucklers, *1:* 46, 199–200, 200 (ill.). *See also under* Adventure
Swayze, John Cameron, *3:* 605, 650
Sweater girl, *3:* 510
Sweatshop labor, *4:* 795–96, 804
Sweets family, *2:* 239
Swift, Tom. *See Tom Swift* series
Swimsuits, *Sports Illustrated, 3:* 725
Swing music, *1:* 72, 123–24; *2:* 368, 425
"Swinging sixties," *1:* 197
Swing-jazz orchestras. *See* Big bands
Swit, Loretta, *4:* 1050
"Swoosh," *4:* 800
Sword and sorcery, *2:* 321
Sycom II, 3: 780
Sydow, Max von, *4:* 965
Synchronized sound, *2:* 275–76, 278–79, 279 (ill.)
Syndicated columnists, *2:* 241
Syphilis, *4:* 1094
Syrups, *1:* 8–9, 9 (ill.), 67
Systems of combat, *4:* 937–38

T

Tabloids, *3:* 707–8, 708 (ill.)
Taco Bell, *2:* 285
Taft, William Howard, *1:* 145
Taggart Baking Company, *2:* 291
Tajiri, Satoshi, *5:* 1322
Takagi, Kisaburo, *5:* 1142
Talk radio, *2:* 343; *5:* **1193–94,** 1225–26
"Talkies" (talking motion pictures), *1:* 46; *2:* 275–76
Talk-show hosts
Carson, Johnny, *4:* 896–97
daytime talk shows, *4:* 897–900, 898 (ill.)
Leno, Jay, *3:* 763; *4:* 897; *5:* 1185
Letterman, David, *5:* 1185–86, 1186 (ill.)
Tall tales, urban legends, *5:* 1217–18
Tamagotchi electronic pets, *4:* 1072
Tandy TRS-80, *4:* 1086
Tango, *1:* 124; *2:* 280
Tanning, *4:* **1096–98,** 1097 (ill.)
Tarantino, Quentin, *5:* 1244
Target stores, *4:* 798
Tarkington, Booth, *2:* 237; *3:* 582
Tartikoff, Brandon, *5:* 1186
Tarzan, *1:* **192–94,** 193 (ill.)
Tata, Joe E., *5:* 1286
Tate, Sharon, *4:* 790
Tattoos, *2:* 260; *5:* 1235
Tatum, Goose, *2:* 330
Tauchnitz (publishers), *2:* 457
Taxi, *4:* **1063–65,** 1064 (ill.)
Taxi Driver, 3: 537–38
Taylor, Cecil, *1:* 74
Taylor, Elizabeth, *3:* 541, 542 (ill.), **542–43,** 661; *4:* 790, 815, 1096
Taylor, Frederick W., *1:* 153
Taylor, James, *4:* 860
Taylor, Mick, *4:* 859
Taymor, Julie, *5:* 1243
Technicolor, *2:* 396, 418
"Techno-hippies," *5:* 1259
Technology, *2:* 345; *5:* 1303
biotechnology, *5:* 1227
Buck Rogers, 2: 304–6, 305 (ill.)

Cold War era, *3:* 638–39
compact discs (CDs), *5:* 1136–37, 1137 (ill.)
electric guitar, *3:* 686–88, 687 (ill.)
Erector sets, *1:* 202–4, 203 (ill.)
Internet, *5:* 1303, 1319–21, 1320 (ill.)
radio, *2:* 339–43, 340 (ill.)
satellites, *3:* 779–80
skyscrapers, *2:* 502–4
television, *3:* 610–13, 611 (ill.)
Tom Swift series, *1:* 194–95
Xerox copiers, *4:* 804–5
Teddy bears, *1:* **30–31,** 31 (ill.)
Teen idols, *3:* 524–25, 563, **632–34,** 633 (ill.), 683, 732 (ill.); *4:* 1056; *5:* 1251
Teenage Mutant Ninja Turtles, *4:* 938; *5:* **1194–95,** 1195 (ill.)
Teenagers
Abercrombie & Fitch, *5:* 1235–36
American Bandstand, 3: 731–32, 732 (ill.)
Andy Hardy movies, *2:* 384–86, 385 (ill.)
anorexia nervosa, *3:* 775
Archie comics, *3:* 568–69, 569 (ill.)
athletic shoes, *1:* 162
bad boy, *4:* 974–75
The Beavis and Butt-Head Show, 5: 1284–85
Beverly Hills 90210, 5: 1225, 1286–87, 1287 (ill.)
Blume, Judy, *4:* 998
bobbysoxers, *3:* 524–25, 525 (ill.)
The Catcher in the Rye, 3: 617, 700–701
cigarettes, *2:* 251–54
dancing, *1:* 124
Dean, James, *3:* 663–64
Friday the 13th, 5: 1127–28
gangs, *5:* 1204–6, 1205 (ill.)
generation X, *5:* 1206–7
Gillis, Dobie, *3:* 737 (ill.), 737–38
goth culture, *5:* 1114–15
grunge, *5:* 1254
Hardy Boys series, *2:* 308–9
jeans, *3:* 658
MAD magazine, *3:* 704, 706
Nancy Drew series, *2:* 455–56
phonograph, *1:* 78
Presley, Elvis, *3:* 689–90, 690 (ill.)
prom, *2:* 345, 358–60, 359 (ill.)
radio, *2:* 343
raves, *5:* 1259–60, 1260 (ill.)
rock and roll, *3:* 690–94, 691 (ill.)
Sassy, 5: 1159–60
Seventeen, 3: 582–83
skateboarding, *3:* 722–24, 723 (ill.)
skinheads, *5:* 1214–15
South Park, 5: 1298–99, 1299 (ill.)
Spears, Britney, *5:* 1261, 1261 (ill.)
teen idols, *3:* 524–25, 563, 632–34, 633 (ill.), 683, 732 (ill.); *4:* 1056; *5:* 1261
Teenage Mutant Ninja Turtles, *5:* 1194–95, 1195 (ill.)
Wayne's World, 5: 1249–50, 1250 (ill.)
Tejano music, *5:* 1251, **1262–63**
Telecaster guitar, *3:* 686
Telecommunications satellites, *5:* 1175
Telecommuting, *5:* 1317
Telegraph, *1:* 140
Telenovella, *2:* 488
Telephone, *1:* 139 (ill.), **139–41;** *2:* 345; *5:* 1308–9, 1309 (ill.)
Televangelists, *1:* 127
Television, *1:* 177–78; *2:* 478; *3:* 514–15, 530, 597, **610–13,** 611 (ill.), 642, 727–28; *4:* 889–90, 951, 1023–24; *5:* 1175, 1277–78. *See also* specific shows and types of shows, e.g., Dramas, TV
advertising, *2:* 246; *3:* 610
Army-McCarthy hearings, *3:* 771
cable TV, *4:* 1027–29. *See also under* Cable TV
cartoons. *See* Cartoons
channels, *3:* 611
commercials, *2:* 374–75; *3:* 595; *4:* 884–85
early, *3:* 514–15, 597
first broadcast news, *2:* 238
holiday special, *3:* 703
Home Shopping Network (HSN), *5:* 1106–7
live drama (Studio One), *3:* 608–9
Music Television (MTV), *5:* 1147–49, 1148 (ill.)
networks, *5:* 1277–78
news and news anchors, *2:* 238; *3:* 604–6; *5:* 1179–80

public debut, *2:* 478
reality TV, *5:* 1292–94, 1293 (ill.), 1294–96, 1295 (ill.)
sitcoms, *3:* 612, 754–56
soap operas, *2:* 486–88
Timex, *3:* 650–51
TV dinners, *3:* 680–82, 681 (ill.)
TV Guide, 3: 714–16, 715 (ill.)
Telstar, 3: 779–80
Temperance, *1:* 213; *2:* 357
Temple, Shirley, *2:* **411–12**
Temptations, *4:* 842, 857 (ill.)
The Ten Commandments, 2: 237–38; *3:* 640, 661
Tennis, *4:* 1009; *5:* 1271
Tennis shoes, *1:* 157, **161–62**
The Terminator, 5: 1119
Terrorism, *3:* 621
Tests, standardized, *2:* **365–66**
Tewes, Lauren, *4:* 1046
Texaco, *1:* 7
The Texaco Star Theater, 2: 483; *3:* 597, 639, 641, 727
Text messaging, *5:* 1315
Thalberg, Irving G., *2:* 277
Thalidomide, *4:* 1091
Thanksgiving Day Parade (Macy's), *2:* **258,** 388 (ill.)
Theater, *1:* 33, *1:* 168; *2:* 384; *3:* 530; *4:* 815; *5:* 1120
Broadway, *1:* 34–36, 35 (ill.). *See also* Broadway
Minstrel shows, *1:* 2, 8, 33, 40–42, 41 (ill.)
vaudeville, *1:* 47–50, 48 (ill.)
Ziegfeld Follies, 1: 50–52
Theaters
Apollo Theater, *2:* 494–95, 495 (ill.)
Broadway, *1:* 34–36, 35 (ill.)
drive-in theater, *2:* 497–99, 498 (ill.)
movie palaces, *1:* 177–78
nickelodeons, *1:* 34, 42–44, 43 (ill.)
Theme music, *2:* 259, 485; *3:* 739
Thimble Theatre, 2: 314
Thinness, diets, *3:* 774–75
Thirteeners (Generation X), *5:* 1206–7
This Is Spinal Tap, 5: 1140
This Is the Army, 3: 530
This Is Your Life, *3:* **758–60**
"This Land Is Your Land," *4:* 851
Thomas, Clarence, *4:* 925
Thomas, Dave, *2:* 285
Thomas, Gerry, *3:* 681
Thomas, Isiah, *5:* 1166
Thomas, Lowell, *2:* 370; *3:* 759
Thomas, Philip Michael, *5:* 1186
Thomas, Richard, *4:* 1066
Thomas the Tank Engine, *5:* 1278, **1299–1300,** 1300 (ill.)
Thompson, Bill, *2:* 482
Thompson, Hunter, *4:* 872
Thompson, James Walter, *1:* 18
Thompson, Jim, *5:* 1244
Thorne-Smith, Courtney, *5:* 1279 (ill.)
Thornhill, Roger, *3:* 668
Thorpe, Jim, *1:* 149, 201
"Thrash" bands, *5:* 1140
"Thrashers," *3:* 723 (ill.), 724
The Three Little Pigs, 2: 271
The Three Musketeers, 2: 237
Three Stooges, *1:* 102, 176; *2:* **412–14,** 413 (ill.)
3-D movies, *3:* **674–76,** 675 (ill.)
3-D photography, *1:* 8, 28–29, 29 (ill.); *3:* 675
Thriller, 5: 1102, 1135, 1141, 1147
Thurman, Uma, *5:* 1244–45
Tiananmen Square massacre, *5:* 1180, 1316
Tickle Me Elmo doll, *4:* 1063
Till Death Do Us Part, 4: 1024
Tillie's Punctured Romance, 1: 147
Tillstrom, Burr, *3:* 603
Tilyou, George C., *3:* 768
Time, *2:* 301, **319–20**
Time-Life, Inc., *4:* 1005, 1006
Timely Comics, *4:* 870
Time-Warner, *2:* 320; *4:* 1028
Timex watches, *3:* 643, **650–51**
Tin Lizzie, *2:* 368
Tin Pan Alley, *1:* 71, 147
Tinker, Grant, *4:* 1049
Tinkertoys, *1:* 211 (ill.), **211–12**
Tinklenberg, Janie, *5:* 1328
Tiny Tim and Miss Vicky, *4:* 897, 898 (ill.)
Titanic, *1:* **228–31,** 229 (ill.); *4:* 963; *5:* 1225
To Have and Have Not, 2: 253
To Kill a Mockingbird, 4: 786, 865
Toast of the Town, 3: 739
Tobacco, *2:* 251–54, 259 (ill.), 259–60
Today, *3:* **760–61;** *4:* 1053
Todman, Bill, *3:* 753
Toho Studios, *3:* 666
Tolan, Eddie, *2:* 467
Toler, Sidney, *2:* 269, 269 (ill.)
Tolkien, J. R. R., *3:* **713–14;** *4:* 1014

Tom Mix, *2:* 370
Tom Swift series, *1:* 188, **194–95**
Tomb Raider, *4:* 1022
Tomlin, Lily, *4:* 893, 911
The Tonight Show, *3:* **761–63,** 762 (ill.); *4:* 1053, 1089
Tonka trucks, *3:* **596**
Tonto, *2:* 485
Tony the Tiger, *1:* 21
Top 40, *3:* **694–95;** *4:* 890
Top Gun, *5:* 1119
Topo Gigio, *3:* 740
Topps Chewing Gum, *2:* 347
Tork, Peter, *4:* 854, 855 (ill.)
Torrio, Johnny, *2:* 350
Touchstone Pictures, *2:* 273–74
Touring ministries, *1:* 115, 127–28, 138; *2:* 240
Tournament of Roses parade, *1:* 114
The Towering Inferno, *4:* 963
Toy Story, *5:* 1237, **1247–49,** 1248 (ill.)
Toys, *1:* 202; *3:* 587, 717–18
  Barbie, *3:* 644–46, 645 (ill.)
  Beanie Babies, *5:* 1306 (ill.), 1306–7
  Cabbage Patch Kids, *5:* 1200–1201, 1201 (ill.)
  construction, *1:* 202
  Cracker Jack prizes, *1:* 59, 59 (ill.), 60
  Erector sets, *1:* 202–4, 203 (ill.)
  Etch A Sketch, *3:* 717, 718, 719 (ill.)
  Fisher-Price toys, *2:* 377–78
  Ghostbusters, *5:* 1130
  G.I. Joe, *4:* 796–97
  Harry Potter series, *5:* 1267 (ill.), 1267–68
  hula hoop, *3:* 777 (ill.), 777–78
  Kewpie dolls, *1:* 66, 86–87
  LEGOs, *3:* 720–22, 721 (ill.)
  Lincoln Logs, *2:* 331–32
  Lionel trains, *1:* 104–6, 105 (ill.)
  plastic, *1:* 25
  Raggedy Ann and Raggedy Andy, *1:* 208–9, 209 (ill.)
  Rambo, *5:* 1133
  Sesame Street, *4:* 1063
  Slinky, *3:* 594–96, 595 (ill.)
  stereoscopic, *1:* 29
  teddy bears, *1:* 30–31, 31 (ill.)
  Teenage Mutant Ninja Turtles, *5:* 1194–95, 1195 (ill.)
  television advertisements, *4:* 915
  Tinkertoys, *1:* 211 (ill.), 211–12
  Tonka trucks, *3:* 596
  Winnie-the-Pooh, *2:* 322, 322 (ill.)
  Yo-Yo, *2:* 336–37, 337 (ill.)
Tracht, Doug, *5:* 1189
Track and field, *2:* 473
Tracy, Dick. *See* Dick Tracy
Trading stamps, *3:* **651–52**
Traffic, *5:* 1212–13
Traf-o-data, *5:* 1232
Trains, *1:* 104–6, 105 (ill.); *5:* 1299–1300, 1300 (ill.)
Trances, *1:* 111
Tranquilizers, *4:* 801–2
Transatlantic and transpacific telephone service, *1:* 154
Transistor radios, *3:* **763–64**
Transportation
  air travel, *2:* 345–46
  Burma-Shave, *2:* 250–51
  Greyhound buses, *1:* 216–17
  highway system, *3:* 775–76
  minivans, *5:* 1208, 1209 (ill.)
  Model T, *1:* 8, 22–23
  road rage, *5:* 1212–13
  Route 66, *2:* 361–63, 362 (ill.)
"Trash fiction," *4:* 997
Trash talk, *5:* 1224
"Travelgate," *5:* 1224
Traveling entertainment. *See* Minstrel shows and Vaudeville
Traveling Wilburys, *4:* 849
Travers, Henry, *3:* 538
Travers, P. L., *4:* 832
Travis, Randy, *4:* 1043
Travolta, John, *1:* 124; *3:* 634; *4:* 957, 974, 975 (ill.), 982, 983; *5:* 1244
Tree, Penelope, *1:* 197
"Treemonisha," *1:* 76
Trekkies, *4:* 919
Trendle, George W., *2:* 485
Trio, *5:* 1103
Trivial Pursuit, *5:* **1170–71**
Troup, Bobby, *2:* 363
Trucks, *3:* 596; *5:* 1215–17, 1216 (ill.)
True Story, *1:* **195–96**
"True-Life Adventure" series, *2:* 273
Truman, Harry S., *3:* 515
Trumbo, Dalton, *3:* 773
Trustbusting, *1:* 7, 153, 155
T-shirts, *1:* 157, **163–64;** *5:* 1249, 1328
Tunney, Gene, *2:* 328

Tupper, Earl S., *3:* 520, 521
Tupperware, *1:* 25; *3:* **520–22,** 521 (ill.)
Tureaud, Lawrence (Mr. T), *5:* 1176, 1177 (ill.)
Turf, *3:* 638
Turner, Lana, *2:* 385 (ill.); *3:* 672
Turner, Ted, *5:* 1179–80
Turturro, John, *5:* 1123
TV. *See* **Television**
TV dinners, *2:* 421; *3:* **680–82,** 681 (ill.)
TV Guide, *3:* **714–16,** 715 (ill.)
Twain, Mark, *3:* 700
Twain, Shania, *5:* 1251
Tweedy, Jeff, *5:* 1253 (ill.)
12 Angry Men, 3: 609
Twelve-step programs, *2:* **504–5**
24/7, *5:* 1224
Twenty-One, 3: 742
"23 Skidoo!," *1:* 2
Twiggy (Leslie Hornsby), *1:* 197; *4:* 790, 807, 812, **813**
The Twilight Zone, *3:* **764–66**
Twin Peaks, 4: 1093
Twist (dance), *1:* 124
Twister (film), *5:* 1237
Twister (game), *4:* **885–87,** 886 (ill.)
2 Live Crew, *5:* 1104, 1135, **1152**
Two-step (dance), *1:* 123
2001: A Space Odyssey, *4:* 788, 815, **838,** 839 (ill.), 939
Ty, Incorporated, *5:* 1306

U

UFO. *See* Unidentified flying objects (UFO)
Uggams, Leslie, *4:* 1057
UHF TV stations, *3:* 611
Ulrich, Skeet, *5:* 1246
Uncle Jim's Question Bee, 3: 741
Uncle Tupelo, *5:* 1252, 1253 (ill.)
Under Cover, 3: 518
Underground bomb shelters, *3:* 620, 623
Underground comics, *2:* 440
Undershirts, *2:* 396
Underwear, *1:* 157, 159–61, 160 (ill.), 163–64
Unger, Felix, *4:* 833
"The Unibomber," *5:* 1227
Unidentified flying objects (UFO), *3:* **635–36,** 636 (ill.), 661–63, 662 (ill.)
Unions, *1:* 7, 149; *2:* 373–74
United Artists (movie company), *1:* 149
United Productions of America (UPA), *2:* 272
United States. *See also* individual government departments, e.g., Federal Bureau of Investigation (FBI)
  Cold War, *3:* 515, 517, 622, 638–40; *4:* 939; *5:* 1100–1102
  government, in film, *2:* 407
  national railroad, *2:* 255
  postal system, *2:* 255
  scouting, *1:* 226–28, 227 (ill.)
  Telstar, 3: 779–80
  turn of the century (1900s), *1:* 1–5
United States Steel Corporation, *1:* 2, 7
Universal Fastener Company, *1:* 164
University of Michigan, *1:* 95
University of Missouri, *4:* 1095
Unser, Al, *1:* 206
Unsub, 4: 1093
The Untouchables, 2: 350
The U.P. Trail, 1: 146
Upchuck, *2:* 236
Updike, John, *2:* 313
UPN network, *5:* 1277
Upper class, *5:* 1115–17, 1116 (ill.)
Urban America, urbanization, *1:* 213; *2:* 238–39
Urban, Joseph, *1:* 51
Urban legends, *5:* **1217–18**
Uris, Leon, *4:* 997
USA Today, *5:* 1101, 1156, **1160–62**
U2, *3:* 688
Utility vehicles, *3:* 519–20

V

Vacuum cleaners, *1:* 126
Valachi, Joe, *4:* 935
Valentino, Rudolph, *1:* 46, 150, 167; *2:* 238, **280–81**
Valium, *4:* 801, **801–2**
Vallee, Rudy, *2:* 389; *3:* 633
Valley of the Dolls, 4: 787, 802, 943
Vampires, Dracula, *2:* 392–93
Van, Bobbie, *3:* 737
Van Alen, William, *2:* 352
Van Doren, Charles, *3:* 742
Van Doren, Philip, *3:* 538
Van Pelt, Linus and Lucy, *3:* 711
Vance, Vivian, *3:* 639, 747

Vanderbilt, Harold S., *1:* 214
Vanity Fair, 1: 157
Variety shows
The Ed Sullivan Show, 3: 739–40, 740 (ill.)
The Gong Show, 4: 1038–39, 1039 (ill.)
Hee Haw, 4: 1042–43
Rowan & Martin's Laugh-In, 4: 911–12, 912 (ill.)
The Texaco Star Theater, 3: 597, 639, 641, 727
Varney, Jim, *4:* 893
"A Vast Wasteland," *4:* 889
Vaudeville, *1:* 2, 33, **47–50,** 48 (ill.), 146
Vaughn, Stevie Ray, *4:* 952
VCR Co-Pilot, *4:* 1072
Vecchio, Mary Ann, *4:* 1085
Vega, Vincent, *5:* 1244
Veidt, Conrad, *3:* 532
Velveeta cheese, *2:* **289**
Vendor Conduct Code, *4:* 796
Ventriloquism, *2:* 391
Ventura, Jesse, *5:* 1173
"Venus," *3:* 641
Vereen, Ben, *1:* 105; 1057
Verushka, *1:* 197
VHF TV stations, *3:* 611
Viacom, *5:* 1147
Viagra, *5:* 1304
Vicious, Sid, *4:* 991, 992, 993
Victor Talking Machine Company, *1:* 147
Victoria, queen of England, *5:* 1202
Victory through Air Power, 2: 272–73
Victrola, *1:* 147–48
Video games, *4:* 1011, **1020–22,** 1021 (ill.); *5:* 1249–50, 1285, 1322
Atari, *4:* 1011–13, 1012 (ill.)
Pac-Man, *5:* 1167–68, 1168 (ill.)
Pokémon, *5:* 1322–23, 1323 (ill.)
Pong, *4:* 1019–20, 1021
Videos, music, *4:* 1029; *5:* 1135, 1141, 1147
Vietnam War, *3:* 622; *4:* 785, 787–88, 797, 822, 841, 922, 945, 1025, 1050, 1083; *5:* 1239
baby boomers, *3:* 617–18
Cronkite, Walter, *3:* 605
Forrest Gump, 5: 1239–40, 1240 (ill.)
Kent State massacre, *4:* 1083–85, 1084 (ill.)
Rambo movies, *5:* 1131–33, 1132 (ill.)
View-Master, *1:* 29
Villechaize, Hervé, *4:* 1036–37, 1037 (ill.)
Vincent, John Heyl, *1:* 118
Violence
Altamont, *4:* 842–43, 843 (ill.)
antiwar movement, *4:* 945–46
Beavis and Butt-Head, 5: 1285
Gunsmoke, 3: 743–44
heavy metal music, *5:* 1141
manga, 5: 1281
Saturday morning cartoons, *4:* 915
Simpson, O. J., *5:* 1324 (ill.), 1324–26
video game, *4:* 1022
Virginia Minstrels, *1:* 41
Virus, computer, *5:* 1318
Visa, *3:* 647
Visakay, Stephen, *2:* 353
Vogue, *1:* **196–97**
Volkswagen Beetle, *3:* 643, **652–55,** 653 (ill.)
Volkswagen Microbus, *3:* 654
Volstead Act, *2:* 357, 419
von Kaltenborn, Hans, *2:* 239
Von Trapp family, *4:* 788
Vorhees, Jason, *5:* 1128
Voting Rights Act, *4:* 924
Vreeland, Diana, *1:* 197
VW. *See* Volkswagen Beetle

W

Waco, Texas, *4:* 1074; *5:* 1307
Wade Advertising Agency, *2:* 375
"Waffle" cones, *1:* 65
Wagner, Honus, *1:* 22; *2:* 347
Wagon Train, 3: 642; *4:* 787
Wait, Pearl B., *1:* 65
Waite, Ralph, *4:* 1066
"Wake Up Little Suzie," *3:* 641
Walken, Christopher, *5:* 1245
Walker, Alice, *4:* 997
Walkman, *4:* **994–95**
Wall Drug, *2:* **505–7,** 506 (ill.)
Wall Street, 5: 1102, 1105
Wallace, Irving, *4:* 997
Wallace, Mike, *3:* 609
Wallace, William Roy DeWitt and Lila, *2:* 317
Wallenda, Karl, *1:* 225
Waller, Robert James, *5:* 1224
Wal-Mart, *4:* 793, 798, **802–4,** 803 (ill.), 1095; *5:* 1328

Walsh, Raoul, *1:* 219
Walt Disney World (Orlando, Florida), *2:* 273; *3:* 769
Walters, Barbara, *3:* 606
Walton, Sam, *4:* 798, 803
The Waltons, *4:* 1023, 1043, **1066–67**
Wanamaker's department store (Philadelphia, Pennsylvania), *2:* 255
War. *See* Civil War; Vietnam War; World War I; World War II
War bonds, *1:* **231–33,** 232 (ill.); *3:* 599
War Games, 5: 1317
The War of the Worlds, *2:* 342, 370, **489–90,** 490 (ill.); *3:* 635
War on Drugs, *4:* 936
War toys, *4:* 796–97
Ward, Arthur Henry Sarsfield, *1:* 188
Ward, Jay, *4:* 914
Warhol, Andy, *1:* 183; *4:* 1046
Warner Bros. (movie studio), *2:* 276; *5:* 1267
Warner Brothers (Harry, Albert, Sam, and Jack), *1:* 44, 45
Warner, Malcolm-Jamal, *5:* 1182 (ill.)
Warner, Sam Bass, *3:* 781
Warners (bras and corsets), *1:* 159
Warren Commission, *5:* 1241
Warshawski, V. I., *2:* 442
Washburn Crosby Company, *2:* 290
Washing machines, *1:* 126
Washington, Booker T., *1:* 170
Washington Wizards, *5:* 1275
Watches, Timex, *3:* **650–51**
Water, carbonated, *1:* 67
Watergate, *4:* 948, 950
Waters, John, *4:* 959
Waters, Muddy, *2:* 295–96; *4:* 858, 871
Watership Down, 4: 949
Watson, John B., *1:* 18
Watson, Thomas Augustus, *1:* 140
Watson, Thomas, Jr., *5:* 1107
Watters, Sam, *4:* 867
Watts, Charlie, *4:* 858, 858 (ill.)
Waukegan, Illinois, *3:* 598
The Way We Lived, *1:* 1–5, 115, 145–51, 213–14; *2:* 235–41, 345, 367–72, 493–94; *3:* 509–15, 615–16, 637–42, 767–68; *4:* 785–92, 921–22, 947–53, 1069–70; *5:* 1099–1104, 1197–98, 1223–28, 1303–4
  cable TV, *4:* 1027–29
  divorce, *4:* 1069, 1075–77
  government, *2:* 407
  highway system, *3:* 775–76
  MTV, *4:* 1029; *5:* 1147–49, 1148 (ill.)
  New Deal construction, *2:* 371–72
  radio "firsts," *2:* 238–39
  suburbs, *3:* 781
  television, *3:* 610–13, 611 (ill.)
Wayne, Bruce, *2:* 434
Wayne, John, *2:* 369, **414–15;** *4:* 979
Wayne's World, *5:* **1249–50,** 1250 (ill.)
WB network, *5:* 1277
WDIA radio (Memphis, Tennessee), *3:* 688
"We Are the World," *5:* 1102–3, 1144
Weary Willie, *1:* 225
Weather Channel, *4:* 1029
Weathermen, *4:* 945, 946
Weathers, Gail, *5:* 1247
Weaver, Dennis, *3:* 743
Weaver, Sigourney, *5:* 1129
Weaver, Sylvester "Pat," *3:* 760; *4:* 898
Weavers, *3:* 640; *4:* 851
Webb, Jack, *3:* 640, 738
"Webcasts," *5:* 1316
"Weekend outlaws," *1:* 16–17
Weight loss diets, *3:* 774–75
Weiners, *1:* 63
Weir, Bob, *4:* 853
Weird Tales, *2:* **320–21**
Weiss, Erich. *See* Houdini, Harry
Weissmuller, Johnny, *1:* 109, 193
Welch, Gillian, *5:* 1252
Welch, Joseph, *3:* 771
Weld, Tuesday, *3:* 737 (ill.)
Welk, Lawrence, *3:* 748–49
Welles, Orson, *2:* 342, 370, 462, 489, 490 (ill.); *3:* 511, 529, 533–34, 534 (ill.)
Wells, Dawn, *4:* 904
Wells, H. G., *2:* 237, 342, 370, 489; *3:* 635
Wembley Stadium (London, England), *4:* 882; *5:* 1143
Wendt, George, *5:* 1178, 1178 (ill.)
Wendy's, *2:* 285
Wenner, Jann, *4:* 787, 871, 872 (ill.)
Wepner, Chuck, *4:* 971
Wertham, Fredric, *2:* 440

West, Adam, *2:* 434
West, Bob, *5:* 1282
West, Mae, *2:* 372
West Side Story, 4: 815; *5:* 1204
The Western, *1:* 147; *2:* **415–16**
Bonanza, 4: 895–96
Cooper, Gary, *2:* 391–92
Gunsmoke, 3: 743–44
Hoover Dam, *2:* 501–2
Lone Ranger, *2:* 485–86
Marlboro Man, *2:* 259 (ill.), 259–60
music, *2:* 426
Shane, 3: 673–74
Wild West Show (Buffalo Bill's), *1:* 36–37
Western Publishing Company, *3:* 577
Westheimer, Ruth, *5:* 1103
WGN (Chicago, Illinois), *2:* 486
WGY (Schenectady, New York), *3:* 610
Whale, James, *2:* 394
Wham-O, *3:* 777; *4:* 881, 1015
Wharton, Edith, *2:* 236
What Every Young Girl Should Know, 2: 310
What Would Jesus Do? (WWJD), *5:* **1328–29**
"Whatever," *5:* 1224
Wheaties, *2:* **289–90**
Wheatstone, Charles, *1:* 29
Wheel of Fortune, 3: 742
Wheeler, Bert, *1:* 49
Wheeler, E. L., *1:* 83 (ill.)
Wheeler, Harvey, *4:* 819
Wheeler-Nicholson, Major Malcolm, *2:* 439
When We Were Very Young, 2: 237
When Worlds Collide, 2: 450
Where the Boys Are, 3: 632
Where the Wild Things Are, 4: 865
"Where's the Beef?," *5:* 1100
Whiffle Hen, *2:* 315
Whirlaway (horse), *1:* 103
Whist, *1:* 214
White, Betty, *4:* 1049
White Castle, *2:* 284 (ill.), 284–85
White, David, *4:* 894
White, Edmund, *4:* 1083
White Fang, 1: 88
White Star shipping line, *1:* 229–30
White supremacy, *1:* 169, **217–20,** 218 (ill.); *2:* 240
Whiteman, Paul, *1:* 72; *2:* 240, 293
Whitewater investigation, *5:* 1225
Whitman, Walt, *3:* 699
Whitney, Harry Payne, *1:* 103
Whitney, Phyllis A., *4:* 997
Who (musical group), *3:* 687; *4:* 841
Who Wants to Be a Millionaire, *1:* 74; *5:* **1300–1302,** 1301 (ill.)
Whole Earth Catalog, *4:* 787, **875**
Who's Afraid of Virginia Woolf?, 3: 542; *4:* 816
"Who's on First?," *3:* 531
"Why don't you come up and see me some time?," *2:* 372
Whyte, William H., *3:* **710**
Wickman, Carl Eric, *1:* 217
Wide World of Sports, *4:* 878, **887–88**
Wife Beware, 2: 497
Wigs, *1:* 132
Wilco, *5:* 1252, 1253 (ill.)
Wilcox, Daeida, *2:* 400
Wilcox, Harlow, *2:* 482
Wild West Show (Buffalo Bill Cody), *1:* 4, 33, **36–37**
Wilder, Laura Ingalls, *4:* 1043
Wile E. Coyote and Road Runner, *3:* **606–8,** 607 (ill.)
Will & Grace, 4: 927; *5:* 1277
Will the Circle Be Unbroken, 5: 1252
Willard, Jess, *1:* 102, 202; *2:* 328
William, Warren, *2:* 458
Williams, Anson, *4:* 1040, 1041 (ill.)
Williams, Barry, *4:* 1026
Williams, Bert, *1:* 49
Williams, Esther, *2:* 376
Williams, Guy, *1:* 199
Williams, Hank, *3:* 513, 557
Williams, Hank, Jr., *4:* 1019
Williams, John, *4:* 968, 978
Williams, Kathlyn, *1:* 147
Williams, Lucinda, *5:* 1252
Williams, Otis, *4:* 857 (ill.)
Williams, Paul, *4:* 857 (ill.)
Williams, Robin, *2:* 316
Williams, Roy, *3:* 752
Williams, Serena, *5:* 1228, 1271
Williams, Spencer, *2:* 479 (ill.)
Williams, Ted, *1:* 97
Williams, Tennessee, *3:* 530
Williams, Vanessa, *2:* 355 (ill.), 356
Williams, Venus, *5:* 1228, 1271
Williamson, Kevin, *5:* 1247
Willis, Bruce, *5:* 1157, 1245
Wills, Chill, *3:* 664

Willys-Overland jeeps, *5:* 1216
Wilson, Anthony H., *5:* 1114
Wilson, Brian, *4:* 789–90, 844–45, 845 (ill.)
Wilson, Carl, *4:* 844, 845, 845 (ill.)
Wilson, Dennis, *4:* 844, 845, 845 (ill.)
Wilson, Dooley, *3:* 532
Wilson, Flip, *4:* 949
Wilson, Sloan, *3:* 657
Wilson, Teddy, *2:* 428
Wilson, William Griffith, *2:* 504
Wilson, Woodrow, *1:* 145, 153, 190, 216; *2:* 364
Wimpy, *3:* 680
Winchell, Walter, *2:* 240, 307, 372
Windows, *5:* 1233
Winfield, J. R., *4:* 959
Winfrey, Oprah, *4:* 899
Winged Victory, 3: 530
Winkler, Henry, *4:* 1040, 1041, 1041 (ill.)
Winn, Matt, *1:* 103
Winnie-the-Pooh, *2:* **321–22,** 322 (ill.)
Winsor, Kathleen, *3:* 511
Winston Cup series, *2:* 474
Winston, Sam, *4:* 866
Wintour, Anna, *1:* 197
Wireless communication, *5:* 1308–9, 1309 (ill.)
Wise, Brownie, *3:* 521
Wise, Robert, *3:* 663
The "Wish Book," *1:* 26
"Witch hunts," *2:* 360–61
Witches, TV, *4:* 893–95
The Wiz, 5: 1141
The Wizard of Oz, *2:* 370, **417–18**
WNEW (New York City), *3:* 684
Wo Fat, *4:* 905
Wolfe, Tom, *4:* 947, 1069; *5:* 1155–57, 1156–57, 1219
Wolfman Jack, *3:* 683
Woman's Day, 2: 433
Women
  Avon, *1:* 116
  Baker, Josephine, *2:* 267–68, 268 (ill.)
  Barbie, *3:* 644–46, 645 (ill.)
  bra, *1:* 157, 159–61, 160 (ill.); *5:* 1271
  cigarettes, *2:* 252, 260
  Clairol hair coloring, *2:* 377
  Cosmopolitan, 4: 867–68
  Didrikson, Babe, *2:* 468–69, 469 (ill.)
  diets, *3:* 774–75
  divorce, *4:* 1069, 1075–77
  Equal Rights Amendment, *4:* 921, 1069, 1080–82, 1081 (ill.)
  flappers, *1:* 133; *2:* 261–63, 262 (ill.)
  Gibson Girl, *1:* 84–85, 85 (ill.)
  Good Housekeeping, 1: 84–85, 85 (ill.)
  hairstyles, *1:* 133–34
  Lilith Fair, *5:* 1257–58
  The Mary Tyler Moore Show, 4: 1046–49, 1047 (ill.)
  Miss America Pageant, *2:* 355 (ill.), 355–56
  National Organization for Women (NOW), *4:* 940–41, 941 (ill.)
  nylon stockings, *2:* 380–82, 381 (ill.)
  the Pill, *3:* 778–79
  sexually transmitted diseases (STDs), *4:* 1094
  sports, *3:* 587; *5:* 1271
  suffrage movement (right to vote), *1:* 213, 221; *2:* 252, 263
  True Story, 1: 196
  Vogue, 1: 196–97
  women's rights, *4:* 940–91, 1076
  Wonder Woman, *3:* 583–85
Women's Christian Temperance Union, *2:* 357
Women's Home Companion, 1: 88
Women's liberation movement, *1:* 160–61; *4:* 790, 807, 921, 998, 1004, 1024, 1025, 1076; *5:* 1209. *See also* Equal Rights Amendment; Feminist movement
Women's National Basketball Association (WNBA), *5:* 1271
Women's rights, *4:* 940–91, 1076
Women's sports, *3:* 587; *5:* 1271
Wonder Bread, *2:* **290–91**
Wonder, Stevie, *4:* 842
Wonder Woman, *2:* 440; *3:* **583–85**
Wood, Ron, *4:* 859
Wooden, John, *4:* 878
Woodruff, Ernest and Robert, *1:* 57
Woods, Donald, *2:* 458
Woods, Tiger, *2:* 290, 334; *5:* 1228, 1271, **1275–76**
Woodstock, *3:* 617; *4:* **862–63,** 863 (ill.); *5:* 1256
Woodward, Bob, *4:* 949
Woodward, Orator Francis, *1:* 65
Woolsey, Robert, *1:* 49

Woolworth, Frank Winfield, *1:* 12–13
Woolworth's stores, *1:* 8, 12 (ill.), 12–13
Wopat, Tom, *4:* 1034
Word games, *2:* 327
Works Progress Administration, *2:* 384, 425
World Book Encyclopedia, *1:* 188, **197–98**
World Hockey Association (WHA), *5:* 1166
"World of Tomorrow," *1:* 142
World Series, *1:* 3, 95, 97; *4:* 877
World Trade Center (New York City), *2:* 503–4; *3:* 621
World War I, *1:* 54, 146–47, 213–14
  cigarettes, *2:* 252
  economy, *1:* 153–54
  Harley-Davidson, *1:* 16
  movies about, *1:* 147
  Red scare, *2:* 360–61
  standardized testing, *2:* 365
  war bonds, *1:* 232, 232 (ill.)
World War II, *1:* 68; *2:* 319, 381; *3:* 509–11, 615, 625; *5:* 1262. *See also* Postwar period
  baby boom, *3:* 616–18
  Casablanca, *3:* 531–32
  Coca-Cola, *1:* 57
  comic books, *4:* 870
  Lindbergh, Charles, *2:* 354
  M & M's, *3:* 547, 547 (ill.)
  martial arts, *4:* 937
  news, *3:* 567
  propaganda films, *2:* 272–73; *3:* 599–600, 702
  rationing, *3:* 523
  sports, *3:* 587
  T-shirts, *1:* 163
  war bonds, *1:* 232–33
World Wide Web (WWW), *1:* 220; *4:* 1029, 1087; *5:* 1227, 1229, 1303, 1319, 1320
World Wrestling Federation, *5:* **1171–73,** 1172 (ill.)
World's Fairs, *1:* 3, 60, **142–43;** *2:* 318, 381, 478
Wouk, Herman, *3:* 638
Wozniak, Steve, *4:* 1070
WQED (Pittsburgh, Pennsylvania), *4:* 908
Wray, Fay, *2:* 403
Wrestling, *5:* 1171–73, 1172 (ill.)
Wright Brothers, *1:* 3, 8, 194; *2:* 345
Wright, George, *3:* 626
Wright, John Lloyd, *2:* 331
Wright, Richard, *3:* 514
Wristwatches, *3:* 650–51
Writing instruments, *2:* 375–76
WSM Barn Dance, *2:* 238, 297. *See also Grand Ole Opry*
Wuornos, Aileen, *4:* 1092
WWJD?: Think About It, *5:* 1328
WWJD? (What Would Jesus Do?), *5:* **1328–29**
WWW (World Wide Web), *5:* 1320
WXYZ (Detroit, Michigan), *2:* 485
Wylie, Philip, *2:* 451
Wyman, Bill, *4:* 858, 858 (ill.)
Wynne, Arthur, *2:* 327

X

X Games, *3:* 724; *5:* 1272, 1273–74
Xerox copiers, *4:* **804–5,** 1086
X-ers (Generation X), *5:* **1206–7,** 1224, 1290–92, 1291 (ill.)
The X-Files, *3:* 625

Y

Yank, *3:* 511
Yankee Doodle Dandy, *2:* 390; *3:* 511
Yankee Stadium (Bronx, New York), *2:* 325
Yasgur, Max, *4:* 862
Yastrzemski, Carl, *2:* 469
The Yearling, *2:* 369
"The Yellow Kid," *1:* 81
Yellowstone National Park, *4:* 1079
Yentl, *4:* 861
"Yo!," *4:* 948
Yodeling, *2:* 299; *3:* 556
Yokum, Abner, *2:* 455
York, Dick, *4:* 894
Yosemite National Park, *4:* 1079
You Bet Your Life, *2:* 406
You Only Live Twice, *4:* 937
Young, Alan, *4:* 906
Young, Cy, *1:* 97 (ill.)
Young, Murat, *2:* 436
Young, Neil, *1:* 106; *5:* 1138
Young, Robert, *4:* 949
Young, Sean, *5:* 1122
"Your Cheatin' Heart," *3:* 557
Your Erroneous Zones, *4:* 949
"You're a Grand Old Flag," *1:* 3
Youth culture, *3:* 767; *4:* 791, 820
  Abercrombie & Fitch, *5:* 1235–36

alternative rock, *5:* 1253–54
antiwar movement, *4:* 922
athletic shoes, *1:* 162
baby boomers, *5:* 1206
Beatniks and the Beat movement, *3:* 698–99, 699 (ill.), 709
The Beavis and Butt-Head Show, 5: 1284–85
bell-bottoms, *4:* 807–9, 808 (ill.)
Beverly Hills 90210, 5: 1286–87, 1287 (ill.)
British, *4:* 994
The Catcher in the Rye, 3: 617
communes, *4:* 1073
Dean, James, *3:* 663–64
Doc Martens, *4:* 809–10
Easy Rider, 4: 820–21, 821 (ill.)
flappers, *1:* 133; *2:* 261–63, 262 (ill.)
gangs, *5:* 1204–6, 1205 (ill.)
Generation X, *5:* 1206–7
grunge, *5:* 1254
Nirvana, *5:* 1258
Pokémon, *5:* 1322–23, 1323 (ill.)
preppy, *5:* 1115–17, 1116 (ill.)
Presley, Elvis, *3:* 689–90, 690 (ill.)
punk, *4:* 992–94
raccoon coats, *2:* 264–65
raves, *5:* 1259–60, 1260 (ill.)
The Real World, 5: 1292–94, 1293 (ill.)
scouting, *1:* 226–28, 227 (ill.)
sexual revolution, *4:* 941–44
sexually transmitted diseases (STDs), *4:* 1093–94
skateboarding, *3:* 722–24, 723 (ill.)
skinheads, *5:* 1214–15
South Park, 5: 1298–99, 1299 (ill.)
Spears, Britney, *5:* 1261, 1261 (ill.)
spring break, *3:* 631–32
Teenage Mutant Ninja Turtles, *5:* 1194–95, 1195 (ill.)
Volkswagen Microbus, *3:* 654
Wayne's World, 5: 1249–50, 1250 (ill.)
Whole Earth Catalog, 4: 875
yuppies, *5:* 1218–20
zines, *5:* 1162–64
zoot suit, *3:* 525–27, 526 (ill.)
Yo-Yo, *2:* **336–37,** 337 (ill.)
Y2K scare, *5:* 1304, **1329–30**
Yukon Basin, *1:* 88
Yuppies, *3:* 618; *5:* 1099, 1100, 1104, 1197, 1203, **1218–20,** 1279
preppy, *5:* 1115–17, 1116 (ill.)
Starbucks, *5:* 1110–11, 1111 (ill.)

Z

Zaharias, Babe Didrikson. *See* Didrikson, Babe
Zaharias, George, *2:* 469
Zamora, Pedro, *5:* 1293
Zapruder film, *5:* 1241
Zenith Corporation, *3:* 576
Zeppelins, *2:* 346
Zero Hour, 5: 1120, 1121
Ziegfeld, Florenz, *1:* 50
Ziegfeld Follies, *1:* **50–52,** 146
Ziegfeld Girls, *1:* 51
Ziering, Ian, *5:* 1286, 1287 (ill.)
Zimmer, Kim, *2:* 484
Zimmer, Norma, *3:* 749
Zimmerman, Robert Allen, *4:* 848
Zines, *5:* 1162–64
Zip Coon, *1:* 40
Zipper, *1:* **164–65**
Zodiac Killer, *4:* 1092
Zondervan publishing company, *5:* 1328
Zoot suit, *3:* **525–27,** 526 (ill.)
Zorro, *1:* **199–200,** 200 (ill.)
Zucker, David and Jerry, *5:* 1121
Zukor, Adolph, *1:* 44
Zwicker, Ralph, *3:* 770